2002

CHAUCER STUDIES XXVIII

SOURCES AND ANALOGUES OF
THE CANTERBURY TALES

Volume I

This is the first in a new two-volume edition of the sources and major analogues of all the *Canterbury Tales* prepared by members of the New Chaucer Society. This collection, the first to appear in over half a century, features such additions as a fresh interpretation of Chaucer's sources for the frame of the work, chapters on the sources of the *General Prologue* and *Retractions*, and modem English translations of all foreign language texts. Chapters on the individual tales contain an updated survey of the present state of scholarship on their source materials. Several sources and analogues discovered during the past fifty years are found here together for the first time, and some other familiar sources are re-edited from manuscripts closer to Chaucer's copies. *Volume I* includes chapters on the Frame and the tales of the Reeve, Cook, Friar, Clerk, Squire, Franklin, Pardoner, Melibee, Monk, Nun's Priest, Second Nun and Parson. Chapters on the other tales, together with the General Prologue and Retractions, will appear in Volume Two.

Professor ROBERT CORREALE teaches at Wright State University, Ohio. Professor MARY HAMEL teaches at Mount St Mary's College, Maryland.

CHAUCER STUDIES
ISSN 0261–9822

Previously published volumes in this series
are listed at the back of this book

SOURCES AND ANALOGUES OF
THE CANTERBURY TALES

Volume I

ROBERT M. CORREALE
General Editor

MARY HAMEL
Associate General Editor

D. S. BREWER

First published 2002
D. S. Brewer, Cambridge

ISBN 0 85991 628 6

D. S. Brewer is an imprint of Boydell & Brewer Ltd
PO Box 9, Woodbridge, Suffolk IP12 3DF, UK
and of Boydell & Brewer Inc.
PO Box 41026, Rochester, NY 14604–4126, USA
website: www.boydell.co.uk

A catalogue record for this book is available
from the British Library

Library of Congress Cataloging-in-Publication Data

Sources and analogues of the Canterbury tales / Robert M. Correale, general editor;
Mary Hamel, associate general editor.
    p. cm – (Chaucer studies ; 28)
    Includes bibliographical references and index.
    ISBN 0-85991-628-6 (alk. paper)
    1. Chaucer, Geoffrey, d. 1400. Canterbury tales – Sources. 2. Literature,
Comparative – Themes, motives. 3. Literature, Medieval – Themes, motives.
    4. Literature, Medieval. I. Correale, Robert M., 1932– II. Hamel, Mary, 1936– III. Series.
PR1912.A2 S68 2002
821'.1–dc21
                                                        2001037783

This publication is printed on acid-free paper

Printed in Great Britain by
St Edmundsbury Press Ltd, Bury St Edmunds, Suffolk

Contents

Preface

Bryan and Dempster's *Sources and Analogues of Chaucer's Canterbury Tales*, first published in 1941, has been one of the most important reference tools in Chaucer studies. It has played a leading role in helping scholars understand and assess how Chaucer handled the many classical, patristic and medieval sources he used in fashioning his masterpiece. In the past sixty years, however, there have been many new developments in the field, and a revised and expanded edition has long been needed. This new *Sources and Analogues of The Canterbury Tales* is a collaborative effort by an international team of scholars to meet this need. Its purpose is essentially the same as that of its distinguished predecessor – to present the sources in the forms that Chaucer knew them, and where sources are unknown, to present the closest analogues to the tales in the forms with which Chaucer was presumably acquainted.[1]

There are, however, several important differences in content and format between Bryan and Dempster's work and this volume. Several new sources and analogues of the *Tales* discovered in the past half century (e.g. *Friar's Tale*, *Second Nun's Tale*) are printed here together for the first time. Some well-known sources of others (e.g. *Man of Law's Tale*, *Wife of Bath's Prologue*) are re-edited from manuscripts closer to those Chaucer presumably knew and used. Some source texts in Bryan and Dempster have been omitted, including especially Sercambi's *Novelle*, now known to have been written too late to have influenced Chaucer's idea for the frame of the *Tales*. The most noticeable difference is the appearance of modern English translations of all sources and analogues in foreign languages. This addition, which will make these texts more accessible to scholars and students of Chaucer, as well as to a larger audience of interested readers of the *Tales*, has also required expansion of this edition to two volumes.

This first volume begins with a fresh examination of the sources of the frame of the work. Helen Cooper's assertion that Boccaccio's *Decameron* is the one text "that can stake a primary claim to being Chaucer's model for the Tales" represents a major shift of opinion among a number of scholars who are now willing to credit the influence of this work on *The Canterbury Tales*, and also

---

[1] W. F. Bryan and Germaine Dempster, eds., *Sources and Analogues of Chaucer's Canterbury Tales* (1941; rpt. Humanities Press, Atlantic Highlands, New Jersey, 1958), p. vii. Additional analogues are printed and discussed by Larry D. Benson and Theodore M. Andersson, eds., in *The Literary Context of Chaucer's Fabliaux* (Indianapolis, IN, and New York, 1971), and in the earlier *Originals and Analogues of Some of Chaucer's Canterbury Tales*, ed. F. J. Furnivall, et al., Chaucer Society, 2nd series, nos 7, 10, 15, 20, 22 (London, 1872).

signals another distinct change from Bryan and Dempster. Stories from the *Decameron* appear here as analogues, for example, to *The Reeve's Tale* and *The Franklin's Tale*. In all, chapters on twelve tales are included in Volume I, ending with a completely revised and augmented discussion of the sources of *The Parson's Tale*. The sources of the remaining twelve tales will be treated in Volume II, which will also have newly added chapters on the *General Prologue* and the *Retractions*, and also contain sizeable portions of the *Teseida,* the direct source of the *Knight's Tale*, to replace the summaries of Boccaccio's work in Bryan and Dempster. In both volumes the chapters follow the order in which the tales appear in *The Riverside Chaucer.*

Our primary aim throughout has been to present the texts of Chaucer's sources and analogues as accurately as possible, leaving questions of how he adapted them for his own artistic purposes to be answered by literary critics. Each chapter, however, contains an introductory discussion of such matters as the origin and transmission of the sources, evidence for Chaucer's indebtedness to them, and a review of research done on them during the past half-century. Though the general editors and other readers have offered suggestions and criticisms of each chapter, the contributors themselves are finally responsible for their contents. They have been given freedom to select the source texts, and allowed to decide whether to reproduce them from printed editions or re-edit them from original manuscripts according to current standard practice, with abbreviations silently expanded and punctuation and capitalization modernized. They have also been allowed to choose what variant readings to present, what textual notes to include, and whether to use their own translations of the foreign language sources or translations made by others. Middle English texts appear in their original forms, but the brief marginal summaries of them in Bryan and Dempster have been removed in favor of modern English glosses of hard words and phrases. It is our hope that all these additions and changes will provide Chaucer scholars – as well as a wider audience of interested readers – with an updated, user-friendly resource that will accurately reflect the present state of knowledge about the sources and analogues of *The Canterbury Tales,* and will nourish and assist research on Chaucer's poem well into the present century.

Preparation of this edition, like projects of similar size and scope, has taken a number of years to complete, and the persons who have aided our efforts are too many to mention all of them suitably by name. Mary Hamel, the associate general editor, in addition to writing the chapter on *The Pardoner's Tale* and preparing the general index, has rendered invaluable assistance in countless ways while performing a variety of other administrative and editorial chores. We are particularly grateful to Derek Brewer, one of our earliest and most enthusiastic supporters, who has remained a source of sound advice and continual encouragement. Derek Pearsall has also been an early and zealous promoter of this project, even assuming leadership of it for a brief period and playing a crucial role in moving it forward. We are also thankful for the support of the members and officers of the New Chaucer Society, especially to John H. Fisher, Robert W. Frank Jr., Christian K. Zacher, and V. A. Kolve, who were

instrumental in bringing the project to the attention of the Society and obtaining its official endorsement.

The members of the Advisory Board have given generously of their time and expertise to read and critique drafts of chapters and to help solve numerous other problems. A number of other scholars have provided various kinds of assistance that is acknowledged by individual contributors in their chapters. We are also greatly indebted to the contributors themselves for volunteering their time and knowledge to assist with this project, for their cooperation with the editors during the writing, and the often burdensome task of revising their work, and to several of them for their Job-like patience while waiting for its publication.

We are indebted to many persons at Wright State University for their generous assistance over the years. A Research Incentive Grant provided funds to get the project underway, and a professional leave afforded the general editor time to do the final editing of this first volume. Dean (now Provost) Perry Moore and Dean Mary Ellen Mazey of the College of Liberal Arts at Wright State have provided generous financial help including the cost of all communication and travel expenses. Henry Limouze, English department chair and Chaucer devotee, has been an ardent supporter of the project from the outset and has given unselfishly of his time and resources to advance it. We are grateful to the department's secretarial staff – Leanne Moeller, Jennifer Sheets and Lynn Morgan – for their numerous personal and professional kindnesses on our behalf. Victoria Chadbourne and Marijane James provided timely help with computer problems, especially by their late-night "conversions" in cyber-space. We would also like to thank the staff at Boydell & Brewer, particularly Caroline Palmer for her patience, determination and good advice, especially when we faltered or lost momentum; and to Pam Cope for her careful reading of the text and her help in improving its layout.

I owe special thanks to my wife Jeanne, who has encouraged and assisted me in countless ways during every stage of the project, and in particular for reading the text and saving me from a number of errors.

Finally, we are grateful to Laurel Broughton and Edward Wheatley for agreeing to take over chapters begun by two former colleagues. Sumner Ferris (*Prioress's Tale*) and George Reinecke (*Manciple's Tale*), members of our original roster of contributors, died while this volume was in preparation, and we greatly lament their passing.

Acknowledgements

The editors, contributors and publishers are grateful to all the institutions and journals listed below for permission to reprint, or to quote from, the materials for which they hold copyright. Every effort has been made to trace the copyright holders; apologies are offered for any omission in this regard, and the publishers will be pleased to add any necessary acknowledgement in subsequent editions.

Frame

Helen Cooper, "Sources and Analogues of The Canterbury Tales: Reviewing the Work," *Studies in the Age of Chaucer* 19 (1997): 183–210. By permission of the editor of *Studies in the Age of Chaucer*.

Reeve's Tale

Decameron IX, 6 from *Il Decamerone*, ed. Vittore Branca (Firenze, 1965), pp. 1062–7. By kind permission of Casa Editrice Le Monnier.

Friar's Tale

British Library, MS Add. 38654, fols. 39–39v; MS Cotton Cleopatra D VIII, fol. 110; MS Harley 4894, fols. 103v–104. By permission of the British Library.

Clerk's Tale

"Historia Griseldis," Peterhouse MS 81, fols. 185–187v; by permission of the Master and Fellows of Peterhouse, Cambridge.

J. Burke Severs, *The Literary Relationships of Chaucer's Clerkes Tale* (New Haven, 1942), pp. 255–89. Copyright Yale University Press, 1942. By permission of Yale University Press.

"Le Livre Griseldis," from Boston Public Library, Rare Books Department, MS Med. 91, fols. 87–93v. By Courtesy of the Trustees.

Squire's Tale

H. Braddy, "Cambyuskan's Flying Horse and Charles VI's 'Cerf Volant,'" *Modern Language Review* 33 (1938): 41–4; reproduced by permission of the Modern Humanities Research Association.

Albert D. Menut and Alexander J. Denomy, *Nicole Oresme, Le Livre du Ciel et du Monde* (Madison, 1968), pp. 400–5; reprinted by permission of The University of Wisconsin Press.

Richard C. Dales, "The Text of Robert Grosseteste's *Questio de fluxu et refluxu maris* with an English Translation," *Isis* 57 (1966): 455–74 (quotation from pp. 460–3, 470); reprinted by permission of the University of Chicago Press.

Lynn White, Jr., "Eilmer of Malmesbury, an Eleventh Century Aviator," *Technology and Culture* (1961): 97–111; reprinted by permission of the Johns Hopkins University Press.

Roger Bacon, *Opus Majus*, trans. Robert Belle Burke (University of Pennsylvania Press, 1928), vol. 1, pp. 161, 408–10; copyright University of Pennsylvania Press, 1928; reprinted by permission.

Roger Bacon, *Opus Majus,* ed. J. S. Brewer (1964), vol. 1, p. 140; vol. 2, pp. 392, 394; reprinted by permission of Minerva Gmbh, Wissenschaflicher und Buchhandlung.

Charles Burnett, ed., *Adelard of Bath: Conversations with His Nephew* (Cambridge, 1998), pp. 79–80; reprinted by permission of Cambridge University Press.

N. F. Blake, ed., *The History of Reynard the Fox*, EETS OS 263 (1970), pp. 79–80; reprinted by permission of the Council of the Early English Text Society.

M. C. Seymour, ed., *On the Properties of Things: John Trevisa's Translation of Bartholomaeus Anglicus De Proprietatibus Rerum* (Oxford, 1975), vol. 1, p. 590; and M. C. Seymour, ed., *Mandeville's Travels* (Oxford, 1967), pp. 169–71, 177, 180. Reprinted by permission of Oxford University Press.

Félix LeCoy, ed., *Le Roman de la Rose*, CFMA (Paris, 1965–70)
vol. 1, pp. 182–3, lines 5917–47
vol. 2, p. 239, lines 16066–71
vol. 3, p. 23, lines 17432–5, 17443–50; p. 36, lines 17855–61; p. 39, lines 17963–70; pp. 40–1, lines 18000–020; pp. 41–2, lines 18031–40; p. 47, 18217–22.
Reprinted by permission of Éditions Honoré Champion.

Guillaume de Lorris, *The Romance of the Rose*, trans. Charles Dahlberg (Hanover, NH, and London, 1983), extracts from pp. 119, 272–3, 292, 298–9, 300, 303. Reprinted by permission of Princeton University Press.

Albert C. Friend, "The Tale of the Captive Bird and the Traveler: Nequam, Berechiah, and Chaucer's Squire's Tale," *Medievalia et Humanistica*, n. s. 1 (1970): 58–9, 63n. By permission of the editor of *Medievalia et Humanistica.*

Franklin's Tale

Félix LeCoy, ed., *Le Roman de la Rose*, CFMA (Paris, 1965–70), vol. 2, p. 7, lines 8425–36; pp. 36–7, lines 9391–424; pp. 171–2, lines 13845–68. Reprinted by permission of Éditions Honoré Champion.

"The Middle English *Lai le Freine*," ed. Margaret Wattie, *Smith College Studies in Modern Languages* 10.3 (1929): 1.

Monk's Tale

Boethius, *De consolatione philosophiae*, 4m 7.13–31. Reprinted by permission of

Nun's Priest's Tale

Second Nun's Tale

Parson's Tale

The Frame[1]

HELEN COOPER

The *Canterbury Tales* is a framed story-collection, a form that originated in the East, was adopted with enthusiasm in the medieval West, and that reached its peak of popularity in European literature in the fourteenth century. In the *Tales*, the frame takes the form of a pilgrimage with the pilgrims as storytellers, and the tales are told in competition with each other; both these elements have sources and analogues of their own that are independent of the generic nature of the whole work as a collection of tales. In addition, the relationships established between the stories as they pick up related themes and motifs from each other, sometimes from adjacent tales, sometimes from more distant ones, is a process that interlocks with the frame of the work but that also has much in common with debate, itself a widespread literary form but also found much more widely in medieval culture.

This survey of sources and analogues will attempt to cover all four of these areas – story-collections and how they organize their constituent tales; debate; poetic contests; storytelling pilgrims – to give some idea of the origins of the large structures of the whole work. The problems attendant on such a survey are rather different from those for the individual tales. There are works that we know from other evidence that Chaucer read, and that may have set him thinking – as the articulation of the stories within Ovid's *Metamorphoses*, for instance, may have done – but that do not offer models for the solutions he himself adopted; there are others that offer closer parallels to Chaucer's solutions but where the clinching evidence that would prove direct debt has been in dispute, Boccaccio's *Decameron* being the most striking instance. Specific topics of debate, such as pro- and antifeminism, can be thoroughly documented as they occur in sections of the *Tales* such as the Wife of Bath's Prologue; but Chaucer's informing principle of structuring his story-collection by analogy with a series of dialectical debating positions derives from more general conventions of debate literature, and from the wider usages of disputation in medieval culture, in the law courts, the schools, Parliament and so on, where

---

[1] This chapter first appeared in substantially similar form as a harbinger of the new *Sources and Analogues* in *Studies in the Age of Chaucer* 19 (1997), 183–210, and is reprinted here by permission.

specific source texts are beside the point. Some of the evidence for pilgrims' habits of storytelling and for poetic contests is historical rather than literary, so surviving written sources can only poorly represent what may have been Chaucer's direct inspiration.

If any one work can stake a primary claim to being Chaucer's model for the *Tales*, it is the *Decameron*. The possibility of Chaucer's knowledge of the work has been much debated, and the arguments are outlined below. It was rejected as a source by R. A. Pratt and Karl Young in their contribution to Bryan and Dempster's *Sources and Analogues of Chaucer's Canterbury Tales* on the grounds that "its basic conception is that of a succession of aristocratic garden scenes rather than of a moving pilgrimage of diverse and discordant personalities," and they regarded "storytelling in the course of a moving pilgrimage" as "fundamental in the design" of the *Tales*.[2] Furthermore,

> we have no decisive evidence that Chaucer was acquainted with it. . . . Chaucer does not mention the *Decameron*, he borrows no stories directly from it, and no copy of it can be traced in England during the period of his life.   (p. 20)

They therefore proposed as Chaucer's model the *Novelle* of Giovanni Sercambi, which Chaucer likewise does not mention, from which he borrows no stories directly, and which was barely known in Italy (there is only one surviving manuscript), let alone England; but it does contain a collection of stories told on a journey, by a single first-person narrator.

Sercambi's claims were always tenuous; they were put beyond consideration by more recent research, which has established that the work was not composed until 1400 or later, too late for Chaucer to have known it.[3] Its removal from the scene allows space for the *Decameron* to re-enter, and its claims to be re-appraised. The shift of critical emphasis that has taken place over the last fifty years allows a new stress on the literary over the literal, the dynamics of articulating a story-collection over the choice of a journey to provide the occasion for the storytelling; and with the shift, Boccaccio's work looks an increasingly certain candidate as the inspiration behind the *Tales*. Even Pratt and Young's claim that it never functions as Chaucer's immediate source for individual tales is open to question; and although it does not furnish the model for every aspect of Chaucer's work, such as the pilgrimage and the organization as a competition, those can, as has been indicated, be supplied from other sources more immediately available to Chaucer.

---

[2] R. A. Pratt and Karl Young, "The Literary Framework of the *Canterbury Tales*," in W. F. Bryan and Germaine Dempster, eds., *Sources and Analogues of Chaucer's Canterbury Tales* (1941; repr. New York: Humanities Press, 1958), pp. 20–1.

[3] *Giovanni Sercambi: Il novelliere*, ed. Luciano Rossi (Rome: Salerno, 1974), I: xix–xx. Rossi also disproves the existence of a hypothetical lost short form of the work supposedly dating from c. 1374.

I.i *Story-collections*

Story-collections were a distinct genre to themselves in the Middle Ages, with their own conventions of organization, content, purpose and audience expectation. They do not, however, constitute a homogenous form.[4] They vary in structure from collections of brief narratives assembled without any kind of introduction or attempt at linking, to collections that are articulated in the most elaborate ways. Most were concerned with giving moral instruction; but exemplary tales are designed to make morals attractive, and the didactic can easily find itself subsumed by the entertaining. There is a broad correlation between simple structure and moral emphasis at one end of the spectrum of story-collections, and literary complexity and a greater stress on pleasurableness at the other; and it is to this latter variety that the *Canterbury Tales* belongs.

Given this range of models, the distinctiveness of the *Tales*, and with that the likelihood of its having a source identifiable from among the many collections circulating in the fourteenth century, can best be brought out by a rapid survey of the different kinds of story-collections in existence, and in particular those known to Chaucer or that were compiled within the sphere of English, Anglo-French or Anglo-Latin culture. The simplest kind of collection has either no frame at all or just a prologue: Chaucer himself produces examples of the form in the *Legend of Good Women* (though the elaboration of the prologue distinguishes the poem from most such collections) and the *Monk's Tale*. Most commonly, collections of this kind contain stories of a single genre – narratives of abandoned or suffering women in the *Legend*, tragedies in the *Monk's Tale*. Chaucer's main source for the *Legend*, Ovid's collection of letters from abandoned women, the *Heroides*, belongs to this category; it also gets a mention in the Man of Law's survey of story-collections in the Introduction to his tale (II.54–5). Such collections may be secular in nature, especially those that are Classical or modelled on the Classics – not only the *Legend*, but early humanist works such as the stories of famous women in Boccaccio's *De claris mulieribus*; even these, however, often have an exemplary function, most explicit in works such as the first-century *Factorum et dictorum memorabilium libri novem* of Valerius Maximus that the Wife of Bath's Jankin included among his reading.[5]

There is a handful of secular story-collections of this simple structure that originate in the Middle Ages, such as the *Lais* of Marie de France; but most of those compiled in this period, including the most widely disseminated examples, were religious or didactic, or both. Collections of saints' lives and of beast fables, where each story carries an accompanying *moralitas*, are usually structured in this way. The best known instances of the form were collections of

---

[4] For a broader survey, see Helen Cooper, *The Structure of the Canterbury Tales* (London: Duckworth, 1983; Athens, Georgia: Georgia University Press, 1984), pp. 8–55.

[5] *Valerii Maximi factorum et dictorum memorabilium libri novem*, ed. Carolus Kempf, Bibliotheca Teubneriana (1888; repr. Stuttgart: Teubner, 1966); and see *Canterbury Tales* III.642–9 (*The Riverside Chaucer*, general ed. Larry D. Benson [Boston: Houghton Mifflin, 1987]).

exempla for use by preachers. Foremost among these is the *Gesta Romanorum*, a ragbag of assorted stories of which the order and even the contents vary extensively from manuscript to manuscript.[6] It originated early in the fourteenth century, probably in England; both Gower and Hoccleve draw on it, and Chaucer occasionally mentions stories it contains although he may have derived them from other sources. In preaching collections of this sort, the stories may potentially be of mixed kinds but the moral or allegorical purpose overrides any development of variety for its own sake.

A rare exception to the single-genre nature of most of these collections with minimal frames is the *Novellino*, an Italian collection of a hundred brief narratives with a prologue dating from around 1300 that was one of Boccaccio's models for the *Decameron*;[7] mixed in with its short *novelle* (which include one of the closest analogues of the *Merchant's Tale*) are episodes from Arthurian tales, beast fables, and moral tales, including a version of the story that the Pardoner tells of meeting death in the form of a hoard of gold.

There is a further group of story-collections that provides a simple linking mechanism between tales in addition to providing a prologue announcing the nature of the work, though there are not many examples of this kind that appear to have been known to Chaucer; Boccaccio's *De casibus virorum illustrium*, which may have been the inspiration for the *Monk's Tale* (the scribe of the Ellesmere manuscript suggests as much), is the main possible exception. In this, those who have fallen from high estate into misery pass before Boccaccio's eyes to tell their stories and allow the opportunity for moralization; its content, of posthumously recounted biographies, recalls Dante's *Inferno*, though here it is the ghosts of the dead that move past while their recorder stays still. The work decisively entered English culture early in the fifteenth century, when Lydgate translated it, by way of an intermediary French translation, as *The Fall of Princes*.[8] Another such loosely linked collection, the *Disciplina clericalis* of Petrus Alfonsi,[9] has its roots in Arabic traditions through its origins in Spain; it may have been written around 1110, when he was working in England as physician to Henry I.[10] The work was widely disseminated throughout Europe, but although this too was translated into English in the fifteenth century,[11]

---

[6]   See the edition by Hermann Oesterley (Berlin: Weidmann, 1872). A Middle English translation was made early in the fifteenth century (ed. Sidney J. H. Herrtage, EETS E.S. 33 [1879]).

[7]   *Il Novellino*, ed. G. Favati (Genoa: Bozzi, 1970). The work is often known by the title given by its first printed edition in 1525, *Le ciento novelle antike*.

[8]   *Giovanni Boccaccio: De casibus virorum illustrium*, ed. P. G. Ricci and V. Zaccaria (Milan: Mondadori, 1983); *Lydgate's Fall of Princes*, ed. Henry Bergen, EETS E.S. 121–4 (1924–27).

[9]   *Petrus Alfonsi: Disciplina Clericalis*, ed. Alfons Hilka and W. Söderhjelm (Heidelberg: C. Winter, 1911); *The "Disciplina Clericalis" of Petrus Alfonsi* trans. and ed. Eberhard Hermes, trans. into English by P. R. Quarrie (London: Routledge and Kegan Paul, 1977).

[10]   See John Tolan, *Petrus Alfonsi and his Medieval Readers* (Gainesville: University of Florida Press, 1993), pp. 10–11. The work is given a more elaborate history by Thomas D. Cooke in *A Manual of the Writings in Middle English, 1050–1500*, vol. 9 (New Haven: Connecticut Academy of Arts and Sciences, 1993), XXIV: Tales, 3326.

[11]   *Peter Alphonse's Disciplina Clericalis*, ed. William Henry Hulme, Western Reserve Studies I.5 (Cleveland, Ohio: Western Reserve University Press, 1919).

Chaucer probably knew it only at second hand through quotations in Albertanus of Brescia's *Liber consolationis et consilii*, the source of *Melibee*. Its frame is very loose, consisting of little more than statements such as "A father said to his son –" or "A master said to his pupil –," and offers none of the dynamics found in the *Tales*.

More suggestive are works that develop the frame to make a story in its own right. In some works from which Chaucer draws stories or examples, such as histories, the Bible, the *Roman de la rose*, and the *Divina commedia*, the stories become incidental to the larger frame in the sense that the overarching structure does not exist exclusively for their sake and takes precedence over them. Such works turn into story-collections in texts such as William of Waddington's Anglo-Norman *Manuel des Pechiez* and its English adaptation, Robert Mannyng of Bourne's *Handlyng Synne*, where the stories are told to illustrate the major topics of Christian instruction: the Ten Commandments, the seven deadly sins, the seven sacraments and so on.[12] Mannyng began his version in 1303, so the work belongs with the great fourteenth-century flowering of story-collections. It is paralleled in its structure from the end of the century by Gower's *Confessio amantis* with its architecture of the seven sins against love. This was certainly known to Chaucer; Gower includes a greeting to him, put into the mouth of Venus, at the end of the earliest version of the poem,[13] and Chaucer's own reference to incestuous stories in the Introduction to the *Man of Law's Tale* (II.77–85) is generally taken as an allusion to the *Confessio*. The early stages of the composition of the *Tales* would have overlapped with the writing of the *Confessio*, but there is no surviving evidence that either poet was inspired to write a story-collection by the example of the other, and they handle the problems and opportunities of the form very differently. Gower's use of a single narrator to offer instruction appears at first glance to be close to Mannyng's *Handlyng Synne*, but Mannyng speaks as narrator in his own voice; Gower's fictional instructor Genius and his first-person interlocutor Amans, who is a fictionalized version of Gower himself, move a step closer to Chaucer's practice in the *Tales* but still offer a very different kind of framing dynamic. There are in addition some works with multiple narrators who tell tales within more fully autonomous frames. Two by Boccaccio have indeed been proposed as models for the *Tales*: the *Ameto*, in which an assembly of minimally allegorical nymphs recount their sexual histories (one of these, an account of the grotesque love-making of a *senex amans*, offers some overlap in subject with the *Merchant's Tale*); and the *Filocolo*, an immensely long retelling of the romance of Floris and Blancheflour that includes an episode in which the characters propose conundrums on the topic of love, *demandes d'amour*, some of which set up the problem at issue by telling stories (one of these, retold

---

[12] *Robert of Brunne's "Handlyng Synne,"* ed. by Frederick J. Furnivall, EETS O.S. 119, 123 (1901, 1903), gives the Anglo-Norman text in parallel.
[13] *Confessio* VIII.2941*–57*, in *The English Works of John Gower*, ed. G. C. Macaulay, EETS E.S. 81–2 (1900–1).

in the *Decameron*, constitutes an analogue to the *Franklin's Tale*). Chaucer could have known either, or indeed both; but even for the *Filocolo* the evidence is very weak, and the latest scholarship on the subject does not claim indebtedness on Chaucer's part.[14] Story-collections with autonomous frames originate much earlier than this, however: the *Seven Sages of Rome*, Oriental in origin, was some two millennia old by the time it reached the West in the mid-twelfth century. It was very widely disseminated in many languages, including an English translation made probably in the late thirteenth century.[15] It is included in the Auchinleck manuscript, which it has been suggested that Chaucer knew;[16] but even if he had read the work, he made little or no use of it (he makes oblique references to one of its stories at III.231–4 and in the *Manciple's Tale*, but tales of this kind often circulated independently), and none at all in terms of structure. The relation of the frame of the *Seven Sages* to the stories it contains is very different from the *Tales*: a prince is accused of sexual misconduct by his step-mother, and the tales are told to the king by his teachers and his stepmother alternately to preserve or threaten his life. The frame, in fact, could exist without the stories, as the Canterbury pilgrimage could not.

Oriental story-collections[17] developed the most sophisticated methods of articulating their constituent tales, but only isolated examples were known in the medieval West. They offer a highly complex structure in which stories are recessed within stories: the supreme example of the form, the *Thousand and One Nights*, makes the fact that no tale is ever complete before several more are under way into the object of the frame story. This particular work was not known in Europe until much later, but some other examples of the form made their way into Western culture by way of Spain: *Kalila and Dimna*, also known as the *Fables of Bidpai*, entered by this route, becoming known through its Latin translation, the *Directorium vitae humanae*.[18] Although Chaucer does not base his work on collections of this kind, he does use stories of Oriental origin on occasion, most particularly in the *Squire's Tale*; and both there and more largely over the whole work he shows signs of a concern to get away from presenting

---

[14] See Barry Windeatt, *Oxford Guides to Chaucer: Troilus and Criseyde* (Oxford: Clarendon Press, 1992), pp. 47, 147: he perceives congruence of story rather than "actual textual borrowing." For a broader discussion of "what larger, more abstract concepts and ideas Chaucer might have derived from such a text," see David Wallace, *Chaucer and the Early Writings of Boccaccio*, Chaucer Studies 12 (Cambridge: D. S. Brewer, 1985), pp. 39–72.

[15] On its history, see Killis Campbell, *The Seven Sages of Rome* (Boston: Ginn & Co., 1907). The various Middle English versions probably all derive from the same translation; there is an edition by Karl Brunner, *The Seven Sages of Rome*, EETS O.S. 191 (1933).

[16] See the two essays by Laura Hibbard Loomis on "Chaucer and the Breton Lays of the Auchinleck Manuscript" and "Chaucer and the Auchinleck MS: *Thopas* and *Guy of Warwick*," reprinted in her *Adventures in the Middle Ages* (New York: Burt Franklin, 1962), pp. 111–49.

[17] On these see Katherine Slater Gittes, "The *Canterbury Tales* and the Arabic Frame Tradition," *PMLA* 98 (1983): 237–51.

[18] *Johannis de Capua Directorium vitae humanae*, ed. Joseph Derenbourg, Bibliothèque des Hautes Études 72 (Paris: F. Vieweg, 1887–89). The work did not appear in any version in English until the sixteenth century, when Sir Thomas North translated an Italian translation of a Spanish translation of John of Capua's Latin (*The Morall Philosophie of Doni*, 1570; edited by Joseph Jacobs as *The Fables of Bidpai* [London: David Nutt, 1888]).

tales simply as a sequence of autonomous stories, and he too will experiment with techniques of recession and insetting.

Another work that offers a similarly elaborate configuration of its constituent tales and that he most certainly did know is the *Metamorphoses* of Ovid. Chaucer himself appears to suggest a parallel between his own work and Ovid's in the Introduction to the *Man of Law's Tale*, where he has the Man of Law claim,

> Me were looth be likned, douteless,
> To Muses that men clepe Pierides –
> *Methamorphosios* woot what I mene;
> But nathelees, I recche noght a bene
> Though I come after hym with hawebake.
> I speke in prose, and lat him rymes make.   (II.91–6)

The reference appears to be to the daughters of Pierus who challenged the Muses, themselves also known as the Pierides, to a singing contest and were turned into chattering magpies for their presumption.[19] In a typically backhanded way, Chaucer appears to be setting himself up as Muse in comparison to the Man of Law's magpie, even while he is himself the ventriloquist behind the Man of Law. In a very broad sense, the *Metamorphoses* kind of story-collection, which offers a frame that exists to justify the telling of the stories and that both introduces and links the tales, represents the category to which the *Canterbury Tales* itself belongs; but the absence of any plot to its frame (which is constituted as an arrangement rather than a story, starting with the Golden Age and working through to Augustus) and its lack of a distinctive group of narrators telling *all* the stories make it a very different work.[20] It was known in two major forms in the fourteenth-century West, in its original Latin, often accompanied by moralizing commentaries, and in the French *Ovide moralisé*,[21] which incorporated substantial moralities into the poetry. Chaucer will occasionally use material from the Latin glossators, for instance in his descriptions of the pagan gods in the *Knight's Tale*; but in contrast to these medievalized versions of Ovid, his own reading of him concentrates to a remarkable degree on the stories alone, not on any exemplary or allegorical function they might be made to bear.

I.ii *The Decameron*

Two points emerge from such a survey of generic analogues to the *Canterbury Tales*: first, that Chaucer's own story-collection participates in a widespread

---

[19] *Ovid: Metamorphoses*, ed. and trans. Frank Justus Miller, Loeb Classical Library (Cambridge, Mass.: Harvard University Press; London: Heinemann, 1944, 1951), 5.295–345, 669–78.

[20] It has none the less been proposed as Chaucer's primary model for the *Tales* by Judson Boyce Allen and Theresa Anne Moritz, *A Distinction of Stories: Chaucer's Fair Chain of Narratives for Canterbury* (Columbus, Ohio: Ohio State University Press, 1981).

[21] Ed. C. de Boer, *Verhandelingen der Koninklijke Akademie van Wetenschappen te Amsterdam: Adfeeling Letterkunde,* Nieuwe Reeks, 15, 21, 30, 37, 43 (1915–38). There is no clear evidence that Chaucer knew the work.

current fashion for such works; and second, that it is strikingly different from most in the dynamics offered by its frame story, in the articulation of its tales, and in its refusal to offer any consistent moralization. Very few works offer any detailed resemblance; and of those that do, the *Decameron* is by far the closest, to the point where deliberate imitation, not coincidence, becomes the only plausible explanation.

The widespread past resistance to recognizing the *Decameron* as a source for, or even an influence on, the *Canterbury Tales* may have ideological as well as scholarly causes: the *Tales* were seen as representing Chaucer's quintessential Englishness.[22] The case against Chaucer's knowledge of the work is based on the lack of specific verbal parallels such as are characteristic of his borrowings from other works of Boccaccio's, notably the *Filostrato* and the *Teseida*. He never gives the impression of working extensively with a copy in front of him; he often uses a source other than Boccaccio even when he is telling a tale that also appears in the *Decameron*. There are, however, more parallels of both idea and phrasing in the two works than have generally been recognized, and those occur in precisely those areas that are unique to these two collections: in their handling of a frame for their storytelling that includes both multiple tellers and a fictional audience; in the interplay both writers invite between that fictional audience and their implied readers, and between fictional tellers and their self-presentation as authors; in their comments on the nature and function of fiction; and in their articulation of a story-collection that forgoes the more obvious kinds of thematic unity.

There is a big difference between acknowledging that Chaucer was not working with a copy of the *Decameron* on his desk, and denying that he knew it at all. A theory between the two has recurrently been proposed, that Chaucer had read or heard the *Decameron* while in Italy – conceivably even from an Italian merchant in London[23] – but did not have a copy of his own to set in front of him while he was writing.[24] This would explain his tendency to work from

---

[22] For further discussion, see Leonard Michael Koff's *Introduction* to *The Decameron and the Canterbury Tales: New Essays on an Old Question*, ed. Leonard Michael Koff and Brenda Deen Schildgen (Madison: Fairleigh Dickinson University Press; London: Associated University Presses, 2000), pp. 14–15.

[23] David Wallace, *Giovanni Boccaccio: Decameron* (Cambridge: Cambridge University Press, 1991), pp. 108–9, notes that as early as 1373 the work was "moving around the European trade routes with the merchant classes who figure so prominently in its pages"; on its links with the *Tales*, see p. 111.

[24] This possibility was put forward by R. K. Root in 1911 ("Chaucer and the *Decameron*," *Englische Studien* 44 [1909]: 1–7), and has been argued since by various other critics including J. S. P. Tatlock ("Boccaccio and the Plan of Chaucer's *Canterbury Tales*," *Anglia* 37 [1913]: 69–117); occasionally a closer connection has been argued, for instance by Donald McGrady ("Chaucer and the *Decameron* Reconsidered," *Chaucer Review* 12 [1977]: 1–26). For a more sceptical survey of the relationship between the works, see Robin Kirkpatrick, "In the Wake of the *Commedia*: Chaucer's *Canterbury Tales* and Boccaccio's *Decameron*," in *Chaucer and the Italian Trecento*, ed. Piero Boitani (Cambridge: Cambridge University Press, 1983), 201–30. Much of the belief that Chaucer did not know the *Decameron* can be traced back to the doubt expressed by Hubertis M. Cummings, *The Indebtedness of Chaucer's Works to the Italian Works of Boccaccio: A Review and Summary*, University of Cincinnati Studies, 10 (Cincinnati: University of Cincinnati, 1916), pp. 176–97, but his arguments are neither sufficiently detailed nor decisive. Peter G. Beidler provides an extensive review of past scholarship in

different sources for analogous stories, and the freedom of treatment he gives himself where no alternative source is known; but his deployment of similar methods and dynamics in articulating a collection would not require a text of the *Decameron* to hand, and the closest parallels show the kind of creative reinvention that would more plausibly come from thinking about Boccaccian ideas than from reworking his precise words.

The parallels can be summarised as follows.

(1) The *Decameron* is the only story-collection prior to the *Tales* where the stories are told by a series of narrators who agree to tell tales to each other as a pastime, and where these stories (unlike in the *Filocolo* and *Ameto*) are the *raison d'etre* of the work. In both, the *brigata* or *compaignye* who are to tell the stories are introduced in a naturalistic fashion that gives them an illusion of historical authenticity in contrast to their overtly fictional tales. Both groups are described as meeting up by chance (in the church of Santa Maria Novella, at the Tabard Inn); they agree to spend time together (to leave Florence for a succession of country houses, to travel to Canterbury as a group) and to tell stories under the direction of a master of ceremonies (a sovereign elected for each day in the *Decameron*, the Host in the *Tales*).

(2) Five of the Canterbury tales – the Reeve's, Clerk's, Merchant's, Franklin's and Shipman's[25] – have analogues in the *Decameron* (Reeve, Day IX,6; Clerk, X,10; Merchant, VII,9 (and see also II,10); Franklin, X,5; Shipman, VIII,1). In addition, there is a more distant analogue to the *Man of Law's Tale* (V,2); and both the *Pardoner's Prologue* (VI,10) and the *Miller's Tale* (III,4, with more distant links to VIII,7 and VII,4) share motifs with the *Decameron*. Two of these tales, the Shipman's and Franklin's, may well be using the *Decameron* as their immediate source; and fully a quarter of the tales in Chaucer's collection have analogues in the work. None of his other known or possible sources, nor any other medieval or Classical story-collection, comes near to offering such a high proportion of parallel stories.

The doubt over Chaucer's knowledge of the work results from the fact that in most of these instances either closer versions to Chaucer's are known from other sources, or else the similarities are too loose to prove direct indebtedness. This last is true even of the two *novelle*, VIII,1 and X,5, that provide the closest analogues known for the *Shipman*'s and *Franklin*'s *Tales*: in both, the plot outlines are the same but the details are extensively changed. One is therefore faced with a choice between an implausible coincidence in the proportion of

---

"Just Say Yes, Chaucer knew the *Decameron*: or, Bringing the *Shipman's Tale* out of Limbo," in Koff and Schildgen, eds, *The Decameron and the Canterbury Tales*, pp. 25–46. A detailed survey of the similarities between the two works is made by N. S. Thompson, *Chaucer, Boccaccio and the Debate of Love* (Oxford: Clarendon Press, 1996); and much of David Wallace's *Chaucerian Polity: Absolutist Lineages and Associational Forms in England and Italy* (Stanford: Stanford University Press, 1997) is devoted to the dialectic that can be constructed between them.

25 See Peter G. Beidler, "Chaucer's *Merchant's Tale* and the *Decameron*," *Italica* 50 (1973): 266–84, and his "Just say yes," for a full discussion of the extent of the work's possible contribution to the *Merchant's* and *Shipman's Tales*.

analogues, and the indisputable evidence in many instances for rival sources. The theory of memorial reconstruction would resolve this dilemma: Chaucer could have read or heard the *Decameron* (or parts of it: it is striking that the closest connections are with the tales of days VII, VIII, IX and X, and the *Conclusione*), and then sought out versions of the same stories to retell when he was working on the *Tales*.

(3)   In both works, the author remains as a first-person presence alongside the storytellers, and although this is done in very different ways (Boccaccio retains his separate identity outside the frame, Chaucer puts himself within it as part of his own fiction) they both use their presence to justify their work in strikingly similar terms. Boccaccio reminds his audience of his presence on three occasions: at the start; in an intervention before the Fourth Day's story-telling, when he tells a story of his own, so dissolving some of the distance between himself as author and his fictional narrators in a way that Chaucer takes much further; and in the *Conclusione dell'autore*. In the last of these he presents the most detailed defence of his work, using arguments that reappear in Chaucer's mouth in the *Tales*. Both insist that the broadness of some of their stories is due to the need for true reporting, that "Whoso shall telle a tale after a man,/ He moot reherce as ny as evere he kan/ Everich a word" (I.731–3), or that "io non pote' né doveva scrivere se non le raccontate," "I could not and ought not to have written them other than they were told";[26] and, like Chaucer, Boccaccio denies that he made the stories up himself, being rather a mere transcriber (*Conclusione* 1258.17). Both remind their readers that they may skip offensive tales, and that if they do not it is their fault (I.3176–86, in the *Miller's Prologue*, which does at least appear before the first of Chaucer's scurrilous stories; Boccaccio mischievously leaves his warning until the end,[27] though, as he also notes, he does provide summaries before each story that indicate something of the content – one could say, not enough). They both thus stress the moral responsibility of the reader over the author: "Blameth nat me if that ye chese amys," as Chaucer puts it (I.3181).

Both authors also stress from the start the pleasure and profit that their stories may bring. Boccaccio insists several times, from the *Proemio* forwards, that his stories are both entertaining and profitable, full of *sollazzevoli cose* and *utile consiglio* (*Proemio* 7.14), pleasurable matters and useful advice; Chaucer puts the same idea into the Host's requirement for *sentence* and *solaas* (I.798), but

---

[26] *Decameron*, ed. Vittore Branca, 2nd edn (Turin: Einaudi, 1984), *Conclusione* 1258.16; a closely similar remark is made earlier, "Se alcuna cosa in alcuna n'è, la qualità delle novelle l'hanno richiesta . . . se io quelle della lor forma trar non avessi voluto, altramenti raccontar non poterlo" (*Conclusione* 1255.4): "if anything in any [of the stories] is [unseemly], the nature of the tales required it . . . if I did not wish to distort their nature, I could not have told them otherwise." Compare the passage around the quotation given from the *Tales*, *GP*, I.725–36, and *MilP*, I.3173–5.

[27] "Chi va tra queste leggendo, lasci star quelle che pungono e quelle che dilettano legga," "You who go along reading these tales, leave aside the ones that give offence and read the ones that please" (*Conclusione* 1259.19); compare Chaucer's invitation to "turne over the leef and chese another tale" if one finds *harlotrie* offensive (*MilP*, I.3176–86).

restores the traditional order of the two (profit first, pleasure second) that Boccaccio inverts. That literature combines the profitable and the pleasant is of course a commonplace of long standing, but the contexts in which both authors use it are closely similar: the association of story-collections with exemplary tales and preaching anthologies means that their inclusion of distinctly immoral stories requires particular justification. Boccaccio explicitly stresses the therapeutic value of such recreation,[28] both by the setting in the Black Death and in the *Conclusione*; the tales of the pilgrimage are told as part of a celebration of recovery from sickness (I.18).

Boccaccio's disingenuous defence of polite language for impolite things is also an issue taken up in the *Tales* (*Conclusione* 1254–5.3–5, *CT* I.725–42). Boccaccio claims that his use of double-entendre avoids unseemliness, so that nothing he writes is *disonesta*; Chaucer denies *vileynye* on his own part, and blames his fictional pilgrims. Boccaccio attacks objectors who are more concerned about immoral words than deeds; Chaucer cites Plato to justify "large" language as "cosyn to the dede." Both, rather startlingly, conclude their apologies with references to Christ, Boccaccio with an appeal to be allowed the same *auttorità* as the painter who represents Christ's maleness (*Conclusione* 1256.6), Chaucer with an appeal to Christ's own example in speaking "ful brode" (*CT* I.739). There is another parallel to this passage of Boccaccio's, where he goes on to insist that the difference in representations of the Crucifixion does not affect the underlying truth, in Chaucer-pilgrim's excursus on literary theory in the prologue to *Melibee*, where he argues that the *sentence* of the Gospels is one although the words vary (VII.943–51).

To summarize: in both works, the authors use their presence to offer the same justifications for writing, the same excuses for their stories not all being moral, the same transferring of ethical responsibility to their audience or readers, and similar discussions of the relation of word to meaning.

(4)   Although the *Tales* goes much further than the *Decameron* in its generic and stylistic diversity,[29] which in turn reflects its greater variety of narrators, both offer a wider range of tales than the typical single-genre medieval story-collection, and both stress this diversity through giving varied audience reactions within the work. Although Boccaccio's tales are all assimilated to the *novella* while Chaucer highlights generic difference, he makes the variations within that form explicit: his narrators talk diversely of diverse things ("diverse cose diversamente parlando," Day IV,7, p. 547.5), and occasionally react in different ways (after Lauretta's song at the end of Day III, "diversamente da

[28] See Glending Olson, *Literature as Recreation in the Later Middle Ages* (Ithaca: Cornell University Press, 1982), especially pp. 155–83.

[29] On these qualities in the *Decameron*, see Thompson, *Chaucer, Boccaccio*, pp. 8–19, and Vittore Branca, *Boccaccio Medievale e nuovi studi sul Decamerone* (Florence: Sansoni, 1981), pp. 83–133, where he writes of the "bifrontalità del *Decamerone*, nei 'temi' e negli 'stili'" (p. 133), towards the comic on the one hand and the lyric or tragic on the other; the elegance and elaboration of style is however continuous, as he himself demonstrates (pp. 45–82).

diversi fu intesa," p. 456.18; compare Chaucer's "Diverse folk diversely they seyde," I.3857).[30]

Boccaccio's tales are stylistically more homogenous than Chaucer's, but both will mix styles for parodic purposes. Interestingly, both the *Merchant's Tale* and its Boccaccian analogue, VII,9, combine a high romance-style opening with bawdy content. Boccaccio further distinguishes his serious, pitiful and comic stories from each other by audience reaction, of debate (IV,4, X,4, 5 and 10), praise (X,8, 9), compassion (IV,2), or laughter (*passim*). Chaucer's wider range of genres is accompanied by a meticulous deployment, or parody, of rhetorical decorum, high-style genres being assigned to the *gentils* and low-style *cherles tales* to the low-born; and like Boccaccio, he sometimes underlines these differences by giving audience reactions: appreciation of the nobility of the Knight's, laughter after the Miller's, soberness after the Prioress's. When such a general response is not given, the Host often steps in with a reaction of his own, usually a notably inappropriate or inadequate one, so that the *Decameron* pattern of beginning the link to the next story with a response to the previous one is maintained.

(5)   To counter the risks created by this diversity of the collections flying apart, both Boccaccio and Chaucer develop connections of theme and motif between tales. In the *Decameron* this is done most explicitly through the setting of a specific topic for each day (the first and ninth excepted), though it is often treated with wit or parody. In II,1, for instance, the very first story told under this regime of prescribed theme, the specified reversal from misfortune to happiness is illustrated by the story of a man who narrowly avoids execution; in IV,2, the prescribed gloomy topic is subverted. Similar processes of parody and subversion occur in the Knight's and Miller's tales, on the pursuit of one woman by two men; in the Monk's and Nun's Priest's treatments of Fortune; and in the "marriage group" and all the other tales on the nature of women. Chaucer does not, in the work as we have it, divide his tales into separate days, though the pilgrimage schema would make such a division possible; but the groups of tales he did leave work on a principle of interrelatedness[31] less explicit than Boccaccio's but otherwise closely similar.

In addition, Boccaccio's tellers will often point out a specific connection with the previous story as a trigger for their own, or sometimes refer back some distance to a common motif (e.g. dreams in IV,5 and 6 and IX,7), in ways comparable to Chaucer's picking up of motifs across tales: he too places dreams at significant points in the *Monk's* and *Nun's Priest's Tales,* the Wife of Bath is recalled in the Clerk's Envoy and by Justinus in the *Merchant's Tale.* Boccaccio takes this reappearance of characters much further than Chaucer, but confines them within the *novelle*: the adventures of Calendrino and his companions recur on several occasions (VIII,3, 6, 9; IX,3, 5). Chaucer by contrast goes further in

---

[30] The point is developed by Thompson, *Chaucer, Boccaccio,* p. 17.
[31] See Cooper, *Structure,* pp. 108–207.

creating some kind of interplay between the characters of his frame and their counterparts within the tales, as tellers use their stories for purposes of insult to wives, friars, summoners, millers and so on. Even this has an approximate parallel in the *Decameron*, when the start of the sixth day's storytelling is delayed by the dispute between the servants Licisca and Tindaro over a story strikingly similar to those narrated by their masters and mistresses; and this event in the frame affects the later *novelle* when Dioneo recalls it in the evening in order to prescribe the topic of the storytelling for the seventh day.

Some of the connections between *novelle* are more casual: that two tales of the same day may be set in the same area or town, for instance. VII,3 is a story of fornication between a mother and her child's godfather, set in Siena; in the tenth tale of the day, Dioneo recalls this to introduce his own story with the same plot elements and setting. A similar relationship is found in the *Tales* between the Miller's and Reeve's tales of adultery with their Oxford and Cambridge settings; Chaucer inherited the Lombard setting of the *Clerk's Tale* from Petrarch, but he changed the location of the *Merchant's Tale* to match, presumably in order to pair with it.

Chaucer's tales are often linked by contrast within a larger similarity – the *Knight's* and *Miller's Tales*, the *Second Nun's* and *Canon's Yeoman's* – and this too is a principle already made explicit in the *Decameron*, where, for instance, stories of tricks played on men by women will be countered by one played by a man on a woman (VIII,1). He is also fond of motifs of overgoing, where the aesthetic competition between stories turns into requital or revenge; and here too there are parallels in the *Decameron*, not between tellers – who in contrast to Chaucer's are consistently polite and courteous, more given to denigrating themselves than each other – but in the stories themselves. So VIII,7, about a guiler beguiled, is capped by VIII,10, in which Dioneo promises to surpass the pleasure already given by such stories by telling of the deception of the greatest deceiver so far. Here the *Tales* offer parallels in such connections between stories as the Reeve's tale of two students' sexual revenge on their deceiver, itself told as revenge against the Miller's tale of one student's successful adultery, and the Friar's and Summoner's tales of the deception of their venal *alter teipse*.

None of these many and various parallels in Boccaccio offers an indisputable *verbal* source for any of the tales or framing material found in Chaucer. What they do show, over and over again, is a convergence of interpretations as to what a story-collection might be, and of solutions to the problem of how to articulate such a very diverse array. The most obvious interpretation of this convergence is that it represents Chaucer's own elaboration of a model he recalled from the *Decameron*. The alternative possibility, that Boccaccio and Chaucer independently invented similar connective schemes for their tales and told many of the same stories, appears increasingly untenable as the parallels mount up. The *Decameron*, it may safely be said, is Chaucer's primary model for his collection of stories.

II. *Debate*

The social and moral variety of Chaucer's pilgrims and the stylistic and generic diversity of their tales are not ends in themselves. They enable Chaucer to set up a series of different and opposed assumptions about human existence and experience, and to present various attitudes to specific issues that were matters of dispute in the larger world. The narrative articulation of the tales works through the Host's calling on one pilgrim to follow another; but the tales are also connected as a series of elements in a debate, or in several debates. The "marriage debate" is the most familiar of these, but it has tended to be treated as an autonomous unit within the larger work; in fact, the whole of the *Canterbury Tales* participates in that fascination with opposites that characterizes the Middle Ages, and that found expression in the debates of the law courts, royal and baronial councils, Parliament, and the schools, in the entire academic method established by works such as Peter Lombard's *Sentences*, and in debate poetry.[32] Debate thus took up a far larger space in the ordinary conduct of life than in the modern age, being the medium of much intellectual activity and of the procedures of administration, and extending beyond serious public life into the realm of entertainment, debate for its own sake. This happened even within the schools, where positions in a disputation were often assigned, so that whether or not the disputant believed in the thesis he was arguing was irrelevant; it was the quality of the argument that was all-important. So, in 1407, the "Scholar-Errant" John Argentyn of Strasbourg arrived in the University of Cambridge and challenged all comers to dispute with him.[33] That such debates took place in public underlines the fact that they were occasions for enjoyment as well as for the practice of professional skills; exercise and display, indeed, took priority over the discovery of a concluding or conclusive truth.

Such a shift of dialectic towards the aesthetic is taken a large step further in the fashion for debating *demandes d'amour*; and in debate poetry, the popularity of which spans the Middle Ages from the ninth century to the fifteenth. Jean de Meun's continuation of the *Roman de la rose* itself constitutes an extended debate in narrative form. Of formal debate poems, some, such as the *Thrush and the Nightingale*, come to a conclusion: the question disputed by the birds, of whether women are a good thing or not (a perennial favourite, also extensively debated over the *Tales* well beyond the limits of the "marriage group"), is resolved by the Nightingale's appeal to the example of the Virgin. Many others are not resolved: the *Owl and the Nightingale* ends before the judgement is given, and it is hard to see what decision could do justice to the issues set out in

---

[32] See Thomas L. Reed, jr, *Middle English Debate Poetry and the Aesthetics of Irresolution* (Columbia, Missouri: University Missouri Press, 1990), pp. 41–96, for a study of the institutional context of literary debates. John W. Conlee's Introduction to his *Middle English Debate Poetry: A Critical Anthology* (East Lansing: Colleagues Press, 1991) notes how a "preoccupation with the interaction of opposites" was a "fundamental habit of mind" (p. xi). For the Latin tradition of debate poetry, see Hans Walther, *Das Streitgedicht in der lateinischen Literatur des Mittelalters* (Munich: Beck, 1920).

[33] Reed, *Debate Poetry*, p. 52.

the poem. Various specific topics are argued in the course of the birds' dispute, but the overarching issue is an irreconcilable difference of attitudes represented in the poem by the fact that owls are owls and nightingales nightingales, and neither is wrong to be so. Chaucer is highly unlikely to have known the work, but in the *Parliament of Fowls* he offers an analogous scheme, in which a specific *demande d'amour* as to which of the three birds of prey (noble birds, in the medieval hierarchy of species) should win the hand of the formel is hijacked by the array of views on courtship, love and faithfulness presented and represented by the lower birds. The cuckoo's or the goose's solutions would be wrong for the eagle or the turtle dove; but their rightness for a cuckoo or a goose constitutes at least part of the point of the poem. The lack of any answer to the initial *demande* may have some topical reference, but more significant within the text is the natural and continuing irreconcilability of different mind sets, different assumptions about behaviour, beliefs, priorities, and the metaphysics of the universe: precisely the same differences that characterize the Canterbury pilgrims and the tales they tell.

The *Parliament* is especially interesting in relation to the *Tales* in that it illustrates how debate can be conducted on both overt and latent levels. Explicit are the rival claims of the birds of prey to have the formel's hand, a debate conducted by all the disputants on the same premises of desert and reward; and also the opposing attitudes to the whole idea of courtship and service, which emerge out of contrasting assumptions about the conduct of life and love. Implicit is the dialectic set up by the structure of the poem, with its opposition between the deathly sensuality of the Temple of Priapus and the regenerative sexuality of the Hill of Nature – though the dialectic is announced by the double inscription over the gate, of the entrance as the way to destruction and death or fertility and bliss. The *Canterbury Tales* takes such a structure much further. The different social estates and their views on the world take the place of the hierarchy of birds. Some specific topics are debated: the "woman question" is unusual in the work for the degree of self-consciousness accorded to it as a debate, with the Wife of Bath directly challenging the orthodox line-up of traditional opponents in her Prologue. Others are recognizable from their familiarity as issues of dispute in broader medieval culture: for instance, the issue of fortune *versus* fate *versus* Providence, debated between (among others) the prisoner "Boethius" and Philosophy, or, as the Nun's Priest notes, by Bishop Bradwardine (VII.3242), is discussed as an issue in itself in the *Knight's Tale*, but then pursued more generally through the way in which later tales assume one principle or another in presenting their action: chance in the *Miller's Tale*, Fortune in the *Monk's Tale*, rival principles of fate (in the shape of the stars, II.190–203, 295–315) and Providence in the *Man of Law's Tale*, the absolute divine control of events in the *Second Nun's Tale*.

This last debate is itself one aspect of a wider issue in the *Tales*, of secular and spiritual attitudes to life, the claims of the world against the claims of God; and here too a tradition of debate poetry encloses the *Tales*, with debates on the subject between the Soul and the Body, or between the Part Sensitive and the

Part Intellective.[34] The positions adopted in such explicit debates within the *Tales* are endorsed by the implicit oppositions set up by the larger dialectic structures of the work that oppose romance to saint's life, saint's life to fabliau. Opposed genres and tellers similarly foreground sublimated love or virginity or amoral animal sexuality or plain lust. The women who come close to embodying the cardinal and theological virtues – Custance's fortitude, Virginia's temperance, Prudence's prudence, Griselda's justice (shown in her rendering of due obedience, which was taken as a primary expression of justice in the Middle Ages), Cecilia's faith, hope and charity[35] – present a silent dialectic opposition to the Wife's enthusiastic espousal of carnality, insubordination to one's husband and all the rest of the charges traditionally laid by men against women.

These large oppositions of this world against the next, fleshly caricature against spiritual sublimation, Carnival against Lent, have a history that goes deep into medieval culture. Of the debates that express such a dichotomy, one of the most thought-provoking in relation to the *Tales* is the *Dialogue of Solomon and Marcolphus*. This consists of a series of aphorisms delivered by the wise king Solomon and capped – Chaucer's term *quited* would be more accurate – by one-liners from the witty and subversive churl Marcolphus. The *Dialogue* originated in Latin some time before the eleventh century;[36] it was not translated into Middle English until the late fifteenth century, but the work was familiar enough in England for the *Proverbs of Hendyng*, widely known in the fourteenth century, to describe Hendyng as "Marcolves sone," and John Audelay and Lydgate also refer to Marcolphus.[37] There is no firm evidence that Chaucer knew the work, but its method, of juxtaposing "official" and "unofficial" views of the world and everything in it, constitutes an epitome of the structural methods of the *Tales*. Solomon speaks with the sober authority of orthodoxy: the four evangelists uphold the world. Marcolphus responds with a total refusal to be impressed and a measure of cheerful obscenity: four props hold up the latrine to keep men from falling.[38] Solomon's views on women, both in favour and (most often) against, were part of the standard antifeminist debates of the Middle Ages, and Chaucer cites the Biblical ones frequently; the *Dialogue* adds others, and counterpoints the king's conventional wisdom with the churl's sardonic streetwiseness. So Solomon's sententious

> A good wyf and a fayre is to hir hosbande a pleasure

is quitted by Marcolphus'

---

[34] For Middle English debates between body and soul, see Conlee, *Debate Poetry*, pp. xxiv–vii and 3–62; for the *Dialogue between the Part Sensitive and the Part Intellective*, see pp. 193–9.

[35] On the secular heroines, see Denise N. Baker, "Chaucer and Moral Philosophy: The Virtuous Women of *The Canterbury Tales*," *Medium Ævum* 60 (1991): 241–56; on Cecilia, see *SNP*, VIII.110, 96–7, 118.

[36] *Salomon et Marcolfus*, ed. Walter Benary (Heidelberg: C. Winter, 1914), p. vii.

[37] *The Dialogue or Communing between the Wise King Salomon and Marcolphus*, facsimile of Gerard Leeu's edition of 1492 ed. E. Gordon Duff (London: Lawrence and Bullen, 1892), p. xviii.

[38] *Salomon*, ed. Benary, p. 9 #38.

A potfull of mylke must be kept wele from the katte.[39]

The shift in register from formality to low-style animal imagery, and in focus from ideals of marriage to appetite and availability, is closely analogous to the stylistic and thematic counterpointing of the *Knight's* and *Miller's Tales*. In the more discursive part of the work, Marcolphus brings in a woman to answer Solomon's antifeminism; she points out to him that it makes much better sense to allow women rather than men to have multiple spouses, since a man cannot manage seven wives but a woman with seven husbands would have no trouble.[40] The same thought seems to have crossed Chaucer's mind, with his heptagamous and henpecked Chauntecleer and the Wife of Bath's continuing enthusiasm for finding husband number six.

Solomon and Marcolphus is a powerfully suggestive analogue to Chaucer's methods in the *Tales*, but not necessarily more than that. The history of debate poetry, and of debates within poetry, is so dense as to make the identification of specific sources for Chaucer's various procedures near to impossible. Some sources and analogues can be identified for the bird debates of the *Parliament*, but by the time one reaches the *Tales*, the *Parliament* itself is a much closer ana-logue than any of its own sources. A number of those are none the less sugges-tive in relation to the *Tales* in that the topic that their birds debate is the merits of one estate against another, whether knights or clerks make better lovers.[41] Chaucer's Clerk is at odds, not with the Knight, but with the virago Wife of Bath, with her sharp spurs and buckler-sized hat; and it has been suggested that her successive treatments of the love-making of a clerk (the sexually adept Jankin) and of a knight (the initially brutal, later reluctant, protagonist of her tale), and their conversion into compliant and respectful lovers, may owe some-thing to these debates.[42] Other debate poems use different estates or professions as protagonists – clerk and husbandman, sailor and farmer, courtier and soldier.[43] Chaucer too sets representatives of the social estates at odds – Miller and Reeve, Summoner and Friar – but for reasons that have their origins in real-life professional rivalries rather than in literary texts: it is he himself who turns their prologues and tales into what amount to paired debate poems.

---

[39] *Dialogue*, ed. Duff, f. 4a; *Salomon*, ed. Benary, p. 6 #8, " 'Mulier bona et pulchra ornamentum est viro suo' – 'Olla plena de lacte debet a catto custodiri.' "

[40] *Salomon*, ed. Benary, p. 39, cap. XV: "Quid faciet, si septem habuerit? Supra vires hominis est istud facere. Melius est enim, ut unaqueque mulier septem habeat maritos."

[41] They are collected in translation in *Chaucer's Dream Poetry: Sources and Analogues*, ed. and trans. B. A. Windeatt, Chaucer Studies 7 (Cambridge: D. S. Brewer, 1982), pp. 85–119; the texts are edited by Charles Oulmont, *Les Débats du clerc et du chevalier dans la littérature populaire du Moyen-Age* (Paris: Champion, 1911). Two of these, *Melior et Ydoine* and *Blancheflour et Florence*, are Anglo-Norman.

[42] Paule Mertens-Fonck, "Life and Fiction in the *Canterbury Tales*: A New Perspective," in *Poetics: Theory and Practice in Medieval English Literature*, ed. Piero Boitani and Anna Torti, J. A. W. Bennett Memorial Lectures, 7th series (Cambridge: D. S. Brewer, 1991), pp. 105–15: see especially pp. 108–9. John Alford has further suggested that the Clerk and Wife are presented so as to recall the tradi-tional rivalry between Logic and Rhetoric: see "The Wife of Bath *versus* the Clerk of Oxford: What their Rivalry Means," *Chaucer Review* 21 (1986): 108–32.

[43] Conlee, *Debate Poetry*, pp. xvi, 210–15.

Chaucer's avoidance of any conclusion, or any judgement between them, is itself broadly typical of one major element of the debate genre. Thomas L. Reed's study has shown how unresolved debates characteristically stress the multiple, the temporal, the mimetic, the ambivalent, the irreverent, and the recreational.[44] The rival speakers, rival tales and rival ideas put forward in the *Tales* replay such a model on a grand scale.

III. *Poetic contests*

The *Canterbury Tales* is unique among story-collections in being organised as a competition, with a prize: a *soper at oure aller cost* on the pilgrims' return to the Tabard. This is not an element found in the *Decameron*, despite the *brigata*'s occasional capping of each other's tales; its probable sources lie elsewhere, in medieval poetic traditions previously connected with lyrics rather than story-collections, and which are known through both literary texts and historical records. It may appear one of the more fanciful elements of the frame, but it has antecedents in real life as well as literature.

Poetic contests have a long history, stretching back at least as far as Theocritus and the Greek dramatists. The literary history of medieval contests takes three major forms. The Virgilian pastoral singing-match, itself derived from Theocritus, converged with debate in the early Middle Ages, so that the rivalry between singers extended both to the quality of song and to the quality of argument.[45] Examples of such Classically-derived pastoral singing-matches could conceivably have been known to Chaucer (Boccaccio's *Ameto*, for instance, contains one, in which rival shepherds sing in support of the worldly *versus* the ascetic life, or perhaps the active *versus* the contemplative[46]); but if they were, he did not develop the possibilities they offered. Poetic contests and competitions that owed nothing to Classical models were central to Welsh culture in the fourteenth century,[47] though England was generally much less permeable to Welsh culture than it was to French. Provence, France and England invented their own forms of contest in the *tenso* and the *jeu-parti*, which again combined debate with poetic skill, and the flyting, which stressed the skilful deployment of abusive rhetoric. Such forms were given an acknowledged place in courtly, academic and even ecclesiastical settings. In the late twelfth century, London schoolboys engaged in verse contests of both the intellectual and vituperative kinds; and a more elaborate flyting between Michael of

---

[44] Reed, *Debate Poetry*, pp. 38–9, gives a summary of the opposing qualities of resolved and unresolved debates; he discusses the "aesthetics of irresolution" over the course of the whole book.

[45] Helen Cooper, *Pastoral: Mediaeval into Renaissance* (Ipswich: D. S. Brewer, 1977), pp. 13–15.

[46] *Commedia delle Ninfe Fiorentine (Ameto)*, ed. Antonio Enzo Quaglio (Florence: Sansoni, 1963), pp. 47–52.

[47] See A. O. H. Jarman and Gwilym Rees Hughes, *A Guide to Welsh Literature* Vol. I (Swansea: Christopher Davis, 1976), pp. 134, 144, on the competitions (first recorded in 1176); the two winners, one poet and one musician, were rewarded with a chair and a prize. On the contest between Dafydd ap Gwilym and Gruffudd Gryg, see Rachel Bromwich, *Dafydd ap Gwilym*, Writers of Wales (Cardiff: University of Wales Press, 1974), pp. 66–71.

Cornwall and Henry of Avranches, which took the form of a mock law-suit in rhyming Latin couplets, was reputedly performed by the poets over the course of three separate occasions in 1254–5 before judges including the Abbot of Westminster, the Dean of St Paul's, the Chancellor and Masters of the University of Cambridge, and assorted bishops.[48] Later vernacular poets with as high an opinion of their writings as Skelton and Dunbar were as anxious to preserve their flytings as they were their more courtly or polite poetry. Similarly, tales in Chaucer that compete in ill-will and abuse – the Miller's and Reeve's, the Friar's and Summoner's – can do so with no concomitant downgrading of their rhetorical skill. The "debate" element is subsumed into the larger idea of the contest.

The close connection of debate with poetic rivalry is most strikingly illustrated in the *jeux-partis*, in which two poets would argue a *demande d'amour*. Most of the surviving French examples come from a single source, the "confrerie des jongleurs et bourgeois d'Arras," a fraternity that existed to promote poetry and song.[49] Such societies, familiar as the *Meistersinger* in Germany and known in French as *puys* (probably because the earliest, dating from 1229, met at Notre Dame du Puy at Valenciennes), were founded in a number of European towns in the thirteenth and fourteenth centuries, including London. The form taken by the London Puy is especially interesting in relation to the *Tales*, for its annual assembly consisted of a competition for the best song, both music and words being judged; and those members who came provided with a song received their dinner free, at the expense of the rest of the *compaignye* – the statutes use the same word for the society as Chaucer does for his association of pilgrims.[50]

These details, together with a great many more about the conduct of the *confrerie*, are known from its surviving statutes, which were twice supplemented[51] to put the financial, poetic and religious provisions of the society (for it, like devotional and parish guilds,[52] had pious aims too) on a clearer footing. The fraternity and its associated annual assembly, "une feste ke hom apele 'Pui,'" were founded in the late thirteenth century by merchants of the city,

---

[48] A. G. Rigg, *A History of Anglo-Latin Literature 1066–1422* (Cambridge: Cambridge University Press, 1992), pp. 188–91, 193–8.

[49] *Recueil général des jeux-partis français*, ed. Arthur Långfors, Societé des Anciens Textes Français (Paris: Firmin Didot, 1926); he gives biographies of the participants from the Arras *confrerie*, pp. xxvi–lii.

[50] On the London Puy, see Anne F. Sutton, "Merchants, Music and Social Harmony: the London Puy and its French and London contexts, *circa* 1300," *London Journal* 17 (1992): 1–17. The statutes and supplementary articles are printed in the *Liber Custumarum*, in Vol. II part I of the *Monumenta Gildhallae Londoniensis*, ed. Henry Thomas Riley, Rolls Series (London: Longman, 1860), pp. 216–28 (see in particular pp. 225, 216); a summary is given on pp. cxxix–xxxi. The later articles express a concern that the contest is turning into a poetry competition, and insist that music is required too (p. 225).

[51] There is a new set of articles introduced by a fresh proem, *Liber*, p. 219, but these still speak of the founding of a chapel as a pious hope for the future; by p. 227, the chapel has been founded, and the concern is with its financing.

[52] On the activities of these in the later Middle Ages, see Eamon Duffy, *The Stripping of the Altars* (New Haven and London: Yale University Press, 1992), pp. 141–54.

en le honour de Dieu, Madame Seinte Marie, touz Seinz, e toutes Seintes; e en
le honour nostre Seignour le Roy e touz les Barons du pais; e por loial amour
ensaucier. Et por ceo qe la ville de Lundres soit renomee de touz biens en tuz
lieus; et por ceo qe jolietes, pais, honestez, douceur, deboneiretes, e bon
amour, sanz infinite, soit maintenue.   (*Liber custumarum*, 216)

[To the honour of God, our Lady Saint Mary, and all saints male and female;
and in honour of our lord the King and all the barons of this land; and for the
promotion of loyal friendship. And in order that the city of London may be
renowned for all good things in all places; and in order that good fellowship,
peace, and sweet and courtly pastimes, and true love, may be maintained
without limit.]

Its members and benefactors included the great merchant Henry le Waleys,
mayor of the city on numerous occasions (1273–74, 1281–84, 1297–99); he had
close connections with continental Europe too – he was also mayor of Bordeaux
in 1275 – and it may have been such international links that inspired the founding of the fraternity: its statutes make careful provision about the subscriptions
of members who are out of the country on the occasion of the *feste*. A prince
was appointed each year to head the *confrerie dou Pui* and sort out quarrels
between its members. He and his successor, together with selected assessors,
would judge the songs; a copy of the best one was hung on the wall of the hall
below the prince's blazon, and its composer crowned. One of the winning
songs, by one Renaus de Hoiland, survives in the Public Record Office, with a
rough crown drawn onto it.[53] At the conclusion of the feast (for which a not too
expensive menu is prescribed in the later articles, to avoid excessive costs), the
winning poet, having enjoyed his free meal, rode through the city between the
outgoing and incoming princes to the latter's house, where all the members
would dance, drink once, and then return home on foot.

In its broader organization, the London Puy resembled a devotional guild, of
the kind that Chaucer's Guildsmen belong to: an association for the purposes of
piety and mutual benevolence. The fraternity was associated with the building
of the chapel of the Guildhall in 1299, and Henry le Waleys gave the Puy an
annuity of five marks to maintain a chaplain there.[54] It did however differ from
many religious guilds in one particular, in that it did not admit women to its
feste: although, as the supplementary articles that introduce this rule note, ladies
will be the subject of every *chaunt roiale*, members must be reminded by their
absence that they are bound to honour all ladies at all times and in all places,
when they are present as well as when they are not.

---

[53] PRO E 163/22/1/2. The words and music of the first stanza, which begins "Si tost c'amis entant a bien
amer," are printed by Christopher Page in *The Cambridge Guide to the Arts in Britain*, Vol. II, ed.
Boris Ford (Cambridge: Cambridge University Press, 1988), p. 237; Page notes that "the musical notes
are messy and seem to have been copied too soon after a feast." See also John Stevens, "Alphabetical
check-list of Anglo-Norman Songs c. 1150–c. 1350," *Plainsong and Medieval Music* 3 (1994): 1–22
(15–17).
[54] *Calendar of Letter-Books preserved among the Archives of the Corporation of the City of London
at the Guildhall*, 11 vols., ed. Reginald R. Sharpe (London: printed by John Edward Francis for the
Corporation, 1899–1912), *E* 1–2 (flyleaf).

It is not known how long the Puy continued. Henry le Waleys died in 1301;[55] another early member, the vintner John of Cheshunt, who had been its third prince, was dead by 1310;[56] the last reference to the Puy in the records is from 1304.[57] It may well, however, have been a later generation of members who revised the statutes so as to prevent the excessive expenditure of earlier princes;[58] it could have survived a couple of decades into the fourteenth century, closer to the date when the *Liber Custumarum* was completed, or conceivably even longer. What is clear is that the idea of writing in competition was not only current on the continent in the fourteenth century, but was prominent in England in the generation of Chaucer's London grandparents, and among the same social group of merchants and vintners from which he himself took his origins. His Canterbury pilgrims form a looser fraternity, but of a not dissimilar kind: they agree to associate as a *compaignye* gathered for a mixture of literary and pious purposes; they are headed by a temporary lord who will judge their poetry, and who endeavours to maintain goodwill between its members (III.1288); and the climax of their association will be the prize supper.

IV. *Pilgrimages and storytelling*

The evidence for pilgrims amusing themselves with storytelling is largely literary but need not therefore be fictional. The scenario offered by the *Tales*, of thirty mounted pilgrims listening to a narration by one of their number, is not naturalistic, but it is probably an exaggeration of a historical practice. One of the references closest to Chaucer occurs in the Prologue to *Piers Plowman*, a work he probably knew. There, the pilgrims are one of the many estates represented on the Field of Folk:

> Pilgrymes and palmeres plighten hem togidere
> To seken Seint Jame and seintes in Rome;

[55] For a recent summary biography of Henry le Waleys, see Gwyn A. Williams, *Medieval London: From Commune to Capital*, corrected edn (London: Athlone Press, 1970), pp. 333–5.

[56] John of Cheshunt is named as the third prince in the *Liber Custumarum*, p. 219, where it is noted that he instituted the custom of presenting a candle at St Martin's le Grand. Of three Johns of Cheshunt in the records (a taverner; a feathermonger who moved into the wine trade, which was wide open to entrepreneurs, and who became one of the leading citizens of London; and a weaver who appears rather later), he is almost certainly to be identified with the second. He is described as "late vintner" in a record of 1310 relating to his heir (*Letter-Book B*, 254 (fol. 112)). Anne F. Sutton suggests that his tavern might have been a possible location for the Puy, in "The *Tumbling Bear* and its patrons: a venue for the London Puy and Mercery," in *London and Europe in the Later Middle Ages*, ed. Julia Boffey and Pamela King, Westfield Publications in Medieval Studies 9 (London: Centre for Medieval and Renaissance Studies, Queen Mary and Westfield College; Turnhout: Brepols, 1995), pp. 85–110.

[57] In *Letter-Book C*, 138–9 (fol. 84b), John le Mirouer was ordered to pay 100 shillings to the work of the Chapel of the Blessed Mary of the Pui. This case provides one tenuous link between those associated with the Puy and the Chaucer family: among those who imposed the fine was William de Leyre, who in 1301 claimed rent against a tenement from members of the Heyron family, including Chaucer's step-grandfather; the property eventually passed to Chaucer's father in 1349 (Vincent B. Redstone and Lilian J. Redstone, "The Heyrons of London: A Study in the Social Origins of Geoffrey Chaucer," *Speculum* 12 [1937]: 182–95, pp. 190, 184–5).

[58] *Liber Custumarum*, pp. 225–6.

Wenten forth in hire wey with many wise tales,
And hadden leve to lyen al hire lif after.[59]

"Telling tales" here refers first to storytelling on the road and then to tall stories told afterwards, travellers' tales of the kind Chaucer also ascribes to pilgrims in the *House of Fame* (2122–3). The casualness of these references indicates that the association of pilgrims and storytelling was a familiar one. Non-poetic testimony to the dual practice of entertainment on the road and tall stories afterwards comes from the Lollard William Thorpe, who describes pilgrims as given to singing "rowtinge songis" and playing bagpipes (both practices that the Archbishop of Canterbury, his interrogator, defended) and afterwards being "greete iangelers, tale tellers and lyeris."[60]

Some of these exaggerations and inventions – not all of which were recognized as such – survive to form a body of pilgrimage literature, in which pilgrims recount their real or, more often, imaginary experiences in exotic places: *Mandeville's Travels* was the runaway success in this field. It was not necessary even to go to Jerusalem to acquire such a fund of travellers' tales: Thorpe and Langland suggest that Galicia, Italy or even England would do just as well. Against this background, the *Canterbury Tales* is most distinctive for its difference from the genre to which at first glance it might seem to belong;[61] but this generic expectation became something of a self-fulfilling prophecy, since by the sixteenth century "canterbury tale" had become a synonym for a cock-and-bull story.[62] Chaucer himself associates his pilgrims' tales with pastimes rather than lies; but he also differentiates the illusory naturalism of the frame from the overt fabulousness of the stories. In telling pilgrims' tales, he is by implication entering a larger debate about the status of fiction, fable and lying.

---

[59] *William Langland: The Vision of Piers Plowman, A Complete Edition of the B-Text*, ed. A. V. C. Schmidt, second edn (London: J. M. Dent, 1995), Prologue 46–9. The passage appears in almost identical form in all three versions of the text.

[60] *The Testimony of William Thorpe, 1407*, in *Two Wycliffite Tracts*, ed. Anne Hudson, EETS O.S. 301 (1993), pp. 64–5.

[61] Donald R. Howard, *Writers and Pilgrims: Medieval Pilgrimage Narratives and their Posterity* (Berkeley: University of California Press, 1980), pp. 77–103.

[62] *OED*, s.v. Canterbury, A.1.

The Reeve's Tale

PETER G. BEIDLER

One of the most popular fabliaux in medieval Europe was the story of two young men who trick their host, one by seducing his daughter and the other by making love to his wife after the shifting of a cradle containing his baby. Chaucer clearly did not invent the broad outlines of what is sometimes called the "cradle-trick story" that he adapted for his own literary purposes in the *Reeve's Tale*. Though none of the analogues – at least not in the forms that survive – can be said to represent "the source" of Chaucer's tale, the story itself was apparently so widely known that it is almost certain that Chaucer had read at least one, and quite possibly more than one, of the versions presented here. In addition to the cradle-trick story in the *Reeve's Tale*, there are three surviving versions of it in French, one in Flemish, one in Italian, and two in German, all of them almost surely predating Chaucer. There are also several later analogues. A central scholarly problem in dealing with so many analogues is determining which among them are closest to the *Reeve's Tale*.

Frederick Furnival attempted to solve the problem by publishing two French analogues, Text A of *Le meunier et les .II. clers* and Jean Bodel's *De Gombert et des deus clers*.[1] In an influential study, Germaine Dempster later stated that only the two French texts of *Le meunier et les .II. clers* (A and B) should be

---

[1] *Originals and Analogues of Some of Chaucer's Canterbury Tales*, orig. 1892, rpt. by the Chaucer Society, 2nd Series, vol. 7 (London: Oxford UP, 1928), pp. 87–102.

seriously considered by Chaucerians interested in working with "the source" of the *Reeve's Tale*, and she concluded that some near relative of Text B was most likely Chaucer's source.[2] Dempster's arguments persuaded W. M. Hart to disregard all other known analogues and present only texts A and B of *Le meunier* in his chapter on the *Reeve's Tale* in Bryan and Dempster.[3] More recently, however, scholars have taken a broader view of the relationship of Chaucer's tale to the other versions of the story. Rather than focus their attention on discovering "the source" of the tale, they study its relationship to several possible sources. Benson and Andersson, in their extensive survey of the *Reeve's Tale* and five of its analogues, compare the various treatments of several common features, including the setting for the tale, the trip of the young men, their lodging, the theft of their grain, their lovemaking with the host's daughter and wife, the tussle with the host, and the beating of the host.[4] Although Benson and Andersson do not print the Flemish *Een bispel van .ij. clerken* (which they erroneously call "a translation" of *De Gombert* [p. 85]), they print Text A of *Le meunier* (along with seven bracketed lines inserted from Text B), Bodel's *De Gombert*, the two German analogues, and two shorter post-medieval analogues: a Latin anecdote and a Danish ballad.

The last two of these, both because they clearly postdate Chaucer and because they are distant in plot, characterization, and literary approach from the *Reeve's Tale*, are not included here. Nor do I include the two German tales, *Das Studentenabenteuer* and *Irregang und Girregar*. There is no evidence that Chaucer knew German, was familiar with German literature, or traveled in Germany. More important, the plots of the German analogues are so far from that of the *Reeve's Tale* that no good case can be made for direct influence. Instead, I have chosen to print, for reasons discussed below, four analogues to the *Reeve's Tale* that Chaucer could quite easily have known: the two texts of the French *Le meunier et les .II. clers*, the Flemish *Een bispel van .ij. clerken*, and the sixth tale of the ninth day of Boccaccio's Italian *Decameron*.

The importance of the two versions of the French *Le meunier et les .II. clers* has been acknowledged by all scholars who have examined the relationship of the *Reeve's Tale* to its possible sources.[5] These fabliaux are the closest analogues to Chaucer's story, and it is likely that he knew some form of one or both of them. Only in these two texts is the host, like Chaucer's Simkyn, a

---

[2] "On the Source of the *Reeve's Tale*," *Journal of English and Germanic Philology* 29 (1930): 473–88.

[3] "The Reeve's Tale" in *Sources and Analogues of Chaucer's Canterbury Tales*, ed. W. F. Bryan and Germaine Dempster (Chicago: University of Chicago Press, 1941; rpt. New York: Humanities Press, 1958), pp. 124–47.

[4] Larry D. Benson and Theodore M. Andersson, *The Literary Context of Chaucer's Fabliaux: Texts and Translations* (Indianapolis: Bobbs-Merrill, 1971), pp. 79–201. They present these comparisons in a four-page facing chart format on pp. 80–3. See also Erik Hertog's *Chaucer's Fabliaux as Analogues* (Leuven: Leuven University Press, 1991) for a somewhat different analysis of the plot elements in the *Reeve's Tale* as compared with its various possible sources. Hertog gives us in chart-format (pp. 66–76) variations on several large and small narrative sequences.

[5] See, for example, W. M. Hart, "The Reeve's Tale: A Comparative Study of Chaucer's Narrative Art," *PMLA* 23 (1908): 1–44, and Roger T. Burbridge, "Chaucer's *Reeve's Tale* and the Fabliau 'Le meunier et les .II. clers,'" *Annuale Médiévale* 12 (1971): 30–6.

miller who robs the grain that the two young men, like Chaucer's John and Aleyn, bring to his mill to be ground. Text A of *Le meunier* is the more complete and has a more polished style than Text B, which, as Dempster notes, "spoils its text by uncalled-for repetitions of previous lines, which in their new surroundings do not always make sense, omits some lines indispensable for the understanding of what follows, and makes a sad mess of rimes" (p. 473). On the other hand, B has several plot elements lacking in A that are similar to those in Chaucer's tale, such as the clerks' suspicions about the miller, the miller's snoring, the miller's theft of the clerks' grain as motivation for their retaliation through sex, and the mention of a cradle. Whatever may be the exact relationship of the two texts of *Le meunier* to each other and to Chaucer, because both are of prime importance for the study of possible sources of the *Reeve's Tale*, I include them here.

Another important analogue is Jean Bodel's late twelfth-century *De Gombert et des deux clers*, which Glending Olson has argued should be considered as a possible source for Chaucer's tale.[6] Olson does not dispute the importance of the two versions of *Le meunier*, but he identifies five narrative features that are not present in either text of *Le meunier*, but are found in both Bodel's and Chaucer's poems: (1) the host is solicitous of his guests, (2) his daughter sleeps in a bed instead of in a bin or cupboard, (3) one of the parents leaves the bedroom to urinate, (4) the baby in the cradle does not cry out, and (5) the host does not realize that his wife has cuckolded him.

My view is that Chaucer is more likely to have known the Flemish *Een bispel van .ij. clerken*, a fourteenth-century derivative of Bodel's *De Gombert*, than to have known *De Gombert* itself. The Flemish analogue contains all five parallels noted by Olson, but it also has eight other plot elements found in the *Reeve's Tale* but not in *De Gombert*. In *Een bispel* and Chaucer's tale the clerks are (1) clever, (2) fun-loving, and (3) polite; in both poems (4) drinking precedes urination and (5) snoring occurs; and in both there is (6) a dangerous father, (7) a sleepy wife, and (8) a bloody fight. Moreover, Chaucer is known to have had dealings in London with Flemish merchants, to have traveled to the Low Countries, and to have had at least some acquaintance with their literature. Indeed, the closest analogue to the *Miller's Tale*, to which the Reeve angrily responds in his own tale, is the Flemish tale of an Antwerp prostitute named Heile. More important, though, the parallels between *Een bispel* and the *Reeve's Tale* provide stronger evidence of his having read it than of his having read *De Gombert*, and I have therefore chosen it instead of its French parent.[7]

---

6 "The *Reeve's Tale* and *Gombert*," *Modern Language Review* 64 (1969): 721–5. Reliable transcriptions of the four MSS of *De Gombert* and a composite edition can be found in Willem Noomen and Nico van den Boogaard, *Nouveau recueil complet des fabliaux*, vol. 4 (Assen/Maastrict, Pays-bas: Van Gorcum, 1988): 281–301.

7 For an elaboration on the evidence, see my "Chaucer's *Reeve's Tale* and Its Flemish Analogue," *Chaucer Review* 26 (1991): 286–95.

In her discussion at the beginning of this volume, Helen Cooper has presented a strong case in favor of Chaucer's familiarity with Boccaccio's *Decameron* and his use of it in developing his ideas for the frame of the *Canterbury Tales*. I believe that Chaucer could also have found in *Decameron IX, 6* a source for certain features in his own cradle-trick tale that he could not have found in the French or Flemish analogues. Among them are Boccaccio's way of (1) setting the stage for the action, (2) differentiating the two young men from one another, (3) making class distinctions among the various characters, (4) placing the host's house near the home of the two guests, (5) making the two guests be previously acquainted with the host, (6) giving the daughter an emotional attachment with the young man who seduces her, (7) having the child be a nursing baby, (8) having the two guests provide their own food, (9) having the guests go to bed at a slightly different time from the host and his family, (10) giving the consumption of alcohol a key function in the plot, (11) reporting that the wife nearly makes a mistake when she returns from her trip outside and almost gets into the "wrong" bed, and (12) giving the wife an active role in the climactic events at the end of the tale.[8]

Perhaps after having read or heard a number of these many versions of the cradle-trick story over the years, Chaucer drew upon his memory of several of them to fashion his own wonderful story of pride, revenge, lust, and deception that he gives to the Reeve "to quyte" the Miller and his tale. In doing so, of course, Chaucer would have combined elements from his literary sources in fresh ways and added to them elements not in any of those sources: the questionable lineage of Simkyn's wife, the dual effects of pride and revenge in the actions of the various characters, the play of the horses in the fens, the daughter's going out for food and drink and her later decision to reveal the location of the stolen flour, the wife's role in bashing her husband, and so on – not to mention the darker tone it acquires when assigned to the sardonic old Reeve. Derivative though it certainly is, Chaucer's *Reeve's Tale* is not quite like anything that came before.

---

[8] For a discussion of these elements and an elaboration of the reasons why I do not consider the two German analogues to be likely candidates as sources of Chaucer's tale, see my "Chaucer's *Reeve's Tale, Decameron IX, 6*, and Two 'Soft' German Analogues," *Chaucer Review* 28 (1994): 237–51. For a discussion of the general likelihood that Chaucer had read the *Decameron*, see my "Just Say Yes: Chaucer Knew the *Decameron*" in *The Decameron and the Canterbury Tales: New Essays on an Old Topic*, ed. Leonard Michael Koff and Brenda Deen Schildgen (Madison, NJ: Fairleigh Dickinson University Press, 2000), pp. 25–46.

I

The Miller and the two Clerks: **Text A**[9]

There once were two poor students
born in the same city and the same land.
They were companions and deacons
in a grove where they lived
5   and where they had been raised.
When hard times burst forth on them
as it does pretty soon and frequently,
it is a hardship for the poor people.
The students saw the misery,
10   and their hearts were heavy with it,
nor did they know what to do
because they did not know how to earn anything
either in their land or in another.
They were ashamed to beg for bread,
15   as much for their honor as for other things.
They had no wealth at all
from which to draw sustenance,
and they did not even know where to flee.
One Sunday after having eaten,
20   they went before the monastery
and there they met.
Then they went out of the city
to tell a little of their secret affairs.
One said to the other: "Listen to me.
25   We don't know what course to take
because we don't know how to earn anything,
and here hunger oppresses us.
It's something that vanquishes all;
no one can protect himself from it,
30   nor do we have anything to draw on anywhere.

---

[9] The translation is by Catherine Bodin.

I

Le meunier et les .II. clers: Text A[10]

(from MS 354 Bibliothèque de Berne, 1275–1300)

Dui povre clerc furent jadis.   fol. 164v
Né d'une vile et d'un païs.
Conpeignon et diacre estoient
En un boschage, o il menoient,
5   O il orent esté norri.
Tant c'uns chiers tans lor i sailli,
Con il fait mout tost et sovant,
C'est domage à la povre gent.
Li clerc virent la mesestance,
10   Si en orent au cuer pesance,
Ne il ne sevent conseillier,
Car ne sevent rien gaaignier
N'en lor païs, n'en autre terre.
Honte avroient de lor pain querre,
15   Tant por lor hordre, et tant por el.
Il n'avoient point de chatel
Don se poïssent sostenir,
Ne il ne sevent où ganchir.
.I. diemanche, après mangier,
20   Sont alé devant lo mostier
Illuec se sont entretrové.
Puis s'an sont de la vile alé,
Por dire .I. po de lor secroi.
Li uns dist à l'autre, "Antan moi.
25   Nos ne nos savon conseillier
Car ne savon rien gaaignier,
Et voiz là fain qui nos destraint,/
C'est une chose qui tot vaint.   fol. 165r
Nus ne se puet de li deffandre,
30   Ne nos n'avon rien nule o prandre.

---

[10] The text is based on W. M. Hart's in Bryan and Dempster. I have checked the text against the more recent printed versions by Jean Rychner in *Contribution a l'etude des fabliaux: variantes, remaniements, dégradations*, vol. 2 (Genève: Droz, 1960), pp. 152–60, and by Willem Noomen in *Nouveau recueil complet des fabliaux*, vol. 7 (Assen/Maastrict, Pays-bas: Van Gorcum, 1993): 273–305. Both Rychner and Noomen call my Text A their "Text B," and my Text B their "Text C." I have generally followed Hart's text unless there seemed to be good reason to adopt readings from Rychner or Noomen. All punctuation is mine, including all direct quotations in quotation marks. A linguistic analysis by Catherine Bodin, who translated the text, suggests that the French dialect of both the A and the B texts, though slightly different, is northern, influenced by western, Norman, and Picard forms. Because there is no title given in the Berne MS, I have used what has come to be the almost universally accepted form of the title.

Have you put aside a single thing
by which we might maintain ourselves?"
The other replied, "By St. Denis,
I don't know how to bring this up
35   but I have a certain friend.
I suggest that we go to him
to borrow a measure of wheat,
to sell it at the going price,
and he will credit me the money
40   for a long time and willingly,
until the feast of St. John,
to shelter us in this bad year."
The other said thereupon,
"That comes about very neatly,
45   for I have, likewise, a brother
who has a big fat mare.
I'll borrow it to take the wheat
and we'll become bakers.
People should take upon themselves any shame
50   to protect themselves in this bad year."
So they did it without further ado.
They brought their wheat to the mill.
The mill was so far from them,
there were more than two leagues to go.
55   It was a water mill with a mill race,
situated alongside a little grove.
There was not thereabouts
cabin, or city, or house,
except for only the miller's
60   and the miller knew his trade too well.
The students quickly opened his door,
they threw their sack of grain inside,
after which they put their mare
into the meadow, alongside the mill race.
65   The one stayed to guard everything.
The other went to pursue the miller,
when he came out before them,
but he went away to hide.
He had very well seen the students coming
70   (I think he wanted to get away from them).
He came running into the miller's house.
He found the lady spinning.
"Lady," he said, "by St. Martin,
where is the lord of the mill?
75   It's sure that he was ahead of us."
"Lord clerk, it's no worry of mine.
You can find him in these woods,
if it pleases you to go,
it is alongside this mill."

As tu nule rien porveü
Par quoi nos soions maintenu?"
L'autre respont, "Par saint Denise,
Je ne te sai faire devise,
35   Mais que jo ai un mien ami.
Je lo que nos aillon vers li
Por prandre .I. setier de fromant,
A la vante que l'an lo vant,
Et il m'an querra les deniers
40   Mout longuemant et volantiers
Jusq'à la feste saint Johan,
Por nos giter de cest mal an."
Li autres a lors respondu,
"Il nos est très bien avenu;
45   Car j'ai un mien frere ensemant,
Qui a une grasse jumant.
Je la prandrai pran lo setier,
Et si devandron bolangier.
L'an doit toute honte endosser
50   Por soi de cest mal an giter."
Ensi lo font, plus n'i atant.
Au molin portent lor fromant.
Li molins si loin lor estoit,
Plus de .II. liues i avoit.
55   C'estoit lo molin à choisel,
Si seoit juste un bocheel.
Il n'ot ilueques environ
Borde, ne vile, ne maison,
Fors sol la maison au munier,
60   Qui trop savoit de son mestier.
Li clerc ont tost l'uis desfermé,
Si ont lo sac dedanz gité,
Après ont mis en un prael
La jumant, joste lo choisel.
65   Li uns remest por tot garder.
L'autre ala lo munier haster,
Que il les venist avancier,
Mais il s'an fu alé mucier.
Bien ot les clers veü venir
70   (Je cuit à aus voldra partir).
Chiés lo munier en vient corant.
La dame a trovée filant.
"Dame," fait il, "por saint Martin,
O est li sires do molin?
75   Bien fust que il nos avançast."
"Sire clers, point ne m'an pesast.
En ce bois lo porroiz trover,
Se il vos i plaist à aler,
Qui ci est joste ce molin."

80   And the clerk got on his way,
      because he had seen him very clearly.
      It bothered his companion, who awaited him,
      That he stayed away so long.
      He came running into the house.
85   "Lady," he said, "for the love of God,
      where has my companion gone?"
      "Sire, on my honor,
      he's gone away to look for my lord
      who would have gone out over there."
90   She really loved this job of hers.
      She sent one clerk after the other,
      and the miller went his way.
      He went straight to the mill,
      took their sack off their mare,
95   with his wife, who was helping him,
      and brought everything into his house.
      When he had everything hidden in his house,
      he returned to the mill,
      and the clerks had gone so far,
100   that they returned to the mill.
      "Miller," they said, "God be with you!
      For the love of God, come out to us."
      "Lords," he said, "why should I?"[11]
      "Faith, for our wheat, which is here."
105   When they went to take up the grain,
      they found neither sack nor mare.
      The one looked at the other.
      "What's this? Have we been robbed?"
      "Yes," said the other, "so it looks to me!
110   Sin has brought us to ruin."
      Each one cried out, "Alas, alas!
      Help us out, St. Nicholas!"
      The miller said, "What's the matter with you?
      Why are you crying out so loud?"
115   "Miller, we have just lost everything.
      Suffering has befallen us,
      because now we have neither mare nor anything else.
      It was our only property."
      "Lords," he said, "I don't know anything about it."
120   "Sir," they said," don't let it weigh on you,
      except insofar as to tell us
      where we can go
      to seek out and recover our loss."
      "Lords," he said, "in this wood.
125   I don't know how to counsel you,
      but go look in this wood,

---

[11] Emend "et je de quoi?" to "ai-je . . .?" Lit., "Do I have reason?"

80 Et li clers se mest au chemin,
    Querre lo vait mout vistemant.
    A son conpeignon, qui l'atant,
    Poise mout qu'il demore tant.
    En la maison en vient corant:
85 "Dame," fait il, "por amor Dé,
    O est mon conpeignon alé?"
    "Sire, si aie je hanor,/
    Il en vait querre mon seignor   fol. 165v
    Qui orandroit issi là hors."
90 Ele ot bien ce mestier amors.
    L'un des clers après l'autre envoie,
    Et li muniers aquiaut sa voie.
    Si vient au molin auramant,
    Lo sac lieve sor la jumant,
95 O sa fame qui li aida,
    En sa maison tot enporta.
    Tant a en sa maison mucié,
    Puis est au molin repairiez,
    Et li clerc ont tant cheminé
100 Que il sont au molin torné.
    "Munier," font il, "Deus soit o vos!
    Por amor Deu, avanciez nos."
    "Seignor," fait il, "et je de quoi?"
    "De nostre blé qu'est ci, par foi."
105 Qant durent prandre lo fromant,
    Ne trovent ne sac ne jumant.
    L'uns d'aus a l'autre regardé.
    "Qu'est ice? Somes nos robé?"
    "Oïl," fait ce l'uns, "ce m'est vis!
110 Pechiez nos a à essil mis."
    Chascuns escrie: "Halas! halas!
    Secorez nos, saint Nicolas!"
    Fait li muniers: "Qu'est ce c'avez?
    Por quoi si durement criez?"
115 "Munier, ja avon tot perdu.
    Malemant nos est avenu,
    Car n'avons ne jumant ne el.
    Tot i estoit notre chatel."
    "Seignor," fait il, "n'en sai noiant."
120 "Sire," font il, "ne vos apant,
    Fors tant que de nos asener
    Quel part nos poïssiens aler
    Querre et tracier nostre domage."
    "Seignor," fait il, "en cest boschage.
125 Ne vos sai je pas conseillier,
    Mais en cel bois alez cerchier,

which adjoins this mill."
Then they went on their way
And entered the wood,
130   and the miller went away.
The one clerk talked to the other.
"Certainly," he said, "there's truth in what they say,
one's a fool to work in vain.
Possessions come and go like straw.
135   Let's go look now for lodging."
"Us? In what place?" "At the miller's.
Let's go into this mill.
God grant us St. Martin's lodging!"
They went to the miller's home.
140   He did not appreciate their coming,
so he asked them right away,
"What did St. Nicholas do for you?"
"Miller," they said, "neither one thing nor the other."
"Well, now get some more property.
145   Because you are too far from a source,
You won't have it in this need."
"Miller," they said, "that may well be.
Lodge us, by St. Silvester,
we don't know where to go today."
150   And the miller began to think
that he would be worse than a dog
if he didn't do them some good
out of their own property, for he could well afford to.
"Lords," he said, "there's only the floor
155   you see here, you'll have nothing more."
"Miller," they said, "it's enough."
The villain had no great wealth.
He had only himself, and in his household,
his daughter, who was worth attention,
160   his wife, and a little child.
The girl was beautiful and graceful,
And the miller who wasn't, not a bit,
put her in a trunk[12]
every night, where she lay,
165   and he locked it up on top
and gave her, through the keyhole,
the key, and then went off to sleep.
But we should get back to our clerks.
That night, when supper time came around,
170   The miller had them brought
bread and milk and eggs and cheese,
that's the fare of the woodlands.

---

[12] "huche" indicates trunk, cashbox, cupboard, and hutch. Because of the size and the top-lock, "trunk" seems to be the best translation.

Qui ci est joste cest molin."
Li clerc se mestent au chemin.
Maintenant sont el bois entré,
130 Et li muniers s'an est alé.
Li uns clers à l'autre parla.
"Certes," font il, "voir dit i a,
Fous est qui en vain se travaille.
Avoir vient et va comme paille,
135 Alons nos huimais herbergier."
"Nos? en quel leu?" "Chiés lo munier,
O no alon en cel molin,
Deus nos doint l'ostel saint Martin!"
Errant vindrent chiés lo munier.
140 Lor venir n'avoit il point chier,
Ainz lor demande aneslopas,
"Que vos a fait saint Nicolas?"
"Munier," font il, "ne .I. ne el."
"Or gaaignez autre chatel.
145 Car de cest estes vos trop loing,
Ne l'avroiz pas à cest besoing."
"Munier," font il, "ce puet bien estre./
Herbergiez nos, por saint Servestre,   fol. 166r
Ne savon maishui o aler."
150 Et li muniers prant à panser
Or seroit il pire que chiens,
S'il ne lor faisoit aucun bien
Del lor, car il lo puet bien faire.
"Seignor," fait il, "nient fors l'aire
155 Ice avroiz, se plus n'en avez."
"Munier," font il, "ce est assez."
Li vilains n'ot pas grant cointie.
Il n'ot que soi, cart de maisnie,
Sa fille q'an doit metre avant,
160 Sa fame, et un petit enfant.
La fille estoit et bele et cointe,
Et li muniers, qu'el ne fust pointe,
En une huche la metoit
Chascune nuit, o el gisoit,
165 Et l'anfermoit par de desus
Et li bailloit, par un pertuis,
La clef, et puis s'aloit cochier.
A noz clers devons repairier.
La nuit, qant ce vint au soper,
170 Li muniers lor fait aporter
Pain et lait et eués et fromage,
C'est la viande del bochage.

He gave enough of it to the clerks.
One ate with the girl,[13]

175   the other with the lady and the miller.
In the fireplace there was an andiron
that had a little ring
that they often took on and off.
The one who ate with the girl

180   took the ring off the andiron
and made sure he hid it well.
That night when they were abed
the student took great notice of her.
He saw well where the miller put her

185   when he packed her into the trunk
and locked it up from the top,
how he gave her the key
through a keyhole, dropped it in to her.
When they were all settled in,

190   he nudged his friend.
"Friend," he said, "I want to go
and talk to the daughter of the miller,
who's locked up in the trunk."
"Do you want," that one said, "to cause a fight

195   And upset this household?
The truth is, you are a scoundrel,
all this could go very badly for us."
"I wouldn't want, for anything,
to go away without knowing

200   if she could be worth something to me."
He went straightaway to the trunk,
Gave a little scratch, and heard her speak.
"What's that," she said, "outside there?"
"It's the one who for your body

205   is so afflicted and suffering,
that if you don't have mercy on him,
he'll never have any joy.
It's the one who ate with you,
who brings to you a golden ring.

210   Never have you had such a treasure.
It is proven and well known
that the stone in it has such a power
that any woman, no matter how easy
and however much she's been a run-around,

215   however impure and unvirginal she is,
she will be by morning, if she has it on her finger.
Here, I'll make a present of it to you."
Straightaway she offered him the key
and straightaway he unlocked the trunk.

---

[13] That is, out of the same trencher or ewer.

Aus .II. clers assez en dona.
L'un o la pucele manja,
175 L'autre o la dame et lo munier.
En l'aitre ot un petit andier
O il avoit un anelet
Que l'an oste sovant et met.
Cil q'o la pucele manja
180 De l'andier l'anelet osta
Bien l'a et repost et mucié.
La nuit qant il furent cochié
Li clers de li grant garde prist.
Bien vit que li muniers li fist
185 Con en la huche la bouta
Et par de desus l'anferma,
Con il li a la clef bailliée,
Par un pertuis, li a lanciée.
Qant il furent aseüré,
190 Il a son conpaignon bouté:
"Conpainz," fait il, "je voil aler
A la fille au munier parler,
Qui est en la huche enfermée."
"Viaus tu," fait cil, "faire mellée
195 Et estormir ceste maison?
Verité est, tu iés bricon,
Tost nos en porroit mal venir."
"Je ne voldroie, por morir,
Que ne m'en aille à li savoir
200 S'el me porroit de rien valoir."
A la huche vient erraumant,
.I. petit grate, et el l'antant.
"Q'est ce," fait ele, "là defors?"
"C'est celui qui por vostre cors
205 Est si destroiz et mal bailli,
Se vos n'avez de lui merci,
Jamais nul jor joie n'avra.
C'est celui qui o vos manja,/
Qui vos aporte un enel d'or.
210 Onques n'aüstes tel tresor.
Bien est esprové et saü
Que la pierre en a tel vertu
Que ja fame, tant soit legiere,
Ne tant par ait esté corsiere,
215 Qui chaste et pucele ne soit,
S'au matin en son doi l'avoit.
Tenez, gel vos en faz presant."
Errant cele la clef li tant
Et il desferme errant la huche.

fol. 166v

220   He got in and she grasped him to herself.
      Now they could have their fun
      and they found nothing to annoy them.
      The miller's wife, before daybreak,
      got up from beside her lord,
225   went into the yard perfectly naked.
      She passed by the low bed
      of the student, who was lying on the floor.
      The clerk saw her pass by.
      When he saw her, he looked at her.
230   He remembered his companion then
      who, in the trunk, was having a good time.
      He really wanted to have one too.
      He thought that he would deceive her
      as she passed back by, if he could.
235   Then he thought he would do no such thing,
      all this could go very wrong.
      Another trick occurred to him.
      It was near his heated-up bed.
      He went straight to the other bed,
240   there where the miller lay.
      He took the child with all his wrappings,[14]
      and when the lady entered at the door
      the clerk pulled the child's ear.
      The infant awoke and cried.
245   The wife went to his bed right off
      when she heard where the infant was.
      She turned right away
      to where the child cried.
      She found his swaddling-clothes, was reassured,
250   then pulled back the covers
      and lay down beside the student.
      And he embraced her tight,
      drew her to himself in a big hug,
      and made her crazy with his sport.
255   He "suffered" quick, then lay back in amazement.
      And the other student got ready,
      when he heard the cock crow,
      because he feared to stay too long.
      He got out of the trunk,
260   then went straight up to his bed,
      Found the swaddling clothes, and was surprised.
      And it is not strange that he was.
      He was afraid, but nonetheless
      went forward a little bit,

---

[14] W. M. Hart in Bryan and Dempster translates "briez" as cradle. The line is perhaps more properly read, "He took the child with all his britches" or swaddling clothes. See, however, the note to line 231 in the translation of Text B, below.

220 Dedanz se met, ele s'acluche.
Or puent faire lor deduit
Car ne trovent qui lor anuit.
La fame o munier, ainz lo jor,
Se leva d'enprès son seignor,
225 Tote nue vait en la cort.
Par de devant lo lit trescort
Au clerc, qui en l'aire gisoit.
Li clerc au trespasser la voit.
Qant il la vit, si l'esgarda.
230 De son conpaignon li manbra
Qui, en la huche, fait ses buens.
Mout convoite faire les suens.
Pansa que il la decevroit
Au revenir, se il pooit.
235 Puis repansoit no feroit mie,
Tost en porroit sordre folie.
.I. autre angin li est creüz.
S'anprès est de son lit chaüz.
A l'autre lit s'an va tot droit,
240 Là o li muniers se gisoit.
L'anfant à tot lo briez aporte,
Et qant la dame entre en la porte.
Li clers tire à l'anfant l'oroille.
Et l'anfes crie, si s'esvoille.
245 Cele ala à son lit tot droit
Qant ele oït o cil estoit.
Puis est erraument retornée
Au cri de l'anfant est alée.
Lo briez trove, don s'aseüre,
250 Puis solieve la coverture
Dejoste lo clerc s'est cochiée.
Et cil l'a estroit enbraciée,
Vers soi l'atrait formant l'acole,
A son deduit tote l'afole.
255 Si sofre tot, si se mervoille.
Et l'autres clers si s'aparoille,
Qant il oït le coc chanter,
Car il cuidoit trop demorer.
De la huche s'an est issuz,
260 Puis est droit à son lit venuz,
Lo briez trove, si s'esbaïst.
N'est pas mervoille s'il lo fist.
Il ot peor, et neporqant
.I. petit est alez avant,/

265 and when he found two heads in that bed
he turned away right off.
To the other bed, where lay
the miller, he went straightaway.
He got into bed beside him,
270 and, not yet awake,
he didn't notice it.
"Friend," said the clerk, "what are you doing?
One who is always silent is worthless.
Oh, I know well, God save me,
275 that I've had a good night.
That girl is really a joy,
our miller's daughter.
Forbidden pleasures are fun,
and fucking in a trunk is first-rate.
280 Friend, go to it, if you can conceal it,
and get your piece of the bacon.
There's plenty to go around.[15]
I've ridden[16] her seven times this night,
so by now she'll be a good ride.[17]
285 And for nothing except the ring off the andiron!
I've really done a good night's work."
When the miller heard of this trick,
he seized the clerk by the throat
and the clerk, when he got the picture, seized him.
290 In a minute he got the miller in such a grip
that he almost made his heart burst,
and the lady began to nudge
the other student who was lying with her.
"Sire," she said, "what'll we do?
295 If it please you, let's get up quick,
for these students are strangling each other."
"Don't fret," he said, "let it go,
let the scoundrels kill each other."
For well he knew, and he was not proven wrong,
300 that his friend was the stronger.
When the miller managed to escape,
he ran straight off to light the fire,
and when he saw his wife,
who was lying with the clerk,
305 "Up from there," he said, "you proven whore!
Who led you there?
I'll easily fix you!"
"Sire," she said, "go about this differently.
Because if I'm a proven whore,

---

[15] Lit., "up to the cord" from which the bacon is hung.
[16] Lit., "I've curved her [bent her?] seven times this night."
[17] Lit., "l'asnée," a measure of the load an ass can bear.

265 Et qant .II. testes a trovées,
    Erraumant les a refusées.
    A l'autre lit, o se gisoit
    Li muniers, s'an va cil tot droit.
    De joste li s'estoit cochiez,
270 Ne s'est pas encore esveilliez.
    Ne ne s'est mie aparceüz.
    "Compainz," fait li clers, "que fais tu?
    Qui toz jorz se tait rien ne valt,
    Or sai je bien, se Deus me salt,
275 Que j'ai aü boene nuitiée.
    Mout est la pucele envoisiée,
    La fille à cest nostre munier.
    Mout par si fait mal anvoisier,
    Et si fait trop bon foutre en huche.
280 Conpeignon, car va, si t'i muce,
    Et si pran do bacon ta part.
    Assez en a jusq'à la hart.
    Par .VII. foiz l'ai anuit corbée,
    Dès or sera boene l'asnée,
285 El n'a fors l'anel de l'andier!
    Si ai je fait bien mon mestier."
    Qant li muniers entant la bole,
    Tantost prant lo clerc par la gole
    Et li clers lui, qui s'aparçoit,
290 Tantost lo met en si mal ploit
    A po li fait lo cuer crever,
    Et la dame aquialt à boter
    L'autre cler qui o lui gisoit.
    "Sire," fait ele, "ce que doit?
295 Si viaus, car nos levon tost sus,
    Ja s'estranglent cil cler laissus."
    "Ne te chaut," fait il, "lai ester,
    Lai les musarz entretuer."
    Il savoit bien, si n'ot pas tort,
300 Que ses conpainz ere plus fors.
    Qant li muniers pot eschaper,
    Tantost cort lo feu alumer,
    Et qant il sa fame aparçoit,
    Qui avoc lo clerc se gisoit:
305 "Or sus," fait il, "pute provée!
    Qui vos a ici amenée?
    Certes, il est de vos tot fait!"
    "Sire," fait ele, "autrement vait.
    Car se je sui pute provée,

310   I was turned into one by a trick.
      But you are a proven thief
      who robbed these students of
      their sack of wheat and their mare,
      for which you could swing in the wind.[18]
315   It's all put up in your barn."
      The two clerks took hold of the villain.
      They battered and threshed him
      until he was almost milled himself.
      Then they had their grain milled elsewhere.
320   They had the "St. Martin's hostel"[19]
      and conducted their affair so well
      that they earned their keep for the bad year.

II

The Miller and the two Clerks: Text B[20]

      Once there were two clerks
      born in the same land and region.
      They were companions and deacons
      in a woods, where they lived
5   and where they had been raised.
      When hard times come upon them,
      as it happens so often,
      it is a great suffering for poor people.
      Famine aggrieved the poor people,
10   and the country declined greatly.
      The clerks saw their ill condition
      and had heavy hearts because of it.
      For neither in their land nor in their region

---

[18] That is, "be hanged."

[19] The expression, "St. Martin's hostel" seems to suggest charity, or free hospitality.

[20] The translation is by Catherine Bodin. For explanations of some of the words – St. Martin's hostel, the "huche" or trunk, eating from the same trencher or ewer, and eating bacon all the way up to the cord – see the notes to the translation of Text A, above.

310   Par engin i fui atornée.
      Mais vos estes larron prové
      Qui en cez clers avez emblé
      Lor sac de blé et lor jumant,
      Dont vos seroiz levez au vant.
315   Tot est en vostre granche mis."
      Li dui clers ont lo vilain pris.
      Tant l'ont folé et debatu
      Par po qu'il ne l'ont tot molu.
      Puis vont modre à autre molin.
320   Il orent "l'ostel saint Martin,"
      Et ont tant lor mestier mené
      Q'il se sont do mal an gité.

II

Le meunier et les .II. clers: Text B[21]

(from Hamilton MS, Berlin, 1275–1300)

      De .II. clers qui fuerent jadis   fol. 50v
      Nez d'une terre et d'un païs.
      Conpainon diacres estoient
      En .I. boscage, ou il manoient
5   Ou il orent esté norri.
      Tant c'un chier tens les asailli,
      Comme ci fet cest mout sovent,
      C'est grant domage a povre gent.
      La fein la povre gent greva,
10   Le païs mout en enpira.
      Les clers virent leur mesestance,
      Si en orent au cuer pesance.
      Qu'en leur païs ne en lor terre

---

[21] This edition follows mostly Text B of the Hart edition in Bryan and Demspter, though I have consulted also the Rychner and Noomen editions (see notes to Text A for the full citations). I have adopted a number of the readings from what Rychner and Noomen call "Text C." My Text B is somewhat garbled, with some lines repeated nearly verbatim (compare lines 57–8 and 67–8, lines 130 and 135, and lines 215–16 and 243–4). Other lines, to judge from the evidence of crippled couplets, appear to have been skipped. I have not adopted Hart's interpolation into Text B of an emended line from Text A (line A 52 after B 43). I have followed Rychner in inserting elipses, numbered as separate lines, after lines B 43, 55, 80, 195, and 250 to indicate that at these points the MS is almost certainly faulty since the rhyme scheme is broken. Because I follow this practice, my line numbering matches Rychner's rather than Hart's after line 195. As with Text A, all punctuation is mine, including all direct quotations in quotation marks. In the Hamilton MS there is no title for this tale.

did they dare, out of shame, to beg for bread,
15   as much for their honor as for other things.
Neither had any property.
Nor did they know any trade
whereby they might earn anything.
One Sunday after eating
20   they went up in front of the monastery
to tell a little of their private affairs.
"Friend," said one, "listen to me.
Have you now provided a way
by which we might sustain ourselves?"
25   He told him, "By St. Denis,
I don't know how to relate this,
except that I have a friend
who all year has been after me
to take one measure of grain
30   at the price that they sell it,
and he'll credit me the money,
very generously and willingly,
even until the feast of St. John,
to shelter us in this bad year."
35   Eloquently the other replied,
"This has come about well for us
because I have a brother of my own likewise,
who has a good mare.
I will take her, take the grain,
40   and we will become henceforth bakers."
And so they did it, waiting for nothing else,
took the mare and the grain
went right away to the mill.
. . .
45   The mill was far from there,
two good leagues away,
and for around a good league or so
there was neither hut nor house,
nothing more than that of the miller
50   who knew pretty much about his trade.
When the miller saw them approach
he knew that he would want to go away from them.
So he hid himself in his bedroom.
One led the mare to the pasture,
55   The other went to rouse the miller.
. . .
Then the miller came out and went away.
He found the wife spinning.[22]

---

[22] These next eighteen lines, from 57 through 74, are obviously somewhat corrupt. The "he" in line 59 is one of the clerks, while the "he" in line 69 is his companion. The French text makes it sound as if it is the miller who comes both times to find his wife spinning.

N'osent por honte lor pein qerre,
15 Tant por lor ordre et tant por el.
Ne il n'orent point de chatel.
Ne ne savoient nul mestier
Ou il peüsent gaagnier.
.I. diëmenche aprés mengier
20 S'en vienent devant le moustier
Por dire .I. poi de lor segroi.
"Conpains," fet l'un, "entent a moi.
T'ies tu ore rien porveü
De quoi nos soion soustenu?"
25 Il li respont, "Par seint Denise,
Je ne t'en sai fere devise,
Ne mes que j'ai .I. mien ami
Qui tot oan m'a asailli
De prendre .I. seter de froment
30 A la vente que hom le vent,
Et il m'en crerra les deniers,
Mout bonement et volentiers,
Si qu'a la feste seint Jehan,
Por nos geter de cest mal en."
35 Enroment l'autre a respondu,
"Mout nos est or bien avenu
Car j'ai .I. mien frere ensement,
Qui a une bonne jument.
Je la prendrai, pren le setier,
40 Si devendronmes boulengier."
Einsi le font, plus n'i atendent,
La jument et le setier pranent
Au molin en vienent errant.
    . . .
45 Le molin loing d'iluec estoit,
.II. bones leues i avoit,
Et d'une fort leue environ
N'avoit ne borde ne meson,
Ne mes sans plus cele au mounier
50 Qui mout savoit de son mestier.
Quant le mounier les vit venir
Bien sot qu'a eus voudra partir.
Lors s'est en la chambre mucié.
L'un mena la jument en pré,
55 L'autre ala le mounier haster.
    . . .
Ques le mounier en vint errant.
Si trueve sa fame filant.

"Lady," he said, "by St. Martin,
60   where is the lord of the mill?"
"Sir," she said, "by St. Omer,
you can find him in these woods,
right nearby this mill."
So the clerk went after him.
65   For his companion, who was waiting for him,
knew this: it was a great bother.
Then the miller came back on his way
and found the wife spinning.
"Lady," he said, "by St. Omer,
70   where did my friend go?"
"Lord," she said, "on my honor,
he went to look for my lord
in these woods next to that mill."
So the clerk went on his way.
75   She sent one off after the other.
The miller retraced his steps.
He took the sack off the mare,
and he took it away promptly,
and his wife helped him.
80   He hid it all in his barn.

. . .

And then went back.
The clerks found the miller.
Now they spoke.
85   "Sire," said the one, "by St. Thomas,
it was well that you came ahead of us!"
"Came ahead, for God's sake? And do I have reason?"
"You'll see now!" "All right, I'm so disposed."
They went right off to the mill,
90   but found neither sack nor mare.
One looked at the other.
"What's this, by God? Is someone making fun of us?"
"Yes," said the other, "that's what I think!"
"Fraud has put us here."
95   They cried, "Alas! Alas!
What will we do, St. Nicholas?"
The miller said, "What's wrong with you?"
"Surely, we've been badly treated.
Sir, we have lost everything.
100   A great misfortune has befallen us.
We've found neither sack nor mare."
The miller said, "I don't see any."
"Sir, don't let any of this weigh on you,
I tell you truthfully,
105   except that maybe you will show us
where we can go to look for
our loss and our damages."

"Dame," fet il, "por seint Martin,
60 Ou est li sire du molin?"
"Sire," fet el, "par seint Omer,
En cel bois le poëz trover,
Tres par dejouste cel molin."
Or est li clerc mis au chemin.
65 A son conpaignon, qui l'atent,
Sachiez, anuie mout forment.
Ques le mounier revint errant
Et trueve sa fame filant.
"Dame," fet il, "por seint Omé,
70 Ou est mon conpaignon alé?"
"Sire," fet ele, "par m'aneur,
Il ala qerre mon seigneur
En cel bois, jouste cel molin."
Or s'est li clers mis au chemin.
75 L'un clerc aprés l'autre en envoie.
Le mounier raprise sa voie.
Le sac lieve sus la jument
Et le trouse delivrement,
Et sa fame li a edié.
80 Tot en sa granche a lancié.

    . . .

Puis est ariere reperié.
Les clers ont le mounier trové./
Meintenant l'ont aresoné.   fol. 51r
85 "Sire," dist l'un, "por seint Thommas,
Bien fus que l'en nos avanchast!"
"Avanchast, Diex? Et je de quoi?"
"Ja le verrés!" "Et je l'otroi."
Au molin en vienent errant,
90 Ne truevent ne sac ne jument.
L'un clerc a l'autre regardé.
"Qu'est ce, Diex? Sommes nos gabé?"
"Oïl," dist l'autre, "ce m'est vis!"
"Mau pechié nos a ici mis."
95 Il s'escrïent: "Elas! Elas!
Que feron nos, seint Nicolas?"
Dist le mounier, "Et que avés?"
"Certes, nos sommes mal menés.
Sire, nos avon tot perdu.
100 Mau pechié nos est avenu.
Ne trovon ne sac ne jument."
Dist le mounier, "N'en vi noient."
"Sire, de riens a vos n'apent,
Ce vos di bien veroiement,
105 Fors que nos voilliez enseignier
Ou peüson aler cerchier
Nostre perte et nostre damage."

The miller said, "Everything here is woods,
for which reason I don't know how to instruct you.
110   But I counsel you to search the wood
all alongside this mill."
So the clerks started off.
They went so far, high and low,
that the sun went down,
115   and that one called the other.
"Friend," he said, "it's true what they say.
Only a crazy man works in vain.
Possessions come and go like straw.
We could do a certain thing
120   which would give ourselves a rest.
I suggest we go take shelter
until tomorrow with the miller
or else we enter this mill.
God give us St. Martin's hostel!"
125   When the miller saw them coming,
you know he did not dare escape.
So he said right away,
"What did St. Nicholas do for you?"
"He didn't do either this or that for us."
130   "I should think not, by St. Omer!
Now go get more capital.
Let it please you, though it may be beautiful or ugly,
because here it is very far-off from you,
you won't have it in this need."
135   "I think it so, by St. Omer!
Could we have lodging?"
Then the miller thought to himself:
"We have no need of it now."
But he would be worse than a dog
140   if he did not do them some good
out of their own goods, when he could afford it.
The miller said, "There's only the threshing floor,
but such lodging you will have, if nothing else."
"Sir, that's plenty enough for us!"
145   The miller had no great household,
himself and his wife and a daughter
who was so beautiful and agreeable.
And so that she did not agree to too much,
he made her sleep in a trunk
150   and locked it through the top and gave her
the key, and then he went off to sleep.
When it came time to eat that night,
he had enough food prepared for them,
everything they needed,
155   bread and eggs and milk and cheese,
that's the fare of the woodlands.

Dist le mounier, "Tot est boscage,
Par quoi ne vos sai enseignier.
110 Mes cel bos vos lo a cerchier
Tres par dejouste cel molin."
Or sunt li clers mis au chemin.
Tant ont en haut et bas alé,
Que le soleil fu escoussé.
115 Et que li .I. l'autre apela.
"Conpaing," fet il, "voir dit i a.
Fous est qui en vein se travaille.
Avoir vient et va comme paille.
Nos porriön fere tel chose
120 De quoi nos nos dondriön pose.
Je lo nos aillon herbegier
Jusqu'a demein ches le mounier,
Ou nos entron en cel molin.
Diex nos doint l'ostel seint Martin!"
125 Quant le mounier les vit venir,
Sachiez que il n'osa guenchir.
Einz s'escria inelepas,
"Que vos a fet seint Nicolas?"
"Ne nos a fet ne ce ne el."
130 "Je le croi bien, para seint Omel!
Or gaagniez autre chatel.
Que bien vos siet, ou let ou bel,
Car icestui vos est mout loing,
Pas ne l'arez a cest besoing."
135 "Je le croi bien, par seint Omel!
Porriön nos avoir l'ostel?"
Lors se porpense le mounier:
"Nos n'avon ore del mestier!"
Mes trop seroit pire d'un chien
140 Se ne lor fesoit aucun bien
Du leur, quant il le puet bien fere.
Dist le mounier: "N'i a fors l'ere,
L'ostel arez, se plus n'avez."
"Sire, c'est a mout grant plentez!"
145 Le mounier n'ot pas grant mesnille,
Lui et sa fame et une fille,
Qui tant estoit et belle et cointe.
Por ce qu'ele ne fust trop cointe,
En une huche la couchoit
150 Et par deseure li bailloit
Le clef, et puis s'aloit couchier.
Quant ce vint au soir au mengier,
Asez lor fist apareillier,
Tot quant qu'i lor estoit mestier,
155 Pein et oés et let et formage,
C'est la viande du boscage.

One of them ate with the girl
and, all having been said, he nudged her with his foot.
And the other ate with the miller and his wife.
160 In the hearth there was an andiron,
and the andiron had a ring,
which often was put on and off.
The one who ate with the girl
took from the andiron the ring,
165 which was placed alongside the fire,
and took it and hid it.
And when they were supposed to go sleep,
because it was after the meal,
he saw his open sack and his grain,
170 which the miller had taken from them.
After, he saw the miller who hid
his daughter in a trunk.
He hid her there and often trembled,
having great fear that someone might steal her.
175 And the girl, so sweet,
received the key through the keyhole.
Thereupon he went to bed and snored loudly,[23]
this miller, and quickly fell asleep.
One of the clerks who listened to this
180 nudged the other clerk with his hand.
"Friend," he said, "I want to go
talk to the miller's daughter."
"What the hell? Are you mad?"
"Is it of no matter to you
185 that the miller stole our grain?"
"Do you want us to shame
and turn this house upside down?
In truth, you are a glutton."[24]
"I would not leave off for anything
190 that presently I might not go find out."
He leaped up from his bed on the spot.
He came up to the trunk, as in a romance.
He stopped right alongside the trunk,
and scratched a little bit,
195 and heard her very well say,

. . .

"What is this, by God? Who is out there?"
"It is he who for your body
is so destroyed and ill-treated,
200 that if you have no mercy on him,
never will he have any pleasure.[25]

---

[23] The snoring does not appear in Text A. In this regard, Text B is closer to Chaucer's version (see 4163).
[24] Perhaps our modern phrase "glutton for punishment" is implied in the expression.
[25] The modern English word is "joy," but implicit in the French word "jouissance" is sexual pleasure.

L' .I. o la pucele menja
Et tot dis du pié la bouta,
Et l'autre o li o sa moillier.
160 En l'aitre si ot .I. landier,
El landier ot .I. anelet,
Que l'en oste sovent et met.
Le clerc qui o la pucele menja
Du landier l'anelet osta,
165 Qui les le feu iert aprochié,
Si l'a bien repus et muchié.
Tant com se dut aler coucher,
Car il estoit aprés mengier,
Son sac vit apert et son blé,
170 Que le mounier lor ot emblé.
Aprés vit le mounier qui muche
Sa fille dedenz une huche.
Iluec la muce et sovent tremble,
Grant paour a c'on ne li emble.
175 Et la pucele, tot soëf,
Par le pertus reçoit la clef.
Adont se couche et ronfle fort,
Icel mounier, et tost s'endort.
.I. des clers qui ce escouta
180 De sa mein l'autre clerc bouta.
"Conpaing," fet il, "je veil aler
A la fille au mounier parler."
"Qu'est ce, deäble? Es tu desvé?"/
"Ne t'est or gueres de nos blé   fol. 51v
185 Que le mounier nos a enblé?"
"Nos veus tu ci fere honir
Et estormir ceste meson?
Veritez est, tu es gloton."
"Or nel leroie por avoir
190 Qu'orendroit ne voise savoir."
De son lit saut inellement,
A la huche vienent, enroment.
A la huche s'est acosté,
Si a .I. petitet graté,
195 Et el l'avoit mout bien oï,
. . .
"Qui est ce, Diex? Qui est la hors?"
"C'est celi qui por vostre cors
Est si destruit et maubailli,
200 Se vos n'avez de li merci.
Jamés nul jor joie n'avra.

It is the student you ate with,
who brings you a ring of gold.
God himself did not make so rich a treasure.
205   Its stone is of such a power,
well have I proved it and known it,
that any woman on earth, however easy,
however much she's run around the earth,
should she have this ring on her finger,
210   she'll always be a virgin.
Here, I'll make you a present of it!"
He gave it to her, and she offered him the key.
Now the trunk was unlocked
and he was in it with the girl.
215   Now he could have his delight
because now he found nothing to stop him.
The miller's wife, before daybreak,
got up from her lord's side,
went into the courtyard completely naked,
220   and the clerk trembled at this.
The clerk saw her pass by.
He remembered his friend
who was having his fun in the trunk,
and he was having so little himself
225   that he swore to God and St. Thomas
that he would stop her on the way back.
Then he thought he would do no such thing.
All this could turn out so crazy.
Another trick occurred to him.
230   He got up naked from his bed.
He carried off the cradle[26] and child in it.
And the lady closed the door.
She came to the bed right away,
where her husband was lying.
235   He pulled the infant's ear.
When it cried she was astonished.
She turned back.
She went towards the child's cry,
found the cradle, and reassured herself.
240   She pulled back the cover
and she enveloped herself inside it.
And he tightly embraced her.
Now he could have his fun
because he found nothing to stop him.

---

[26] The word in Text A (line 241) is "briez" which means "britches" or swaddling clothes, not cradle. Here, in Text B, the word is "berz" or cradle. In this regard the B-version is closer to Chaucer's "cradel" (A 4212). There may, however, be some scribal or linguistic confusion between the "briez" and the similar form "berz," so it is possible that Text A originally had the baby transported in a cradle rather than merely in swaddling or bedclothes.

Le cler qui avec vos menja,
Qui vos aporte .I. anel d'or.
Diex ne fist si riche tresor.
205 La pierre en est de tel vertu,
Bien l'ai esprové et seü,
Qu'il n'est souz ciel fame legierre,
Qui par terre eit esté corsiere,
Se l'anelet a en son deit,
210 Que toz jorz pucele ne soit.
Tenez, je vos en faz present!"
Cil li baille, la clef li tent.
Or a la huche desfermée,
Avec la pucele est entrée.
215 Or en puet fere son delit
Car or ne trueve qui li nuit.
La fame au mounier, ainz le jor,
Se lieve d'ovec son seignor,
Tote nue vet en la court,
220 Et le clerc si fremist trestot.
Le clers au trespasser la vit.
De son conpaignon li sovint
Qui en la huche fet ses bons,
Et il a si petit des soens
225 Qu'il jure Deu et seint Thommas
C'au revenir la retendra.
Il repense nen fera mie.
Tost l'en porroit venir folie.
.I. autre engin li est creü.
230 De son lit se lieve tot nu.
Le berz a tot l'enfant enporte.
Et la dame a reclos la porte.
Au lit est venue tot droit,
La ou son mari se gesoit.
235 S' a tiré a l'enfant l'oreille.
Il bret et ele s'esmerveille.
Si est ariere retornée.
Au bret de l'enfant est alée,
Le bers trueve, si s'aseüre.
240 Li souzlieve la coverture
Et el s'estoit dedenz mucée.
Et il l'a estroit enbracée.
Or en puet fere son delit
Car il ne trueve qui li nuit.

245   That one heard the cock crow
       who was lying in the trunk.
       He came out of the trunk very quickly.
       He took leave of the girl,
       and went straight back to his bed
250   where his friend was lying.

       . . .

       He carefully examined
       the two heads he found there,
       and immediately turned away.
255   So he went right back to the other bed,
       there where the miller was lying.
       "Good friend," he said, "what are you doing?
       How did your night go?
       I had such a good night of it.
260   That girl is really a lot of fun,
       the daughter of our miller.
       Sleeping with her is great!
       I've had her six times this night,
       with her lying in my arms completely naked.
265   Sleeping in a trunk is great fun.
       Friend, go and see if you can hide
       And get your piece of the bacon.
       There's plenty enough left."
       When the miller heard the trickery
270   he took the clerk by the throat.
       And when the clerk felt this,
       he got him in such a grip
       That he all but strangled him.
       But the miller escaped
275   when he saw that he could escape.
       He went straight to light the fire,
       then came straight back to the bed
       where his wife was lying.
       "Are you his fallen woman?"
280   and entered into deep thought.
       "By God, you are easily fixed.
       You have started a bad fight."[27]
       "If I have become a fallen woman,
       I was brought to it by deception.
285   But you are a proven thief,
       who have robbed the two students
       of their sack of wheat and their mare.
       You ought to be strung up in the wind."
       When the clerks heard of this trickery,
290   they took the miller by the throat.
       They so much beat him, so much threshed him,

---

[27] "Mauplet," from Latin "placitum," suggests an evil quarrel or lawsuit.

245 Celui oï le coc chanter
    Qui en la huche se gesoit.
    De la huche ist inellement.
    A la pucele congié prent,
    Au lit s'en est venu tot droit
250 La ou son conpaignon gesoit.
    . . .
    Si a tot belement tasté
    Les .II. testes i a trovées,
    Enroment les a refusées.
255 A l'autre lit revint tot droit,
    La ou le mounier se jesoit.
    "Beau conpaing," fet il, "que fes tu?
    Comment t'est anuit avenu?
    Mout ai eü bone nuitiée.
260 Mout est la pucele envoisiée,
    La fille a cest nostre mounier.
    Mout fet bon avec li couchier!
    Et .VI. foiz l'ai anuit eüe,
    Entre mes bras trestote nue.
265 Mout par fet bon couchier en huche.
    Compains, car va et si t'i muche
    Et si pren du bacon ta part.
    Mout en i a jusqu'a la hart."
    Quant le mounier entent la boule
270 S'avoit le clerc pris a la goule.
    Et quant le clerc dont s'aperchoit,
    Si l'avoit mis en si mal ploit
    Qu'a poi que ne l'a estranglé.
    Mes le mounier est eschapé
275 Quant vit que il pot eschaper.
    Errant vint le feu alumer.
    Au lit s'en est venu tot droit,
    La ou sa fame se gesoit.
    "Estes vos sa fame desvée?"
280 Et entre en grande pensée.
    "Par Deu, il est de vos tot fet.
    Vos avez commencé mauplet."
    "Que se je sui fame desvée,
    Par enging i fui amenée.
285 Mes vos estes lerre prové,
    Qui avez au .II. clers enblé
    Leur sac de blé et leur jument.
    S'en devez estre mis au vent."
    Quant les clers entendent la boule,
290 S'ont le mounier pris a la goule.
    Tant l'ont foulé, tant l'ont batu,

that he gave back all their grain.
Then they conducted their business so well
that they got themselves out of the bad year.
295   To God and St. Nicholas
they give thanks from high and low.

III

A Moral Tale about Two Clerics[28]

We often hear bawdy verses
in which we can easily learn
wisdom as well as foolishness.
I was once told
5   about two clerics who had returned
from Paris, having learned
both wisdom and how to enjoy themselves,
as is still the custom there.
I was also told
10   that they had spent all their money.
They traveled by highways and byways
until late one evening,
just before sundown,
they came up to a man
15   and asked him, for pity's sake,
to give them shelter for the night.
The good fellow did so
and took them into his house.
One of the clerics immediately noticed
20   the man's wife and promptly
fell in love with her. She was a fine woman,
with eyes sparkling like crystal.
Then the daughter appeared,
and the other cleric was tempted

[28] I am grateful to Therese Decker, to T. M. Guest, to Erik Hertog, and to Carol A. N. Martin for help with the translation.

Que tot lor blé lor a rendu.
Puis ont lor mester tant mené
Qu'il se sunt du mal en geté.
295 A Deu et a seint Nicolas
En rendent grasces haut et bas.

III

Een bispel van .ij. clerken[29]

(from MS KB 15.589–623, Royal Library, Brussels
"Hulthem Collection," 1350–75)

Men heeft ghehoert in ghedichte   fol. 113va
Depllijcheit daer men bi lichte
Verstoet vroetscap ende sothede.
Ic quam eens daer men mi sede
5 Van twe clerken, die waren gekeert
Van parijs ende die geleert
Hadden spel ende wijsheit mede,
Ghelijc dat daer noch es die sede.
Oec soe liet men mi verstaen
10 Dat si haer gote hadden verdaen.
Si ghingen stratem ende pade,
Dat si quamen eens sauons spade,
Als die sonne te dalen began
Ende achter haelden enen man
15 Dien si baden op ghenade
Dat hi hen herberghe dade.
Die goode man heuet ghedaen
Ende heeft se in sijn huus ontfaen.
Stappans heeft die clerc versien
20 Des goets mans wijf, die hi mettien
Minnende wert. Si was noyael,
Haer oghen blicten als een cristael.
Hier na quam die dochter voert,
Die ander clerc wert becoert

[29] The text of the Middle Dutch poem is based on a transcription of the fourteenth-century manuscript in Brussels. Comparisons were made with the most recent printed text in C. Kruyskamp, *De middelnederlandse boerden* ('S-Gravenhage: Martinus Nijhoff, 1957). For an earlier printed text, see Eelco Verwijs, *Dit sijn x goede boerden* ('S-Gravenhage: Martinus Nijhoff, 1860). The MS has the title given above, as well as a short subtitle, "Ene goede boerde" translated as "a fine humorous tale." For the sake of simplicity the subtitle is not included as part of the title here. I am grateful to Erik Hertog for his help in transcribing the MS in Brussels. All punctuation, of course, is mine.

25   and quite obsessed by love for her,
      but he dared not let her know of it,
      though he would gladly have seduced her.
      There was a child lying in the cradle.
      The woman took a pot
30   and meal and milk from a jug
      and set about making porridge.
      The cleric quickly went
      and sat next to her by the fire,
      then surreptitiously stole from the pot-hanger
35   a ring from which
      the pot was suspended;
      it was made of iron, if I understood correctly,
      and the cleric took it.
      The host had by then prepared
40   butter, milk properly warmed,
      and some excellent stewed fruit.
      It was good rustic food.
      The cleric could not restrain himself
      from watching the wife
45   the whole time as she sat eating
      beside her husband.
      She made him very uneasy,
      but Gobert did not notice that.
      He made up for his two guests
50   a bed which he put by the wall
      next to his own and his daughter's.
      Then he took off his shoes
      and warmed himself, for it was cold.
      They were burning straw, not wood.
55   The husband went to bed.
      His wife got up when he did.
      She took the cradle, believe me,
      and set it next to her bed.
      The daughter too went to bed,
60   and so did the two strangers,
      who had drunk plenty of whey.
      The host started snoring,
      and soon the hostess did too.
      The one cleric stood up,
65   with his heart trembling and beating hard.
      He went timidly to the daughter,
      feeling cold with fear.
      As soon as she felt him,
      she said, very nervously,
70   "If my father wakes up, you're a dead man.
      Get away from here, as quick as you can.
      I think you must be crazy."
      The cleric answered courteously,

25 Met hare minnen ende beseten,/
    Ende hi en dorste haer niet laten weten,   fol. 113vb
    Maer gherne soude hi se bedrieghen.
    Daer lach een kint inder wieghen.
    Die vrouwe nam een panne
30 Bloeme ende melc uut eenre kannen
    Ende ginc ene pap ghereiden.
    Die clerc quam sonder beiden
    Neuen haer sitten biden colen
    Ende heeft haer heimelijc ghestolen
35 Vanden stele enen rinc,
    Daer die panne mede hinc,
    Yseren was hi na mijn verstaen,
    Die clerc heeften op ghedaen.
    Die weert hadde doen ghereet
40 Boter, melc, te maten heet,
    Ende compost van goeden prise,
    Dit was goede dorper spise.
    Di clerc en conste hem niet ontien,
    Hi en moeste op die vrouwe sien
45 Al die wile dat si sat
    Bi haren goeden man ende at.
    Si dede hem wel groet verdriet,
    Maer her Gobert en merkes niet.
    Hi maecte sine gasten beiden
50 Een bedde dat hi bi wants leide
    Aen tsine ende sijnre dochter mede.
    Daer na hi sine scoen uut dede
    Ende ginc hem wermen want het was cout.
    Men berde daer stoppelen sonder hout.
55 Slapen es die man gegaen.
    Sijn wijf es met hem op gestaen.
    Si nam die wieghe, geloues mi,
    Ende settese haren bedde bi.
    Die dochter ginc oec slapen,
60 Ende beide die vremde knapen,
    Die weys ghenoech hadden gedroncken.
    Ende die weert ginc liggen roncken,
    Ende die weerdinne oec wel saen.
    Die een clerc es op ghestaen,
65 Dien therte beuede ende verscoet.
    Hi ginc ter dochter wert al bloet,
    Van vresen was hi al vercoelt.
    Tierst dat sine heeft ghevoelt,
    Sprac si met sorgen groet,
70 "Ontsprinct mijn vader ghi sijt doot./
    Vliet henen hets meer dan tijt.   fol. 114ra
    Mi dunct dat ghi verscouen sijt."
    Die clerc antworde hoefschelike,

"Take pity on me, my love!
75   I have not the power
to part from you.
I can't hide my feelings for you.
Hush now; if your father woke up,
he might think we had done
80   what we have not yet thought of,
and that I had had my way with you.
So keep quiet,
for he would certainly think that.
This ring of red gold
85   is yours, if you want it.
It is worth almost ten pounds.
It is too big for me, but I couldn't find a smaller."
Then he put it on her finger
and it slipped over her knuckle.
90   Then he said and solemnly swore,
"It is yours. Feel the weight of it."
With that he settled himself closer to her
and played a game with her.
If I told you which one, you would know it well.
95   This cleric lay there thoroughly enjoying himself.
His companion was suffering torments,
lying there thinking about the woman.
The one had pleasure, the other sorrow,
as many a one has had.
100   Meanwhile, up rose
Master Gobert from his bed,
badly wanting to piss.
He went and took a leak outside the door.
The second cleric got up
105   and went to where the cradle stood
and picked it up
and carried it secretly
to the bed where he himself had been lying.
Then he came back
110   to where he knew the woman was
and began to make love to her.
She thought it was her husband,
for she was barely awake.
She let the young man do as he wished.
115   Now Master Gobert
came back to bed.
He did not suspect any trickery,
but felt for the cradle,
as he habitually did
120   when he came back after pissing.
He came straight to the bed.
When he couldn't find the cradle,

"Hebt mijns ghenade, suuerlike!
75 Ic en hebbe niet die cracht
Dat ic van u scheiden macht.
Ic en mach mi jegen u niet veizen.
Swijght, u vader mocht peisen,
Ontspronghe hi, dat wi hadden gewracht
80 Dies wi nocht sijn ombedacht,
Ende ic ghedaen hadde minen wille.
Hier bi soe swighet stille,
Want hijs seker wanen soude.
Dit vingherlijn van roden goude
85 Es uwe, op dat ghijt ghert.
Hets min dan .x. pond weert.
Hets mi te groet, in vant geen minder."
Doen stac hijt haer anden vingher
Dat ouer hare cnokel voer.
90 Daer seide hi ende swoer,
"Hets uwe. Proeuet wat dat weeght."
Mettien hi hare bat nare leeght
Ende spelde met hare een spel.
Seidict u, soe wistijt wel.
95 Dese clerc lach met groten spele.
Sijn gheselle leet commers vele,
Die lach en peinsde om die vrouwe.
Die een hadde spel die ander rouwe,
Als menich heeft gedaen.
100 Hier binnen soe es op ghestaen
Van sinen bedde her Gobert
Die te pissene sere beghert.
Voer die dore ginc hi staen leken.
Dander clerc es op gestreken
105 Daer hi die wieghe staende vant
Ende namse metter hant
Ende heeftse heimelijc gedregen
Ten bedde daer hi hadde gelegen.
Daer na es hi weder comen
110 Daer hi die vrouwe heeft vernomen,
Met hare te spelene dat hi began.
Si waende hebben haren man,
Want si qualijc was ontsprongen.
Si liet ghewerden den jonghen.
115 Nu es weder her Gobert
Te sinen bedde weert ghekeert./
Hine hoedde hem niet van bedrieghe,   fol. 114rb
Maer ginc tasten na die wieghe,
Van costumen hi dit leerde
120 Wanneer dat hi van pissen keerde.
Te sinen bedde quam hi te hant.
Doen hi die wieghe niet en vant,

he said to himself,
"I must be half-witted.
125   Has the devil brought me here,
or has some will of the wisp led me astray?
I've ended up at my guests' bed."
Then he began feeling around,
stepping softly,
130   and came eventually to where the cradle stood.
He found the bed still warm.
He promptly stretched out his arm
for his wife, who was not there.
Then he thought, "Surely she has
135   gone out to the privy."[30]
With that thought he went to sleep.
The cleric was now with the woman,
who looked after him very well.
He thought he was very fortunate.
140   He tuned her strings three times.
Master Gobert was lucky
to have married a thresher like that,
who had learned to winnow so well.
Then the woman[31] said, "Master Gobert,
145   although you are old and dried up,
you will still do very nicely.
Though your face is full of wrinkles,
your prick is greatly improved.
Is this usual with old men,
150   or are you afraid sex will not be allowed old people?"
The cleric did not say a word
and let her say what she wanted.
The other cleric was with the daughter,
making love to his heart's content.
155   When he had played with her up and down,
he went back to his bed
before dawn should break – back to the bed
in which Master Gobert was sleeping.
The cleric lay down next to
160   Master Gobert, believe me,
thinking it was his companion,
and poked him in the ribs.
Master Gobert immediately woke up
and soon came to understand
165   that the cleric had deceived him,
which did not please him very much.
Softly he said,
"Where have you been? Tell me that.

---

[30] Lit., "to pick flowers."
[31] The word "man" in the MS is surely a copyist's error for "vrouw" or woman.

Seide hi te hem seluen dit waert,
"Ic mach wel sijn een musaert.
125 Heeft mi die necker bracht hier,
Of verleyt mi dwaes fier?
Ic ben geraecht te minen gasten."
Doen ginc hi elder wert tasten,
Al sachte sette hi voert den voet,
130 Doch quam hi daer die wieghe stoet.
Dat bedde vant hi noch al waerm.
Mettien stac hi voert den arm
Na sijn wijf die daer niet en was.
Doen peinsde hi, "Sijt seker das
135 Dat si ware gegaen bloemen lesen."
Doe wert hi in slape met desen.
Die clerc nu bider vrouwen es,
Die hem dede goet ghetes.
Hem dochte hi hadde wel ghevaren.
140 Hi vertemperde III werf haer snaren.
Her Gobert was daer doe wel an,
Dat hi dien derscher ghewan,
Die soe wel wannen hadde gheleert.
Doe seide die man, "Her Gobert,
145 Al sidi out ende tay,
Ghi selt noch wesen herde fray.
Al heeft u anschijn menege runtse,
Ghebetert es wel sere u fluntse.
Pleghet dus den ouden lieden,
150 Of waendi dat ment sal verbieden?"
Die clerc sweech emmer stille
Ende liet haer segghen haren wille.
Dander die bider dochter lach,
Ende hare minne goetlijc plach.
155 Als hi gespelt hadde op ende neder
Keerde hi te sinen bedde weder,
Eer hem verclaerde die dach,
Daer her Gobert in slape lach.
Die clerc es gelegen bi
160 Her Gobert, gheloues mi,
Ende waende sinen geselle hebben
Ende gincken stoten in sijn rebben./
Stappans her Gobert ontspranc
Ende doe wisti eer yet lanc
165 Dat hem die clerc hadde bedroghen,
Dies hi luttel was in hoghen.
Binnens monts sprac hi,
"Wanen comdi dat? Seght mi?

fol. 114va

You seem so utterly exhausted."
170   The cleric said, "I've been making love
to the daughter of our host here.
I gave her that good ring
that the pot was hanging from.
I said it was a finger-ring,
175   so I got her to keep quiet
and did everything I wanted.
I bored a hole in her barrel!"
"God curse you for that,"
said Master Gobert furiously,
180   and then struck him with his fist.
The cleric hit him back,
so that he fell off the bed
into the ashes on the hearth.
The host promptly jumped up again.
185   They went for each other hammer and tongs,
pummeling each other
hard with their fists, good fighters.
Each aimed at the other's weapons.[32]
No one ever saw such good jousting
190   in so short a time as these two provided,
without weapons or leather tunics.
Their family jewels were oozing blood,
for they were both stark naked.
Suddenly the wife awoke at the noise
195   the two of them were making.
"Master Gobert," she said, "go and separate them,
for they are fighting terribly.
But take great care, my dear lord.
It is dark and some accident might befall you.
200   Keep one hand in front of your balls,
I beg you, my dear friend.
You served me so well just now
that truly, not for ten pounds
would I want you to be hit there."
205   "Gladly, lady," he said at once.
He got to his feet
and went to where
his companion was lying on the ground.
He quickly grabbed the host
210   and threw him on a bench,
so that he went cross-eyed.
Master Gobert was badly beaten up
and his hair pulled out.
The poor fellow defended himself

---

[32] The word "wapene" can refer to the genitals as "weapons" of a kind. In any case, the clerk and the host are clearly "fighting dirty," as the next several lines show.

Ghi schijnt soe sere vermoyt."
170   Dander sprach, "Ic hebbe ghesoyt
     Des weerts dochter van hier binnen.
     Den goeden rinc liet ic haer winnen
     Daer di panne mede hinc.
     Ic seide het was een vingherlijnc,
175   Dus dedic haer swighen stille
     Ende dede al gader minen wille.
     Ic boerde ene bonne in haer vat!"
     "Dies moetti heben godsat,"
     Sprac her Gobert metter druust,
180   Ende sloechen daer na metter vuust.
     Die clerc sloeghen weder,
     Dat hi viel vanden bedde neder
     In die aschen op den hert.
     Met desen vaert op die weert.
185   Elc scoet andren in sijn haer,
     Mallic ginc andren gheuen daer
     Metten vuusten wel ghedicke.
     Elc hadde van wapene een ansichte.
     Men sach noit soe wel tornieren
190   Hem tween in soe corter vren,
     Sonder wapene ende sonder coryeren.
     Van bloede sepen haer parueren,
     Want si waren beide al naect.
     Stappans es die vrouwe ontwaecht
195   Om tgheruchte van hem beiden.
     "Her Gobert," sese, "gaetse sceiden,
     Want si vechten herde sere.
     Maer emmer huedt u, lieue here.
     Hets doncker het mochte u mesvallen.
200   Houdt u een hant voer u scallen,
     Des biddic u, wel lieue vrient.
     Soe wel hebdi mi nu ghedient,
     In wonde om .x. pond in trouwen
     Dat ghi daer ane waert te blouwen."
205   "Gherne vrouwe," seide hi saen.
     Voer voets es hi op ghestaen
     Ende es comen te ghemoete/
     Daer sijn ghesele lach onder voete.   fol. 114vb
     Hi nam den weert eer iet lanc
210   Ende werpen op ene banc,
     Dat hem die oghen sijn verwandelt.
     Her Gobert was sere meshandelt
     Ende sijn haer ghetoghen uut.
     Nochtan soe werde hem die cornuut,

215   as best he could, but he was too slow.
     They pushed him and pounded his back,
     so that he became limper than his own belly.
     Master Gobert did not have much luck.
     At daybreak, after they had
220   beaten him up like this, they left.
     Master Gobert remained behind in great distress.
     This tale teaches us
     that those who have bold wives
     should not put much trust in,
225   nor have anything to do with,
     those who shave their pates.
     If they do, they will regret it.
     For while they are busy earning a living,
     and don't feel like making love,
230   the clerics, who mostly
     desire other men's wives,
     and waste their goods as well, are ready and waiting.
     And I have seldom heard
     that they take responsibility for their offspring.

IV

Decameron IX, 6[33]

In the valley of the Mugnone there was, not so long ago, a good man who earned his keep by providing food and drink to travelers. Although he was poor and his house small, he would in time of emergency put up for the night, not everyone, but those he knew. Now it so happens that this man had a pretty enough wife who had given him two children; one was a lovely young girl of great charm, of about fifteen or sixteen years of age, who still had no husband; the other was a tiny boy who was not even a year old, and was still nursed by his mother. The young woman had caught the eye of a charming, pleasing, and altogether elegant young man from our city, who was in the habit of traveling about the countryside when he fell violently in love with her. At the same time, she was enormously flattered to have gained such attention from such a swain and exerted herself to retain his love by providing him many sweet glances. She similarly fell in love with him. There were many times the mutual desire of each of the partners would have reached its natural climax, if Pinuccio, which was the name of this young man, had not been revolted

---

[33] The translation is by Teresa A. Kennedy.

215 Soe hi best can hi en was niet vlugge.
　　Si stieten ende sloegen sinen rugge,
　　Dat hi wert weker dan sijn buc.
　　Her Gobert hadde clein gheluc.
　　Doen hi dus was gheslagen,
220 Ghinghen si wech het ginc daghen.
　　Her Gobert bleef in groten sere.
　　Dit exempel gheeft ons lere
　　Die hebben stouten vrouwen
　　Dat si te vele niet en betrouwen
225 Noch te vele niet hanteren
　　Die ghene die crune scheren.
　　Doen sijt het sal hem schinen.
　　Want als si om neringhe pinen,
　　Ende hem te minnen niet en lust,
230 Sijn die clerke wel gherust
　　Die al meest mans wiuen begheren,
　　Ende somwile haer goet verteren.
　　Selden hebbic oec verstaen
　　Dat si gheuaderen bidden gaen.

IV

Decameron IX, 6

(ed. Vittore Branca [Firenze, 1965], pp. 1062–7, c. 1350–60)[34]

　　Nel pian di Mugnone fu, non ha guari, un buono uomo, il quale a' viandanti dava
pe' lor danari mangiare e bere; e come che povera persona fosse e avesse piccola
casa, alcuna volta per un bisogno grande, non ogni persona, ma alcun conoscente
albergava. Ora aveva costui una sua moglie assai bella femina, della quale aveva
due figliuoli: e l'uno era una giovanetta bella e leggiadra, d'età di quindici o di
sedici anni, che ancora marito non avea; l'altro era un fanciul piccolino che ancora
non aveva uno anno, il quale la madre stessa allattava. Alla giovane aveva posti gli
occhi addosso un giovanetto leggiadro e piacevole e gentile uomo della nostra città,
il quale molto usava per la contrada, e focosamente l'amava; ed ella, che d'esser da
un così fatto giovane amata forte si gloriava, mentre di ritenerlo con piacevoli
sembianti nel suo amor si sforzava, di lui similmente s'innamorò; e più volte per
grado di ciascuna delle parti avrebbe tale amore avuto effetto, se Pinuccio (che così

---

[34] I do not reproduce here, or in the translation, the "frame" material from Boccaccio – the brief plot
summary and the account of the situation leading up to the tale proper. In any case, the frame materials
here are not extensive. The narrator of this sixth tale of the ninth day is Panfilo, whose only transition to
the previous story is that the name of one of the women in that story is Niccolosa, which reminds him of
a different story about a woman who happens to have that same name. Just before starting his story,
Panfilo says that it shows how a good woman's cleverness prevented a scandal.

by the idea of the censure that would have led to the dishonor of both their reputations. But as the days passed his ardor reached a peak and there came such desire to Pinuccio to be with her again that he fell into thought, seeking a way that he could lodge overnight at her father's house, with the understanding that, as he was familiar with the layout of the girl's house, if he could manage to stay he could come to her, without anyone else the wiser. Once this idea came to him he took immediate measures to put his plan into action.

So he, together with a close friend named Adriano, who knew all about his passion, took off late one afternoon with two livery stable nags, packed themselves two cases, maybe filled with straw, and left Florence, and by a circular route arrived in the valley of the Mugnone, riding in after nightfall, and making it appear that they were returning from Romagna, knocking at the door of the good man who, since he was quite familiar with both of them, opened the door quickly. And to him Pinuccio said: "Look, put us up for the night; we thought we could get back to Florence, and although we gave it our best shot, we've only gotten this far at this hour, as you can see."

To this the host replied: "Pinuccio, you can understand that I am a bit worried about how I can put such men as you in my home, but now since at this hour you have arrived and there is really nowhere else you could go, I am delighted to house you as well as I am able."

Therefore the two young men dismounted and stepped into the little lodging, after stabling their nags, and then, having brought with them a nice supper, they ate together with the host. Now the host only had a little bedroom in which there were three small beds arranged to the best of the host's ability, which meant that there was hardly any space left between them. Two of these beds stood along one wall of the room and the third stood against another, with the result being that only with difficulty could one move about. Of these three beds the host made up the least uncomfortable for the two comrades and invited them to lie down. Then, after a little time, while they pretended to sleep, though neither of them did sleep, the host tucked his daughter into one bed, and he and his wife climbed into the other, alongside of which she had placed the cradle where her young son slept. And they were arranged in this way. Pinuccio, having carefully scoped everything out, and after waiting until he was sure everyone was sleeping, slowly got up and went to the little bed where his beloved lay sleeping, and got into bed to lie down beside her. She, although at first frightened, was quickly reconciled to his presence, and with him took such pleasures as they both most desired. While Pinuccio thus occupied himself with the girl, along came a cat which caused something or other to fall, which awoke the wife when she heard it. For this reason she got up, with some timidity of course, as dark as it was, and went towards the place where she had heard the noise. Adriano got up for a different reason. As luck would have it he had to answer nature's call. He also arose and set off on his expedition. He found the cradle where the wife had left it, and not being able to pass without moving it, took it from the side of the bed where it had been placed and put it alongside the bed where he had been sleeping. After doing what he had risen to do he returned, forgetting about the cradle, and got back into bed.

The wife, after looking around and finding out that what had fallen was of no importance, did not even bother to light a lamp. She cursed at the cat, returned to the bedroom and picked her way straight to the bed where her husband was sleeping. Not finding the cradle, she said to herself, "O for heaven's sake, what an idiot! Look at what I'm doing. Only for the love of God have I not gone straight into the bed of

aveva nome il giovane) non avesse schifato il biasimo della giovane e 'l suo. Ma pur di giorno in giorno multiplicando l'ardore, venne disidero a Pinuccio di doversi pur con costei ritrovare, e caddegli nel pensiero di trovar modo di dover col padre albergare, avvisando, sì come colui che la disposizion della casa della giovane sapeva, che, se questo facesse, gli potrebbe venir fatto d'esser con lei, senza avvedersene persona; e come nell'animo gli venne, così sanza indugio mandò ad effetto.

Esso, insieme con un suo fidato compagno chiamato Adriano, il quale questo amor sapeva, tolti una sera al tardi due ronzini a vettura e postevi su due valigie, forse piene di paglia, di Firenze uscirono, e presa una lor volta, sopra il pian di Mugnone cavalcando pervennero, essendo già notte; e di quindi, come se di Romagna tornassero, data la volta, verso le case se ne vennero, e alla casa del buon uom picchiarono, il quale, sì come colui che molto era dimestico di ciascuno, aperse la porta prestamente: al quale Pinuccio disse: "Vedi, a te conviene stanotte albergarci: noi ci credemmo dover potere entrare in Firenze, e non ci siamo sì saputi studiare, che noi non siam qui pure a così fatta ora, come tu vedi, giunti."

A cui l'oste rispose: "Pinuccio, tu sai bene come io sono agiato di poter così fatti uomini, come voi siete, alberare; ma pur, poi che questa ora v'ha qui sopraggiunti, né tempo ci è da potere andare altrove, io v'albergherò volentieri com'io potrò."

Ismontati adunque i due giovani e nello alberghetto entrati, primieramente i loro ronzini adagiarono, e appresso, avendo ben seco portato da cena, insieme con l'oste cenarono. Ora non avea l'oste che una cameretta assai piccola, nella quale eran tre letticelli messi come il meglio l'oste avea saputo; né v'era per tutto ciò tanto di spazio rimaso, essendone due dall'una delle facce della camera e 'l terzo di rincontro a quegli dall'altra, che altro che strettamente andar vi si potesse. Di questi tre letti fece l'oste il men cattivo acconciar per li due compagni, e fecegli coricare: poi, dopo alquanto, non dormendo alcun di loro, come che di dormir mostrassero, fece l'oste nell'un de' due che rimasi erano coricar la figliuola, e nell'altro s'entrò egli e la donna sua, la quale allato del letto dove dormiva pose la culla nella quale il suo piccolo figlioletto teneva. Ed essendo le cose in questa guisa disposte, e Pinuccio avendo ogni cosa veduta, dopo alquanto spazio, parendogli che ogn'uomo addormentato fosse, pianamente levatosi, se n'andò al letticello dove la giovane amata da lui si giaceva, e miselesi a giacere allato: dalla quale, ancora che paurosamente il facesse, fu lietamente raccolto, e con essolei di quel piacere che più disideravano prendendo si stette. E standosi così Pinuccio con la giovane, avvenne che una gatta fece certe cose cadere, le quali la donna destatasi sentì: per che levatasi, temendo non fosse altro, così al buio come era, se n'andò là dove sentito avea il romore. Adriano, che a ciò non avea l'animo, per avventura per alcuna opportunità natural si levò, alla quale espedire andando, trovò la culla postavi dalla donna, e non potendo senza levarla oltrepassare, presala, la levò del luogo dove era e posela allato al letto dove esso dormiva; e fornito quello per che levato s'era e tornandosene, senza della culla curarsi, nel letto se n'entrò.

La donna, avendo cerco e trovato che quello che caduto era non era tal cosa, non si curò d'altrimenti accender lume per vederlo, ma, garrito alla gatta, nella cameretta se ne tornò, e a tentone dirittamente al letto dove il marito dormiva se n'andò; ma, non trovandovi la culla, disse seco stessa: "Oimè, cattiva me, vedi quel che io faceva! in fé di Dio, che io me n'andava dirittamente nel letto degli osti miei"; e,

my guests." Groping around a bit further ahead, she found the cradle and got into bed next to Adriano, thinking all the while that she was lying next to her husband. Adriano, who had still not fallen back to sleep, feeling her next to him, received her well and cheerfully, and without making any conversation started sailing tight to the wind, to the great delight of the woman.

And such was the situation when Pinuccio, not wanting sleep to overtake him while in bed with his girl, having had such pleasures as he desired, got up from her side to return to his own bed to sleep, and there he went. Finding the cradle, he thought that it must be the bed of his host, and therefore went a little further, and lay down with his host, who woke up at the arrival of Pinuccio. Pinuccio, believing he was lying by Adriano, said: "I'll tell you there never was such sweetness as that of Niccolosa! By the body of God, I've had with her the greatest delight that a man ever had with a woman, and I tell you that I've visited six times at her house since I left you here."

The host was none too happy at hearing this news. At first he said to himself: "What the hell is going on?" Then, with more anger than wisdom, he said: "Pinuccio, you have committed a terrible crime, and I don't know why you have done this to me. But by the body of God, I'll pay you back."

Pinuccio, who was not the savviest guy in the world, perceived his error but made no effort to gloss over the situation as best he could. He said: "How are you going to pay me back? What can you do to me?"

The host's wife, who thought she was in bed with her husband, said to Adriano: "O my God! Listen to how our guests are having words with each other."

Adriano laughingly replied: "Let them do it, goddamn them. Those two had too much to drink last night."

The wife, already suspecting she heard the voice of her husband cursing, recognized Adriano's voice and unhappily realized where she was and with whom. At this point, having a brain, without saying another word, she quickly got up, taking the cradle of her little son, and since no light penetrated the darkness of the room, sneaked with it as best she could to the bed where her daughter was sleeping and lay down next to her. As if she had been awakened by her husband's loud grumbling, she called out and asked what he and Pinuccio were arguing about. The husband replied: "Didn't you hear what he said he's been doing to Niccolosa?"

The wife answered: "He's lying through his teeth, for he certainly hasn't been anywhere near Niccolosa, since I've been lying here beside her all night, and haven't been able to get to sleep, and you're a fool to believe him. You fools drink all night, then dream and sleepwalk, imagining your marvelous sexual prowess. It's too bad that you haven't fallen and broken your necks! And what is Pinuccio doing in bed with you? Why isn't he in his own bed?"

From the other side of the room Adriano, seeing with what cunning the wife hid her embarrassment and that of her daughter, said: "Pinuccio, I've told you a hundred times that you shouldn't wander around sleepwalking, and then make all kinds of claims that you've only dreamed about. It's going to get you in big trouble one of these days. Come back here, damn you!"

The host, hearing what his wife and Adriano said, began to believe that Pinuccio had been dreaming, and grabbing his shoulder, shook him and called him, saying: "Pinuccio, wake up. Go back to your bed."

Assimilating all that had been said, Pinuccio started to act like a man who was dreaming and began to babble nonsense, at which the host got the biggest laugh in

fattasi un poco più avanti e trovando la culla, in quello letto al quale ella era allato insieme con Adriano si coricò, credendosi col marito coricare. Adriano, che ancora raddormentato non era, sentendo questo, la ricevette bene e lietamente, e senza fare altramenti motto, da una volta in su caricò l'orza con gran piacer della donna.

E così stando, temendo Pinuccio non il sonno con la sua giovane il soprapprendesse, avendone quel piacer preso che egli desiderava, per tornar nel suo letto a dormire le si levò dal lato, e là venendone, trovando la culla, credette quello essere quel dell'oste: per che, fattosi un poco più avanti, insieme con l'oste si coricò, il quale per la venuta di Pinuccio si destò. Pinuccio, credendosi essere allato ad Adriano, disse: "Ben ti dico che mai sì dolce cosa non fu come è la Niccolosa! al corpo di Dio, io ho avuto con lei il maggior diletto che mai uomo avesse con femina, e dicoti che io sono andato da sei volte in su in villa, poscia che io mi partii quinci."

L'oste, udendo queste novelle e non piacendogli troppo, prima disse seco stesso: 'Che diavol fa costui qui?', poi, più turbato che consigliato, disse: "Pinuccio, la tua è stata una gran villania, e non so perché tu mi t'abbi a far questo; ma, per lo corpo di Dio, io te ne pagherò."

Pinuccio, che non era il più savio giovane del mondo, avveggendosi del suo errore, non ricorse ad emendare come meglio avesse potuto, ma disse: "Di che mi pagherai? che mi potrestù fare tu?"

La donna dell'oste, che col marito si credeva essere, disse ad Adriano: "Oimè! odi gli osti nostri che hanno non so che parole insieme."

Adriano ridendo disse: "Lasciali fare, che Iddio gli metta in mal anno: essi bevver troppo iersera."

La donna, parendole avere udito il marito garrire e udendo Adriano, incontanente conobbe là dove stata era e con cui: per che, come savia, senza alcuna parola dire, subitamente si levò, e presa la culla del suo figlioletto, come che punto lume nella camera non si vedesse, per avviso la portò allato al letto dove dormiva la figliuola e con lei si coricò; e quasi desta fosse per lo rumore del marito, il chiamò e domandollo che parole egli avesse con Pinuccio: il marito rispose: "Non odi tu ciò ch'e' dice che ha fatto stanotte alla Niccolosa?"

La donna disse: "Egli mente bene per la gola, ché con la Niccolosa non è egli giaciuto: ché io mi ci coricai io in quel punto che io non ho mai poscia potuto dormire; e tu se' una bestia che gli credi. Voi bevete tanto la sera, che poscia sognate la notte e andate in qua e in là senza sentirvi, e parvi far maraviglie: egli è gran peccato che voi non vi fiaccate il collo! Ma che fa egli costi Pinuccio? perché non si sta egli nel letto suo?"

D'altra parte Adriano, veggendo che la donna saviamente la sua vergogna e quella della figliuola ricopriva, disse: "Pinuccio, io te l'ho detto cento volte che tu non vada attorno, ché questo tuo vizio del levarti in sogno e di dire le favole che tu sogni per vere ti daranno una volta la mala ventura: torna qua, che Dio ti dea la mala notte!"

L'oste, udendo quello che la donna diceva e quello che diceva Adriano, cominciò a creder troppo bene che Pinuccio sognasse: per che, presolo per la spalla, lo 'ncominciò a dimenare e a chiamar, dicendo: "Pinuccio, destati: tornati al letto tuo."

Pinuccio, avendo raccolto ciò che detto s'era, cominciò a guisa d'uom che sognasse ad entrare in altri farnetichi: di che l'oste faceva le maggior risa del

the world. At last, after sufficient shaking, he pretended to waken, and calling Adriano, said, "Is it already morning, that you're waking me?"

Adriano replied: "Yes, get over here."

At this, feigning disorientation and behaving like one still half asleep, he finally got up from the side of the host and returned to bed with Adriano. In the morning when they got up, the host began to laugh and make fun of Pinuccio and his dreams. And after a few more witticisms, the two young men saddled their horses, packed their bags, had a drink with their host, remounted, and took themselves back to Florence, just as happy with the way things had turned out as with what had actually happened.[35] And soon after, finding a new method, Pinuccio and Niccolosa were reunited, she always swearing to her mother that Pinuccio had been dreaming. Because of this, the wife, remembering the embraces of Adriano, said to herself that only she had been awake after all.

---

[35] That is, were as happy with the way they had escaped the accusations as they had been with their sexual exploits with the daughter and mother.

mondo. Alla fine, pur sentendosi dimenare, fece sembiante di destarsi, e chiamando Adrian, disse: "È egli ancora dì, che tu mi chiami?"

Adriano disse: "Sì, vienne qua."

Costui, infignendosi e mostrandosi ben sonnocchioso, al fine si levò dal lato all'oste e tornossi al letto con Adriano; e, venuto il giorno e levatisi, l'oste incominciò a ridere e a farsi beffe di lui e de' suoi sogni. E così d'uno in altro motto, acconci i due giovani i lor ronzini e messe le lor valigie e bevuto con l'oste, rimontati a cavallo se ne vennero a Firenze, non meno contenti del modo in che la cosa avvenuta era, che dello effetto stesso della cosa. E poi appresso, trovati altri modi, Pinuccio con la Niccolosa si ritrovò, la quale alla madre affermava lui fermamente aver sognato; per la qual cosa la donna, ricordandosi dell'abbracciar d'Adriano, sola seco diceva d'aver vegghiato.

The Cook's Tale

JOHN SCATTERGOOD

When the Cook intervenes in the storytelling contest of the *Canterbury Tales* he emerges in considerable detail. What is said about him and what he says about himself are consistent with the description of him in the *General Prologue*, but enrich and develop it. In the *General Prologue* he is associated with London (I[A], 382), which he twice refers to later as "oure citee" (4343, 4365). It also emerges that he has a shop in London (4352), and that his name is Roger of Ware (4336, 4353). It may be that he is based on a certain Roger Knight of Ware, Cook, who appears to be the man accused of being a "common night-walker," that is, one who broke the curfew, in 1373 and who is named in pleas of debt in 1377 and 1384.[1] If it were the case that Chaucer's model for this character was called "Knight" it would make sense of what appear to be two jokes about the Cook: he is once called by Harry Bailly "gentil Roger" (4353), and in the *Manciple's Prologue* when he falls off his horse in a drunken stupor he is referred to ironically as "a fair chyvachee of a cook" (IX[H], 50) – both of which connote a nobility which he fails to live up to. It is probably no accident that he is involved in two altercations with Harry Bailly, the innkeeper from Southwark, again a character based on a real person from the metropolis: enmity between cooks and innkeepers was traditional.[2] It looks as though Chaucer had a fairly secure sense of how he saw the Cook, possibly because the Cook was based on somebody known to him. And when he begins the *Cook's Tale* there is the same precise concentration on local detail. It is set in London, and Cheapside, one of its principal thoroughfares, and Newgate, one of its main prisons, are both mentioned (4377, 4402). The story also involves an apprentice in one of the London victuallers trades (4365–6). Chaucer is on familiar territory, which makes it all the stranger that he appears to stop after 58 lines: all that remains is a description of Perkyn Revelour and his unruly lifestyle (4365–98), an account of how he left his master after being discharged from his

---

[1] For these records see Edith Rickert, "Chaucer's Hodge of Ware," in (London) *Times Literary Supplement*, 20 October 1932, p. 761; and Earl D. Lyon, "Roger of Ware, Cook," *Modern Language Notes* 52 (1937): 491–4.

[2] For the traditional enmity between cooks and innkeepers see F. J. Tupper, "The Quarrels of the Canterbury Pilgrims," *Journal of English and Germanic Philology* 14 (1915): 256–70.

apprenticeship (4399–412), and a few lines about how he took up lodgings with a similarly riotous friend whose wife kept a shop for the sake of appearances ("contenaunce") but actually made a living from prostitution (4415–22).

E. G. Stanley has argued that the tale is complete as it stands, and that its brevity is part of the Cook's instinct for reducing everything to its lowest essentials.[3] That is not, however, the impression formed by J. M. Manly and Edith Rickert: "That Chaucer wrote thus far and stopped is difficult to believe. He seems not only master of a matchless technique but too thoroughly master of his story-material to stop. Only sudden illness or some other insurmountable interference could have prevented him from going on."[4] They appear to believe that material may have been lost, a view recently restated by M. C. Seymour, who argues that at some early stage of the transmission of the Canterbury sequence the page or pages containing the rest of the *Cook's Tale* went missing.[5] Donald R. Howard has a more colourful version of this explanation: "Possibly it was finished but too scurrilous to be transcribed, and so went underground. Possibly Chaucer or someone else suppressed it, ripped it out of an early copy leaving only what was on the same folio with the ending of the Reeve's Tale."[6] This is an attractive idea, and possible, but not very likely. The scurrility of the Miller's and Reeve's tales did not prevent their survival; and Chaucer's suggestion that anyone who was offended by the "harlotrie" of his low-life tales should "Turne over the leef and chese another" (3177) could as well have applied to whatever the Cook may have told. The evidence of the early copyists is ambiguous. The Hengwrt copyist seems to think that the tale was not finished: "Of this Cokes tale Chaucer made na moore," he writes in the margin where it breaks off, as if he had searched unsuccessfully for a completed version. But he is not altogether sure, it appears, for he leaves the rest of the page and part of the following page blank, as if allowing for the possibility that something may turn up. The Ellesmere copyist also leaves space for more text, should it become available.

Recently, however, Richard Beadle has raised the possibility that there may never have been any intention on Chaucer's part to continue the story of Perkyn Revelour, or, at least, not at this point in the storytelling sequence.[7] He draws on material in Sir Francis Kinaston's commentary on *Troilus and Criseyde* in Oxford, Bodleian Library MS Additional C 287 and in Sir John Selden's *De Synedriis Praefecturis Judicis Veterum Ebraerorum* (1653), both of which make use of a manuscript, once belonging to Selden but now lost, which preserved a version of the *Cook's Prologue* and *Tale* which is significantly different from that to be found anywhere else. Most manuscripts divide the Prologue

---

[3]   See "Of This Cokes Tale Maked Chaucer Na Moore," *Poetica* 5 (1976): 36–59.

[4]   See *The Text of the Canterbury Tales*, ed. J. M. Manly and Edith Rickert, 8 Vols. (Chicago: University of Chicago Press, 1940), III. 446 (note to line 4433).

[5]   See "Hypothesis, Hyperbole, and the Hengwrt Manuscript of the *Canterbury Tales*," *English Studies* 68 (1987): 214–19; and "Of This Cokes Tale," *Chaucer Review* 24 (1990): 259–62.

[6]   *The Idea of the Canterbury Tales* (Berkeley: University of California Press, 1976), p. 244.

[7]   See "'I wol nat telle it yit': John Selden and a Lost Version of the *Cook's Tale*," in *Chaucer to Shakespeare: Essays in Honour of Shinsuke Ando*, ed. Toshiuki Takamiya and Richard Beadle (Cambridge: D. S. Brewer, 1992), pp. 55–66.

from the Tale at line 4365, "A prentys whilom dwelled in oure citee . . .": some specifically designate what has gone before as "prologue" and what follows as "tale." But Selden's manuscript had no division there and ran the material dealing with Perkyn Revelour on from the badinage between the Cook and Harry Bailly. In this version, the break comes after the account of Perkyn Revelour, not before it:

> . . . A Shop and swived for her sustenance
> And ther withall he lough and made chear
> And said his tale as ye shullen after here
> Here beginneth the Cokes tale of Gamelin . . .

Beadle argues that there is a case for seeing the material about Perkyn Revelour not as the beginning of the Cook's story but as a "feint," a ploy which is meant to indicate to Harry Bailly that he could respond to the innkeeper's criticisms of his cookshop with a scurrilous story about "herbergage" (Harry Bailly's profession) if he so wished, "But nathelees I wol nat telle it yit" (4361). This is interesting and a possible reading: it makes sense of some of the features of the remaining text. But Chaucer uses "whilom" and a description of place and characters in the opening lines of many of his tales, including two of the three that precede the *Cook's Tale* and the one which immediately follows it (see I[A], 859–61; 3187–8; II[B1], 134–5). So it looks as though line 4365 is the opening of a story: "A prentys whilom dwelled in oure citee . . ." This is the way most copyists saw the material: even if they do not specifically and separately designate the "prologue" and the "tale" they often begin this line with an emphatic decorative capital.

But copyists hate a vacuum, and in twenty five manuscripts, the earliest of which are London, British Library MS Harley 7334 and Oxford, Corpus Christi College MS 198, the *Tale of Gamelyn* is used to supply the deficiency left by the tale Chaucer evidently began but did not complete. Eight manuscripts have no transitional material, but simply begin the tale where Chaucer left off. Most, however, like London, British Library, Egerton MS 2863, make some pretence of deferring the story of Perkyn Revelour and beginning something else:

> But here of I wil passe as now
> And of yonge Gamelyn I wile telle yow.

The copyist of London, British Library Lansdowne MS 851, no doubt referring back to the argument about scurrilous tales which preceded the Miller's offering (I[A] 3167–86) repudiates what the Cook had written already as "harlotrie" and offers the *Tale of Gamelyn* as something more respectable

> Fye ther one, it is so foule, I wil nowe tell no forthere
> ffor shame of the harlotrie that seweth after.
> A velany it were there of more to spell,
> Bot of a knyghte and his sonnes my tale I wil forthe tell.

In London, British Library MS Royal 17 D XV the copyist, remembering that the pilgrims were originally meant to tell more than one tale (I[A] 788–95), allows what the Cook has said so far to constitute a "tale" and includes the story of Gamelyn as his second offering: "Her endeth o tale of the cooke and her folowyth a nother tale of the same cooke." The *Tale of Gamelyn* is a violent provincial romance, dealing with quarrels about inheritance and land in a gentry family.[8] How and why it came to be associated with the Cook of London in a collection of tales written by a poet whose habitual milieu was the royal court and the metropolis is not known and is difficult to imagine. Skeat speculates:

> It is quite clear that some scribes preserved it because they thought it worth preserving, and that it must have been found amongst Chaucer's MSS in some connection with his *Canterbury Tales*. We can hardly doubt that he had obtained a copy with a view to making good use of it, and the various copies now extant all agree so closely that they may have been due to a single original . . .[9]

He suggests that Chaucer may have intended to work the story up for telling by the Yeoman, which is plausible enough since he is the most obvious "green-wood" character on the pilgrimage, though it seems equally likely to me, if he did have a copy, that Chaucer may have used it as part of his source material for his parody of old-fashioned romance in *Sir Thopas*. Of course, he may not have had a copy and the poem may owe its inclusion among the tales to an early copyist, desperate to fill an embarrassing lacuna in his text. Unlikely as it may appear, two things could have suggested a suitability of this story for the Cook – like the material he has already used in relation to Perkyn Revelour, this story involves crime, justice, and the law, and its hero is a young man seeking to make his way in a world controlled by his elders. But other than this, it is hard to see much appropriateness.

Since the manuscripts can tell us comparatively little about what sort of story the *Cook's Tale* was likely to be, we are forced back on the evidence of the text which has survived, fragmentary though it may be, for pointers. And there are several. It looks as though he intended to centre his story on the dissipated London apprentice Perkyn Revelour, a type-figure with a significant and indicative name, and that the story would be short and comic: he describes it as "a litel jape" (4343).[10] If we accept at face value his intention to reserve for later any tale about an "hostileer" as part of the quitting of Harry Bailly, some of the possibilities that remain are the following. First, the Cook could have picked up the moral of the Reeve's previous tale, which had interested him, that "herberwynge by nyghte is perilous" (4332) and developed it: his fragment ends

---

[8]   For an account of this poem see my essay "*The Tale of Gamelyn*: The Noble Robber as Provincial Hero," in *Reading the Past: Essays on Medieval and Renaissance Literature* (Dublin: Four Courts Press, 1996), pp. 80–113.

[9]   See *The Tale of Gamelyn*, ed. W. W. Skeat (Oxford: Clarendon Press, 1884), p. xvi.

[10]   What follows in this paragraph summarizes points made in more detail in my article "Perkyn Revelour and the *Cook's Tale*," *Chaucer Review* 19 (1984): 14–23; reprinted in *Reading the Past: Essays on Medieval and Renaissance Literature*, pp. 183–91.

with Perkyn Revelour taking up residence with a friend ("he sente his bed and his array" [4418]) who has a wife who is a prostitute. Second, it may be that the issue of social class was present in Chaucer's mind. A point frequently made by those who satirize urban wastrels like Perkyn Revelour is that they assume life-styles beyond their substance and rank, and Chaucer adverts to this idea in the lines:

> Revel and trouthe, as in a lowe degree,
> They been ful wrothe al day, as men may see.   (4397–8)

Third, the factor of age may have been important in the Cook's story. Charac-ters such as Perkyn Revelour tend to be young, and the victims of their exploita-tion are usually older and settled into more prosperous lifestyles. There is a hint of this already in the lines:

> For sikerly a prentys revelour
> That haunteth dys, riot, or paramour,
> His maister shal it in his shoppe abye,
> Al have he no part of the mynstralcye.   (4391–4)

Fourth, it is possible that the story may have turned on trickery, or even crime. Usually, characters such as Perkyn Revelour prey on unsuspecting innocents, but they are also prone to quarrels between themselves. Perhaps Chaucer's intro-duction of a "compeer" who "lovede dys, and revel, and disport" (4419–20) means that he envisaged the *Cook's Tale* as involving rivalry between people who look as though they ought to have similar interests. The characters in Chaucer who conform most closely to the type represented by Perkyn Revelour are the three young men of the *Pardoner's Tale*: they are several times described as "riotoures" (VI[C] 661, 692, 716) and they spend their time in "riot, hasard, stywes, and tavernes" (465). One of the central ironies of this story is that it begins with a pact of sworn brotherhood between the three (696–704) but ends in mutual treachery and death. A fifth possibility, therefore, is that the Cook would tell a story on this theme – one that had already been raised in the *Knight's Tale* (I[A] 1128–86) in a courtly setting, but which could have been developed at a different social level. Earl D. Lyon in 1941 found that "Parallels to the story elements . . . taken singly, are as abundant as one might expect, especially in the humorous stories of Renaissance England and of fifteenth-century Germany . . ." and he cites analogous material involving unruly appren-tices or servants, like Perkyn Revelour, whose unsavoury adventures take place in the sort of urban setting suggested for his tale.[11] But the attempt to find a source or analogue which incorporated the elements of Chaucer's story in a sig-nificantly similar way proved, as he said, "fruitless."

More recently, there have emerged two suggestions for seeing the Cook's

---

[11] "The Cook's Tale," in *Sources and Analogues of Chaucer's Canterbury Tales*, ed. W. F. Bryan and Germaine Dempster (New York: Humanities Press, repr. 1958), p. 149.

fragment, and any possible tale that may have followed it, in a more political light. Paul Strohm associates the emphasis on "revel" with the way in which, according to the Westminster chronicler, the dissident peasants of 1381 described their activities as "A revelle! A revelle!" He believes that the *Cook's Tale* "participates ontologically in a larger system of narratives treating revelry and rebuke in the sense that it draws upon their narrative and symbolic energy and shares a portion of their social work" though he does not think that the story is "an allegory of the 1381 Rising or even necessarily a reference to it."[12] So one may recognize a sixth possibility, that the story may have dealt with politics and social dissidence, however indirectly or directly articulated. More generally, David Wallace has written on the strains and tensions in the social fabric of London in the late fourteenth century and sees what Chaucer has written in the Cook's fragment as being symptomatic of this lack of urban identity: "There is no idea of a city for all the inhabitants of a space called London to pay allegiance to; there are only conflicts of associational, hierarchical, and anti-associational discourses, acted out within and across the boundaries of a city wall or the fragments of a text called *The Canterbury Tales*."[13] So there may be a seventh possibility in a story which articulates the fragmented nature of the urban culture of England's capital city.

However, the assumption that the story the Cook is to tell will necessarily be scurrilous and comic has been challenged by V. A. Kolve, who finds, along with all the evidence which points to a fabliau-like developement, another and very different voice in the surviving text – one that is sententious and moralistic.[14] This represents the view of events as seen by the master victualler to whom Perkyn Revelour is apprenticed:

> But atte laste his maister hym bithoghte,
> Upon a day, whan he his papir soghte,
> Of a proverbe that seith this same word:
> "Wel bet is roten appul out of hoord
> Than that it rotie al the remenaunt."
> So fareth it by a riotous servaunt;
> It is ful lasse harm to lete hym pace,
> Than he shende alle the servantz in the place.
> Therfore his maister yaf hym acquitance,
> And bad hym go, with sorwe and with meschance!   (4403–12)

He points out that since the Cook had a "shoppe" (4352) in London he must have been a citizen, and that he is associated with the five guildsmen (379), who

---

[12] See "'Lad with revel to Newegate': Chaucerian Narrative and Historical Meta-Narrative," in *Art and Context in Late Medieval English Narrative: Essays in Honor of Robert Worth Frank, Jr.*, ed. Robert R. Edwards (Cambridge: D. S. Brewer, 1994), pp. 136–76. The quotation is from p. 174.

[13] See "Chaucer and the Absent City," in *Chaucer's England: Literature in Historical Context*, ed. Barbara A. Hanawalt, *Medieval Studies at Minnesota*, Vol. 4 (Minneapolis: University of Minnesota Press, 1992), pp. 59–90. The quotation is from p. 84.

[14] See *Chaucer and the Imagery of Narrative: The First Five Canterbury Tales* (London: Arnold, 1984), pp. 258–85.

are patterns of bourgeois probity and ambition: it is possible but not certain that he is to cook for them on the pilgrimage. "The part of the Cook's performance that projects an imaginative self-identification with the values of the master victualler is grounded in a linked professional and civic identity."[15] This voice in the Cook's fragment sets forth the ethos of trade, and has to do with profit and respectability. It is clear that this is the aspect of the fragment to which some of the fifteenth-century copyists responded, for some finished off the fragment for themselves by providing a moral outcome for the interrupted story. These can be very brief, such as the following from University of Chicago, McCormick MS:

> And thus with horedom and bryberye
> Togeder thei used till thei honged hye;
> For who so euel byeth shal make a sory sale.
> And thus I make an ende to my tale.[16]

Even so, it is interesting that even a perfunctory ending such as this should include a proverb about mercantile practice (Whiting, S29). Another spurious conclusion, some forty lines long, from Oxford, Bodleian Library, MS Bodley 686, is much more circumstantial, but basically makes the same point. It contains proverbial maxims such as "Euelle sponne wolle at the laste wolle come oute" (Whiting, W571), and has one of the two male characters hanged and the other committed to prison, before it moralizes itself:

> And therfore yonge men, lerne while ye may,
> That with mony dyuers thoghtes beth prycked al the day.
> Remembre you what myschefe cometh of mysgouernaunce:
> Thus mowe ye lerne worschep and come to substaunce.
> Thenke how grace and gouernaunce hath broght hem a boune.
> Many pore mannys sonn ches state of the toune . . .[17]

Young men are to turn their attentions, whatever their other daily distractions may be, to "worschep" and "substaunce," that is, to respectability and wealth: in an urban context, says the continuator, that is the way to get on in the world. Kolve suggests that Chaucer may have intended to tell a prodigal-son type of story, ". . . which might have flattered the values of the guilds even better than a narrative of justice strictly conceived. It might have celebrated at the end, as it does at the beginning, the master victualler's patience and discretion, adding to those virtues a demonstration of his Christian capacity to forgive and be charitable of heart."[18] This proposal, however, is hardly consistent with the "litel jape" which has been promised. And no specific story of a morally improving kind has been proposed for the Cook.

---

[15] See Kolve, *Chaucer and the Imagery of Narrative*, p. 275.
[16] Printed in Manly and Rickert, *The Text of the Canterbury Tales*, II. 169.
[17] See Manly and Rickert, *The Text of the Canterbury Tales*, V. 434–7.
[18] See Kolve, *Chaucer and the Imagery of Narrative*, p. 277.

Two other scholars have developed Kolve's interest in MS Bodley 686. David Lorenzo Boyd has argued that the version included in this manuscript is significantly conditioned by its codicological context: ". . . in this expensively produced codex linking the maintenance of social order and moral precepts to the wealth, power, and status of its owners, Perkyn's anarchic threat becomes instead an important opportunity for containing the transgressive and justifying the social order."[19] The rewriting makes the story an exemplary piece against disobedience. Daniel J. Pinti, however, argues that the "continuation" and "revision" of the tale in this manuscript renders it more open. "The scribe reading and rewriting Chaucer's tale takes pains to distinguish his voice from the author's, to juxtapose two complementary literary voices and thereby create a version of the *Cook's Tale* that not only pretends to completion and even moralization, but also reimagines the themes in significant ways and functions as a commentary on the idea of Chaucerian authority in the fifteenth century."[20]

But it may well be that it is pointless to search for sources and analogues for the *Cook's Tale* which are literary narratives: perhaps when Chaucer says that he will tell of something that "fil in oure citee" (4343) he means, literally, that the story will be based on something which actually occurred in London. The only other Canterbury tale to be set in London, the *Canon's Yeoman's Tale,* deals also with the seamier side of the life of the capital, and concentrates on the fraudulent tricks of alchemists (VIII[G] 1012). No source has been found for this tale either, and it may be that Chaucer, when he dealt with contemporary London affairs, preferred to use material he knew at first hand or local stories he had heard. There is some indication that this may be the case because the materials on which the surviving part of the Cook's fragment is based appear to be contemporary legal documents relating to apprenticeship – instructions, oaths, and indentures – and contemporary satirical poetry. Once this is recognized the duality of tone of the remaining text becomes easier to understand: both of these types of material are implicitly or explicitly moralistic in that they seek to inculcate and promote good behaviour, but both are specific, as they have to be, as to what constitutes bad behaviour.

However, before looking at documents of this sort in relation to the *Cook's Tale* it is appropriate to say something about Perkyn Revelour's name, because there are several things which are unusual about it. It is relatively unusual in Chaucer for people to be referred to by names consisting of more than one term. When names do have more than one word in them it is usually in specific circumstances: they are sometimes well-known writers (Marcus Tullius Scithero, William Seynt Amour, John Crisostom), or historical figures (Tullius Hostilius, Hugh of Lincoln, Hugolyn de Pyze), or famous comtemporaries (Bernabo Viscounte, Jakke Strawe). He refers to his friends (Bukton, Gower, Graunson,

---

[19] See "Social Texts, Bodley 686, and the Politics of the *Cook's Tale*," *Huntingdon Library Quarterly,* 58i (1995): 81–98. The quotations are from p. 95.
[20] See "Governing the *Cook's Tale* in Bodley 686," *Chaucer Review* 30 (1996): 379–88. The quotations are from pp. 380 and 386.

Scogan, Strode, Vache) by their surnames, and he is himself referred to in this way in the Prologue to the *Man of Law's Tale* II[B1] 47, though the Eagle on the *House of Fame* 729 uses his Christian name. But elsewhere only Harry Bailly and "Hodge of Ware" (the first based on a contemporary figure, and the second probably so) are given anything other than a Christian name – except for Perkyn Revelour. English surnames fall broadly into four categories – those based on family names, those referring to places ("Hodge of Ware"), those indicating trades (Harry Bailly), and descriptive names or nicknames. It is to the last category that "Revelour" (= reveller, rioter, profligate) obviously belongs: indeed, the word "revelour" is once applied to this character (4391) when it is clearly not a name but a description of one of his characteristics.

These names, because they are often derogatory, are not names which people assumed for themselves, but are essentially names given to them by others: most people called "revelour" would no doubt have preferred to be called something else. No Perkyn Revelour has so far been found in the contemporary records, and it may be that Chaucer invented a name which seemed to him appropriate for an unruly apprentice: his use of this word is among the earliest uses recorded. But similar derogatory surnames occur in the London plea and memoranda rolls. On 24 July 1338 "Robert de Stratford, cordwainer, was attached to answer a charge of harbouring Alice Donbely, Alice Tredewedowe and other prostitutes . . ."[21] In a general complaint about disorderly behaviour in the city made by a jury drawn from the wards of the Bridge, Billingsgate and the Tower on 3 July 1340, it was affirmed, amongst other things, that "Agnes de Chedyngfeld and Clarice la Claterballock . . . are women of ill-fame"[22] – the first of these has a placename surname, referring to Chiddingfold (Surrey), the second a highly derogatory nickname. In a list of eight women committed to Newgate on 15 May 1365 for causing an affray in Holborn appears "Joan Stormy."[23] On 27 January 1373, in a list of people who owed "desperate debts" to Joan Northwold, appear "John Lemman" (= darling) and "William Prat 'de la Stowes'": at this date "prat" usually means "trick" or "device", but in view of its use in relation to somebody described as "of the Stews" (= brothel) it may be that it meant "buttocks" as it did later.[24] Either way, it is a derogatory surname. If Chaucer was inventing he was using a name of great plausibility and authenticity. But the possibility remains that he was not inventing. "Revell" in various spellings is now a not particularly uncommon surname, and it was used as early as 1201.[25]

The word "revel" is related to "rebel" etymologically, and the point Chaucer constantly makes about this "prentys revelour" is that he breaks all the rules he

---

[21] *Calendar of Plea and Memoranda Rolls, 1323–1364*, ed. A. H. Thomas (Cambridge: Cambridge University Press, 1926), p. 173.

[22] *Calendar of Plea and Memoranda Rolls, 1323–1364*, p. 125.

[23] *Calendar of Plea and Memoranda Rolls, 1365–1381*, ed. A. H. Thomas (Cambridge: Cambridge University Press, 1929), p. 32.

[24] *Calendar of Plea and Memoranda Rolls, 1365–1381*, p. 169.

[25] See *MED*, revel n. (1), 3. As surname.

is meant to keep. Chaucer constantly measures off Perkyn Revelour's behaviour against what, as an apprentice, he would have been enjoined to do and what he would have sworn to do. *The Chamberlain's Devout Instructions to Apprentices* (c. 1450) lists what is expected:

> You shall constantly and devoutly, every day, morning and evening, on your knees serve God, attending at the public service of the church, and hearing of the word preached, and endeavour the right practice thereof in your life and conversation. You shall be diligent and faithful in your master's service during the time of your apprenticeship and deal truly in what you shall be trusted. You shall often read over the covenants of your Indenture, together with these Instructions, and endeavour to perform the same to the utmost in your power. You shall avoid all evil company, and all occasions which may tend to draw you to the same; and make speedy return when you shall be sent on your master's or mistress's errands. You shall avoid idleness, and be ever employed in God's service, or about your master's business. You shall be of fair, gentle, and lowly speech and behaviour to all men, and especially to your governors; and avoid all manner of gaming, cursing, swearing, drunkenness; and according to your carriage, you must expect your good or evil from God and your friends.[26]

The standard Indenture, which is referred to here, first lists the master's obligations to his apprentice and then those of the apprentice to his master, as follows:

> . . . During the term the apprentice is to keep his master's secrets, to do him no injury, and to commit no excessive waste of his good. He is not to frequent taverns, not to commit fornication, in or out of his master's house, nor make any contract of matrimony nor affiance himself without his master's leave. He is not to play at dice-tables or chequers, or any other unlawful games, but is to conduct himself soberly, justly, piously, well, and honourably, and to be a faithful and good servant, according to the use and custom of London.[27]

It seems fairly clear that Chaucer has these types of document in mind as well as the ethos which underlies them when he constructs the portrait of Perkyn Revelour, who breaks not only the general spirit of his apprenticeship but also every specific rule: the "papir" the master looks for at line 4404 is almost certainly an indenture of this sort Far from looking after his master's goods Perkyn Revelour robs him: "often tyme he foond his box ful bare" (4390). Instead of

---

[26] Quoted from W. N. Hibbert, *A History of the Worshipful Company of Founders of the City of London* (London: Privately Printed, 1925), p. 305. But the instructions were fairly standard over a whole range of trades. And they remained virtually unchanged over several centuries. See, for example, Arthur Pearce, *A History of the Butchers' Company* (London: The Meat Trades' Journal Co. Ltd, 1929), p. 268, where the instructons appear to come from the reign of Queen Anne.

[27] Quoted from C. M. Clode, *Early History of the Guild of Merchant Taylors* (London: Harrison and Sons, 1888), p. 344. It refers to an indenture between John Harrietsham and Robert Lacy dated 20 December 1451. Like the Chamberlain's instructions, indentures of this sort are fairly standard for all trades, and remained virtually unchanged over many years. For one dated 1795 between two butchers, a father and son both called Nathaniel Hearn, see Pearce, *A History of the Butchers' Company*, pp. 266–7.

making "speedy return" when he is sent on errands he spends as much time out of the shop as possible and "wolde nat come ayeyn" (4380) until he had enjoyed himself thoroughly. Though expressly forbidden to do so "He loved bet the taverne than the shoppe" (4376). Similarly, instead of avoiding "fornication" he "was as ful of love and paramour" (4372). He is given to "unlawful games," especially "dys" (4384–7, 4392). And instead of avoiding "evil company" he seeks it: he "gadered hym a meynee of his sort" (4381). Chaucer uses texts which embody the mercantile ethos of contemporary London, which promulgate the high standards of professional and personal behaviour that the citizen-to-be was expected to live up to, and constructs an antitype, a character who breaks every precept, who resists being incorporated into the ethos and uses what opportunities his lifestyle affords him for personal pleasures of an immoral and sometimes criminal sort.

Chaucer also derived something from contemporary satire, perhaps from the macaronic poem usually called *On the Times,* to which Thomas Wright gave the date 1388 but which now appears to be a little earlier.[28] Richard Firth Green has argued, convincingly it seems to me, that some lines of it refer to the equipping of an expedition to France, largely paid for by the prominent London citizen John Philipot, in the summer of 1380, and the absence of John of Gaunt in Scotland ("regna remota") in the autumn of that year.[29] Because of its admiration for "Goode Iak" (i.e. Philipot) and its well-informedness about London and London affairs, it is fair to assume it was probably written in the capital: it certainly promulgates the viewpoint of the responsible and respectable citizenry. A number of contemporary abuses are attacked in this poem including the fashionable dress and immoral lifestyles of "galauntes, purs penyles" – impoverished wastrels who spend their money on fine clothes and their time on a variety of unsavoury pursuits. One passage in particular addresses itself to matters which interest Chaucer in his portrait of Perkyn Revelour. In London, British Library MS Harley 536 it runs as follows:

> Viue la bele thei cri
> fragrantia vina bibentes
> Thei drynke tyl thei drye
> lingua sensuque carentes
> Thei crye felle the bolles
> bonus est liquor hic maneamus
> ffor alle crystyn soulys
> dum durant vasa bibamus
> Whan men reste takis
> noctis sompno recreati
> Such felowes wakis
> ad dampna patra[n]da parati

---

[28] See *Political Poems and Songs Relating to English History*, 2 Vols., Rolls Series 14 (London: Longman, Green, Longman, Roberts, 1859–1861), I. 270–8.
[29] See his article "Jack Philipot, John of Gaunt, and a Poem of 1380," *Speculum* 66 (1991): 330–41.

Armis sydus & blode
horum quidam recitabit
yit whan he is most wode
hunc sermo blandus domabit
Peraventure at an houre
poscunt hij tempora plausis
A contre tenour
cantabit carcere clausis.[30]

["Long live the beautiful one," they cry, drinking the fragrant wine.
They drink until they become thirsty, lacking the use of tongue and
sense. They cry, "Fill the cups. The drink is good. Let us stay here. For
all Christian souls, while the cups last, let us drink." When men take
their rest, refreshed by the sleep of night, such fellows wake, prepared
for doing harm. "Arms, sides, and blood," one of them will repeat. Yet
when he is most angry, a soft speech will vanquish him. Perhaps for an
hour they demand the applause of the times. A counter-tenor he will
sing, locked in jail.]

Chaucer's character is not particularly to be associated with fine and fashionable clothes – though he is described as "Gaillard . . . as goldfynch" (4367), one
of the most highly coloured, as well as one of the most lively, of British birds,
and though he does take a good deal of care over his hair, like other would-be
fashionable young men in Chaucer. But he is, like the gallants described, a
haunter of taverns, and, like them, he has seen the inside of a prison (4402).

Though too little of it has survived for one to be confident about generalizing,
it does appear that in the *Cook's Tale* Chaucer is not using the type of source
material he usually used, but contemporary documents of a non-narrative sort.
That there were strains in the social fabric of London and in the apprenticeship
system in the latter part of the fourteenth century is well-known. It looks as
though Chaucer may have been intending to address some of these issues, in a
tale, perhaps based on a contemporary incident, which is likely to have been
comic, but that he did not get very far with it.

---

[30] The quotation is taken from London, British Library MS Harley 536 fols. 34r–35v, which in my
opinion preserves the best text. There are other copies in British Library MS Harley 941 fols. 21v–23v;
and in Trinity College Dublin MS 516 fols. 108v–110r. The opening eight lines also appear in Oxford,
Bodleian Library MS Rawlinson c 86 fol. 59r. In Trinity College Dublin MS 516 the last but one line of
my quotation, interestingly in view of Chaucer's possible knowledge of the poem, reads "A cownter
tenor at Newgat." In the text given above, where the rhymes are better, there is presumably a pun on
"contre tenour," since the Counter was one of the prisons of London. Earlier in the passage,
"patra[n]da" is emended from the reading in the manuscript which is "patrada." Somewhere in the
transmission of this line a copyist appears to have missed a suspension mark.

The Friar's Tale

PETER NICHOLSON

The story of the devil's seizure of a greedy lawyer or official when he is cursed by one of his own victims first occurs in writing in the early thirteenth century. Some three dozen analogues are known, from both literary and popular sources.[1] The most important for the background of Chaucer's version are a small group of Latin exempla that are found in England in the fourteenth and early fifteenth centuries and that seem to represent a distinct English tradition of the tale.

The two earliest analogues appear at approximately the same time. One is a 224-line Middle High German poem by the Austrian poet Der Stricker, who wrote in the second quarter of the thirteenth century.[2] Though one of the first known examples of the story, it is also one of the most sophisticated, particularly in its use of dialogue to establish the relation between the devil and his victim.

---

[1] The most complete list of analogues is still Archer Taylor's "The Devil and the Advocate," *PMLA* 36 (1921): 35–59. See also Lutz Röhrich, *Erzählungen des Späten Mittelalters und ihr Weiterleben in Literatur und Volksdichtung bis zur Gegenwart* (Berlin: Francke, 1962–67), 2:460–71, who adds some texts, provides an updated bibliography, and offers a very valuable discussion. Röhrich also reprints in convenient form a number of the most important analogues, including some previously unprinted versions (2:251–78).

[2] Ed. Hanns Fischer, *Verserzählungen*, 2nd ed., Altdeutsche Textbibliothek, No. 68 (Tübingen: Niemeyer, 1977), 2:31–42; also in Röhrich, 2:251–6 (from Fischer's first edition), with notes, 2:462–3. Translated by David Blamires in *Medieval Comic Tales*, trans. Peter Rickard et al. (Totowa, NJ and Cambridge: Rowman and Littlefield and D. S. Brewer, 1973), 72–4. Excerpted in Bryan and Dempster, pp. 272–3.

One day a rich and notoriously sinful judge rides out to visit his favorite vine-yard, and on his way back he is met by the devil, who has chosen that day to seek him. The devil is very richly dressed. The judge, not recognizing him, asks who he is and where he is from, and when the devil declines to say, the judge threatens him. When he learns that he is the devil, the judge asks what his business is, and the devil replies that he is to seize that day everything that is given to him sincerely. The judge asks that he be allowed to come along and see. The devil says no, but the judge commands him in the name of God to allow him; and though the devil warns him that it will not be to his profit, the judge angrily insists on accompanying him, however much it costs. The devil at length agrees, and promises that the judge will learn something that he didn't know before, and the judge is delighted:

> «nu lâ belîben dînen zorm»,
> sprach der vervluochte geist,
> «dâ du vil lützel umbe weist,
> des vindest du noch hiute ein teil.»
> dô wart er vrô unde geil,
> daz er dâ wunder solde sehen;
> dâ was im leide an geschehen.

["Now stop being so angry," said the accursed spirit. "Before the day is out you'll learn a bit about what you know next to nothing of." At this the judge became merry and cheerful. He was pleased that he was about to see some marvellous things.][3]

When they arrive at the marketplace, many people offer the judge a drink, and when the judge offers some to the devil, the devil declines. Then they hear a woman cursing a pig. The judge urges the devil to seize the animal, but the devil refuses since the woman is not sincere. They hear another woman cursing her ox, and another cursing her disobedient child; each time the judge urges the devil to seize his winnings, but the devil excuses himself in the same way. Finally a poor, frail and elderly woman sees the judge, and weeping, commits him to the devil for having unjustly taken her only cow. The devil proclaims that she means it, and seizing the judge by the hair, he rises straight into the air and carries him off. Thus the judge thought to gain, but he lost. It is unwise to have anything to do with the devil.

Approximately contemporary with Der Stricker's poem, the tale was also told in the form of a Latin exemplum by Caesarius of Heisterbach in his *Libri VIII Miraculorum*:[4]

---

[3] Text from Fischer, p. 36; trans. Blamires, p. 73.

[4] *Die Fragmente der Libri VIII Miraculorum des Caesarius von Heisterbach*, ed. Aloys Meister, *Römische Quartalschrift für christliche Alterthumskunde und für Kirchengeschichte*, Supplementheft 13 (Rome, 1901), 90–1; reprinted with translation by Larry Benson and Theodore M. Andersson, eds., *The Literary Context of Chaucer's Fabliaux* (Indianapolis: Bobbs-Merrill, 1971), pp. 362–5; also by Röhrich, 2:256–7. Only three books of Caesarius' work survive. The author, who lived between 1180 and 1240, is better known for his widely circulated *Dialogus Miraculorum*. See J.-Th. Welter, *L'Exemplum dans la littérature religieuse et didactique du moyen âge* (Paris: Guitard, 1927), pp. 113–18; J. A. Herbert, *Catalogue of Romances in the Department of Manuscripts in the British*

One day an avaricious and pitiless *advocatus*[5] rides out to collect some fees from a certain town, and along the way he encounters the devil in the form of a man. Realizing from his frightful appearance and from their conversation that his companion is the devil, he tries unsuccessfully to escape by crossing himself and by prayers. When they hear a man curse a pig, he urges the devil to seize the animal, hoping in this way to be free. Similarly when they hear a mother curse her baby; but in each case the devil declines since the curses were not given from the heart. Finally the townspeople, seeing the man approach, commend him to the devil, and the devil, proclaiming that they curse him from their heart, seizes him and carries him off. Those who take advantage of the poor should be warned by this exemplum.

This tale had a long life, particularly in the German-speaking area of Northern Europe. Der Stricker's version evidently had no direct imitators, but Caesarius' was the ancestor of a long series of exempla and tales stretching down into the nineteenth century.[6] There are also several other written versions of the tale that appear to have drawn independently from the same story tradition. Among these are an anonymous exemplum in a fourteenth-century manuscript from Austria,[7] a tale by Johannes Pauli,[8] and another by Hans Sachs,[9] all three of which have been either cited or reprinted as analogues of Chaucer's version. The tale has also been recorded from popular sources in the nineteenth and twentieth centuries, including tales from Denmark, Sweden, Iceland, France, and elsewhere, outside the area in which the earliest written versions are found.[10]

Der Stricker's and Caesarius' versions illustrate the basic elements of the story that remain constant in all these later retellings: the evil victim; the devil's appearance in more or less human guise; his refusal of one or more gifts that are not offered to him sincerely; and his final capture of the victim when the man is cursed by a person or group of people whom he himself has victimized. They also illustrate the kinds of alterations that were possible: in the profession of the victim; in the form in which the devil appears; in the number and order of the

Musuem, 3 (London: British Museum, 1910), pp. 348–9; and Jacques Berlioz and Marie Anne Polo de Beaulieu, eds., *Les Exempla Médiévaux* (Carcassonne: GARAE/Hesiode, 1992), pp. 89–118.

[5] *Advocatus* is usually translated as "lawyer," but as Benson and Andersson point out (363, citing Du Cange, *Glossarium mediae et infimae latinitatis*), it could have a much broader meaning, including the lay bailiffs and administrators of church estates, as it apparently does in this exemplum.

[6] See Taylor, "'The Devil and the Advocate,'" 37–43, and Röhrich 2:462–3. Among the direct imitations of Caesarius is the tale from Johannes Herolt's *Promptuarium exemplorum* (1484) reprinted in *Originals and Analogues*, p. 106, and Bryan and Dempster, p. 271.

[7] British Library MS Add. 15833, fol. 156v; see Taylor, "'The Devil and the Advocate,'" pp. 38–9; also Bryan and Dempster, pp. 269–70, except that it is not correct that the tale "agrees almost verbatim" with Caesarius, as Taylor claims, p. 270.

[8] *Schimpf und Ernst* (1522), ed. Johannes Bolte (Berlin: Stubenrauch, 1924), 1:56–7; reprinted by Röhrich 2:257.

[9] *Sämtliche Fabeln und Schwänke*, ed. Edmund Goetze and Carl Drescher (Halle: Niemeyer, 1893–1913), 3:179–80; reprinted by Röhrich 2:259–60. The poem is dated 1547.

[10] See Taylor, "The Devil and the Advocate," *passim*; and Röhrich, 2:270–8, 465–8. The tale is type 1186 in Aarne-Thompson; it is listed as nos. 1574 and 2204 in Frederic C. Tubach, *Index Exemplorum: An Index of Medieval Religious Tales*, Folklore Fellows Communications, no. 204 (Helsinki: Suomalainen Tiedeakatemia, 1969).

episodes that precede the final seizure; and in the number and identity of the people who deliver the final curse. Variations on each of these elements occur in no consistent pattern in the later versions, and without disturbing the underlying logic of the tale. The victim is almost always someone in a position to exploit the poor – a bailiff, a tax collector, a steward, a judge, or (most often) a lawyer – though in the fourteenth-century Austrian exemplum he is a merely a peasant who has not paid the wages he owes to the woman who delivers the final curse. When the devil appears, he is sometimes disguised, either as a peasant or as a man of wealth, and sometimes he is recognizable, either because of his hoof or because of his horrifying demeanor. The usual number of episodes is three, and the most common arrangement is Caesarius' (pig-child-victim). The pig may be replaced by another animal (a sheep in the Austrian exemplum; a cow or a horse in some other tales); the order of the first two episodes may be reversed (as in Johannes Pauli's); and the number of incidents may be increased (as in Der Stricker's) or reduced to two (as in Hans Sachs'). And the final curse may be delivered by a group of townspeople (as in Caesarius') or more often by an individual: a peasant, a debtor, or a widow.

Variations also occur in the victim's response when he learns the identity of his companion. These are of somewhat greater interest because of the development that some tellers give to the opening section of the tale. In the simplest forms – including Pauli's and Sachs' as well as many of the popular versions – the victim's reaction is not described, but one may infer from his silence that he remains unaware that he is the prey. In the Austrian exemplum he is fearful at first, but he accepts a somewhat ambiguous reassurance from the devil. In Caesarius' version and in the tales that are derived from it, the man is conscious of his danger as soon as the devil's identity is revealed, and when he is given the chance, he tries to free himself by persuading the devil to take another prize. Der Stricker's tale, on the other hand, enlarges on the victim's obliviousness to his danger: he threatens the devil, he insists on accompanying him, he ignores the devil's warning, and he is ironically eager both to learn about the devil's trade and to see that the devil take his proper reward.[11]

When the tale appears in England, it is in the version in which the victim is ignorant that he is the prey. Apart from the *Friar's Tale*, it survives in the form of three apparently independent Latin exempla (one of which exists in two copies) which in nearly all respects provide the closest known analogues to Chaucer's version. These are the three texts that are reprinted below. Though they are similar in basic outline, the differences among these three exempla

[11] See also the modern Pomeranian tale reprinted by Röhrich 2:273–5 (summarized by Taylor, " 'The Devil and the Advocate,' " pp. 49–50), in which the lawyer is curious about the devil's trade. This tale resembles Der Stricker's in a number of details (though not in the extensiveness of the opening conversation), and Röhrich (2:468) uses it to argue that Der Stricker also drew directly from popular tradition. In another modern tale with some similarities to Chaucer's (reprinted by Röhrich 2:270–2; summarized by Taylor, " 'The Devil and the Advocate,' " pp. 43–4) the lawyer, confident that he is not the prey, openly brags of his extortions, and impatient with the devil's scruples, he offers to demonstrate how he gains his winnings in the final scene. Röhrich (2:466) raises some doubts, however, about the tale's authenticity.

demonstrate that some degree of variation was also present in the English tradition of the tale.

The earliest (text I, below) appears in a fragmentary collection of exempla on the virtues and vices from the first half of the fourteenth century, under the heading "De Injustitia."[12] It reappears, in a nearly verbatim copy, in the unique manuscript of the *Speculum Parvulorum*, a collection of pious narratives and other devotional writings compiled by William Chartham, a monk at Christ Church Canterbury (*ob.* 1448).[13] It is the least fully developed of the three Latin examples, but it is unique in the way in which the devil's appearance is described and it offers a unique sequence of opening episodes.

The two other versions appear closer to Chaucer's time. Both preserve the more traditional sequence of episodes as found in Caesarius. Each also offers some interesting similarities to Chaucer's version. In each, it is the devil who initiates the conversation by inquiring "Quo vadis?" and by asking about the victim's profession, reversing the usual pattern. Each also makes explicit the similarity between the devil and his victim that is only implied in all other versions, and each provides separate hints for Chaucer's characterization of the victim. The first of these (text II) occurs in a collection of historical works, exempla, and other miscellaneous pieces (including some verses in English) that was compiled before 1400.[14] This version offers a unique variation on the victim's ignorance of his danger, for despite the warnings that he is given, he never realizes that his companion is the devil. A short time later, the tale appears again in a collection of sermons by the English Benedictine Robert Rypon (text III).[15] Rypon's version makes less of the victim's ignorance, but it presents the victim as a greedy *ballivus* (cf. *FrT* 1389–92), and it provides another analogue for the widow who delivers the final condemnation.

These three exempla – together with whatever similar tales might be dis-

---

[12] British Library MS Add. 38654, fols. 39–39v. See *Catalogue of the Additions to the Manuscripts in the British Museum . . . MDCCCCXI–MDCCCCXV* (London, 1925), pp. 185–6. This tale (and its copy in the Lambeth Palace MS, below) were first described by Siegfried Wenzel, "Chaucer and the Language of Contemporary Preaching," *Studies in Philology* 73 (1976): 142–3. I wish to express my gratitude to Professor Wenzel for his help in providing information about these two MSS.

[13] Lambeth Palace MS 78, fols. 280v–281. See M. R. James, *A Descriptive Catalogue of the Manuscripts in the Library of Lambeth Palace. The Mediaeval Manuscripts* (Cambridge: University Press, 1932), pp. 128–35.

[14] British Library MS Cotton Cleopatra D VIII, fol. 110. On the MS see H. L. D. Ward, *Catalogue of Romances in the Department of Manuscripts in the British Museum*, 1 (London: British Museum, 1883), 200, 249; Herbert 3:638–42; and Peter Nicholson, "The Analogues of Chaucer's *Friar's Tale*," *English Language Notes* 17 (1979): 97. This analogue was first printed (with translation) by Thomas Wright in *Archeologia* 32 (1847): 365. A new transcription appeared in *Originals and Analogues*, p. 105, whence it was reprinted by Skeat 3:450–1. The transcription in Bryan and Dempster, pp. 271–2, contains several errors.

[15] British Library MS Harley 4894, fols. 103v–104. The tale was first described by G. R. Owst, *Literature and Pulpit in Medieval England* (Cambridge, 1933; 2nd ed. New York: Barnes & Noble, 1961), pp. 162–3. See also Peter Nicholson, "The Rypon Analogue of the *Friar's Tale*," *The Chaucer Newsletter* 3, no. 1 (Winter, 1981): 1–2. On fol. 116v of the MS occurs a reference to a comet that appeared during the Lenten season of 1401, and Owst takes this as an approximate date for the compilation of the whole collection; see his *Preaching in Medieval England* (1926; rpt. New York: Russell & Russell, 1965), pp. 207–8.

covered in the future – provide evidence of a tradition of tale that evidently circulated both orally and in written form in fourteenth-century England and that provided the most immediate background for Chaucer's version. None of the three surviving examples is sufficiently like the *Friar's Tale* to have served as Chaucer's "source," nor can any be presumed to have been known to him directly. Taken together, however, they provide nearly all of the features that Chaucer can be shown to have borrowed. The only significant details that they lack are the victim's inquisitiveness about the devil's trade and the promise that he will learn something that day, as found, for instance, in Der Stricker's version. Both motifs are associated, of course, with the form of the story that Der Stricker tells, in which the victim is ignorant that he is the prey, the form that is also represented in the other surviving English versions. In these two details, Chaucer's poem may provide an independent witness of the nature of the English tale tradition from which he drew.

I

Concerning Injustice

There once was a barrister who did not care which side he took for the purpose of gaining a fee. Often he colored falsehood with plausible-sounding reasoning and with man-made laws, and in this way he deprived many of their rightful property. One day it happened that he rode toward a county court, and an ugly rascal came running alongside him. [5] The barrister asked where he was headed. "To the city to which you are going," he said. "And what will you do there?" "I will listen when anyone is consigned to the devil, and I will carry him off." And he: "Who then are you?" "I am the devil." They came to a certain village where a mother was arguing with her daughter, and among other things she committed her to the devil. Then the barrister said to the devil, "Seize her, because she is given to you." [10] "Not at all," said the devil, "because she is not given to me from the heart. For though the mother might have said as much, she does not wish it to happen." They came to another village, where a father was arguing with his son, and committed him to the devil. Then the barrister said as before, and the devil replied as before. Finally they came to the city. Then men and women from every side cursed the barrister, and committed him to the devil. [15] Upon hearing this, the devil said to the barrister, "Come with me, for you are given to me from the heart, and justly." Then the devil carried him off, and nowhere did he appear again.

[20] Therefore let all who plead against justice and a clear conscience and who cloak falsehood under the guise of truth and who defend injustice in the guise of the law watch out for themselves, lest similar in guilt, they also be found similar in punishment.

II

A story about a wicked seneschal

There once was a man, a seneschal and a lawyer, an exploiter of the poor and a plunderer of their goods, who went to court one day in order to raise a dispute and to make some profit. Another came up to him on his journey, saying [5] to him, "Where are you going, and what is your business?" He answered: "I am out to gain some profit." And the second one said, "I am very much like you. Let us go on together." The first one consenting, the second

Variants from Lambeth Palace MS 78, fols. 280v–281:
Title Lambeth: Qualiter diabolus asportavit quendam falsum causatorem
8   **Inter** *Lambeth*
9   **diabolo** *Lambeth*

I

De Injustitia

(from British Library MS Add. 38654, fols. 39–39v,
first half of the fourteenth century)

Erat quidam narrator qui non curavit quam partem teneret ad hoc quod pecuniam adquireret. Sepe falsum rationibus verisimilibus et humanis legibus coloravit, multosque hoc modo jure suo privavit. Accidit quadam die quod versus comitatum equitavit, venitque unus turpis ribaldus currens juxta ipsum.
5 Quesivit narrator quo tenderet. "Ad civitatem," ait ille, "ad quam tu tendis." "Et quid ibi facies?" "Ascultabo quando aliquis traditur diabolo, et ipsum asportabo." Et ille: "Quis nam / es tu?" "Ego sum diabolus." Venerunt per quandam villam ubi mater cum filia contendebat, et in[ter] cetera eam diabo[lo] tradebat. Tunc ait narrator diabolo, "Accipe illam, quia tradita est
10 tibi." "Nequaquam," inquit diabolus, "quia non ex corde mihi tradita est. Quamvis enim mater ita dixerit, ita fore non cupit." Venerunt per aliam villam ubi pater cum filio contendebat, et eum diabolo tradebat. Tunc narrator dixit ut prius, et diabolus respondit ut prius. Tandem venerunt ad civitatem. Tunc homines et mulieres ex utraque parte narratori maledixerunt, et eum diabolo
15 tradiderunt. Quo audito, ait diabolus narratori, "Veni mecum, quia ex corde et juste mihi traditus es." Tunc diabolus ipsum asportavit, et nusquam postea comparuit.

Caveant igitur sibi omnes contra justiciam et sanam conscienciam placitantes et sub specie veri falsum colorantes, ac sub specie juris injuriam
20 defensantes, ne similes in culpa, similes inveniantur in pena.

II

Narracio de quodam senescallo sceleroso

(from British Library MS Cotton Cleopatra D VIII, fol. 110, before 1400)

Erat vir quidam, senescallus et placitator, pauperum calumpniator et bonorum huiusmodi spoliator, qui die quadam forum judiciale causa contencionis faciende et lucrandi adivit. Cui quidam obviavit in itinere, dicens ei, "Quo vadis? Et quid habes officii?" Respondit primus, "Vado lucrari." Et
5 ait secundus, "Ego tui similis sum. Eamus simul." Primo consenciente, dixit

said to him, "What is the source of your gain?" He replied, "Taking advantage of the poor as long as anything remains to them, namely by means of lawsuits, disputes, and ill-treatment, whether just or unjust. Now I have told you where my profit comes from; tell me, I beg you, what is the source of yours?" The second [10] replied, "Whatever is given to the devil in a curse I count for myself as gain." The first man laughed, and scoffed at the second, not realizing that he was the devil. Shortly afterwards, as they passed through the city, they heard a poor man curse a calf that he was taking to sell because it was going crookedly. They heard a similar curse from a woman beating her son. The first man then said to the [15] second, "Look, you can gain something if you wish. Take the boy and the calf." The second replied, "I cannot, because they did not curse from the heart." As they went a short way further, some poor people, coming towards the court, on seeing the seneschal all began to heap curses upon him. And the second said to the first, "Do you hear what they are saying?" "I hear," he said, "but it is nothing to me." And the [20] second one said, "They are cursing from the heart, and they deliver you to the devil. And thus you will be mine." And seizing him at once, he disappeared with him.

III

A Greedy Bailiff

Thirdly in this first main section it remains to say in what way sin is noted in the devil. But perhaps some good men and women dislike hearing the devil named. But it should be noted that there are two ways to speak about the devil, in one way to his pleasure, in another way to his displeasure. They speak to his [5] displeasure who preach about and expose the evils that he inflicts upon mankind, so that these may be guarded against that much more. They speak to his pleasure who, by cursing out of negligence or rancor, or in conjurations and such, name the name of him whose naming pleases him; and more frequently than it is sought, the devil is permitted to carry out these curses and oaths.

[10] So it is told about the bailiff of a certain one, who in collecting the rents of his lord was excessively greedy and eager for his own profit, being less sparing to the poor in particular. One day as he was riding to a certain village on account of his office, it happened that the devil in the form of a young man became his companion on his journey. The devil said to him, "Where are you going?" He replied, "To the next village on the [15] business of my lord." To whom the former: "Do you wish to gain for yourself and for your lord as much as you can, and to receive whatever they might wish to give you?" The bailiff replied, "So I wish, inasmuch as the gift is free." To whom the devil said, "Good; and you do justly." To whom the bailiff said, "Who are you, and where are you from?" "I," he said, "am the devil, and I go about for my profit just as you do for your lord's profit and for your own profit. [20] And I wish to seize not whatever men might give to me, but whatever with

secundus ei, "Quid est lucrum tuum?" Et ille: "Emolumentum pauperum quamdiu aliquid habent, ut per lites contenciones et vexaciones sive juste sive injuste. Modo dixi tibi lucrum meum unde est. Dic mihi queso: unde est et tuum?" Respondit secundus dicens, "Quicquid sub maledictione traditur
10 diabolo, computo mihi pro lucro." Risit primus, et derisit secundum, non intelligens quod esset diabolus. Paulo post cum transirent per civitatem audierunt quendam pauperem maledicere cuidam vitulo quem duxit ad vendendum quia indirecte ibat. Item audierunt consimilem de muliere fustigante puerum suum. Tunc ait primus ad secundum, "Ecce potes lucrari si
15 vis. Tolle puerum et vitulum." Respondit secundus, "Non possum, quia non maledicunt ex corde." Cum vero paululum processissent, pauperes euntes versus judicium videntes illum senescallum ceperunt omnes unanimiter maledictiones in ipsum ingerere. Et dixit secundus ad primum, "Audis quid isti dicunt?" "Audio," inquit, "sed nichil ad me." Et dixit secundus, "Isti
20 maledicunt ex corde et te tradunt diabolo. Et ideo meus eris." Qui statim ipsum arripiens, cum eo disparuit.

III

Robert Rypon, A Greedy Bailiff

(from British Library MS Harley 4894, fols. 103v–104, c. 1401)

Tertio in ista prima parte principali restat dicere quomodo peccatum in diabolo denotatur. Sed forsan aliqui boni viri et mulieres abhorrent audire diabolum nominatum. Sed notandum quod est loqui dupliciter de diabolo, uno modo ad suam complacentiam, alio modo ad suam displicentiam. Illi locuntur
5 ad suam displicentiam qui sua maleficia que infert humano generi predicant et exponunt ut tantius caveantur. Illi locuntur ad suam complacentiam qui maledicendo ex negligencia vel rancore aut in conjurationibus et huiusmodi nominant eius nomen cuius nominatio sibi placet, et frequentius quod petitur, permittitur diabolus adimplere.
10 Sicut narratur de quodam ballivo cuiusdam, qui colligendo firmas eius domini fuit nimis cupidus lucro proprio et intentus, presertim pauperibus minus parcens. Qui dum quadam die causa sui officii ad quandam villam equitaret, contigit diabolum in forma adolescentis sibi comitem fieri vie sue. Qui diabolus dixit ei, "Quo vadis?" Respondit, "Ad villam proximam in
15 negotio domini mei." Cui ille, "Visne lucrari tibi et domino tuo quam potissimus et recipere quicquid voluerint tibi dare?" Respondit ballivus, "Ita volo, quia donum est liberum." Cui diabolus "bene" inquit; "et juste facis." Cui ballivus "quis" inquit, "et unde es tu?" "Ego" ait "sum diabolus, et circueo circa lucrum meum sicut et tu circa lucrum domini tui et tuum lucrum.
20 Et volo capere non quicquid homines dederint mihi, sed quicquid cum corde et voluntate mihi donaverint libentius acceptabo." Respondens ballivus, "justissime" inquit "facis." Procedentes itaque venerunt prope dictam

heart and will they might give to me very freely I will accept." Replying, the bailiff said, "You do most justly." Proceeding thus, they came near to the said village, and they saw coming towards them some nearly untamed oxen on a plough, which going more often crookedly and off the track, the farmer commended to the devil. "Here," [25] said the bailiff. "These are yours." "No, because they are by no means given from the heart." Then coming into the village they heard a baby cry, and the angry mother, not able to pacify it, said, "Be quiet or let the devil take you." Then the bailiff said, "This is yours." He replied, "Not at all, because she does not wish to give up her child." Finally reaching the edge of the village, a certain poor widow whose [30] only cow he had seized the day before saw them, who perceiving the bailiff, with knees bent and hands outstretched exclaimed, "To all the devils of hell I commend you." Then said the devil, "Certainly this one is mine, because it is given to me sincerely. Thus I wish to have you." And he led the bailiff he had received off to hell.

This story, I say, though in part humorous, is also a warning against certain evils. [35] For first man is taught that he not name the devil out of negligence or rancor. Second, that he not commend anything to him, for such a commendation can perhaps be put into effect. Third, that the officers of lords should not be too greedy. Fourth, that they should not do injustice to the poor or to others by harming their persons or extorting their goods, lest perhaps it happen to them in the end as it happened to the aforesaid bailiff.

34 **revocatio** *MS* revocatiam

villulam, et viderunt boves pene indomitos in aratra contraitantes, quos sepius indirecte incedentes et exorbitantes, agricola diabolo commendavit. "Ecce"
25 inquit ballivus; "illa tua sunt." "Non, quia minime dantur ex corde." Deinde in villam venientes audiverunt infantulum plorare, quem mater non potens mitigare, offensa dixit, "Sileas aut demon te habeat."/ Tunc ballivus "hoc est" inquit "tuum." Respondit, "Nequaquam, quia suo filio carere nollet." Tandem accedentes ad finem ville, vidit quedam vidua paupercula cuius vaccam
30 unicam pridie rapuisset, que ballivum prospiciens, flexis genibus et expansis manibus exclamavit, "Omnibus inferni diabolis te comendo." Tunc ait diabolus, "Certe hoc meum est, quia cordialiter mihi datum. Volo ideo te habere." Et acceptum ballivum duxit ad infernum.

Ista inquam narratio, licet in parte jocosa, tum est a certis malis revocati[o].
35 Primo enim docetur homo ne cum necligentia aut rancore diabolum nominet. Secundo, ne sibi aliquid comendet, quia forsan talis comendatio potest sortiri effectum. Tertio, ne officiarii dominorum sint nimis cupidi. Quarto, ne injuriam faciant pauperibus aut aliis, eorum personas ledendo aut illorum bona extorquendo, ne forsan eis finaliter contingat sicut ballivo contigit antedicto.

The Clerk's Tale

THOMAS J. FARRELL and AMY W. GOODWIN

Chaucer's *Clerk's Tale* is the first English rendering of the Griselda story, which by the end of the fourteenth century had also captured the imagination of many other writers and readers in Western Europe.[1] In adapting this story for the *Canterbury Tales*, Chaucer was part of a broad pattern of response to its simple plot, another participant in the tale's transmission across cultures, languages, and national boundaries. J. Burke Severs established definitively that Chaucer's principal sources for the *Clerk's Tale* were Petrarch's Latin *Historia Griseldis* and *Le Livre Griseldis*, an anonymous French translation of Petrarch.[2] His excellent scholarship soon made comparison of the *Clerk's Tale* to the Latin *Historia Griseldis* a standard practice in most modern criticism. In the last twenty years, however, scholars have broadened their interest to include other versions of the tale, in part because it is likely that Chaucer had some knowledge of them and in part because they can tell us about the tale's cultural value

---

[1] For the transmission of Petrarch's Griselda story in Europe, see Raffaele Morabito, "La Diffusione della Storia di Griselda dal XIV al XX Secolo," *Studi sul Boccaccio* 17 (1988): 237–85; Judith Bronfman, *Chaucer's Clerk's Tale: The Griselda Story Received, Rewritten, Illustrated* (New York: Garland, 1994); Lee Bliss, "The Renaissance Griselda: A Woman for All Seasons," *Viator* 23 (1992): 301–43. The most comprehensive study of the story in France remains that of Elie Golenistcheff-Koutouzoff, *L'Histoire de Griseldis en France du XIVe au XV siècle* (1933; Geneva: Slatkine, 1975), which contains texts of several French versions of Petrarch's Griselda story.

[2] *The Literary Relations of Chaucer's Clerkes Tale* (1942; Hamden, CT: Archon, 1972). On the "title" of Petrarch's work see Charlotte Cook Morse, "What to Call Petrarch's Griselda," *The Uses of Manuscripts in Literary Studies: Essays in Memory of Judson Boyce Allen,* Studies in Medieval Culture 31 (Kalamazoo: Medieval Institute Publications, 1992). Morse demonstrates that "Historia Griseldis" rubrics far outnumber those like the "Obedientia Uxoris" one that Severs used for his title (270). But Petrarch himself debated whether Boccaccio's tale should be considered an *historia* or a *fabula*, finally opting rather diffidently for the latter term. Questions of genre are evident in other rubrics calling the tale *fabula, narracio, exemplum,* and *vita* (270).

in the late Middle Ages. The tale's many redactors gave the story a variety of interpretive contexts, addressed divergent audiences, and refashioned Griselda to exemplify numerous virtues and behaviors. These competing versions can contribute to our understanding of the narrative possibilities of the material Chaucer took up and his achievement in the *Clerk's Tale*.

The Griselda Story in Italy

Thomas J. Farrell

Many folktales paralleling the Griselda story (Aarne-Thompson Type 887) are in fact derived from early written versions. Other folktales once adduced as antecedents, particularly "Monster Bridegroom" stories (Aarne-Thompson Type 425A) are unlikely sources because they do not occur in the Mediterranean. Bettridge and Utley have identified a folk tradition they call the "The Patience of a Princess," which is more likely to have influenced Boccaccio.[3] This story takes many forms, but always focuses on an impoverished bride specifically associated with the virtue of patience, who is tested by her husband, an imperious padishah. The tests may include the isolation of the bride, the removal of her children by their father, and the reputed cannibalism of the husband/father. The bride often constructs a doll to whom she recites her sorrows, and the story ends with the reunion of the family.

The last story in Boccaccio's *Decameron* (1352) is the first known written version of the Griselda. In it, the folk elements have been fully assimilated into the author's cultural context. Given the increasing likelihood that Chaucer knew the *Decameron*, it is clear that Boccaccio's treatment of the Griselda may have influenced Chaucer's understanding of the tale.[4] The evidence of Boccaccian influence on the language of the *Clerk's Tale* remains very slight, but the likelihood that Boccaccio's version – especially, perhaps, his conclusion – was present in Chaucer's memory as he worked on the *Clerk's Tale* gives the *Decameron* a relevance greater than that of any other analogue.

Addressed specifically to "ladies," Boccaccio's collection was conceived as recreational literature for the bourgeoisie of Florence, who aspired to the lifestyle of its main characters, the city's young aristocrats. The Griselda story is told by the ironic narrator Dioneo, in response to the topic specified for the final day of storytelling, "those who have acted generously or magnificently in affairs of the heart or other matters."[5] All of the basic elements of the story are present in Boccaccio's version: Gualtieri's disinclination to marry is overcome by an appeal from his subjects; he discusses marriage with Griselda and then leads his

---

[3] William Edwin Bettridge and Francis Lee Utley ("New Light on the Origin of the Griselda Story," *Texas Studies in Literature and Language* 13 [1971]: 153–208) discuss the folktale analogues thoroughly. On the "Monster Bridegroom," see Dudley Griffith, *The Origin of the Griselda Story* (Seattle: U Washington P, 1931), and Wirt Cate, "The Problem of the Origin of the Griselda Story," *Studies in Philology* 29 (1932): 389–405.

[4] On Chaucer and Boccaccio, see Helen Cooper's opening chapter in this volume. John Finlayson ("Petrarch, Boccaccio, and Chaucer's *Clerk's Tale*," *Studies in Philogy* 97 [2000]: 255–75) makes a specific argument that Chaucer knew and was influenced by the *Decameron*.

[5] Giovanni Boccaccio, *Decameron*, ed. Vittore Branca (Milan: Arnoldo Mondadori, 1985), p. 800: "di chi liberalmente o vero magnificamente alcuna cosa operasse intorno a' fatti d'amore o d'altra cosa."

entourage to her on the wedding day; he tests her patience sequentially by pretending to murder their children, by banishing her, and by asking her to prepare for his pretended new bride; finally, he restores her to full honor. Dioneo criticizes Gaultieri's conduct harshly, calling him "more suited to watch over pigs than to rule over men" and he expresses both admiration and incredulity at Griselda's patient submission, joking in conclusion that she might instead have "allowed another man to warm her wool in order to get herself a nice-looking dress out of the affair."[6]

Giovanni Sercambi followed Boccaccio's tale closely in his *Novelliere* (now dated after 1399). Like some other analogues, Sercambi's version treats the Griselda simply: his renaming of the heroine "Gostantina" signals his sole interest. Sercambi increases direct narration at the expense of characters' speeches and abridges the tale slightly, especially by reducing commentary on it. In doing so he eliminates the complexity of response so noticeable in other versions: he is content to conclude that Count Artú "devoted himself to enjoying life with Constantina; and so they lived to a ripe old age."[7]

Petrarch's response to Boccaccio, coming much earlier, shows more of the complexity that would intrigue other readers, including Chaucer. In 1373, Petrarch translated and carefully reworked the tale, prefacing it with a discussion of his friend's work. The translation was sent to Boccaccio as part of a series of letters that was recopied a year later with additional comments (in yet another letter) about the Latin tale's reception.[8] Petrarch changes the plot only slightly, elaborating the opening scenes and emphasizing Walterus' power by leaving Griselda unaware of his plans until he arrives with the wedding entourage. The more important changes come in audience, style, and purpose. Petrarch writes to a broader but more select audience of intellectuals across Europe, and his style is correspondingly weighty: more sober in itself and also elaborated with religious and classical allusions.[9] In the final paragraph of XVII.3 he casts the tale as an exemplum of the Christian's devotion to God rather, or at least more, than as a model for wives; elsewhere he wavers in his evaluation of it: in XVII.4 he rejects a friend's dismissal of Griselda as "just a story," arguing that "Some people proclaim a thing impossible for anyone simply because they find it difficult themselves. Thus they judge everyone by their own standard, so that none can surpass them, when there have been

---

[6] *Decameron*, p. 903 "più degni di guardar porci che d'avere sopra uomini signoria"; p. 904: "si a un altro fatto scuotere il pillicione che riuscito ne fosse una bella roba."

[7] Giovanni Sercambi, *Il Novelliere*, ed. Luciano Rossi, vol. 3 (Rome: Salerno, 1974), 223 "con Gostantina si dié buon tempo. E finiro i lor dí in vecchiessa." On the date of the *Novelliere*, see the *Introduzione*, vol. 1, p. xix.

[8] *Epistolae Seniles* XVII contains four letters in all: a letter of transmission (XVII.1), a negative response to Boccaccio's suggestion that Petrarch reduce his literary work (XVII.2), the Griselda tale with introductory comments and concluding moralization (XVII.3) and a report on the tale's reception (XVII.4). XVII.1–3 were composed in 1373; XVII.4, a year later. We print XVII.3. See Severs for details of the composition (7–11).

[9] Anne Middleton, "The Clerk and his Tale: Some Literary Contexts," *Studies in the Age of Chaucer* 2 (1980): 128–9.

and may still be a great many who do easily what is commonly held to be impossible."[10]

Severs' edition in Bryan and Dempster was reprinted a year later with full apparatus and commentary in *The Literary Relationships of Chaucer's Clerkes Tale*. His claim to have established the Petrarchan text of *Seniles* XVII.3 has been borne out, but the complementary claim that such a text also represented the text that Chaucer translated (p. 110) is clearly incorrect, since the glosses from Petrarch copied into early manuscripts of the *Canterbury Tales* contain many variants and correlate best with CC2, a manuscript denigrated by Severs.[11]

For this edition I have collated an additional eight manuscripts – listed below before the Latin text – and have recollated CC2, looking for a manuscript whose text of Petrarch contained the kind of variation exhibited in both CC2 and the glosses to Chaucer's poem, but one with a more Petrarchan text than CC2; such a text will best approximate Chaucer's source manuscript. Peterhouse College (Cambridge) MS 81 (henceforth Pe), a collection of Petrarch's works that includes the complete *Seniles*, copied early in the fifteenth century and quite possibly in England, meets those criteria and is therefore used as the base manuscript for this edition. While it is somewhat more Petrarchan than the manuscript Chaucer used, Pe frequently agrees with CC2 and the glosses, especially in the first half of its text.[12] The text printed here is therefore distinct from Severs' in many readings, although the differences rarely affect meaning substantially.[13] Paragraphing is based on Pe's marginal division of the text into fairly regular units.[14] Such divisions are rare in manuscripts of Petrarch's letter, however, and Pe's divisions are more numerous than those in any text described by Severs (p. 196). Punctuation is my own, but based on the practices of the Pe scribe, who clearly was concerned to make Petrarch's sometimes complex sentence structure more comprehensible by marking off grammatical units from one another. As a result, sentences are generally shorter here than in Severs's edition.[15]

---

[10] "Esse nonnullus qui quecumque difficilia eis sint, impossibilia omnibus arbitrentur: sic mensura sua omnia metientes ut se omnium pr[i]mos (Pe "promos") locent, cum tamen multi fuerint forte et sint quibus essent facilia que vulgo impossibilia viderentur."

[11] Germaine Dempster, "Chaucer's Manuscript of Petrarch's Version of the Griselda Story," *Modern Philology* 41 (1943): 6–16.

[12] For a description of Pe see M. R. James, *A Descriptive Catalogue of the Manuscripts in the Library of Peterhouse* (Cambridge, 1899), pp. 99–8. Dempster argued that Chaucer's manuscript must have been, like CC2, part of family *b*. My collations indicate instead that CC2 is a more anomalous manuscript than either Severs or Dempster thought. Pe is basically a family *a* manuscript, but it contains some readings from the *b* and *c* families. Among the manuscripts I have collated, Pe, Ba, Bod2, Har7, and Har6 were also known to Severs but not collated by him. As Morse shows, there are still at least 150 uncollated manuscripts of the text.

[13] The goals of this edition are more fully explained in Thomas J. Farrell, "Philological Theory in *Sources and Analogues*," *Medieval Perspectives* 15.2 (2000): 34–48.

[14] The text also appears with small gaps in the line, normally corresponding to the marginal letters. At lines 192, 232, 279, and 292, such spaces occur in distinction to the alphabetical *ordinatio*: these might be considered alternative locations for a modern paragraph.

[15] A. C. Spearing read an earlier version of my edition and translation of Petrarch. The present text is much improved by his helpful suggestions.

The apparatus provides variants in two forms: (1) emendations of Pe and (2) readings from the glosses to early *Canterbury Tales* manuscripts where they contain a reading different from the reading of Pe. In the first case, all the authorities for the emendation are listed first, followed by Pe's reading and then other readings occurring in the eight additional manuscripts I have collated. Most of the emended readings are also found in Severs' edition, and are therefore cited first in the list of variants as "Severs." In the second case, the reading of Pe is given in the lemma, followed in order by variants from the glosses as recorded in Hengwrt (Hg) and Ellesmere (El), then variants from Severs' edition, and from the other manuscripts I have collated. Variant readings from the other manuscripts that Severs collated are omitted here, but can be found in his critical edition. I have disregarded minor variations of word order within sentences, and the Pe scribe's extraneous "et," occurring especially near the end of the text. Information on the most important variants is provided in the notes to the text. The manuscripts I have collated for this edition are as follows:

Pe   Peterhouse College (Cambridge) MS 81, fols. 185–187v (base text)
CC2   Corpus Christi College (Cambridge) MS 275, fols. 163–168v.
Ba   Balliol College (Oxford) MS 146b, fols. 54–59v.
Bod2   Bodleian Library MS Canonici misc. 297, fols. 98–108.
Po   Indiana University Lilly Library MS Poole 26, fols. 46–52.
G4   Glasgow University Library MS Hunter 480, fols. 1–5v (2 leaves missing between fols. 3–4).
G1   Glasgow University Library MS Gen. 1125, fols. 218–220.
Har7   British Library MS Harley 2678, fols. 89–92v.
Har6   British Library MS Harley 2268, fols. 6v–10v.

The Story of Griselda

Petrarch's Epistolae Seniles XVII.3

To Giovanni Boccaccio: A preface or prologue to the Story of Griselda.

I saw your book in our mother tongue, though I don't know how or when it came to me. You published it some time ago, I believe, when you were young. I would be lying if I were to say that I read it, since it is very lengthy and written in vernacular prose for the masses. There was also much work to do and my time was limited. As you know, even if I remain distant from the disturbance of battles all around, I cannot be unmoved by restlessness in the state. What should I say? I skimmed through the book like a hurried tourist, glancing here and there, but not stopping. Rumor had it that the wrath of critics had hounded the book, though it was always defended splendidly by your voice and scepter. I was not surprised, for I knew the power of your imagination, [10] and I know that such people have proved arrogant and despicable: they chastise others for accomplishing whatever they lack the will, or the knowledge, or the ability to do, being learned and voluble in this one respect, though mute about everything else.

I was delighted with my browsing, and as for the rather frankly uninhibited events that cropped up, your age when you wrote it is enough excuse, as are the style and the idiom, for levity is suitable in the stories and in those who would read them. Your audience makes all the difference: the range of their conduct pardons the stylistic diversity. Among many stories which are, to be sure, amusing and slight, a few more pious and serious ones caught my attention. But even about those I have no definitive opinion, for nowhere did I read carefully all the way through. Like most such skimmers, I considered the beginning and end of the book more closely than the rest. [20] In that first place you described accurately and lamented nobly (in my opinion) the state of our country in that time of plague, which our age finds sorrowful and piteous beyond all others.

But at the other end you have placed last – and in great contrast to much of what precedes it – a story that so pleased and engaged me that, amid enough duties to

---

7   **Excucurri** Severs Ba; Excuturi Pe; Excurri Po Har7 Har6; Excurritor Bod2; *om* CC2 G4 G1.
14   **excusabat** Severs Ba Po Har7 Har6; excusabit Pe Bod2; *om* CC2 G4 G1.
18   **quod** Severs Ba Har7 Har6; quid Pe Po; que Bod2; *om* CC2 G4 G1.
23   **precedencium** Severs Ba Har6; pendencium Pe; precedentibus Bod2 Po Har7; *om* CC2 G4 G1.

Historia Griseldis
Petrarch's Epistolae Seniles XVII.3

(from Cambridge University Peterhouse College MS 81)

Ad eundem prefacio seu prologus in Historiam Grisildis.[16]

(fol. 185a) [L]Ibrum[17] tuum, quem nostro materno eloquio, ut opinor, olim iuvenis edidisti, nescio quidem unde vel qualiter ad me delatum vidi.[18] Nam si dicam legi, menciar. Siquidem ipse magnus valde, et ad vulgus et soluta scriptus oratione, et occupacio mea maior et tempus angustum erat. Idque
5   ipsum, ut nosti, bellicis undique motibus inquietum, a quibus et si animo procul absim, nequeo tamen fluctuante re publica non moveri.[19] Quid ergo? [Excucurri] eum, et festini viatoris in morem, hinc atque hinc circumspiciens, nec subsistens. Animadverti alicubi librum ipsum canum dentibus lacessitum, tuo tamen baculo egregie tuaque voce defensum. Nec miratus sum. Nam et
10   vires ingenii tui novi, et scio expertus esse hominum genus et insolens et ignavum, qui, quidquid ipsi vel nolunt vel nesciunt vel non possunt, in aliis reprehendunt, ad hoc unum docti et arguti, sed elingues ad reliqua.
   Delectatus sum ipso in transitu. Et siquid lascivie liberioris occurreret, [excusabat] etas tunc tua dum id scriberes, stilus, ydioma, ipsa quoque rerum
15   levitas et eorum qui lecturi talia videbantur. Refert enim largiter quibus scribas, morumque varietate stili varietas excusatur. Inter multa sane iocosa et levia, quedam pia et gravia deprehendi, de quibus tamen diffinitive quid iudicem non habeo, ut qui nusquam totus inheserim. At [quod] fere accidit eo more currentibus, curiosius aliquanto quam cetera libri principium finemque
20   perspexi. Quorum in altero patrie nostre statum, illius scilicet pestilentissimi temporis, quod pre omnibus nostra etas lugubre ac miserum mundo vidit, meo quidem iudicio et narrasti proprie et magnifice deplorasti.
   In altero autem historiam ultimam et multis [precedencium] longe dissimilem posuisti, que ita michi placuit meque detinuit ut, inter tot curas

---

[16] Boccaccio is the addressee of all the letters in *Seniles* XVII. The rubric erroneously identifies the text that follows as "Epistola secunda," although it has already identified the beginnings of *Seniles* XVII.1 and XVII.2 on fol. 183b. The prefatory section ("Librum tuum") is part of the same letter (XVII.3) as the tale proper ("Est ad ytalie"). The rubric before "Est ad Ytalie" correctly notes "Tertia."
   A useful distinction has evolved in source study of the *Clerk's Tale* between the name of Chaucer's heroine – Grisilde – and "Griselda" as the name of the heroine of narrative material he inherited, especially in Petrarch. The translation preserves that distinction although Pe usually records her name in a way similar to Chaucer's spelling.

[17] Space has been left here for a seven line initial capital that was never executed. Similarly, a four line capital was not completed for the narrative "Est ad Ytalie" at line 50.

[18] Boccaccio published the *Decameron* when he was about 40, a calculation we base largely on Petrarch's testimony about the year of his birth. Petrarch may have thought of the *Decameron* as a youthful work simply because it was Boccaccio's last major vernacular opus; almost all of his subsequent work was in Latin and, in Petrarch's eyes, *ipso facto* more mature.

[19] Because Venice and Padua had been at war since October 1372, Petrarch retreated from his house at Arquà to the greater security of Padua. In September 1373 he was part of the delegation sent to Venice to negotiate peace.

make me almost forget myself, I wanted to memorize it, so that I might recall its pleasures as often as I wished and retell it in conversation with my friends, as the opportunity might arise. When, not long after, I had done so and seen that it pleased my audience, suddenly it occurred to me that this beautiful story would perhaps also delight those ignorant of Italian. [30] After all, it had consistently pleased me for many years after I first heard it and you liked it, I felt, well enough to give it the final position in your Italian book, where the art of rhetoric teaches us to place whatever is more important.

And so one day I was as usual dividing my thoughts in many ways. Angry at them and myself, as I was saying, I tossed aside routine business and addressed myself to write this story of yours. I certainly hoped to make you glad by translating your work on my own initiative. Love of you and the story impelled me to what I would hardly have done for anyone else. Not forgetting Horace's advice in the *Ars Poetica* – "Do not force yourself to translate too faithfully, word by word" – [40] I have unfolded your story in my own way, freely changing or adding a few words throughout. I believed that you would not merely have accepted this strategy, but encouraged it. The translation has been praised and sought by many, but I return it to you, dedicated to no one but you. Whether the change of vestment has disfigured it or perhaps adorned it, you be the judge. It returns to where it began, knowing its judge, its home, and the way there. You and whoever reads it know that you (not I) must answer for what you have written. If anyone asks me whether the story is true – whether I have written a history or a fable – I will respond with Sallust's words: "Credibility must be sought with the author," that is, my friend Giovanni. Having said that, I begin.

Also to Boccaccio: Extraordinary Wifely Obedience and Trust

[50] On the western side of Italy, a lofty mountain named Vesulus reaches its peak out of the Apennines and into the rarified air above the clouds. This mountain, famous in its own right, is most renowned as the source of the Po. The river falls from a small spring on the mountainside and, carried toward the rising sun, is quickly swollen in a brief space by numerous tributaries. Thus it becomes not only one of the great streams but (as Virgil calls it) the king of rivers. It rushes through the Ligurian rapids; from there it bounds Emilia, Flaminia, and Venice and finally descends to the Adriatic Sea in a great delta. That part of the country about which I spoke first, surrounded by a graceful plain and scattered hills and mountains, is both pleasant and happy. Taking its name from those mountains whose foot it lies under,

25   **fecere** Severs Ba Bod2 Har6; facere Pe; fecerant Po; fecerunt Har7; *om* CC2 G4 G1.
27   **confabulantibus** Severs Ba Bod2 Po Har7 Har6; confabulatibus Pe; *om* CC2 G4 G1.
29   **eciam** Severs Ba Bod2 Po Har7 Har6; et Pe; *om* CC2 G4 G1.
39   **obliviscerer** Severs Bod2 Po Har6; obliviscer Pe; obliviscar Ba; olivisceret Har7; *om* CC2 G4 G1.
40   **imo** Severs Ba Po; uno Pe Har6; ideo Bod2; *om* Har7; *om* CC2 G4 G1.
42   **expetita** Severs Ba Po Har7; expectata Pe; expedita Bod2 Har6; *om* CC2 G4 G1.
50   **unus** *om* Hg El CC2; *om* G1
51   **liquido sese** Severs Hg El CC2 Ba Bod2 G4 Har7 Har6; liquidose se Pe; liquidoso se Po; *om* G1.
52   **eius a** *om* El; eius e Severs Ba G4 G1 Har7; eius CC2; ei e Bod2; *ms defective* Hg.
58   **planicie** planicies Hg El Ba.

25 pene mei ipsius que immemorem me [fecere], illam memorie mandare
voluerim, ut et ipse eam animo quociens vellem non sine voluptate repeterem,
et amicis ut fit [confabulantibus] renarrarem. Si quando tale aliquid incidisset,
quod cum brevi postmodum fecissem gratamque audientibus cognovissem,
subito talis interloquendum cogitacio supervenit, fieri posse ut nostri [eciam]
30 sermonis ignaros tam dulcis historia delectaret, cum et michi semper ante
multos annos audita placuisset, et tibi usque adeo placuisse perpenderem ut
vulgari eam stilo tuo censueris non indignam et fine operis, ubi Rethorum
disciplina validiora quelibet collocari iubet.

Itaque die quodam, inter varios cogitatus animum more solito discerpentes,
35 et illis et michi, ut sic dixerim, iratus, vale omnibus ad tempus dicto, historiam
ipsam tuam scribere sum aggressus, te haut dubie gavisurum sperans, ultro
rerum interpretem me tuarum fore. Quod non facile alteri cuicumque
prestiterim, egit me tui amor et historie. Ita tamen, ne horacianum illud
poetice artis [obliviscerer] – Nec verbum verbo curabis reddere fidus interpres
40 – historiam tuam meis verbis explicui, [imo] alicubi aut paucis in ipsa
narracione mutatis verbis aut additis, quod te non ferente modo sed favente
fieri credidi. Que licet a multis et laudata et [expetita] fuerit, ego rem tuam tibi
non alteri dedicandam censui. Quam quidem an mutata veste deformaverim
an for(fol. 185b)tassis ornaverim, tu iudica. Illic enim orta, illuc redit; notus
45 iudex, nota domus, notum iter, ut unum et tu noveris et quisquis hoc leget: tibi
non michi tuarum rationem rerum esse reddendam.[20] Quisquis ex me queret
an hec vera sint, hoc est an historiam scripserim an fabulam, respondebo illud
Crispi: Fides penes auctorem meum scilicet Iohanem sit. Hec prefatus,
incipio.

Ad eundem. Insignis obedientia et fides uxoria. Tertia.

50 [E]st ad Ytalie latus occiduum Vesulus ex Appennini iugis mons unus
altissimus, qui, vertice nubila superans, [liquido sese] ingerit etheri, mons
suapte nobilis natura, Padi ortu nobilissimus, qui eius a latere fonte lapsus
exiguo, orientem contra solem fertur, mirisque mox tumidus incrementis brevi
spacio decurso, non tantum maximorum unus amnium sed fluviorum a
55 Virgilio rex dictus, Liguriam gurgitem violentus intersecat; dehinc Emiliam
atque Flamineam Veneciamque discriminans, multis ad ultimum et ingentibus
hostiis in Adriaticum mare descendit. Ceterum pars illa terrarum de qua
primum dixi, que et grata planicie et interiectis collibus ac montibus
circumflexis, apta pariter et iocunda est, atque ab eorum quibus subiacet pede
60 montium nomen tenet, et civitates aliquot et oppida habet egregia. Inter

---

[20] Similarly, the Clerk insists that the Griselda tale is Petrarch's story, especially at IV, 56 and 1147.

[60] it contains many towns and notable cities. The land of Saluzzo lies among the others at the root of Vesulus, full enough of villages and castles ruled by the will of certain noble marquises. The first and greatest, it is said, was a certain Walter, to whom the rule of his estate and the whole land belonged. Young and handsome, no less noble in behavior than in blood, he was in short an admirable man in every way, except that, content with his present lot, he gave no thought to the future. Accordingly he gave himself so fully to hunting and pleasure that he almost ignored everything else. To the even greater discomfort of his people, meanwhile, he also shrank from any mention of marriage.

[70] For a while they were silent, but eventually approached him as a group. One of them, either more assured or more eloquent, and better acquainted with his lord, spoke. "Because of your kindness, O great marquis, we dare, whenever the need demands it, to approach you individually and speak in firm confidence. Now let my voice deliver to your ears the silent wishes of all. (Not that I have any special role in this matter, but with many signs you have shown me to be dear to you among the others.) Certainly, all of your deeds please us, and always have pleased us, so that we consider ourselves fortunate in such a lord. But if you allow one petition, and respond to our intercession, we will surely be the happiest people in all the neighboring lands: I mean that you should turn your mind to marriage and lay your [80] neck (not merely free but imperial) under that lawful yoke, and do so before all else. The rapid days fly by, and even in the flower of your youth, silent and relentless age always stalks that flower: death is near at any age. No one is exempt from this duty; all must die. And while so much is certain, no one knows when death shall come. Therefore receive the prayers of those who have never rejected your authority. Leave the work of finding a wife to us, and we shall secure one worthy of your merit, and born of such splendid parents that through her the highest hopes may be fulfilled. Free us all from this nagging worry, lest, if anything mortal should befall, you might leave no heir, [90] and your people be left without an avowed ruler."

These pious prayers moved the heart of the man, and he said, "You urge me, friends, toward something which never entered my mind. I was accustomed to enjoy my freedom, which is rare in marriage. Even so, I submit myself freely to the will of my subjects, confident in your prudence and faith. But as for your offer to select a wife for me, I release you from that labor, and place it upon my own shoulders. What does one person's nobility convey to another? Children are often unlike their parents. Whatever good is in a person comes from God. So I will commit the fate of my rank and my marriage to him, trusting in his usual faithfulness; he will find what is best for my peace and well-being. And therefore, because it pleases you, I will choose a wife. I promise it in good faith, [100] and will neither frustrate nor delay your wish. You in return must promise one thing – and keep your promise: you must accept whatever wife I choose with full honor and veneration, and none of you must dispute or question my choice. For you, I, the freest man I have known, submit

---

67   **futurorum erat** Severs Ba Bod2 Po G4 G1 Har7 Har6; *om* Pe; futurorum fuit CC2.
68   **egre** Severs CC2 Ba Bod2 Po G4 G1 Har7 Har6; egie Pe.
82   **senectus** Severs CC2 Ba Bod2 Po G4 G1 Har7 Har6; subvectus Pe.
88   **solicitudine** Severs CC2 Ba Bod2 Po G4 G1 Har7 Har6; solitudine Pe.
92   **enim mea** CC2; enim in ea Pe; omni Ba Bod2 G4 Har6; omnimoda Severs Po G1 Har7.
100 **nec** Severs Ba Bod2 Po G4 G1 Har7 Har6; non Pe CC2.

cetera, ad radicem Vesuli, terra Saluciarum vicis et castellis satis frequens, marchionum arbitrio nobilium quorundam regitur virorum, quorum unus primusque omnium et maximus fuisse traditur Walterus quidam, ad quem familie ac terrarum omnium regimen pertineret; et hic quidem forma virens
65 atque etate, nec minus moribus quam sanguine nobilis, et ad summam omni ex parte vir insignis, nisi quod presenti sua sorte contentus, incuriosissimus [futurorum erat]. Itaque venatui aucupioque deditus, sic illis incubuerat ut alia cuncta pene negligeret; quodque in primis [egre] populi ferebant, dum ab ipsis quoque coniugii consiliis abhorreret.
70 Id aliquamdiu cum taciti pertulissent, tandem catervatim illum adeunt quorum unus cui vel auctoritas maior erat vel facundia maiorque cum suo duce familiaritas, Tua, inquit, humanitas, optime marchio, hanc nobis prestat audaciam; ut et tecum singuli quociens res exposcit devota fiducia collo- quamur, ut nunc omnium tacitas voluntates mea vox tuis auribus invehat, non
75 quod singulare habeam ad hanc rem, nisi quod tu me inter alios carum tibi multis indiciis comprobasti. Cum merito igitur tua nobis omnia placeant, semperque placuerint, ut felices nos tali domino iudicemus. Unum est, quod si a te impetrari sinis teque nobis exorabilem prebes, plane felicissimi finitimorum omnium futuri sumus: ut coniugio scilicet animum applices,
80 collumque non liberum modo sed imperiosum legitimo subicias iugo, idque quam primum facias. Volant enim dies rapidi, et quamquam florida sis etate, continue tamen hunc florem tacite [senectus] ingreditur, morsque ipsa omni proxima est etati. Nulli muneris huius immunitas datur, eque omnibus moriendum est; utque id certum, sic est illud ambiguum quando eveniat.
85 Suscipe igitur eorum preces qui nullum tuum recusarent imperium. Querende autem coniugis studium nobis relinque, talem enim tibi procurabimus que te merito digna sit, et tam claris orta par(fol. 185va)entibus ut de ea spes optima sit habenda. Libera tuos omnes molesta [solicitudine], ne si quid humaniter forsan accideret, tu sine tuo successore abeas, ipsi sine votivo rectore
90 remaneant.
Moverunt pie preces animum viri, et Cogitis, inquit, me, amici, ad id quod michi in animum nunquam venit. Delectabar enim [mea] libertate,[21] que in coniugio rara est. Ceterum subiectorum michi voluntatibus me sponte subicio, et prudencie vestre fisus et fidei. Illam vobis quam offertis querende curam
95 coniugis remitto, eamque humeris meis ipse subeo. Quod unius enim claritas confert alteri? Sepe fillii dissimilimi sunt parentum. Quicquid in homine bonum est, a deo est: illi ergo et status et matrimonii mei sortes, sperans de solita sua pietate, commiserim; ipse michi inveniet quod quieti mee sit expediens ac saluti. Itaque quando vobis placitum est ita uxorem ducam: id
100 vobis bona fide polliceor. Vestrumque desiderium [nec] frustrabor equidem nec morabor. Unum vos michi versa vice promittite ac servate: ut quam- cumque coniugem ipse delegero, eam vos summo honore ac veneracione prosequamini, nec sit ullus inter vos qui de meo unquam iudicio aut litiget aut queratur. Vestrum fuerit me omnium quos novissem liberimum iugo

---

[21] Severs prints the Petrarchan *Delectabar omnimoda libertate*. Pe's unique reading *enim in ea* is obvi- ously a version of the *enim mea* found in CC2, echoed in the Clerk's "my liberte" (IV, 145).

to the yoke of matrimony. But the choice in this marriage must be mine, and whoever she is, my wife must be your lady, just as if she were the daughter of a Roman prince." Unanimously and joyfully, they promised never to fall short. Like those who scarcely thought it possible to see the hoped-for wedding day, they eagerly received his command to prepare magnificently the chosen day. Thus Walter left the discussion, [110] gave responsibility for the wedding to his own servants, and announced the date for it.

Not far from the palace was a tiny village of a few poor farmers, the poorest of whom was named Janicula. But heavenly grace, which sometimes lights on even the poorest dwellings, had touched his only child, named Griselda. Her body was fair enough, but no one surpassed the beauty of her conduct and spirit. With little food, growing up in the worst poverty, ignorant of all comfort, she had learned not to dream about soft and tender things: a mature, manly spirit lay hidden in her virginal breast. Comforting the age of her father with immeasurable love, she used to graze his few sheep, wearing away her fingers meanwhile by spinning thread. [120] Returning again to the house, she would prepare home-grown meals according to their lot before lying down on her hard bed. In sum, she performed in their narrow cottage the whole duty of filial obedience and piety. Yet Walter, periodically riding past, fixed his eyes, not youthfully lascivious but maturely considerate, on the virtue of this maid, excellent beyond her age and gender. His keen insight had penetrated the obscurity in which her commonness hid her. Thus it happened that, despite his earlier disinclination, he decided simultaneously to marry, and to marry this woman and no other.

The day of the wedding was approaching and since no one knew where the bride would be found, no one failed to wonder. Walter meanwhile was collecting golden rings, crowns and baldrics. [130] He ordered costly dresses and shoes – everything of the sort needed – prepared to the measure of another girl who was quite like Griselda in stature. When the awaited day had come, and no hint about the bride had been heard, the astonishment of all reached new heights. The hour of the banquet arrived, and now the whole house bustled with tremendous preparation. Walter set out as if to meet an approaching bride, and left the palace attended by a throng of noble men and women. Griselda, unaware that all these things were being prepared for her, and having done what was necessary in the house, was bringing water from a distant well, so that, her other work being completed, she could with her friends prepare for a glimpse of her lord's wife. As she was crossing her father's threshold, Walter approached deep in thought and, [140] calling her by name, asked where her father was. Reverently and humbly she replied that he was at home. "Tell him to come to me," he said. When the old man came, Walter grasped his hand, took him aside for a moment, and said quietly, "I know, Janicula, that I am dear to you, and I know you are a faithful man, and I think that you would wish for whatever pleases

---

108   **apparandis** Severs Ba Bod2 G4 G1 Har7 Har6; apparendis Pe CC2 Po.

112   **incolarum** Severs Ba Bod2 Po G4 G1 Har7 Har6; vicolorum Pe; in quo larum CC2.

125   **abscondebat** Severs CC2 Bod2 Po G4 G1 Har7 Har6; om Pe; abscordebat Ba.

134   **Tum** Severs CC2 Ba G4 G1 Har7; Cum Pe Har6; Tunc Bod2 Po.

138   **visendam** visendum Hg; videndum El.

139   **properaret** prepararet Hg El Bod2 Har6; preparet G4. **Dum** Quam Hg El CC2 G1; Tum Severs Har7; tunc Bod2.

140   **incedens** cedens El.

144   **velle** Severs CC2 Ba Bod2 Po G4 G1 Har7 Har6; ille Pe.

105 subiecisse coniugii; mea sit ipsius coniugii electio; quecumque uxor mea erit,
illa, seu romani principis filia, domina vestra sit. Promittunt unanimiter ac lete
nichil defuturum, ut quibus vix possibile videretur optatum diem cernere
nupciarum, de quibus diem certum magnificentissime [apparandis] domini
iubentis edictum alacres suscepere. Ita e colloquio discessum est, et ipse
110 nichilominus eam ipsam nupciarum curam domesticis suis imposuit, edixitque
diem.

Fuit haut procul a palacio villula paucorum atque inopum [incolarum],
quorum uni omnium pauperimo Ianicula nomen erat: sed ut pauperum quoque
tugurria non numquam gratia celestis invisit, unica illi nata contigerat
115 Grisildas nomine, forma corporis satis egregia, sed pulcritudine morum atque
animi adeo speciosa ut nichil supra. Hec parco victu, in summa semper inopia
educata, omnis inscia voluptatis, nil molle nil tenerum cogitare didicerat, sed
virilis senilisque animus virgineo latebat in pectore. Patris senium inestimabili
refovens caritate, et pauculas eius oves pascebat, et colo interim digitos
120 atterebat; vicissimque domum rediens, oluscula et dapes fortune congruas
preparabat, durumque cubiculum sternebat, et ad summam angusto in spacio
totum filialis obediencie ac pietatis officium explicabat. In hanc virgunculam
Walterus, sepe illuc transiens, quandoque oculos non iuvenili lascivia sed
senili gravitate defixerat, et virtutem eximiam supra sexum supraque etatem,
125 quam vulgi oculis condicionis obscuritas [abscondebat], acri penetrarat
intuitu. Unde effectum vel uxorem habere, quam nunquam ante voluerat, et
simul hanc nullamque aliam habere disponeret.

Instabat nupciarum dies; unde autem ventura sponsa esset, nemo noverat,
nemo non mirabatur. Ipse interim et anulos aureos et coronas et balteos
130 conquirebat, vestes autem preciosas et calceos et eius generis necessaria
omnia ad mensuram puelle alterius, que stature sue persimilis erat, preparari
faciebat. Venerat expectata dies, et cum nullus sponse rumor audiretur,
admiracio omnium vehementer excreverat. Hora enim prandii aderat, iamque
apparatu ingenti tota domus fervebat. [Tum] Walterus adventat velut sponse
135 obviam pro (fol. 185vb) fecturus, domo egreditur, prosequente virorum ac
matronarum nobilium caterva. Griseldis, omnium que erga se prepararentur
ignara, peractis que peragenda domi erant, aquam e longinquo fonte
convectans, paternum limen intrabat, ut, expeditis curis aliis, ad visendam
domini sui sponsam cum puellis comitibus properaret. Dum Walterus,
140 cogitabundus incedens eamque compellans nomine, ubi nam pater eius esset
interogavit; que cum illum domi esse reverenter atque humiliter respondisset,
Iube, inquit, ad me veniat. Venientem seniculum, manu prehensum, parumper
abstraxit ac submissa voce, Scio, ait, me, Iannicula, carum tibi, teque
hominem fidum novi, et quecumque michi placeant [velle] te arbitror. Unum

me. Still, I wish to know one thing in particular: whether you wish me, your lord, to become your son-in-law, by giving me your daughter as wife." Stunned by this unexpected proposition, the old man froze; he could barely murmur this reply: "I must neither desire nor shun anything, except what may be pleasing to you, who are my lord." "Let us go in together, then," he said, "so that I may ask her certain questions in your presence."

[150] While the people waited and wondered, they entered and found the girl more than occupied in serving her father and stunned by the unaccustomed arrival of such a guest. Walter approached her with these words. "It pleases both your father and me that you should be my wife. I believe that this would also please you. But I must ask whether, when what will soon be done has been done, your willing spirit is prepared never to dissent from my will in any thing which concerns you and me; whether you will permit me to do whatever I wish with you, without any resistance in your face or your words, with a willing spirit?" Trembling at this extraordinary idea, she replied, "I know myself unworthy of such an honor, my lord. But if this is your will and my fate, I will never knowingly do – no, I will not even think anything contrary to your will. [160] Nor will you do anything to which I will object, even if you command my death." "Enough," he said. And leading her outside and showing her to the people he said, "This is my wife; this is your lady: cherish her, love her, and, if you hold me dear, you must hold her most dear." Then, so that she might bring no relics of her old fortune to her new house, he commanded her to be stripped and decked with new clothes from head to foot. The surrounding ladies, taking her to their hearts in turn, modestly and quickly fulfilled his orders. The uncouth girl was thus clothed, her tangled hair rearranged by hand and hurriedly smoothed. Adorned with gems and a crown, suddenly she appeared transformed, so that people hardly recognized her. Walter solemnly wedded her with a precious ring he had brought for the purpose. [170] He commanded her to be led to the palace on a snow-white horse, while the people attended her and rejoiced. The marriage was celebrated in this way, making the day most joyful.

Very shortly there shone from the poor bride such divine favor that she seemed to have been brought up and educated in an imperial court rather than a shepherd's cottage. She was extraordinarily beloved and venerated among the people; it was scarcely possible to persuade even those who knew her from birth that she was Janicula's child. The grace of her life and manners and the gravity and sweetness of her words bound her to every soul with great love. Not only within her own country

---

145 **nominatim** Severs CC2 Ba Bod2 Po G4 G1 Har7 Har6; nominatum Pe.

146 **Inopino** Severs CC2 Ba Bod2 Po G4 G1 Har7 Har6; In optimo Pe.

151 **invenere** invenit Hg El CC2; invenire Har7 Har6.

156 **repugnancia** impugnatione Hg El CC2.

159 **nil** Hg El CC2; nec Pe; nichil Severs Ba Bod2 Po G4 G1 Har7 Har6. **eciam** Severs Ba Bod2 Po G4 G1 Har7 Har6; et Pe; nec etiam G4.

163 **Hinc** Dehinc Hg El CC2 Po G1 Har7 Har6.

164 **novam** Severs CC2 Bod2 Po G4 G1 Har7 Har6; novo Pe; nova Ba. **inferret** inferat Hg El; infert CC2; ferret Bod2. **iussit** iusserit El.

167 **comptamque** Severs Ba Bod2 Po G4 Har7; compertamque Pe; comptam coopertam CC2; cohopertamque G1; comptam Har6.

175 **esset vixque** est vix quod Hg El; est vixque CC2 G4 Har6.

176 **illam ab origine** illius originem Hg El CC2; eius originem G1; ab origine Har6. **erat** *om* Hg El.

177 **morum** Severs CC2 Ba Po G4 G1 Har6; erat morum Pe Har7; tantus morum Bod2. **ac** atque Hg El CC2; et Har7.

145 tamen [nominatim] nosse velim: an me, quem dominum habes, data michi hac
tua in uxorem filia, generum velis? [Inopino] negocio stupefactus, senex
obriguit, et vix tandem paucis hiscens, Nichil, inquit, aut velle debeo aut
nolle, nisi quod placitum tibi sit, qui dominus meus es. Ingrediamur soli ergo,
inquit, ut ipsam de quibusdam interogem, te presente.

150 Ingressi igitur, expectante populo ac mirante; puellam circa patris
obsequium satagentem et insolito tanti hospitis adventu stupidam invenere,
quam hiis verbis Walterus aggreditur: Et patri tuo, inquit, placet et michi ut
uxor mea sis. Credo idipsum tibi placeat. Sed habeo ex te querere, ubi hoc
peractum fuerit quod mox erit, an volenti animo parata sis ut de omnibus
155 tecum michi conveniat, ita ut in nulla unquam re a mea voluntate dissencias
et, quicquid tecum agere voluero, sine ulla frontis aut verbi repugnancia te ex
animo volente michi liceat. Ad hec illa miraculo rei tremens, Ego, mi domine,
inquit, tanto honore me indignam scio; ac si voluntas tua, sique sors mea est,
[nil] ego umquam sciens, ne dum faciam, sed [eciam] cogitabo, quod contra
160 animum tuum sit; nec tu aliquid facies, et si me mori iusseris, quod moleste
feram. Satis est, inquit ille. Sic in publicum eductam populo ostendens, hec,
ait, uxor mea, hec domina vestra est; hanc colite, hanc amate. Et si me carum
habetis, hanc carissimam habetote. Hinc nequid reliquiarum fortune veteris
[novam] inferret in domum, nudari eam iussit, et a calce ad verticem novis
165 vestibus indui, quod a matronis circumstantibus ac certatim sinu illam
gremioque foventibus verecunde ac celeriter adimpletum est. Sic horridulam
virginem, indutam, laceramque comam recollectam manibus [comptamque]
pro tempore, insignitam gemmis et corona velut subito transformatam, vix
populus recognovit; quam Walterus anulo precioso, quem ad hunc usum
170 detulerat, solempniter desponsavit. Niveo equo impositam, ad palacium
deduci fecit, comitante populo et gaudente. Ad hunc modum nupcie celebrate,
diesque ille letissimus actus est.

Brevi dehinc inopi sponse tantum divini favoris affulserat, ut non in casa
illa pastoria sed in aula imperatoria educata atque edocta videretur. Atque
175 apud omnes supra fidem cara et venerabilis facta esset, vixque hiis ipsis qui
illam ab origine noverant persuaderi posset Iannicole natam esse. Tantus erat
vite, tantus [morum] decor, ea verborum gravitas ac dul(fol. 186a)cedo, quibus
omnium animos nexu sibi magni amoris astrinxerat. Iamque non solum intra

but through all the neighboring provinces, her name was renowned with praise. [180] Men and women ran to see her with burning eagerness. Thus Walter, graced by a humble but worthy and prosperous marriage, lived in great peace at home and in the highest favor of men. Because he had recognized so clearly the extraordinary virtue concealed by her poverty, his prudence was widely praised. And the bride was wise not only in womanly and domestic matters. When affairs required it, she took up public duties in the marquis' absence, resolving the country's controversies and the feuds of the nobility with such authoritative opinions and with such maturity and equity of judgment that everyone said the woman had been sent from heaven for the common welfare.

Not long after, she became pregnant, and the people waited anxiously. [190] Then she delivered a very beautiful girl and (however much they would have preferred a boy) this proof of her fertility made not only the marquis, but the whole country happy. As can happen, however, Walter was seized by a desire – wiser heads will call it more amazing than worthy. When the child had stopped nursing, he decided to test further the already proven faithfulness of his dear wife, and to repeat the test again. He therefore took her privately into his chamber, and spoke with a troubled face. "You know, O Griselda – for I believe that in your present fortune you are not forgetful of your former station – you know, I say, how you came into this house. You are very dear and beloved to me, but not to my nobility, especially since you began to bear children; their spirits are grieved at serving a plebeian lady. Desiring peace with them, [200] I must submit to an external judgment about your daughter, not my own. I must do what pains me more than anything else could. Yet I would do nothing without your knowledge: I wish you to align your mind with me, and to show that patience which you promised at the beginning of our marriage." Having heard this, moved neither in speech nor in expression, she replied, "You are our lord. Both I and this little daughter are yours: do as you like about your affairs. Nothing can please you which will displease me. There is nothing I deeply desire to possess or fear to lose, except you. I have fixed this resolve in the core of my heart; it will never be moved by either passing time or death. Anything else may happen before my mind will be changed." He was happy with her response, but departed masked in melancholy.

[210] A bit later, he called one of his most faithful retainers to him, whose efforts he was wont to use in matters of some consequence, showed him what he should do, and sent him to his wife. The servant came to her at night, saying, "Forgive me, my lady, and do not blame me for what I am forced to do. You know, most wise lady, what it means to be a servant; to someone with your insight, however inexperienced,

179 **per finitimas** Severs CC2 Bod2 Po G4 G1 Har7; finitinas et Pe; per finitas Ba Har6.
182 **honestatus** honestatis Severs Hg El. **domi** dei Hg El CC2.
187 **dirimens** *add* atque componens Severs Hg El CC2 Ba Bod2 Po G4 G1 Har6; *add* ac componens Har7.
186 **nobiliumque** nobilium Hg El CC2.
191 **fecunditate** Severs CC2 Ba Bod2 Po G4 G1 Har7 Har6; facunditate Pe.
192 **Cepit** Ceperit Hg El.
193 **laudabilis** Severs CC2 Ba Bod2 G4 Har7 Har6; *add* cupiditas Pe; laudabilem Po G1. **doctiores iudicent** *om* El CC2; iudicent matrone G4; doctores satis iudicent G1; *ms defective* Hg.
194 **iterum** *add* atque iterum Severs El Ba Bod2 Po G4 G1 Har7; *add* atque CC2; iterumque iterum Har6; *ms defective* Hg.
203 **mota** *om* El.
214 **inexperte** Severs CC2 Bod2 Po G1 Har7 Har6; inexperta Pe Ba; *om* G4.

patrios fines, sed [per finitimas] quasque provincias suum nomen celebri
180 preconio fama vulgabat, ita ut multi ad illam visendam viri ac matrone studio
fervente concurrerent. Sic Walterus, humili quidem sed insigni ac prospero
matrimonio honestatus, summa domi in pace,[22] extra vero summa cum gratia
hominum, vivebat; quodque eximiam virtutem tanta sub inopia latitantem tam
perspicaciter deprehendisset, vulgo prudentissimus habebatur. Neque vero
185 solers sponsa muliebria tantum ac domestica, sed ubi res posceret, publica
etiam subibat officia, viro absente, lites patrie nobiliumque discordias
dirimens tam gravibus responsis tantaque maturitate et iudicii equitate, ut
omnes ad salutem publicam demissam celo feminam predicarent.

Nec multum tempus affluxerat, dum gravida effecta, primum subditos
190 anxia expectacione suspendit. Dehinc, filiam enixa pulcherimam, quamvis
filium maluissent,[23] tamen votiva [fecunditate] non virum modo sed totam
patriam letam fecit. Cepit, ut fit, interim Walterum, cum iam ablactata esset
infantula, mirabilis quedam quam [laudabilis] doctiores iudicent cupiditas,
satis expertam care fidem coniugis experiendi altius et iterum retemptandi.
195 Solam ergo in thalamum sevocatam, turbida fronte sic alloquitur: Nosti, O
Griseldis – neque enim presenti fortuna te preteriti tui status oblitam credo –
Nosti, inquam, qualiter in hanc domum veneris. Michi quidem cara satis ac
dilecta es; ac meis nobilibus non ita, presertim ex quo parere incepisti, qui
plebeie domine subesse animis ferunt iniquissimis. Michi ergo, qui cum eis
200 pacem cupio, necesse est de filia tua non meo sed alieno iudicio obsequi, et id
facere quo nil michi posset esse molestius. Id enim vero te ignara nunquam
fecerim; volo autem tuum michi animum accomodes, pacienciamque illam
prestes quam ab inicio nostri coniugii promisisti. Hiis auditis, nec verbo mota,
nec vultu, Tu, inquit, noster es dominus. Et ego et hec parva filia tue sumus.
205 De rebus tuis igitur fac ut libet. Nil placere enim tibi potest quod michi
displiceat. Nichil penitus vel habere cupio vel amittere metuo, nisi te; hoc ipsa
in medio cordis affixi, nunquam inde vel lapsu temporis vel morte vellendum.
Omnia prius fieri possunt quam hic animus mutari. Letus ille responso, sed
dissimulans visu mestus abscessit.

210 Et post paululum unum suorum satellitum fidissimum sibi, cuius opera
gravioribus in negociis uti consueverat, quid agi vellet edoctum, ad uxorem
misit. Qui ad eam noctu veniens, Parce, inquit, o domina, neque michi
imputes quod coactus facio. Scis, sapientissima, quid est esse sub dominis,
neque tali ingenio predite quamvis [inexperte] dura parendi necessitas est

---

[22] With 396, this line gives the clearest evidence of Chaucer's ties to a manuscript even closer to CC2
than Pe. Only Hg El CC2 read *summa dei in pace* corresponding to "In Goddes pees" (IV, 423).

[23] Chaucer assigns the wish for a son to Griselda at IV, 444 ("Al had hir levere have born a knave child"),
probably because his MS agreed with five MSS (including CC2) in reading *maluisset.*

the hard necessity to obey is not unknown. I am commanded to take this child and –." He cut his speech short, as if expressing his bloody assignment silently. The man's reputation was suspect. His expression was suspect. The time was suspect and his demand was suspect, so that she understood clearly that her dear daughter was going to be killed; nevertheless, she neither sighed nor wept. Such behavior would be very stern in a nurse, not to mention a mother. [220] But taking the little girl with a tranquil countenance, she gazed at her a while, then, kissing her, blessed her, and marked her with the sign of the holy cross, and gave her to the retainer, saying, "Go, and carry out whatever orders our lord has given you. I ask one thing: take care that wild beasts or birds do not mutilate this little body, unless you are commanded to the contrary."

He returned to the marquis, explaining what he had said and what reply was made, and showed him the child. A father's devotion moved Walter's feelings deeply, but he did not bend from the rigorous course of his intention. He commanded the retainer to carry the child with all possible secrecy to Bologna, wrapped in cloths, hidden in a basket, and carried on the back of a mule. [230] There Walter's sister, the wife of the Count of Panago, would give maternal attention to her nourishment and moral development while taking utmost care that no one should know whose child she was. So the retainer went, and faithfully performed his charge. Meanwhile Walter, though he considered the countenance and speech of his wife often, never found any indication of a changed spirit: an invariable alacrity and diligence, her accustomed obedience and the very same love remained. There was no grief, no mention of her daughter; never, either deliberately or in passing, was her name heard on her mother's lips.

Four years passed in this way, until Griselda conceived and bore a most fine son, to the great joy of the father and all his friends. When the child stopped nursing after two years, however, the father returned to his former inquisitiveness, [240] and spoke to his wife again: "For some time, you have heard that my people are unhappy with our marriage, especially since you showed yourself fertile, but most off all since you bore a son. They say – and this murmur comes often to my ears – 'When Walter dies, the offspring of Janicula will lord it over us, so noble a land subject to such a ruler.' Every day, many such notions are tossed about among the people. For these reasons, still desirous of peace and – to speak truly – fearing for myself, I am moved to arrange for this child what I arranged for his sister. I tell you this lest the sudden sadness should disturb you." She replied, "And I have said, and I repeat: I can neither desire nor shun anything except what you do; I have no part in these children except the labor. You are my lord and theirs: [250] exercise your authority in your affairs. You should not seek my consent, because in entering your house I discarded my preferences and inclinations along with my clothes: I have assumed yours. Just so, whatever you desire, I desire, in every situation. If I had foreknown your will, I would certainly have begun to wish and desire what you do

---

227 **propositi non** Severs CC2 Ba Bod2 Po G1 Har6; propositumque Pe; propositum n. Har7; *om* G4.

232 **quod** Severs CC2 Ba Bod2 Po G1 Har7 Har6; quid Pe; *om* G4.

234 **sedulitas** sedalitas Hg El; *om* G4. **obsequium** obsquium El; *om* G4.

235 **nulla** tristicia *om* Hg El G4.

238 **leticiam** Severs CC2 Ba Bod2 Po G1 Har7 Har6; letissimam Pe; *om* G4.

240 **affatur** Severs CC2 Ba Bod2 Po G1 Har7 Har6; afferat Pe; *om* G4. **ait** *om* El G4

215 ignota. Iussus sum hanc infantulam accipere, atque eam – .[24] Hic sermone
arrupto, quasi crudele ministerium silencio exprimens, subticuit. Suspecta viri
fama, suspecta facies, Suspecta hora, suspecta erat oracio, quibus etsi clare
occisum iri (fol. 186b) dulcem filiam intelligeret, nec lacrimulam tamen ullam
nec suspirium dedit. In nutrice quidem, ne dum in matre, durissimum.
220 Sed tranquilla fronte puellulam accipiens, aliquantulum respexit, et simul
osculans, benedixit ac signum sancte crucis impressit, porrexitque satelliti et
Vade, ait, quodque tibi dominus noster iniunxerit exequere. Unum queso: cura
ne corpusculum hoc fere lacerent aut volucres, ita tamen nisi contrarium sit
preceptum.
225   Reversus ad dominum, cum quid dictum quidve responsum esset exposuisset
et ei filiam obtulisset, vehementer paterna animum pietas movit;[25] susceptum
tamen rigorem [propositi non] inflexit. Iussitque satelliti obvolutam pannis,
ciste iniectam, ac iumento impositam, quieto omni quanta posset diligencia
Bononiam deferret ad sororem suam, que illic Comiti de Panico nupta erat.
230 Eamque sibi traderet alendam materno studio, et caris moribus instruendam,
tanta preterea occultandam cura, ut cuius filia esset a nemine posset agnosci.
Ivit ille illico, et solicite [quod] impositum ei erat implevit. Walterus interea,
vultum coniugis ac verba considerans, nullum umquam mutati animi
perpendit indicium: par alacritas atque sedulitas, solitum obsequium, idem
235 amor, nulla tristicia, nulla filie mencio, nunquam sive ex proposito sive
incidenter nomen eius ex ore matris auditum.
        Transiverant hoc in statu anni iiii[or], dum ecce, gravida iterum, filium
elegantissimum peperit, [leticiam] patris ingentem atque omnium amicorum,
quo nutricis ab ubere post biennium subducto, ad curiositatem solitam
240 reversus pater, uxorem rursus [affatur]: Et olim, ait, audisti populum meum
egre ferre nostrum connubium, presertim ex quo te fecundam cognovere,
nunquam tamen egrius quam ex quo marem peperisti. Dicunt enim – et sepe
ad aures meas murmur hoc pervenit – Obeunte igitur Waltero, Iannicole nepos
nostri dominabitur, et tam nobilis patria tali domino subiacebit. Multa cotidie
245 in hanc sentenciam iactantur in populis. Quibus ego, et quietis avidus et – ut
verum fatear – michi metuens, permoveor ut de hoc infante disponam quod de
sorore disposui. Id tibi prenuncio ne te subitus dolor turbet. Ad hec illa Et
dixi, ait, et repeto: nichil possum seu velle seu nolle nisi quod tu, neque vero
in hiis filiis quicquam habeo preter laborem. Tu mei et ipsorum dominus; tuis
250 in rebus iure tuo utere, nec consensum meum queras. In ipso enim tue domus
introitu ut pannos sic et voluntates affectusque meos exui, tuos indui:
quacumque ergo de re quicquid tu vis, ego eciam volo. Nempe que si future
tue voluntatis essem prescia, ante etiam quicquid id esset et velle et cupere

---

[24] Petrarch's normal Latin syntax with the verb in the final position is more chilling than either Middle or
Modern English can be: the object *eam* is stated, and a verb describing her fate is strongly implied.
Har6 completes the sentence graphically: *eam Iugulabo*: "I will cut her throat." Chaucer's sergeant
simply says that he will take the child (IV, 533).

[25] The *pietas* is unmistakably Walter's in Petrarch. Chaucer does not render the passage closely, but the
common variant *paternum* for *paterna* (it appears in 14 MSS including CC2) at least suggests locating
the piety in someone else. Certainly Chaucer seems more interested in Grisilde's *pietas* than Walter's.

before you wished it; but since I cannot anticipate your resolve, I follow it freely now. Show me that my death would please you, and I die willingly: in the end nothing, not even death itself, would have been equal to our love." Admiring the woman's steadfastness, he left with a disturbed countenance.

And immediately he sent his retainer to her a second time. Having at length excused himself because of the necessity of obedience, and at length having asked her indulgence if he had done or were to do anything disturbing to her, [260] the servant demanded the infant as if about to perform a terrible atrocity. With the same countenance as always, whatever her state of mind, she picked up her son. Anyone would have found him as loveable for his disposition and his beauty as his mother did. Signing him with the cross and blessing him as she had her daughter, she drank him in with her eyes for a few moments and kissed him. With no apparent sign of inward sorrow, she gave him to the retainer. "See that you do what you are commanded," she said. "One more thing I pray: that – if it may be – you protect this beautiful child's delicate limbs from disturbance by birds and beasts." He returned with this charge to the marquis. Walter was more and more astonished. Had he not known her to have loved the children greatly, Walter might have suspected this feminine strength to proceed from some kind of savagery of spirit. But much as she loved them all, [270] none was more beloved than her husband. Walter had the boy carried to Bologna by the same man who had taken his sister.

These proofs of conjugal good will and faithfulness might have been enough for the most demanding husband; but some people, having begun a course of action, will not desist. No, they press on further, clinging to their plan. With his eyes therefore fixed on his wife, Walter carefully considered whether any change toward himself had occurred, but he was wholly unable to find any, unless she became daily more faithful and obedient to him. They seemed but one mind – not one common to both, but simply the man's mind. The wife had resolved, as regards herself, neither to desire anything nor to refuse anything. Gradually, ugly rumors began to spread about Walter: [280] because of his wild and inhuman harshness, humiliated by remorse and shame of his wife, it was said, he had ordered the children murdered. For the children were nowhere to be seen and no one had heard where they were. In this way a man otherwise beloved and illustrious made himself notorious and hated by many. Yet his harsh spirit was not deflected; he persevered in his established sternness and his cruel desire to test Griselda.

And so when the twelfth year from the birth of his daughter had passed, he sent messengers to Rome, who brought back counterfeit papal letters. These, it was commonly believed, gave him permission from the Pope to put aside his first wife, for the contentment of himself and his people, and to marry another; it was by no means difficult to persuade the ignorant peasants of any story. [290] When this rumor came to Griselda, she was sad, I imagine. But always firm about herself and her lot, she remained unaffected, awaiting the decision of the man to whom she had given

265 **ut si fieri potest** Severs CC2 Ba Bod2 Po G1 Har6; *add* ut Pe; si fieri potest Har7; *om* G4.
269 **animi** Severs CC2 Ba Bod2 Po G1 Har7 Har6; omnium Pe; *om* G4.
275 **ullam** Severs CC2 Bod2 Po Har7 Har6; illam Pe Ba; ulla G1; *om* G4.
277 **isque** Severs CC2 Po Har7 Har6; idque Pe; is Ba; hiisque Bod2 G1; *om* G4.
279 **Ceperat** Ceperit Hg El; *om* G4.
284 **experiendique** Severs CC2 Ba Bod2 Har7 Har6 expediendique Pe; experiendi Po G1; *om* G4.
286 **simulatas** Severs Ba Bod2 G1 Har7 Har6; sigillatas Pe; dissimulatas CC2; similatas Po; *om* G4.
291 **semel** Severs CC2 Ba Bod2 Po G1 Har7 Har6; senilis Pe; *om* G4

inciperem, quam tu velles; nunc animum tuum, quem prevenire non possum,
255 libens sequor. Fac senciam tibi placere quod moriar, volens moriar, nec res
ulla denique nec mors ipsa nostro fuerit par amori. Admirans femine
constanciam, turbato vultu abiit.

Confestimque satellitem olim missum ad eam remisit, qui multum excusata
necessitate parendi, multumque petita venia si quid ei molestum aut fecisset
260 aut faceret, quasi immane scelus acturus poposcit infantem. Illa eodem quo
semper vultu, qualicumque animo, filium forma corporis atque indole non
matri (fol. 186va) tantum sed cunctis amabilem in manus cepit, signansque
eum signo crucis et benedicens ut filiam fecerat, et diuticule oculis inherens,
atque deosculans, nullo penitus signo doloris edito, petenti obtulit. Et tene,
265 inquit, fac quod iussus es. Unum eciam nunc precor: ut, si fieri [potest], hos
artus teneros infantis egregii protegas a vexacione volucrum ac ferarum. Cum
hiis mandatis reversus ad dominum, animum eius magis ac magis in stuporem
egit, ut nisi eam nosset amantissimam filiorum, paulominus suspicari posset
hoc femineum robur quadam ab [animi] feritate procedere. Sed cum suorum
270 omnium valde, nullus erat amancior quam viri. Iussus inde Bononiam
proficisci, eo illum tulit quo sororem tulerat.

Poterant rigidissimo coniugi hec benivolencie et fidei coniugalis experimenta sufficere. Sed sunt qui, ubi semel inceperint, non desinant; imo
incumbant hereantque proposito. Defixis ergo in uxorem oculis, an ulla eius
275 mutacio erga se fieret contemplabatur assidue, nec [ullam] penitus invenire
poterat, nisi quod fidelior illi indies atque obsequencior fiebat. Sic ut duorum
non nisi unus animus videretur, [isque] non communis amborum sed viri
dumtaxat unius, uxor enim per se nichil velle, ut dictum est, nichil nolle
firmaverat. Ceperat sensim de Waltero decolor fama crebrescere: quod videli-
280 cet effera et inhumana duricie, humilis penitencia ac pudore coniugii, filios
iussisset interfici. Nam neque pueri comparebant, neque ubinam gencium
essent ullus audierat; quo se ille vir alioquin clarus et suis carus multis
infamem odiosumque reddiderat. Neque ideo trux animus flectebatur, sed in
suscepta severitate [experiendique] sua dura illa libidine procedebat.
285 Itaque cum iam ab ortu filie xii[us] annus elapsus esset, nuncios Romam
misit, qui [simulatas] litteras apostolicas inde referrent, quibus in populo
vulgaretur datam sibi licenciam a Romano Pontifice, ut pro sua et suarum
gencium quiete, primo matrimonio reiecto, aliam ducere posset uxorem; nec
operosum sane fuit aggrestibus rudibusque animis quod libet persuadere. Que
290 fama cum ad Griseldis noticiam pervenisset, tristis, ut puto. Sed ut que
[semel] de se suisque de sortibus statuisset, inconcussa constitit, expectans

herself and everything that was hers. Walter sent to Bologna, and asked his kinsman to lead back his children, spreading the rumor that he intended to take this young girl as his wife. Faithfully doing what was asked, the count set forth on the appointed day with the girl – now old enough to marry, beautiful and distinguished in her splendid array – her seven-year-old brother, and a choice company of nobles.

Meanwhile Walter, with his usual urge to test his wife again, to push her sorrow and shame to the utmost, led her into an audience before many people. "I used to be happy enough in marriage with you, [300] focusing on your character and not your origin. Now, however, I see that every great fortune is a great servitude: what is permissible for some farmer is not permissible for me. My people impel me, and the Pope consents, to take another wife. She is on her way here, and will arrive soon. Therefore be strong in spirit: give place to your successor, take back your dowry, and return to your old home in peace. The lot of humans is never stable." She replied, "My lord, I always knew that there was no parallel between your greatness and my lowness. I never held myself worthy to be your – I do not say wife – but servant, and in this house, where you made me the lady, I swear before God that I always was a servant in spirit. Therefore I thank God and you [310] for this period of great honor with you, far beyond my merit. For the rest, I am prepared with a good and tranquil mind to return to my father's house, to grow old and die where I spent my youth, always a happy and honorable widow, who had been the wife of such a man. Willingly I make way for your new wife, and may she come to you in joy! Whenever you please, I will leave without reluctance this place where I used to live most happily.

"But since you command that I take my dowry with me – I note what sort it is, and it was not lost when I came to you, stripped of my own clothes and reclothed in yours, on the threshold of my father's house. I brought you no other dowry but faithfulness and nakedness. See therefore, I shed this gown and restore this ring, with which you married me. The other rings, clothes, and jewels which you gave me, and which made me ripe for envy, are in your chamber. [320] Naked I came from my father's house; naked I shall return there, except that I consider it unworthy that this womb, which contained the children that you begot, should appear naked to the people. And so if it pleases you, and not otherwise, I pray and beseech that in exchange for the virginity that I brought here and do not take away, you command that one shift be left to me of those I used to wear in your house, with which I will cover the womb of your former wife." Tears welled up in the man; he could no longer be contained. Turning his face, Walter said in a trembling voice, "I grant you a single shift," and left weeping. She stripped herself in front of all; content in just her shift, she left with naked head and naked feet. Many followed her, lamenting and blaming Fortune; [330] with dry eyes and in noble silence, the venerable woman returned alone to her paternal home.

The old man had always considered his daughter's marriage dubious and never held out much hope for it. He always expected that so powerful a man, proud in the fashion of the nobility, his gorge rising at so lowly a wife, would surely dismiss her

---

300 **quoniam** Severs CC2 Ba Bod2 Po G1 Har7 Har6; ipsum Pe; *om* G4.
307 **tuo** Severs CC2 Ba Bod2 Po G1 Har7 Har6; *add* nunquam Pe; *om* G4.
324 **earum** Severs CC2 Ba Po G4 G1 Har7 Har6; earumque Pe; *om* Bod2.
333 **sacietate** Severs CC2 Bod2 Po G4 G1 Har6; saciate Pe; saciente Ba; societate Har7.

quid de se ille decerneret cui se et sua cuncta subiecerat. Miserat iam ille Bononiam, cognatumque rogaverat ut ad se filios suos adduceret, fama undique diffusa virginem illam sibi in coniugium adduci. Quod ille fideliter
295 executurus, puellam iam nubilem, excellentem forma preclaroque conspicuam ornatu, germanumque simul suum annum iam septimum agentem ducens, cum eximia nobilium comitiva, statuto die iter arripuit.

Hec inter Walterus, solito ut uxorem retemptaret ingenio, pudoris ac doloris ad cumulum, in publicum adducte coram multis, Satis, inquit, tuo coniugio
300 delectabar, mores tuos non originem respiciens. Nunc [quoniam], ut video, magna omnis fortuna servitus est magna, non michi licet quod cuilibet liceret agricole. Cogunt mei, et papa consentit, uxorem me alteram habere. Iamque uxor in via est statimque aderit. Esto igitur forti animo, dansque locum alteri, et dotem tuam referens, in antiquam domum equa mente revertere. (fol. 186vb)
305 Nulla hominum perpetua sors est. Contra illa, Ego, inquit, mi domine, semper scivi inter magnitudinem tuam et humilitatem meam nullam esse proporcionem. Meque nunquam [tuo], non dicam coniugio, sed servicio dignam duxi. Inque hac domo, in qua tu me dominam fecisti, deum testor, animo semper ancilla permansi. De hoc igitur tempore quo tecum multo cum honore longe supra
310 omne meritum meum fui, deo et tibi gracias ago; de reliquo, parata sum bono pacatoque animo paternam domum repetere, atque ubi puericiam egi senectutem agere et mori, felix semper atque honorabilis vidua, que viri talis fuerim uxor. Nove coniugi volens cedo, que tibi utinam felix adveniat. Atque hinc ubi iocundissime degebam quando ita tibi placitum est, non invita discedo.
315 At quod iubes dotem meam mecum ut auferam, quale sit video, neque enim excidit ut paterne olim domus in limine spoliata meis, tuis induta vestibus ad te veni, neque omnino michi alia dos fuit quam fides et nuditas. Ecce igitur ut hanc vestem exuo, anulumque restituo quo me subarrasti. Reliqui anuli et vestes et ornamenta quibus te donante ad invidiam aucta eram, in thalamo tuo
320 sunt. Nuda de domo patris egressa, nuda ibidem revertar, nisi quod indignum reor ut hic uterus in quo filii fuerunt quos tu genuisti, populo nudus appareat. Quam ob rem si tibi placet, et non aliter, oro atque obsecro ut in precium virginitatis quam huc attuli quamque non refero, unicam michi camisiam linqui iubeas [earum] quibus uti soleo tecum, qua ventrem tue quondam
325 uxoris operiam. Habundabant viro lacrime, ut contineri amplius non posset. Itaque faciem avertens, Et camisiam tibi unicam habeto, verbis trementibus vix expressit, et sic abiit illacrimans. Illa, coram cunctis sese exuens, solam sibi retinuit camisiam, qua contenta, nudo capite pedibusque nudis, egreditur; atque ita prosequentibus multis et flentibus fortunamque culpantibus, siccis
330 una oculis et honesto veneranda silencio, ad paternam domum remeavit.

Senex, qui has filie nuptias semper suspectas habuerat neque umquam tantam spem mente conceperat semperque hoc eventurum cogitaverat, ut, [sacietate] sponse tam humilis exorta, domo illam quandoque vir tantus et

from the house. So her father had saved a place for her worn old tunic, hidden in a corner of his cottage. Now, hearing not his silent daughter but the noisy crowd, he ran to meet her at the threshold and covered her half-nakedness in this old dress. She remained with her father for a few days in equanimity and remarkable humility, with no sign of sadness in her spirit, and showed no trace of her more prosperous fortune. As much might have been expected, [340] since she always lived amidst riches humble and poor in spirit.

Now the Count of Panago was approaching, and the story of the new bride was everywhere. The count sent one of his people to announce when they were going to arrive in Saluzzo. The day before, Walter called Griselda to him (she came devotedly) and said, "I desire that this girl be received magnificently at a banquet here tomorrow. Let each guest be welcomed to the feast – she and her entourage, and my own people in the same way – and let their welcome and placement honor the worthiness of each guest appropriately. I do not have in my house enough women for this work; thus you (who know my habits best) must assume the duties of receiving and installing the guests, however poorly dressed you may be." "I am not just willing," she said, "but eager [350] to do this and whatever I understand to be your pleasure. I will never tire or slacken in this while any traces of life remain." Having spoken, she seized the accoutrements of a servant and began to rearrange the house, order meals, lay out the bedding, and exhort the other women in the manner of a most faithful servant. The count arrived about mid-morning, and immediately all began to marvel at the beauty and manners of the girl and her brother. Some said that Walter had made a wise and happy exchange, that this bride was more delicate and noble, and her splendid kinsman only added to her luster. As the banquet's preparations neared readiness, Griselda, busy everywhere and solicitous of all, was neither depressed by the turn of events nor shamed by her shabby clothes. With a clear countenance she stood in front of the entering girl, and said, [360] "Welcome, my Lady."

She received the other guests with cheerful looks and remarkably graceful words. She managed the whole house with so many skills that everyone, especially those newly arrived, wondered greatly that such dignified behavior and prudence could be found in such mean attire. Griselda was unable to say enough in high praise of both the girl and the boy, but in turns she described now her elegance, now his. Walter, seating himself at the meal, turned towards her and as if jesting said to her in a loud voice in front of everyone, "What do you think of my bride? Is she noble and beautiful enough?" "Clearly, none more beautiful or noble could be found," she replied. "If you are ever able to lead a peaceful and happy life, [370] it will be with her. I hope and desire it will be so. Yet in good faith I ask and urge one thing. Do not sting her with the goads you used on another woman. For she is younger and more delicately raised, and I imagine that she cannot endure so much."

He looked at her cheerfulness, and considered the constancy of the woman, so

---

336 **antiqua** Severs CC2 Ba Bod2 G1 Har7 Har6; antiquam Pe Po G4.

362 **disponeret** Severs CC2 Ba Bod2 Po G4 G1 Har7 Har6; disponere Pe.

366 **infantilem** Severs CC2 Bod2 Po G4 G1 Har7 Har6; infantulam Pe; infantilam Ba.

369 **pulcrior** Severs CC2 Ba Bod2 Po G4 G1 Har7 Har6; pulchra Pe. **nulla** Severs CC2 Ba Bod2 Har7; ulla Pe G4 Har6; *om* Po G1.

372 **enutrita** nutrita Hg El CC2. **quantum** Severs Hg El CC2 Ba Po G4 G1 Har7 Har6; quam cum Pe; in q. Bod2.

373 **auguror** ut reor Hg El CC2; augurior Bod2 Har7; ut augurior G1.

more nobilium superbus abiceret, tunicam eius hispidam et attritam senio
335 abditam parve domus in parte servaverat. Audito ergo non tam filie tacite
redeuntis quam comitum strepitu, occurrit in limine et seminudam [antiqua]
veste coperuit. Mansit illa cum patre paucos dies equanimitate atque
humilitate mirabili. Ita ut nullum in ea signum animi tristioris, nullum
vestigium fortune prosperioris extaret. Quippe cum in mediis opibus inops
340 semper spiritu vixisset atque humilis.

Iam panici Comes appropinquabat, et de novis nupciis fama undique
frequens erat. Premissoque uno de suis, diem quo sallucias perventurus esset
acceperat. Pridie igitur Walterus, ad se Griseldim evocans, devotissime
venienti, Cupio, ait, ut puella cras huc ad prandium ventura magnifice
345 accipiatur, virique et matrone qui secum sunt, simulque et nostri qui convivio
intererunt, ita ut locorum verborumque honor singulis pro dignitate servetur.
Domi tamen feminas ad hoc opus ydoneas non habeo. Proinde tu, (fol. 187a)
veste quamvis inopi, hanc tibi, que mores meos nosti optime, suscipiendorum
locandorumque hospitum curam sumes. Non libenter modo, inquit, sed cupide
350 et hoc et quecumque tibi placita sensero faciam semper, neque in hoc
umquam fatigabor aut lentescam dum spiritus huius reliquie ulle supererunt.
Et cum dicto, servilia mox instrumenta corripiens, domum vertere, mensas
instruere, lectos sternere, hortarique alias ceperat, ancille in morem fidelissime.
Proxime lucis hora tercia, comes supervenerat. Certatimque omnes et puelle et
355 germani infantis mores ac pulcritudinem mirabantur. Erantque qui dicerent
prudenter Walterum ac feliciter permutasse, quod et sponsa hec tenerior esset
et nobilior, et cognatus tam speciosus accederet. Sic fervente convivii
apparatu ubique presens, omnium solicita Griseldis, nec tanto casu deiecta
animo nec obsolite vestis pudore confusa, sed sereno vultu intranti obvia
360 puelle, Bene venerit domina mea, inquit.

Dehinc ceteros dum convivas leta facie et verborum mira suavitate
susciperet, et immensam domum multa arte [disponeret], ita ut omnes et
presertim advene unde ea maiestas morum atque ea prudencia sub tali habitu
vehementissime mirarentur, atque ipsa in primis puelle pariter atque infantis
365 laudibus saciari nullo modo posset. Sed vicissim modo virgineam, modo
[infantilem] eleganciam predicaret. Walterus, eo ipso tempore quo assidendum
mensis erat in eam versus, clara voce coram omnibus, quasi illudens, Quid tibi
videtur, inquit, de hac mea sponsa? Satis pulcra ac honesta est? Plane, ait illa,
nec [pulcrior] ulla nec honestior inveniri potest. Aut cum [nulla] umquam, aut
370 cum hac tranquillam agere poteris ac felicem vitam; utque ita sit cupio et
spero. Unum bona fide te precor ac moneo: ne hanc illis aculeis agites quibus
alteram agitasti. Nam quod et iunior et delicatius enutrita est, pati [quantum]
ego auguror non valeret.

Talia dicentis alacritatem intuens, atque constanciam tociens tamque acriter

often and roughly offended. Taking pity on the ignoble fate of a woman so undeserving of it, and unable to bear it any longer, he said, "Enough, my Griselda. Your faithfulness is known and proved to me. I do not imagine that there is anyone under heaven who has known such great tests of marital love." As he said this, he embraced his dear wife in his loving arms. Overwhelmed by the shock of joy, she felt as if awakened from a troubled sleep. [380] "You," he said, "only you are my wife; I never have had, nor will have, another. This girl, whom you thought to be my bride, is your daughter; this boy, whom you believed to be my kinsman, is your son. Those who seemed lost separately, you have recovered together. Let those who believed the opposite know me painstaking and testing, not impious. I have proved my wife rather than condemning her and hidden my children rather than killing them."

His words produced almost unbearable joy and frantic devotion: Griselda rushes with the happiest tears to embrace her children, wearies them with kisses, and bedews them with maternal tears. Quick and doting women hurriedly surround Griselda, remove her stained clothes, and cover and adorn her with her accustomed garb. Happy applause and auspicious words from all surround them. That day was renowned for its great joy and tears [390] even more than the day of marriage was. They lived for many years in marvelous peace and concord. Walter ordered the poor father-in-law (whom he had thus far seemed to neglect, not to spoil the test he had conceived) conducted to the royal house in honor. He arranged a magnificent and noble marriage for his daughter, and left his son as the successor to his kingdom. Thus Walter was happy in both his wife and offspring.

I thought it fitting to re-tell this story in a different style, not so much to urge the matrons of our time to imitate the patience of this wife (which seems to me almost unchanging) as to arouse readers to imitate her womanly constancy, so that they might dare to undertake for God what she undertook for her husband. God is the appropriate tester of evils, [400] as the Apostle James said; but he tempts no one himself. Nevertheless he tests us. Often he allows us to be belabored with heavy stings, not so that he might know our spirit – he knew us before we were created – but so that our fragility might be shown to us by clear and familiar signs. I would have rated among the most steadfast of men one of whatever station who endured without complaint and for God what this little country wife endured for her mortal husband.

375   **merite** Severs CC2 Ba Bod2 Po G4 G1 Har6; merito Pe Har7.
376   **ac** Severs CC2 Ba Bod2 Po G4 G1 Har7 Har6; *add* eciam Pe.
383   **impium** Severs CC2 Ba Bod2 Po G4 Har7 Har6; novi impium Pe; in ipsum G1.
385   **amens** Severs CC2 Ba Bod2 Po G4 Har7; *om* Pe; amoris G1; merens Har6.
396   **alio** alto Hg El CC2; *ms defective* Har6. **tam** tamen Hg El CC2 Bod2 Po; *om* Har6.
397–98   **michi vix mutabilis** michi inimitabilis Hg El; michi vix imitabilis Severs Ba Bod2 Po G4 G1 Har7; sibi inimitabilis CC2; vix michi mirabilis Har6.
399   **excitarem** excitarentur Hg; excitarent El; excitare CC2; exercitarem Har7; excitacerem Har6.
399–400   **audeant qui licet** audeat quilibet Hg El CC2; audeant Ba; audeat licet Bod2; ardeant qui licet Har7.
401   **temptet** temptat Hg El CC2 G1 Har7.

375 offense mulieris examinans, et indignam sortem non sic [merite] miseratus,
[ac] ferre diucius non valens, Satis, inquit, mea Griseldis, cognita et spectata
michi fides est tua. Nec sub celo aliquem esse puto qui tanta coniugalis amoris
experimenta percepit. Simul hec dicens, caram coniugem leto stupore
perfusam et velut de sompno turbido experrectam, cupidis ulnis amplectitur.
380 Et tu, ait, tu sola uxor mea es. Aliam nec habui, nec habebo. Ista autem quam
tu sponsam meam reris, filia tua est; hic qui cognatus meus credebatur, tuus
est filius. Que divisim perdita videbantur, simul omnia recepisti. Sciant qui
contrarium crediderunt me curiosum atque experientem esse, non [impium];
probasse coniugem, non dampnasse; occultasse filios, non mactasse.
385 Hec illa audiens, pene gaudio exanimis et pietate [amens] iocundissimisque
cum lacrimis, suorum pignorum in amplexus ruit, fatigatque osculis, pioque
gemitu madefacit. Raptimque matrone alacres ac faventes circumfuse, vilibus
exutam suis, solitis vestibus induunt exornantque. Plausus letissimus et fausta
omnium verba circumsonant, multoque cum gaudio et fletu ille dies
390 celeberimus fuit, celebrior quoque (fol. 187b) quam dies fuit nupciarum.
Multosque post per annos ingenti pace concordiaque vixere; et Walterus
inopem socerum, quem hactenus neglexisse visus erat, ne quando concepte
animo obstaret experiencie, suam in domum translatum in honore habuit,
filiam suam magnificis atque honestis nupciis collocavit, filiumque sui
395 dominii successorem liquit, et coniugio letus et sobole.
Hanc historiam stilo nunc alio retexere visum fuit, non tam ideo, ut matronas
nostri temporis ad imitandam huius uxoris pacienciam, que michi vix
mutabilis[26] videtur, quam ut legentes ad imitandam saltem femine constanciam
excitarem, ut quod hec viro suo prestitit, hoc prestare deo nostro audeant, qui
400 licet ut Iacobus ait Apostolus intemptator malorum sit, et ipse neminem
temptet: probat tamen. Et sepe nos multis ac gravibus flagellis exerceri
sinit, non ut animum nostrum sciat, quem scivit ante quam crearemur. Sed ut
nobis nostra fragilitas notis ac domesticis indiciis innotescat. Habunde ego
constantibus viris asscripserim, quisquis is fuerit, qui pro deo suo sine murmure
405 paciatur quod pro suo mortali coniuge rusticana hec muliercula passa est.[27]

---

[26] In general, the manuscripts of *Seniles XVII.3* present a good text of the narrative: variants are not extremely numerous and rarely affect the meaning substantially. As this paragraph changes the rhetorical focus to commentary on Griselda, however, that faithfulness to Petrarch's text also changes. Scribes produced many and widely divergent versions of Petrarch's statement about his purpose and moral. I have printed Pe's unique reading "mutabilis" to emphasize the extraordinarily large number and critical importance of those variants (others listed in Severs 326–7). Hg El CC2 remark the "stilo nunc alto" of the tale; three other mss. claim that it is told "stilo non alio" from Boccaccio's; while Griselda's behavior is "michi vix imitabilis" in most MSS (and Severs), it is "michi vix mutabilis" in Pe, "michi inimitabilis" in Hg El, "sibi imitabilis" in CC2, and "vix michi mirabilis," or "michi vix immutabilis" elsewhere. Although there are explanations for most of these variants in normal scribal practice – Pe's *mutabilis* is distinguished from *imitabilis* only because the scribe consistently marks "i" – their sudden appearance here and their non-correspondence to familial affiliations suggest more tolerance of scribal variation in this part of the text.

Thus, particular attention must be paid to the five variants in Hg El, which indicate the reaction to the story in Chaucer's MS. In the case of *audeat quilibet*, the variant forces re-analysis of the syntax: in Pe as in Severs' text *legentes* is the subject for *audeant*, and *qui licet* depends from *deo*. But in the gloss the indefinite *quilibet* – not the highly specific Petrarchan "readers" – must be the subject of *audeat*.

[27] The text of XVII.3 in Pe ends with "et responsio" introducing XVII.4 which follows immediately. Charlotte C. Morse in "Exemplary Griselda," *Studies in the Age of Chaucer* 7 (1985): 64–5 explains why Chaucer is unlikely to have known XVII.4.

The Griselda Story in France

Amy W. Goodwin

Petrarch's Latin Griselda story eclipsed Boccaccio's and was transmitted to
other countries in the form of Latin copies, adaptations, and vernacular translations. The moral conclusion contributed to its appeal, making the work acceptable in collections of religious writings.[28] By the sixteenth century there were
translations and adaptations of Petrarch's Griselda story in Italian, Catalan,
Spanish, Czech, Dutch, German, Polish, Portuguese, Hungarian, French, and
English.[29] But the tale's earliest route of transmission was to France, where in
little over a decade after Petrarch's death (1374), there were two different
French translations, one by Philippe de Mézières, entitled *Le Miroir des Dames
Mariées* (1385–89), and the other the anonymous *Le Livre Griseldis*.[30]

Both of these translations bear on our understanding of Chaucer's *Clerk's
Tale*. Severs clearly showed that Chaucer's principal French source was the
anonymous Griselda story, from which Chaucer often translated lines verbatim.
Yet Severs also recognized that a few correspondences between the *Clerk's
Tale* and Philippe's Griselda story suggested that Chaucer was familiar, at the
very least, with a version of Philippe's *Miroir des Dames Mariées*. Additional
evidence makes it even likelier that Chaucer drew a few details and, perhaps,
some inspiration from Philippe de Mézières.[31] The two French translations are
linked, moreover, in other important ways. A number of correspondences
between them in lexicon, sentence structure, and innovations suggests that the
anonymous translator knew Philippe's translation and borrowed from it in
minor ways.[32] Both use the tale as an exemplum addressed to wives and broaden

---

[28] F. N. M. Diekstra discusses the inclusion of Petrarch's *Historia Griseldis* in manuscripts containing
moral treatises. See his *A Dialogue Between Reason and Adversity: A Late Middle English Version of
Petrarch's De Remediis* (Assen: Van Gorcum, 1968), pp. 29–31.

[29] See Morabito's catalogue in "La Diffusione," pp. 241–77.

[30] For the approximate dating of Philippe's translation, see Philippe de Mézières, *Le Livre de la Vertu du
Sacrement de Mariage*, ed. Joan B. Williamson (Washington, D.C.: Catholic University Press of
America, 1993), p. 9. Future references to Philippe's text will be cited by page numbers in this edition.
The date of the anonymous translation is unknown, presumably occurring sometime after Philippe's
translation and before Chaucer's *Clerk's Tale*.

[31] Anne Middleton suggests some possible similarities between Philippe's remarks in his prologue to the
translation about his relationship to Petrarch and his own style and Harry Bailly's advice to the Clerk in
the Prologue to the *Clerk's Tale*. See "The Clerk and his Tale: Some Literary Contexts," *Studies in the
Age of Chaucer* 2 (1980): 141–7.

[32] Although not impossible, it is unlikely that Philippe borrowed from the anonymous translator because
Philippe's Griselda story is so thoroughly contextualized by the books preceding it. Here are some of
the correspondences. Both omit the geographical prologue and preface the tale with similar praise of
Petrarch: Philippe introduces Petrarch with the following phrase: "vaillant et solempnel docteur poete,
maistre Fransoys Patrac" (358); the anonymous translator with this phrase: "un tres vaillant et moult
solennel poete, appellez François Petrach" (ll. 5–6). Both use hunting as a transition to place Walter in

the tale's application to include other constituencies. However, very different stylistic values and didactic aims inspire these two translations, which adumbrate distinct but overlapping traditions of the Griselda story in France.

Philippe translated the Griselda story for inclusion in his *Le Livre de la Vertu du Sacrement de Mariage*. Yet his translation also circulated independently and is often included with manuals intended to instruct wives on proper conduct (9 of 17 MSS).[33] *Le Livre de la Vertu du Sacrement de Mariage* is itself a sort of conduct book for wives. But unlike *Le Ménagier de Paris* and *Le Livre du Chevalier de la Tour Landry*, the two other fourteenth-century marriage manuals in or with which his Griselda story appears, Philippe's book is almost never concerned with the daily, domestic aspects of marriage, such as the chores involved in running a household. He is, instead, always concerned with spiritual resources and remedial virtues, which he urges wives to cultivate.[34] For Philippe, spiritual marriage is the greatest worldly union that one can have within the Catholic faith because the union between a husband and wife figures within itself three other mystical marriages: (1) God's marriage to the rational soul, (2) Christ's marriage to humanity, (3) and Christ's marriage to the church, which is figured as Mary. In marrying, one owes to one's spouse Christ's commitment to humanity and Mary's devotion to Christ (70). Philippe's *Livre* prepares his readers to see Griselda's behavior allegorically and encourages them to accept suffering willingly in conformity with Christ. Placed in the fourth and final book of the *Livre*, Griselda embodies the precepts that Philippe has elaborated at length. She is like both Christ and Mary, and these associations are created by her selfless devotion to her husband and her suffering and, more emphatically, through the use of diction with which Philippe has already described Christ and Mary in his first two books. Book Three contains a remedial or medicinal manual examining the

---

Griselda's vicinity; in both Griselda is carrying a crock of water when Walter arrives to marry her. In the passages below, the French translators seem to be in dialogue with each other, contesting whether Griselda's humble behavior when she returned to her father's house was marvelous, with Philippe insisting on the marvel and the anonymous translator commenting that her equanimity was in keeping with her behavior all along: Philippe: "Quelle mervaille! car quant elle avoit esté si longuement dame en milieu des richesses et des honnours, si s'estoit elle toujours tenue povre d'esperit et tres humble en conversation" (372–3). Anon. translator: "et ce n'estoit pas merveille, comme en ses grans richesses tousjours en pensee humble eust vescu et fust maintenue" (ll. 349–51). Petrarch makes no mention of this marvel. Severs probably recognized that these translations were not quite independent of each other. He notes many correspondences between these two translations not found in Petrarch in his chapter establishing Chaucer's use of the anonymous translation (135–76).

33 Golenistcheff-Koutouzoff describes the manuscripts containing Philippe's translations in *L'Histoire*, pp. 34–42.

34 For a discussion of the complex organization of *Le Livre*, Philippe's didactic aims, and the work's reception, see Carolyn P. Collette, "Chaucer and the French Tradition Revisited: Philippe de Mézières and the Good Wife," *Medieval Women: Texts and Contexts in Late Medieval Britain*, ed. Arlyn Diamond, et al. (Brepols, 2000), pp. 151–68; Joan B. Williamson, "Philippe de Mézières' Book for Married Ladies: A Book from the Entourage of the Court of Charles VI," *The Spirit of the Court: Selected Proceedings of the Fourth Congress of the International Courtly Literature Society (Toronto, 1983)*, ed. Glyn S. Burgess and Robert A. Taylor (Cambridge: D. S. Brewer, 1985), pp. 393–408; Elie Golenistcheff-Koutouzoff, *Etude sur Le Livre de la Vertu du Sacrement de Mariage de Philippe de Mézières* (Belgrade: Svetlost, 1937).

spiritual maladies that afflict wives and discussing the cures.[35] Here, Philippe has firmly insisted that a wife must love her husband – even though he may be her enemy – and that God may test a wife by giving her a bad husband (225–6, 304–5). These preceding books crucially contextualize Griselda's behavior.[36]

Philippe expands his source with commentary and details.[37] He claims to translate Petrarch loosely, capturing the substance but not the elegant style, a claim that conceals in part the substantive changes that he makes (358). He thoroughly reprioritizes Petrarch's text. Prizing Griselda's ability to overcome herself, that is, her human and feminine nature (356), he differs strategically from Petrarch and the anonymous translator in revealing the stark contrast between Griselda's calm, dutiful obedience to her husband and her inner turmoil. He presents Griselda as an historical figure, overlooked by chroniclers, and although he offers Griselda as a model for wives and as a model for all Christians of the rational soul who chooses God, he is also aware of the various difficulties her behavior poses for those who might try to emulate it. He counsels his readers that just like archers who shoot for the bull's eye but do not always hit it, they, too, should strive to be like Griselda (357). Yet he also allows readers to use discretion in determining what to imitate, advising them, like Chaucer's Nun's Priest, but without jocularity, to take the grain and leave the chaff (358).

Unlike Petrarch, Philippe does not mute his criticism of Walter; Chaucer's own harsh criticism of Walter may have been inspired by Philippe's treatment of him. In *Le Miroir des Dames Mariées*, Walter does not have any allegorical association with God; he is a bad husband. The narrator condemns Walter's "perilous" curiosity (367), refers to his tests as "torment" (369), and describes his behavior as "cruel" (370). In his moral conclusion, moreover, he spells out even more clearly the distinction between God and Walter:

> Et est assavoir que maistre François Petrac (ms. Periat), poete couronné, à la fin de ceste merveilleuse et gracieuse histoire dist ainsi: "Ceste histoire," dist-il, "j'ay voulu escrire à mon stille publiquement à la mémoire des homes, et non tant seulement à la fin que les matrones et dames de nostre temps doivent ensuir la marquise de pacience, laquelle pacience semble aussi comme impossible à porter, maiz à fin que les lisans de ceste histoire se doivent efforcier à la constance de ceste femme, c'est assavoir ce qu'elle fist à son mary de vertu de pacience, ilz la vueillent fere à Dieu, combien que Dieu ne tempte pas les hommes, selon ce que dit saint Jacques l'apostre, comme fist le marquis s'espouse, mais aucuneffoiz les vuels bien esprouver et consent

---

[35] For the importance of the remedial or medicinal virtues in Boccaccio's Griselda story, see Victoria Kirkham, "The Last Tale of the *Decameron*," *Medievalia* 12 (1989): 205–19.

[36] For the importance of the Griselda story for Philippe's entire project, see Collette, pp. 163–6.

[37] See Kevin Brownlee, "Commentary and the Rhetoric of Exemplarity: Griseldis in Petrarch, Philippe de Mézières, and the *Estoire*," *The South Atlantic Quarterly* 94 (1992): 865–74. Robert R. Edwards also discusses Philippe's adaptation, particularly the importance of his interpretive framework; see his "'The Sclaundre of Walter': The *Clerk's Tale* and the Problem of Hermeneutics," *Mediaevalitas: Reading the Middle Ages*, eds. Piero Boitani and Anna Torti. The J. A. W. Bennett Memorial Lectures, 9th Series (Cambridge: Brewer, 1996), pp. 21–3.

que nous soions bien souvent exité par tribulacions, et non pas pour congnoiste nostre couraige, comme fist le marquis à sa femme, car avant que nous feussions créez, il savoit et scet clerement quelz nous devons estre, mais il seuffre à ce que par les tribulacions continuelz nostre propre fragilité nous soit monstrée et de nous bien congnue. Et pour ce," dit le noble poete, "je l'attribueray à tres merveilleux, illustres hommes et constans, quiconques sera celui qui pour son Dieu sanz murmurer souffrera ce que ceste povre femme, née en grant povreté entre les menues genz, sans honneur et science souffry pour son mortel mary."

[At the end of this marvellous and gracious story, the crowned poet, master Francis Petrarch, said the following: "This story," said he, "I wished to make known in my own style for the edification of men and not only to the end that wives and ladies of our times should imitate this marchioness's patience, which also seems impossible to bear, but to the end that the readers of this story should strive for the constancy of this wife; that is, what she did for her husband by virtue of patience they would do for God; however, God does not tempt men, according to Saint James the apostle – as this husband did his spouse – but sometimes he wishes to test them and allows us often enough to be vexed with tribulations, and not in order to know our hearts – as did this marquis his wife – for before we were created he knew and knows clearly what we should become, but he allows that by continual tribulations our own fragility be shown to us and known by us. And for this," the noble poet said, "I count as wonderful, illustrious, and constant men whoever he be who for his God without murmuring would suffer what this poor woman, born in great poverty among obscure people, without honor or learning, suffered for her mortal husband."] [38]

Chaucer may have known Philippe de Mézières. After a lengthy career as a crusader and Chancellor of Cyprus, he returned to France and became a prominent figure in the court of Charles V, whose son Charles VI he tutored. He became a prolific writer of religious texts in his old age. He also wrote *Letter to King Richard*, urging marriage between Richard and Isabel to bring peace to France and England and wishing for Richard a wife like Griselda.[39] Severs suggested that Chaucer may have been familiar with the adaptation of Philippe's translation by the compiler of *Le Ménagier de Paris*, for there are a few details contained in the *Clerk's Tale* some which originate in Philippe's translation and others which are thought to be unique to *Le Ménagier de Paris*. These correspondences include the following: musicians accompany Walter to Griselda's home (*Le Ménagier*); Griselda kneels when Walter approaches her (*Le Ménagier*); Janicula is weeping when he meets Griselda upon her return (both texts); Griselda clutches her children so tightly that it is hard to remove them

---

[38] Golenistcheff-Koutouzoff lists eleven manuscripts containing the moral conclusion. See *L'Histoire*, p. 54. For the moral conclusion cited above, see pp. 180–2. The translation is mine.

[39] Philippe de Mézières, *Letter to King Richard*, trans. G. W. Coopland (New York: Barnes & Noble, 1975), p.42. Although there is no hard evidence linking Philippe and Chaucer, as Carolyn Collette has observed, there is quite an accumulation of "circumstantial detail[s]," which she discusses, pp. 153–4.

from her grasp when she swoons (both texts).[40] There are two additional correspondences between Chaucer's moral conclusion and Philippe's. Like Philippe,
Chaucer begins his moral conclusion reminding his readers of the tale's source,
Petrarch. Like Chaucer's Clerk, who calls Griselda's humility "inportable" (l.
1144), in his own moral conclusion Philippe presents Griselda's patience as
unbearable (*impossible à porter*). Both of these correspondences are lacking in
the anonymous translation and the adaptation by the compiler of *Le Ménagier*.

It is not clear which version of Philippe's translation Chaucer may have
known since Philippe's moral conclusion does not appear in the sole manuscript
of *Le Livre de La Vertu du Sacrement de Mariage*. The Clerk's insistence on his
own source in Petrarch suggests that regardless of Chaucer's knowledge of
other sources, he had no interest in advertising the growing continental popularity of this tale or its different versions. If aspects of Philippe's remarkable translation and certain details appealed to Chaucer, he nonetheless chose as his
principal French source *Le Livre Griseldis*, the translation that is most faithful to
Petrarch's Griselda story.

The anonymous translator restores the focus of Petrarch's narrative to
Griselda's patience and constancy in adversity. He points out these virtues in his
brief prologue and returns to them in the moral conclusion. In late fourteenth-
century France, there was a nascent Petrarchan following which perceived
Petrarch as a moral philosopher.[41] In 1361 in Paris, Charles V heard Petrarch
deliver an oration on the vicissitudes of fortune. Charles later commissioned
Jean Daudin to translate Petrarch's *De Remediis Utriusque Fortune*, which
Daudin completed in 1378.[42] The anonymous translator may well see the
Griselda story as a fictional counterpart to Petrarch's *Remedies*. Griselda treats
with equanimity the vertiginous changes which Fortune (in the guise of Walter)
thrusts upon her; moreover, through her virtuous conduct she exceeds the
expectations of her husband and kingdom.[43]

The faithfulness of the anonymous translation may indicate a higher valuation
of the Griselda story as a Petrarchan text. This conservative translation attempts
to imitate Petrarch's style. The translator is interested in the formal qualities of
the work, dividing it into six sections, to draw out its Petrarchan structure. Each
division begins with an initial focus on Walter, whose perception of Griselda
guides the reader's deepening understanding of her virtues. Only the second
section appears to break this pattern, but, here, the division highlights the

---

[40] See Severs, pp. 126–27, n4; 174; 176, n8.

[41] See Charlotte Morse, "The Exemplary Griselda," *Studies in the Age of Chaucer* 7 (1985): 64.

[42] Ernest Hatch Wilkins, *Life of Petrarch* (Chicago: University of Chicago Press, 1961), pp. 174–5. For a
discussion of Charles V's interest in translating important texts into French, see Léopold DeLisle,
Recherches sur La Librairie de Charles V, Roi de France, 1337–1380, vol. 1 (1907; Amsterdam:
Gérard Th. van Heusden, 1967) pp. 82–5, and for information on Jean Daudin, pp. 92–4.

[43] For a discussion of the techniques of the anonymous translator, see Wendy Harding, "Griselda's Translation in the *Clerk's Tale*," *The Medieval Translator* 6 (1998): 194–210.

parallel between Janicula, who is so virtuously served by his daughter, and Walter, who searches for just such a wife.

The minor changes the translator makes seem aimed at adapting the tale to his audience of women. Unlike Philippe, who apostrophizes to queens, princesses, and marchionesses, the anonymous translator is self-effacing and deferential to what may be a similarly noble audience. He eliminates Walter's speech preferring natural virtue to noble blood; he eliminates Janicula's disparaging comment to the effect that Walter's behavior in rejecting Griselda was typical of the nobility. Like Philippe, he eliminates a few details that might have appeared to slight women or to oppose the work's exemplary aim to include them. In the anonymous translation, Griselda's virtues surpass those of other women her age, not as in the Latin text in which her virtues surpass those of both her age and gender. Perhaps because Griselda will be stripped naked before being married, in the anonymous translation alone, only noble women accompany Walter from the palace in his wedding entourage. Like Philippe, he has Walter and the kingdom rejoicing in the birth of the daughter for her own sake, rather than as a sign of her mother's fertility.

Severs pointed out other important details that the anonymous translator added, many of which Chaucer retained, for example, the description of the wedding preparations, the noblewomen's reluctance to touch Griselda's poor garment, and the poor fit of her ragged, old clothes when she returns home to her father. Despite these realistic details, in general, the anonymous translator seems to guard against engaging the reader too deeply in the tale's suspense and pathos. Although Griselda faints after Walter has revealed her children and taken her back as his wife, there is no reunion scene between Griselda and her children. The anonymous translator rejected both Petrarch's unrealistically joyful scene and Philippe's disturbingly painful one. He fashions a less mimetic Griselda than either Philippe's or Petrarch's, but she is more philosophically consistent, never revealing feelings that might be at odds with Walter's stated wishes.

Griselda's femaleness in France was particularly important, yet rather than constraining the tale's interpretation, it opened it up. Some manuscripts emphasize her status as a wife, but others her extraordinary and enabling virtues. Adaptations of both translations proliferated into the fifteenth and sixteenth centuries, forming a rich group of analogues that attests to the ability of the Griselda story to accommodate significantly different interpretations and to address social, philosophical, and religious issues. Space permits only a few examples of the variety among the manuscript contents and the internal adaptations of the story itself.

Only one extant manuscript places the anonymous translation alongside the conduct manual *Le Livre du Chevalier de la Tour Landry*. Although in this manuscript the Griselda story has been adapted for concision, the scribe has made a few telling changes. He addresses the work to married women and those about to marry. Within the tale, while Griselda tends her sheep, she mends her clothes. Her ability to settle disputes in the kingdom when Walter is absent has

been eliminated. The moral conclusion opening up the tale's application to all readers has also been omitted.[44] Two other manuscripts of the anonymous translation owned by women imply different interests in the story. The philosophical orientation of a manuscript owned by Jeanne de France, Duchess of Auvergne (BNP ms. fr. 12459), does not suggest exclusively female interests. The anonymous Griselda story is included with *Les Moralités du Gieu d'Éschés, Melibée et Prudence*, and *Chaton en François*. But the manuscript owned by Loise de la Tour, Dame de Crequy (BNP ms. fr. 20042), seems like a woman's reader, containing *Le Roman de Melibée et Prudence*, *L'Histoire de Apolonius Roi de Tyr, Le Romant de Grisillidis* and *La Vie de Sainte Marguerite en Prose*. This collection, with its impressive line-up of indomitable, resourceful, and pious women, offers a range of exemplary female behaviors and widely different models of wives.

Both French translations occur in contexts that champion women. Philippe's version was adapted by Christine de Pizan for her *Livre de la Cité des Dames*, but Christine does not include the Griselda story as a marriage exemplum, citing instead her exemplary love for her father (II. 11. 2) and recounting the tale as an example of a woman of strong character (II. 50). The anonymous translation appears alongside the dialogue "Against the Slanderous Mouth," a defense of women against their detractors. Yet in religious collections, Griselda exemplifies virtues all Christians should emulate. Some of these manuscripts may have been intended as devotional reading for a lay audience, and some with a homiletic orientation suggest a clerical audience. In two of the latter, the anonymous translation follows *Livre de Bonnes Meurs* by Jacques LeGrand, a treatise on the seven deadly sins and the remedial virtues.[45]

The variety among the different adaptations of the Griselda story in late medieval France should inform contemporary disagreements over the meaning or significance of Chaucer's *Clerk's Tale*. By 1395, Philippe's translation had been adapted for the play *L'Estoire de Griseldis*. By the mid-fifteenth century, adaptations appeared which mixed details from both translations.[46] As Golenistcheff-Koutouzoff observed, the Griselda story was in "vogue" in Paris. The compiler of *Le Ménagier de Paris* apologizes to his wife for Walter's cruelty, but he recommends the narrative because, among other reasons, people are reading the work and she should know what they are talking about.[47]

---

44 BNP ms. fr. 1505 The variants I have paraphrased are as follows: "A lexemple des femmes mariees et autres a marier" (fol. 126r); "recoudre sa povre robe" (fol. 128r); Griselda's ability to settle disputes is lacking from the description of her virtues once she is married on fol. 130r; the work ends without any moral commentary on fol. 134v.

45 "La Bouche Médisant" appears in Arsenal ms. fr. 2076. See *L'Histoire*, p. 92. Golenistcheff-Koutouzoff does not mention *Livre de Bonnes Meurs* in his descriptions of these manuscripts, BNP ms. fr. 24434, p. 90; Grenoble 817, p. 93. See *Bibliothèque Nationale Catalogue Général, Anciens Petits Fonds*, vol. II (Paris, 1897–1902), pp. 370–2; and *Catalogue Général des Manuscrits des Bibliothèques Publiques de France*, vol. 7 (Paris, 1885–1924), p. 264.

46 *L'Estoire de Griseldis*, ed. Barbara M. Craig, Humanistic Studies 31 (Lawrence, Kansas: University of Kansas Publications, 1954). See *L'Histoire* for a discussion of "contamination," pp. 134–5.

47 For Golenistcheff-Koutouzoff's comment, see p. 124. "Mais l'istoire est telle, et ne la doy pas corriger ne faire autre, car plus sage de moy la compila et intitula; et desire bien que puis que autres l'ont veue,

Fourteenth-century French readers recognized the chameleon-like quality of the Griselda story, and part of the pleasure and challenge of adapting it and reading it must surely have been in construing it in new ways.

The following edition of *Le Livre Griseldis* slightly revises and updates Severs' edition in *The Literary Relationships of Chaucer's Clerkes Tale*. Severs chose as the base manuscript Bibliothèque Nationale ms. fr. 12459 (PN3), and I have also used this manuscript as the base text because it alone among the twenty-one manuscripts of the anonymous translation contains the divisions Chaucer used in the *Clerk's Tale*. It also contains a full text, not marked by omissions and paraphrases. Severs made only thirty-five emendations, most of them very minor, adding words or parts of words that had been left out, only occasionally changing a word, and in two places changing a whole phrase. This edition retains his emendations, which are well attested by the six other manuscripts Severs used in his edition; it makes no new emendations, and reproduces Severs' accurate transcription of PN3.

To his edition, I have added an eighth manuscript, Boston Library MS f. Med. 91 (BPL), whose existence Severs only discovered after his *Literary Relationships* was already in galley proofs. This manuscript has been dated as late fourteenth century.[48] It is also quite a full manuscript, showing clear evidence of the anonymous translator's fidelity to Petrarch as well as his innovations. BPL also has a few readings that are closer to those in Chaucer's text than those of PN3. For example, Griselda requests that her children's bodies be protected from wild beasts and birds, rather than from just beasts as in PN3. Janicula is alerted to Griselda's return by the noise of the people at his door, rather than by his coming to meet the people on horseback as in PN3. At the end of the story, Griselda is taken off into a chamber to be reclothed, instead of being reclothed in front of everyone as in PN3. In contrast to PN3, the Boston manuscript also has fewer doublets. Many texts of the anonymous translation eliminate doublets ostensibly for concision. The age and completeness of the Boston manuscript may suggest that some of the doublets in PN3 could themselves be additions, perhaps the result of polishing by a later scribe.

The Boston manuscript also contains three readings that Chaucer either did not have in his source text or chose not to use. Following Golenistchef-Koutouzoff, Severs recognized two families of manuscripts that were primarily distinguished by slightly different endings to the story. Family 1, from which Severs selected the base manuscript and all others for his edition, follows

---

que aussi vous la veez et sachez de tout parler comme des autres." *Le Mesnagier de Paris*, eds. Georgina E. Brereton and Janet M. Ferrier (Livre de Poche, 1994), p. 232.

[48] Severs mentions BPL in *Literary Relationships*, p. 181, n2. It is described in Margaret Munsterberg, "The Sayings of the Philosophers," *More Books: The Bulletin of the Boston Public Library* 16 (1941): 315–21, and contains in the following order *Les Dits Moraulx des Philosophes, Appollonius de Tyre, Le Livre Griseledis* and *Le Miroir des Pecheurs*.

Germaine Dempster (*Modern Philology* 40 [1943]: 286) lamented that Severs had not consulted the fourteenth-century Chartres manuscript in preparing his edition. This manuscript was so badly damaged by fire that it is unreadable except in a few places. Photographic reproductions of the illegible manuscript can be obtained, but the manuscript itself cannot be handled.

Petrarch faithfully. In contrast, Family 2 departs slightly from the Petrarchan ending: rather than just bringing Janicula to the palace at the end of the story, Walter knights him and his son.[49] Apart from containing this fanciful innovation, the Boston manuscript in other respects ranks among the best Severs used for his edition. This manuscript also contains two unique variants, each consisting of merely a word or short phrase: (1) Walter and Griselda go to a temple on the way to the palace after he has married her. (2) In the moral conclusion, one finds that "*estimable*" has been substituted for "*ensuivable*" so that Griselda's patience and constancy are judged to be hardly worthy, rather than hardly imitable. Yet the scribe still follows the Petrarchan moral closely, adding only at the end that Griselda's patience is that shown to us by God the Father, Son, and Holy Spirit. Slight elaborations of the moral conclusion are found throughout the manuscripts of the anonymous translation.

The major difference between this edition and Severs' is in the selection of variants. In addition to giving the variants among the manuscripts when he emended the text, Severs also gave variants in places where he thought a manuscript might contain a reading closer to the reading in Chaucer's source. Instead of using this principle of selection, I have selected variants that give a fuller picture of the variety among the eight manuscripts where they differ in interpreting the story, and I have tried to indicate by them the flavor or character of each manuscript.[50] There is a great deal of linguistic variation across these manuscripts, which my set of variants will not reveal. Readers interested in all variants of the mss. in Severs' edition should consult his "Corpus of French Variants" in his *Literary Relationships* (pp. 328–57).

Every emendation of PN3 has support in at least one of the other manuscripts listed below. When emending this text, I cite first all manuscripts having the emended reading, then the reading of PN3, followed by the readings of all other manuscripts. Elsewhere variants are cited following the order of the manuscripts listed below.[51]

PN3   Bibliothèque Nationale, Paris. ms. fr. 12459. Fifteenth century, fols. 135r–142v (base text).

PN2   Bibliothèque Nationale, Paris. ms. fr. 1165. Early fifteenth century, fols. 85r–93v.

PN7   Bibliothèque Nationale, Paris. ms. n.a. fr. 4511. Fifteenth century, fols. 7r–23v.

BB   Stadtbibliothek, Bern. ms. 209. Fourteenth or fifteenth century, fols. 1r–4v.

PN4   Bibliothèque Nationale, Paris. ms. fr. 20042. Fifteenth century, fols. 50v–60r.

---

[49] See *L'Histoire*, pp. 98–102, for a description of Family 2.

[50] I have filled out some of the variant readings from my own transcriptions and photographic reproductions. In the few places where Severs' list of variants differed from mine, in some cases I have deferred to him and in other rare places I have silently corrected what seemed to me to be errors.

[51] I am grateful for the helpful comments on this essay and translation offered by Lisa J. Kiser, Chantal Marechal, Mark Parker, Charlotte C. Morse, and Carolyn P. Collette. I received generous support for the different parts of this project from the National Endowment for the Humanities in the form of a summer seminar fellowship, directed by Martin Stevens, and from Randolph-Macon College in the form of Walter W. Craigie Research Grants and a Rashkind Faculty Grant.

BPL Boston Public Library. MS f. Med. 91. Fourteenth century, fols. 86v–93v.

PN1 Bibliothèque Nationale, Paris. ms. fr. 1505. Late fifteenth century, fols. 126r–134v.

PA Bibliothèque de l'Arsenal, Paris. ms. 2076. Fifteenth Century, fols. 225r–238r.

The Book of Griselda

[Preface]

At the request and under the guidance of my master, and as an example for married women and all other women, I have put into French from Latin, according to my short wit and understanding, the following story of Griselda, of the marvellous constancy and patience of a woman. This story was translated from Lombard into Latin by a very worthy and much celebrated poet named Francis Petrarch. God rest his soul. Amen.

And the first chapter begins in this way.

[I]

At the foot of the mountains on one side of Italy is the land of Saluzzo, which formerly was quite populated with loyal towns and castles, in which were many great lords [10] and noblemen, the first and greatest of whom was a marquis, whose first name was Walter, and to whom principally belonged the governance and rule of this land. This lord was handsome and young, of very noble lineage, and had more than enough good manners. In sum, he was noble in all ways, except that he only wished to play and amuse himself [15] and to spend his time never thinking about time or things to come. So only in hunting and hawking did he take sport and pleasure because all other things mattered little to him. And moreover, he had no intention to marry, for which above all other things the people were so troubled that one time as a group they went to him. One of them, with the greatest authority [20] and eloquence and on close terms with the lord, said to him: "Your kindness, lord marquis, gives us courage so that anytime that we have need, we speak to you loyally and boldly; and see here that I wish to speak to you on behalf of all of your men and subjects. Not that I have any special part in this thing, except that among the others you have honored me with your favor, which in many ways I have experienced. [25] And since all of your deeds please us and have always pleased us, for good reason we consider ourselves quite happy to have you for a lord. But there is one thing, to which if you agree with us and consent, we will be, it seems to us, the

---

Title: **Le Livre Griseldis** *om* PN2 PA; La pacience de grizelidiz PN7; Ci commence listoire de griseldis BB; Chy commence le rommant de Grisillidis PN4; Cy comence le livre griselidis autrement appelle lexemplaire des femmes BPL; Cest le Romant de Griselidis Marquise de Saluce PN1.

1–6 **Au ... Amen** *om* BB PN4. 1–2 **Au ... j'ay** A lexemplaire des femmes mariees et de toutes autres jay BPL; A lexemple des femmes mariees et autres a marier ay icy PN1. 2–3 **petit engin** advis PA. 5 **et ... poete** homme PN2; orateur et poete BPL PN1; poete qui fut PA. 6 **Amen** *om* PN2 PN7 BPL PN1 PA. 7 **Et ... chappitre** Cy apres commence Grisillidis PN2; *om* PN7 BB PN4 BPL PN1 PA. 13 **plus** plain PN1. 16 **prenoit** *add* tout PA. **car** que PN2 PN7 BB PN4 BPL; plus que PN1; mes PA. 17–18 **peu ... autres choses** *om* PN4. 18 **estoit** *add* fort PN1; *add* moult PA. 19 **un** PN2 PN7 BB PN4 BPL; *om* PN3; lun PN1 PA. **de ... auctorité** des plus sages PN1. 21 **nous fait** nous est nous PN7 BB PN1 PA. 22 **et hardiement** *om* PN4 BPL. 23–4 **aucune ... manieres** puissance ne aucune seigneurie plus que ung autre Tu maymes si comme maintes foiz PN1. 28 **aises** eureux PN2 BPL PN1. 31 **viellesce ... chasse** PN2 BB BPL PA; enveillist sans dire mot et la suit et chasse villesce PN3; svelle(?) sanz dire mot la suit et chasse PN7; viellesse sans dire la suit et chasse PN4; vieillesse sans sonner mot la suit et chasse PN1.

Le Livre Griseldis

(from Paris, Bibl. Nationale, ms. franc. 12459)

[Preface]

(fol. 135r) Au commandement et soubz la correccion de mon maistre, et a
l'exemplaire des femmes mariees et toutes autres, j'ay mis, selon mon petit
engin et entendement, de latin en françois l'ystoire de Griseldis qui cy aprés
s'ensuit de la constance et pacience merveilleuse d'une femme. Laquelle
5   hystoire translata de lombart en latin un tres vaillant et moult solennel poete,
appellez François Petrach, dont Dieux ait l'ame. Amen.
Et commence le premier chappitre.

[I]

Au pié des mons en un costé d'Ytalie est la terre de Saluces, qui jadis estoit
moult peuplee de bonnes villes et chastiaulx, en laquelle avoit plusieurs grans
10   seigneurs et gentilz hommes, desquelz le premier et le plus grant on treuve
avoir esté un marquis appellez en son propre nom Wautier, auquel princi-
paument appartenoit le gouvernement et dominacion d'icelle terre. Bel et jeune
seigneur estoit, moult noble de lignaige et plus assez en bonnes meurs, et en
somme noble en toutes manieres, fors tant qu'il ne vouloit que soy jouer et
15   esbatre et passer temps ne ne consideroit point au temps ne es choses a venir. Et
ainsy tant seulement a chacier et a voler prenoit son desduit et plaisir, car de
toutes autres choses peu lui chaloit. Et mesmement ne se vouloit point marier,
dont sur toutes les autres choses le peuple estoit courroucié, en tant que une fois
(fol. 135v) tous ensemble alerent a lui, desquelz [un] de plus grant auctorité,
20   beau parleur et bien privez dudit seigneur, lui va dire: "Ton humanité, sire
marquis, nous donne hardiesse que, toutesfois que besoing nous fait, parlions a
toy feaublement et hardiement; et veez cy que je te veul dire de par tous tes
hommes et subgez. Non pas que j'aye aucune singularité a ceste chose, fors que
entre les autres tu m'as chier de ta grace, comme en maintes manieres je l'ay
25   approuvé. Et comme, doncques, et a bonne cause, tous tes fais nous plaisent et
tousjours nous aient pleu, si que nous nous tenons pour moult eureux que
t'avons a seigneur. Mais une chose est, laquelle se tu nous veulz accorder et
ottroier, nous serons, ce nous semble, les plus aises de tous noz voisins: c'est
assavoir que tu te vueilles marier sans plus attendre, car le temps passe et s'en
30   va. Et ja soit ce que soyes jeune et en fleur de jeunesce, toutesfois ceste fleur
[viellesce, sans dire mot, la suist et chasse], et est la mort prochaine a tout aage,

most contented of all our neighbors: this is, that you would be willing to marry without delay, for time passes and is gone. [30] And although it is true that you are young and in the flower of youth, all the while old age, without saying a word, follows and chases this flower, and death is close at hand to every age; no one escapes it. And so, each must die, the one like the next; and no man knows where or when or how. Therefore, receive and accept, we beg you, the prayers and requests of those who would refuse none of your commands. [35] And if you wish to entrust us with finding you a wife, we will procure for you such a one as to be worthy of you and of such good and high rank that you should have reason to expect the best of her. Deliver us therefore, we beseech you, from our great worry, so that if you were to die we would not dwell without a lord and ruler."

Then, the sweet words of his subjects moved the lord, and he responded: "You constrain me, my friends," said he, "to that which I have never had in mind. I delight in liberty, which is not often found in marriage, but now I wish to submit to the good intentions and counsel of you, my subjects, trusting in your faith, loyalty, and prudence. [45] And, as to your offer, I release you of the duty and worry of finding me a wife. Since it pleases you, I will marry, and this I promise you in good faith, nor will I delay. Yet there is one promise that you will make me and keep: that whomever I elect and take for a wife, you will honor her sovereignly and not a one of you will speak ill of my [50] judgment, or complain or murmur in any way. And I desire that it be my choice and free will to choose such a wife as I please. And whoever she be, you will honor and revere her and treat her as a lady, as if she were the daughter of an emperor or king."

And then all promised him, consenting quite eagerly, [55] like those to whom it had not seemed likely that they would ever see the wedding day. And then a day was chosen and appointed on which, the marquis said and promised, he would marry; and so with their meeting finished, they departed. Then the marquis commissioned and entrusted to his personal and intimate retainers the preparation of the nuptials.

[II]

How the marquis wished to marry the maiden Griselda, daughter of Janicula, and how and in what manner the nuptials took place.

Near the city and palace where the marquis dwelled was a small village where a few poor people lived, among whom the poorest was named Janicula. But just as the grace of God sometimes [65] descends into a small house and household, this good man had a daughter named Griselda, who was sufficiently beautiful in her shape and features but who could not possibly be more full of goodness, manners, and virtues.

---

33 **comment** *add* ne en quelle maniere ne a quelle heure PN1. 33–4 **nous te supplions** *om* BPL. 34 **et requestes** *om* BPL. 34–5 **nulz . . . refuseroient** nul tien commandement ne refuseroient PN2 PN7 BB PN4; quelconque le tien commendement ne refuseroient BPL; nulle foiz refuseroi(?) ton commandement PN1. 38 **cusençon** affection PN7; amour PN1. 40 **parolles** prieres PN2 PN7 BB BPL; *add* et prieres PN4 PN1 PA. **seigneur** marquiz PN7. 42 **souvent** forment PN4; *om* PN1. 45 **vous y offrez** moffres PA. 46–7 **en bonne** par ma PA. 48 **garderez** *om* PN1. 49 **mesparlera** mesplaira BPL. 50 **aucunement** en aucune maniere au contraire PN1. 54 **promistrent . . . voulentiers** promistrent joyeusement et voulentiers et dun consentement BPL. **d'un** *all other mss*; du PN3. 56 **et ordonné** *om* BPL. 57 **et se departirent** *om* BPL. 60–1 **Comment . . . nopces** *om all other mss*. 63–4 **estoit . . . povre** en avoit un tres povre BPL. 65 **descent** chiet et descent BPL PN1. **un** *om all other mss*.

ne aucun ne lui eschappe. Et ainsy fault il mourir l'um comme l'autre; et ne scet homme ou, ne quant, ne comment. Or, doncques, reçoys et accepte, nous te supplions, les prieres et requestes de ceulx qui nulz tiens commandemens ne
35 refuseroient. Et nous vueilles chargier de toy querir femme; et nous la te procurerons telle que sera digne de toy avoir, et de si bon et si grant lieu que, par raison, devras esperer tout bien d'elle. Delivres nous doncques, nous t'en prions, de grant cusençon affin que se tu mouroies nous ne demourissions sans seigneur et gouverneur."

40 Lors esmeurent les doulces parolles de ses subgetz ledit seigneur, et respondi: "Vous me contraignez, mes amis," dist il, "a ce que je n'euz oncques en pensee. Je me delittoye en franchise, qui peu souvent est en mariage, mais je me vueil soubmettre maintenant aux bonnes voulentez et conseil de vous mes subgez, moy confiant de vostre foy, loyauté, et prudence.
45 Et vous laisse la cure et cusençon, comme vous vous y offrez, de moy querir femme. Et puis qu'il vous plaist, je me marieray, et je le vous promés en bonne foy, ne pas n'atendray longuement. Une chose toutesfois vous me promettrez et garderez: que quelconque que je esliray et prandray a femme, vous l'onnourerez souverainement, ne ja aucun de vous ne mesparlera de mon
50 jugement, plaindra ne murmurera (fol. 136r) aucunement. Et vueil qu'il soit en mon chois et voulenté de prendre telle femme comme il me plaira. Et quelconque qu'elle soit, vous l'aurez en honnour et reverence et pour dame la tendrez, comme se elle estoit fille d'emperiere ou de roy."

Et lors tous lui promistrent et [d'un] consentement moult voulentiers,
55 comme ceulx a qui il ne sembloit pas que ja peussent veoir le jour des nopces. Et fut pris et ordonné un jour, dedens lequel le marquis dist et promist qu'il espouseroit; et ainsy leur parlement fina et se departirent. Et commist et encharga ce dit seigneur a aucuns siens privez et familliers l'appareil des nopces.

[II]

60 Comment le marquis voult avoir en mariage la pucelle Griseldis, fille de Janicole, et comment et la maniere des nopces.

Pres de la cité et du palais ou demouroit ledit marquis, avoit une villette ou habitoient et demouroient peu de gens et povres, entre lesquelz estoit un et le plus povre, appellez Janicolle. Mais comme aucune foiz la grace de Dieu
65 descent en un petit hostel et mainnaige, ledit bon homs avoit une fille, appellee Griseldis, de beauté de corps et de membres assez belle, mais de bonté et

This maiden had been raised in great poverty and did not know what ease was, nor had she learned to prize anything soft or anything delicate; and all the while a mature and ancient courage was hidden [70] and enclosed in her virginity, and with very great affection and reverence she took care of her father in his old age. Now I don't know how many sheep there were that she led to pasture; in tending them she was always doing something, such as spinning or stripping flax, and when returning, she would carry cabbages or other kinds of greens for them to live on. And thus she took care of this poor man, her father, very affectionately and [75] tenderly. In short, she had all proper and pious deference that in a daughter is possible.

On this virginity the marquis often cast his eyes each time he passed by her to go hunting or hawking. He looked at her not out of youthful gallantry or evil lust but, rather, with great wisdom he often considered and noted her great virtue, which could not be surpassed in a [80] woman of such youth, and which the people had not noticed. Since it was so that he was to take a wife, that which he had never wanted before, this one alone and no other was he disposed and determined to wed. The day of the aforesaid marriage was approaching rapidly, and no one yet knew or had heard say what woman the marquis would take, for which [85] everyone marvelled. And he, in the meantime, had rings, crowns, dresses, and jewels made to the measurements of another girl who was the same size and shape as she whom he wished to take as his wife. The wedding day came, and the dinner hour was approaching quickly. At the palace a magnificent display had been arranged of decorations, food, and all else belonging to the occasion. And, [90] look there, the marquis, as if he went to meet his wife, leaves his home accompanied by many good noble women. Griselda knew nothing of all that was being done for her, but having heard that her lord should get married, she set out to do early and quickly all that she had to do in their cottage and was already coming back from fetching a [95] vessel of water from afar. And just as she was to enter their house, the marquis, looking pensive, comes before her asking where her father was, to which she responded humbly and with great reverence: "My lord, in our home."

"Go tell him," he says, "that he should come speak to me."

And when this good man came, he took him by the hand and drew him aside and

---

67 **estoit . . . povoit** *om* PN1. 68 **riens mol** PN2 PN7 BB; *om* PN3 PN1 PA; *add* ne dur BPL; riens mot PN4. 68–9 **ne riens tendre** *om* BPL. 71 **ne . . . quans** quatre ou cinq PN7. **menoit** *add* chacun jour PN7; *add* chacun jour aux champs PN1. 73 **chanve** *add* ou de recouldre sa pouvre robe PN1. 75–8 **doulcement . . . vouler** icelle ledit marquis regardoit molt forment quant il passoit par illecques en allant et retournant de chasser et PN1. 75 **fille** bonne fille PA. **puet** *om* PN4; *add* ou doit PA. 79 **par . . . vertu** pour la grant patience et la grant vertu quil avoit en elle PN4; mais par grant sapience et memoire considerant les grants vertus que estoient en elle PN1; pour grant sapience et par les grans vertus qui estoient en elle PA. **sapience** PN2 PN7 BB; pacience PN3; *add* et sagesse BPL. 80 **tel** *all other mss*; ce PN3. 81–2 **nottoit . . . et celle** notoit sa contenance par laquele elle BB; nestoit dont que voulente ot de femme avoir que navoit oncques voulu par avant et celle BPL; nottoit dont ce venoit qui lavoit esmu a femme prandre consideroit quil ne lavoit oncques voulu par avant et ycelle PN1; souvent sa contenance Par laquelle contenance elle PA. 82 **et celle** PN2 PN7 PN4; celle PN3. **se** *all other mss*; *om* PN3. 86 **couronnes** *add* chapeaulx PN1. 87 **et fourme** *om* BB. **et fourme . . . vouloit** que le marquis faignoit de voloir prendre PA. 90 **veez cy** *om* PN1. **ist** il yssit PN1. 91 **sa maison** la cite PN1. **nobles** *om* BB. **bonnes dames** damoiselles PN2; *add* et damoezelles PN7; hommes et bons gens PN1; dames PA. 93 **seigneur** *add* terrien PN1. 94 **en une** une PN7. 95 **croche** boie PN7; vesseau PN1. **de l'eaue** *om* PN4. 96 **leur** sa PN1. 96–7 **ou . . . laquelle** Dy va ou est ton pere laquelle BPL; Dy moi ou est ton pere et elle PN1. 98 **Monseigneur** Seigneur PN2 BB PN4; Sire PA. 100 **fut venus** PN2 PN7 BB PN4 PN1 PA; *om* PN3; feust venus BPL.

de meurs et vertus tant reamplie estoit que plus ne povoit. Ceste pucelle avoit
esté nourrie en grant povreté et ne savoit que c'estoit d'aise, [riens mol] ne
riens tendre n'avoit apris; et toutesfoiz courage meur et ancien estoit muciez
70   et enclos en sa virginité, et en tres grant chierté et reverence nourrissoit son
povre pere en sa viellesce. Et ne sçay quans brebis avoient, qu'elle menoit en
pasture, et en menant faisoit tousjours aucune chose comme filler ou tillier
chanve, et au retour apportoit des chouz ou autre maniere d'erbettes pour eulx
vivre. Et ainsy gouvernoit ce povre homme, son pere, moult charitablement et
75   doulcement. Briefment, toute obeïssance de bien, de pitié, qui en fille puet
estre, estoit en elle.

    En ceste virginité ledit (fol. 136v) marquis, la aucune foiz passant pour aler
chacier ou vouler, maintes foiz gettoit ses yeux, non pas par jeune mignotise
ou delectacion mauvaise, mais par grant [sapience] sa grant vertu, plus que en
80   femme de [tel] aage ne seult avoir, que le peuple n'avisoit pas, souvent
consideroit ledit marquis et nottoit, dont fut fait que il a femme avoir, ce que
oncques n'avoit voulu par avant, [et celle] seule et nulle autre [se] disposa et
determina a prendre. Le jour des nopces devant dit s'approuchoit desja fort, et
nul encores ne savoit ne oioit dire quelle femme ledit marquis prandroit, dont
85   chascun se merveilloit. Et il, ce temps pendant, faisoit faire aneaulx,
couronnes, robes, et joyaulx a la mesure d'une autre pucelle, qui estoit de la
grandeur et fourme d'icelle que prandre vouloit a femme. Vint le jour des
nopces, et l'eure du disner se approuchoit fort, et avoit on fait grant appareil
ou palais de paremens, viandes, et autrement, comme au fait appartenoit. Et
90   veez cy le marquis, ainsi comme s'il alast au devant de sa femme, ist hors de
sa maison acompaignié de plusieurs nobles bonnes dames. Ne Griseldis de
tout ce que pour elle se faisoit riens ne savoit, mais bien avoit oÿ dire que son
seigneur se devoit marier; et pour ce s'estoit hastee et avancee de faire ce
qu'elle avoit a faire en leur maisonnette, et venoit desja de querir en une
95   croche de l'eaue de bien loing. Et tout ainsy qu'elle vouloit entrer en leur
maison, le marquis, tout pensis, vient au devant d'elle, en lui demandant ou
estoit son pere; laquelle lui respondi humblement et en tres grant reverence:
"Monseigneur," dist elle, "en nostre hostel."

    "Ou lui dis," fait il, "qu'il viengne parler a moy."
100   Et quant ce bon homs [fut venus], il le prist par la main et le tira a part et en

in a low voice told him: "I know, Janicula, that you love me and hold me dear, and that you are my faithful subject, and that whatever things please me, you wish them too, and are pleased with them. Yet there is one thing in particular that I want to know: if it would be acceptable to you that I take your daughter as a wife, and if you agreed to have me as your son-in-law." [105] Then the good man, who knew nothing of this thing, was astonished; dumbfounded, he flushed and was so shaken that he could hardly say, "Nothing, lord, must I desire but that which pleases you, who are my rightful lord."

"Let us go in alone then," said the marquis, "to your room, for I wish to ask your daughter certain questions in your presence." Then they entered, the [110] people waiting outside and marvelling at the care the girl showed for her father, managing in her humility and poverty the arrival of such a great lord. The marquis addressed her in this manner: "Griselda," said he, "it pleases your father and me also that you should be my wife. I believe that this should please you too, but I have something to ask you and I wish to know from you yourself, since what will be done [115] will be done soon: if with a good heart and free will you are ready and willing, and that all be permissible to me, and that I be able to do with you anything without you ever contradicting my will in any manner, and that you desire and be pleased with whatever pleases me."

To these things, altogether trembling at this marvellous event, she responded: "My lord," said [120] she, "I know certainly that I am neither worthy nor sufficient for such a great honor. Yet if this thing is your desire and my fortune, never will I do or think anything within my power that is against your will or pleasure; nor could you do anything, even make me die, that I would not suffer patiently."

"That is enough," said he; and then he led her before all those assembled and said to the people: "This," said he, "is my wife and your lady. Honor her, love her. And if you hold me dear, I pray you, hold her very dear." And straightaway he commanded her to disrobe until she was naked, and he bade the good ladies who were there to reclothe her splendidly from head to toe in new dresses. This [130] thing they did quite shame-facedly because of the contrast between the coarse, poor clothing they took off her and the precious ones with which they reclothed her. And

---

101 **bien** *om* PN4. 102 **quelconques** toutes les PA. **me plaisent** *add* je scay certainement que PA. 103 **especiaulment** *om* PN4 BPL PN1. 104 **bien** *om* PN7 BPL. 106 **en tremblant** et tout en tremblant et tellement qu PA. **dire** *add* mot PN7 PN1 PA. 110 **soy merveillant** se merveilla moult le marquis PA. 111 **pere** pouvoir PN1. **l'ordonner** le gouverner PN7. 112 **il** *all other mss*; y PN3. 113–14 **je . . . aussy** *om* PN7. 115 **tantost** *add* si dieu plaist PA. **vouloir** *all other mss*; vouloie PN3. 115–17 **le . . . voulenté** veulx que tout fait que feray avecques toy tu le feras et vouldras a ma volente PN1; le vieulx aussi que quelconque chose que je vaudray faire avec toy tu ne contrediras a ma volente PA. 116 **en . . . maniere** tant que tu vives BPL. 117 **quanqu'il** PN2 BPL PA; quanqui PN3; tout ce quil PN7; quant quil BB; quelconque PN4; tout fais qui PN1. 120 **ne souffisant** *om* PN1. 121 **de . . . honneur** pour toi BB PA. **toutesfois . . . eur** te plaist toutesfois ta volente est mon cuer ne PN2; te plaist toutesfois se ta volonte et mon eur y est PN7; toutesfoiz te agree et eur est BB; toutesfois est mon eur BPL; ta volonte y est et mon cueur aussi y est PN1; tagree et mon eur est PA. 122 **quelque chose** *om* PN2; chose BB PA. 124 **seuffre** *add* et la fist PN7; *add* et porte reverence PA. **amez . . . chiere** lamez vous la et la cherissez vous se amez chier mon honneur et ma personne PN1. 128–9 **devestir . . . richement** vestir et la fist vestir de robbes neuves tres ricement PN4; devestir toute nue ainsi comme elle yssit du ventre sa mere et puis la fist vestir de robes tres chieres PN1. 128 **revestir** vestir PN2 PN7 BPL. 130 **moult honteusement** bien vergoigneusement BPL PN1. **vestemens** robes PN2 PN7 BB PN4 BPL PA; draps PN1. 133 **transmuee** tresmuee PN7; tresallee PN1. **changié** toute changiee PN2 BB BPL; toute chargie PN4; chacun PN1; changee de tous poins PA.

basse voix lui dist: "Je sçay," dist il, "Janicole, que tu m'ainmes et as bien chier, et es mon homme feable, et que quelconques choses me plaisent, tu les veulz et te plaisent. Une chose toutesfoiz especiaulment vueil savoir: se il te plaist bien que j'aye ceste tienne fille a femme et me vueille avoir ton
105 gendre." Dont li bon homs, qui riens ne savoit de ce fait, fut moult esmerveilliez; et tout rougis et esbaÿs, en tremblant, a paine pot dire: "Riens," dist, "sire, vouloir ne doy que ce qui te plaist, qui es mon droiturier seigneur."

"Entrons doncques," dist le marquis, "seulz en ta chambre, car je veil faire (fol. 137r) a ta fille certaines demandes, toy present." Lors y entrerent, le
110 peuple attendant et soy merveillant des services que la pucelle faisoit a son pere de l'ordonner en sa petitesce et povreté a la venue de si grant seigneur. Laquelle ledit marquis arrengna en ceste maniere: "Griseldis," dist il, "[il] plaist a ton pere et a moy aussi que tu soies ma femme. Je croy que ce te plaist aussy, mais je t'ay a demander et veil savior de toy, se puis que ce sera fait qui
115 sera tantost, se de bon cuer et plain [vouloir] tu es preste et le veulx, et que tout me loise, et puisse faire avec toy si que jamis en quelconque maniere tu ne contrediras a ma voulenté et que tu vueilles et te plaise [quanqu'il] me plaira."

A ces choses, de ce fait merveilleux toute tremblant, respondi: "Je," dist
120 elle, "monseigneur, sçay certainement que je ne suis pas digne ne souffisant de si grant honneur. Et se ceste chose toutesfois est ta voulenté et mon eur, jamais riens ne feray ne penseray quelque chose a mon povoir qui soit contre ta voulenté ou plaisir, ne tu ne feras ja chose, et me feisse mourir, que je ne seuffre pacienment."
125 "C'est assez," dist il; et ainsy la fist amener devant tous en publique et dist au peuple: "Ceste," fait il, "ma femme et vostre dame est. Honnourez la, amez la. Et se vous m'avez chier, je vous prie, aiez la tres chiere." Et incontinent la commanda a devestir toute nue et du pié jusques au chief la fist revestir de neuves robes tres richement par les bonnes dames qui la estoient. Laquelle
130 chose firent moult honteusement pour le regart des vilz et povres vestemens qu'elles lui desvestoient aux precieuses que on lui vestoit. Et ainsi ordonnee et paree de couronne et de pierrerie tres grandement, comme soudainement transmuee et changié, a paine la recongnust le peuple. Laquelle le marquis

when she was so very grandly arrayed and adorned with a crown and gems, as if suddenly transformed and changed, the people could hardly recognize her. The marquis solemnly wedded her with a precious ring that he had had made [135] especially for this purpose. He then had her put on a handsome palfrey and led to the palace, the people accompanying her and making a great and joyful celebration. The wedding took place, and the day was spent very joyfully and happily.

Then everyone believed that God had sent such grace to this woman that she seemed not to have been born and raised in a poor village home but in a royal residence. [140] And everyone held her so dear and in such great honor and love that those who knew who she was and who were acquainted with her since birth could hardly believe that she was the daughter of Janicula; she had within her such propriety, decorum, good manners, wisdom, and eloquence that all delighted to hear her. And not only in her own country but in [145] neighboring countries and regions her good name and her great praise and good reputation spread and grew, so that many men and women came to see her for her worthiness. And so the marquis, humbly but virtuously married, lived in true peace within his home and in great favor without. Since he had perceived such great and excellent virtues hidden in such great poverty, [150] each held him to be wise, for not only did the good creature do the work and chores belonging to a wife, but when the case required it, she attended to and oversaw the state; her lord being absent and away, the discord of the land and the strife arising between nobles or other people she abated and appeased very wisely. Such eloquent and wise words [155] and answers, so much discretion and high judgment did she have, that many held her to be and said that she was sent from heaven to address the general welfare of the people. And it was not long before she was pregnant and gave birth to a beautiful daughter. However much one would have preferred a son, still the marquis and all of the country rejoiced greatly.

[III]

How the marquis wished to try and test Griselda his wife in diverse ways and to see her great constancy.

Now look, I do not know where the marquis got the strange notion, which some wise men wish to praise, to assay his wife and to test her more than before, whom he

---

135 **mener** *add* au temple BPL. 137–8 **liément . . . envoia** liement en priant dieu pour elle que elle se governast sagement et finablement dieu envoya PA. 138 **Or . . . envoia** et donna nostre seigneur PN1. 139–40 **estre . . . nee** avoir este nee et nourrie PN2 PN7 BB PN4 BPL PA. 143–4 **se . . . ouÿr** prenoit grant plaisir de la veoir et ouir BPL; prenoit grant plaisir de la regarder et ouyr PN1. 144 **pays et** PN2 PN7 BB PN4 PA; pays PN3 PN1. 144–5 **pays . . . regions** bonnes villes BPL. 145–7 **son . . . veoir** *om* PN1. 145 **d'elle** *om* PN2 PN7 BB PN4 BPL PA. 146 **croissoit** disoit PN2 PN7 BB BPL; disoient PN4; *om* PA. 146–7 **le . . . bien** la grant bonte BB. 147 **humblement** *all other mss*; humble PN3. **mais** et PN7 PN4 BPL PN1 PA. 147–8 **virtueusement** gracieusement BPL. 149–54 **lequel . . . saigement** *om* PN1. 149–50 **en . . . prins** PN2; en si grant amitie leust pris PN3; en si tres grant povrete misere eust prins PN7; *om* BB PA; en si grant povrete muchie eust PN4; en si grant povrete mucee tant sagement eust prins BPL. 150–1 **et mesnages** PN2 BB PN4 BPL PA; en marriage PN3; et mesnage PN7; *om* PN1. 152 **absent et** presens ou PN7. 153–4 **contencions . . . autres** *om* PN4. 154 **gens** des gens PN4. 155 **grant . . . et** *om* PN1. 156 **estre** *add* anonciee et BB. **des cielz** *om* PN1. **salut** *add* et proufit BPL PN1. 157 **publique** et publique PN2 PN7 BB PN4 BPL PA et bien publique PN1. 158 **amé** *add* quelle eust enffante PN7. 159 **grandement** *om* PN2 PN7 BB PN4 BPL PN1; moult PA. 160–1 **Comment . . . constance** *om all other mss*. 162 **veez . . . je** PN2 BB PN4; veez ce que je BPL; assez tost apres lenffantement PN7; apres ce ung petit de temps je PN1; voiez ci PA.

solennelment espousa de l'anel precieux que a cest usaige et pour ce
135 especiaument il avoit fait faire. Et la fist mettre sur un beau palefroy et mener
au palays, le peuple la acompaignant et faisant grant feste et liesce, et furent
faites les nopces et passa le jour moult joyeusement et liément.

Or crut Dieu et envoia tant grace en celle femme que non pas en povre
maison de villaige mais en hostel royal sembloit estre nourrie et avoir esté
140 nee. Et l'ost chascun tant chiere et en si grant honneur et amour que ceulx qui
savoient qui elle estoit et qui la congnoissoient de nativité a paine povoient
croire qu'elle (fol. 137v) feust fille a Janicole, tant avoit en elle de honnesteté,
belle vie, bonne maniere, sagesse, et doulceur de parler que chascun se
delittoit a la ouÿr. Et ja non pas tant seulement en son pays, mais es [pays et]
145 regions voisines son bon nom et la grant louenge et la bonne renommee d'elle
se publioit et croissoit, tellement que mains hommes et femmes pour le grant
bien d'elle l'aloient veoir. Et ainsi le marquis, [humblement] mais virtueusement mariez, vivoit en bonne paix en sa maison et en grant grace dehors;
lequel, comme si tres grant et excellant vertus, [en si grant povreté mucié, eust
150 prins], chascun l'en tenoit a saige; car non pas tant seulement euvres [et
mesnages] appartenans a femme ladicte bonne creature faisoit, mais, ou le cas
le requeroit, la chose publique adresçoit et pourveoit; son seigneur absent et
dehors, les descors du pays et contencions si s'esmouvoient entre nobles ou
autres gens, abaissoit et appaissoit tres saigement. Tans beaux et saiges parlers
155 et responses, tant grant discrecion et hault jugement avoit en elle, que
plusieurs la tenoient et disoient estre envoiee des cielz au salut du bien
commun publique. Et ne demoura gueres qu'elle fut grosse et enfanta une
belle fille. Combien que on eust mieulx amé un filz, toutesfoiz le marquis et
tout le pays s'en esjoÿrent grandement.

[III]

160 Comment ledit marquis voult essaier et approuver Griseldis sa femme par
diverses manieres et veoir sa grant constance.

Et veez cy que je ne sçay quelle ymaginacion merveilleuse print ledit
marquis, laquelle aucuns saiges veulent louer, c'est assavoir de experimenter

had already tried and tested enough, [165] and to tempt her again in diverse ways. One night he came to her in her bedroom and, as if quite distraught and troubled, he says to her: "You are well aware, Griselda – and I believe that the office I have put you in has not made you forget the condition I took you out of – you know well enough how you came into this house. You are certainly very dear to me and I love you well enough, as you [170] know; but my noblemen do not – especially since you have given birth to a daughter. They think it is quite ignoble to be subject to such a common woman as you are. Therefore, since I desire with all my heart to appease them and to live in peace with them, it is now necessary for me to arrange and do with your daughter not according to my desire and pleasure but according to the counsel [175] and judgment of others. Yet I do not wish to do anything without your knowing; therefore, I want you to give me your consent and accord, and show the patience that you promised me at the beginning of our marriage."

Having heard this matter, shaken in neither her expression nor her words, she responded to him maturely and wisely: "You are my lord," said she, "and this [180] little girl and I are yours; therefore, do with your things as you please. Certainly nothing that can please you could displease me; I could neither covet nor regret to lose anything – I have no doubt – except you. And this I have placed perfectly in my heart so that it will never be removed by the passing of time or by death. And all else can happen before my heart will change."

The marquis rejoiced at this response, but he dissembled his feelings and pretended that he was angry and sad, and took his leave of her. A little later, he sent to her a servant of his, a sergeant who was faithful to him and whom he had tested in greater things, and he informed him exactly how he should act. This sergeant came to her at night. "Pardon me, my lady," he said, "do not blame me at all or [190] hold against me what I am constrained to do. You know what it is to be subject to great lords and how one must obey them. I have been commanded to take this child." And in saying this, gesturing as if he would do a cruel and evil thing, he took the child in a rough and clumsy manner. This sergeant was held to be a cruel man, and had an ugly face, [195] and had come at a suspicious hour, and spoke like a man full of ill-will. And so the good and simple lady believed that he would do an evil deed to her little girl, whom she loved so much; yet she neither shed tears nor sighed – who

164–5 et essaier . . . tenter *om* PN4. 164 **assez essayee et** assez PN2 BB PA; *om* PN7 BPL PN1. 165 **approuvee . . . encores** esprouvee mais nonobstant tout il la voult encores tempter PA. 166 **de nuit** *om* PN7. 167 **dire** *add* en ceste maniere PA. 169 **bien . . . bien** moult agreable et taime PA. 170 **nobles gens** ne me nobles PN7. 170–1 **a enfanter** *all other ms*; *om* PN3. 171 **une fille** *om* PN2 BB PN4 BPL PN1 PA. 172 **telle** une telle PN7. **femme** dame PN2. **de peuple** PN2 PN7 BB PN4 BPL PA; *om* PN3; de peuple commun PN1. **qui desire** *all other mss*; cuidoie PN3. **estre** *om all other mss*. 173 **appaisie et** estre et PN2 PN7 BB PN4 BPL PA; a PN1. **necessité** auctorite PN7. 173–4 **m'est a** est orendroit de BPL. 174 **et faire** *om* PN1. **pas a ma** mie a ta PN1. 175 **ton sceu** ton consentement PN7; que tu le saiches PN1. 180 **ta** *all other mss*; *om* PN3. 182 **toy** *add* et ton amour PN1; *add* en ce monde PA. **mis** *om* BB. 183 **ne par laps de** ne par PN2; ne par passement de PN7; de couvrement de BPL; par espace de PN1. **ne par mort ne** *om* PN1. 188 **plus . . . choses** plus grant chose PN2 BB PN4 PA; bien grans choses PN7; plusieurs choses BPL; plusieurs manieres PN1. 190 **fay** suis BB PN4 BPL PN1 PA. **contraint** cy venu PN4. **Tu scez** vous scavez PN1. 192 **faire** *all other mss*; *om* PN3. 193 **chose** *all other mss*; *om* PN3. **comme . . . signes** *om* PN1. 193–4 **par rude . . . maniere** *om* PN7. 193 **lourde** laide PN1. 194 **de . . . figure** lait de visaige et de figure BPL; lait de visage et cruel de maniere PN1. 195 **souspessonneuse** *add* a heure de menuit BPL; *add* entre jour et nuit PN1. **estoit venuz** *om* BPL. **plain** *om* PN4; *add* de mauvaistie et BPL. 197 **plours** plains PN7.

et essaier sa femme plus avant, laquelle il avoit desja assez essayee et
165 approuvee, et de la tenter encores par diverses manieres. Vint une fois a elle
de nuit en sa chambre, aussy comme tout courrouciez et troublez, et lui va
dire: (fol. 138r) "Tu sces bien, Griseldis, – et je croy que la dignité ou je t'ay
mis ne te fait oublier l'estat ou je te pris, – tu scez assez comment tu vins en
ceste maison. Tu m'es certainement bien chiere et si t'aime bien, comme tu
170 scez; mais ce ne font pas mes nobles, mesmement quant tu as commencié [a
enfanter] une fille, lesquelz se dient estre moult villenez qui soient subgés a
telle femme [de peuple] comme tu es. Or, doncques, je [qui desire] estre de
tout mon cuer appaisié et vivre en paix avec eulx, maintenant neccessité m'est
a ordonner et faire de ta fille non pas a ma voulenté et plaisir, mais au conseil
175 et jugement d'autruy. Toutesfoiz, je n'en veil riens faire sans ton sceu; je veil,
doncques, que tu me prestes ton consentement et accort, et aies celle pacience
que tu me promis des l'encommencement de nostre mariage."
Laquelle chose oyee, de visaige ne de parler ne s'esmeut, mais meurement
respondi a lui et saigement: "Tu es," dist elle, "mon seigneur, et je et ceste
180 petite fillette sommes tiennes; doncques fais de [ta] chose comme il te plaist.
Certainement riens ne te puet plaire qui me desplaise, ne riens ne couvoite a
avoir ne a perdre ne ne doubte que toy. Et cecy ay je mis parfaitement en mon
cuer, ne jamais ne par laps de temps ne par mort ne s'en partira. Et toutes
autres choses se puent avant faire que ce courage a moy muer."
185 Le marquis de ceste response fut moult liez en cuer, mais il dissimula et
faingny qu'il feust courroucié et triste et se party d'elle. Et un peu aprés
envoia a elle un sien serviteur et sergent a lui feable, qu'il avoit esprouvé en
plus grans choses, et l'enforma bien comment il feroit, lequel vint de nuit a
elle. "Pardonne moy," dist il, "ma dame, ne point ne me metz sus ne ne me
190 saches mauvais gre de ce que je fay contraint. Tu scez que c'est d'estre soubz
grans seigneurs, et comment il fault a eulx obeïr. Commandé m'est de prandre
cest enffant." Et en ce disant, ainsi qu'il voulsist [faire] crueuse et mauvaise
[chose], comme le monstroit par signes, prist l'enfant par rude et lourde
maniere. Ce sergent estoit tenuz pour crueux homme, et estoit de laide figure,
195 et a heure souspessonneuse estoit venuz, et parloit comme homme plain de
mauvaise voulenté. Et aussi cuidoit la bonne dame et simple qu'il alast faire
mauvais fait de sa fillette que (fol. 138v) tant amoit; toutesfoiz ne plours ne

doubts this would be a difficult thing even for a nurse? And with a calm face, she took up her child and looked at her for a little while, kissed and blessed her, made [200] the sign of the cross, and handed her over to the sergeant. "Go," she said, "do and execute that which my lord has entrusted to you. Yet I beseech you," she said, "to do what is within your power to keep wild beasts from devouring and tearing up this child's body unless you have been enjoined to do the contrary."

When the sergeant returned to his lord and told him of his wife's [205] response and presented him with his daughter, he was moved to great pity. Nonetheless, he still did not desist from his purpose, and he ordered the sergeant to bundle up the little girl well and securely and to take her secretly to Boulogna la Grasse to his sister, the wife of the count of Panango, to hand her over to her to raise for him and to teach her learning and [210] morals, as her own daughter, and to keep her so discreetly that no one would be able to recognize or figure out who she was. And he went right away and carefully carried out what he was ordered to do. And after this the marquis often noted and regarded the expression, the words, the bearing, and the behavior of his wife to see if in any way she made reference to her daughter, but he did not see or [215] perceive her to be changed or altered in any manner whatsoever. Such happiness, such obedience, such service and love, as she had always shown before, she rendered him. No sign of sadness nor any mention of her daughter did she make either on purpose or by accident.

In this state four years passed before she was pregnant and gave birth to a very beautiful son, for which the father and all of his friends were very joyful. When the child [220] was two years old and had finished nursing, the marquis once again came to his wife and said to her: "Wife, you have heard before how my people are discontented and murmur about our marriage, and especially now since they see that you are able to bear children and are disposed and inclined to have heirs, and that you even have a male. And they often say: 'Once our marquis is dead, the [225] grandson of Janicula will be our lord, and so noble a land will be subject to such a lord' and the people have often said many such words. These things and words make me – I, who wish to live in peace yet fear for my life – preoccupied and melancholy. So I am determined to do with this child as I did with the other. And I make this known to you first so that the [230] sudden sadness not trouble or hurt you too much."

To this she said, "I have told you and I remind you that I cannot wish or not wish for anything except what you wish. Nor do I have any part in these children except their birth. You are lord of them and of me: use your things according to your right;

198 **sospirs** *add* ne semblans de coroux elle PN1. **dobt estre** eust deu estre PN2 BB PN4; est PN7; eust este BPL; devroit estre PN1 PA. **tenue** *om* BPL. **en ... nourrice** et tres merveilleuse a une telle dame et mere PN1. 199 **le baisa** PN2 BB PN4 PA; la baisa PN3; baisa PN7 BPL PN1. 199–200 **le baisa ... croix** puis le laissa et baisa et lui fist le signe de la croix trois foix sur luy PN1. 200 **elle** *add* ou nom de dieu et de sa puissance et PN1. 202 **sauvaiges** *add* ou oyseaulx BPL. 205 **il fut** PN2 PN7 BB PN4 BPL; dont il fut PN3; adonques fut PN1; et lors il fut PA. **neantmoins** *om* PN7. 206 **toutesfoiz** *om* PN2 BPL PN1 PA. 207 **fillette** enffant PN7 PN1; fille BB PN4 BPL PA. 210 **meurs** bonne meurs PN1; bonnes manieres PA. 210–11 **et si ... feust** *om* BPL. 211 **il y** ledit sergent ly PN7; le serviteur PN1. 214 **quelconque maniere** nulle maniere du monde PA. 215 **muee** yrer PN4. 216 **tousjours ... rendoit** devant PN2 BB PN4 BPL PA; devant elle luy faisoit PN7; elle avant luy faisoit PN1. 216–17 **ne nulle ... faisoit** *om* PN1. 218 **tant** *om* PN2 PN7 BB PN4 PN1; que veez BPL; avant PA. 224 **masle** enfant masle BPL PN1 PA. 225–6 **et sy ... seigneur** *om* PA. 226–41 **et maintes ... amour** et luy dist ledit marquis comme il avoit fait de son autre enffant et quil vouloit ainsi faire de celluy Et la bonne dames luy fist encores plus gracieuses responces que par devant PN1. 226 **souvent** *om* BPL. 228 **vivre** souvent estre PN2 BB PN4 BPL PA; estre PN7. **Sy ... meu** si vault mieulx PN4; *add* de verite ou non BPL. 229 **premierement** *om* BPL. **affin** *om* PN2 PN7 BB PN4 BPL. 232 **ces enffans** cest enfant PN2; tes enffans PN7. 233 **choses** enffans PN7.

sospirs ne fist, qui dobt estre tenue a tres dure chose en une nourrice. Et de
plain front prist son enffant et le regarda un pou et [le baisa] et beneist, et fist
200 le signe de la croix, et le bailla audit sergent. "Va," dist elle, "fay et excecute
ce que monseigneur t'a enchargié. Je te prie, toutesfoiz," dist elle, "que tu
gardes a ton povoir que les bestes sauvaiges ne devourent ou menguent le
corps de cest enffant, se le contraire ne t'est enjoint."

Lequel sergent quant il fut retournez a son seigneur et lui raconta la response
205 de sa femme et lui presenta sa fille, [il fut] meu de grant pitié. Neantmoins
toutesfoiz ne desista il point de son propos, et commanda audit sergent qu'il
envelopast ladicte fillette bien et seurement et qu'il la portast secretement a
Bouloingne la grasse a une sienne suer, qui estoit la mariee au conte de
Paniquo, et a lui la baillast a nourrir de par lui et a enseignier de science et de
210 meurs, comme sa fille, et si celeement la gardast que nul ne sceust ne ne peust
congnoistre ou apparcevoir qui elle feust. Et il y ala tantost et soingneusement
accomplist ce que commis lui estoit. Et le marquis aprés ce souvent avisoit et
consideroit la chiere, les parolles, le semblant, et le maintien de sa femme se
point lui feroit semblant de sa fille, mais en quelconque maniere ne la vit ou
215 apparçut changié ou muee. Telle liesce, telle obeïssance, tel service et amour,
comme tousjours faisoit par avant, lui rendoit, ne nulle tristesce, ne nulle
mencion de sa fille de propos ou par accident ne faisoit.

En cest estat se passerent iiii ans, tant qu'elle fut grosse et enfanta un tres
beau filz, dont le pere et tous les amis furent moult joyeux. Lequel enfant puis
220 qu'il ot deux ans et qu'il fut sevré de la nourrice, le marquis de rechief vint a
sa femme et lui dist: "Femme, tu as oüy autrefoiz comment mon peuple est
mal content et murmure de nostre mariage, et maintenant especiaument, puis
qu'ilz voient que tu portes et es disposee et encline a avoir lignié, et
mesmement que tu as masle. Et dient souvent: 'Nostre marquis mort, le
225 nepveu de Janicole sera nostre seigneur, et sy noble pays sera subjet a tel
seigneur;' et maintes telles parolles dist souvent le peuple. Lesquelles choses
et parolles je, qui veil vivre en paix et en doubtant aussi de ma personne, me
font vivre pensif et merancolieux. (fol. 139r) Sy suy meu que de cest enfant
face comme j'ay fait de l'autre. Et ce je te fay premierement assavoir, affin
230 que la douleur soudaine ne te troublast trop ou nuisist."

A ce, "Je t'ay fait," elle dist, "et je le te recorde que je ne puis riens vouloir,
fors ce que tu veulx, ou non vouloir. Ne je n'ay riens en ces enffans que
l'enffantement. Tu es seigneur d'eulx et de moy: use de tes choses a ton droit,

neither ask nor require my consent in this thing. When I entered over the threshold of your house – there is [235] nothing more true – I stripped off my clothes and also my desires and dressed in yours. Whatever you wish, therefore, whatever it be, I wish it. And certainly, if I could know your will even before you, I would desire and do it even before you; therefore, [240] I will now willingly follow and carry out your desire, which I could not know before you told me. And if it pleased you that I die, I would die very willingly, for death could not compare to our love."

[IV]

How the marquis then sent his sergeant to his wife Griselda to seize her son, as he had done with her daughter, and how benevolently, without making any show of anger, she handed him over.

When the marquis thus perceived and recognized the great constancy of his wife, he was greatly astonished and, very troubled, he departed from her and immediately sent the sergeant whom he had sent to her before. This sergeant, excusing himself for being obliged to obey, then, as if intending to commit an act of great cruelty, asked for the child as he had the other; and she responded with good [250] cheer, though it must have been that she was greatly afflicted in her heart. Her son, so beautiful and sweet, she took in her arms, and blessed him and made the sign of the cross, as she had done with her daughter, and for a little while she looked at him and kissed him without showing a sign of grief, and handed him over to the messenger. "Here," she said, "do that which you were sent for. One thing, though, I kindly request of you, if I may, that [255] if you are able to, you try to preserve and protect the body and limbs of this noble child, so that fierce beasts do not devour or ravage him." Carrying off the child, the sergeant returned to the marquis and told him how he had found his wife, at which the marquis marvelled more and more, and so much so that if he had not known that she loved her children perfectly, he would have held her to be a suspect and [260] wicked woman and believed that this hardness and constancy came from the workings of some cruel will; but he was sure that she loved nothing more besides himself than them. He sent this son to Bologna to be raised and kept secretly as he had done with his daughter.

235 **seul** *add* de luis PN7. 236 **Quanque** Tant que PN2. 236–7 **comment . . . soit** *om* PN7. 236 **que** PN2 BB PN4 BPL PA; qu PN3. 237 **je veil** et je le vueil aussi et dois voloir PA. 238 **je . . . meismes** *om* BPL. **que . . . meismes** *om* PN7. 239 **maintenant** *add* fay BB. **je ne puys** je puis PN7 BPL. 240 **j'ensuivray et feray** je le feray BPL. 242–4 **Comment . . . bailla** *om all other mss.* 245 **Quant . . . ainsi et** et apres plusieurs parolles et remonstrances ledit marquis PN1. **grant** *om* PN7. **constance** *add* et pacience et fermete PN1. 245–53 **sa . . . envoié** la bonne dame dont il fut encores plus joyeulx mais encores appella celluy servant querir lenffant devers la marquise laquelle luy bailla moult gracieusement toutesfoiz quelle fust bien corroucee en cueur PN1. 246 **tout troublé** *om* PN2 BPL. 247 **sergent en** *om* BPL. **en** *om* PN2 PN7 BB PN4 PA. 249 **comme . . . l'autre** *om* BPL. **respondy** *om* PN2 PN7 BB PN4 BPL PA. 250 **cuer** *add* et moult triste BPL. 251 **doulcet** moult doulcet PA; *add* tant que plus ne povoit BPL. 252 **sans** *add* oncques PA. **monstrer** monstrer PN2 PN7 BB PN4 BPL PA; monstre PN3. 254–8 **une . . . femme** Et dist audit serviteur quelle le gardast de toutes bestes sauvages et oyseaulx sil estoit possible PN1. 256 **mauvaises** *add* ou oyseaulx BPL. **devourent ou** *om* BPL. 257–8 **ce qu'il . . . sa** les requestes et prieres de sa BPL. 258 **en plus** *all other mss*; en plus en plus PN3. 259 **qu'elle . . . parfaitement** parfaitement lamour que elle avoit en lui et en PA. **parfaitement** *om* BPL. 260–1 **et eust . . . voulonté** *om* PN1. 260 **fermeté** seurte BB PN4 PA. 261–2 **apres lui** *om* BPL. 262 **lui** *om* PN4. 262–6 **Il . . . plus** *om* PN1. 262 **a nourrir . . . secretement** *om* BPL.

ne en ce ne demande ou requier mon consentement. Quant j'entray, il n'est
235   riens plus vray, ou seul de ta maison, je devesty mes robes et aussy mes
voulentez et vesti les tiennes. Quanque tu veulx, doncques, comment [que] ce
soit, je veil. Et pour certain, se je povoie avant savoir ta voulenté que toy
meismes, je la vouldroye et feroye avant que toy meismes; doncques
maintenant ta voulenté, que je ne puys devant savoir que la me dies,
240   j'ensuivray et feray voulentiers. Et s'il te plaist que je muire, je vueil morir
tres voulentiers, ne la mort ne se pourroit comparer a nostre amour."

[IV]

Comment ledit marquis envoia secondement son sergent a sa femme
Griseldis pour lui oster son filz, comme il avoit fait sa fille, et comment
benignement, sans faire nul semblant de courrous, elle lui bailla.
245   Quant le marquis apparçut ainsi et congnut la grant constance de sa femme,
se esmerveilla moult et, tout troublé, se parti d'elle, et tantost envoia ce
sergent que autresfois avoit envoié a elle. Lequel sergent, en soy excusant
comment il lui convenoit obeïr, ainsi comme se il voulsist faire une grande
inhumanité, demanda l'enfant comme il avoit fait l'autre, et elle respondy de
250   bonne chiere, ja fust ce que bien estoit courroucee en cuer. Son filz moult bel
et doulcet prist entre ses bras et le beneist et seigna, comme elle avoit fait la
fille, et un petit longuement le regarda et le baisa, sans [monstrer] signe de
douleur, et au messaige le bailla. "Tien," dist elle, "fay ce a quoy tu es envoié.
Une chose, toutesfoiz, te requier chierement tant que je puis: (fol. 139v) que,
255   se tu pues faire, tu vueilles garder et deffendre le corps et membres de ce
noble enffant, que bestes mauvaises ne le devourent ou menguent." Lequel,
enportant ledit enfant, retourna au marquis et lui raconta ce qu'il avoit trouvé
en sa femme, dont de plus [en plus] se merveilla, et tellement que, s'il n'eust
sceu qu'elle amast parfaitement ses enffans, il l'eust tenue pour suspette et
260   mauvaise femme, et eust creu celle fermeté et constance venir de couraige
d'aucune crueuse voulenté; mais seur estoit qu'elle riens plus n'amoit aprés
lui. Il envoia ce filz a Bouloingne a nourrir et a garder secretement, comme il
avoit fait sa fille.

Now, I entreat you, couldn't these trials of obedience and marital fidelity [265] quite suffice for this lord? But there are some who when they have begun something or have it in mind persist in it nevertheless. Then the marquis considered more than before whether his wife was changed towards him or made reference in any way to her children; but in nothing was she altered: she was more constantly faithful to him, more obedient and attentive than before. [270] Then a wicked rumor about the marquis began to spread: that out of shame for marrying so poorly, he must have been moved by an evil spirit to arrange to have his children killed and murdered, for no one saw either of them nor did anyone know or hear where they were; and so he, who was so noble and so loved by his subjects, in another way made himself hated and [275] notorious among his people. Yet not even for this did his hard resolve change, but he proceeded and continued even more than before in his madness with his cruel notion to test his wife, so that when twelve years had passed since the birth of his daughter, he sent messengers to Rome who brought him back forged letters by which he led the people to believe that to make peace between him and [280] his people the pope had given him leave and dispensation to divorce his wife and to take another. And it was not hard to make these simple and ignorant people believe what he pleased. When this news came to Griselda's attention, she was not afflicted by it or altered in any manner or changed, waiting until he, to whom she had yielded in all her acts, would announce his will. [285] He had already sent to Bologna and had written to his sister's husband to send him his children. The rumor, indeed, spread everywhere that the marquis would marry a great lady. And this Count of Panango, who was good friends with the marquis, was already on the way, accompanied by many noblemen in a great train and procession, bringing the [290] marquis's daughter, who was very beautiful and of marriageable age, and this girl's brother, who was around seven years old.

[V]

How the marquis said to his wife Griselda that he must take another wife, and how he sent her to her father naked except for only a poor shift, and how Janicula, her father, [295] came to meet her and handed her her poor old clothing that he had kept.

During this time the marquis, wishing to test and tempt his wife more than before,

266 **tousjours plus** *add* fort que devant PN7; *add* pour penser BB; *add* affaire PN4; tousjours de plus en plus quils pourront encore faire PA. 267 **lui** li son courage PA. 269–70 **ne . . . avant** ne le survinst et honnorast encores plus que devant PN1. 269 **fust plus** feust PN2 PN7 BB PN4; feust de jour en jour et BPL. **lui** *add* plus PN2 PN7 BB PN4 BPL. **obeissante et** reverant plus BPL. 270 **courir** *add* et acroistre BPL PN1. 274 **si amez** sage PN1. 275 **dur** *om* PN2 PN1. **mua** voust(?) muer ne changer PA. 277–85 **si . . . voulenté** Et envoia a Romne messages pour avoir dispensacion de se departir de sa femme affin quil eust paix de son peuple et eut ladicte dispensacion PN1. 278 **ses messages** messaige BPL. **apporterent** apporta BPL. **faintes** faites BB PN4 PA. 283 **mua** *add* couleur PN7; *add* ne changa PA. 283–4 **ne ne . . . cil** Ains attendoit touzjours moult humblement que cellui PA. 284 **a** *repeated* PN3. **soubmis** commis PN7. 285–91 **Il . . . ans** Et envoia ambassadeurs et gens devers le conte de harmuz pour avoir une sienne fille a femme et leut et fut amenee devers ledit marquise PN1. 288 **qui . . . marquis** et autres lesquelz estoient moult amis et feaulx ensemble BPL. **moult** grant PN2; *add* grant PN7 BB PN4. 290 **fille** femme PN4. 292–5 **Comment . . . gardé** *om all other mss.* 296–306 **Et . . . estat** Et lors il ala devers griseldis et luy dist de rechef la maniere comment il failloit quil se fist pour avoir paix a son peuple et quelle eust pacience et print tout en gre PN1.

Povoient, je vous prie, a ce seigneur ces experimens d'obeïssance et de foy
265 de mariage bien souffire? Mais y sont aucuns que quant il ont aucune chose
commancié ou en propos qui continuent tousjours plus. Or avisa plus que
devant ledit marquis se sa dicte femme se mueroit envers lui ou feroit
semblant en aucune maniere de ses enffans; mais en riens ne se changa qu'elle
ne fust plus continuelment a lui feable, plus obeïssante et serviciable que par
270 avant. Si commençoit du marquis une mauvaise renommee a courir: qu'il
n'eust ce de mauvais esperit meu, et pour honte de ce qu'il c'estoit si
petitement mariez, fait faire et fait perir et occirre ses enffans, car on n'en
veoit aucun ne on ne savoit ne oyoit dire ou ilz estoient; dont il, qui estoit si
noble et estoit si amez de ses subgés, en autre maniere se faisoit haynneux et
275 notter de son peuple. Et toutesfoiz ja pour ce son dur couraige ne mua, mais
en sa merancolie et dure ymaginacion de approuver sa femme proceda et
continua encores plus avant; si que comme depuis la nativité de sa fille eust
xii ans, il envoia a Romme ses messages qui lui apporterent lettres faintes, par
lesquelles il donnoit a entendre au peuple que le pape pour la paix de lui et de
280 ses gens lui avoit donné congié et dispensacion de soy departir de sa femme et
prandre une autre. Et ne fut pas fort de le donner a entendre a ses gens simples
et rudes ce qu'il lui pleut. Laquelle chose quant elle vint a la congnoissance
Griseldis, elle ne s'en esbaÿst ne mua en aucune maniere ne ne changa soy,
attendant que cil, [a] qui elle avoit soubmis tous ses fais, en ordonnast a sa
285 voulenté.(fol. 140r) Il avoit desja envoié a Bouloingne et avoit escript au mari
de sa suer que il lui amenast ses enfans. La renommee courroit ja partout que
le marquis devoit prendre a femme une grant dame. Et ycellui conte de
Paniquo, qui estoit moult amis dudit marquis, en grant appareil et ordonnance,
et moult bien acompaignié de nobles, estoit desja au chemin, et amenoit ycelle
290 fille du marquis, moult belle et en point de marier, et le frere d'icelle fille, qui
avoit environ sept ans.

[V]

Comment ledit marquis dist a sa femme Griseldis qui'il failloit qu'il preist
autre femme qu'elle, et comment il la renvoia chiez son pere toute nue,
excepté tant seulement une povre chemise, et comment Janicole, son pere, lui
295 vint au devant, qui lui bailla ses povres vestemens qu'il avoit gardé.

Et ce temps pendant le marquis, vueillant sa femme plus que devant essaier

came to her and said: "Griselda, I do not wish to hide anything from you, and I want you to know that I have greatly enjoyed having you as a wife for the goodness and virtue that I know to be in you, and not for your lineage, as you [300] must know; but I recognize now that in all great fortune and lordship there is great servitude, for what is permitted and possible for a poor man is not permitted to me. My people constrain me – with the pope's consent – to take another wife, who is already en route and will be here soon. Therefore, take heart and be strong; make way for another, and take the dowry that you brought with you [305] and return with it to your father's home. Such is the way things are: no one can be sure of his lot."

To this she said: "I have always known and held that between your magnificence and my humbleness and poverty there was no comparison, nor did I ever even think of myself as your wife, for I did not consider myself worthy to be your chambermaid. [310] And I call on God, who knows all, as my witness: in this place, your home, where you made me a lady, in my heart I always considered myself as your chambermaid and servant. For this time, then, when without merit I was more honored than I certainly deserved, I give thanks to God and to you. As to the rest, I am ready and [315] willing to return to my father's where I was raised in my childhood; and to be there in my old age and to die there pleases me, the blessed and honorable widow of such a great lord as you. And willingly will I give way to your new wife: I wish with all my heart that she be your happiness and fortune. And from here where I have been and lived in great pleasure, since it pleases you, [320] I will leave willingly. As to your command that I take back with me my dowry, what it was I recall. Nor have I forgotten how, when long ago you wished to take me as a wife, on the threshold of my father's home, I was stripped of the poor clothes that I wore and was clothed in your great precious ones; no other dowry at all did I bring to you than faith and loyalty. [325] Therefore, look, since it pleases you, I take this off, your dress, and return the ring with which you wedded me. The other rings, clothes, crowns, and ornaments that fortune has lent me for a space of time with you – and, in making and reconciling her debts, removes them from me and takes them back – are in your coffers. I came naked from my father's house, and I will return

---

297 **vint** vient PN2 BB PN4 PA. **celer** *add* a mon pouvoir BB. 298 **grant** moult grant PA. **biens** grans biens PA. 298–9 **biens et vertus** bonnes meurs BPL. 299 **estre** et veoie PN7. 300 **grande fortune** fortune grandeur BB. 301 **est grant** nest que PN7. **il . . . me loise** je nose mie faire PA. 301–2 **loise ce . . . homme** loist pas faire ce que ung povre homme feroit en tel cas PN7. 305 **des choses** *add* de ce monde BPL PA. 307–20 **A . . . partiray** Ladicte griseldis fut aussi paciente que davant et luy respondit quil fist tout a son plaisir et vouloir PN1. 307 **elle** *add* monseigneur PN2 PN7 BB PN4 BPL PA. **tenu** veu PN4. 312–13 **De ce . . . j'en** Et depuis en moy honnorant ay plus eu de merites et de biens qua moy nappartenoit dont je PA. 312 **sans** sus PN2 BPL; sur PN7 BB. 313 **ne vail** nay PN2; ne vueil BB PN4 BPL. 314 **graces** *add* et mercy PN7. **prompt** propre PN2. 315–17 **d'y . . . vesve de** la demourer en ma veillesce me plaist moult bien et suis bien eureuse et honnorable destre vesve dun PA. 317 **voulentiers** tres voulentiers BPL. 319–20 **Et . . . partiray** et men partiray BB; *om* PA. 320 **A . . . toutesfoiz** Mais quant ad ce que PA. 320–34 **A quoy . . . femme** Alors ledit marquis la fist devestir de tous les habillements quelle avoit et lui dist quelle sen restournast chez son pere ou point quil lavoit prinse Et apres plusieurs parolles et requestes par elle faiz envers ledit marquis luy pria que pour elle mucer et couvrir sa char quil luy laissast une des chemises quelle vestoit quant on lappelloit sa femme et en honneur du pucelage que ledit marquis avoit eu delle PN1. 320 **commande** demandes BPL. 321–2 **quel . . . quant** tel quil est. Tu scez bien comment je vins en ta compaignie quant PA. 321 **je le . . . oublié** certes il me souvient bien PN7. **je le voy ne** *om* BPL. 322 **seul de** *add* luis a lostel a PN7. 323 **robes** robelaletes BPL. 324 **autre douaire** *om* PN7. 325 **Veez cy** *om* PN7. **puis . . . plaist** *om* BPL. 328 **tes** *add* coffres et PN4.

et tenter, vint a elle et lui dist: "Griseldis, je ne te veul riens celer, et vueil que
tu saches que j'avoye grant plaisir de toy avoir a femme pour les biens et
vertus que je savoye estre en toy, et non pas pour ton lignaige, comme tu le
300   dois savoir; mais je congnois maintenant que toute grande fortune et
seigneurie est grant servitute, car il ne me loise ce qu'il loise et puet faire un
povre homme. Mes gens me contraingnent, et le pape consent, que je preigne
une autre femme, qui est ja en voie et sera tantost cy. Aies doncques bon
couraige et fort; fay lieu a l'autre, et pren le douaire que tu apportas avecques
305   moy et t'en retourne en la maison de ton pere. Ainsi est des choses: nul n'est
seur en son estat."

     A ce dist elle: "J'ai tousjours sceu et tenu que entre ta grant magnificence et
mon humilité et povreté n'avoit nulle comparoison, ne moy oncques je ne dis
mie seulement d'estre ta femme, mais d'estre ta chamberiere ne me reputay
310   digne. Et j'en appelle Dieu en tesmoing, qui scet tout, en ceste tienne maison
ou (fol. 140v) tu m'as fait dame, ay tousjours en cuer et me suy tenue pour ta
chamberiere et servente. De ce temps, doncques, que sans mes merites et trop
plus que je ne vail certainement moy honnourant j'ay esté avec toy, j'en rens
graces a Dieu et a toy. Quant au remenant, je suy preste de bon et prompt
315   courage de retourner chiez mon pere, ou j'ay esté nourrie en m'enfance; et d'y
estre en ma villesce, et la morir bien me plaist, bieneureuse et honnourable
vesve de si grant seigneur comme tu es. Et voulentiers feray lieu a ta nouvelle
femme, laquelle soit en ton boneur et aventure, comme de tout mon cuer le
desire. Et de cy, ou j'estoie et demouroie en grant plaisir, puis qu'il te plaist,
320   voulentiers me partiray. A quoy, toutesfoiz, me commande tu que je reporte
avec moy mon douaire, quel il l'est je le voy, ne je n'ay pas oublié comment,
quant pieça tu me voulz prendre a femme, je fus desvestue sur le seul de mon
pere des povres robes que j'avoye vestues, et fus vestue des tiennes grandes
precieuses, ne en tout n'aportay avec toy autre douaire que foy et loyauté.
325   Veez cy, doncques, puis qu'il te plaist, je te desvests ceste tienne robe et rens
l'aneau de quoy tu m'espousas. Les autres aneaux, vestures, couronnes, et
autres ornemens, que fortune m'avoit presté une espasse de temps avec toy et,
en faisant et paiant son deu, les me toust et reprent, sont en tes escrins. Nue

there naked unless you consider and hold it for a base and [330] ungracious thing, as I believe you would, that this womb here that carried the children you engendered be seen naked or uncovered by the people. For which reason, if it pleases you and not otherwise, I beg you: in recompense for the virginity that I brought to you, which I do not take back, permit me one of the shifts that I had when I was called your wife."

Then the marquis wept so hard from pity that he could hardly contain himself; and so turning away his face and in a very troubled voice, he was barely able to say, "Then stay in that which you are wearing." And so she departed without crying; and before everyone she undressed; and only kept the shift that she was wearing, and with her head completely uncovered and shoeless, she goes off. And in this [340] state several follow her, weeping and slandering fortune, and she alone neither wept nor said a word. And thus she returned to the house of her father. And this good man, her father, who from the start had suspected the marriage and never felt sure about it, but rather was always uncertain about what would happen in the future, came to meet the people on horseback at his door, and with the poor dress that [345] all the while he had kept for her, covered her with great difficulty, for the woman had grown up and filled out, and the poor dress had become stiff and ragged. And she lived for a number of days with her father in wondrously great humility and patience, such that no sign of sadness or of regret over the prosperity that she had had did she make or show in any way. And this was not [350] surprising, for in her great wealth in spirit she had always lived and borne herself humbly.

Now the Count of Panango was coming from Bologna and quickly approaching, and the news of the new nuptials continued to spread throughout the land; then this count sent word to the marquis to say the day he would be there. And a little before he [355] came, the marquis sent for Griselda, who came quite willingly to obey his commands, and he said to her: "Griselda, I greatly desire that this maiden, who should be here tomorrow to be my wife, those who will come with her, and also all those who will be at dinner be received properly and perfectly and that each be regaled and attended to according to his worth and rank. [360] Yet I have no one here who knows how to do this properly; for this reason, then, although you are

329 **ne repute** repputes PN7. 330 **et malgracieuse** *om* BPL. 332 **je ... et** *om* BPL. **pour** que par BPL. 333 **laisse moy** il te plaise a moy laisier PA. 334 **j'estoie ... femme** je estoie ta femme et ton espouse BPL. 335–42 **Lors ... de son pere** Et donc ploura ledit marquis de sa femme forment de pitie quil eut delle et devant tous sen ala en sa chemise seulement et sen retourna en la maison de son pere PN1. 335 **forment** moult forment PA. 336 **parler ... troublé** parlant tout tremblant BPL. **tout** *om* PN7. **dire** *add* mot PN2 PN7. 337 **celle** elle PN7 BPL; Griseldis PA. **sans** *add* oncques PA. 338 **plourer** *add* plus BB. 338–9 **la ... avoit** une de ses chemises de laquelle se couvry au mieulx que elle post BPL. 339 **et deschausse** *om* PN2; et deschavellee PN4. **va** ala PN7. 340 **plusieurs** *add* gens PN2; *om* BPL. **fortune** *add* les bonnes gens de la ville BPL. 341 **mie** point PN2 PN7 BB PN4 BPL PA. **retourna** retourne PN2 BB PN4 BPL PA. 342–51 **Et ... maintenue** Et quant le bon homme vit ainsi sa fille nue il la couvoit de sa robe vieille quil avoit tousjours gardee et par ainsi ladicte marquise demoura par aucuns jours avecques son pere en grande humilite et pacience PN1. 344 **vint** vient PN2 BB BPL PA. **des ... cheval** delle et des gens qui la suyvoient PN7; a la noise des gens BPL. **seul** *add* de son huys PN7. **robette** robelete PN2 PN7 BB PN4 BPL PA. 345 **femme** Griseldis PA. 346 **et embarnie** *om* BB; femme PA. 347 **jours** temps PA. 349 **maniere** *add* semblant PN2. 350–1 **richesses ... maintenue** richesses et honneurs elle avoit touziours vescu en grant humilite PA. 350 **humble** humblement BB; *add* et benigne BPL. 351 **vescu et** este vestue et se PN7. 352–6 **Et ... Griseldis** Et ledit conte de paniquo le jour quil deut arriver le marquis manda Griseldis laquelle vint moult volentiers devers luy en obeissance et lui dist le marquis PN1. 356 **moult voulentiers** *om* BPL. 358–9 **et aussy ... estat** estre honnorablement serviez chacun selon sa personne PN1. 359 **grandement** *add* et honnorablement PA. **ordonné** assiz BPL. 360–2 **Toutesfoiz**

vins de chiez mon pere, et nue la retourneray, se tu ne repute et tien chose vil
330　et malgracieuse, comme je croy que tu feroyes, que ce ventre cy, qui a porté
les enffans que tu as engendrez, soit veu nus ne descouvert au peuple. Pour
laquelle chose, s'il te plaist et non autrement, je te supplie que, ou pris et pour
la virginité que je apportay avec toy, laquelle je n'en reporte mie, laisse moy
une des chemises que j'avoie quant j'estoie appellee ta femme."

335　　Lors ploura forment de pitié le marquis si que a paine contenir se povoit; et
ainsi, en tournant son visaige, en parler tout troublé, a paine peust dire,
"Doncques te demeure celle que tu as vestue." Et ainsi se party celle sans
plourer; et devant chascun se devesti, et seulement retint la chemise que
vestue avoit, et la teste toute descouverte et deschausse s'en va. Et en cest
340　estat la suivent plusieurs, plourans et maudisans fortune, et elle seule ne
(fol. 141r) plouroit mie ne ne disoit mot. Et ainsy s'en retourna en l'ostel de
son pere. Et le bon homs son pere, qui adés avoit eu le mariage suspet ne
oncques n'en avoit esté seur, ains doubtoit tousjours que ainsy n'en avenist,
vint a l'encontre des gens a cheval sur son seul; et de la povre robette, que
345　tousjours lui avoit gardee, la couvry a grant mesaise, car la femme estoit
devenue grande et embarnie et la povre robe enrudiee et empiree. Et demoura
avec son pere par aucuns jours en merveilleusement grant humilité et
pacience, si que nul signe de tristesce, nulz remors de la prosperité qu'elle
avoit eu ne faisoit ne monstroit en aucune maniere; et ce n'estoit pas
350　merveille, comme en ses grans richesses tousjours en pensee humble eust
vescu et fust maintenue.

　　Et ja le conte de Paniquo venoit de Bouloingne et approchoit fort, et des
nouvelles nopces se continuoit et publioit la renommee par tout le pays; sy
envoia ledit conte au marquis dire le jour qu'il seroit a lui. Et un peu devant
355　qu'il venist, le marquis manda Griseldis, qui venist pour obeïr a ses commandemens moult voulentiers, et lui dist: "Griseldis, je desire moult que celle
pucelle, qui doit demain estre cy pour estre ma femme, et ceulx qui vendront
avec elle, et aussy tous ceux qui seront au disner, soient receus bien et
grandement, et que chascun soit festoyé et ordonné selon sa personne et estat.
360　Toutesfoiz, ceans [n'ay] a present qui proprement sceut ce faire; pourquoy,

poorly and badly dressed, take charge of this, you who know my ways and the layout of the house."

"Now," said she, "not only willingly but also with a very happy heart, this and anything else that I feel would please you I will always do. [365] Never will I renounce this or grow tired of it as long as I live." And in so saying, she starts to get busy, as in sweeping up the house, setting the tables, making beds, and putting everything in order, and bidding the other chambermaids each in her own way to do her very best.

It was about nine o'clock in the morning when the count, who was bringing the daughter and [370] son, arrived, and everyone eagerly examined the beauty of the two children and marvelled among themselves. Then there were some who said that the marquis was only being wise to let his first wife go and to take this beautiful young wife, mainly since she was so noble and her brother so beautiful. And so, the preparations for dinner were well underway; and this Griselda went running about everywhere, [375] without being ashamed that she was so poorly dressed, or that she had been cast down from her high marriage in such a way, but with cheerfulness and joy she went to meet the maiden and said, "Welcome, my lady." And in this manner with a joyful expression, sweetly, and benevolently, she greeted the lords, ladies, and damsels who were there to dine, distributing them [380] throughout the palace and putting them in such good order that each of them, and especially the foreigners, wondered at the source of such manners and so much good sense beneath such clothing, and they professed their great astonishment and above all things were not able to look at her enough. Nor could Griselda praise enough her two children: now the maiden, now [385] the son she commended for their beauty and conduct. And the marquis, just as everyone was to sit down to dinner, said to Griselda in a loud voice in front of everyone, as if making fun of her: "Say, Griselda, what do you think of my wife? Isn't she beautiful?"

"Yes, quite," she said, "nor do I believe that you could find one prettier or more noble. You will live in peace and happiness with her – as I pray [390] God that you

---

... **l'ostel** Et pour ce griseldis que tu congnois mes condicions et la maison de ceans et nen sauroie a qui baillir la charge non obstant que tu soies mal habillee Tu en prandras la charge PN1. 360 **n'ay** PN2 BB PN4 BPL PA; na PN3; ny a PN7. **proprement** *om* BPL. **faire** *add* aucune belle ordranance PA. 360–1 **pourquoy ... ce** je vueil combien PA. 361 **pren** que tu preignes le soing et PA. 363 **tant seulement** *om* PN7. 364 **cuer** *add* et joyeux PN1. 364–5 **et ce ... vive** *om* PN1. 364 **quelconque** aultre PN4. **tousjours** tres voulentiers BB; voulentiers PN4. 365 **ne m'ennueray** mais me suyvra PN2; ne men mueray PN7. 366–73 **a ... bel** a laborer et nectoier leaus et ordonner ce quelle povoit et prioit es autres que chacun en droit soy fist le mieulx quil peust PN1. 367 **chamberieres** *om* BPL. **chascune** chascun BPL. 368 **qu'elle pourroit** quil peust BPL. 371 **deux** *add* beaux PN2. 372 **femme** PN7 BB PN4 PA; *om* PN3 PN2 BPL. 372–3 **et ... femme** *om* PN4. 373 **bel** belle que grant merveilles estoit de les veoir PA. 374 **l'appareil** la prest PN2 PN7 BB. **l'appareil ... disner** leure du mengier BPL. 375 **couroit** *add* a mont et a val PA. 375–6 **si ... mariage** si mue et mal vestue PN1. **mal ... ainsy** *om* PN2. 378–85 **qui ... recommandoit** et tres doulcement les salua et les estrangiers fort se esmerveilloient dont si grant sens et honeur venoit de dessoubz si petit estat et habit PN1. 379 **benignement** courtoisement BPL. 379–80 **du ... palays** de tout son povoir BB PA. 380–1 **et especiaument ... estrangiers** *om* BPL. 381 **se merveilloient** PN2 PN4; *om* PN3 BB; disoient PN7; sen merveilloit BPL; sesbaissoient grandement PA. **dont** *add* plusieurs sen esbaissoient dont BPL. **grant sens** *om* BPL. 382 **et s'en ... esbaÿssement** *om* BPL. 382–3 **ne se ... aussy** *om* PN2 PN7 BB PN4 BPL PA. 384 **parler ... louenges** louer BPL. **vierge** pucelle BPL; fille PA. 385 **beauté et** *add* le contenance PN4. **recommandoit** moult mervoilleusement recommandoit PA. **Et le** Et vez cy le BPL. 386 **table** la messe PN1. **en ... voix** *om* BPL. **devant tous** *om* BB PA. **ainsi comme** *om* PN1. 387 **belle** *add* et doulce PN1. 388 **plainement** vrayment PN1; *add* certe PA. 389–90 **Tu vivras ... faces** Si requiers dieu que en bonne pays puisses tu vivre avec elle BPL. 389 **euresement** joie PN1.

doncques, ja soit ce que tu soies mal vestue et povrement, pren la cusançon de cecy, qui congnois mes meurs et les estres de l'ostel."

"Maintenant," dist elle, "non pas voulentiers tant seulement mais de tres lié cuer, et ce et quelconque chose que je sentiroie qui te pleust feray tousjours.
365 Ne ja de ce ne me laisseray ne m'ennueray tant que vive." Et en ce disant, commence a besoingnier, comme de baloier la maison, mettre tables, faire liz, et ordonner tout et prier aux autres chamberieres que chascune en droit soy feist au mieulx qu'elle pourroit.

Il estoit ja environ tierce du jour que le conte, qui avoit amené et la fille et
370 le filz, estoit venuz, et chascun regardoit tres fort et voulentiers la beauté de ses deux enfans, et se merveilloient tous. Et estoient ja aucuns qui disoient que le marquis faisoit que saige de laissier la premiere [femme] et de prendre celle belle jeusne femme, mesmement qu'elle estoit tant noble et son frere tant bel. Et ainsy s'avançoit fort l'appareil du disner; et par tout aloit (fol. 141v) et
375 couroit celle Griseldis, sans avoir honte de ce qu'elle estoit si mal vestue, ne de ce qu'elle estoit ainsy abaissié de son hault mariage, mais de bonne chiere et liee vint a l'encontre de celle pucelle et dist, "Bien soiez venue, ma dame." Et en ceste maniere les seigneurs, dames, et damoiselles qui la devoient disner de liee chiere tres doulcement et benignement elle recevoit et ordonnoit du
380 tout ce palays et mettoit a point tellement que chascun, et especiaument les estrangiers, [se merveilloient] dont telles meurs, tant grant sens soubz tel abit venoient, et s'en donnoient grant esbaÿssement, et sur toutes choses ne se povoient souler de la regarder. Ne aussy ne se povoit souler Griseldis de parler des louenges de ses deux enffans: maintenant de la vierge, maintenant
385 du filz la beauté et maintien recommandoit. Et le marquis, tout ainsy que on devoit aler a table, en haulte voix dist a Griseldis devant tous, ainsi comme en soy jouant: "Dy, Griseldis, que te semble il de ma femme? Est elle belle?"

"Plainement," dist elle, "ouy; ne je ne croy mie que plus belle ne plus gente tu puisses trouver. Tu vivras en paix et euresement avec elle, comme je prie a

do and I have hope that you will – or never with anyone else. One thing, though, I wish to ask and request of you: that you do not goad her as you did the other, for she is younger and was raised more delicately; I believe that she will not be able to bear suffering."

[VI]

How the marquis reclaimed his wife Griselda and restored her to her position [395] with him, and how he showed her her two children whom she believed he had had killed and murdered.

And when the marquis saw the complete good will of this wife, her constancy and great patience, this wife whom so many times and so cruelly he had afflicted and who had thus responded, he said in a loud voice: "This is enough, Griselda. I have fully [400] seen and recognized your good faith and true humility, nor do I believe that there is anyone under the sun who has seen or experienced as much true love and obedience in marriage as I have in you." And in so saying, he took her in his arms very gently, and she was stupefied, just as if she had awakened from a dream. "You are," he said, "my only wife. I have had no other, nor will I ever. This one here, [405] you see, whom you believed to be my wife is your daughter, and the child your son. These children whom you believed to have lost two times, you have now recovered all at once. All who believed the contrary should know that I did what I did only to test and try you, never planning to have my children killed, God forbid; nor since [410] I married you was my intention ever other than to keep you and regard you as my wife." Upon hearing this news, Griselda was dizzy and about to faint, and just as the marquis took her in his arms, she crumpled. Then without delay, the good ladies who were there stripped her of the poor clothes she wore, reclothed her in her good ones, and adorned her splendidly. And then all [415] began to cheer up and be joyful, for the lord wished it and entreated all to do so. There was a greater celebration than there had been at the first wedding. And then for a very long time, the marquis and Griselda lived together in great peace and true love. Then this marquis also brought

390 **le faces** soit PN1; soit il et adviegne PA. 390–1 **et . . . requerir** Mais dune chose te prie PN1. 390 **autre** *add* ne vivras en paix PN4; *add* fame tu ne devroiez avoir bien ne joye PA. 391 **poingnes** compaignes PN4; pugnisses pas PN1. 392 **que . . . as** dont tu mas PA. **l'autre** *om* PA. 393 **souffrir . . . pourroit** et pour ce elle ne le porroit souffrir comme je croy PN1; et croy certainement quelle ne pourroit riens souffrir PA. 394–6 **Comment . . . occirre** *om all other mss.* 397 **regarda** regarde toutes ces choses et ot advise PA. 397–8 **regarda . . . pacience** ot bien veu et apparceu la bonne voullente la constance et la pacience de sa bonne femme BPL. 399 **respondoit** humble tousjours estoit et doulcement respondoit BPL; respondit humblement et doulcement il PA. 400 **bonne** *add* volonte PN4. 401–2 **de mariage** *om* PN1. 402 **en ce . . . disant** ce dit BPL. 402–3 **tres doulcement** PN2 PN7 BB PN4 BPL PA; *om* PN3; tres debonairement PN1. 403 **et elle . . . songe** *om* BLP. 404 **femme** *add* et nulle PN1; *add* en verite et PA. **ceste** *add* pucelle PA. 405 **femme** *add* en verite elle PA. 406–7 **tu les . . . tout** *om* PN1. 406 **recouvré** retrouve PN4 BPL. 407 **ensemble** *add* Et les a nourriz ma suer et introduis abier et a tout honneur faire comme tu le pues appercevoir BB. 407–8 **ce . . . fait** *om* BB. 408 **et non . . . voulu** et neuz oncques entencion ne voulente de PA. 409 **ne fu** *add* heure BPL PN1. 410 **t'espousay** PN2 PN7 BB PN4 BPL PN1 PA; tespousa PN3. **femme** *add* et vraye espouse BPL. 411 **nouvelles** *add* elle cheyt PN1; bonne nouvelles PA. **pasmee** pensive PN2. 412 **dames** femmes et les bonnes dames BB. 413 **estoient la** *add* prindrent gracieusement et PN7. **estoient** *add* lamenerent en sa chambre et BPL; *add* apres ce quelle fut revenue de paulmoisons PA. 414 **revestirent** *add* tres honnorablement et en grant reverence PN7. **bonnes** *add* robes royaulx BPL. **grandement** *add* et richement PN7; *add* et ce fait fu ramenee au palays et assise a la destre du marquis BPL; *add* de robe riches et honnorables PN1. **chascun** *om* PN7. 415–16 **vouloit . . . chascun** vouloit ainsi et chascun len prioit tres affectueusement PN7. 416 **on plus** greigneur

390 Dieu que ainsy le faces, et ay esperance que ce feras tu, ou jamais avec autre.
Une chose toutefoiz te vueil prier et requerir: que tu ne la poingnes des
aguillons que tu as pointe l'autre, car et plus jeune est et plus delicieusement
nourrie; souffrir, comme je croy, ne le pourroit."

[VI]

Comment le marquis rappella sa femme Griseldis et la remist en son estat
395 avec lui, et comment il lui monstra ses deux enfans qu'elle cudoit qu'il eust
fait morir et occirre.

Et quant le marquis regarda la bonne et entiere voulenté de celle femme, la
constance et grant pacience, que tant de fois et tant durement courroucié avoit,
et qui ainsy respondoit, dist a haulte voix: "C'est assez, Griseldis, j'ay a plain
400 veu et congneu ta bonne foy et vraye humilité, ne je ne croy mie que soubz le
ciel soit aucun qui tant ait veu ne approuvé de vraie amour et obeïssance de
mariage que (fol. 142r) j'ay en toy." Et en ce faisant et disant l'embraissa [tres
doulcement], et elle s'esbahyt tout ainsy que s'elle s'esveillast d'un songe.
"Tu es," dist il, "seule ma femme; autre n'ay eu, ne ja n'auray. Ceste cy, voy
405 tu, que tu cuidoies estre ma femme est ta fille, et l'enfant ton filz. Yceulx
enffans que tu cudoies avoir perdu a deux foiz, tu les as maintenant recouvré
tout ensemble. Saichent tous qui le contraire ont cudié, moy avoir fait ce que
j'ay fait pour toy approuver et essaier tant seulement, et non pas avoir voulu
faire tuer mes enffans, dont Dieu me gart, ne oncques ne fu, puis que
410 [t'espousay], que pour ma femme ne te tenisse et reputasse." Et quant
Griseldis oÿ ces nouvelles, toute pasmee et avenoiee, ainsi que le marquis
l'avoit embrassié, se laissa cheoir. Et lors tantost les bonnes dames qui la
estoient la devestirent de ses povres robes qu'elle avoit vestue, et la
revestirent de ses bonnes et parerent tres grandement. Et adoncques chascun
415 commença a faire bonne chiere et joyeuse, car le seigneur le vouloit et en
prioit chascun. Et fist on plus grant solennité que on n'avoit fait aux nopces

his poor father-in-law to his home and held him in great honor, for he had not attended to him until then in order to test his wife better. [420] And his daughter married very nobly; and his son succeeded him in great and true prosperity as his heir.

This story of the patience of this wife has been told not only so that I might stir the wives of today to imitate this [425] patience and constancy, which to me seems hardly imitable and possible, but also to stir the readers and listeners to imitate and consider for themselves at least the constancy of this wife to the end that what she suffered for her mortal husband they do and perform for God. And as the Apostle St. James says, He tempts no one, but many times tests us and makes us suffer grievous punishment. Not because He does not [430] know our heart and intention before we were born, but so that by clear judgment and proof we recognize and see our own frail humanity. Also this story is written especially for steadfast men, if there are any who for our creator and redeemer Jesus Christ could suffer and patiently endure what, for her mortal husband, this poor little wife endured. Explicit

chiere et plus BPL. **solennité** *add* et plus grant feste et plus joyeuse PN7. 417–20 **Et . . . honneur** et apres disner manda le marquis Jeh Nicole pere de sa femme auquel il navoit oncques fait nul bien pour mieulx esprouver sa femme mais adont le fist seoir a grant honneur et le fist chevalier avec son filz et depuis le tint tousjours en grant honneur et chiere tant quil vesquis en son hostel BPL. 417 **grant . . . long** celle sollempnite PN7. **ensemble** *add* par grant espace de temps PN7. 417–18 **Et . . . amour** bonne et vraye amour et tranquillite PN7; et en parfaite amour PA. 418–22 **ledit . . . heritier** Et fist venir le pere de sa femme avecques luy et maria sa fille Et luy succeda son filz Et vesquit apres luy comme son heritier PN1. 419 **serorge** sire PN2; et tres petit serourge PA. **tenu compte** fait ne compte ne mencion se pou non PN7. **pour** afin de PN7. 421–2 **tres . . . heritier** haultement et grandement et tres honnorablement selon son estat et apres ledit marquis succeda son filz en grant prosperite et puissance au gre du pais et fut son heritier et seigneur de la terre PN7. 423–35 **Ceste . . . femmelette** *om* PN1. 423 **recité** raconte BB; recontee PN4 BPL PA. **pacience** *add* et constance PN7. **femme** *add* grizelidiz PN7. 424 **femmes** autres femmes PN4. 425 **que a** qui a PN2 PN7 BB PN4 BPL PA. **ensuivable** ensuyable BB; estimable BPL; ensuutable PA. 425–6 **mais aussy** *add* pour esmouvoir BPL; mais pour ce que PA. **mais . . . oyans** *om* PN7. 426 **oyans** voians PN4. **a . . . constance** puissent considerer et avoir en memoire la constance PA. **mains** moins PN7 BB BPL. 427–8 **ce . . . Dieu** tout ainsi comme elle souffri les adversitez paciemment pour son mortel mary Nous vueillons aussi paciemment porter et souffrir les adversitez et tribulacions de ce maniere en rendant graces a dieu de tout ce quil nous envoye PA. 427 **rendent** *add* graces PN4. 428 **Dieu** *add* graces BPL. **nul** *add* ne nulle PA. 429 **tres griefment** *om* PN7. **griefment** bien PN4; grandement BPL PA. 430 **congnoisse** *add* et saiche bien PN7; *add* bien BPL PA. **entencion** mencion BPL. 431 **clers et evidens** chers PN4. 431–2 **fragile humanité** fragillite humaine PN2 PN7 BB PN4 BPL PA. 432–5 **aux . . . femmelette** pour donner constance et pacience a toute creature et endurer paciemment toute adversite qui lui puet venir pour lamour de son creatour ainsi comme ceste povre famelette fist pour son mortel mari la quelle pacience nous ottroit le pere le filx et le saint esperit BPL. **se . . . femmelette** quilz seuffrent endurent pour nostre createur et redempteur toutes tribulacions paciemment a lexemple de ceste pouvre femellete qui souffrit et endura pour son mortel mary ce que vous aves oy ci dessus PA. 434 **paciemment** *om* PN7. **mortel** PN2 PN7 BB PN4 BPL PA; *om* PN3. 435 **femmelette** femme PN2. 435 **Explicit** Cy fine grisillidis PN2; Explicit la constance et pacience grizelidis PN7; Explicit de Grisillidis PN4; Explicit Griseledis BPL; Explicit griseldis PN1; *om* BB PA.

premieres. Et depuis grant temps et long furent ensemble en grant paix et bonne amour ledit marquis et Griseldis. Et depuis, ce marquis son povre serorge, duquel n'avoit tenu compte jusques alors pour mieulx faire son
420 experiment de sa femme, fist venir en sa maison, et le tint en grant honneur. Et maria sa fille tres haultement; et succeda en grande et bonne prosperité son filz comme son heritier.

Ceste hystoire est recité de la pacience de celle femme, non pas tant seulement que les femmes qui sont aujourd'uy je esmeuve a ensuir ycelle
425 pacience et constance, que a paine me semble ensuivable et possible, mais aussy les lisans et oyans a ensuiir et considerer au mains la constance d'icelle femme, afin que ce qu'elle souffrist pour son mortel mary, facent et rendent a Dieu. Lequel, comme dist Saint Jaque l'Apostre, ne tempte nul, mais bien appreuve et nous sueffre maintes foiz tres griefment pugnir. Non pas qu'il ne
430 congnoisse nostre couraige et entencion devant que soyons nez, mais pour que par jugemens clers et evidens recongnoissions et veons nostre fragile humanité. Et en especial est ce escript aux constans hommes, se il est aucun qui pour nostre createur et redempteur Jhesu Crist seuffre et endure pacienment ce que pour son mary [mortel] endura ceste (fol. 142v) povre
435 femmelette. Explicit

The Squire's Tale

VINCENT DiMARCO

With the exception of the long Confession of Nature in the *Roman de la Rose*, half a dozen passages of which Chaucer adapts at various points in the *Squire's Tale*, no close literary source of the poem has come to light, and the fragmentary nature of the narrative, as well as the strong likelihood of Chaucer's dependence on oral reports and reminiscences of travelers and merchants, renders the possibility of finding a written source for the story unlikely indeed. Nonetheless, the miscellaneous quality of the tale and its wide range of allusion and reference to particular personages, topics and motifs suggest both the broadly intellectual and specifically literary traditions to which Chaucer was indebted, and which here are illustrated largely through analogues, rather than sources.

Thomas Percy[1] and Richard Hole[2] early noted general similarities of the

---

[1] Thomas Percy in a letter to Thomas Warton, 26 August 1762, as cited by Donald C. Baker, *The Squire's Tale, A Variorum Edition of the Works of Geoffrey Chaucer*, vol. 2, part 12 (Norman, OK, and London, 1990), p. 9; see further William L. Alderson and Arnold C. Henderson, *Chaucer and Augustan Scholarship*, University of California Publications, no. 35 (Berkeley, 1970), p. 223.

[2] Richard Hole, *Remarks on the Arabian Nights' Entertainments; in which the Origin of Sinbad's*

Squire's Tale to the "Tale of the Enchanted Horse" in the *Thousand and One Nights*, and although this vast collection of stories as we know it today was unavailable to Chaucer,[3] some form of this story – one of the oldest in the anthology – doubtless circulated in western Europe in the late thirteenth century, as is made clear by independent redactions of it in two Old French romances, the *Cleomadés* of Adenet le Rois and the *Meliacin* of Girart d'Amiens.[4] The oriental tale itself is known today in three versions that represent medieval forms of the story: the two similar versions designated, respectively, Boulaq (B) and Habicht (H), and a somewhat more independent one, communicated to the orientalist Galland (G) early in the eighteenth century, which likewise appears to preserve much earlier materials.[5] With individual variations, the story can be summarized as follows:

> The king of Persia, father of three daughters and one son (G: one daughter, one son) celebrates a seasonal feast (B: unspecified occasion) at which three sages (G: one sage) appear. The sages bear gifts: a golden peacock that along with its chicks tells the hour of day; a statue of a trumpeter who blows his instrument at the approach of an enemy; and a horse of ebony, or ebony and ivory, that flies (G: the horse is not at first intended as a gift). After the sages demonstrate the automata they ask for the princess in marriage. The king agrees (H), hesitates (G), or merely accepts the first two gifts (B). The royal prince is indignant over the possibility of his sister marrying a hideous sage and wishes to test the horse. He impatiently flies off without receiving the instructions of the sage (G), or is allowed to ascend by the magician who tells him only how to make the horse rise by turning a pin, but not how to control the contrivance once airborne. The prince vanishes; the sage is imprisoned. In time the prince discovers how to control the horse mechanically. He lands on the roof of a palace and finds a beautiful princess asleep guarded by a eunuch. The young people are soon mutually attracted, but when her father, alerted by the eunuch, hastily arrives, the prince convinces the king that he will fight his entire army on horseback for the hand of his daughter; once on the back of the magic steed, he flies home.

Voyages, and Other Oriental Fictions, Is Particularly Considered (London, 1797), pp. 239–42; and see Vincent DiMarco, "Richard Hole and the *Merchant's* and *Squire's Tales*: An Unrecognized Eighteenth-Century (1797) Contribution to Source and Analogue Study," *Chaucer Review* 16 (1981): 171–80.

3   Duncan B. Macdonald, "A Bibliographical and Literary Study of the First Appearance of the *Arabian Nights* in Europe," *Literary Quarterly* 2 (1932): 387–420.

4   Albert Henry, ed., *Les Oeuvres d'Adenet le Roi*, t. 5: *Cleomadés* (Brussels, 1971); and Antoinette Saly, ed., *Girart d'Amiens[,] Meliacin ou le Cheval de Fust* (Aix-en-Provence, 1990).

5   For the Boulaq edition (1835), see Nikita Elisseeff, *Thèmes et motifs des Mille et une Nuits; essai de classification* (Beirut, 1949), p. 66. Boulaq's version of the story serves as the basis of the translation of E. W. Lane, *The Thousand and One Nights, Commonly Called, the Arabian Nights' Entertainments* (London, 1841), 2:517–48. Habicht compiled a new recension of materials from various manuscript sources that had never before existed together; his version of the tale of the Enchanted Horse was furnished by a Tunisian, Mordecai ibn an-Najjar. For the history of Galland's translation of the *Nights* see H. S. V. Jones, "The *Cléomadés*, the *Méliacin*, and the Arabian Tale of the 'Enchanted Horse,'" *Journal of English and Germanic Philology* 6 (1907): 234–6; and Elisseeff, *Thèmes*, pp. 69–76.

After a time, and against the wishes of his father, the prince flies back to his lady, who persuades him to take her away with him. They fly to Persia, where he leaves her in a garden to inform his father of their arrival. But the evil sage, who had been released from prison through the intercession of the prince on his earlier return, discovers both princess and horse while he gathers simples. He poses as a messenger of the prince, persuades her to mount the horse with him, and abducts her. They arrive in *Cachemire* (G), *Roum* i.e., Asia Minor (B), or China (H), where the reigning monarch imprisons the sage, who has tried unsuccessfully to pass off the woman as his wife, and falls in love with her himself. She feigns madness. The prince, meanwhile, searches widely before learning of her whereabouts. He impersonates a doctor specializing in mental afflictions, and arranges for her "cure" by bringing her to the horse. They escape and fly to Persia. His father breaks the horse in pieces and destroys its works. The young lovers marry; the prince is reconciled to his wife's father and succeeds to the throne on the death of his own father.

During the last two decades of the thirteenth century, Adenet le Rois and Girart d'Amiens, working independently – most probably from French *abrégés* of the story as it had passed into Spanish oral tales – produced the long and rather similar romances of *Cleomadés* and *Meliacin*. Both of the immediate sources of these romances incorporated details from more than one of the extant versions of the oriental story. These *abrégés* were similar, but not identical, Girart apparently remaining more faithful to his source than Adenet.[6] Comparing the *Squire's Tale* to the extant versions of the oriental story and the two romances suggests that, with the exception of the flying horse controlled by mechanical pins, Chaucer probably took little beyond the general setting and situation and perhaps occasional hints for possible narrative development. In the *Squire's Tale* Cambyuskan has *two* sons and one daughter; the visitor bears *four* magic gifts (the ring and the sword having no counterparts in the oriental tale or the French romances); the visitor is an emissary, neither a sage nor the actual creator of the gifts; and there is no correspondence of names or places. Moreover, the stranger in Cambyuskan's court is never referred to as ugly, and although the prospect of Canacee's future rescue by her brother Cambalo (*SqT* 667–9) may hint at complications not inconsistent with a forced marriage or abduction, both the oriental tale and the romances employ this motif only as a springboard to the romantic adventures of the brother of the princess. Indeed, the closest narrative similarity seems to lie in the forecast that Algarsyf, Canacee's other brother, will win a wife after great, but unspecified, adventures with the magic horse (*SqT* 663–6). And there is nothing in either the oriental tale or the French romances to correspond to the piteous story told to Canacee by the falcon in Part Two of Chaucer's story.

---

6 See the table of correspondences assembled by Henry, *Cleomadés*, pp. 609–59, and Antoinette Saly, "Les sources du *Meliacin* de Girart d'Amiens," *Travaux de linguistique et de littérature* (Université de Strasbourg) 17.2 (1979): 23–46, which go beyond the earlier study of Paul Aebischer, "Paléozoologie de *l'Equus clavileñus*, Cervant," *Etudes de lettres* (Université de Lausanne), série 2, t. 6 (1962): 93–130.

Adenet, Girart, and their works were certainly known in England, though none of the extant manuscripts of the two romances is found in the British Isles.[7] The *Cleomadés*, apparently the more popular of the two, is explicitly mentioned by Froissart, one of Chaucer's favorite contemporary authors, in his *Espinette Amoureuse*, a poem that also contains an analogue of the magic mirror of the *Squire's Tale*. Chaucer may have known one or both of the romances, but the absence in either of any convincing verbal parallels to the *Squire's Tale* strongly suggests the poet's general familiarity with the story, rather than his close working knowledge of actual texts. Nevertheless, at a number of points the *Squire's Tale* seems closer to the plot of the *Meliacin* than to the *Cleomadés*, both when the two romances depart from the oriental story as we have it, and when the *Meliacin* agrees with the oriental story against the changes introduced by Adenet. Both romances differ from the oriental tale in designating the monarch's birthday as the occasion of the feast, but only in *Meliacin* and the *Squire's Tale* does the monarch himself ordain this commemoration: festivities are planned in the *Cleomadés* by the chief lords of the realm. Moreover, only in the *Meliacin* and the *Squire's Tale* (290–301) is a religious observance mentioned as part of the festivities. Further, the scene in the *Meliacin* and the *Squire's Tale* is laid far from western Europe, with Nubien ruling the court of "Grand Ermenie," but in *Cleomadés* Marcadigas reigns in Spain. The *Meliacin*, again like the *Squire's Tale*, gives the audience no reason to expect the king's feast will be interrupted by the arrival of magic gifts, whereas the *Cleomadés* has an earlier scene in which the evil sage Crompars plans the stratagem to trap the king through a rash boon of gratitude. The visitors in *Cleomadés* are kings, while Clamazart, who brings the magic horse in *Meliacin*, is a nobleman, and the messenger of the "kyng of Arabe and of Inde" is repeatedly referred to as a knight in the *Squire's Tale*. Moreover, both the *Meliacin*, and the Habicht and Galland versions of the oriental tale, agree with the *Squire's Tale* against the *Cleomadés* in presenting a scene in which the power of the magic horse is demonstrated and/or explained in advance. Finally, the opening scene of the *Squire's Tale* is developed as directly as its counterpart in *Meliacin*, both poets moving from a description of the monarch's beautiful daughter to a description of the feast honoring the father, without, as in *Cleomadés*, any lengthy intervening account (lines 320–1852) of the *enfances* of prince Cleomadés. Jones, in Bryan and Dempster (364–74), printed extracts of the *Cleomadés* instead of the then-unedited *Meliacin*. But here I present lines from the *Meliacin* as representative of the form of the story closer to the one Chaucer might have known.

Whatever the form and extent of Chaucer's knowledge of the story of the Enchanted Horse, he re-drafted it for an historical setting and milieu different from those of its original and/or romance re-workings, specifically as a fictionalization of relations between the court of Sarai, the fourteenth-century capital of the Golden Horde or the Mongols of Russia, and the kingdom "of

---

[7] Girart dedicated his *Escanor* to Eleanor of Aquitaine, wife of Henry II; Edward I awarded Adenet a grant in 1297.

Arabe and of Inde," i.e., Middle India (or Lesser India, India Minor), an area extending from southern Arabia all the way to the Indus delta, and as such largely co-terminous in the fourteenth century with the empire of the Mamluks and its sphere of activity. Centered in Cairo, and in full possession of the Holy Land since the fall of Acre in 1291, the Mamluks were eager to extend their influence into Nubia and Ethiopia – identified with India as the kingdom of Prester John – while retaining their considerable holdings down the Arabian coast as far as South Yemen and exerting strong influence over the tribes of the interior Arabian peninsula.[8] In an effort to form an alliance against Hulegu and the Ilkhanids of Persia, who had taken Baghdad and abolished the Caliphate, there had been diplomatic relations in 1261–63 between the Mamluk sultan Baibars and the devout Muslim Khan of the Golden Horde, Berke, with gifts from Cairo delivered to the Mongol court on the Volga, leading to the reported marriage of Berke's daughter to the Mamluk potentate. But the closest historical analogue to the *Squire's Tale* involves relations between the two long-reigning fourteenth-century monarchs Sultan el-Melik en Nasir (ruled 1291–92, 1298–1308, 1309–40), and Uzbek Khan of the Golden Horde (ruled 1313–41), a devout Muslim who nonetheless enjoyed the reputation in the West as practicing tolerance toward Christians.[9] Apparently concerned with what appeared to be Egypt's gestures of rapprochement with Persia, Uzbek dispatched an embassy in 1314 bearing gifts to Nasir; two years later the Mamluk sultan sent rich presents to Uzbek at Sarai with the request that a princess be furnished as bride to the Sultan. On 17 October 1319 Princess Tulunbeg sailed for Egypt, was received there after a lavish lay-over in Constantinople as guest of Andronicus II, and was married in 1320. Later reports indicated that Nasir had divorced her after only a few days and had given her to one of his emirs. The Mongols were naturally offended, but Nasir succeeded in keeping the Golden Horde as allies, while maneuvering at the same time toward a peace treaty with the Ilkhanids, and thus effectively undermining any western European hopes for a Christan-Mongol alliance to regain the Holy Land.

Various names in the *Squire's Tale* have been thought to derive from star charts and hence to furnish the grounds for ingenious astrological allegorizing,[10] but the presence of the Greek name Theodora (*SqT* 664) as future wife of Algarsyf, son of Cambyuskan, suggests Chaucer's knowledge of Mongol/ Muslim-Orthodox Christian alliances through marriage, as for example that of

---

[8] Vincent DiMarco, "The Historical Basis of Chaucer's *Squire's Tale*," *Edebiyât* ns 1, no. 2 (1989): 1–22, enlarging on a suggestion of R. A. Pratt, ed., *The Tales of Canterbury* (Boston, 1966), p. 375, note to *SqT* 110.

[9] There is a series of papal letters (1317, 1321, 1323, 1330, 1338, 1340) to Uzbek and his court at Sarai, thanking the Khan for his benevolent treatment of Christians, urging him to protect Christians from Muslim strictures, and at one point (1340) urging his wife and son to convert to Christianity; see DiMarco, "Historical Basis," p. 10.

[10] See for example J. D. North, *Chaucer's Universe* (Oxford, 1988), pp. 263–88, partially superseding J. D. North, "Kalenderes Enlumyned Ben They: Part II," *Review of English Studies* ns 20 (1969): 257–62. See also Dorothee Metlitzki, *The Matter of Araby in Medieval England* (New Haven and London, 1977), pp. 74–80.

1257 between Prince Gleb of Rostov and the daughter of Mongke Khan, who was re-named at baptism Theodora, or that of 1346, when Theodora, daughter of John VI Cantacuzenus, married the Ottoman Sultan Orkhan. Chaucer's Cambalo (or Cambalus) (*SqT* 31, 656, 667) has been thought to be a reminiscence of Cambalus, Kublai Khan's capital, or of Kambala (properly, Kammala), Kublai's grandson.[11] But Cembalo, modern Balaklava on the Crimean peninsula, was an important trading center which Uzbek ceded to the Venetians. Indeed, it may be more than coincidental that in one respect in which the *Squire's Tale* differs from the oriental story of the Enchanted Horse and both Old French romances, in representing the monarch as father of *two* sons and one daughter, there is an historical correspondence, for Uzbek had two sons and one daughter.[12] That his daughter was a paternal half-sister to Uzbek's sons may even bear on the suggestion of incest in Cambalo's struggle to "wynne" Canacee (*SqT* 669).

The attention paid in modern interpretive criticism of the *Squire's Tale* to supposed narrational confusion and the rhetorical limitations of the story and its teller has obscured, in my opinion, the extent to which Chaucer not only historicizes, with an unusual degree of cultural relativism, the exotic world beyond Christian Europe, but consistently suggests in his treatment of the marvelous and magical a new, largely "rational" and "scientific" spirit that has no recourse to traditional supernatural explanations (divine or demonic) and clearly seeks to inquire beyond the court entertainments of illusionists.[13] Similarly, the tale consistently disparages an uninformed appreciation of magic relying on allusion to classical myth (e.g. the Pegasus, the sword of Thelophus, the Trojan horse) in favor of a more learned audience's knowledge of how such things *really* work. Even if the narrator cannot always claim to possess such knowledge himself (*SqT* 246), he points his audience toward the disciplines where he confidently believes such knowledge resides. Thus we find the magic horse described as a mechanical contrivance controlled by pins, the far-seeing magic mirror presented in the context of perspectivist optics, and the medicinal qualities of the magic sword discussed with reference to the chemical processes of tempering metals. Even the magic ring, which seems least conducive to a scientific or pseudo-scientific explanation, is put forward in the context of recognizable scientific transmutation, to which glass-making and common meteorological phenomena are analogous. Thus, in the relevant sections to follow, I present material representative of the tradition of scientific speculation and experiment regarding such "magical" phenomena, arguing implicitly that the First Part of the *Squire's Tale* owes much to the tradition and genre of

---

[11] By Skeat and Robinson, respectively, in their notes to the tale; see also Carmel Jordan, "Soviet Archeology and the Setting of the *Squire's Tale*," *Chaucer Review* 22 (1987): 128–40.

[12] *The Travels of Ibn Battuta A. D. 1325–1354*, trans. H. A. R. Gibb (London, 1961), 2:502–6.

[13] For Chaucer's possible debt to the tradition of court entertainments, see Merle Fifield, "Chaucer the Theater-goer," *Papers on Language and Literature* 3, Supplement (1967): 67–9.

"Question" or "Problem" literature, including *quodlibeta*, that rationalize marvels and aim to explain phenomena naturally.[14]

The Second Part of the tale (347–670), containing the falcon's piteous complaint of the faithless tercelet, Canacee's ministrations (aided by the magic ring), and the prospect of the birds' future reconciliation through the power of the ring and the intervention of Cambalus, suggests in part Chaucer's re-working of what is probably earlier material, from an unidentified source in his own *Anelida and Arcite*, and perhaps a general indebtedness to Machaut's *Dit de l'alerion*.[15] For the exemplary material illustrating the proverb of "alle thyng, repeirynge to his kynde, / Gladeth hymself" (*SqT* 608–9ff.), Chaucer again turns to material he uses elsewhere, but seems to have directly adapted the ultimate source,[16] Boethius' *Consolation of Philosophy*, rather than to have used Jean de Meun's treatment of the Boethian figures as he does in the *Manciple's Tale* (163ff.). The story of the tercelet's perfidy, the fact that Canacee, obviously affected by the falcon's history, causes a mew to be decorated with images of traditionally faithless birds, and the prospect nonetheless of a happy ending, led Braddy to the identification of another story in the *Thousand and One Nights* as a possible source.[17] In "Princess Dunya and Prince Taj al-Muluk" (*Nights* 133–35) a woman who hates men on the basis of a dream in which a male bird abandons his mate caught in a net (even though the female had earlier saved him from the same predicament) is later convinced by the hero after he commissions paintings showing the male bird killed by the fowler while delivering his mate. This analogue may indeed be relevant, though nowhere in the *Squire's Tale* fragment does Canacee evince any antipathy toward men, and earlier she has been shown to have gone "on the daunce" with the strange visitor to court in an atmosphere of romantic gaiety (*SqT* 277–88). The story of Princess Dunya in the *Thousand and One Nights* forms part of the long "family romance" of King Umar al-Numan, who, like Cambyuskan, has two sons (really paternal half-brothers) and a daughter who at one point unwittingly marries her half-brother; but there appears on the surface no other correlation with the *Squire's Tale* of the incidents that compose this long story-group, either with respect to the main narrative thread or to the various interspersed stories. Metlitzki, however, has argued the relationship of the Umar al-Numan cycle to the Greek narratives connected with Omar of Melitene and the (eleventh-century) Byzantine epic of

---

[14] For this "genre," which includes *problemata*, books of natural questions, commentaries, and *quodlibeta*, see William Eamon, *Science and the Secrets of Nature: Books of Secrets in Medieval and Early Modern Culture* (Princeton University Press, 1994); the valuable commentary in Brian Lawn, *The Prose Salernitan Questions* (London, 1979), an edition of an anonymous Latin collecton dealing with science and medicine (c. 1200); and Bert Hansen, *Nicole Oresme and the Marvels of Nature* (Toronto, 1985), an edition and translation of Oresme's *De causis mirabilium*.

[15] For which correspondences see Baker, *Squire's Tale*, pp. 21–3 and notes to the tale.

[16] Baker, *Squire's Tale*, pp. 230–31, and that same author's *The Manciple's Tale, A Variorum Edition of the Works of Geoffrey Chaucer*, vol. 2 (Norman, OK, and London, 1984), pp. 103–5.

[17] Haldeen Braddy, "The Oriental Origin of Chaucer's Canacee-Falcon Episode," *Review of English Studies* 31 (1936): 11–19; and Braddy, "The Genre of Chaucer's *Squire's Tale*," *Journal of English and Germanic Philology* 41 (1942): 279–90.

Digenes Akrites, a "family romance" likewise comprised of the adventures of a warrior father, mother, two chief sons and a daughter, in which, among many episodes, the hero, Digenes, fights for his love against two brothers (cf. *SqT* 668–9) and brings her home on an extraordinary, albeit living horse, which may represent a rationalization of a magic flying horse.[18] But if Chaucer had in mind a story like that of Princess Dunya, it might have come to him in a form more closely resembling the analogue in the (tenth-century) *Katha Sarit Sagara (Ocean of Story)* of Somadeva.[19] In this tale, the wooing of the lady is accomplished through paintings of a faithful male swan that overcome the princess' memories of male deceit in her former life as a swan; and the wooing serves as a frame within which *other* episodes and adventures are inserted into the narrative, similar to the way such events are suggested at the end of Part Two of the *Squire's Tale*. Moreover, in the *Katha Sarit Sagara* the hero is able to find the princess, and eventually escape with her, by means of a flying mechanical contrivance.

Finally, in speculating on how the falcon would come to find her mate again, Friend pointed to an eastern tale, attested to in various medieval Persian and Hebrew texts, and Alexander Nequam's *De naturis rerum* (c. 1197–1204), in which a bird feigns death to escape its cage and rejoin its mate.[20] Those versions of English provenance are reprinted below, to complete what little can be brought forward regarding the Second Part of the *Squire's Tale*.

Meliacin

(From Girart d'Amiens, *Meliacin ou le Cheval de Fust*, ed. Antoinette Saly [Aix-en-Provence, 1990], lines 115–75, 570–628, pp. 5–7; 20–2; my translation.)

Uns jours fu de sollempnité	115
Que cis rois ot a grant plenté	
Chevaliers et dames ensamble,	
Car coutume estoit, ce me samble,	
Que chascuns rois en ramenbrance	
Avoit le jour de sa naissance	120
Comme de sa nativité,	
Et metoit en auctorité	
Cel jour plus que nule autre feste:	

[18] Metlitzki, *Matter of Araby*, pp. 144–53.

[19] *The Ocean of Story being C. H. Tawney's Translation of Somadeva's Katha Sarit Sagara (or Ocean of Streams of Story)*, ed. N. M. Penzer (London, 1925), 3:281–300. In the Persian *Thousand and One Days*, the frame is likewise supplied by the princess' reluctance to love, based on a similar animal dream, as Braddy, "Genre," p. 89, noted. Here the nurse of the princess tells her many stories in an effort to change her mind; the last tale in the collection, "The Story of the Princess of Cashmire," persuades her through the device of the paintings. See *The Thousand and One Days: Persian Tales*, trans. Justin Huntly McCarthy (London, 1892), 1:1–7; 2:252–88.

[20] Albert C. Friend, "The Tale of the Captive Bird and the Traveler: Nequam, Berechiah, and Chaucer's *Squire's Tale*," *Medievalia et Humanistica* ns 1 (1970): 57–65.

Et portoit couroune en sa teste
Et tenoit feste merveilleuse   125
Et court riche et mout plentüeuse.
. . .
Li qeu ne firent lonc sejour
De faire le mengier haster;
Cil se coururent aprester
Qui servoient d'autres offices.   165
Aprés ce que li sacrefices
Fu fais de cele gent paiene,
Chascuns cele partie assene
Ou il se devoit atourner
Puis reprisent a retourner;   170
Vers le roi qui les atendoit,
Qui a riens nee n'entendoit
Qu'a faire a chascun son plaisir,
Si que chascuns avoit desir
De faire tous tans son service.   175
. . .
"Sire, j'en sui tous aprestés,   570
Dist li maistre, de l'esprouver.
Se vous volés de ci lever,
Le pooir vous en mousterrai,
Kar devant tous l'essaierai,
Puis si verrés ce que sera."   575
Li rois dist volentiers ira
Veoir se c'est voirs que il dit.
Nus des autres n'i mist desdit.
Et cil les degrés jus avale;
Tout s'en issent hors de la sale   580
Pour regarder ce que seroit
Et que cis maistres mousterroit.
Li philosophez devala
Jus des degrés, et tant ala
Qu'a son cheval vint tot suant;   585
De monter s'ala essaiant,
Et tant fist et tant se coita
Qu'a grandes paines i monta.
Adont fist ce dont il ert duis,
Kar el cheval ert ses deduis,   590
Et pour ce miex s'i atorna.
Une cheville adont tourna
Ki el col du cheval ert mise,
Et li chevaus ot plus tost prise
Sa voie qu'oisiaus ne volast.   595
Si croi que riens si tost n'alast
Comme li chevaus s'en aloit
Partout ou ses maistres voloit,
Une eure tost, puis belement,

Com cil qui par enchantement   600
Estoit et ouvrés bastis;
Kar cil n'estoit mie aprentis
Ki fait l'ot si soutivement.
Mais or vous voeil dire comment
Ceste nigremance ert si gente: 605
Li philosophes, qui s'entente
Metoit mout es chosez soutilles,
I ot mises .IIII. chevilles
Que par nigremance avoit faites
Et si soutivement entraites   610
Que, se ne fust par aventure,
Nus hom n'i conneüst jointure.
El col fu mise la premiere
Et l'autre, en la crupe, derriere;
L'autre cheville, el flanc senestre,   615
Et la quarte refu el destre.
Tout ainsi furent atachiez
El cheval de fust et fichiez,
Ne nus, pour art ne pour savoir,
Ne peüst le cheval mouvoir   620
Tant c'un pas le peüst mener,
S'avant ne seüst assener
As chevilles et metre a droit.
Mais tant furent en mal endroit
Et a trouver et a cerchier   625
Qu'a paine i peüst adrecier
Nus hom s'aucuns ne li desist,
Se Fortune ne le fesist.

[There was one day of solemnity   115
when this king assembled
knights and ladies in great number;
for it was the custom, it seems to me,
that each king held the day
of his birth in remembrance   120
as of his nativity,
and he imputed more authority to that day
than to any other feast,
and he bore the crown on his head,
and made a marvelous feast   125
and richly held a great court.
. . .
The cooks did not long delay
to cause the meal to be expedited;
those who were serving in other offices   165
rushed to make ready.
After the sacrifice
was made by that pagan people,

each was directed towards that place
where he was expected to go.
Afterwards they began to return   170
to the king who was awaiting them,
and who aimed at nothing else
than to give pleasure to each one,
so that each desired
to do his service continually.

. . .
". . . Sire, I am all ready,"   570
said the master, "to prove it.
If you wish to rise from here
I will show you the power for that,
for I will try it before you;
then you will see what will be."
The king said he would go willingly
to see if what he said was true.
None of the others contradicted,
and the king descended the steps.
All issue forth from the hall   580
in order to see what would happen
and what the master would show.
The philosopher went down the steps
so that he came
perspiring to his horse.
He went about trying,
worked so hard, throwing his legs over the beast,
so that with great difficulty he mounted.
Then he did that which he had arranged,
for he took delight in the horse,   590
and for that reason the better he prepared.
He turned a pin
which was placed in the neck of the horse
and the horse took up its way
faster than a bird flies,
so that I think nothing goes as fast
as that horse was going,
everywhere its master wished
for an hour
like that which was made
and constructed through enchantment.   600
For he was not at all an apprentice
who had made it so subtly.
But now I wish to tell you how
this very noble magic was done.
The philosopher, who put his pleasure in ingenious things,
had placed there four pins
which were made through necromancy,
and so subtly designed

that, if it was not by chance,
no one might ever learn the construction.
The first was placed in the neck;
and the second, behind, in the croup;
and the third pin was in the left flank; 615
and the fourth was in the right.
They were attached and fixed in the horse of wood,
so that no one, through art or knowledge, could move the horse
so as to lead it as much as a foot,
if beforehand he did not know how to control
and place the pins correctly.
But they were in such awkward places
to find or to seek out
that a man could scarcely locate them
if he were not helped,
unless Fortune brought it about.]

CANACEE AND THE FALCON

(From *Boethius[,] The Theological Tractates[,] De Consolatio Philosophiae*, ed. H. F. Stewart, E. K. Rand, and S. J. Tester, Loeb [Cambridge, MA, and London, 1978], 3.m2.21–6, p. 238; trans. Chaucer, *Boece* 3.m2.21–31.)

Ludens hominum cura ministret,
Si tamen arto saliens texto
Nemorum gratas viderit umbras,
Sparsas pedibus proterit escas,
Silvas tantum maesta requirit,
Silvas dulci voce susurrat.

[And the janglynge brid that syngeth on the heghe braunches (that is to seyn, in the wode), and after is enclosed in a streyte cage, althoughe that the pleyinge bysynes of men yeveth (hym) honyed drynkes and large metes with swete studye, yit natheles yif thilke bryd skippynge out of hir streyte cage seith the agreables schadwes of the wodes, sche defouleth with hir feet hir metes ischad, and seketh mornynge oonly the wode, and twytereth desyrynge the wode with hir swete voys.]

In *SqT* 409, the image of the tree "for drye as whit as chalk" from which the falcon cries, may have been suggested by the *Roman de la Rose* (ed. Félix Lecoy, *Le Roman de la Rose*. CFMA [Paris, 1965–70], lines 5917–47, 1:182–3; trans. Charles Dahlberg, *The Romance of the Rose* [Hanover, NH and London, 1983], p. 119).[21]

---

[21] The passage follows closely upon *RR* 5914: "a l'espee de sa froidure" (with the sword of [the north wind's] cold); cf. *SqT* 57, "Agayn the swerd of wynter, keene and coold."

La roche porte un bois doutable,
don li arbre sunt merveillable:
l'une est brahaigne et riens ne porte,
l'autre en fruit porter se deporte,   5920
l'autre de foillir ne refine,
l'autre est de foilles orfeline;
et quant l'une en sa verdor dure,
les pluseurs i sunt sanz verdure;
et quant se prent l'une a florir   5925
au pluseurs vont les fleurs morir.

. . .

Li roussigneus a tart i chante;
mes mout i bret, mout s'i demante
li chahuans o sa grant hure,   5945
prophetes de malaventure,
hideus messagier de douleur.

[There is a strange wood on the rock; the trees in it are wondrous. One is
sterile and bears nothing; another delights in bearing fruit. One never stops
producing leaves; another is bare of foliage. . . . There the nightingale rarely
sings, but the screech-owl with his great beard, the prophet of misfortune and
hideous messenger of sorrow, cries out and raves.]

The Tale of the Captive Bird and the Traveler (from Alexander Nequam, *De
Naturis rerum* (c. 1197–1204), ed. Thomas Wright, *Chronicles and Memorials
of Great Britain* (London, 1863), pp. 87–9; quoted by Albert C. Friend, "The
Tale of the Captive Bird and the Traveler: Nequam, Berechiah, and Chaucer's
Squire's Tale," *Medievalia et Humanistica* ns 1 (1970), p. 63n, and translated,
pp. 58–9.

Erat igitur in Britannia Majore miles psittacum habens magnae generositatis,
quem tenerrime diligebat. Peregre autem proficiscens miles, circa montes
Gelboe psittacum vidit, et sui quem domi habebat recordatus inquit, "Psittacus
noster cavea inclusus te salutat, tibi consimilis." Quam salutationem audiens
avis, morienti similis corruit. Indoluit miles, fraude deceptus aviculae, et
itinere peregrinationis completo domum revertens, visa retulit. Militis vero
psittacus diligenter relationi domini sui aurem adhibuit, et dolorem simulans e
pertica cui insidebat morienti similis cecidit. Miratur tota domus familia,
super casu repentino ingemiscens. Jubet dominus autem sub divo reponi, ut
salubri aura frueretur, quae temporis nanciscens opportunitatem evolat
[evolavit] perniciter haud reversura. Ingemuit dominus, et se delusam esse
tota domus conqueritur. Reducunt ad memoriam multiplex solatium quid eis
psittacus conferre consueverat, et avi montanae tantae fraudis repertrici
saepius imprecantur.

[There was a knight in Great Britain who had a parrot to whom he was greatly
attached. And once during a journey . . . in the vicinity of the mountains of
Gelboa, he came upon a parrot which reminded him of the bird he had left at

home, and he said, "We have a bird like you at home in a cage who sends you greetings." Upon hearing this the bird dropped down as if dead. The knight was saddened, for he was deceived by the bird's deathlike appearance. When he reached home, he told to the household what he had seen, and the caged parrot listened intently to every word. Not long thereafter the grieving parrot dropped from its perch as if dead. The entire household mourned its apparent illness, and the knight directed that the parrot be taken from its cage and placed in the open air. Once freed, the bird took wing and flew away leaving behind the members of the household, at first saddened by their loss and then angered by the ruse of the distant mountain bird.][22]

In concluding this section I note from two unpublished doctoral dissertations a number of lines from Dante's *Divina Commedia* that bear some resemblance to lines describing the falcon and her situation.[23]

THE MAGIC STEED OF BRASS

The magic steed is said to be capable of transporting its rider wherever he desires in the space of twenty-four hours. Constructed under the proper astrological conditions, it is controlled both by the turning of various pins and by verbal directions (*SqT* 115–31; 314–34). While some onlookers seek to explain its magic with reference to legend and myth (*SqT* 204–11) and others seek to rationalize it as an illusion (*SqT* 217–19), the possibility is raised of a more subtle explanation (*SqT* 183–8).

There are several Eastern analogues to the mechanical flying horse. In an Indian story, for example, a prince mounts a magic horse of wood and brass, learns to control its motion through verbal commands and manipulation of a silver stud between the ears, finds a beautiful princess and flies away with her.[24]

---

[22] Friend, "Tale of the Captive Bird," pp. 59–62 includes a translation by Moses Hadas of a similar, late twelfth-century (?) fable, "Starling and Princess" of Rabbi Berechiah ben Natroni Krespia haNakdan (*Mishle Shualim* [*Hebrew Fox Fables*]).

[23] *Inf.* 5.116–19, cf. *SqT* 414–17; *Inf.* 5.100–2, cf. *SqT* 504–20; *Inf.* 5.103–5, cf. *SqT* 5229–31; *Inf.* 5.140–2, cf. *SqT* 56, 582, 630–1; cited by Edwin Lee Conner, "The *Squire's Tale* and Its Teller: Medieval Tradition and Chaucer's Artistry of Allusion," Diss. Vanderbilt University, 1985, p. 301. *Purg.* 33.130–4, cf. *SqT* 567–71; cited by J. P. Bethel, "The Influence of Dante on Chaucer's Thought and Expression," Diss. Harvard University; see Howard H. Schless, *Chaucer and Dante: A Revaluation* (Norman, OK, 1984), p. 203.

[24] Mark Thornhill, *Indian Fairy Tales* (London, 1889), pp. 108–45. For other Eastern analogues see Berthold Laufer, *The Prehistory of Aviation* Field Museum of Natural History, Anthropological Series 18, no. 1 (Chicago, 1928), pp. 47–8 (*Twenty-five Tales of a Vetala*); p. 50 (Bana's *Harshacharita*); pp. 55–6 (*Thirty-two Tales of the Lion-throne* or *Tales of King Vikramaditya*); and pp. 62–3 (*Panchatranta* 1.5).

Epistola de secretis operibus artis et naturae

(From *Fr. Rogeri Bacon*, ed. J. S. Brewer, Rolls Series 360 [London, 1859], p. 533; translated by T. M., *Friar Bacon his Discovery of the Miracles of Art, Nature, and Magic* [London, 1618], pp. 17–18.)

Item possunt fieri instrumenta volandi, ut homo sedeat in medio instrumenti revolvens aliquod ingenium, per quod alae artificialiter compositae aërem verberent, ad modum avis volantis. . . . Haec autem facta sunt antiquitus, et nostris temporibus facta sunt, ut certum est; nisi sit instrumentum volandi, quod non vidi, nec hominem qui vidisset cognovi; sed sapientem qui hoc artificium excogitavit explere cognosco. Et infinita quasi talia fieri possunt. . . .

[It's possible to make Engines for flying, a man sitting in the midst whereof, by turning onely about an Instrument, which moves artificial Wings to beat the Aire, much after the fashion of a Birds flight. . . . Such Engines as these were of old, and are made even in our dayes. These all of them (excepting only that instrument of flying, which I never saw or know any, who hath seen it, though I am exceedingly acquainted with a very prudent man, who hath invented the whole Artifice) with infinite such like inventions, Engines and devices are feasable.][25]

Nicole Oresme, Le livre du ciel et du monde (completed 1377)

(From *Nicole Oresme. Le Livre du ciel et du monde*, ed. Albert D. Menut and Alexander J. Denomy; trans. Albert D. Menut [Madison, WI, 1968], pp. 400–5.)

. . . un vaissel de matiere pesante et ouquel fust matiere pesante, si comme un honme ou pluseurs, estoit sus la superfice convexe de l'element de l'aer laquelle est presque sperique comme dit est et sanz perturbacion, tel vaissel pourroit lasus reposer aussi naturelment come une nef repose en Seine. . . . tel vessel reposeroit lasus aussi naturelment comme une nef repose en une eaue et samble que ce soit sanz violence. Et appert par ce que se elle estoit perpetuele, elle y reposeroit perpetuelment.

[. . . a vessel of heavy material loaded with heavy objects such as a man or several men, standing upon the nearly spherical convex surface of the element of the air, and with no perturbation, could remain up there as naturally as a ship rests on the Seine. . . . a vessel would remain up there just as naturally as a boat floating at rest in the water and probably without requiring any

---

[25] In *Communia mathematica fratris Rogeri*, Bacon declares that instruments of flying or driving at incomparable speed in chariots or on animals ("instrumenta volandi et deferendi in curribus sive in animalibus in incomparabili velocitate") have in fact been created; see *Opera hactenus inedita Rogeri Bacon*, ed. Robert Steele (Oxford, 1940), fasc. 16, pp. 43–4. John Wilkins, *Mathematicall Magick* (London, 1648), p. 199, discusses the mechanics of flying chariots.

violence. It seems that, if the receptacle were perpetual, it would remain there eternally.]

The flight of Eilmer of Malmsbury, c. 1010, as recounted by William of Malmsbury, *De gestis regum Anglorum* (from *Willelmi Malmesbiriensis monachi De gestis regum Anglorum libri quinque*, ed. William Stubbs, Rolls Series 90 [London, 1887], 1:276–7; trans. Lynne White, Jr., "Eilmer of Malmesbury, an Eleventh Century Aviator," *Technology and Culture* 2 [1961]: 97–111.)

> Is erat litteris, quantum ad id temporis, bene imbutus, aevo maturus, immanem audaciam prima juventute conatus: nam pennas manibus et pedibus haud scio qua innexuerat arte, ut Daedali more volaret, fabulam pro vero amplexus, collectaque e summo turris aura, spatio stadii et plus volavit; sed venti et turbinis violentia, simul et temerarii facti conscientia, tremulus cecidit, perpetuo post haec debilis, et crura effractus. Ipse ferebat causam ruinae quod caudam in posteriori parte oblitus fuerit.

> [He was a man learned for those times, of ripe old age, and in his youth had hazarded a deed of remarkable boldness. He had by some means, I scarcely know what, fastened wings to his hands and feet so that, mistaking fable for truth, he might fly like Daedalus, and, collecting the breeze on the summit of a tower, he flew for more than the distance of a furlong. But, agitated by the violence of the wind and the swirling of air, as well as by the awareness of his rashness, he fell, broke his legs, and was lame ever after. He himself used to say that the cause of his failure was his forgetting to put a tail on the back part.][26]

The two following illustrations of non-mechanical flying animals are note-worthy analogues:

Froissart's *Chronicles*

(Quoted by Haldeen Braddy, "Cambyuskan's Flying Horse and Charles VI's 'Cerf Volant,'" *Modern Language Review* 33 [1938]: 41–4; trans. Sir John Bourchier, Lord Berners, 1523–25 [London, 1901], 3:338–9.)

The king dreams that a falcon given him by the Earl of Flandres has flown from his control, and that he is unable to retrieve it:

> ... et à elles, apparoit à iaulx en issant hors de ce fort bois et venoit en celle lande, et s'enclinoit devant le roi; et li rois dissoit au connestable, qui regardoit ce cerf à mervelles et en avoit grant joie: "Connestables, demorés

---

[26] Cf. the flight of Bladud, the legendary father of Lear, as recounted by Geoffrey of Monmouth, in *The Historia Regum Britanniae of Geoffrey of Monmouth with Contributions to the Study of Its Place in Early British History*, ed. Acton Griscom and R. E. Jones (New York, 1929), pp. 261–2.

ichi; je monterai sus che cerf qui se represente à moi, et sieurai mon faucon."
Li connestables li acordoit. Là montoit li jones rois de grant volenté sus che
cerf volant, et s'en aloit à l'aventure après son faucon; et chils chers, comme
bien dotrinés et avissés de faire le plaisir dou roi, le portoit par desus les grans
bois et les haulx arbres. Et veoit que ses faucons abatoit oisiaux à si grant
plenté que il en estoit tous esmervilliés comment il pooit ce faire, et sambloit
au roi que, quant cils faucons ot asés volet et abatu de hairons et de oisiaux
tant que bien devoit souffire, li rois reclama son faucon; et tantos cils faucons,
comme bien duis, s'en vint assir sus le poing dou roi. Et estoit vis au roi que il
reprendoit le faucon par les longnes et le metoit à son devoir, et cils cers
ravaloit par desus ces bois et raportoit le roi en la propre lande là où il l'avoit
encargié et où li connestables de France le atendoit, qui avoit grant joie de sa
venue. Et, sitos comme li rois fu là venus et descendus, li cers s'en raloit et
rentroit au bois, et ne le veoient plus.

[And at this poynt, the kynge thought that there apered sodenly before hym a
great hart with wynges, and enclyned himselfe before hym, wherof he had
great joye, and thought howe he sayd to the constable, Sir, abyde you here,
and I wyll mount on this hart, and so folowe my faucon. And so the kynge
thought he mounted on this flyeng hart, and howe the hart acordyng at the
kynges desyre dyde beare hym over all the great wodes and trees, and ther he
sawe howe his faucon beate downe great plentie of foules, so that it was
marveyle to beholde. And than it semed to the kynge, whan his faucon had
long flyen and beaten downe many herons, than he thought he called her, and
incontynent the faucon came and sat her downe on his fyst. And than the hart
flewe agayne over the wodes, and brought the kyng to the same launde where
as the constable taryed for hym, who had great joye of his comynge; and as
soone as he was alyghted, he thought the hart departed, and than never sawe
hym after.]

Ou-yang Hsüan, *Ode on the Heavenly Horse*

(The marvelous horse given by John of Marignolli as a gift from the Pope to
Toghon Temür, Great Khan 1333–68, on 19 August 1342 became the subject of a
poem by the famous Chinese scholar Ou-yang Hsüan; from I. de Rachewiltz,
Papal Envoys to the Great Khans [Stanford, 1971], p. 194.)

The Son of Heaven is humane and sage
and all the nations have submitted to him.
The Heavenly Horse has come
from the west of the West.
Dark clouds cover its body,
it has two hoofs of jade.
It is more than five feet high
and twice as much in length.
In crossing seven oceans
its body seemed to fly.
The seas were like its retinue

and thunders followed by.
When the Emperor was in the Hall
of Goodness and Humanity, at daybreak,
suddenly the west wind rose
and the Heavenly Horse appeared,
With dragon head, and phoenix breast,
and eyes that darted lightning.

THE MAGIC MIRROR

The mirror presented to Canacee has the power to reveal future adversity for a king and his kingdom (*SqT* 132–5), to distinguish friends and allies from enemies (*SqT* 136), and to expose a lover's dissimulation (*SqT* 137–41). An explanation of the mirror's powers based on optical science is suggested (*SqT* 228–35); the authorities "Alocen," "Vitulon," and Aristotle are invoked; and reference is made to the supposed construction in Rome of such a mirror. The mirror, along with the magic sword, is carried to the high tower (*SqT* 174–7). Later (*SqT* 371–2), the sleeping Canacee, "right for impressioun / Of hire mirour," has a vision.

The source of the magic mirror in Western literature is the Pharos Lighthouse in the harbor of Alexandria, built by Ptolemy Soter, and regularly described as one of the Wonders of the World. Apparently possessed of sophisticated optical apparatus featuring a large concave mirror that reflected the image of ships far out to sea, this lighthouse served as the subject of legends and hyperbolic accounts by dozens of Arab historians, geographers, and travelers from the ninth century onwards.[27] Reports of European travelers, merchants, and visitors to the tomb of St. Mark in Venice, where the Pharos is depicted in mosaic, disseminated notice of it in the West, with the lighthouse's magic mirror introduced into Western European literary tradition, as illustrated here.[28]

Roman d' Eneas (1155–60)

(From *Eneas; roman du XII siècle*, ed. J. J. Salverda de Grave, CFMA [Paris, 1929], lines 7604–14, 2:51–2; trans. John A. Yunck, *Eneas* [New York and London, 1974], p. 204.)

De dedus ot un mireor;
iluec poënt tres bien veor,   7605

---

[27] Hermann Tiersch, *Pharos. Antike Islam und Occident* (Leipzig and Berlin, 1909), pp. 90–6.
[28] Cappella Zen, vault, west half; see Otto Demus, *The Mosaic Decoration of San Marco, Venice*, ed. Herbert L. Kessler (Chicago and London, 1988), p. 180, fig. 88.

quant l'an les vendra aseor,
ou fust par mer ou fust par terre;
ja ne fussent conquis par guerre;
bien veoit an el mireoir
qui ert asis desus la tor   7610
lor enemis vers aus venir,
donc se pooient bien garnir,
aparoillier aus a deffandre;
n'erent legier pas a sorprendre.

[Over (the peak of the roof) was a mirror, in which they could see very well when someone was coming to attack them, whether by sea or land. They would never be conquered in war; whoever was seated at the foot of the tower could see in the mirror their enemies coming toward them. Thus they could supply themselves well and prepare themselves for defense; they would not be easy to surprise.]

Epistola Presbyteri Johannis ad Emmanuelem *(The Letter of Prester John)*, Interpolation C *(ante* 1221)

(From Friedrich Zarncke, ed., "Der Priester Johannes," *Abhandlungen der philologisch-historischen Classe der königlich sächsischen Gesellschaft der Wissenschaften* 7 [1879], p. 920.)

In summitate vero supremae columpnae est speculum, tali arte consecratum, quod omnes machinationes et omnia, quae pro nobis et contra nos in adiacentibus et subiectis nobis provinciis fiunt, a contuentibus liquidissime videri possunt et cognosci. Custoditur autem a XII milibus armatorum tam in die quam in nocte, ne forte aliquo frangi possit aut deici.

[On the top of the topmost column is a mirror, constructed by such art that all machinations and all things that are done for us or against us in adjacent or subject provinces are able to be seen clearly by watchers, and I know. It is guarded by twelve thousand soldiers day and night, lest it be broken or thrown down.][29]

During the thirteenth century, the *salvatio urbis* legend was appropriated by the tradition of Virgil as sage and magician, whose contrivances were reputed to have preserved Naples and, more popularly, Rome:

---

[29] The legend was also introduced into the Alexander cycle; see *Secretum Secretorum cum glossis et notulis*, ed. Robert Steele, in *Opera hactenus inedita Rogeri Bacon*, facs. 5 (Oxford, 1920), p. 260.

The Seven Sages of Rome

(From *The Seven Sages of Rome*, ed. Killis Campbell [Boston, 1907],
lines 2207–14, p. 75.)

In myddes Rome Virgil made a stage,
and þare he set anoþer ymage;
A merure had he in his hand,
þat þai of Rome myght se ilk land   2210
þat seuin daies iornay about þam ere,
Who wald þam pese and who wald were,
þus war þai warned ilka day
When any fase wald þam affray.[30]

Cleomadés

(From Albert Henry, ed., *Les Oeuvres d'Adenet le Roi*, t. 5: *Cleomadés*
[Brussels, 1971], lines 1691–8, p. 61.)

A Ronme fist, c'est verités,
Virgiles plus grant chose assez,
car il i fist un mireoir
par quoi on povoit bien savoir,
par ymage qu'il y avoit,   1695
se nus vers Ronme pourchaçoit
ne fausseté ne traÿson
de ceaus de leur subjectïon.[31]

[At Rome Virgil, it is true, made numerous great things, for he made a mirror
there through which one could well know by the image that was there if
anyone of their subjects was occupied with treachery or treason.]

---

[30] Unfortunately, the King of Poyl sends spies to Rome as envoys who surreptitiously bury gold beneath
the tower that supports the mirror. They then persuade the king to dig for the treasure; the tower is
undermined and the mirror falls to pieces. The King of Rome is punished by having molten gold poured
down his throat.

[31] Cf. the similar wording in *Le Roman de Renart le Contrefait*, ed. Gaston Raynaud and Henri Lemaitre
(Paris, 1914), 2:71, lines 29391–8.

l'Espinette amoureuse

(From *Jean Froissart[,] l'Espinette amoureuse*, ed. Anthime Fourrier [Paris, 1963], lines 2590–3, 2628–31, 2715–24; pp. 123–4, 126–7); translations are my own and that of Donald C. Baker, *The Squire's Tale, A Variorum Edition of the Works of Geoffrey Chaucer,* vol. 2, part 12 [Norman, OK, and London, 1990], p. 198, note to *SqT* 368–72.)

This poem, which makes explicit allusion to the *Cleomadés*, refers to the go-between who passes on a lady's mirror to her lover as

> . . . le mestre   2590
> Qui fist le mireoir a Romme
> Dont estoient veü li homme
> Qui cevaucoient environ

[the master who constructed at Rome the mirror by means of which are seen the men who ride in those environs].

The lover often gazes into this mirror after departing the country, hoping to find her image therein. One night, it happens:

> "De mon mireoir me prens garde
> Que g'i voi l'impression pure
> De ma dame et de sa figure,   2630
> Qui se miroit ou mireoir"

[Of my mirror I take heed, because I see in it the pure impression of my lady and her form which is reflected in the mirror.]

She is not physically present, of course, but the lover insists on the reality of her image in the mirror, and recounts the supposedly Ovidian tale of Papirus, who, when leaving Ydoree, constructed two mirrors such that each person could see the image of the other while they were separated:

> Car, quant il venoit en agree   2715
> Que ens se miroit Ydoree,
> Elle y veoit son ami chier,
> Papirus, pour li solacier,
> Et Papirus otretant bien
> Veoit Ydoree ens ou sien.   2720
> . . .
> Encores en voit on l'exemple
> A Romme, de Minervee ou temple.

[. . . for, when it was to her liking
that Ydoree looked into the mirror

she saw there her dear friend,
Papirus, in order to solace her;
and Papirus in the same way
saw Ydoree within his mirror.

. . .

One can still see an example of this
In Rome, in the temple of Minerva.]   2720

Caxton's *History of Reynard the Fox*, translated by him from a Middle Dutch
prose version of the Reynard story printed by Gerard Leeu in 1479 at Gouda,
which was closely dependent on a poetic version (RII) produced in the second
half of the fourteenth century, likewise brings together the magic mirror and an
allusion to the *Cleomadés*, here with explicit reference to the flying horse.[32]
Reynard, in an effort to divert attention from the murder of Kywart the hare,
digresses before the king to describe his various lost treasures:

The History of Reynard the Fox

(From *The History of Reynard the Fox*, ed. N. F. Blake, EETS os 263 [London,
1970], pp. 79–80.)

Now ye shal here of the mirrour/ the glas that stode theron was of suche vertu
that men myght see therin/ all that was don within a myle/ of men of beestis
and of al thynge that me wold desire to wyte and knowe/ and what men loked
in the glasse had he ony disseace/ of prickyng or motes/ smarte or perles in his
eyen he shold be anon heled of it. . . . The tree in whiche this glas stode was
lyght and faste and was named cetyne/ hit sholde endure euer er it wold rote
or wormes shold hurte it/ and therfore kynge salamon seelyd his temple wyth
the same wode withynforth/ Men preysed it derrer than fyn gold hit is like to
tre of hebenus/ of whiche wode kynge Crompart made his horse of tree for
loue of kynge morcadigas doughter that was so fayr/ whom he had wende for
to haue wonne/ That hors was so made within/ that wo someuer rode on hit
yf he wolde/ he shold be within lesse than on hour/ an hondred myle thens/
And that was wel preuyd For cleomedes the kynges sone wolde not byleue
that/ That hors of tree had suche myght and vertue/ He was yonge/ lusty and
hardy/ And desyred to doo grete dedes of prys for to be renomed in this world/
And leep on this hors of tree/ Crompart torned a pynne that stode on his brest/
And anon the horse lyfte hym vp and wente out of the halle by the wyndowe
and er one myght saye his pater noster/ He was goon more ten myle waye
cleomedes was sore aferd and supposed neuer to haue torned agayn/ as
thistorye therof telleth more playnly/ but how grete drede he had/ and how
ferre that he rood vpon that horse made of the tree of hebenus er he coude
knowe the arte and crafte how he shold torne hym/ and how Ioyeful he was

---

[32] For the Middle Dutch text, see W. Gs. Hellinga, *Van den Vos Reynaerde: I Teksten* (Zwole, 1952),
pp. 274–5 (MS P, lines 4282–332).

whan he knewe it/ and how men sorowed for hym/ and how he knewe alle this and the ioye therof when he cam agayn al this I passe ouer for losyng of tyme.

Virgil's mirror was often moralized, either without reference to the theme of romantic falseness or as the means whereby a lover's perfidy is discovered:

Le Roman de la Rose

(From Félix Lecoy, ed., *Le Roman de la Rose*, CFMA [Paris, 1965–70], lines 17432–50, 3:23; trans. Charles Dahlberg, *The Romance of the Rose* [Hanover, NH, and London, 1983], p. 292.)

soit a fere a champ ou a vile,	
soit honeste ou desavenant,	
si la voit Dex des maintenant	
ausinc con s'el fust avenue	17435
. . .	
An cest biau mirouer poli,	
qu'il tient et tint tourjorz o li,	
ou tout voit quan qu'il avandra	17445
et tourjorz presant le tandra,	
voit il ou les ames iront	
qui leaument le serviront	
et de ceus ausinc qui n'ont cure	
de leauté ne de droiture.	17450

[(Let ten years go by, or twenty or thirty, in fact five hundred or a hundred thousand, and whether the event occurs in the country or in the city, whether it is honest or something that one should not do,) still God sees it from this very moment as if it had taken place. . . . In this beautiful polished mirror, which He keeps and has always kept with Him, in which He sees all that will happen and will keep it always present, He sees where the souls will go who will serve Him loyally; He sees also the place of those who have no concern for loyalty or justice.]

Confessio Amantis

(From *The English Works of John Gower*, ed. George C. Macaulay, EETS es 82 [Oxford, 1957], 5.2225–30, p. 8.)

Wherof, mi Sone, thou miht hiere,	2225
Whan Covoitise hath lost the stiere	
Of resonable governance,	

Ther falleth ofte gret vengance.
For ther mai be no worse thing
Than Covoitise aboute a king. . . .[33]   2230

Gesta Romanorum

(From *The Early English Versions of the Gesta Romanorum*, ed. Sidney J. H.
Herrtage, EETS es 33 [London, 1879], pp. 4–5.)

In a story in the *Gesta Romanorum*,[34] a knight on pilgrimage to Rome is
deceived by his young wife, who conspires with her lover, a necromancer, to
arrange for his death by fabricating an image of him into which the necromancer
will shoot an arrow. But a Roman clerk – in the earliest version, Virgil – foils
the plan by presenting the husband with a magic mirror that enables him to see
what is planned and to know when the arrow is shot, so he can submerge
himself in water. His image is safe; the arrow returns on its flight to kill the necromancer; the wife is executed for her crimes; and the knight re-marries. The
allegory in the Middle English version is as follows:

> "The wife that lovith not hire husbond is þi flesch, þat dispisith all werkis that
> þe spirite lovith." The necromancer, i.e., the Devil, conspires with the flesh
> whenever one ceases from works of penance. The Virgil-figure is a "discrete
> confessour or a prechour . . . Which techith a man How þat he shall defende
> him aȝenst þe dartys of þe devill." The image is reason; the arrow, envy or
> avarice; the defense offered by the mirror, holy doctrine. Holding one's head
> under water is to subject oneself to the yoke of penance. "And thenne þou
> shalt take a new wife, *scil.* a spirit obediente to a new gouernaunce; And
> thenne per consequens þou shalt have euermore lastyng lif."

Roman de la Rose

(From Félix Lecoy, *Le Roman de la Rose*, CFMA [Paris, 1965–70] lines 18031–40,
3:41–2; trans. Charles Dahlberg, *The Romance of the Rose* [Hanover, NH, and
London, 1983], p. 300.)

Mars et Venus, qui ja pris furent
ansamble ou lit ou il se jurent,
s'il, ainz que seur le lit montassent,
en tex mirouers se mirassent,
mes que leurs mirouers tenissent   18035

---

[33] For other such moralizations, see the *Gesta Romanorum*, ed. Hermann Oesterley (Berlin, 1872), p. 590,
no. 186, germ. 18; and the *Scala celi* of Jean Gobi le Jeune, excerpted in Jacques Berlioz, "Virgile dans
la litterature des *exempla* (XIIIe–XVe siècles)," in *Lectures médiévales de Virgile*, Actes du colloque
organisé par l'Ecole française de Rome (Rome, 1985), pp. 118–19.

[34] *Gesta Romanorum*, ed. Adelbert Keller (Stuttgart and Tübingen, 1842), pp. 153–5, no. 102.

si que le lit dedanz veïssent,
ja ne fussent pris ne lïez
es laz soutilz et delïez
que Vulcanus mis i avoit,
de quoi nus d'aus riens ne savoit.   18040

[If Mars and Venus, who were captured in the bed where they were lying together, had looked at themselves in such a mirror before they got up on the bed, provided that they held their mirror so that they could see the bed in it, they would never have been captured or bound in the fine, thin nets that Vulcan had placed there and that neither of them knew anything about.]

As noted by Koeppel,[35] the optical description of the properties of the mirror (*SqT* 228–35) is most probably derived from the *Roman de la Rose* (from Félix Lecoy, *Le Roman de la Rose*. CFMA [Paris, 1965–70], lines 18000–222, 3:40–1, 47; trans. Charles Dahlberg, *The Romance of the Rose* [Hanover, NH, and London, 1983], pp. 300, 303.)

et li convandroit prandre cure   18000
d'estre deciples Aristote,
qui mieuz mist natures en note
que nus hon puis le tans Caÿn.
Alhacem, li nieps Huchaÿn,
qui ne refu ne fos ne garz,   18005
cist fist le livre des *Regarz*:
de ce doit cil sciance avoir
qui veust de l'arc en ciel savoir,
car de ce doit estre juigierres
clers naturex et regardierres,   18010
et sache de geometrie,
don necessaire est la metrie
au livre des *Regarz* prover.
Lors porra les causes trover,
et les forces des mirouers,   18015
qui tant ont merveilleus pouers
que toutes choses tres petites,
letres grelles tres loing escrites
et poudres de sablon menues,
si granz, si grosses sunt veües   18020
. . .
Mes ne vueill or pas metre cures
en desclarïer les figures
des mirouers, ne ne dirai
conment sunt reflechi li rai,   18220
ne leur angles ne vueil descrivre
(tout est ailleurs escrit an livre).

[35] E. Koeppel, "Chauceriana," *Anglia* 14 (1892): 258.

[One would have to take the trouble to be a disciple of Aristotle, who had made better observations of nature than any man from the time of Cain. Alhazen, the nephew of Huchain, was neither a fool nor a simpleton, and he wrote the book of *Observations*, which anyone who wants to know about the rainbow should know about. The student and observer of nature must know it and he must also know geometry, the mastery of which is necessary for the proofs in the book of *Observations*. There he will be able to discover the causes and the strength of the mirrors that have such marvelous powers that all things that are very small – thin letters, very narrow writing, and tiny grains of sand – are seen as so great and large. . . . But I do not now want to take the trouble to clarify the shapes of mirrors, nor do I want to tell how rays are reflected or to describe their angles. Everything is written elsewhere in a book.]

Roger Bacon in particular was a leading theorist of the magic mirror, and was reputed to have actually constructed the device:

Epistola Fratris Rogerii Baconis de Secretis operibus Artis et naturae, et de nullitate magiae (ante 1248)

(From *Rogeri Bacon*, ed. J. S. Brewer, Rolls Series 360 [London, 1859], pp. 534–5; trans. anon. in *The Admirable Force and Efficacy of Nature* [London, 1597], rept. in *The Mirror of Alchimy Composed by the Thrice-Famous and Learned Friar, Roger Bachon*, ed. Stanton J. Linden [New York and London, 1992], pp. 57–8.)

Possunt enim sic figurari perspicua ut longissime posita appareant pro-pinquissima, et e converso; ita quod ex incredibili distantia legeremus minutissimas literas, et numeraremus res quascunque parvas, et stellas faceremus apparere quo vellemus. Sic enim aestimatur Julius Caesar super littus maris in Galliis, deprehendisse per ingentia specula dispositionem et situm castrorum et civitatum Britanniae majoris. Possunt etiam sic figurari corpora, ut maxima appareant minima, et e converso; et alta appareant ima et infima, et e converso; et occulta videantur manifesta.

[For so may the perspects be framed, that things most farre off may seeme most nigh unto us, and cleane contrarie. So that we may reade verie small letters, an incredible distance from us, and beholde things how little soever they bee, and make starres to appeare wheresoever wee will. And it is thought that *Julius Caesar* did from the Seacoastes in *Fraunce* marke and observe the disposition and situation of the Castles and Citties of the lesser Brytannie by the helpe of great glasses. Bodyes also may so bee framed, that the greatest things shall appeare to be the least, the highest to bee the lowest, the most secret to bee the most manifest, and in like sort the contrarie.][36]

---

[36] See also Bacon's discussion of the topic in *Opus Maius*, ed. J. S. Brewer (Frankfurt am Main, 1964), Part 5, Concerning Optics, Last Distinction, ch. 3–4, 1:164–5; trans. Robert Belle Burke, *The Opus Maius of Roger Bacon* (Philadelphia, 1928), 2:581–2.

In an account of various Franciscans written 1384–85 by Peter of Trau, Oxford MS Bodley Canon. Misc. 525, fol. 203v, we find that "frater Rogerius dictus Bachon Anglicus" had constructed two mirrors at Oxford,

> in quorum altero quilibet omni hora diei et noctis poterat accendere candelam, in altero vero videre quid agebant homines in quantumcumque remotis constituti partibus. Et quia ad experimentum primi studentes plus stabant candelas accendendo quam in libris studendis, et in secundo multi, visis suis consanguineis et amicis mori, infirmari, aut aliter impediri, de universitate recedentes studium destruebant, eiusdem universitatis communi consilio utrumque est fractum.

> [by one of them you could light a candle at any hour, day or night: in the other you could see what people were doing in any part of the world. By experimenting with the first, students spent more time in lighting candles than in studying books; and seeing in the second their relations dying or ill or otherwise in trouble, they got into the habit of "going down" to the ruin of the university: so by common counsel of the University both mirrors were broken.][37]

THE MAGIC RING

The magic ring given to Canacee enables its possessor to understand the speech of birds and be able to converse with them, as well as to understand the medicinal properties of plants (*SqT* 146–55). The fame of Moses and Solomon with respect to such contrivances is alluded to, and reference is made to other apparent wonders which, once the processes are understood, cease to amaze (*SqT* 247–60). Awakening from her first sleep, Canacee feels joy because of her ring and mirror (*SqT* 367–9); later, she understands and is able to converse with the falcon (*SqT* 432ff.), and prepares herbal medicines for her (*SqT* 470–1). We are told that the ring, along with the "mediacioun of Cambalus," will figure in the successful reconciliation of the falcon and her lost love (*SqT* 652–7).

Solomon's knowledge of animals and the natural world is declared in 1 Kings 4.33, while both the Aggadah and the Koran explictly mention his knowledge of

---

[37] A. G. Little, "Description du manuscrit canonici miscell. 525 de la Bibliotheque Bodléienne," *Opuscules de critique historique*, fasc. 5 (Paris, 1903), p. 267, as cited in G. Molland, "Roger Bacon as Magician," *Traditio* 30 (1974): 47; translation by A. C. Crombie quoted p. 53. For Bacon's enduring reputation as a *savant* of the scientifc basis of magic mirrors, see Robert Record, *The Path-way to Knowledge, containing the First Principles of Geometrie* (London, 1551); facs. ed. Amsterdam and Norwood, NJ, 1974, preface (unpaged). See also Thomas Digges, *An Arithmeticall Treatise named Stratioticos* (London, 1579), p. 189; and Robert Smith, *A Complete System of Opticks* (London, 1738), p. 13.

birds' speech.[38] His ring is famous in the West as either a curative, specifically exorcising device, or as a magical means of securing one's desires:

Historia Scholastica

(From Peter Comestor, *Historia Scholastica*, Liber III Regum, in *PL* 198:1352; my translation.)

Excogitavit etiam characteres, qui inscribebantur gemmis, quae posita in naribus arreptitii, cum radice Salomoni monstrata, statim eum a daemonibus liberabat. Haec scientia plurimum valuit in gente Hebraeorum, et maxime necessaria erat. Ante adventum enim Christi saepius homines a daemonibus vexabantur, quod homines vivos ad infernum quandoque detrudebant. Josephus (8.5) quoque testatur se vidisse quemdam Eleazarum exorcistam coram Vespasiano, et filiis ejus, et tyrannis, in hunc modum praedictum curantem vexatos a daemonibus, et ut probaret eis daemonem egressum per nares cum spiritu anhelantis, vas ponebat in medio, et imperabat daemoni egresso, ut illud everteret in argumentum suae egressionis; et ita fiebat.

[He also devised characters which were inscribed on gems and placed in the noses of the possessed with conspicuous root of Solomon; immediately he freed the possessed from demons. This knowledge was of great value to many in the Hebrew nation, and was greatly necessary. Before the coming of Christ men were often troubled by demons, because they sometimes thrust them down alive into hell. Josephus also testifies that he saw a certain exorcist, Eleazar, before Vespasian and his sons and princes, curing those troubled by demons in this aforesaid manner, and in order to prove to them the leaving of the demon through the nose by the spirit of the breath, he placed a basin in the midst, and ordered the demon as he was leaving to overturn it in proof of his leaving; and thus he did.]

Rings associated with Solomon were considered magical means to secure one's desires, in love or otherwise.[39]

The legend of Moses's magic rings arose out of the troublesome verse Numbers 12.1, from commentary that did not construe the *aethiopissam* there mentioned to refer to Zipporah.[40] While Hebrew commentary insisted that Moses never consummated his marriage in all the years he spent with the Cushite princess before leaving to marry Zipporah, Peter Comestor introduced the magic ring as a device of separation:

---

[38] *Aggadah*, Song R 1:1, no. 9; Tanh. B, Intro, 157; *Koran*, ch. 27.

[39] BL MS Sloane 121 (fifteenth century), cited by Richard Kieckhefer, *Magic in the Middle Ages* (Cambridge, 1989), p. 71, offers instructions for fabricating such a ring, under the heading "Experiments which King Solomon devised for the love and courting of a certain noble queen, and they are experiments of nature." See also George Lyman Kittredge, *Witchcraft in Old and New England* (Cambridge, MA, 1929), pp. 62–3, for a 1532 case involving one R. Jones of Oxford.

[40] This section is drawn in part from Vincent DiMarco, "A Note on Canacee's Magic Ring," *Anglia* 99 (1981): 399–405.

Historia Scholastica

(From Peter Comestor, *Historia Scholastica*, Liber Exodi, ch. 6, in *PL* 198:1144; my translation.)

. . . duas imagines sculpsit in gemmis hujus efficaciae; ut altera memoriam, altera oblivionem conferret. Cumque paribus annulis eas inseruisset, alterum, scilicet oblivionis annulum, uxori praebuit; alterum ipse tulit, ut sicut pari amore, sic paribus annulis insignirentur. Coepit ergo mulier, amoris viri oblivisci, et tandem libere in Aegyptum regressus est.[41]

[. . . he fashioned two images in gems of this power, that the one conferred memory, the other forgetfulness. And when he inserted them into these similar rings, he offered one, namely the ring of oblivion, to (his) wife, and the other he bore; so that they were distinguished by equal rings, just as by equal love. Accordingly, the woman began to forget the love of the man, and finally he returned to Egypt without hindrance.]

In what recalls the earlier rabbinical interpretation of the Cushite woman as Zipporah, Nicholas Trevet in *Les Chronicles* has Moses give his wife *both* rings to comfort her in his absence,[42] whereas Gower has the lover confess his inability to remember what to say when face-to-face with his lady, although he could by no means forget her.

Confessio Amantis

(From *The English Works of John Gower*, ed. George C. Macaulay, EETS es 81 [Oxford, 1957], 4.647–65, p. 319.)

Althogh I hadde on such a Ring,	
As Moises thurgh his enchanting	
Som time in Ethiope made,	
Whan that he Tharbis weddid hade.	650
Which Ring bar of Oblivion	
The name, and that was be resoun	
That where it on a finger sat,	
Anon his love he so foryat,	
As thogh he hadde it nevere knowe:	655
And so it fell that ilke throwe,	
Whan Tharbis hadde it on hire hond,	

---

[41] Peter Comestor's account is the basis of that of Vincent of Beauvais, *Speculum Historiale*, 2.2; Gervais of Tilbury, *Otia Imperialia*, ed. F. Liebrecht (Hanover, 1856), tertia distinctio, no. cxi; and the Middle English *Genesis and Exodus*, ed. R. Morris, lines 2698ff.

[42] BL MS Arundel 56, fol. 9v: "Et [l'un] anel apella memoire, et l'autre obliaunce qar tant come Sephora usa la anel qe fut apelle memoire a nul temps poet oblier son baron Moyses, et quant ele usa l'anel q'estoit apelle obliaunce a nul temps poet survenir ne penser de Moyses."

No knowlechinge of him sche fond,
Bot al was clene out of memoire,
As men mai rede in his histoire;   660
And thus he wente quit away,
That nevere after that ilke day
Sche thoghte that ther was such on;
Al was foryete and overgon.
Bot in good feith so mai noght I.   665

The story of Moses' rings, which was frequently allegorized in exempla and illustrative tales,[43] also served as the subject of scientific speculation:

Opus Maius

(From Roger Bacon, *Opus Maius*, ed. J. S. Brewer [Frankfurt am Main, 1964], Part 4, Astrologia, 2:392, 394; trans. Robert Belle Burke, *The Opus Maius of Roger Bacon* [Philadelphia, 1928], 1:408–10.)

Haec Josephus primo Antiquitatum libro, et magister in historiis, et multi confirmant. Mira res fuit haec, quae animum mulieris immutavit. Salomon vero ordinavit de hujusmodi multis, quae praeter solitum cursum naturae factae sunt, ut dicit Josephus octavo libro. . . . Philosophus igitur voluit quod faceret opera sapientiae per debitas constellationes ad modum Moysis, qui excitavit animam mulieris per coelestes virtutes receptas in materia. Nam qua ratione potuit illa mulier mutari ad castitatem et oblivionem viri per imagines, potuit et ad alios mores moveri non solum ipsa, sed quicunque. . . . Sed quia haec opera videntur vulgo studentium esse supra humanum intellectum, quia vulgus cum suis doctoribus non vacat operibus sapientiae, ideo vix est aliquis ausus loqui de his operibus in publico. Statim enim vocantur magici, cum tamen sint sapientissimi qui haec sciunt.

[Josephus in the first book of the Antiquities states these facts, and the Master in the Histories (Peter Comestor) and many others attest them. This was a wonderful thing that changed the heart of the woman. Solomon, moreover, made regulations respecting many things of this kind, which happened contrary to the ordinary course of nature, as Jospehus states in the eighth book. . . . The philosopher (Aristotle) wished then that (Alexander the Great, who wanted to change the morals of certain tribes) should perform deeds of wisdom by means of the necessary constellations in the manner of Moses, who stirred the mind of the woman by means of the celestial force received in

---

[43] Where, for example, the husband's deception with the ring that causes the wife to forget him is treated as an allegory of the human soul, restrained by the body, but wishing to return to heaven; see *Gesta Romanorum*, ed. Oesterley, no. 10; *The Early English Versions of the Gesta Romanorum*, ed. Sidney J. H. Herrtage, no. 51; Karl Inge Sandred, ed., *A Middle English Version of the Gesta Romanorum edited from Gloucester Cathedral MS 22* (Uppsala, 1971), no. 19. See also Robert Holcot, *Super libros Sapientiae* (Hagenau, 1494), lectio cxii, in which the ring of memory represents the recognition of eternal life, and the ring of oblivion the recognition of death.

the material. For as that woman could be changed to purity and to a forgetfulness of her husband by means of images, so could she have been influenced also to adopt other morals, and not only she, but any other woman. . . . But since these works seem to the rank and file of students to be beyond human intellect, because the throng with its teachers has no leisure for the works of science, scarcely any one has ventured to speak about these works in public. For they are straightway called magicians, whereas they are the very wisest who know these things.]

The matter was apparently a popular one in learned circles, as is suggested in *quodlibeta* such as that of Pierre d'Auvergne, *Quodl.* I (1296), quest. 14 (my translation):

Utrum imagines quae fiunt per astrologos, secundum illorum scientiam habeant efficaciam in naturalibus, puta an annuli oblivionis quos Moyses dicitur fecisse habebant virtutem oblivioni inducendi.[44]

[Whether images which astrologers make according to their knowledge have efficacy on things of nature, for example whether the rings of oblivion which Moses is said to have fabricated had the virtue of inducing forgetfulness.]

Finally, it is curious to discover that Alice Perrers was reputed to have commissioned a friar to produce two such "Mosaic" rings as a gift from her to Edward III.

Monk of St. Albans, *Chronicon Angliae*

(From *Chronicon Angliae, ab Anno Domini 1328 usque ad annum 1388*, ed. E. M. Thompson [London, 1874], pp. 98, 142; translation of BL MS Harley 6217 by Thomas Amyot, printed in *Archaeologia* 22 [1829]: 236, 280.)

Anulos etiam, ut quondam Moyses fecerat, oblivionis et memoriae, et ita iste frater imaginaverat, quibus rex quamdiu uteretur praedictae meretricis recordatione nunquam careret. . . . Undecimo kalendas Junii, videlicet in vigilia Beati Protomartyris Anglorum Albani, magnificus rex Edwardus, anuli decoctus infirmitate, quod tempus sibi credimus a divina pietate concessum ad usum poenitentiae et redimenda peccata, pene tamen improvisus, in fata concessit.

---

[44] P. Glorieux, *La Litttérature quodlibétique de 1260 a 1320* (Kain, 1925), p. 259. See also Nicole Oresme, *Tabula problematum*, in Bert Hansen, *Nicole Oresme and the Marvels of Nature*, p. 369, quest. 37: "Utrum ymagines quas faciunt astrologi habeant aliquam virtutem acquisitam pro sculptura in tali vel tali hora facta. Et quare fuerunt invente? Et videtur quod Moyses fuerit in causa et cetera." [Whether images which astrologers make have any power by being made at a particular time. And how were they made? And is it seen that Moses was the originator, etc.] Oresme also takes up the matter in his *Livre de Divinacions*, where Moses' rings are discussed and allusion made to Solomon's magical expertise; see G. W. Coopland, *Nicole Oresme and the Astrologers: A Study of His "Livre De Divinacions"* (Liverpool, 1952), pp. 62–3.

[. . . he mayde also, as they say Moyses dyd in tymes paste, rynges of memorie
& forgettfulnes, and so the freir imagined, that so long as the kynge sholde use
them, he sholde never want the remembrance of the forsayed harlott. . . . The xi
kalends of Jullii, the vygell of our first martir Seint Albon, the renowned kynge
Edward sodden as it were with the disease of the (MS blank, *annuli* added in
the margin) which tyme we beleve was gyven hym of God to the use of
penitence, and to redeme his synes, had almoaste sodaynly dyed.]

THE MAGIC SWORD

The virtue of the sword is that although it can cut through the thickest armor,
the wound it causes can be healed by the application of the sword's flat edge
(*SqT* 155–67). The story of the wounding, then healing, of Thelophus by
Achilles is recalled, and the narrator alludes generally to the various ways of
tempering metal, but confesses his ignorance of the actual processes involved
(*SqT* 236–46).

The allusion to Thelophus is too general to allow identification of a particular
source, though, as Schless points out, the most detailed account Chaucer may
have known is that of Book 12 of the *Ovide Moralisé*:[45]

Ovide Moralisé

(From *Ovide Moralisé, Poème du commencement du quatorzième siècle publié
d'après tous les manuscrits connus*, ed. C. de Boer, *Verhandelingen der
Koninklijke Akademie van Wetenschappen* 37 [1936], 12.840–6, 4:279; trans.
Howard H. Schless, *Chaucer and Dante* [Norman, OK, 1984], p. 202.)

Telephon eüssé je mort   840
Par ce mien dart, qui le plaia,
Mes cil vers soi me rapaia
Por ce qu'il me cria merci
Si le sauvai par ce fer ci,
Dont je l'avoie à mort feru.   845
Je le bleçai; je l'ai garu!

[Telephon I would have killed with this spear of mine that covered him with
wounds, but because he begged mercy of me, he appeased me, so I saved him
with the very weapon with which I had struck him fatally. I wounded him; I
cured him.]

---

[45] See Howard H. Schless, *Chaucer and Dante*, p. 202.

The scientific context of the *Squire's Tale*, however, suggests as Chaucer's source the account of the Elder Pliny in the *Historia Naturalis,* where, in a discussion of the medicinal properties of various ores and the by-products of their commercial preparation, the author mentions various techniques of tempering as illustrated in the story of Achilles and Thelophus.

Historia Naturalis

(From *Pliny[,] Natural History*, ed. and trans. H. Rackham, Loeb [Cambridge, MA, and London, 1968], 34.41.144–34.46.155, 9:232–9.)

> et fornacium magna differentia est, nucleusque quidam ferri excoquitur in iis ad indurandam aciem, alioque modo ad densandas incudes malleorumve rostra. Summa autem differentia in aqua, cui subinde candens inmergitur. . . . Est et robigo ipsa in remediis, et sic proditur Telephum sanasse Achilles, sive id aerea sive ferrea cuspide fecit; ita certe pingitur ex ea decutiens gladio suo. . . . Potentia eius ligare, siccare, sistere. . . . Squama quoque ferri in usu est ex acie aut mucronibus, maxime simili, sed acriore vi quam robigo.

> [There is also a great difference between smelting works, and a certain knurr of iron is smelted in them to give hardness to a blade, and by another process to (give) solidity to anvils or the heads of hammers. But the chief difference depends on the water in which at intervals the red hot metal is plunged. . . . The list of remedies even includes rust itself, and this is the way in which Achilles is stated to have cured Telephus, whether he did it by means of a copper javelin or an iron one. . . . The effect of rust is to unite wounds and dry them and staunch them. . . . Scale of iron, obtained from a sharp edge or point, is also employed, and has an effect extremely like that of rust only more active.][46]

Finally, the Squire's professed ignorance of actual hardening techniques mirrors the secrecy surrounding arcane and often complex recipes for preparing the metal: Theophilus, *On Divers Arts*, calls for the scrapings of burnt ox horn to be sprinkled over the hot metal before quenching, and elsewhere recommends quenching in the urine of a goat or of a red-haired boy.[47] Germanic smiths added goose dung to the charcoal to assist the hardening (by adding nitrogen?), as in the saga of *Theodoric of Berne*, where an unsatisfactory sword is broken up, fed to geese, recovered, and re-manufactured.[48] Bandini's *Fons memorabilium,*

---

[46] Cited by Vincent DiMarco, "Richard Hole and the *Merchant's* and *Squire's Tales*: An Unrecognized Eighteenth-Century (1797) Contribution to Source and Analogue Study," *Chaucer Review* 16 (1981): 171–80. Elsewhere in the *Historia Naturalis* (25.42) Pliny offers two alternative theories: that Thelophus was healed by the herb *archilleos* (milfoil or yarrow), which had been discovered by Achilles, or by *aerugo*, verdigris prepared from the rust of a spear.

[47] Theophilus, *On Divers Arts*, trans. John G. Hawthorne and Cyril Stanley Smith (New York, 1963), pp. 93–4 (3.18) and p. 95 (3.21).

[48] See Joseph Needham, *The Development of Iron and Steel Technology in China*, Second Biennial Dickinson Memorial Lecture to the Newcomen Society, 1956 (Cambridge, 1964), p. 43n.

silently following the recipe of Albertus Magnus, states that a sword tempered in the juice of a radish mixed with the juice of earthworms will cut all iron as if it were lead.[49]

METEOROLOGICAL SCIENCE

As soore wondren somme on cause of thonder,
On ebbe, on flood, on gossomer, and on myst,
And alle thyng, til that the cause is wyst.   (*SqT* 258–60)

Chaucer in these lines continues to rely on the Confession of Nature from the *Roman de la Rose*, which has served as the direct source of the passage immediately preceding regarding the production of glass from fern ashes (see below).

By Chaucer's time, informed opinion favored the Aristotelian explanation (*Meteorologica* 2.9) of thunder as the result of dry "exhalations" or vapors drawn from the earth by the sun's heat becoming trapped in the region where air in the process of cooling is forcibly ejected as clouds condense, and then neighboring clouds are struck. This explanation is echoed in the *Roman de la Rose*, in the same section that offers a poetic description of gossamers, i.e., the product of convection currents caused by the sun's rays increasing the ground temperature, evaporating the dew, and carrying aloft the threads of spider webs.

Roman de la Rose

(From *Le Roman de la Rose*, ed. Félix Lecoy [Paris, 1965–70], CFMA, lines 17855–970, 3:36, 39; trans. Charles Dahlberg, *The Romance of the Rose* [Hanover, NH, and London, 1983], pp. 298–9.)

Les vanz font il contrarier,   17855
l'air anflamber, brere et crier,
et esclater an maintes parz
par tonnairres et par esparz,
qui tabourent, timbrent et trompent
tant que les nues s'an derompent   17860
par les vapeurs qu'il font lever.[50]

---

[49] See also *The Pirotechnia of Vannoccio Biringuccio* (published posthumously, 1540), trans. Cyril Stanley Smith and Maria Teach Gnudi (Cambridge, MA and London, 1942), pp. 371–6, which lists such secret tempering preparations as herbal juices, rams' horns, and oxen's hooves.

[50] For a more detailed exposition of the theory of the formation of thunder, see the romance of *Syrac and Boctus*, known in fourteenth-century England in a French version, *La Fountaine de toutes sciences*, and in an English translation by Hugo of Caumpeden, *The history of kyng Boccus & Sydracke*. See BL MS Lansdowne 793, fols. 79r–79v, and the text as edited by T. L. Burton, *Sidrak and Bokkus*, EETS os 311 (Oxford, 1998), 1:319–20.

...
et metent leur toisons sechier
au biau soleill plesant e chier,
et les vont par l'air charpissant   17965
au tens cler et replandissant;
puis filent, et quant ont filé,
si font voler de leur filé
granz agulliees de fil blanches
ausinc con por coudre leur manches.   17970

[The (celestial) influences make the winds blow against one another, make the air break out in flame, yell and cry out, and burst out in many parts with thunder and lightning that rumble, drum, and trumpet until the clouds are burst open by the vapors that they have raised. . . . (The clouds) put out their fleeces to dry on the pleasant warmth of the beautiful sun and in the clear, resplendent weather, they go about teasing and carding them. They spin, and when they have spun, they set flying, with their spinning, great spindlefuls of white thread as if it were for sewing up their sleeves.]

Chaucer departs from the *Roman* to make mention of tidal action which, given its association with other meteorological phenomena influenced by the radiation of energy (specifically light and heat), effects physical changes in the receiving material. In this he was probably influenced by the most important medieval theorist on the matter, Robert Grosseteste, who developed the lunar theory that classical and early Christian authors (Posidonius, Pliny, Augustine, Ambrose, Bede) had approached:

Questio de fluxu et refluxu maris

(From Richard C. Dales, "The Text of Robert Grosseteste's *Questio de fluxu et refluxu maris* with an English Translation," *Isis* 57 [1966]: 455–74; lines 77–118, pp. 460–3, 470.)

. . . sol autem habet significationem super temperamentum aeris principaliter tunc et luna habebit principaliter significationem super temperamentum aque cum in hiis duabus speris fiat generatio et corruptio omnium animantium et hec duo luminaria sint principalia principia omnis generationis et corruptionis. . . . Cum oritur luna in orizonte alicuius maris tunc primo infundit radios luminares in medio maris et fortiter imprimens suam virtutem movet hoc mare augeturque hec motio quousque pervenerit luna ad circulum meridionalem. Cum autem transierit circulum meridionalem minoratur virtus effectiva et recedit mare ad canales proprios quousque pervenerit luna ad occidentem. . . . Sicut ergo tempus revolutionis lune ab ortu ad ortum excedit tempus diei et noctis, ita tempus duarum accessionum et duarum reversionum diversarum et perfectarum excedit tempus diei et noctis.

[. . . the sun is primarily responsible for motions which take place in the air, and the moon for those which take place in water, since in these two spheres (i.e., air and water) the generation and corruption of all living things take place, and these two luminous bodies are the principal causes of every generation and corruption. . . . When the moon rises on the horizon of any sea, it first casts its luminous rays on the center of that sea and, strongly impressing its power, it moves this sea, and this motion increases until the moon arrives at the meridian. But when it passes over the meridian its effective power is diminished, and the sea recedes towards its original place until the moon has set. . . . And thus in one revolution of the moon from rise to rise, two high tides occur in that place over whose horizon the moon has risen.]

In the *Opus Maius* Roger Bacon refined and developed Grosseteste's theory of lunar rays by describing tidal action with reference to geometry, i.e., "Naturelly, by composiciouns / Of anglis" (*SqT* 229–30):

Opus Maius

(From Roger Bacon, *Opus Maius*, ed. J. S. Brewer [Frankfurt am Main, 1964], 1:140; trans. Robert Belle Burke, *The Opus Maius of Roger Bacon* [Philadelphia, 1928], 1:161.)

Propter quod considerandum est, quod quando luna ascendit super mare alicujus regionis, ejus radii cadunt ad angulos obliquos, ut quilibet qui novit casum angulorum potest hoc scire. Et quia cadunt ad angulos tales, oportet quod sint debilis virtutis, ut prius ostensum est. Et ideo solum possunt elevare vapores a fundo maris, et ampullas tumentes, et ingurgitantes aquas maris, ut expellantur a canalibus suis, quos vapores non possunt radii ad aerem extrahere nec consumere propter debilitatem suam; et ideo oportet ut aqua fluat a sedibus suis, donec durat hujusmodi ebullitio vaporum. Sed cum luna accedit ad medium coeli, cadunt magis et magis radii ejus ad angulos rectos, et fortificantur super corpus maris, ac extrahunt vapores ad aerem et consumunt, unde debilitatur fluxus paulatim, secundum quod luna appropinquat lineae meridiei; et quando venit ad illam lineam sunt vapores castigati et consumpti, ita ut statim dum luna descendit ad aliam quartam coeli incipiat refluxus, quia cessante causa cessat effectus.

[Wherefore we must consider that when the moon rises over the sea of any region, its rays fall at oblique angles, as any one acquainted with the incidence of angles knows. And because they fall at such angles, the rays are necessarily of weak force, as has been shown before. And therefore they are only able to raise vapors from the depth of the sea, like swelling bottles, and overflowing waters of the sea, so that they are driven from their channels. These vapors the rays cannot draw out to the air nor consume them because of their weakness; and therefore of necessity the water flows from its resting places, as long as

this kind of ebullition lasts. But when the moon approaches the middle of the sky, the rays fall more and more at right angles and become strong over the body of the sea and draw forth the vapors to the air and consume them, whence the flow grows weaker little by little according to the moon's approach to the meridian; and when she reaches it, the vapors are kept in check and consumed, so that at once while the moon is descending to another quarter of the heavens, the reflux begins, since the effect ceases when the cause ceases.]

Lastly, Aristotle, *Meteorologica* 1.9.346 describes mist as a by-product of condensation, i.e. as a vapor that is not condensed by the sun's rays into cloud and rain. But Bartholomaeus Anglicus understands it as the result of dissolving clouds, the product of evaporation by the sun:

On the Properties of Things

(From *On the Properties of Things: John Trevisa's Translation of Bartholomaeus Anglicus De Proprietatibus Rerum*, ed. M. C. Seymour [Oxford, 1975], 1:590.)

Myst is impressioun imade of resolucioun and tofallinge of cloudes þat beþ tofalle, as Aristotel seiþ. For vapoures so resolued and tofalle, and toschedde and tospred into alle þe parties of þe eire, brediþ and gendreþ myst. . . . And whanne myst is al ismyte of wiþ þe bemes of þe sonne it falliþ donward and turneþ ageyne into þe matiere þat it come of, and vanyschiþ and failiþ; and so þe eyre is ipurgid, and þanne it bodiþ faire wedir and cliere.

MARVELS AND CAUSES

Commenting on the reactions of the crowd to the horse of brass – their considering it a "fairye" (i.e., a marvel; *SqT* 201) or an illusion of magic (*SqT* 217) – the narrator notes the tendency of those ignorant of true causes to imagine the worst. With regard to the magic mirror, some believe an explanation is available in books (*SqT* 235). The narrator remarks (*SqT* 256–60) that marvels become familiar when the cause is known.

Such sentiments draw on a long-lived tradition, comprehensively detailed by Hansen, of explaining marvels naturally, without recourse to magic or divine (or demonic) causation.

Adelard of Bath, *Questiones Naturales*

(From *Adelard of Bath, Conversations with his Nephew*, ed. and trans. Charles Burnett [Cambridge, 1998], pp. 202–5; text cited by Hansen, *Nicole Oresme*, p. 66.)

Quid stupes? Quid dubitas? Quid nunc hac nunc illac nutans inconstantie vultum prestas? Atqui scio qua tenebra teneris, que universos qui de rerum ordine dubitant involvit, errorem inducit. Ammiratione enim insolentiaque indutus, animus, dum rerum effectus sine causis abhorrens a longe aspicit, numquam se dubitatione exuit. Propius intuere, circumstantias adde, causas prepone, et effectum non mirabere.

[Why are you stunned? Why are you in doubt? Why now swaying this way, now that, do you give the appearance of a lack of constancy? But I know by what darkness you are held captive – it is that which envelops all those who doubt about the order of things and brings in error. For, veiled by the wonderfulness and strangeness of the matter, the mind, while it recoils from effects in things which do not have causes and gazes from afar, never casts off its doubt. Look more closely! Add the circumstances! Lay down the causes first, and you will not be surprised by the effect!]

Epistola de secretis operibus artis et naturae

(From *Fr. Rogeri Bacon*, ed. J. S. Brewer, Rolls Series 360 [London, 1859], p. 525; trans. anon. in *The Admirable Force and Efficacy of Nature* [London, 1597], rept. in *The Mirror of Alchimy Composed by the Thrice-Famous and Learned Friar, Roger Bachon*, ed. Stanton J. Linden [New York and London, 1992], pp. 50–1.)

. . . nam quaedam sunt omnino irrationabilia quae philosophi adinvenerunt in operibus naturae et artis, ut secreta occultarent ab indignis. Sicut si omnino esset ignotum quod magnes traheret ferrum, et aliquis volens hoc opus perficere coram populo, faceret characteres et carmina proferret, ne perciperetur quod totum opus attractionis esset naturale.

[After this maner there are many thinges hidden in the Philosophers bookes, wherein a wise man must beware, that neglecting the Charmes and Characters, he onely attend and make tryall of the worke of Nature and Art. And then he shall perceyve things living, and without life, to concurre and agree in Nature, for the conformitie and likenesse of their Natures, and not by vertue of the Charme or Character: whereas the simple people suppose manie things to bee wrought by Magicke, which are nothing else but the secretes of Art and Nature.]

Roman de la Rose

(From Félix Lecoy, ed., *Le Roman de la Rose* [Paris, 1965–70], lines 16066–71,
2:239; trans. Charles Dahlberg, *The Romance of the Rose* [Hanover, NH, and
London, 1983], pp. 272–3.)

> Ne voit l'an conment de fouschiere
> font cil et cendre et vairre nestre
> qui de veirrerie sunt mestre,
> par depuracion legiere?
> Si n'est pas li vairre fouschiere,   16070
> ne fouschiere ne rest pas vairre.[51]

[Do we not see how those who are masters of glass-blowing create from fern,
by means of a simple process of purification, both ash and glass? And neither
is the glass fern, nor does the fern remain glass.]

MONGOL CUSTOMS

1. Cuisine

SqT 67–71 most probably derives from *Mandeville's Travels*, as was first
argued by Bennett,[52] largely on the strength of Chaucer's reference "as tellen
knyghtes olde" (*SqT* 69), which seems to separate Mandeville's account of
admittedly traditional material from all others conceivably available to the poet
in the written records of missionaries and other religious.

Mandeville's Travels

(*From Mandeville's Travels* [Cotton Text], ed. M. C. Seymour [Oxford, 1967],
ch. 26, p. 180.)

In a section devoted to "the lawe and the customs of the Tartarienes duellynge
in Chatay":

> And thei eten houndes, lyouns, lyberdes, mares, and foles, asses, rattes, and
> mees, and alle maner of bestes grete and smale, saf only swyn and bestes that
> weren defended by the olde lawe. And thei eten alle the bestes withouten and
> withinne, withouten castynge awey of ony thing saf only the filth. And thei

---

[51] These lines were identified as a source of *SqT* 253–7 by F. de Tollenaere, "'To Maken of Fern-Asshen Glas,'" *English Studies* 31 [1950]: 97–9.
[52] Josephine Waters Bennett, "Chaucer and *Mandeville's Travels*," *MLN* 68 (1953): 69–72.

eten but litille bred but yif it be in courtes of grete lordes. And thei haue not in many places nouther pesen ne benes ne non other potages but the broth of the flessch, for litille ete thei ony thing but flessch and the broth.

Simon of Saint-Quentin, *Historia Tartarorum*

(Preserved in Vincent of Beauvais, *Speculum Historiale*, 29.78 ["De victu eorum"]; my translation.)

In carnibus autem equinis plus delectantur quam in alijs. Rattos etiam, & canes edunt, & cattos libentissime comedunt, vinum libentissime bibunt quando habere possunt, lacte iumentino, quod ipsi Camous vocant, quotidie sicut & homines caeteri vino forti se inebriant. . . . Carnes autem humanas deuorant vt leones, assas igni & elixas comedentes.[53]

[They take delight more in horse flesh than in any other foods. Moreover, they eat rats and dogs and cats most willingly; they get drunk on mares' milk, which they call kumiss, every day, just as certain men do on strong wine. . . . They devour human flesh, however, like lions, eating it roasted and boiled.]

2. Incest and marriage relations

SqT 667–9, which seems to refer to the romantic conquest of Canacee by "Cambalo," identified in *SqT* 30 as son of Cambyuskan, may indicate Chaucer's knowledge of the Mongols' liberal understanding of consanguinity as an impediment to marriage:

Mandeville's Travels

(From *Mandeville's Travels* [Cotton Text], ed. M. C. Seymour [Oxford, 1967], ch. 25, p. 177.)

In that contree sum man hath an c. wyfes, summe lx., summe mo, summe lesse. And thei taken the nexte of hire kyn to hire wyfes, saf only that thei out taken hire modres, hire doughtres, and hire sustres of the moder syde. But hire sustres on the fadir syde of another womman thei may wel take, and hire bretheres wyfes also after here deth, and here stepmodres also in the same wyse.[54]

---

[53] Cf. the accounts of the Mongols' cuisine in the "Letter of Archbishop Peter" (1241–4), John of Plano Carpini, *Ystoria Mongolorum* (1247), and C. de Bridia, *Tartar Relation* (1247), in Gregory C. Guzman, "Reports of Mongol Cannibalism in the Thirteenth-Century Latin Sources: Oriental Fact or Western Ficton?" in Scott D. Westrem, ed., *Exploring New Worlds: Essays on Medieval Exploration and Imagination* [New York and London, 1991], pp. 31–68, esp. 31–40.

[54] Cf. William of Rubruck, *Itinerarium*, ch. 7, trans. Christopher Dawson, *Mission to Asia* (New York, 1955), p. 104.

3. Magic at the Mongol court

In her edition of the *Squire's Tale*, D. Bethurum calls attention to accounts in the narratives of Odoric of Podernone and Marco Polo of Mongol magicians causing goblets of wine to rise untouched.[55] Mandeville's version is as follows:

Mandeville's Travels

(From *Mandeville's Travels* [Cotton Text], ed. M. C. Seymour [Oxford, 1967], ch. 25, pp. 169–71.)

And at o syde of the emperours table sitten many philosofres that ben preued for wise men in many dyuerse sciences, as of astronomye, nigromancye, geomancye, piromancye, ydromancye, of augurye, and many other sciences. . . . And than comen iogulours and enchauntoures that don many meruaylles. For thei maken to come in the ayr the sonne and the mone be semynge to euery mannes sight. And after thei maken the nyght so derk that no man may see nothing, and after thei maken the day to come ayen fair and plesant with bright sonne to euery mannes sight. And thanne thei bryngen in daunces of the faireste damyselles of the world and richest arrayed. And after thei maken to comen in other damyselles, bryngynge coupes of gold fulle of mylk of dyuerse bestes, and yeuen drynke to lordes and to ladyes. And than thei make knyghtes to iousten in armes fulle lustyly, and thei rennen togidre a gret raundoun, and thei frusschen togidere fulle fiercely and thei breken here speres so rudely that the tronchouns flen in sprotes and peces alle aboute the halle. And than thei make to come in huntyng for the hert and for the boor with houndes rennynge with open mouth. And many other thinges thei don be craft of hire enchauntementes, that it is merueyle for to see.[56]

---

[55] *The Squire's Tale*, ed. Dorothy Bethurum (Oxford, 1965), note to line 219.

[56] I wish to thank Helen Cooper, Ernest Gallo, David O'Connell, and Robert Correale, the General Editor of this volume, for their careful reading of various early drafts of this chapter.

The Franklin's Tale

ROBERT R. EDWARDS

The *Franklin's Tale* incorporates several kinds of literary sources in a story centering on the folklore motif of the "rash promise."[1] Nineteenth- and early-twentieth-century scholars traces the roots of the story to Oriental precursors.[2] Medieval versions of the story appear in Jean de Condé's *Chevalier à la manche* and Don Juan Manuel's *Conde Lucanor* as well as in Matteo Boiardo's *Orlando innamorato*. Chaucer's sources for the *Franklin's Tale* divide into three groups. His major narrative source is a story that Boccaccio included in a sequence of "Questioni d'amore" (Love Questions) in the *Filocolo* and then retold in shortened form and with new thematic emphases in the *Decameron*. Menedon's story in the Love Questions of Book 4 of the *Filocolo* is closest to the *Franklin's Tale* in narrative elements and details, although some scholars have argued recently for the thematic influence of Emilia's tale from *Decameron* 10.5.[3] A second group of sources furnishes topical references and materials used for thematic elaboration in the tale. The third group comprises echoes and reminiscences of various Latin and vernacular works. This chapter focuses on the first two kinds of sources, leaving aside verbal echoes and parallels in phrasing.

The question of Chaucer's major source is complicated historically by the Franklin's announced intention to retell a Breton lay that he has "in remembraunce" (V.709–15). Relying on the prologue, scholars from the late eighteenth century onward assumed that Chaucer must have worked from the text of a lay, yet no extant lay in French or English corresponds to the details of Chaucer's poem.[4] Thirty-four lays survive in French, beginning with Marie de France's twelfth-century collection, which defined many, though not all, characteristics of the genre.[5] Eight English lays besides the *Franklin's Tale*

---

[1] Antti Amatus Aarne, *The Types of the Folk-tale: A Classification and Bibliography*, trans. and rev. Stith Thompson, FF [Folklore Fellows] Communications 74 (Helsinki, 1928), M223.

[2] W. A. Clouston, "The Damsel's Rash Promise: Indian Original and Asiatic and European Versions of the *Franklin's Tale*," *Originals and Analogues of Some of Chaucer's Canterbury Tales*, ed. F. J. Furnivall, Edmund Brock, and W. A. Clouston, Chaucer Society Publications, 2nd series, nos. 7, 10, 15, 20, and 22 (London, 1872–88), pp. 289–340; Pio Rajna, "Le origini della novella narrata del 'Frankeleyn' nei *Canterbury Tales* del Chaucer,", *Romania* 32 (1903): 204–67; Anselm Aman, "Die Filiation der 'Frankeleynes Tale' in Chaucers Canterbury Tales," Diss. Munich (Erlangen, 1912); J. Schick, "Die ältesten Versionen von Chaucers Frankeleynes Tale," *Studia Indo-Iranica: Ehrengabe für Wilhelm Geiger*, ed. Walther Wüst (Leipzig, 1931), pp. 89–107.

[3] N. S. Thompson, *Chaucer, Boccaccio, and the Debate of Love: A Comparative Study of "The Decameron" and "The Canterbury Tales"* (Oxford, 1996), pp. 251–69; and Karla Taylor, "Chaucer's Uncommon Voice: Some Contexts for Influence," *The "Decameron" and the "Canterbury Tales": New Essays on an Old Question*, ed. Leonard Michael Koff and Brenda Deen Schildgen (Madison, NJ, 1999), pp. 47–82.

[4] Thomas Tyrwhitt, *The Canterbury Tales of Chaucer*, 5 vols. (London, 1775–78), argues for a lost source while treating the *Filocolo* and *Decameron* as imitations of it: "The Lay itself is either lost, or buried, perhaps for ever, in one of those sepulchres of Mss. which, by courtesy, are called Libraries; but there are two imitations of it extant by Boccace, the first in the vth Book of his *Philocopo*, and the second in the *Decameron*, D.x. N.5" (I quote from the 2nd ed., 2 vols. [Oxford, 1798], I: 100–2).

[5] For general discussion of the *lai* as a narrative form, see Jean Charles Payen, *Le Lai narratif*, Typologie des sources du moyen âge occidental, fasc. 13, pt. 2 (Turnholt, 1975); see, for the *Franklin's Tale*, Emily Yoder, "Chaucer and the 'Breton Lay,'" *Chaucer Review* 12 (1977): 74–7; and A. C. Spearing, "Marie de France and her Middle English Adapters," *Studies in the Age of Chaucer* 12 (1990): 117–56.

survive. They divide into two groups formally and chronologically.[6] Four lays written in couplets, including the lays of the Auchinleck MS, date from the first half of the fourteenth century; four tail-rhyme lays date from the second half. The thematic resemblances to the French lays and their English imitations led scholars like W. H. Schofield to propose that Chaucer worked from a poem now lost.[7] Laura Hibbard Loomis suggested, however, that Chaucer's knowledge of the genre came largely from the Auchinleck MS.[8] Later scholars have tended to regard the Franklin's invocation of the Breton lay as a rhetorical strategy rather than an authorial definition of the poem's genre. Like Dorigen's name and the mention of Armorik, Pedmark, and Kayrrud, it seeks to create the literary atmosphere of a romantic Breton past.[9]

As Pio Rajna demonstrated, Chaucer's major source is the tale Menedon recounts as the fourth of thirteen Love Questions in Book 4 of the *Filocolo*.[10] The Love Questions form a separate, cohesive collection of tales within the *Filocolo*. Scholars see in them a precursor of the narrative frame (*cornice*) that Boccaccio will later employ in the *Decameron*. Menedon's story and the sequence as a whole are set within an intricate pattern of framing devices. The Love Questions are debated in a pastoral setting by an aristocratic company of young men and women, who amuse themselves and pass the heat of the afternoon by telling stories that illustrate the predicaments occasioned by love. Within the *Filocolo*, this sequence of tales occupies a moment of leisure and repose during Florio's long quest to recover and marry Biancifiore. The larger story of love, separation, and reunion in marriage is contained, in turn, within a narrative of cultural transformation, for it begins in pagan antiquity and ends with conversions to Christianity. Boccaccio offers the still larger fictional pretext that the entire story was recorded in Greek by one of the characters and has been translated by him into the vernacular at the request of his beloved. The *Filocolo* is a vast, sprawling romance. Scholars like Helen Cooper doubt whether Chaucer read it all, though David Wallace has argued that Chaucer may have been influenced by a cursory reading.[11] The *Filocolo* has an extensive manuscript tradition, and from at least the fifteenth century the Love Questions circulated as an independent collection of stories (they were translated as such

6   Texts in Anne Laskaya and Eve Salisbury, eds., *The Middle English Breton Lays*, TEAMS (Consortium for the Teaching of the Middle Ages), Middle English Texts Series (Kalamazoo, MI, 1995); see also Thomas C. Rumble, ed., *The Breton Lays in Middle English* (Detroit, 1965); and Mortimer J. Donovan, *The Breton Lay: A Guide to Varieties* (Notre Dame, IN, 1969).

7   W. H. Schofield, "Chaucer's *Franklin's Tale*," *PMLA* 6 (1901): 405–47.

8   Laura Hibbard Loomis, "Chaucer and the Breton Lays of the Auchinleck MS," *Studies in Philology* 38 (1941): 14–33.

9   On Brittany as a pagan setting, see Kathryn L. Hume, "Why Chaucer Calls the *Franklin's Tale* a Breton Lai," *Philological Quarterly* 51 (1972): 365–79; Alastair J. Minnis, *Chaucer and Pagan Antiquity* (Cambridge, 1982); and Minnis, "From Medieval to Renaissance? Chaucer's Position on Past Gentility," *Proceedings of the British Academy* 72 (1986): 205–46.

10 Pio Rajna, "Le origini." See also "L'Episodio delle questioni d'amore nel *Filocolo* del Boccaccio," *Romania* 31 (1902): 28–81.

11 Helen Cooper, *The Canterbury Tales*, Oxford Guides to Chaucer (Oxford, 1989), pp. 233–4; and David Wallace, *Chaucer and the Early Writings of Boccaccio* (Cambridge, 1985), pp. 39–60.

into other European vernaculars during the Renaissance).[12]

Menedon's story in the *Filocolo* provides the main narrative elements of the *Franklin's Tale*: the lady's request for an apparently impossible feat; the lover's employment of a magician; the obligation to keep a promise; the three successive acts of generosity by the husband, unwanted suitor, and magician; and the final question about which of the three was the most generous ("the mooste fre" V.1622). The *Filocolo's* version differs from the retelling in the *Decameron* in several respects.[13] The *Decameron* omits the elaborate account of the would-be lover's despondent journey to secure help in fulfilling the lady's request, and it lacks the extensive description of the magician's preparations to create a May garden in January, which is the impossible task she has set. At the end, it also emphasizes the lover's abandonment of sexual desire in favor of charity and friendship, whereas the *Filocolo* stresses the *demande* that Chaucer takes up with variation: "which of the three men acted most generously?" In her introductory chapter to this volume, Helen Cooper reviews the evidence for Chaucer's knowledge of the *Decameron*. She argues for structural and thematic parallels, though not verbal resemblances, between the *Decameron* and the *Canterbury Tales*. If Chaucer knew or knew of the *Decameron* but did not have a copy of the text at hand, he might have found an inspiration for the framing device of the *Tales* but not a direct source for the *Franklin's Tale* itself.[14] N. S. Thompson suggests an alternative that admits both sources. Chaucer, he says, may have known the story from both the *Filocolo* and the *Decameron*, and may have added the *Decameron's* concern with compassion into the narrative structure of his own tale. A further alternative is that Chaucer read the story in a collection of the Love Questions excerpted from the *Filocolo*.[15]

A second group of sources introduces new details to the basic story and provides suggestions for Chaucer's thematic elaboration. Geoffrey of Monmouth's *Historia Regum Britanniae* gives the names of the two principal male characters. Arviragus, whose name is a Latinized form from Celtic, is the second son of Cymbeline. He makes peace with the Emperor Claudius, joins him in his campaign to subjugate the Orkneys and the provincial islands to Roman rule, and marries Claudius's daughter Genuissa. Aurelius is the elder brother of Uther Pendragon, and he causes the Carole of the Giants to be moved from Ireland to

---

[12] For discussion of the textual tradition, which serves as the basis for his critical edition of the *Filocolo*, see Antonio Enzo Quaglio, "Tra fonti e testo del *Filocolo*," *Giornale storico della letteratura italiana* 140 (1963): 321–63, 489–551; and "La tradizione del testo del 'Filocolo,'" *Studi sul Boccaccio* 3 (1965): 55–102.

[13] For discussion, see Robert R. Edwards, "Rewriting Menedon's Story: *Decameron* 10.5 and the *Franklin's Tale*," *The "Decameron" and the "Canterbury Tales": New Essays on an Old Question*, pp. 226–46.

[14] See also Donald McGrady, "Chaucer and the *Decameron* Reconsidered," *Chaucer Review* 12 (1977): 1–26; and Peter G. Beidler, "Just Say Yes, Chaucer Knew the *Decameron*: Or, Bringing the *Shipman's Tale* out of Limbo," *The "Decameron" and the "Canterbury Tales": New Essays on an Old Question*, pp. 25–46.

[15] Robert R. Edwards, "Source, Context, and Cultural Translation in the *Franklin's Tale*," *Modern Philology* 94 (1996): 141–62.

Stonehenge. Geoffrey, or perhaps the chronicle histories he spawned in French and English, is a probable source as well for other elements in Chaucer's tale, such as Arveragus's worldly ambition and the miraculous removal of the stones from the coast of Brittany, which is Dorigen's impossible request to Aurelius.

Geoffrey's description of Arviragus's military prowess in initially resisting the Romans gives some background for Arveragus's wish in the *Franklin's Tale* to go to England in order "[T]o seke in armes worshipe and honour" (V.811). Geoffrey also emphasizes Arviragus's deep love for Genuissa, the presumed model for Dorigen. Jerome W. Archer contends, however, that the case for treating Geoffrey as the direct source is by no means secure. He proposes, more-over, that the theme of *trouthe*, which figures so prominently in the *Franklin's Tale*, may derive from a passage in Layamon's *Brut*, which has no parallel in Geoffrey or his Anglo-Norman imitator Wace.[16] In this passage (4887–914), Genuis exhorts Arviragus to respect his pledge (*quides, fore*) of loyalty to Rome when he revolts against Claudius. Geoffrey is the likely source for an episode that parallels the "magyk natureel" (V.1155) by which the clerk of Orléans causes the rocks to disappear temporarily from the coast. Merlin uses his craft and powers to remove the rocks set by the giants in Ireland so that Aurelius can erect a fitting memorial at Stonehenge. Though the details vary from the clerk's "merveille," Geoffrey and Wace share with the *Franklin's Tale* a common interest in the capacity of ingenuity to overcome physical limits. Thomas and Mary Reisner have argued that the legend surrounding the Northumbrian anchorite St. Balred and the Bass Rock offers a more appropriate parallel that Chaucer might have known, but Peter Lucas has shown that Chaucer did not know the legend and that the location is incorrect.[17]

In retelling the story from the *Filocolo*, Chaucer significantly modifies the marriage theme. In Boccaccio there is no doubt that the husband is the governor of the marriage. The lady makes a point of hiding Tarolfo's continued solicita-tions. Part of the debate between Menedon and Fiammetta, which follows the story in the *Filocolo*, has to do with the wife's overstepping her prerogatives by making a contractual promise without her husband's agreement. Chaucer re-defines the marriage in order to emphasize its mutuality and reciprocity. The chief means for doing so is to reject *maistrie*. The speech on marriage which the Franklin inserts into his narrative, much like the marriage encomium of the *Merchant's Tale* (IV.1267–1392), asserts the right of each partner to be free

[16] Jerome W. Archer, "On Chaucer's Source for 'Arveragus' in the 'Franklin's Tale,'" *PMLA* 65 (1950): 318–22.

[17] Thomas A. Reisner and Mary Ellen Reisner, "A British Analogue for the Rock-Motif in the *Franklin's Tale*," *Studies in Philology* 76 (1979): 1–12; and Peter J. Lucas, "Chaucer's Franklin's *Dorigen*: Her Name," *Notes & Queries* n.s. 37 [235] (1990): 398–400. For earlier discussion of the landscape, see J. S. P. Tatlock, *The Scene of the Franklin's Tale Visited*, Chaucer Society Publications, 2nd series 51 [1911] (London, 1914).

from constraints and to exercise liberty while demonstrating patience.[18] Although church doctrine nominally supported companionate marriage, the source closest to the arguments made by the Franklin is the *Roman de la Rose*. In Jean de Meun's portion of the *Rose*, Ami's description of the natural equity that existed in the Golden Age finds a counterpart in marriage (8425–36), and Ami's reproof of the jealous husband (9391–424) advances the case for equality in marriage. The related claim that women are born free and desire liberty comes from Nature's speech later in the *Rose* (13845–68). These propositions, excerpted from Jean's satire, prepare for the thematic complications that result when Arveragus in fact exercises *maistrie* by insisting that Dorigen should redeem her promise to Aurelius. A similar complication arises in Chaucer's borrowings from St. Jerome's *Adversus Jovinianum* for Dorigen's complaint. As Germaine Dempster demonstrated, the complaint is a carefully constructed piece.[19] Chaucer's tale exploits not only the pathetic effects of Jerome's recital of virtuous women driven to death before (and sometimes after) dishonor but also the dramatic discrepancy between the innocent victims of antiquity and the predicament Dorigen has created for herself.

The selections in this chapter present texts and translations of the major narrative elements of the *Franklin's Tale*. References to echoes and reminiscences of Latin and vernacular works can be found throughout the critical literature on the poem.[20] In their version of the chapter in Bryan and Dempster (pp. 377–97), Tatlock and Dempster included a great deal of material relating to the Breton lay.[21] Since these materials provided parallels but not detailed correspondences to Chaucer's text, I have removed them and allowed the prologue shared by *Lay*

---

[18] Discussion in Robert P. Miller, "The Epicurean Homily on Marriage by Chaucer's Franklin," *Mediaevalia* 6 (1980): 151–86; Gerald Morgan, "Boccaccio's *Filocolo* and the Moral Argument of *The Franklin's Tale*," *Chaucer Review* 20 (1986): 285–306; James I. Wimsatt, "Reason, Machaut, and the Franklin," *The Olde Daunce: Love, Friendship, Sex and Marriage in the Medieval World*, ed. Robert R. Edwards and Stephen Spector (Albany, NY, 1991), pp. 201–10.

[19] Germaine Dempster, "Chaucer at Work on the Complaint in the *Franklin's Tale*," *MLN* 52 (1937): 16–23; and "A Further Note on Dorigen's *Exempla*," *MLN* 54 (1939): 137–8.

[20] D. C. Baker, "A Crux in Chaucer's *Franklin's Tale*: Dorigen's Complaint," *Journal of English and Germanic Philology* 60 (1961): 56–64; Robert Cook, "Chaucer's *Franklin's Tale* and *Sir Orfeo*," *Neuphilologische Mitteilungen* 95 (1994): 333–6; Mortimer J. Donovan, "The *Anticlaudian* and Three Passages in the *Franklin's Tale*," *Journal of English and Germanic Philology* 56 (1957): 52–9; Mary Hamel, "*The Franklin's Tale* and Chrétien de Troyes," *Chaucer Review* 17 (1983): 316–31; Kevin J. Harty, "Chaucer and the Fair Field of Anglo-Norman," *Les Bonnes Feuilles* 5 (1975): 3–17; Roger Sherman Loomis, "A Parallel to the Franklin's Discussion of Marriage," *Philologica: The Malone Anniversary Papers*, ed. Thomas A. Kirby and Henry Bosley Woolf (Baltimore, 1949), pp. 191–4; John Livingston Lowes, "The *Franklin's Tale*, the *Teseide* and the *Filocolo*," *Modern Philology* 15 (1917–18): 689–728; Bruce A. Rosenberg, "The Bari Widow and *The Franklin's Tale*," *Chaucer Review* 14 (1980): 344–52; Jesús L. Serrano Reyes, *Didactismo y moralismo en Geoffrey Chaucer y Don Juan Manuel: Un estudio comparativo textual* (Córdoba, 1996); Charles Witke, "*Franklin's Tale*, F 1139–51," *Chaucer Review* 1 (1966): 33–6; C. L. Wrenn, "Chaucer's Knowledge of Horace," *Modern Language Review* 18 (1925): 286–92; Constance S. Wright, "On the *Franklin's Prologue*, 716–21, Persius, and the Continuity of the Mannerist Style," *Philological Quarterly* 52 (1973): 739–46; and Karl Young, "Chaucer's Use of Boccaccio's *Filocolo*," *Modern Philology* 4 (1906–7): 169–77.

[21] See also L. Foulet, "Le Prologue du *Franklin's Tale* et les lais bretons," *Zeitschrift für Romanische Philologie* 30 (1906): 698–711.

le Freine and *Sir Orfeo* to stand as a historical example of what Chaucer might plausibly have understood as characteristic of the genre. Menedon's story from the *Filocolo* is printed from Antonio Enzo Quaglio's edition, which provides the first truly critical edition of a work with a complex textual and editorial history. The nature of Chaucer's borrowing is such that we cannot determine to which part of the textual tradition the manuscript he read might have belonged. Given the tenuous links between the *Filocolo* and other possible references in Chaucer's poetry, I suspect that he might well have read the story in an excerpted collection of the Love Questions, much like the ones executed in the fifteenth century. The variants recorded from the Love Question manuscripts suggest how Boccaccio's concluding question about generosity (*liberalità*) might have transformed into the Franklin's question about freedom (*libertà*). *Decameron* 10.5 is included so as to provide a means for comparing alternate versions of the story and for studying Boccaccio and Chaucer's successive rewritings of the same text. The sections from Geoffrey of Monmouth are substantially those in Bryan and Dempster. Chaucer's knowledge of Geoffrey is shown in his reference to "Englyssh Gaufride" (*House of Fame* 1470). I have added corresponding passages from Wace to show the vernacular tradition of chronicle history and indicate some of the elaborations that the later chroniclers make. Wace amplifies the theme of ingenuity over strength ("engin surmunte vertu") and leaves it intentionally ambiguous whether Merlin operates by magic or science. Similarly, the section from Layamon has been added to show the elaboration of the theme of *trothe*. The passages from the *Roman de la Rose* are another addition. Dempster and Tatlock offer no sources for the Franklin's speech about marriage, but the passage has become a significant focus in more recent criticism. The selection from Jerome's *Adversus Jovinianum* is printed from the critical edition by Ralph Hanna III and Traugott Lawler prepared for The Chaucer Library.[22] Hanna and Lawler's edition supersedes the two editions of Pembroke College, Cambridge MS 234 by Daniel Silvia and John Brennan, Jr., which sought to present a text close to the kind Chaucer would have known.[23] Hanna and Lawler argue on the basis of conjunctive errors that their base manuscript (Cambridge, University Library MS Ii.vi.39) is the closest representative to Chaucer's text. They point out, however, that Chaucer may have gone to a complete text of Jerome rather than relied on excerpts.

[22] Ralph Hanna III and Traugott Lawler, eds., *Jankyn's Book of Wikked Wives*, vol. 1: The Primary Texts, The Chaucer Library (Athens, GA, 1997).

[23] Daniel S. Silvia Jr., "Chaucer's Use of Jerome's *Adversus Jovinianum*, with an Edition of Book I, Chapters 40–49, based on Medieval Manuscripts," Diss. University of Illinois, 1962, *Dissertation Abstracts* 23 (1963), cols. 4345–6; and John Patrick Brennan Jr., "The Chaucerian Text of Jerome's *Adversus Jovinianum*: An Edition Based on Pembroke College, Cambridge, MS 234," Diss. University of California, Davis, 1967, *Dissertation Abstracts* 28 (1968), cols. 4622A–3A. See also Silvia, "Glosses to the *Canterbury Tales* from St. Jerome's *Epistola Adversus Jovinianum*," *Studies in Philology* 62 (1965): 28–39.

I.

Lay le Freine, 1–20

(from Auchinleck Manuscript [Edinburgh, Advocates Library, MS 19.2.1], fol. 261r and from "The Middle English *Lai le Freine*," ed. Margaret Wattie, *Smith College Studies in Modern Languages* 10.3 [1929], p. 1)[24]

	We redeþ oft & findeþ ywrite,	
	& *þis clerkes wele it *wite,	these know
	layes þat ben in harping	
	ben yfounde of *ferli þing.	marvelous
5	Sum *beþe of *wer & sum of wo,	are war
	& sum of ioie & mirþe also,	
	& sum of trecherie & of gile,	
	of old auentours þat *fel *while;	happened once
	& sum of *bourdes & ribaudy,	jests
10	& mani þer beþ of *fairy.	enchantment
	Of al þinges þat men seþ,	
	mest o loue for soþe *þai beþ.	they
	In Breteyne bi *hold time	olden
	þis layes were wrouȝt, so seiþ þis rime.	
15	When kinges miȝt *our yhere	anywhere
	of ani meruailes þat þer were,	
	þai token an harp in *gle & game,	mirth
	& maked a lay & ȝaf it name.	
	Now of þis auentours þat weren yfalle	
20	y can tel sum *ac nouȝt alle.	but

1   **ywrite** te
11   **þinges** þingeþ
12   **mest** maist

[24] The same passage appears at the beginning of the version of *Sir Orfeo* preserved in MS Harley 3810, with some difference in wording and line order and with an additional couplet in an altered passage after line 12 of the Auchinleck MS; see *Sir Orfeo*, ed. A. J. Bliss, 2nd ed. (Oxford, 1966). The version of *Sir Orfeo* in Oxford, Bodleian Library, MS Ashmole 61 also opens with a definition of the topics of the lay; see Bliss, pp. 3–4.

II

Il Filocolo, 4.31–4

The noble lady seemed happy from her appearance, when Menedon, who was seated near her, said, "Most exalted queen, the turn now falls to me to propose a question in your presence, which with your permission I shall ask. And if hereafter I extend myself too far in my speech, [5] I beg pardon from you and the others here with me. But what I intend to ask could not be understood fully if it were not preceded by a story, which may perhaps not be short." And after these words he began to speak as follows.

In the land where I was born, I remember there was a very rich and noble gentleman who, loving a lady of the city with a perfect love, [10] took her for his wife. Another gentleman named Tarolfo fell in love with this lady, since she was very beautiful; and he loved her with so much love that he had eyes only for her and desired nothing more. He undertook to gain her love in many ways, such as often passing in front of her house, or jousting, or fighting in tournaments, or other deeds; and he often sent her messengers, perhaps to promise her very great gifts and to learn her intention. [15] The lady bore all these things quietly, without giving a sign or favorable response to the gentleman, saying within herself, "Once this man realizes that he can obtain no favorable response or good act from me, perhaps he will stop loving me and bothering me." But through all this Tarolfo still did not stop, [20] following the teachings of Ovid who said that a man should not stop persevering because of a lady's hardness, since by persistence soft water works its way through hard rock. But the lady, fearing that these things might come to her husband's notice and that he then might think it happened through her wishes, decided to tell him about it, but she was swayed by a better idea and said, "I [25] might, if I told him, start something between them that would never let me live happily again; this should be handled some other way." And so she hit upon a devious trick. She sent word to Tarolfo as follows: if he loved her as much as he claimed, she would like a gift from him which, once she had received it, she swore by her gods and by that loyalty gentle ladies should possess that she would satisfy his every [30] pleasure; but if he did not want to give her what she asked, he should determine not to bother her further, unless

Variants: Of the variants listed below, readings from B, RL, Vo, and Vr1 are taken from independent collections of the Love Questions; Vch is a manuscript of the *Filocolo* belonging to a subgroup in the family that Quaglio regards as a less reliable source for Boccaccio's work.

B   Kraków, Biblioteka Jagiellońska, Cod. Ital. gu. 16, s. xv
RL   Rome, Biblioteca dell'Accademia dei Lincei, Codex 44, E, 31 (Rossi 184), s. xv (1443 or 1444)
Vch Rome, Biblioteca Apostolica Vaticana, Chigi L, VI, 233, s. xv
Vo   Rome, Biblioteca Apostolica Vaticana, Ottoboni Latinus 2151, s. xv
Vr1 Rome, Biblioteca Apostolica Vaticana, Rossi 936, s. xv

II

Il Filocolo, 4.31–4

(from *Il Filocolo*, ed. Antonio Enzo Quaglio,
Vol. 1 of *Tutte le opere di Giovanni Boccaccio*, ed. Vittore Branca
[Milan: Mondadori, 1964–83], 396–410)

Era nella vista contenta la gentil donna, quando Menedon, che appresso di
lei sedea, disse, "Altissima reina, ora viene a me la volta del proporre nel
vostro cospetto, ond'io con la vostra licenza dirò. E da ora, se io troppo nel
mio parlare mi stendessi, a voi e appresso agli altri circunstanti dimando
5   perdono, però che quello ch'io intendo di proporre interamente dare non si
potrebbe a intendere, se a quello una novella, che non fia forse brieve, non
precedesse." E dopo queste parole così cominciò a parlare.
   Nella terra là dov'io nacqui, mi ricorda essere un ricchissimo e nobile
cavaliere, il quale di perfettissimo amore amando una donna nobile della terra,
10   per isposa la prese. Della quale donna, essendo bellissima, un altro cavaliere
chiamato Tarolfo s'innamorò; e di tanto amore l'amava, che oltre a lei non
vedeva, né niuna cosa più disiava, e in molte maniere, forse con sovente
passare davanti alle sue case, o giostrando, o armeggiando, o con altri atti,
s'ingegnava d'avere l'amore di lei, e spesso mandandole messaggieri, forse
15   promettendole grandissimi doni, e per sapere il suo intendimento. Le quali
cose la donna tutte celatamente sostenea, sanza dare o segno o risposta buona
al cavaliere, fra sé dicendo, "Poi che questi s'avedrà che da me né buona
risposta né buono atto puote avere, forse elli si rimarrà d'amarmi e di darmi
questi stimoli." Ma già per tutto questo Tarolfo di ciò non si rimanea,
20   seguendo d'Ovidio gli amaestramenti, il quale dice l'uomo non lasciare per
durezza della donna di non perseverare, però che per continuanza la molle
acqua fora la dura pietra.[25] Ma la donna, dubitando non queste cose venissero
a orecchie del marito, e esso pensasse poi che con volontà di lei questo
avvenisse, propose di dirgliele; ma poi mossa da miglior consiglio disse, "Io
25   potrei, s'io il dicessi, commettere tra costoro cosa che io mai non viverei lieta:
per altro modo si vuole levare via," e imaginò una sottile malizia. Ella mandò
così dicendo a Tarolfo, che se egli tanto l'amava quanto mostrava, ella volea
da lui un dono, il quale come l'avesse ricevuto, giurava per li suoi iddii, e per
quella leanza che in gentile donna dee essere, che essa farebbe ogni suo
30   piacere; e se quello che domandava, donare non le volesse, ponessesi in cuore
di non stimolarla più avanti, se non per quanto egli non volesse che essa
questo manifestasse al marito. E 'l dono il quale ella dimandò fu questo. Ella
disse che volea del mese di gennaio, in quella terra, un bel giardino e grande,

---

[25] Ovid, *Ars amatoria* 1.475–76 and *Epistulae ex Ponto* 4.10.5; cf. Hans Walther, ed., *Proverbia
sententiaeque latinitatis medii aevi: Lateinische Sprichwörter und Sentenzen des Mittelalters in
alphabetischer Anordnung,* 9 vols. (Göttingen, 1965–69), 5599a.

he wanted her to reveal this to her husband. And the gift she asked for was this. She said she wanted a beautiful and large garden in the city during the month of January, full of grass and flowers and trees and fruit, as if it were the month of May. [35] She said to herself, "This is something impossible: I shall rid myself of him this way." When Tarolfo heard this, though it seemed impossible to him and he understood perfectly why the lady had requested it, he answered that he would never rest or come again into her presence until he could give her the gift she had asked. He left the city with the [40] company that he wanted to keep and searched all the western world looking for counsel about how to fulfill his desire, but finding no one, he searched the hottest regions and came to Thessaly, where he was sent for this purpose by a prudent man. When he had stayed there a few days, not having found what he had been seeking, it happened that as he was almost despondent about his purpose [45] he arose one morning before the sun was ready to rise in the dawn and began to walk all alone across the miserable plain that had once been tinged with Roman blood. And after he had gone a long ways, he saw a man before him at the foot of a mountain; he was not young nor too old, bearded – his clothes indicated that he must be poor – [50] small in stature and very thin. He was going along gathering herbs and using a small knife to dig up different roots with which he filled the hem of his gown. When Tarolfo saw him he was amazed and was not sure what he might be; but after he was certain he was a man, he drew near to him and greeted him, asking him who he was and [55] where he came from and what he was doing in that place at such an hour. The little old man answered, "I am from Thebes, and Tebano is my name; and I go collecting herbs in this plain to make from their juices some things necessary and useful in different illnesses, which is how I make a living, and necessity rather than pleasure compels me to come at this hour. But who are you, who [60] seem so noble in appearance and walk here alone?" Tarolfo replied to him, "I am a very wealthy gentleman from the far west, and because I am overwhelmed and troubled by thoughts of an undertaking of mine, which I cannot achieve, I go walking alone this way so I can grieve better without restraint." Tebano said to him, "Don't you know the nature of the place? Why did you not take another [65] way beforehand? You might easily be attacked by evil spirits here." Tarolfo answered, "God's power is the same everywhere. Here as elsewhere he has my life and my honor in his hands; let him do with me as he pleases. Death would truly be a most rich treasure to me." Then Tebano said, "What is your undertaking, which leaves you so sorrowful because you cannot achieve it?" [70] Tarolfo answered him, "It is such that it seems impossible to me ever to bring it off, since I have found no advice here." Tebano said, "Do you dare say what it is?" Tarolfo replied, "Yes, but to what good?" "Perhaps none," said Tebano, "but what is the harm?" Then Tarolfo said, "I am searching for advice about how in the coldest month I can have a garden full of flowers, fruits, and grass, [75] beautiful as if it were the month of May; I can find no one to give me help or advice about it that is true." Tebano stood suspended a moment without answering and then said, "You and many others judge the knowledge and power of men according to their clothes. If my robe had been like yours or if you had found me among rich princes [80] instead of gathering herbs, you would not have found it diffi-cult to tell me your need; but often the greatest treasure of knowledge is

d'erbe e di fiori e d'alberi e di frutti copioso, come se del mese di maggio
35 fosse, fra sé dicendo, "Questa è cosa impossibile: io mi leverò costui da dosso
per questa maniera." Tarolfo, udendo questo, ancora che impossibile gli
paresse e che egli conoscesse bene perché la donna questo gli domandava,
rispose che già mai non riposerebbe né in presenza di lei tornerebbe, infino a
tanto che il dimandato dono le donerebbe. E partitosi della terra con quella
40 compagnia che a lui piacque di prendere, tutto il ponente cercò per avere
consiglio di potere pervenire al suo disio; ma non trovato lui, cercò le più
calde regioni, e pervenne in Tesaglia, dove per sì fatta bisogna fu mandato da
discreto uomo. E quivi dimorato più giorni, non avendo ancora trovato quello
che cercando andava, avvenne che essendosi egli quasi del suo avviso
45 disperato, levatosi una mattina avanti che 'l sole s'apparecchiasse d'entrare
nell'aurora, incominciò tutto soletto ad andare per lo misero piano che già
tinto fu del romano sangue.[26] E essendo per grande spazio andato, egli si vide
davanti a' piè d'un monte un uomo, non giovane né di troppa lunga età,
barbuto, e i suoi vestimenti giudicavano lui dovere essere povero, picciolo di
50 persona e sparuto molto, il quale andava cogliendo erbe e cavando con un
picciolo coltello diverse radici, delle quali un lembo della sua gonnella avea
pieno. Il quale quando Tarolfo il vide, si maravigliò e dubitò molto non altro
fosse;[27] ma poi che la stimativa certamente gli rendé lui essere uomo, egli
s'appressò a lui e salutollo, domandandolo appresso chi egli fosse e donde, e
55 quello che per quello luogo a così fatta ora andava faccendo. A cui il
vecchierello rispose, "Io sono di Tebe, e Tebano è il mio nome, e per questo
piano vo cogliendo queste erbe, acciò che de' liquori d'esse faccendo alcune
cose necessarie e utili a diverse infermità, io abbia onde vivere, e a questa ora
necessità e non diletto mi ci costringe di venire; ma tu chi se' che nell'aspetto
60 risembri nobile, e quinci sì soletto vai?" A cui Tarolfo rispose, "Io sono
dell'ultimo ponente assai ricco cavaliere, e da' pensieri d'una mia impresa
vinto e stimolato, non potendola fornire, di qua, per meglio potermi sanza
impedimento dolere, mi vo così soletto andando." A cui Tebano disse, "Non
sai tu la qualità del luogo come ella è? Perché inanzi d'altra parte non pigliavi
65 la via? Tu potresti di leggieri qui da furiosi spiriti essere vituperato." Rispose
Tarolfo, "In ogni parte puote Iddio igualmente: così qui come altrove gli è la
mia vita e 'l mio onore in mano; faccia di me secondo che a lui piace:
veramente a me sarebbe la morte un ricchissimo tesoro." Disse allora Tebano,
"Quale è la tua impresa, per la quale, non potendola fornire, sì dolente
70 dimori?" A cui Tarolfo rispose, "È tale che impossibile mi pare omai a
fornire, poi che qui non ho trovato consiglio." Disse Tebano, "Osasi dire?"
Rispose Tarolfo, "Sì, ma a che utile?" "Forse niuno," disse Tebano, "ma che
danno?" Allora Tarolfo disse, "Io cerco di potere aver consiglio come del più
freddo mese si potesse avere un giardino pieno di fiori e di frutti e d'erbe,
75 bello sì come del mese di maggio fosse, né trovo chi a ciò aiuto o consiglio mi
doni che vero sia." Stette Tebano un pezzo tutto sospeso sanza rispondere, e
poi disse, "Tu e molti altri il sapere e le virtù degli uomini giudicate secondo i
vestimenti. Se la mia roba fosse stata qual è la tua, tu non m'avresti tanto

---

[26] Near Pharsalus, the site of the battle between Caesar and Pompey celebrated in Lucan's epic poem the
   Pharsalia.
[27] Not a ghost or phantom from the battle.

hidden under the filthiest cloth, and so no one should hide his need to anyone who offers counsel and help, provided that it cannot hurt him to have it known. But what will you give the person you are looking for to bring this off for you?" Tarolfo stared at his face as he was saying these words and wondered if he were making fun of him, [85] since it seemed unbelievable to him that he should be able to wield such power, unless he were God. Nonetheless, he answered thus, "I am lord over many castles in my land and much treasure because of them, all of which I will divide in half with whoever does me this favor." "Surely if I do this," said Tebano, "I won't need to go gathering herbs." [90] "Certainly," said Tarolfo, "if you are the one who promises to accomplish this and then brings it off, you won't have to exert yourself any more to become rich, but how or when can you do this for me?" Tebano said, "When is up to you; don't concern yourself with the how. I shall come with you, trusting in the word of the promise you make me, and when we arrive where you want to be, [95] command what you wish – I shall provide it without fail." Tarolfo was so happy within himself because of this development that he could have been scarcely happier if he had held his lady in his arms then, and he said, "Friend, for me it is getting late to do what you promised, so let us leave without delay and go where it must be done." Tebano threw aside the herbs and, [100] taking up his books and the other things needed for his art, took to the road with Tarolfo, and in a short time they came to the city they sought, rather close to the month when the garden had been requested. They rested there quietly and in hiding until the appointed time, but when the month arrived, Tarolfo ordered that the garden be made ready so that he might give it to his [105] lady. As soon as Tebano had the order, he waited for night and, when it came, he saw the moon turn its horns into a full circle and shine its full radiance over the familiar countryside. Then he went out from the city, leaving his clothes and shoes, with his hair thrown over his bare shoulders, all alone. The erratic stages of night passed; birds, animals and men rested without any murmur; [110] and above the mountains the unfallen leaves were without movement, and the damp air rested in peace. Only the stars were shining, when, having walked around the city many times, he came to the place which he had chosen for the garden, which was next to a stream. There he raised his arms toward the stars, turning toward them three times, and bathed his white hair in the running water as many times, [115] calling as often for their help with a loud voice. Then kneeling on the hard earth, he began to say: "O night, truest secret of high things, and you, o stars, who follow the resplendent day together with the moon, and you, o greatest Hecate, who come as helper to the things we have begun, and you, o holy Ceres, renewer of the full face of the [120] earth, and all you verses, o arts, o herbs, and you, earth, producing powerful plants, and you, breezes and winds and mountains and rivers and lakes, and each god of the woods or secret night, through whose help I have already turned the running rivers back to their sources and made moving things stand still and still ones start moving and who already gave my verses the power to hunt the oceans [125] and search their depths without doubt and to brighten cloudy weather and fill up the clear

100 **maesterio** misterio BVo

penato a dire la tua bisogna, o se forse appresso de' ricchi prencipi m'avessi
80   trovato, come tu hai a cogliere erbe; ma molte volte sotto vilissimi drappi
grandissimo tesoro di scienza si nasconde: e però a chi proffera consiglio o
aiuto niuno celi la sua bisogna, se, manifesta, non gli può pregiudicare. Ma
che doneresti tu a chi quello che tu vai cercando ti recasse ad effetto?" Tarolfo
rimirava costui nel viso, dicendo egli queste parole, e in sé dubitava non
85   questi si facesse beffe di lui, parendogli incredibile che, se colui fosse stato
Iddio, ch'egli avesse potuto fare virtù. Non per tanto egli li rispose così, "Io
signoreggio ne' miei paesi più castella, e con esse molti tesori, i quali tutti per
mezzo partirei con chi tal piacere mi facesse." "Certo," disse Tebano, "se
questo facessi, a me non bisognerebbe d'andare più cogliendo l'erbe."
90   "Fermamente," disse Tarolfo, "se tu se' quelli che in ciò mi prometti di dare
vero effetto, e davelo, mai non ti bisognerà più affannare per divenire ricco;
ma come o quando mi potrai tu questo fornire?" Disse Tebano, "Il quando fia
a tua posta, del come non ti travagliare. Io me ne verrò teco fidandomi nella
tua parola della promessa che mi fai, e quando là dove ti piacerà saremo,
95   comanderai quello che tu vorrai: io fornirò tutto sanza fallo." Fu di questo
accidente tanto contento in se medesimo Tarolfo, che poca più letizia avria
avuta se nelle sue braccia la sua donna allora tenuta avesse, e disse, "Amico, a
me si fa tardi che quello che imprometti si fornisca: però sanza indugio
partiamo e andiamo là ove questo si dee fornire." Tebano, gittate via l'erbe, e
100 presi i suoi libri e altre cose al suo maesterio necessarie, con Tarolfo si mise al
cammino, e in brieve tempo pervennero alla disiderata città, assai vicini al
mese del quale era stato dimandato il giardino. Quivi tacitamente e occulti
infino al termine disiderato si riposarono; ma entrato già il mese, Tarolfo
comandò che 'l giardino s'apprestasse, acciò che donare lo potesse alla sua
105 donna. Come Tebano ebbe il comandamento, egli aspettò la notte, e, venuta,
vide i corni della luna tornati in compiuta ritondità, e videla sopra l'usate terre
tutta risplendere.[28] Allora egli uscì della città, lasciati i vestimenti, scalzo, e
con i capelli sparti sopra li nudi omeri, tutto solo. I vaghi gradi della notte
passavano, gli uccelli, le fiere e gli uomini riposavano sanza niuno mormorio,
110 e sopra i monti le non cadute frondi stavano sanza alcuno movimento, e
l'umido aere in pace si riposava: solamente le stelle luceano, quando egli, più
volte circuita la terra, pervenne al luogo, il quale gli piacque d'eleggere per lo
giardino, allato ad un fiume. Quivi stese verso le stelle le braccia, tre volte
rivoltandosi ad esse, e tante i bianchi capelli nella corrente acqua bagnò,
115 domandando altretante volte con altissima voce il loro aiuto; poi poste le
ginocchie sopra la dura terra, cominciò così a dire: "O notte, fidatissima
segreta dell'alte cose, e voi, o stelle, le quali al risplendente giorno con la luna
insieme succedete, e tu, o somma Ecate, la quale aiutatrice vieni alle cose
incominciate da noi, e tu, o santa Cerere, rinnovatrice dell'ampia faccia della
120 terra, e voi qualunque versi, o arti, o erbe, e tu qualunque terra producente
virtuose piante, e voi aure, e venti, e monti, e fiumi, e laghi, e ciascuno iddio
de' boschi o della segreta notte, per li cui aiuti io già rivolsi i correnti fiumi
faccendogli tornare nelle loro fonti, e già feci le correnti cose stare ferme, e le
ferme divenire correnti, e che già deste a' miei versi potenza di cacciare i mari

---

[28] Boccaccio's description of Tebano's magic is based on Ovid's account of Medea's effort to save the
life of Aeson, Jason's aging father, in *Metamorphoses* 7.179–293.

sky with dark clouds at my whim, making the wind cease and come as I pleased, and who break the hard jaws of the frightful dragons, making as well the standing forests move and the high mountains tremble and the shades return from the Stygian swamps into their dead bodies and go out alive [130] from their tombs, and sometimes take you, o moon, from your roundness, which in former times the sounding horns used to help you do, sometimes also making the bright face of the sun grow pale – be present and give me your assistance. I have need now of juices and herbs by which the dry earth, despoiled of its flowers, fruits, and grasses first by autumn and then by the coldest winter, [135] might be made to return flowering, showing springtime before its proper season." This much said, he quietly added many other things to his prayers. Then he fell quiet, and the stars did not shed their beams in vain, but faster than the flight of a bird, a chariot drawn by two dragons came before him; he climbed into it, and took the reins that guided the two dragons into his hands, and mounted up into the [140] air. Taking his way through the high regions, he left Spain behind and set out for the island of Crete; from there he sought Pelion, Ocris and Ossa, Mount Nero, Pacchino, Peloro, and the Appenines all in short course, plucking out and cutting the roots and herbs he wanted with his sharp sickle, nor did he forget those he was picking when Tarolfo found him in Thessaly. He took stones [145] from the top of Mount Caocaso and gathered the tongues of poisonous snakes from the sand of the Ganges and Libya. He saw the wet banks of the Rhône, the Seine, Amphrysus and Ninfeo, the mighty Po, the imperial Tiber, the Arno, the Don, and the Danube, taking from these, too, the herbs that seemed necessary to him, and he added them to the others gathered from the summits of the wild [150] mountains. He sought out the island of Lesbos and that of Colchis and Delphos and Patmos, and whatever others he felt would be useful to his purpose.

With these things, he came back before the third day was over to the place from which he had left; and the dragons, which had merely smelled the aroma of the herbs he had gathered, throwing off the old scales of many years, were rejuvenated and [155] made young again. He dismounted there and made two altars of grassy earth, the one on the left for Hecate, the one on the right for the goddess of renewal. When this was done and votive fire had been lit on them, he began to walk around them with his hair thrown over his old shoulders and with an uneasy murmur; time and again he dipped burning wood into the blood he had gathered. Then putting them back on the altars and sometimes using [160] them to water the earth he had chosen for the garden, he sprinkled this same earth three times with fire, water, and sulfur. Then, having placed an immense vase full of blood, milk, and water on the burning flames, he made it boil for a long time, adding the herbs and roots gathered from the strange places, putting in various seeds and the flowers of [165] unknown herbs, and adding stones found in the far east, hoar-frost gathered from the previous nights, together with the flesh and wings of starved witches, the last part of a wolf's testicles, the scales of a Libyan snake, and the skin of a watersnake, and finally a liver of a very old stag along with all the lungs; and to these he added a thousand other things, either without names or with names so strange that memory fails me. [170] Then he took a branch from a dried olive tree and began to mix all these things together with it. As he did this, the dry branch began to turn green and quickly it sent out leaves, and not much

125   e di cercare sanza dubbio i loro fondi, e di rischiarare il nuvoloso tempo, e il
chiaro cielo riempiere a mia posta d'oscuri nuvoli, faccendo i venti cessare e
venire come mi pareva, e con quelli rompendo le dure mascelle degli
spaventevoli dragoni, faccendo ancora muovere le stanti selve e tremare gli
eccelsi monti, e ne' morti corpi tornare da' paduli di Stige le loro ombre e vivi

130   uscire de' sepolcri, e tal volta tirare te, o luna, alla tua ritondità, alla quale per
adietro i sonanti bacini ti soleano aiutare venire, faccendo ancora tal volta la
chiara faccia del sole impalidire: siate presenti, e 'l vostro aiuto mi porgete. Io
ho al presente mestiere di sughi e d'erbe, per li quali l'arida terra, prima
d'autunno, ora dal freddissimo verno, de' suoi fiori, frutti e erbe spogliata,

135   faccia in parte ritornare fiorita, mostrando, avanti il dovuto termine,
primavera." Questo detto, molte altre cose tacitamente aggiunse a' suoi
prieghi. Poi tacendo, le stelle non dieron luce invano, ma più veloce che volo
d'alcuno uccello un carro da due dragoni tirato gli venne avanti, sopra il quale
egli montò, e, recatesi le redine de' posti freni a' due dragoni in mano, suso in

140   aria si tirò. E pigliando per l'alte regioni il cammino, lasciò Spagna e cercò
l'isola di Creti: di quindi Pelion, e Ocris e Ossa, e 'l monte Nero, Pacchino,
Peloro e Appennino in brieve corso cercò tutti, di tutti svellendo e segando
con aguta falce quelle radici e erbe che a lui piacevano, né dimenticò quelle
che divelte avea quando da Tarolfo fu travato in Tesaglia. Egli prese pietre

145   d'in sul monte Caocaso, e dell'arene di Gange e di Libia recò lingue di
velenosi serpenti. Egli vide le bagnate rive del Rodano, di Senna, d'Amprisi e
di Ninfeo, e del gran Po, e dello imperial Tevero, e d'Arno, e di Tanai, e del
Danubio, di sopra da quelle ancora prendendo quelle erbe che a lui pareano
necessarie, e queste aggiunse all'altre colte nelle sommità de' salvatichi

150   monti. Egli cercò l'isola di Lesbos e quella de' Colchi e Delfos e Patimos, e
qualunque altra nella quale sentito avesse cosa utile al suo intendimento.
    Con le quali cose, non essendo ancora passato il terzo giorno, venne in quel
luogo onde partito s'era: e i dragoni, che solamente l'odore delle prese erbe
aveano sentito, gittando lo scoglio vecchio per molti anni, erano rinnovellati e

155   giovani ritornati. Quivi smontato, d'erbosa terra due altari compose, dalla
destra mano quello d'Ecate, dalla sinistra quello della rinnovellante dea.[29] I
quali fatti, e sopr'essi accesi divoti fuochi, co' crini sparti sopra le vecchie
spalle, con inquieto mormorio cominciò a circuire quelli: e in raccolto sangue
più volte intinse le ardenti legne. Poi riponendole sopra gli altari e tal volta

160   con esse inaffiando quel terreno il quale egli avea al giardino disposto, dopo
questo, quello medesimo tre volte di fuoco e d'acqua e di solfo rinnaffiò. Poi,
posto un grandissimo vaso sopra l'ardenti fiamme, pieno di sangue, di latte e
d'acqua, quello fece per lungo spazio bollire, aggiungendovi l'erbe e le radici
colte negli strani luoghi, mettendovi ancora con esse diversi semi e fiori di

165   non conosciute erbe, e aggiunsevi pietre cercate nello estremo oriente, e brina
raccolta le passate notti, insieme con carni e ali d'infamate streghe, e de'
testicoli del lupo l'ultima parte, con isquama di cinifo e con pelle del chelidro,
e ultimamente un fegato con tutto il polmone d'un vecchissimo cervio: e, con
queste, mille altre cose, o sanza nomi o sì strane che la memoria nol mi ridice.

170   Poi prese un ramo d'un secco ulivo e con esso tutte queste cose cominciò a

---

[29] Ceres.

after that, covered with them, one could see it was loaded with black olives. When Tebano saw this, he took the boiling liquid and began to pour it out and spread it over the spot of land he had chosen and on which he had placed [175] sticks for the number and kinds of trees he wanted. The earth no sooner felt this than everything began to bloom, producing new and beautiful grasses, and the dry sticks became green plants and all of them were fruitbearing. When this was done, Tebano went back to the city, returning to Tarolfo, who was somewhat fearful that he had been [180] tricked by him because of the long time that he had been away, and Tebano found him very pensive. He said to him, "Tarolfo, what you have asked has been done, and it is at your pleasure." This pleased Tarolfo well enough, and since the next day was a most solemn feastday in the city, he went to his lady, who had not seen him for a very long time, and he said to her, "My lady, after a long [185] labor, I have produced what you commanded; when it pleases you to see it and take possession, it is at your disposal."

The lady marveled much at seeing him and even more hearing what he said; and not believing it, she answered, "That pleases me well; let me see it tomorrow." On the following day, Tarolfo went to the lady and said, [190] "My lady, may it please you to go to the garden, which you asked of me in the cold month." The lady went then, accompanied by many people, and came to the garden; they entered through a beautiful gateway, and the air inside felt mild and sweet, not cold like outside. The lady walked around everywhere, admiring and gathering herbs and flowers, of which there seemed to be many; and [195] moreover the power of the liquids that had been sprinkled around caused fruits usually seen in August to be produced and made all the trees beautiful there in the fierce season; and many people, walking with the lady, ate them. This seemed a most beautiful and marvelous thing to the lady, and no other had ever seemed so beautiful to her. And when she was sure in many ways that this was a true garden [200] and that the gentleman had satisfied what she had requested, she turned to Tarolfo and said, "Without a doubt, my sir, you have gained my love, and I am prepared to stand by what I promised you. I truly wish one favor – that you be willing to delay submitting me to your desire until my husband goes hunting or some place else outside the city so that you [205] can take your pleasure more safely and without worry." This pleased Tarolfo and leaving the garden, he departed from her very nearly contented. This garden was made known to all the people in the area, except no one knew until much later how it came to be. But the noble lady who had received it and was sorrowful because of this, left and returned to her bedroom full of sad dejection. [210] Wondering how she might renege on what she had promised and finding no acceptable excuse, she felt more sorrow. Her husband saw this many times and began to marvel much and ask her what was bothering her. Too ashamed to reveal to her husband the promise made for the gift she had asked, the lady said it was nothing, fearing that her husband might think her wicked. [215] Finally, not being able to resist the questions of her husband who still wanted to know the cause of her

240 **liberalità** liberta RLVch
260 **liberalità** liberata *corr* liberalita Vrl
284 **liberalità** liberta RLVo

mescolare insieme. La qual cosa faccendo, il secco ramo cominciò a divenire verde e in brieve a mettere le frondi, e, non dopo molto, rivestito di quelle, si poté vedere carico di nere ulive. Come Tebano vide questo, egli prese i boglienti liquori, e sopra lo eletto terreno, nel quale di tanti legni avea fatti
175 bastoni quanti alberi e di quante maniere voleva, e quivi quelli liquori incominciò a spandere e ad inaffiare per tutto: la qual cosa la terra non sentì prima, ch'ella cominciò tutta a fiorire, producendo nuove e belle erbette, e i secchi legni verdi piantoni e fruttiferi divennero tutti. La qual cosa fatta, Tebano rientrò nella terra tornando a Tarolfo, il quale quasi pauroso d'essere
180 stato da lui beffato per la lunga dimoranza dimorava, e trovollo tutto pensoso. A cui egli disse, "Tarolfo, fatto è quello che hai dimandato, e è al piacere tuo." Assai piacque questo a Tarolfo, e dovendo essere il seguente giorno nella città una grandissima solennità, egli se n'andò davanti alla sua donna, la quale già era gran tempo che veduta non l'avea, e così le disse, "Madonna, dopo lunga
185 fatica io ho fornito quello che voi comandaste: quando vi piacerà di vederlo e di prenderlo, egli è al vostro piacere."

La donna, vedendo costui, si maravigliò molto, e più udendo ciò che egli diceva; e non credendolo, rispose, "Assai mi piace; faretecelo vedere domane." Venuto il seguente giorno, Tarolfo andò alla donna, e disse,
190 "Madonna, piacciavi di passare nel giardino, il quale voi mi dimandaste nel freddo mese." Mossesi adunque la donna da molti accompagnata, e pervenuti al giardino, v'entrarono dentro per una bella porta, e in quello non freddo come di fuori, ma uno aere temperato e dolce si sentiva. Andò la donna per tutto rimirando e cogliendo erbe e fiori, de' quali molto il vide copioso: e
195 tanto più ancora avea operato la virtù degli sparti liquori, che i frutti, i quali l'agosto suole producere, quivi nel salvatico tempo tutti i loro alberi facevano belli: de' quali più persone, andate con la donna, mangiarono. Questo parve alla donna bellissima cosa e mirabile, né mai un sì bello ne le pareva avere veduto. E poi che essa in molte maniere conobbe quello essere vero giardino,
200 e 'l cavaliere avere adempiuto ciò che ella avea domandato, ella si voltò a Tarolfo e disse, "Sanza fallo, cavaliere, guadagnato avete l'amore mio, e io sono presta d'attenervi ciò che io vi promisi; veramente voglio una grazia, che vi piaccia tanto indugiarvi a richiedermi del vostro disio, che 'l signore mio vada a caccia o in altra parte fuori della città, acciò che più salvamente e sanza
205 dubitanza alcuna possiate prendere vostro diletto." Piacque a Tarolfo, e lasciandole il giardino, quasi contento da lei si partì. Questo giardino fu a tutti i paesani manifesto, avvegna che niuno non sapesse, se non dopo molto tempo, come venuto si fosse. Ma la gentil donna, che ricevuto l'avea, dolente di quello si partì, tornando nella sua camera piena di noiosa malinconia. E
210 pensando in qual maniera tornare potesse adietro ciò che promesso avea, e non trovando licita scusa, in più dolore cresceva. La quale vedendo il marito più volte, si cominciò molto a maravigliare e a domandarla che cosa ella avesse: la donna dicea che niente avea, vergognandosi di scoprire al marito la fatta promissione per lo dimandato dono, dubitando non il marito malvagia la
215 tenesse. Ultimamente, non potendosi ella a' continui stimoli del marito, che pur la cagione della sua malinconia disiderava di sapere, tenersi, dal principio

despondency, she told him from beginning to end why she continued to be sad. Hearing the account, the gentleman thought a long time and, knowing in his mind the lady's purity, he said the following, "Go and secretly keep your promise; give Tarolfo freely what [220] you promised. He has earned it reasonably and with great labor." The lady began to lament and say, "May the gods keep such a blemish far from me; in no way will I do this. I would rather kill myself than do something that would be dishonorable or displeasing to you." The gentleman said to her, "Lady, I do not want you to kill yourself over this or [225] even give yourself a single moment of sadness. It will not displease me; go and do what you promised, for I shall not hold you less dear. But once you have done this, beware of these kinds of promises next time, even if you think the gift you ask for is impossible to have."

When the lady saw her husband's wish, she adorned herself and made herself beautiful and, taking an [230] entourage, she went to Tarolfo's lodging; and painted with shame, she presented herself before him. When he saw her, Tarolfo rose from beside Tebano with whom he was sitting; and he went to meet her full of wonder and joy and received her honorably, asking the reason for her coming. The lady replied to him, "I have come to be wholly at your pleasure; do with me what you please." Then [235] Tarolfo said, "You make me wonder endlessly, considering the hour and the company with which you have come. This could not happen without discussion between you and your husband. Tell me about it, I pray you." Then the lady told the story completely to Tarolfo, just as the things were in order. When he heard this, Tarolfo began to marvel more than before and to ponder, and he began to realize [240] the great generosity shown to him by the husband who had commanded her to go to him, and he said to himself that whoever would think of committing an ignoble act to such a generous man would be worthy of great censure. Speaking to the lady, he said, "Noble lady, you have discharged your obligation loyally and as a valiant woman, for which I take as received what I desired from you. And so when you please, [245] you may return to your husband and thank him on my behalf for such a favor and ask him to hold me excused for the folly which I showed earlier, assuring him that never in the future will such things be undertaken by me."

The lady thanked Tarolfo very much for such courtesy and left happy, returning to her husband, to whom she recounted everything that happened from beginning to end. But when [250] Tebano returned, he asked Tarolfo how things had turned out for him. Tarolfo told him, and Tebano said, "Because of this have I then lost what you had promised me?" Tarolfo answered, "No, on the contrary, whenever you want, go and take half of my castles and treasure, just as I promised you, for I hold myself fully served by you." Tebano responded to this, "May the gods forbid that [255] I should be less than courteous when a gentleman was so generous to you with his wife and you did not act basely toward him. More than all the things of the world it pleases me to have served you, and I wish that what I might have received in recompense for service should remain yours just as it was," and he would not take anything from among Tarolfo's possessions.

[260] Now the question is, which of them showed the greater generosity:

330 **liberalità** liberata *corr* liberalita Vr1

infino alla fine gli narrò perché dolente dimorava. La qual cosa udendo il
cavaliere lungamente pensò, e conoscendo nel pensiero la purità della donna,
così le disse, "Va, e copertamente serva il tuo giuramento, e a Tarolfo ciò che
220 tu promettesti liberamente attieni: egli l'ha ragionevolmente e con grande
affanno guadagnato." Cominciò la donna a piangere e a dire, "Facciano
gl'iddii da me lontano cotal fallo; in niuna maniera io farò questo: avanti
m'uccíderei ch'io facessi cosa che disonore o dispiacere vi fosse." A cui il
cavaliere disse, "Donna, già per questo io non voglio che tu te n'uccida, né
225 ancora che una sola malinconia tu te ne dia: niuno dispiacere m'è, va e fa
quello che tu impromettesti, ch'io non te ne avrò di meno cara; ma questo
fornito, un'altra volta ti guarderai di sì fatte impromesse, non tanto ti paia il
domandato dono impossibile ad avere."
Vedendo la donna la volontà del marito, ornatasi e fattasi bella, e presa
230 compagnia, andò all'ostiere di Tarolfo, e di vergogna dipinta gli si presentò
davanti. Tarolfo come la vide, levatosi da lato a Tebano con cui sedea, pieno
di maraviglia e di letizia le si fece incontro, e lei onorevolmente ricevette,
domandando della cagione della sua venuta. A cui la donna rispose, "Per
essere a tutti i tuoi voleri sono venuta; fa di me quello che ti piace." Allora
235 disse Tarolfo, "Sanza fine mi fate maravigliare, pensando all'ora e alla
compagnia con cui venuta siete: sanza novità stata tra voi e 'l vostro marito
non può essere; ditemelo, io ve ne priego." Narrò allora la donna interamente
a Tarolfo come la cosa era tutta per ordine. La qual cosa udendo, Tarolfo più
che prima s'incominciò a maravigliare e a pensare forte, e a conoscere
240 cominciò la gran liberalità del marito di lei che mandata a lui l'avea, e fra sé
cominciò a dire che degno di gravissima riprensione sarebbe chi a così
liberale uomo pensasse villania; e parlando alla donna così disse, "Gentil
donna, lealmente e come valorosa donna avete il vostro dovere servato, per la
qual cosa io ho per ricevuto ciò che io di voi disiderava; e però quando piacerà
245 a voi, voi ve ne potrete tornare al vostro marito, e di tanta grazia da mia parte
ringraziarlo, e scusarglimi della follia che per adietro ho usata, accertandolo
che mai per inanzi più per me tali cose non fiano trattate."
Ringraziò la donna Tarolfo molto di tanta cortesia, e lieta si partì tornando
al suo marito, a cui tutto per ordine disse quello che avvenuto l'era. Ma
250 Tebano ritornato a lui, Tarolfo domandò come avvenuto gli fosse; Tarolfo
gliele contò; a cui Tebano disse, "Dunque per questo avrò io perduto ciò che
da te mi fu promesso?" Rispose Tarolfo, "No, anzi, qualora ti piace, va, e le
mie castella e i miei tesori prendi per metà, come io ti promisi, però che da te
interamente servito mi tengo." Al quale Tebano rispose, "Unque agl'iddii non
255 piaccia che io, là dove il cavaliere ti fu della sua donna liberale, e tu a lui non
fosti villano, che io sia meno che cortese. Oltre a tutte le cose del mondo mi
piace averti servito, e voglio che ciò che in guiderdone del servigio prendere
dovea, tuo si rimanga sì come mai fu," né di quello di Tarolfo volle alcuna
cosa prendere.
260 Dubitasi ora quale di costoro fosse maggiore liberalità, o quella del

the gentleman who acceded to sending his wife to Tarolfo; or Tarolfo who sent back to her husband untouched that lady whom he had always desired and for whom he had done so much to bring things to the point to which it had come, when the lady came to him, as he had wanted; or [265] Tebano who, abandoning his country as an old man and coming thence to earn the gifts he had been promised and undertaking to accomplish what he had promised and having been rewarded, then gave everything back, remaining himself as poor as before?

"The story and your question are most gracious," said the queen, "and in truth [270] each one was very generous, and considering them carefully, the first was generous with his honor, the second with his sexual appetite, and the third with what he had acquired. And so, wanting to know who showed the greater generosity or courtesy, it is appropriate to consider which of these three things is the most valuable. When we know that, we shall certainly know who was most generous, since he who gives the most should be regarded as the most generous. [275] Of these three things, one is precious – that is to say, honor – which Lucius Aemilius Paulus, after conquering Perseus the king, wanted more than the treasures he had won. The second – carnal intercourse – should be avoided, according to the sayings of Sophocles and Xenocrates, who hold that lechery should be avoided like a raging tyrant. The third should not be desired – namely, riches – insofar as these are [280] most often troubling to the virtuous life and a man can live virtuously with a certain amount of poverty, just as Marcus Curtius and Marcus Atilius Regulus and Publius Valerius Publicola demonstrate in their works. Therefore, if honor alone is precious in these three and nothing else is, then he who gave that showed the greater generosity, even if he did so unwisely. He was still foremost in generosity, for which [285] the others followed behind him. And so, in my opinion, he who gave the lady, in whom his honor consisted, was more generous than the others."

"I agree," said Menedon, "that it should be as you say, insofar as it is said by you,[30] but to my mind each one of the others was more generous; please hear why. It is quite true that the first gave up the lady, but in doing so he did not show such [290] generosity as you say, for if he had wanted to refuse her, he could not justly do so because of the promise made by the lady, which had to be observed. He who gives what he cannot refuse does well, insofar as he does it generously, but he gives little. And so, as I said, each one of the others was more generous, since, as I just said, Tarolfo had desired the lady for a long time already [295] and loved her above all things, and had long endured to have her and devoted himself to satisfying her demand to search for things almost impossible to have, which, when found, earned him the right to enforce the sworn word. Having this, as we have said, there is no doubt that the husband's honor, and returning what she promised, was in his hands. [300] This is what he did and therefore he was generous with the husband's honor, the wife's promise, and his own long desire. It is a great thing to have endured a long thirst and then come to the fountain and not drink in order to let another drink. The third was still more generous because, seeing that poverty is one of the most irksome things in the world to bear, inasmuch as it

---

[30] May also be construed: "I agree that things are as you say, insofar as you go. . . ."

cavaliere che concedette alla donna l'andare a Tarolfo, o quella di Tarolfo, il quale quella donna cui egli avea sempre disiata, e per cui egli avea tanto fatto per venire a quel punto che venuto era, quando la donna venne a lui, se gli fosse piaciuto, rimandò la sopradetta donna intatta al suo marito; o quella di
265 Tebano, il quale, abandonate le sue contrade, oramai vecchio, e venuto quivi per guadagnare i promessi doni, e affannatosi per recare a fine ciò che promesso avea, avendoli guadagnati, ogni cosa rimise, rimanendosi povero come prima.

"Bellissima è la novella e la dimanda," disse la reina, "e in verità che
270 ciascuno fu assai liberale, e, ben considerando, il primo del suo onore, il secondo del libidinoso volere, il terzo dell'acquistato avere fu cortese: e però volendo conoscere chi maggiore liberalità overo cortesia facesse, conviene considerare quale di queste tre cose sia più cara. La qual cosa veduta, manifestamente conosceremo il più liberale, però che chi più dona più liberale
275 è da tenere. Delle quali tre cose l'una è cara, cioè l'onore, il quale Paulo, vinto Persio re, più tosto volle che i guadagnati tesori.[31] Il secondo è da fuggire, cioè il libidinoso congiugnimento, secondo la sentenza di Sofoldeo e di Senocrate, dicenti che così è la lussuria da fuggire come furioso signore. La terza non è da disiderare, ciò sono le ricchezze, con ciò sia cosa che esse sieno
280 le più volte a virtuosa vita noiose, e possasi con moderata povertà vivere virtuosamente, sì come Marco Curzio e Attilio Regolo e Valerio Publicola nelle loro opere manifestarono. Adunque, se solo l'onore è in queste tre caro, e l'altre no, dunque quelli maggiore liberalità fece che quello donava, avvegna che meno saviamente facesse. Egli ancora fu nelle liberalità principale, per la
285 cui l'altre seguirono: però, secondo il nostro parere, chi diè la donna, in cui il suo onore consisteva, più che gli altri fu liberale."

"Io," disse Menedon, "consento che sia come voi dite, in quanto da voi è detto, ma a me pare che ciascuno degli altri fosse più liberale, e udite come. Egli è ben vero che 'l primo concedette la donna, ma in ciò egli non fece tanta
290 liberalità quanto voi dite; però che se egli l'avesse voluta negare, giustamente egli non poteva, per lo giuramento fatto dalla donna, che osservare si convenia: e chi dona ciò che non può negare ben fa, in quanto se ne fa liberale, ma poco dà. E però, sì com'io dissi, ciascuno degli altri più fu cortese, però che, come io già dissi, Tarolfo avea già lungo tempo la donna
295 disiderata e amata sopra tutte le cose, e per questa avere avea lungamente tribolato, e mettendosi per satisfazione della dimanda di lei a cercare cose quasi impossibili ad avere, le quali pure avute, lei meritò di tenere per la promessa fede: la quale, sì come noi dicemmo, tenendo, non è dubbio che nelle sue mani l'onore del marito, e il rimetterle ciò che promesso gli avea,
300 stava. La qual cosa egli fece: dunque dell'onore del marito, del saramento di lei, del suo lungo disio fu liberale. Gran cosa è l'avere una lunga sete sostenuta, e poi pervenire alla fontana e non bere per lasciare bere altrui. Il terzo ancora fu molto liberale, però che, pensando che la povertà sia una delle moleste cose del mondo a sostenere, con ciò sia cosa ch'ella sia cacciatrice

---

[31] The references to classical figures in Fiammetta's speeches are taken from Valerius Maximus, *Factorum et dictorum memorabilium libri IX*, principally the chapters on abstinence and continence and on poverty.

drives out [305] happiness and peace, banishes honor, takes possession of virtue, and leads to bitter worries, each person naturally endeavors to flee it with a burning desire. This desire to live splendidly in leisure burns so much for many people that they give themselves over to dishonest gains and unseemly enterprises, perhaps not knowing or not being able to realize their desire any other way. For [310] this reason sometimes they deserve to die or to suffer eternal exile from their city. Therefore, how pleasant and dear it must be for a man to earn and possess it in the proper way! And who will deny that Tebano was extremely poor, since he left his nightly rest and went gathering herbs and digging up roots in dangerous places in order to sustain his life? And it can be believed that [315] this poverty obscured his virtue, when we hear that Tarolfo thought himself deceived by him, when he saw him dressed in filthy clothes. We can believe he was eager to leave that misery and become rich, knowing that he came from Thessaly into Spain, setting out on unknown and uncertain aerial ways with dangerous things to fulfill the promise he made and [320] to receive what the other pledged. Undoubtedly, we must believe that whoever submits himself to such things and to so many of them in order to flee poverty knows it is full of every sorrow and tribulation. And the more he escapes poverty and enters the rich life, the more it is pleasing to him. Therefore, for someone who came from poverty into wealth and thereby into a pleasing life, how much and what kind of generosity [325] is it that he should give it up and agree to return to the condition he fled from with such effort? Very great and generous things are done, but this seems to me the greatest of all, considering moreover the age of the giver who was an old man, inasmuch as greed is usually thought to have more power over the elderly than the young. Therefore, I claim that each of the two others [330] showed more generosity than the first and the third more than any."

"You defend your position as well as anyone could," said the queen, "but I intend briefly to show you how you should follow my opinion rather than your own. You propose that the husband showed no generosity in giving up his wife, since he had to [335] by right, because of the promise made by the wife. That would be the case, if the promise were binding; but because the lady, inasmuch as she is part of the husband or rather the same body with him, could not make that promise without the consent of the husband; and if she did, it would be invalid, for no subsequent promise can contravene an earlier promise properly made and [340] especially not those promises made improperly for improper reasons. It is the practice in matrimonial bonds for the husband to swear to be always content with the lady and the lady with the man and never for one to change the other for another. Therefore, the lady could not make a promise; and if she did, as we have already said, she made it improperly, and being contrary to her first promise, it was not [345] valid; and not being valid, it should not hand her over to Tarolfo except at her husband's wish; and if she were handed over to Tarolfo, it was the husband who was generous with his honor and not Tarolfo as you say. Nor could he be generous in sending her back, since the promise was invalid; thus Tarolfo remained generous only in his carnal desire. This is something that everyone should rightly [350] do because we are all obliged for every reason to abandon vices and follow virtues. And he who does what he is bound to do by reason, as you have said, is not generous in anything; but whatever good beyond that is done,

305 d'allegrezza e di riposo, fugatrice d'onori, occupatrice di virtù, adducitrice d'amare sollecitudini, ciascuno naturalmente quella s'ingegna di fuggire con ardente disio. Il quale disio in molti per vivere splendidamente in riposo s'accende tanto, che essi a disonesti guadagni e a sconce imprese si mettono, forse non sappiendo o non potendo in altra maniera il lor disio adempiere: per
310 la qual cosa tal volta meritano morire, o avere delle loro terre etterno essilio. Dunque, quanto deono elle piacere e essere care a chi in modo debito le guadagna e possiede! E chi dubiterà che Tebano fosse poverissimo, se si riguarda ch'egli, abandonati i notturni riposi, per sostentare la sua vita, ne' dubbiosi luoghi andava cogliendo l'erbe e scavando le radici? E che questa
315 povertà occupasse la sua virtù ancora si può credere, udendo che Tarolfo credeva da lui essere gabbato, quando di vili vestimenti il riguardava vestito; che egli fosse vago di quella miseria uscire e divenire ricco, sappiendo ch'egli di Tesaglia infino in Ispagna venne, mettendosi per li dubbiosi cammini e incerti dell'aere alle pericolose cose per fornire la 'mpromessa fatta da lui e
320 per ricevere quella d'altrui, in sé si può vedere: chi a tante e tali cose si mette per povertà fuggire, sanza dubbio si dee credere che egli quella piena d'ogni dolore e d'ogni affanno essere conosce. E quanto di maggiore povertà è uscito e entrato in ricca vita, tanto quella gli è più graziosa. Adunque, chi di povertà è in ricchezza venuto, e con quella il vivere gli diletta, quanta e quale liberalità
325 è quella di chi quella dona, e nello stato, ch'egli ha con tanti affanni fuggito, consente di ritornare? Assai grandissime e liberali cose si fanno, ma questa maggiore di tutte mi pare: considerando ancora alla età del donatore che era vecchio, con ciò sia cosa che ne' vecchi soglia continuamente avarizia molto più che ne' giovani avere potere. Però terrò che ciascuno de' due seguenti
330 aggia maggiore liberalità fatta che 'l primo, e 'l terzo maggiore che niuno."
   "Quanto meglio per alcuno si potesse la vostra ragione difendere, tanto la difendete ben voi," disse la reina, "ma noi brievemente intendiamo dimostrarvi come il nostro parere deggiate più tosto che il vostro tenere. Voi volete dire che colui niuna liberalità facesse concedendo la mogliere, però che
335 di ragione fare gliele convenia per lo saramento fatto dalla donna: la qual cosa saria così, se il saramento tenesse; ma la donna, con ciò sia cosa ch'ella sia membro del marito, o più tosto un corpo con lui, non potea fare quel saramento sanza volontà del marito, e se 'l fece, fu nullo, però che al primo saramento licitamente fatto niuno subsequente puote derogare, e massi-
340 mamente quelli che per non dovuta cagione non debitamente si fanno; e ne' matrimoniali congiungimenti è usanza di giurare d'essere sempre contento l'uomo della donna, e la donna dell'uomo, né di mai l'uno l'altro per altra cambiare; dunque la donna non poté giurare, e se giurò, come già detto avemo, per non dovuta cosa giurò; e contraria al primo giuramento, non dee
345 valere, e non valendo, oltre al suo piacere non si dovea commettere a Tarolfo, e se vi si commise, fu egli del suo onore liberale, e non Tarolfo, come voi tenete. Né del saramento non poté liberale essere rimettendolo, con ciò sia cosa che il saramento niente fosse: adunque solamente rimase liberale Tarolfo del suo libidinoso disio. La qual cosa di propio dovere si conviene a ciascuno
350 di fare, però che tutti per ogni ragione siamo tenuti d'abandonare i vizi e di seguire le virtù. E chi fa quello a che egli è di ragione tenuto, sì come voi diceste, in niuna cosa è liberale, ma quello che oltre a ciò si fa di bene, quello è da chiamare liberalità dirittamente. Ma però che voi forse nella vostra mente

that is properly called generosity. But perhaps you are thinking silently to yourself, 'what honor can there be in a chaste wife that a husband [355] should hold it so dear?' I shall extend my discussion somewhat, showing you more clearly how neither Tarolfo nor Tebano, about whom I intend to speak, showed any generosity with respect to the gentleman. It is known that chastity along with the other virtues returns no advantage to the possessor except honor, which among other and [360] less virtuous men makes them more excellent. If they maintain this honor with humility, they become God's friend and consequently live and die happily, eventually becoming possessors of eternal goods. If the lady preserves this honor for her husband, he lives happy and certain in his offspring and behaves openly with people, pleased to see her honored among the most exalted women for that virtue; and in his mind it is a [365] clear sign that she is good and God-fearing and loves him, and it must please him not a little knowing that she is given to him as an inseparable companion forever, until death. Because of this blessing, his worldly and spiritual goods seem to multiply continually. And thus by contrast the man whose lady fails in this virtue can pass no hour in consolation; nothing pleases him, [370] and the one wishes the other's death. They hear themselves gossiped about for this shameful vice by the most wretched people, and it seems to him that such things can be believed regardless of who says it. And even if all the other virtues were in him, this vice seems to have the power to contaminate and waste them. Therefore, the greatest honor is that which a lady's chastity confers on a man, and it should be held [375] precious. He to whom such a gift is given as a favor can be called blessed, though we believe there are few who might be envied for such good. But to return to the case at hand, you see how much the gentleman gave, but it has not slipped my mind that you said Tebano was more generous than the others because, having become rich through his efforts, he did not hesitate to return [380] to the misery of poverty by giving away what he had gained. It seems clear that you know little about poverty, which surpasses all wealth if it comes happily. Perhaps it already seemed to Tebano that he was full of bitter and diverse worries because of the riches he had obtained. He already imagined that Tarolfo thought he had wronged him and planned to kill him in order to regain his castles. He [385] lived in fear perhaps of being betrayed by his own people. He began to worry about managing his own lands. He already knew all the deceptions prepared by his tenants for him. He thought himself envied by many for his riches and feared that thieves might secretly take them from him. He was full of so many different thoughts and fears [390] that every rest fled from him. And so thinking of his earlier life and how he led it without such worries, he said to himself, 'I wanted to get rich to have comfort, but I see it is an increase of tribulations and worries and the flight from quiet.' And desirous to return to his former life, he gave the riches back to the one who had given them to him. Poverty is [395] wealth rejected, an unknown good, a flight from cares, which Diogenes knew full well. What nature requires is enough for poverty. The man who lives patiently with it draws near to safety from every envy, and the possibility of great honors coming his way is not taken from him, if he lives virtuously as I have already said; and so if Tebano took this weight off his back, he was not [400] generous but wise. He was generous to Tarolfo to the extent that he wanted to give it to him instead of another, since he could have

tacito ragionate, 'che onore può essere quello della casta donna al marito che
355 tanto debbia esser caro?' noi prolungheremo alquanto il nostro parlare,
mostrandolvi, acciò che più chiaramente veggiate Tarolfo né Tebano, di cui
appresso intendiamo di parlare, niuna liberalità facessero a rispetto del
cavaliere. Da sapere è che castità insieme con l'altre virtù niuno altro premio
rendono a' posseditori d'esse se non onore, il quale onore, tra gli altri uomini
360 meno virtuosi, li fa più eccellenti. Questo onore, se con umiltà il sostengono,
gli fa amici di Dio, e per consequente felicemente vivere e morire, e poi
possedere gli etterni beni. La quale se la donna al suo marito la serva, egli
vive lieto e certo della sua prole, e con aperto viso usa infra la gente, contento
di vedere lei per tale virtù dalle più alte donne onorata, e nell'animo gli è man-
365 ifesto segnale costei essere buona, e temere Iddio, e amare lui, che non poco
gli dee piacere, sentendo che per etterna compagnia indivisibile, fuor che da
morte, gli è donata. Egli per questa grazia ne' mondani beni e negli spirituali
si vede continuo multiplicare. E così, per contrario, colui la cui donna di tale
virtù ha difetto, niuna ora può con consolazione passare, niuna cosa gli è a
370 grado, l'uno la morte dell'altro disidera. Elli si sentono per lo sconcio vizio
nelle bocche de' più miseri esser portati, né gli pare che sì fatta cosa non si
debbia credere a chiunque la dice. E se tutte l'altre virtù fossero in lui, questo
vizio pare ch'abbia forza di contaminarle e di guastarle. Dunque grandissimo
onore è quello che la castità della donna rende all'uomo, e molto da tener
375 caro. Beato si può chiamare colui a cui per grazia cotal dono è conceduto,
avvegna che noi crediamo che pochi sieno quelli a' quali di tal bene sia
portato invidia. Ma ritornando al nostro proposito, vedete quanto il cavaliere
dava: ma egli non ci è della mente uscito quanto diceste, Tebano essere stato
più che gli altri liberale, il quale con affanno arricchito, non dubitò di tornare
380 nella miseria della povertà, per donare ciò che acquistato avea. Apertamente si
pare che da voi è mal conosciuta la povertà, la quale ogni ricchezza trapassa
se lieta viene. Tebano già forse per l'acquistate ricchezze gli pareva esser
pieno d'amare e di varie sollecitudini. Egli già imaginava che a Tarolfo
paresse avere mal fatto, e trattasse di ucciderlo per riavere le sue castella. Egli
385 dimorava in paura non forse da' suoi sudditi fosse tradito. Egli era entrato in
sollecitudine del governamento delle sue terre. Egli già conoscea tutti
gl'inganni apparecchiati da' suoi parziali di farli. Egli si vedea da molti
invidiato per le sue ricchezze, egli dubitava non i ladroni occultamente quelle
gli levassero. Egli era ripieno di tanti e tali e sì varii pensieri e sollecitudini,
390 che ogni riposo era da lui fuggito. Per la qual cosa ricordandosi della preterita
vita, e come sanza tante sollecitudini la menava lieta, fra sé disse, 'Io
disiderava d'arricchire per riposo, ma io veggo ch'elli è accrescimento di
tribulazioni e di pensieri, e fuggimento di quiete.' E tornando disideroso
d'essere nella prima vita, quelle rendé a chi gliele avea donate. La povertà è
395 rifiutata ricchezza, bene non conosciuto, fugatrice di stimoli, la quale fu da
Diogene interamente conosciuta. Tanto basta alla povertà quanto natura
richiede. Sicuro da ogni insidia vive chi con quella pazientemente s'accosta,
né gli è tolto il potere a grandi onori pervenire, se virtuosamente vive come
già dicemmo; e però se Tebano si levò questo stimolo da dosso, non fu
400 liberale, ma savio. In tanto fu grazioso a Tarolfo, in quanto più tosto a lui che
ad un altro gli piacque di donarlo, potendolo a molti altri donare. Fu adunque
più liberale il cavaliere, che il suo onore concedea, che nullo degli altri. E

given it to many others. Therefore, the gentleman who gave away his honor was more generous than any of the others. And think of one thing: the honor he gave them is unrecoverable, which is not the case for many other things such as battles and tests and other things in [405] which it is possible, if something is lost one time, it can be regained another. Let this be enough said about your question."

III

Decameron 10.5

Madonna Dianora asks Messer Ansaldo for a January garden as beautiful as if it were in May; Messer Ansaldo gives it to her by making an arrangement with a magician; her husband permits her to satisfy the pleasure of Messer Ansaldo, who, hearing of the husband's generosity, releases her from her promise, [5] and the magician, without asking anything for himself, releases Messer Ansaldo.

When Messer Gentile had been praised to the heavens by everyone in the happy company, the king commanded that Emilia continue; as if eager to speak, she began very confidently in this way, "Tender ladies, [10] no one will rightly say that Messer Gentile did not act generously, but to claim that no more could possibly be done would not be difficult to discredit, and I intend to show you so with the little story that I will recount for you."
In Friuli, a province somewhat cold but blessed with beautiful mountains, many rivers, and clear fountains, is a town called Udine, in which there was a beautiful and noble [15] lady, named Madonna Dianora, the wife of a great rich man named Gilberto, who was quite pleasant and good natured. And for her worthiness, this lady deserved to be loved greatly by a noble and great baron who had the name Messer Ansaldo Gradense, a man of high reputation known to everyone for both his strength of arms and courtesy. Loving her passionately and doing everything he could [20] so that he might be loved by her and to that end frequently entreating her through his messengers, he nonetheless toiled in vain. The gentleman's entreaties were wearisome to the lady, and seeing that, although she refused everything he asked of her, he continued to love and entreat her, she thought of a marvelous and (to her mind) impossible request that would get rid of him.
[25] She said to one of the women who often came to her on his behalf, "Good woman, you have often sworn to me that Messer Ansaldo loves me above all things and you have offered me marvelous gifts on his behalf, which I wish to remain with him, for they could never induce me to love him or give

pensate una cosa: che l'onore che colui donava è irrecuperabile, la qual cosa
non avviene di molti altri, sì come di battaglie, di pruove e d'altre cose, le
405 quali se una volta si perdono, un'altra si racquistano, e è possibile. E questo
basti sopra la vostra dimanda aver detto."

III

Decameron 10.5

(from *Decameron,* ed. Vittore Branca, Vol. 4 of *Tutte le opere di Giovanni
Boccaccio* [Milan: Mondadori, 1964–83], 877–82)

Madonna Dianora domanda a messer Ansaldo un giardino di gennaio
bello come di maggio; messer Ansaldo con l'obligarsi a uno nigromante
gliele dà; il marito le concede che ella faccia il piacere di messer
Ansaldo, il quale, udita la liberalità del marito, l'assolve della promessa,
5 e il nigromante, senza volere alcuna cosa del suo, assolve messere
Ansaldo.

Per ciascuno della lieta brigata era già stato messer Gentile con somme lode
tolto infino al cielo, quando il re impose a Emilia che seguisse; la qual
baldanzosamente, quasi di dire disiderosa, così cominciò, "Morbide donne,
10 niun con ragion dirà messer Gentile non aver magnificamente operato, ma il
voler dire che più non si possa, il più potersi non fia forse malagevole a
mostrarsi: il che io avviso in una mia novelletta di raccontarvi."
In Frioli, paese quantunque freddo lieto di belle montagne, di più fiumi e di
chiare fontane, è una terra chiamata Udine, nella quale fu già una bella e nobile
15 donna, chiamata madonna Dianora e moglie d'un gran ricco uomo nominato
Gilberto, assai piacevole e di buona aria. E meritò questa donna per lo suo
valore d'essere amata sommamente da un nobile e gran barone, il quale aveva
nome messere Ansaldo Gradense, uomo d'alto affare e per arme e per cortesia
conosciuto per tutto. Il quale, ferventemente amandola e ogni cosa faccendo che
20 per lui si poteva per essere amato da lei e a ciò spesso per sue ambasciate
sollicitandola, invano si faticava. E essendo alla donna gravi le sollicitazioni del
cavaliere, e veggendo che, per negare ella ogni cosa da lui domandatole, esso
per ciò d'amarla né di sollicitarla si rimaneva, con una nuova e al suo giudicio
impossibil domanda si pensò di volerlosi torre da dosso.
25 E a una femina che a lei da parte di lui spesse volte veniva, disse indi così,
"Buona femina, tu m'hai molte volte affermato che messere Ansaldo sopra
tutte le cose m'ama e maravigliosi doni m'hai da sua parte proferti; li quali
voglio che si rimangano a lui, per ciò che per quegli mai a amar lui né a
compiacergli mi recherei. E se io potessi esser certa che egli cotanto

him pleasure. If I could be sure that [30] he loved me as much as you say, surely I would bring myself to love him and do what he wants; and so if he wants to show good faith with what I shall ask, I shall be ready to fulfill his wishes."

The good woman said, "What is it, my lady, that you want him to do?"

[35] The lady answered, "What I want him to do is this: Next January I want a garden made near the city full of green grass, flowers, and leafy trees, as if it were in May. If he does not do this, then neither you nor anyone else should ever petition me further because if he bothers me any more I shall endeavor to get rid of him, complaining to my husband and kinsmen [40] from whom I have hidden everything so far."

When he heard the request and proposal from his lady, the gentleman realized it was a difficult and nearly impossible thing to do, and he understood that the lady had asked for it for no other reason than to turn him from his hopes. Still, he decided to try to do it in so far as he could, and [45] he sought about in the greater part of the world for someone who might help him or give him advice. Finally, there came to hand one man who offered to do it by magic, provided he were paid enough. Messer Ansaldo, having agreed to terms with him for a very large amount of money, happily awaited the time designated by his lady. When it arrived with the greatest cold and everything covered with snow and [50] ice, on the night before the kalends of January, the magician deployed his skills in a most beautiful meadow near the city so that when morning came, according to the testimony of those who saw it, there appeared one of the most beautiful gardens that had ever been seen, with grass and trees and fruits of all kinds. When Messer Ansaldo had happily seen this, he had some of the most beautiful flowers [55] gathered and secretly presented to his lady; and he invited her to see the garden she had commanded, so that she could know by that how much he loved her, and remember the promise made to him and sworn by her oath and how as a true lady she could endeavor to redeem it.

[60] The lady, when she heard about the wonderful garden from many people who had seen the flowers and fruits, began to repent of her promise. But despite her repentance, eager to see strange sights, she went to see the garden with many other women of the city; and commending it greatly in admiration, she returned home more sorrowful than any other woman thinking [65] of what it obligated her to do. And her sorrow was such that she was not able to hide it within her, and when it appeared on the outside her husband naturally took notice and wanted to know the cause. The lady was silent for a long time, out of shame; finally, compelled, she explained everything in the way it had happened.

Hearing this, Gilberto was first very upset. Then, when he thought of his wife's pure [70] intention, he drove away anger with wiser counsel and said, "Dianora, it is not the act of a wise or honest woman to listen to any messages of that sort, nor to bargain her chastity with anyone under any condition. Words received by the heart through the ears have greater power than many people realize, and almost anything becomes possible for a lover. [75] You did wrong first in listening and then in bargaining. But since I know the purity of your heart and mind, in order to free you from the bonds of the promise, I will allow you something perhaps no one else would, being moved also by

30　m'amasse quanto tu di', senza fallo io mi recherei a amar lui e a far quello che
egli volesse; e per ciò, dove di ciò mi volesse far fede con quello che io
domanderò, io sarei a' suoi comandamenti presta."

Disse la buona femina, "Che è quello, madonna, che voi disiderate ch'el
faccia?"

35　Rispose la donna, "Quello che io disidero è questo: io voglio, del mese di
gennaio che viene, appresso di questa terra un giardino pieno di verdi erbe, di
fiori e di fronzuti albori, non altrimenti fatto che se di maggio fosse; il quale
dove egli non faccia, né te né altri mi mandi mai più, per ciò che, se più mi
stimolasse, come io infino a qui del tutto al mio marito e a' miei parenti tenuto
40　ho nascoso, così, dolendomene loro, di levarlomi da dosso m'ingegnerei."

Il cavaliere, udita la domanda e la proferta della sua donna, quantunque
grave cosa e quasi impossibile a dover fare gli paresse e conoscesse per
niun'altra cosa ciò essere dalla donna addomandato se non per torlo dalla sua
speranza, pur seco propose di voler tentare quantunque fare se ne potesse e in
45　più parti per lo mondo mandò cercando se in ciò alcun si trovasse che aiuto o
consiglio gli desse; e vennegli uno alle mani il quale, dove ben salariato fosse,
per arte nigromantica profereva di farlo. Col quale messer Ansaldo per
grandissima quantità di moneta convenutosi, lieto aspettò il tempo postogli; il
qual venuto, essendo i freddi grandissimi e ogni cosa piena di neve e di
50　ghiaccio, il valente uomo in un bellissimo prato vicino alla città con sue arti
fece sì, la notte alla quale il calen di gennaio seguitava, che la mattina
apparve, secondo che color che 'l vedevan testimoniavano, un de' più be'
giardini che mai per alcun fosse stato veduto, con erbe e con alberi e con frutti
d'ogni maniera. Il quale come messere Ansaldo lietissimo ebbe veduto, fatto
55　cogliere de' più be' frutti e de' più be' fior che v'erano, quegli occultamente
fé presentare alla sua donna e lei invitare a vedere il giardino da lei
adomandato, acciò che per quel potesse lui amarla conoscere e ricordarsi della
promission fattagli e con saramento fermata, e come leal donna poi procurar
d'attenergliele.

60　La donna, veduti i fiori e' frutti e già da molti del maraviglioso giardino
avendo udito dire, s'incominciò a pentere della sua promessa, ma con tutto il
pentimento, sì come vaga di veder cose nuove, con molte altre donne della
città andò il giardino a vedere; e non senza maraviglia commendatolo assai,
più che altra femina dolente a casa se ne tornò a quel pensando a che per
65　quello era obligata. E fu il dolore tale, che, nol potendol ben dentro
nascondere, convenne che, di fuori apparendo il marito di lei se n'accorgesse;
e volle del tutto da lei di quello saper la cagione. La donna per vergogna il
tacque molto: ultimamente, constretta, ordinatamente gli aperse ogni cosa.

Gilberto primieramente ciò udendo si turbò forte: poi, considerata la pura
70　intenzion della donna, con miglior consiglio cacciata via l'ira, disse,
"Dianora, egli non è atto di savia né d'onesta donna d'ascoltare alcuna
ambasciata delle così fatte, né di pattovire sotto alcuna condizione con alcuno
la sua castità. Le parole per gli orecchi dal cuore ricevute hanno maggior forza
che molti non stimano, e quasi ogni cosa diviene agli amanti possibile. Male
75　adunque facesti prima a ascoltare e poscia a pattovire; ma per ciò che io
conosco la purità dello animo tuo, per solverti da' legame della promessa,
quello ti concederò che forse alcuno altro non farebbe, inducendomi ancora la
paura del nigromante, al qual forse messer Ansaldo, se tu il beffassi, far ci

fear of the magician, who perhaps Messer Ansaldo, if you make a fool of him, might order to cause us trouble. I want you to go to him and [80] try to gain a release from this promise in any way you can, short of sacrificing your chastity. If you cannot do it otherwise, then this one time you may give him your body but not your heart."

When she heard her husband, the lady wept and refused to accept such a favor from him. However much the lady refused, it pleased Gilberto to have things so. [85] Thus when the sun rose on the following day, the lady, not adorning herself excessively, went to the house of Messer Ansaldo with two family retainers in front of her and a maid behind.

Hearing that his lady had come to him, he marveled greatly; rising up, he called for the magician to be brought to him and said, "I want you to see how [90] much good your art has gained me." He went out to greet her and received her honestly, with reverence and without any uncontrolled appetite. He brought everyone into a beautiful room with a big fire, and after showing her to a seat, he said, "My lady, I pray you, if the long love which I have borne for you merits any reward, do not be put out to explain to me the true cause that has [95] brought you here at this hour and with such company."

Ashamed and as if with tears in her eyes, the lady answered, "Sir, neither love for you nor a solemn promise send me here but my husband's command. Having more concern for the pain of your uncontrolled love than his honor or mine, he has made me come to you; and by [100] his order, I am prepared to give you every pleasure this one time."

Messer Ansaldo at first marveled when he heard the lady, and then he begin to marvel even more. Moved by Gilberto's generosity, his desire began to change to compassion, and he said, "My lady, since things are as you say, God forbid that I be the one who soils the honor [105] of the man who had compassion for my love; and so you may stay here as long as you please, exactly as if you were my sister and you may leave freely at your pleasure, provided that you convey to your husband such thanks as you think appropriate to the courtesy he has shown and regard me in the future as a brother and [110] servant." When the lady heard this, she was happier than ever and said, "Having seen your manners, nothing could ever make me believe that anything could result from my coming to you than what I see you have done.

I shall always be indebted to you for this." Then taking her leave, she [115] returned honorably escorted to Gilberto and recounted for him what had happened. From this event, a very close and loyal friendship joined him and Messer Ansaldo.

When Messer Ansaldo made ready to give him the fee he had promised, the magician, having heard of the generosity of Gilberto to Messer Ansaldo and of Messer Ansaldo to the lady, said, "Since [120] I have seen Gilberto generous with his honor and you with your love, God forbid that I not be just as generous with my payment; and so, knowing it rests well with you, I intend it to stay with you."

The gentleman was embarrassed and tried to make him take it all or at least part, but he petitioned in vain. After the magician had taken away [125] his garden after the third day and wished to depart, he commended him to God. Sexual desire having been extinguished in his heart, there remained the fire of honest charity.

farebbe dolenti. Voglio io che tu a lui vada e, se per modo alcun puoi,
80   t'ingegni far che, servata la tua onestà, tu sii da questa promessa disciolta:
dove altramenti non si potesse, per questa volta il corpo ma non l'animo gli
concedi."

La donna, udendo il marito, piagneva e negava sé cotal grazia voler da lui.
A Gilberto, quantunque la donna il negasse molto, piacque che così fosse: per
85   che, venuta la seguente mattina, in su l'aurora, senza troppo ornarsi, con due
suoi famigliari innanzi e con una cameriera appresso n'andò la donna a casa
messere Ansaldo.

Il quale udendo la sua donna a lui esser venuta si maravigliò forte; e
levatosi e fatto il nigromante chiamare gli disse, "Io voglio che tu vegghi
90   quanto di bene la tua arte m'ha fatto acquistare"; e incontro andatile, senza
alcun disordinato appetito seguire, con reverenza onestamente la ricevette, e
in una bella camera a un gran fuoco se n'entrar tutti; e fatto lei porre a seder
disse, "Madonna, io vi priego, se il lungo amore il quale io v'ho portato merita
alcun guiderdone, che non vi sia noia d'aprirmi la vera cagione che qui a così
95   fatta ora v'ha fatta venire e con cotal compagnia."

La donna vergognosa e quasi con le lagrime sopra gli occhi rispose,
"Messere, né amor che io vi porti né promessa fede mi menan qui ma il
comandamento del mio marito, il quale, avuto più rispetto alle fatiche del
vostro disordinato amore che al suo e mio onore, mi ci ha fatta venire; e per
100   comandamento di lui disposta sono per questa volta a ogni vostro piacere."

Messere Ansaldo, se prima si maravigliava, udendo la donna molto più
s'incominciò a maravigliare: e dalla liberalità di Giliberto commosso il suo
fervore in compassione cominciò a cambiare e disse, "Madonna, unque a Dio
non piaccia, poscia che così è come voi dite, che io sia guastatore dello onore
105   di chi ha compassione al mio amore; e per ciò l'esser qui sarà, quanto vi
piacerà, non altramenti che se mia sorella foste, e quando a grado vi sarà
liberamente vi potrete partire, sì veramente che voi al vostro marito di tanta
cortesia, quanta la sua è stata, quelle grazie renderete che convenevoli
crederete, me sempre per lo tempo avvenire avendo per fratello e per
110   servidore."

La donna, queste parole udendo, più lieta che mai disse, "Niuna cosa mi
poté mai far credere, avendo riguardo a' vostri costumi, che altro mi dovesse
seguir della mia venuta che quello che io veggio che voi ne fate; di che io vi
sarò sempre obligata." E preso commiato, onorevolmente accompagnata si
115   tornò a Gilberto e raccontogli ciò che avvenuto era; di che strettissima e leale
amistà lui e messer Ansaldo congiunse.

Il nigromante, al quale messer Ansaldo di dare il promesso premio
s'apparecchiava, veduta la liberalità di Giliberto verso messer Ansaldo e
quella di messer Ansaldo verso la donna, disse, "Già Dio non voglia, poi che
120   io ho veduto Giliberto liberale del suo onore e voi del vostro amore, che io
similmente non sia liberale del mio guiderdone; e per ciò, conoscendo quello
a voi star bene, intendo che vostro sia."

Il cavaliere si vergognò e ingegnossi di fargli o tutto o parte prendere; ma
poi che invano si faticava, avendo il nigromante dopo il terzo dì tolto via il
125   suo giardino e piacendogli di partirsi, il comandò a Dio: e spento del cuore il
concupiscibile amore, verso la donna acceso d'onesta carità si rimase.

Che direm qui, amorevoli donne? preporremo la quasi morta donna e il già

What shall we say of this, amorous ladies? Shall we place the nearly dead lady and love already tepid through lost hope above this generosity of Messer Ansaldo, who loved more passionately than ever and burned with even greater hope [130] and held in his hands the quarry he pursued so long? It seems to me a foolish thing to believe this generosity could compare to that.

IV

History of the Kings of Britain, 67–8

Claudius feared the daring of the king and the bravery of the Britons; he preferred to subdue them with common sense and wisdom rather than begin an uncertain battle. He therefore proposed a mutual alliance to [Arviragus] and promised to give him his daughter if only he would recognize the kingdom of the Britons to be under Roman authority. [5] Laying aside plans for war, the elders urged Arviragus to be content with Claudius's proposal. They said it would not be a cause of shame to be made subject to the Romans, since they were masters of the empire of the entire world. Calmed by this and many other things, he yielded to their advice and made himself a subject to Caesar. Then immediately Claudius sent to Rome for his daughter [10] and with Arviragus's help subdued the Orkneys and the provincial islands to his power.

At the end of winter, the messengers returned with his daughter and brought her to her father. Genuissa was the girl's name, and she was of such beauty that those who saw her were led into admiration. And when she was joined by lawful marriage, she inflamed the king with such a passionate love that he set her above all other things. [15] Consequently, wanting the place in which he had first married her to be renowned, he suggested to Claudius that they build a city in that place that would furnish memory of such a marriage in future times. Claudius agreed and ordered the city to be called Kaerglou, that is, Gloucester, after his own name, which it is to this day, and it is located within the confines of Cambria and Logres on the river Severn. Some people [20] say that the name was taken from duke Gloius, whom Claudius sired in that city; he succeeded to the dukedom of Cambria after Arviragus's reign. Once the city was built and the island pacified, Claudius returned to Rome and handed over rule of the islands of the province to Arviragus.

rattiepidito amore per la spossata speranza a questa liberalità di messer
Ansaldo, più ferventemente che mai amando ancora e quasi da più speranza
130   acceso e nelle sue mani tenente la preda tanto seguita? Sciocca cosa mi
parrebbe a dover credere che quella liberalità a questa comparar si potesse.

IV

Historia Regum Britanniae, 67–8

(from *The Historia Regum Britanniae of Geoffrey of Monmouth*, I:
Bern, Burgerbibliothek, MS. 568, ed. Neil Wright [Cambridge, 1984], 43–4)

Quippe timebat regis audaciam Britonumque fortitudinem: preferebat ipsos
sensu et sapientia subiugare quam dubium certamen inire. Mandabat ei igitur
concordiam daturumque promittebat sese filiam suam, si tantummodo regnum
Britannie sub Romana potestate recognouisset. Postpositis ergo debella-
5   tionibus suaserunt maiores natu Aruirago promissionibus Claudii adquiescere.
Dicebant autem non ei esse dedecori subditum fuisse Romanis, cum totius
orbis imperio potirentur. His uero et pluribus aliis mitigatus paruit consiliis
suorum et subiectionem Cesari fecit. Mox Claudius misit propter filiam suam
Romam et auxilio Aruiragi usus Orcades et prouinciales insulas potestati sue
10   submisit.
Emensa hyeme deinde redierunt legati cum filia eamque patri tradiderunt.
Erat autem nomen puelle Genuissa eratque ei tanta pulchritudo ut aspicientes
in admirationem duceret. Et ut maritali lege copulata fuit, tanto feruore amoris
succendit regem ita ut ipsam solam cunctis rebus preferret. Unde locum quo
15   primo ei nupserat celebrem esse uolens suggessit Claudio ut edificarent in illo
ciuitatem que memoriam tantarum nuptiarum in futura tempora preberet.
Paruit ergo Claudius precepitque fieri ciuitatem que de nomine eius Kaerglou,
id est Gloucestria, nuncupata usque in hodiernum diem in confinio Kambrie et
Loegrie super ripam Sabrine sita est. Quidam uero dicunt ipsam traxisse
20   nomen a Gloio duce quem Claudius in illa generauerat; cui post Aruiragum
gubernaculum Kambriti ducatus cessit. Edificata igitur urbe ac pacificata
insula rediit Claudius Romam regimenque prouinciarum insularum Aruirago
permisit.

V

Wace's Brut, 5031–92

The armies had already engaged with lances and in armed combat when the wise men and the elders turned to one side; they feared the loss of their own men. They sought the emperor to ask what he would do, whether he wanted peace or battle. He answered them courteously that he had no wish for battle but wanted peace and love and for Rome to have no more trouble. He had no interest in any other objective except that Rome have its rights. He will honor Arviragus; he had a daughter whom he will give him if he wants to become his vassal and hold his fief from Rome. Arvirgaus granted that, and so they were reconciled with each other. They lodged at Winchester; they were friends and got to know each other. From there they sent people to Rome who were charged to make Genoïs ready to travel since Claudius must give her away. Meanwhile, with Arviragus and his help he conquered Orkney and the other islands around there – I can't remember their names. [1–30] The messengers went their way and returned at the beginning of summer; they sent Genoïs, noble in body and beautiful in appearance. The barons of the land between Wales and England were to marry the young girl and seal their agreement on the Severn in a valley which is very rich and abundant. To commemorate that agreement, they made a memorial at the place by founding a city and called it Gloucester. The city has this name because Claudius built it. Others say there are different explanations, which seem reasonable enough. Claudius sired a son there who was named Glois. Glois was the lord of Gloucester and lord of Wales, as I have heard. Because Glois was born there and named its lord, Gloucester is named after him – I find this cause written. Gloucester is the city of Glois; there is no better reason. When Genoïs was married, she was crowned at her wedding. After the wedding was finished, Claudius returned to Rome. [31–62]

V

Wace's Brut, 5031–92

(from *Le Roman de Brut*, ed. Ivor Arnold, I [Paris, 1938], 269–72)

Ja esteient a l'assembler
E al lancier e al geter,
Quant li sage hume e li veillart
Se sunt turné a une part;
5 La perte cremeient des lur,
Si requistrent l'empereür
Pur demander que il fereit,
Si pais u bataille voleit.
E il respondi bonement
10 Que de bataille n'ad talent
Ainz vult la pais e vult l'amur
Ne mais que Rome i ait enur.
De nul altre gaain n'ad cure
Ne mais que Rome ait sa dreiture.
15 Arviragum enorera;
Une fille ad qu'il li durra
Se il vult sis huem devenir
E de Rome sun fieu tenir.
Arviragus l'ad graanté,
20 Si se sunt entr'els acordé.
En Wincestre se herbegierent,
Amis furent si s'acointerent.
D'iluec s'unt a Rome enveied
Cil ki en sunt apareillied
25 Pur Genoïs faire amener
Que Claudius deveit doner.
Entretant cunquist Orchenie
Par Arvirage e par s'aïe,
E altres illes envirun
30 Que jo ne sai coment unt nun.
Li messagier lur veie tindrent

35 E a l'entrant d'esté revindrent;
Si amenerent Genuïs,
Gente de cors, bele de vis.
A la meschine marier,
E a lur covenant fermer,
Furent li baron de la terre
Entre Guales e Engleterre
40 Sur Saverne en une valee
Ki mult est riche e asazee.
Pur cel plai mettre en remembrance
Firent al lieu tel enorance
Que une cité i funderent
45 E Gloëcestre l'apelerent.
La ville pur ço cest nun a
Que Claudius l'edifia.
Altre dient altre achesun
Qui assez bien semble raisun;
De Claudio fu engendrez
50 Uns filz illuec, Glois fu numez.
Gloi fu de Gloëcestre sire
E dux de Guales, ço oi dire.
Pur ço que Gloi fud illuec nez
E que sirë en fu numez,
55 Fu Gloëcestre de lui dite,
Ceste achaisun truis jo escrite.
Gloëcestre c'est cité Gloi,
Unc plus dreite raisun ne soi.
Quant Genuïs fu mariee,
60 A ses noces fu coronee.
Emprés les noces fu la sume
Que Claudius rala a Rome.

VI

Layamon's Brut, 4887–914

All day there the fight lasted to the utmost, until dark night divided their great fight. On both sides knights lay cut to pieces; there was harm of the worst kind before Exeter. The queen named Genuissa beheld that; her heart was sad for her men who fell. She called to her lord who was dear to her heart; the queen spoke thus to King Arviragus: "My lord, think how good your vassals are; you have much faith, steadfast trust, which are the things that befit each king, if he will be honest with good men,[32] rich men and humble. Think on your promises, which you yourself pledged to my father Claudian who was your known friend and did you the honor of giving me to you as your wife. And you are as dear to me as any liege lord. My people are outside here and your people inside. If you break your promises and kill my people, as I have told you the truth, you will be on bad terms with your son. And if my people climb up and bring you down and you and your men fall to ground and if you and your men are killed, then I would be at odds with my son. Peace is better than such discord. And think of your agreement, how you swore to my father to send Rome tribute from your kingdom each year as long as you live. And your life still continues – long may it do so. Therefore, you must observe what you pledged before."

---

[32] Accepting Madden's reading "feon men" for Brook and Leslie's "seoumen" as well as Madden's conjecture "good (?) men."

VI

Layamon's Brut, 4887–914

(from Layamon, *Brut*, ed. G. L. Brook and R. F. Leslie, I [London, 1963], 254–6)

    Alle dæi þer ilæste   fæht mid þan mæste.
    a þet þat þustere niht   to-dælde heore muchele fiht.
    læien a ba halue   cnihtes to-heouwen.
    þær wes hærm mid þon meste   bi-uoren Ex-chæstre.
5   Þat bi-heold þa quene   Genuis i-haten.
    særi wes hire heorte   mid hermen a-fulled.
    cleopede to hire lauerde   þe leof hire wes on heorte.
    to þon kinge Aruiragus   þæ quene spac wið him þus.
    Lauer[d] bi-þenc þe   Þine þeowes beoð gode.
10   þu hauest mucle treow-scipe   treowðe staðeluæste.
    þat beoð þa þingges   þe bi-riseð to ælche kinge
    riche men & hæne   ȝif wið seoumen he wule beon clænen.
    Bi-þenc þu a þine quides   þe þu sulf quiddest.
    wið Claudien minne fader   þe wes þi cudliche freond
15   þe dude þe þa wurhscipe   bi-tahte me þe to wiue.
    & þu ært me swa leof   swa mi kine-lauerd.
    Mi cun is her wið-vten   & þi kun her wið-innen.
    ȝif þu brekest þine quides   & mi cun quellest
    soð ich þe habbe iseid   wið þine sune þu beost iuæid.
20   & ȝif mi cun clembeð   & bi-neoðen þe ibringeð
    & þe seoluen & þin folc   falleð to grunde
    ȝif þu and þine þer wurðeð dæd   þeonne beo ich wið mine sune iued.
    betere weore sæhte   þene swulc vnisibbe.
    & bi-þenc þe of þan fore   hu þu mine fader swore
25   to lasten alche ȝere   al to þine liue
    gauel in-to Rome   of þine kine-dome.
    & ȝet ilæsteð þi lif   swa hit do longe.
    for þi þu most holden   þat þu ær bihæhtest.

VII

Romance of the Rose, 8425–36

Thus we see that good love cannot endure in marriages, when the husband thinks he is wise and scolds his wife and hits her and makes her live in such strife that he tells her she is silly and foolish for staying at the dance and keeping promises so often with attractive young men; they make one another bear so many difficulties when he wants to have mastery of his wife's body and her goods.

VIII

Romance of the Rose, 9391–424

Friend, this was a jealous oaf – his flesh should be fed to the wolves! – who filled himself up with jealousy, as I've just shown you in my example, and made himself lord over his wife, though she should not be his lady but his equal and companion, just as the law joins them; and he likewise should be her companion without making himself her lord and master. When he prepares such torments for her and does not treat her as an equal, making her live in such discomfort, don't you think he displeases her and that the love between them will fail, whatever she might say? Yes, without fail. A man who wants to be called lord will never be loved by his wife, for it properly follows that love dies when lovers want lordship. Love cannot continue and live if it is not free and lively in the heart. [1–22]

And so we see in this way that for all those who first used to love each other *par amours*, when they mutually desire to marry afterwards, contention can come between them so that love cannot hold them together; for he who called himself a sergeant to her who used to be his mistress when he loved *par amours* now calls himself lord and master over the woman who used to be his lady when she was loved *par amours*. [23–30]

VII

Le Roman de la Rose, 8425–36

(from *Le Roman de la Rose*, ed. Félix Lecoy, II [Paris, 1966], 7)

Por ce voit l'en des mariages,
quant li mariz cuide estre sages
et chastie sa fame et bat,
et la fet vivre en tel debat
5 qu'il li dit qu'el est nice et fole
don tant demore a la querole

et don el hante si sovent
des jolis vallez le covent,
que bone amour n'i peut durer,
10 tant s'entrefont maus andurer,
quant cil veut la mestrise avoir
du cors sa fame et de l'avoir.

VIII

Le Roman de la Rose, 9391–424

(ed. Lecoy, II, 36–37)

Conpainz, cist fos vilains jalous,
don la char soit livree a lous,
qui si de jalousie s'ample
con ci vos ai mis en example,
5 et se fet seigneur de sa fame,
qui ne redoit pas estre dame,
mes sa pareille et sa compaigne,
si con la loi les acompaigne,
et il redoit ses compainz estre
10 sanz soi fere seigneur ne mestre,
quant tex tormenz li appareille
et ne la tient conme pareille,
ainz la fet vivre en tel mesese,
cuidez vos qu'il ne li desplese
15 et que l'amor entr'eus ne faille,
que qu'ele die? Oïl, sanz faille:
ja de sa fame n'iert amez

qui sires veust estre clamez;
car il covient amors morir,
20 quant amant veulent seignorir.
Amor ne peut durer ne vivre,
s'el n'est en queur franc et delivre.
Por ce revoit l'en ensement,
de touz ceus qui prumierement
25 par amors amer s'entreseulent,
quant puis espouser s'entreveulent,
enviz peut entr'eus avenir
que ja s'i puisse amors tenir;
car cil, quant par amors amoit,
30 serjant a cele se clamoit
qui sa mestresse soloit estre:
or se claime seigneur et mestre
seur li, que sa dame ot clamee
quant ele iert par amors amee.

IX

Romance of the Rose, 13845–68

Furthermore, women are born free; it is [human] law, depriving them of their freedoms such as Nature had granted them, which has bound women to constraints. For Nature is not so foolish that she makes Marote born only for Robichon nor, if we pay attention to it, Robichon for Mariete or for Agnes or Perrete. Thus she has made us, have no doubt, my son, all women for all men and all men for all women, each woman common to each man and each man common to each woman. Thus when they are engaged and taken by law, and married, in order to avoid profligacy, quarrel, and death and to help raising children, for which both parties are responsible, wives and maidens – whatever they are, ugly or beautiful – strive to regain their freedoms in all ways.

X

History of the Kings of Britain, 130

Merlin came up to the men who were standing around and said, "Use your strength, men, so that in pulling down those stones you might know whether ingenuity bows to strength or strength to ingenuity." At his order, they gave themselves up with one mind to working machines of all kinds and tried to pull down the circle. Some prepared ropes, others cables, still others ladders
5   to bring about what they sought; but in no way could they succeed. When they were all exhausted, Merlin broke into laughter and made his own machines. Then, when he had set out everything necessary, he lifted the rocks more lightly than anyone could believe. When they were set down, he had them carried to the ships and loaded, and so with joy they began to return to Britain
10   and with favoring winds made land and came with the stones to the men's tombs.

IX

Le Roman de la Rose, 13845–68

(ed. Lecoy, II, 171–2)

D'autre part el sunt franches nees;
loi les a condicionees,
qui les oste de leur franchises
ou Nature les avoit mises;
5   car Nature n'est pas si sote
qu'ele face nestre Marote
tant seulement por Robichon,
se l'antandement i fichon,
ne Robichon por Mariete,
10   ne por Agnés ne por Perrete,
ainz nous a fez, biau filz, n'en doutes,
toutes por touz et touz por toutes,
chascune por chascun conmune

et chascun conmun a chascune,
15   si que, quant el sunt affiees,
par loi prises et mariees,
por oster dissolucions
et contenz et occisions
et por aidier les norretures
20   dom il ont ensemble les cures,
si s'efforcent en toutes guises
de retourner a leur franchises
les dames et les damoiseles,
quex qu'el soient, ledes ou
25   beles.

X

Historia Regum Britanniae, 130

(ed. Wright, pp. 91–2)

Circumstantibus itaque cunctis accessit Merlinus et ait: "Utimini uiribus
uestris, iuuenes, ut in deponendo lapides istos sciatis utrum ingenium uirtuti
an uirtus ingenio cedat." Ad imperium igitur eius indulserunt unanimiter
multimodis machinationibus et agressi sunt choream deponere. Alii funes, alii
5   restes, alii scalas parauerunt ut quod affectabant perficerent; nec ullatenus
perficere ualuerunt. Deficientibus itaque cunctis solutus est Merlinus in
risum suasque machinaciones confecit. Denique, cum queque necessaria
apposuisset, leuius quam credi potest lapides deposuit. Depositos autem fecit
deferri ad naues et introponi et sic cum gaudio in Britanniam reuerti ceperunt
10   et prosperantibus uentis applicant sepulturasque uirorum cum lapidibus
adeunt.

XI

Wace's Brut, 8039–64

"If you want to make a lasting work that will be beautiful and proper and that all ages will talk about, bring here the Carole that the giants made in Ireland, a marvelous and great work of stones set in a circle one on top of the other. The stones are of such size and weight that no force of men known until now could carry one of them." "Merlin," said the king laughing, "since the stones are so heavy that no man could move them, who could ever carry them here, as if we had such affection for stones in this kingdom?" "King," said Merlin, "don't you know that ingenuity conquers force? Strength is good and invention is worth more; ingenuity prevails where strength fails. Ingenuity and art create many things that force does not dare begin. Ingenuity can move the stones, and through ingenuity you can have them."

XII

Wace's Brut, 8119–58

When the Britons were disarmed and were well settled, Merlin, who was in their group, sent them to a mountain where the Carole of the giants was placed, which they had sought. Killomar was the name of the mountain on whose top the circle was. They looked at the stones and walked around them. And one said to the other that he had never seen such a work. "How can these stones be lifted and removed?" "Sires," said Merlin, "see if you can remove these stones by the strength you have and if you can carry them." They were on top and behind, in front and to the side of the stones; they pulled and pushed, lifted and shook. Not in the least could they make a turn by force. "Move back," said Merlin, "far away. You will never do anything more by force. Now you will see that ingenuity and knowledge are more powerful than physical strength." Then he went forward, as was proper, looked around, moved his lips like a man saying prayers – I don't know whether or not he said prayers. Then he called again to the Britons. "Come forward," he said, "come! Now you can take the stones, carry them to your ships, and load them." Just as Merlin predicted, just as he said and imagined, the Britons took the stones and carried them to their ships and put them on board.

XI

Brut, 8039–64

(ed. Arnold, pp. 424–6)

"Se tu vuels faire ovre durable,
Ki mult seit bele e covenable
E dunt tuz tens seit mais parole,
Fai ci aporter la carole
5 Que gaiant firent en Irlande,
Une mervelluse ovre e grande
De pieres en un cerne assises,
Les unes sur les altres mises.
Les pieres sunt teles e tantes,
10 Tant ahuges e tant pesantes,
Que force d'ome k'ore seit
Nule d'eles ne portereit."
"Merlin," dist li reis, en riant,

"Des que les pieres peisent tant
15 Que huem nes purreit remuer,
Ki mes purreit ci aporter;
Cume se nus en cest regné
Avium de pieres chierté?"
"Reis," dist Merlin, "dunc ne sez tu
20 Que engin surmunte vertu.
Bone est force e engin mielz valt;
La valt engin u force falt.
Engin e art funt mainte chose
Que force comencer nen ose.
25 Engin puet les pieres muveir
E par engin les poez aveir."

XII

Brut, 8119–58

(ed. Arnold, pp. 428–30)

Quant Bretun furent desarmé
E bien se furent reposé,
Merlin, ki ert en la compaine,
Les mena en une muntaine
5 U la carole esteit assise
As gaianz, qu'il aveient quise.
Killomar li munz aveit nun
U la carole esteit en sun.
Cil unt les pieres esguardees,
10 Assez les unt environees;
E li uns ad a l'altre dit,
Ki unches mais tel ovre vit:
"Cument sunt ces pieres levees
E cument serunt remuees?"
15 "Seinurs," dist Merlin, "assaiez
Se par vertu ke vus aiez
Purrez ces pieres remuer,
E si vus les purrez porter."
Cil se sunt as pieres aërs
20 Detriés, devant e de travers;

Bien unt enpeint e bien buté;
E bien retrait e bien crollé;
Unches par force a la menur
Ne porent faire prendre un tur.
25 "Traiez vus," dist Merlin, "en sus,
Ja par force nen ferez plus.
Or verrez engin e saveir
Mielz que vertu de cors valeir."
Dunc ala avant si s'estut,
30 Entur guarda, les levres mut
Comë huem ki dit oreisun;
Ne sai s'il dist preiere u nun.
Dunc ad les Bretuns rapelez:
"Venez avant," dist il, "venez!
35 Or poëz les pieres baillier,
A voz nefs porter e chargier."
Si come Merlin enseinna,
Si cum il dist e enginna,
Unt li Bretun les pieres prises,
40 As nés portees e enz mises.

XIII

Against Jovinian, 1.41–6

When the Thirty Tyrants of the Athenians had killed Phidon at the banquet, they ordered his virgin daughters to come to them, and to be stripped naked like prostitutes and to sport with indecent gestures on the floor stained in their father's blood. The girls concealed their sorrow for a while, and when they saw the revelers drunk, they went out, as if attending to the [5] needs of nature; they held on to each other and cast themselves into a well so that they might preserve their virginity by death. The virgin daughter of Demotion, chief of the Areopagites, learning of the death of her fiance Leosthenes who caused the war against the Lamians, killed herself, claiming that, although she was untouched in body, nevertheless if she were compelled to accept another man, she would take him as a second husband, since she had promised herself with an earlier pledge [to Leosthenes]. The Spartans and [10] Messenians maintained friendly relations for such a long time that they even sent virgins to each other for certain holy rites. On a certain occasion, when the Messenians tried to violate fifty of the Spartan virgins, none of that number consented to defilement, but all died most willingly for their chastity. On account of this, a serious and very long war resulted, and after a great while [15] Mamertina was destroyed. Aristoclides, the tyrant of Orcomenus, fell in love with a Stymphalian virgin, who took refuge in the temple of Diana when her father was killed and clung to her image and could not be torn away from it by force. She was stabbed to death on the same spot. On account of her death, all Arcadia was shaken by such sorrow that the people made war and avenged the murder of the virgin. [20] When the Spartans had been conquered and night rituals called the Hyacinthia were being celebrated, Aristomenes of Messenia, a most just man, carried off fifteen virgins from the troop of cele-brants, and fleeing the entire night with hurried steps he passed beyond the territory of the Spartans. And when his companions wanted to rape the girls, he warned as long as he could that they should not do it; and in the end he killed some of those disobeying him, while the others were restrained by fear. Ransomed [25] afterwards by their kinsmen, when they saw Aristomenes was going to be charged with a capital offense, the girls would not return to their

Selected variants are from:
I   Cambridge, University Library Ii.vi.39
Pc   Cambridge, Pembroke College, MS 234

17   **eius** *add* manibus suis I Pc.
17–19 **Ob cuius . . . ulcisceretur** *om* I.
21   **choris** *thoris* Pc.
23   **quamdiu** quantum I.

XIII

Adversus Jovinianum, 1.41–6

(from *Jankyn's Book of Wikked Wyves*,
ed. Ralph Hanna III and Traugott Lawler, The Chaucer Library
[Athens: University of Georgia Press, 1997], 163–75)

Triginta Atheniensium tiranni, cum Phidonem necassent in convivio, filias eius virgines ad se venire iusserunt et scortorum more nudari ac super pavimenta, patris sanguine cruentata, impudicis gestibus ludere; que paulisper dissimulato dolore cum temulentos convivas cernerent, quasi ad requisita
5 nature egredientes, invicem se complexe precipitaverunt in puteum ut virginitatem morte servarent. Demotionis Ariopagitarum principis virgo filia, audito sponsi Leosthenis interitu, qui bellum Lamiacum concitarat, se interfecit, asserens quanquam intacta esset corpore, tamen si alterum accipere cogeretur, quasi secundum accipere, cum priori mente nupsisset. Sparciate et
10 Messenii diu inter se habuere amicicias in tantum ut ob quedam sacra etiam virgines ad se mutuo mitterent. Quodam igitur tempore cum l. virgines Lacedemoniorum Messenii violare temptassent, de tanto numero ad stuprum nulla consensit, sed omnes libentissime pro pudicitia occubuerunt. Quamobrem grave bellum et longissimum concitatum est, et post multum temporis
15 Mamertina subversa est. Aristoclides Orcomeni tirannus adamavit virginem Stimphalidem, que cum, patre occiso, ad templum Diane confugisset et simulacrum eius teneret, nec vi posset avelli, in eodem loco confossa est. Ob cuius necem tanto omnis Arcadia dolore commota est ut bellum publice sumeret et necem virginis ulcisceretur. Aristomenes Messenius, vir iustissi-
20 mus, victis Lacedemoniis, et quodam tempore nocturna sacra celebrantibus, que vocabantur Iacincthina, rapuit de choris ludentium virgines xv^cim., et tota nocte gradu concito fugiens, excessit de finibus Spartanorum. Cumque eas comites eius vellent violare, monuit quamdiu potuit ne facerent, et ad extremum quosdam non parentes interfecit, ceteris metu cohercitis. Redempte
25 postea a cognatis puelle, cum Aristomenem viderent cedis reum fieri, tamdiu

homeland until, having fallen to their knees as suppliants, they saw that the defender of their chastity had been acquitted of charges.

How should the daughters of Scedasus from Leuctra in Boeotia be praised? It is told that, when their father was gone, they received two young travelers under the law of hospitality. Giving themselves up too much to wine, the men used force on the virgins during the night. Having lost their chastity and not wanting to go on living, the girls died from wounds they gave each other. And it is right not to be silent about the Locrian virgins, not one of whom gave cause for foul rumor or any tale about the defilement of their virginity, though they were sent to Troy by custom for nearly one thousand years? Who could pass over in silence the seven virgins of Miletus? When the Gauls were laying waste to everything, they fled disgrace through death, lest they suffer anything shameful at the hands of their enemies. They left behind their own example to all virgins: to a noble mind, chastity is a greater concern than life. [28–37]

After Thebes was conquered and destroyed, Nichanor was overcome in love by one of the captured virgins. Seeking marriage with her and the willing caresses that a captive should of course want, he realized that for chaste minds virginity is preferable to a kingdom, and when she had killed herself by her own hand, the lover held her weeping and mourning. The Greek writers recount the story of another Theban virgin whom a Macedonian enemy had spoiled. She concealed her sorrow for a while and afterwards cut the throat of the violator of her virginity as he slept, and then she killed herself joyfully, since she did not want to live after the loss of her chastity nor die before her vengeance had come. [38–45]

[42.] Among the Gymnosophists of India, authoritative opinion reports from one generation to another that a virgin produced Buddha, the founder of their doctrine, from her side. Nor is this to be wondered at among barbarians, since most learned Greece imagined that Minerva was created from the head of Jupiter and Father Bacchus from his thigh. Pseusippus, the son of Plato's sister, and Clearchus in his *Praise of Plato* and Anaxilides in the second book of *Philosophy* say that Periction, the mother of Plato, was taken forcibly by an apparition of Apollo, and they believe that the prince of wisdom was born not otherwise but from a virgin. But Timaeus writes that the virgin daughter of Pythagoras presided over a troop of virgins and taught them the doctrines of chastity. Diodorus the Socratic is said to have had five daughters trained in dialectic and noted for their modesty, about whom Philo, the teacher of Carneades, writes a very full history. And lest Roman power reproach us that the Lord our Savior was born from a virgin, they believe that the founders of their city and people were born from Mars and the virgin Ilia. [46–59]

Jerome against Jovinian on the Chastity of Women

[43.] This rehearsal, running quickly through various histories, has touched on the virgins of the secular world. I shall come to wives who did not want to

---

37   **esse** *add* debere I Pc. **vitam** uictam Pc.
46   **Gimnosophistas** bragmanas gimnosofistas Pc. **per manus** permanens I.
52   **phantasmate** in fores memorie I Pc.

ad patriam non sunt reverse, quamdiu iudicum advolute genibus defensorem pudicitie sue cernerent absolutum.

Quo ore laudande sunt Scedasi filie in Leuctris Boetie? Quas traditum est, absente patre, duos iuvenes pretereuntes iure hospitii suscepisse. Qui multum
30 indulgentes vino, vim per noctem intulere virginibus, que amisse pudicitie nolentes supervivere, mutuis vulneribus conciderunt. Iustum est et Locridas virgines non tacere, que cum Ilium mitterentur ex more per annos circiter mille, nulla obsceni rumoris et pollute virginitatis ullam fabulam dedit. Quis valeat silentio preterire septem Milesias virgines? Que Gallorum inpetu
35 cuncta vastante, ne quid indecens ab hostibus sustinerent, turpitudinem morte fugerunt, exemplum sui cunctis virginibus relinquentes: honestis mentibus magis pudicitiam cure esse quam vitam.

Nichanor, victis Thebis atque subversis, unius captive virginis amore superatus est. Cuius coniugium expetens et voluntarios amplexus, quod
40 scilicet captiva optare debuerat, sensit pudicis mentibus plus virginitatem esse quam regnum, et interfectam propria manu flens et lugens amator tenuit. Narrant scriptores Grecie et aliam Thebanam virginem quam hostis Macedo coruperat dissimulasse paulisper dolorem, et violatorem virginitatis sue iugulasse postea dormientem, seque interfecisse cum gaudio ut nec vivere
45 voluerit post perditam castitatem nec ante mori quam sui ultrix existeret.

[42.] Apud Gimnosophistas Indie, quasi per manus huius opinionis auctoritas traditur quod Buddam, principem dogmatis eorum, e latere suo virgo generarit. Nec hoc mirum de barbaris, cum Minervam quoque de capite Iovis et Liberum Patrem de femore eius procreatos, doctissima finxerit
50 Grecia. Pseusippus quoque sororis Platonis filius et Clearchus in *Laude Platonis* et Anaxilides in secundo libro philosophie Perictionem matrem Platonis phantasmate Apollinis oppressam ferunt, et sapientie principem non aliter arbitrantur, nisi de partu virginis editum. Sed et Thimeus scribit Pytagore virginem filiam choro virginum prefuisse et castitatis eas instituisse
55 doctrinis. Diodorus socraticus quinque filias dialecticas insignis pudicitie habuisse narratur, de quibus et Philo Carneadis magister plenissimam scribit historiam. Ac ne nobis Dominum Salvatorem de virgine procreatum Romana exprobraret potentia, auctores urbis et gentis sue Ilia virgine et Marte genitos arbitrantur.

Iheronimus contra Iovinianum de castitate mulierum

60 [43.] Hec de virginibus seculi currens per multiplices historias et properans sermo perstrinxerit. Veniam ad maritas que mortuis vel occisis prioribus viris

go on living after their first husbands died or were slain, lest they be compelled into a second sexual union, and who loved their first husbands remarkably, for we know that a second marriage was also condemned among primitive heathens. Dido, the sister of Pygmalion, after she had assembled a great mass of gold and silver, sailed to Africa and there founded the city of Carthage; and when she was asked to marry by Iarbas, the king of Libya, she delayed the wedding for a while until she built the city. Not much later, having built a funeral pyre in memory of her former husband Sychaeus, she decided she would rather burn than marry. A chaste wife built Carthage, and in return that city met its end in praise of chastity. For the wife of Hasdrubal, when the city was taken and set afire and she saw she was going to be captured by the Romans, holding her small sons in each hand, leaped into the burning ruins of her own house. [60–71]

[44.] What shall I say of the wife of Niceratus? Unable to endure the wrong to her husband, she committed suicide, so as not to bear the lust of the Thirty Tyrants whom Lysander put in place after Athens was conquered. Artemesia, the wife of Mausolus, is also said to have been notable for her chastity. Although she was queen of Caria and was praised by noble poets and history writers, she is most praised for this–that she always loved her dead husband as if he were alive, and built a tomb so wondrous in size and beauty that even today every costly tomb is called a mausoleum, after his name. Teuta, queen of the Illyrians, though she ruled over strong men for a long time and often overcame the Romans, wondrously deserves to be associated with chastity. [72–81]

The Indians, like nearly all barbarians, have very many wives. Among them it is the law that the most beloved wife be burned with her dead husband. Wives therefore compete among themselves for the love of their husband, and the highest ambition of the rivals and the evidence of their chastity is to be thought worthy of death. And so the winner, dressed in her wedding clothes and ornaments, lies next to the corpse, embracing and kissing it, and, in praise of chastity, despises the fires put underneath her. I think whoever dies this way is not looking for a second marriage. [82–7]

When the Athenians were conquered, Alcibiades, the friend of Socrates, fled to Pharnabazus. Having taken a bribe from Lysander, the prince of the Spartans, Pharnabazus ordered him killed. After he was strangled and his head had been cut off and sent to Lysander as proof the killing was done, the rest of his body lay unburied. Only his concubine, against the order of the most cruel enemy, among strangers and in imminent danger, gave him a proper funeral, she herself being prepared to die for the dead man whom she had loved while he was alive. Let married women, Christian wives in any event, imitate the faithfulness of concubines; and let them, being free, exhibit what she protected as a captive. [88–95]

[45.] Strato, the prince of Sidon, wanted to kill himself with his own hand, lest he become a thing of mockery to the menacing Persians, whose treaty he had slighted for friendship with the king of the Egyptians. He was held back

67 **exstructa** constructa I; structra Pc.
71 **filiis** suis I.
74 **libidinem** iugem libidinis I; iugem libidinem Pc
89 **a Lisandro** ab Alexandro Pc.

supervivere noluerunt, ne cogerentur secundos nosse concubitus; et que mire
unicos amaverunt maritos ut sciamus digamiam etiam aput ethnicos reprobari.
Dido, soror Pigmalionis, multo auri et argenti pondere congregato, Affricam
65 navigavit ibique urbem Kartaginem condidit et cum ab Iarba rege Libie in
congugium peteretur, paulisper distulit nuptias, donec conderet civitatem. Nec
multo post exstructa in memoriam mariti quondam Sichey pyra, maluit ardere
quam nubere. Casta mulier Kartaginem condidit, et rursum eadem urbs in
castitatis laude finita est. Nam Astrubalis uxor, capta et incensa urbe, cum se
70 cerneret a Romanis esse capiendam, apprehensis ex utroque latere parvulis
filiis, in subiectum domus sue devolavit incendium.

[44.] Quid loquar Nicerati coniugem? Que impatiens iniurie viri, mortem
sibi ipsa conscivit, ne xxx^ta. tirannorum, quos Lisander victis Athenis
imposuerat, libidinem sustineret. Artemesia quoque uxor Mausolei insignis
75 pudicitie fuisse peribetur. Que cum esset regina Carie et nobilium poetarum
atque historicorum laudibus predicetur, in hoc vel maxime effertur quod
defunctum maritum sic semper amavit ut vivum, et mire magnitudinis ac
pulchritudinis exstruxit sepulcrum, intantum ut usque hodie omnia sepulchra
pretiosa ex nomine eius "mausolea" noncupentur. Teuta Illiriorum regina, ut
80 longo tempore viris fortissimis imperaret et Romanos sepe frangeret, miraculo
utique meruit castitatis.
Indi, ut omnes pene barbari, uxores plurimas habent. Apud eos lex est ut
uxor carissima cum defuncto marito cremetur. He igitur contendunt inter se de
amore viri, et ambitio summa certantium est ac testimonium castitatis dignam
85 morte decerni. Itaque victrix in habitu ornatuque pristino iuxta cadaver
accubat, amplexans illud et deosculans et suppositos ignes pudicitie laude
contempnens. Puto que sic moritur, secundas nuptias non requirit.
Alciabiades ille socraticus, victis Atheniensibus, fugit ad Pharnabuzum.
Qui, accepto precio a Lisandro principe Lacedemoniorum, iussit eum interfici.
90 Cumque suffocato caput esset ablatum et missum Lisandro in testimonium
cedis explete, reliqua pars corporis iacebat insepulta. Sola igitur concubina
contra crudelissimi hostis imperium, inter extraneos et imminente discrimine,
funeri iusta persolvit, mori parata pro mortuo quem vivum dilexerat.
Immitentur matrone, et matrone Christiane saltem, concubinarum fidem, et
95 prestent libere, quod captiva servavit.

[45.] Strato regulus Sidonis manu propria se volens confodere, ne
imminentibus Persis ludibrio foret, quorum fedus Egiptii regis societate
neglexerat, retrahebatur formidine et, gladium quem arripuerat circum-

by fear, and, terrified, he awaited the approach of the enemy, looking at the sword he had seized. When his wife saw he was going to be captured, she wrenched the sword from his hand and pierced his side. When his body was laid out in the proper way, she threw herself dying on it, lest she be forced to endure intercourse with another after her marriage troth. [96–102]

Xenophon writes in *The Education of Cyrus the Elder* that when her husband Abradatas was slain, Panthea his wife, who loved him with an extraordinary love, lay next to his lacerated body and, having pierced her breast, poured her blood into her husband's wounds. A wife thought it a just reason for killing her husband the king who had shown her naked, unbeknownst to her, to his friend. For she decided she was not loved if she could be displayed to another man. Rhodogune, the daughter of Darius, killed the nurse who urged a second marriage on her after the death of her husband. Stories tell of Alcestis who willingly died in place of her husband Admetus, and Penelope's chastity is the topic of Homer's poem. Laodomia, too, is remembered by the poets for not wanting to go on living after Protesilaus was killed at Troy. [103–11]

Concerning Roman Women

[46.] I shall pass on to the Roman women and put Lucretia first who, not wanting to survive the violation of her chastity, blotted out the stain on her body with her own blood. Duillius, who was the first to triumph in Rome's naval battles, took Bilia as his wife, a virgin of such chastity that she was a model to that world, in which immodesty was an abomination rather than a mere vice. When he grew old and trembling in his body, he was reproached once in a quarrel for his foul-smelling mouth and sadly betook himself home. And when he asked his wife why she had never warned him so that he might alleviate this fault, she said, "I would have, except I thought all men's mouths smelled that way." This chaste and noble woman should be praised either way: whether she ignored the man's illness yet patiently bore it, or the man found out about the misfortune of his body not through his wife's disgust but his enemy's abuse. Certainly a woman who married a second husband could not say this kind of thing. [112–23]

Marcia, the younger daughter of Cato, when she was asked why she was not marrying again after the loss of her husband, answered that she did not find a man who wanted her more than her possessions. This said tastefully, it shows that wealth rather than virtue usually works in selecting wives, and many men marry not with their eyes but with their fingers. Clearly, this is the great prosperity that greed procures! The same woman, when she was mourning her husband, was asked by other wives which day would be the last of her mourning, and she said, "The last day of my life." I think a woman who was lamenting her lost husband in this way was not planning a second marriage. [124–31]

Brutus married Porcia when she was a virgin; Cato married Marcia when she was not a virgin. But Marcia went to and fro between Hortensius and

99   **Quem** Magisque Pc.
107   **posset** est Pc.
120   **pudica** pudicicia Pc

spectans, hostium pavidus exspectabat adventum. Quem iam iamque capien-
100 dum uxor intelligens, extorsit acinacem e manu et latus eius transverberavit.
Compositoque ex more cadaveri se moriens superiecit, ne post virginalia
federa alterius coitum sustineret.

Xenophon in Ciri maioris scribit infantia, occiso Abradate viro, quem
Panthia uxor miro amore dilexerat, collocasse se iuxta corpus lacerum et
105 confosso pectore, sanguinem suum mariti infudisse vulneribus. Iustam
causam regis occidendi putavit uxor quam maritus nudam amico suo et
ignorantem monstraverat. Iudicavit enim se non amari, que et alteri posset
ostendi. Rodogune filia Darii post mortem viri nutricem que illi secundas
nuptias suadebat, occidit. Alcesten fabule ferunt pro Atmeto sponte defunctam,
110 et Penelopis pudicitia Homeri carmen est. Laodomia quoque poetarum ore
cantatur occiso apud Troiam Protesilao noluisse supervivere.

De Romanis mulieribus

[46.] Ad Romanas feminas transeam; et primam ponam Lucretiam, que
violate pudicitie nolens supervivere, maculam corporis cruore delevit.
Duillius qui primus Rome navali certamine triumphavit, Biliam virginem
115 duxit uxorem tante pudicitie ut illo quoque seculo pro exemplo fuerit, quo
impudicitia monstrum erat, non vitium. Is iam senex et trementi corpore, in
quodam iurgio audivit exprobrari sibi os fetidum, et tristis se domum contulit.
Cunque uxorem questus esset quare se nunquam monuisset ut huic vitio
mederetur, "Fecissem," inquit illa, "nisi putassem omnibus viris sic os olere."
120 Laudanda in utroque pudica et nobilis femina, et si ignoravit vitium viri et si
patienter tulit, et quod maritus infelicitatem corporis sui, non uxoris fastidio,
sed maledicto sensit inimici. Certe que secundum ducit maritum hoc dicere
non potest.

Martia Catonis filia minor, cum quereretur ab ea, cur post amissum
125 maritum denuo non nuberet, respondit non se invenire virum qui se magis
vellet quam sua. Quo dicto eleganter ostendit divitias magis in uxoribus eligi
solere quam pudicitiam, et multos non oculis, sed digitis uxores ducere.
Optima sane res quam avaritia conciliat! Eadem cum lugeret virum, et
matrone ab ea quererent quem diem haberet luctus ultimum, ait, "Quem et
130 vite." Arbitror que ita virum querebat absentem de secundo matrimonio non
cogitabat.

Brutus Porciam virginem duxit uxorem; Martiam Cato non virginem; sed
Martia inter Hortensium Catonemque discurrit, et sine Catone vivere potuit;

Cato, and could live without Cato; Porcia could not live without Brutus. For women devote themselves more completely to a single man, and to know no other is a great bond of close affection. When a relative advised Annia that she should marry another man – she was both in her flower and of attractive appearance – she said, "I will never do that. For if I shall find a man as good as the one I had before, I do not want to fear that I will lose him; if I find a bad one, why should it be necessary to put up with a worse one after a good one?" When a certain woman of good character who had a second husband was being praised in her presence, Porcia the younger answered, "A happy and chaste wife never marries more than once." Marcella the elder, asked by her mother whether she was happy to have married, said, "So much that I should not want to again." Valeria, the sister of the two Messalas, having lost her husband Servius, wanted to marry no one. Asked why she would do this, she said that in her mind her husband Servius was always alive. [134–44]

Portia sine Bruto non potuit. Magis enim se unicis viris applicant femine, et
135 nichil aliud nosse magnum artioris indulgentie vinculum est. Anniam cum
propinquus moneret ut alteri viro nuberet–esse enim ei et etatem integram et
faciem bonam – "Nequaquam," inquit, "hoc faciam. Si enim virum bonum
invenero, ut ante habui, nolo timere ne perdam; si malum, quid necesse est
post bonum pessimum sustinere?" Porcia minor, cum laudaretur apud eam
140 quedam bene morata que secundum habebat maritum, respondit, "Felix et
pudica matrona numquam preter semel nubit." Macella maior, rogata a matre
sua gauderetne se nupsisse, respondit, "Ita valde ut amplius nolim." Valeria
Messalarum soror, amisso Servio viro, nulli volebat nubere. Que interrogata
cur hoc faceret, ait sibi semper maritum Servium vivere.

The Pardoner's Prologue and Tale

MARY HAMEL

The Pardoner's Prologue

As original a character as the Pardoner is, his extraordinary self-presentation in his *Prologue* is based to a certain degree on the confession of Faux Semblant in the *Roman de la Rose*, a source that also influenced the portrait of the Friar in the *General Prologue*. The influence is shown here not only by the defiant shamelessness of the two confessions, with their shared themes of hypocrisy and venality, but by a few specific, significant shared ideas and some verbal parallels.

Chaucer's procedure in the *Pardoner's Prologue* was nevertheless eclectic enough to intermingle these echoes with other materials, not least of which is observed actual behavior, by the evidence of sermons and Langland. The parallels to lines 377–88, the Pardoner's "gaude" whereby those guilty of "synne horrible" were forbidden to offer to his relics, were therefore judged too general to constitute real analogues and so are not included here: in the words of Albert C. Friend, "This hoax was a tale widely current in the fourteenth century."[1] For this reason, attention is concentrated here on the *Roman de la Rose*; but a somewhat larger selection from the confession of Faux Semblant is included to demonstrate not only verbal parallels but also parallelism of idea that implies a more general influence.

The choice of text was somewhat problematic; for the most appropriate text to demonstrate Chaucer's source may well be that of the C-fragment of the Middle English *Romaunt of the Rose*, which exemplifies the kind of text Chaucer most likely had access to, whoever was responsible for the translation.[2] For this reason, equivalent line numbers from Fragment C are footnoted below. For the French text, though more recent editions are available, that of Langlois is chosen here as "the one most fully annotated and that provides the greatest number of variants."[3] In particular, two interpolated passages not found in the best manuscripts of the *Roman de la Rose* have some importance for the *Pardoner's Prologue*, and these are printed here from Langlois's notes.

---

[1] "Analogues in Cheriton to the Pardoner and his Sermon," *Journal of English and Germanic Philology* 53 (1954): 384. In addition to the instances cited by Germaine Dempster in Bryan and Dempster 411–14, Friend notes an earlier occurrence from the thirteenth-century preacher Odo of Cheriton: "Similiter quidam praedicator in sermone ait, 'Quecumque habuit rem cum aliquo quasi cum marito nihil offerat ad reliquas istas,' et sic omnes ne viderentur adulterem optulerunt" (Lincoln Cathedral Library MS 11, fol. 5v, col. 2): "And likewise a certain preacher in a sermon says: 'Whatever woman has had an affair with a man as if with her husband, she may offer nothing to these relics,' and so all, that they might not seem guilty of adultery, made their offering" (Friend's text and translation, p. 384).

[2] On the question of authorship, see Alfred David's Explanatory Notes to the *Romaunt*, *Riverside Chaucer* pp. 1103–4; it is generally agreed that the C-fragment was translated not by Chaucer himself but by a fifteenth-century "Chaucerian" (1103).

[3] David 1104. See also David's textual introduction to the *Romaunt*, p. 1199. More recent editions include that of Félix Lecoy, 3 vols., Classiques Français du Moyen Age (Paris, 1965–70).

Jean de Meun
The Romance of the Rose[4]

"But whatever place I come to [11065]
And however I conduct myself there
I hunt for nothing but fraud.
No more than Sir Tibert the cat
5   Attends to anything but mice and rats
Do I attend to anything but fraud.

. . .

"Without fail I am a traitor, [11169]
And God has judged me for a thief.
I am a perjurer, but what I accomplish
10   Is scarcely known before it's done,
For many have come to death through me
Who never recognized my trickery;
And they suffer and will suffer
Who never will recognize it.
15   Whoever does recognize it, if he is wise,
Protects himself from it, or else comes to great harm.
But deception is so powerful
That its recognition is too difficult.
For Proteus, who was accustomed to
20   Change into anything whenever he wanted,
Was never capable of such trickery or fraud
As I practice, for never in a town
Have I entered where I was recognized,
However much I was heard or seen there.
25   I know too well how to change my stripes
To take on some disguise and reject others.

. . .

"And I go through all regions [11213]
Examining all religions;
But from religion, without fail,
30   I leave the grain and take the chaff . . .

. . .

["I make people fall into my traps [*Insert A*]

1–6   Cf. *Romaunt* 6201–06.
7–26 Cf. *Romaunt* 6307–26.
27–30 Cf. *Romaunt* 6351–54.
31–48 See *Romaunt* 6361–69, 6375–82. The three lines "N'i a nul prelat . . . la bouche close" (38–40)
      are not translated in the *Romaunt*.

4 Translated with the help of Catherine A. Bodin.

Jean de Meun
Le Roman de la Rose

(ed. Ernest Langlois, Vol. III, Société des Anciens Textes Français [Paris, 1921])

	Mais en quelque leu que je viegne	[11065]
	Ne coment que je m'i contiegne,	
	Nule rien fors barat n'i chaz;	
	Ne plus que dans Tiberz li chaz	
5	N'entent qu'a souriz e a raz,	
	N'entens je a riens fors a baraz.	

. . .

	Senz faille traitres sui gié,	[11169]
	E pour larron m'a Deus juigié;	
	Parjurs sui, mais ce que j'afin	
10	Set l'en enviz devant la fin,	
	Car pluseur par mei mort reçurent	
	Qui onc mon barat n'aperçurent,	
	E receivent e recevront	
	Qui jamais ne l'apercevront.	
15	Qui l'apercevra, s'il est sages,	
	Gart s'en, ou c'iert ses granz domages;	
	Mais tant est fort la decevance	
	Que trop est grief l'apercevance;	
	Car Protheüs, qui se soulait	
20	Muer en tout quanqu'il voulait,	
	Ne sot onc tant barat ne guile	
	Con je faz, car onques en vile	
	N'entrai ou fusse queneüz,	
	Tant i fusse oïz ne veüz.	
25	Trop sai bien mes abiz changier,	
	Prendre l'un e l'autre estrangier . . .	

. . .

	E vois par toutes regions	[11213]
	Cerchant toutes religions;	
	Mais de religion, senz faille,	
30	J'en lais le grain e preing la paille . . .	

. . .

	[Je faz cheoir dedenz mes pieges	[*Insert A*]

31–48   These lines are an interpolation, printed from Langlois pp. 310–11 (selected lines).

Through my prerogatives;
I can confess and absolve –
No prelate can stop me –
35   All people, wherever I find them.
I know of no prelate who can do this,
Except for the Pope alone.

. . .

"There is no prelate who dares take reprisals
Or grumble against my people:
40   I have closed their mouths well.

. . .

"But it doesn't bother me, however things go:
I have some money, I have some stock.
I have done so much, I have preached so long,
I have taken so much, I have been given so much
45   By everyone in his or her folly,
That I have a nice little life,
Through the simpleness of the prelates
Who fear my snares too much. . .]

. . .

"[William of St. Amour] wanted that I renounce   [11515]
50   Begging and that I work for a living,
If I didn't have enough to live on.
Really he must have believed me drunk –
For working cannot content me;
I'll have nothing to do with working:
55   There's too much effort in working.
I'd rather say prayers before the people
And buckle up my foxiness
In the robe of religious hypocrisy."
"What's this? the Devil! what are you saying?"
60   What did you say just now?"
"What?" "Great, manifest disloyalty.
Then do you not fear God?" "Certainly not,
Since scarcely can one who fears God
Attain to great things in this world;
65   For the good people who flee evil
And loyally live off their own possessions,
And who conform their lives to God,
Scarcely get from one loaf to the next.
Such people drink too much discomfort;
70   There is no life that displeases me so.

. . .

"By my larceny I pile up and amass   [11553]
A great treasure piled up in a mass

49–70 Cf. *Romaunt* 6787–6808.
71–86 Cf. *Romaunt* 6825–40.

Le monde par mes privilieges;
Je puis confessier et assoudre,
Ce ne me peut nus prelaz toudre,
35   Toutes genz, ou que je les truisse.
Ne sai nul prelat qui ce puisse,
Fors l'apostoile seulement,
. . .
N'i a nul prelat qui remordre
Ne groucier contre mes genz ose:
40   Je leur ai bien la bouche close.
. . .
Mais ne me chaut coment qu'il aille,
J'ai des deniers, j'ai de l'aumaille,
Tant ai fait, tant ai sermoné,
Tant ai pris, tant m'a l'en doné,
45   Touz li mondes par sa folie,
Que je meine vie jolie,
Par las simplece des prelaz,
Qui trop fort redoutent mes laz.]
. . .
[Il] voulait que je reneiasse   [11515]
50   Mendicité e labourasse,
Se je n'avaie de quei vivre.
Bien me voulait tenir pour ivre.
Car labourer ne me peut plaire;
De labourer n'ai je que faire:
55   Trop a grant peine en labourer.
J'aim meauz devant les genz ourer
E afubler ma renardie
Dou mantel de papelardie.
– Qu'est ce? diable! quel sont ti dit?
60   Qu'est ce que tu as ici dit?
– Quei? – Granz desleiautez apertes.
Don ne crains tu pas Deu? – Non, certes,
Qu'enviz peut a grant chose ataindre
En cet siecle qui Deu veaut craindre,
65   Car li bon qui le mal eschivent,
E leiaument dou leur se vivent,
E qui selonc Deu se maintienent,
Enviz de pain a autre vienent.
Teus genz beivent trop de mesaise;
70   N'est vie qui tant me desplaise.
. . .
Par ma lobe entas e amasse   [11553]
Grant tresor en tas e en masse,

37   **Fors l'apostoile** le pape tant *some mss.*

That cannot collapse for anything.
For, suppose I have a palace built
75   And fulfill all my pleasures
Among companions or in bed,
With tables full of delicacies,
Then I no longer want any other life.
Let my silver and my gold pile up:
80   For before my treasury might be empty,
The coins come to my rescue.
Don't I make my bears dance well?
Acquisition is all my intention;
My collecting is worth more than my income.
85   Thus though I might be killed or beaten,
I mean to insinuate myself everywhere.
. . .
["I go everywhere to take care of souls –   [*Insert B*]
None can hold out without me –
And to preach and to advise,
90   Without ever working with my hands.
From the Pope I have the bull,
And he does not take me for a fool.]
. . .
"I have no care for poor folk: [11575]
Their condition is neither attractive nor nice.
. . .
95   "And for the saving of souls   [11587]
I seek out lords and ladies
And the properties and the lives
Throughout all their households
And make them believe and put into their heads
100   That their parish priests are beasts
Towards me and my companions.
. . .
"We have yet another custom   [11637]
Concerning those whom we know to be against us.
. . .
"If we see that he can win,   [11643]
105   Through certain people, honor on earth,
Provisions, or possessions,
We concentrate and watch to see
By which stairway he can climb,
And, the better to capture and overcome him,
110   By treachery we defame him

82–82   Make my bears dance – i.e., juggle my affairs.
87–92   Cf. *Romaunt* 6841–48.
93–4   Cf. *Romaunt* 6856–57.
95–101 Cf. *Romaunt* 6869–75.
102–21 Cf. *Romaunt* 6923–44.

Qui ne peut pour riens afonder;
Car, se j'en faz palais fonder,
75 E accomplis touz mes deliz
De compaignies ou de liz,
De tables pleines d'entremès,
Car ne vueil autre vie mais,
Recreist mes argenz e mes ors;
80 Car ainz que seit vuiz mes tresors
Denier me vienent a resours.
Ne faz je bien tomber mes ours?
En aquerre est toute m'entente,
Meauz vaut mes pourchaz que ma rente.
85 S'en me devait tuer ou batre,
Si me vueil je par tout embatre.

. . .

[Par tout vois les ames curer,   [*Insert B*]
Nus ne peut mais senz moi durer
E preeschier et conseillier,
90 Senz jamais des mains traveillier.
De l'apostole en ai la bule,
Qui ne me tient pas pour entule.]

. . .

Je n'ai cure de povres genz: [11575]
Leur estaz n'est ne beaus ne genz.

. . .

95 E pour le sauvement des ames,   [11587]
J'enquier des seigneurs e des dames,
E de trestoutes leur maisnies
Les proprietez e les vies,
E leur faz creire e met es testes
100 Que leur prestre curé sont bestes
Envers mei e mes compaignons . . .

. . .

Une autre coustume ravons   [11637]
Seur ceus que contre nous savons;

. . .

Se nous veons qu'il puist conquerre   [11643]
105 Par queusque genz eneur en terre,
Provendes ou possessions,
A saveir nous estudions
Par quel eschiele il peut monter,
E, pour lui meauz prendre e donter,
110 Par traïson le diffamons

87–92 The second interpolation is printed (six lines of ten) from Langlois p. 322.

To them, since we like him not at all.
The rungs of his ladder
We cut in this way and strip him
Of his friends, so that he will never know
115 By a word how he has lost them.
For, if we censured him openly,
Perhaps we would be blamed for it,
And so would fail in our aim;
Then, if our evil intention
120 He knew, he would defend himself from it,
So that people would censure us for it.

. . .

"But I do not dare to lie to you;   [11969]
Still, if I were able to sense
That you had not perceived it,
125 The lie you would have in your fist;
Certainly I would deceive you,
Nor would I renounce it as a sin . . ."

122–7   Cf. *Romaunt* 7287–92.

Vers ceus, puis que nous l'amons.
De s'eschiele les eschillons
Ainsinc copons, e le pillons
De ses amis, qu'il ne savra
115 Ja mot que perduz les avra;
Car, s'en apert le grevions,
Espeir blasmé en serions,
E si faudrions a nostre esme;
Car, se nostre entencion pesme
120 Savait cil, il s'en defendrait,
Si que l'en nous en reprendrait.
. . .
Mais a vous n'ose je mentir;   [11969]
Mais se je peüsse sentir
Que vous ne l'aperceüssiez,
125 La mençonge ou poing eüssiez;
Certainement je vous boulasse,
Ja pour pechié ne le laissasse.

The Pardoner's Tale

The *Pardoner's Tale* of the three "riotours" who find Death is a version of a folktale with a remarkably wide range, from Chaucer's England to the Near and Far East and sub-Saharan Africa; it very likely originated as a tale of the Buddha as Boddhisatva from the fourth or third century B.C.[5] Developing over such a long period and with such a wide geographical range, the story evolved into several distinct types, all recognizable as versions of the folktale motif "The Treasure Finders Who Murder Each Other."[6] There are five principal types: in one version, Christ or a similar moral leader warns his disciples to have nothing to do with gold they have found by chance; after they leave it, two companions find it (or two disciples linger). Because it is too heavy to carry, one goes for a mule or ass and food while the second guards the gold; the latter stabs the former when he returns and then eats (and feeds the mule) poisoned food brought by his victim. Jesus returns to show his disciples the truth of his warning in the three corpses. A second type shows Jesus actually creating the treasure out of earth as a test; here there are three companions (and no mule), and Jesus again returns at the end to draw the moral and return the gold to earth. The third type begins not with Jesus but with a hermit or similar figure, who warns three companions he encounters by chance that he is fleeing Death and who directs them where to find him; the usual pattern ensues, but the hermit normally does not return at the end. The fourth type has three companions but no warning character, though Jesus or another character appears at the end to draw the moral; the fifth type, with either two or three companions, has neither opening warning-figure nor final moralist.[7]

It is evident that Chaucer's version corresponds most closely to the third type, and this is the primary basis for the selection of analogues included here. Only the *exempla* from British Library MSS Add. 11872 and 27336, included because they are among the earliest in date (ca. 1400 for the former, early fifteenth century for the latter), are Type 1 analogues. The other *exemplum* (1406), the novella (1576), and the play of St. Anthony (mid-15th century) are all Type 3. Though the last two were printed a considerable time after Chaucer's death, they are included because they undoubtedly reflect a much earlier oral circulation of the tale, and moreover have more in common with the *Pardoner's*

---

[5] See F. J. Furnivall, E. Brock, and W. A. Clouston, eds., *Originals and Analogues of Chaucer's Canterbury Tales*, Chaucer Society, 2nd Series (London, 1872–87), pp. 418–22, for texts of Eastern versions.

[6] Antti Aarne and Stith Thompson, *The Types of the Folktale*, 2nd rev. (Helsinki, 1961), Type 763.

[7] See Mary Hamel and Charles Merrill, "The Analogues of the *Pardoner's Tale* and a New African Version," *Chaucer Review* 26 (1991): 175–7, for a full description of this classification and a summary account of analogues published since 1940 (none medieval). For examples of other types, see also Frederick Tupper, "The Pardoner's Tale," in Bryan and Dempster, pp. 415–23.

Tale than any other medieval analogues.[8] It is noteworthy that the play, the novella, and two of the three *exempla* are Italian or from Italian manuscripts. The novella and play – the Italian analogues most similar to the *Pardoner's Tale* – are both associated with Florence;[9] similarities between them suggest that they may have been derived from the same ancestor, though the play's version has of course been considerably adapted to fit into the framework of the saint's legend. This provenance raises the interesting possibility that Chaucer came across the story in the course of his visit to Florence in 1373; certainly no other extant early analogues are English.[10] The three *exempla*, the novella, and the *Play of St. Anthony* are presented in the second section below.

Chaucer's treatment of this story remains unique in many ways, not least of which is its setting as not only the *exemplum* of a sermon (three of the analogues printed here are explicitly that), but of a sermon that digresses widely from its announced theme of avarice to take up the "tavern sins," especially gluttony and drunkenness. Two important sources for the Pardoner's treatment of drunkenness and overeating in the earlier part of his tale are Innocent III's *De miseria humane conditionis* and Jerome's *Adversus Jovinianum*.[11] Because this material

---

[8] Alessandro D'Ancona demonstrated through identification of datable names that the novelle collected in the *Novellino* date from the twelfth through the fourteenth centuries, with those added to the 1572 edition by Borghini (see next note) datable particularly from the late thirteenth and fourteenth centuries: *Studi di Critica e Storia Letteraria*, 2nd ed. (Bologna, 1912), pp. 7–15, especially 10–13. Indeed, three fourteenth-century manuscripts contain novelle corresponding to items in the *Novellino* (see Guido Biagi, ed., *Le Novelle antiche dei Codici Panciatichiano-Palatino 138 e Laurenziano-Gaddiano 193* (Firenze, 1880), pp. xci–xciv, xcviii–ci). The novella printed here is not among those datable by names or early manuscript; but its similarities to the mid-fifteenth-century play suggest a common ancestor from at least the fourteenth century. See also Henry Seidel Canby, "Some Comments on the Sources of Chaucer's 'Pardoner's Tale,'" *Modern Philology* 2 (1905): 479.

[9] The novella was printed by Vincenzo Borghini in Florence in 1572 as #82 of the *Libro de Novelle et di Bel Parlar Gentile*, published by Filippo and Iacopo Giunti; this was a revised edition of the collection *Lo Ciento Novelle Antike*, first published by Carlo Gualteruzzi in Bologna in 1525 (the two editions are known collectively as the *Novellino*). This version replaces a Type 1 novella (#83) in the 1525 edition (printed by Tupper, pp. 416–17) and may have been based on a Florentine manuscript (see below, note 18). D'Ancona argues that the original compiler of the *Novellino* was a Florentine, pp. 47–52. For the history of the Florentine *sacre rappresentazioni* (including that of St. Anthony), see Joseph S. Kennard, *The Italian Theatre from its Beginning to the Close of the Seventeenth Century* (1932; rpt. New York: Benjamin Blom, 1964), pp. 30–63.

[10] Hans Sachs's *Der Dot im Stock*, included by Tupper (pp. 429–36), also corresponds to the *Pardoner's Tale* in a number of details, though none uniquely. See Walter Morris Hart, "'The Pardoner's Tale' and 'Der Dot im Stock,'" *Modern Philology* 9 (1911–12): 17–22, for detailed parallels; most are also in the Italian play, and others are very minor. This is also quite a late text (1554–6); moreover, in an author well-known for his wide reading in vernacular as well as classical texts (e.g., his translation of Boccaccio), there appears a faint possibility that Sach's version of the story might have been influenced by Chaucer's – or even by some version of the Italian novella.

[11] For a detailed account of the parallels between the *De miseria* and the *Pardoner's Tale*, see Robert E. Lewis, ed., *De miseria condicionis humane* (Athens, GA: University of Georgia Press, 1978), pp. 8–12, 71–3. Chaucer's use of the *De miseria* in the *Pardoner's Tale* is interspersed with echoes of St. Jerome; in addition, some elements in this part of the *Tale* may also reflect Chaucer's familiarity with John of Wales's *Communiloquium* (not included here): see Robert A. Pratt, "Chaucer and the Hand That Fed Him," *Speculum* 41 (1966): 619–42, and Lewis, pp. 71–2, nn. 46–8. As Lewis says, "In these passages from the Pardoner's Tale it is often impossible to know exactly where Chaucer got his material, whether from the *De miseria*, from St. Jerome's *Epistola adversus Jovinianum*, from John of Wales's *Communiloquium*, from the Vulgate (directly or indirectly), from another source, or simply from his

appears first in the tale, these sources are presented in the first section of what follows.

Another way in which Chaucer's treatment of the folktale is unique is the figure of the Old Man, which has only a functional resemblance to the hermits of the Type 3 analogues. This character gains an extraordinary and haunting power by Chaucer's inspired borrowing of ideas and language from his only identified source for the portrait, the first Elegy of the sixth-century Roman poet Maximianus. This confession of the speaker's despair and self-disgust at the encroachments of old age also influenced the *Reeve's Prologue*; it introduces a series of six elegies in which the poet's erotic past takes its place among other kinds of experience that age has ruined. It has been shown that the Latin poet's work must have been very familiar to English schoolboys of Chaucer's day, since it was regularly included in the *florilegia* used in schools – surprising though it may seem in view of the erotic nature of the poetry.[12]

A larger selection from the elegy is printed below in the third section than in Bryan and Dempster; beyond the often-cited direct verbal parallel of the old man's cane knocking on his mother's gate the earth, the mood of the elegy seems to pervade the speech of Chaucer's Old Man. The lines chosen include the elegy's description of the physical appearance of the aged; its judgments of sensual pleasures such as eating and drinking; its images of the mockery of age by youth; and its discussion of the avarice of old age, whereby, as the images of Tantalus and the dragon suggest, though the old man is a miser, wealthy in owning riches, he is poor in his inability to use them – as if he were their guardian and not their possessor.

personal knowledge" (11). See also John M. Steadman, "Old Age and *Contemptus Mundi* in *The Pardoner's Tale*," *Medium Ævum* 33 (1964): 125–9.

[12] See George R. Coffman, "Old Age from Horace to Chaucer: Some Literary Affinities and Adventures of an Idea," *Speculum* 9 (1934): 253n, 271. Chaucer's use of this text was first noted by George Lyman Kittredge, "Chaucer and Maximianus," *American Journal of Philology* 9 (1888): 84–5.

I. The Tavern Sins

[17] Of Gluttony[13]

"The beginning of man's life is water and bread and clothing and a house to cover shame." But now the fruits of trees are not sufficient for gluttons, nor the varieties of vegetables, nor the roots of plants, nor the fish of the sea, nor the beasts of the earth, nor the birds of the sky, but they seek for [spices], compare aromas, nurse fattened birds, catch the plump ones, [5] which are carefully prepared by the skill of the cooks, which are splendidly presented by the ceremony of the waiters. One grinds and strains, another mixes and prepares, turns substance into accident, changes nature into art, so that satiety turns into hunger, squeamishness recovers an appetite; to stimulate gluttony, not to sustain nature; not to fill a need, but to satisfy a desire [10]. Yet the pleasure of gluttony is so brief that as to the size of the place it is scarcely four inches, as to length of time scarcely as many minutes. Moderation is condemned, and superfluity is pursued. The appetite knows no limit in diversity of foods and variety of tastes, and greediness exceeds measure. But then the stomach is weighed down, the mind is disturbed, the intellect is overcome; thence not prosperity and health, but sickness and death. [15] Hear the opinion of the wise man on this: "Be not greedy in any feasting, and pour not out thyself upon any meat; for in many meats there will be sickness, and by surfeiting many have perished." "Meat for the belly and the belly for the meats: but God shall destroy both it and them."

[18] Examples against Gluttony

[20] Gluttony demands a costly tribute, but it returns the smallest value, because the more delicate the foods are, the more stinking the excrements are. What goes in vilely comes out vilely, expelling a horrible wind above and below, and emitting an abominable sound. Gluttony closed paradise, sold the birthright, hanged the baker, beheaded the Baptist. Nabuzardan, chief of cooks, burned the temple and destroyed all Jerusalem. [It was] at the banquet [that] Baltazar [25] saw the hand writing against him: "Mane, Thecel, Phares," and he was killed by the Chaldeans the same night. "The people sat down to eat and drink, and they rose up to play," but "yet their meat was in their mouth, and the wrath of God came upon them." "They that were feeding delicately died in the streets." The rich man who "feasted sumptuously every day" "was buried in hell."

---

4   **spices** paints *Lewis.*

[13] Translation by Robert E. Lewis, pp. 164–70. Reprinted by permission.

I. The Tavern Sins

(Lotario dei Segni (Pope Innocent III), *De miseria condicionis humane*, ed. and trans. Robert E. Lewis [Athens, GA, 1978], pp. 165–71).[14]

[17] De Gula

"Inicium vite hominis aqua et panis et vestimentum et domus protegens turpitudinem." Nunc autem gulosis non sufficiunt fructus arborum, nec genera leguminum, nec radices herbarum, nec pisces maris, nec bestie terre, nec aves celi, set querunt pigmenta, comparant aromata, nutriunt altilia, capiunt obesa,
5   que studiose coquantur arte cocorum, que laute parentur officio ministrorum. Alius contundit et colat, alius confundit et conficit, substanciam vertit in accidens, naturam mutat in artem, ut saturitas transeat in esuriem, ut fastidium revocet appetitum; ad irritandam gulam, non ad sustentandam naturam; non ad necessitatem supplendam, set ad aviditatem explendam. Ceterum tam
10   breve est gule voluptas ut spacio loci vix sit quatuor digitorum, spacio temporis vix sit totidem momentorum. Contempnitur mediocritas, et super-fluitas affectatur. In diversitate ciborum et varietate saporum aviditas nescit modum, et voracitas excedit mensuram. Set inde gravatur stomachus, turbatur sensus, opprimitur intellectus; inde non salus et sanitas, set morbus et mors.
15   Audi super hoc sentenciam sapientis: "Noli avidus esse in omni epulacione, et non te effundas super omnem escam; in multis enim escis erit infirmitas, et propter crapulam multi [fol. 95] obierunt." "Esca ventri et venter escis: Deus autem et hunc et has destruet."

[18] Exempla contra gulam

Gula carum tributum exigit, set vilissimum reddit, quia quanto sunt
20   delicaciora cibaria, tanto fetidiora sunt stercora. Turpiter egerit quod turpiter ingerit, superius et inferius horribilem flatum exprimens, et abominabilem sonum emittens. Gula paradisum clausit, primogenita vendidit, suspendit pistorem, decollavit Baptistam. Nabuzardan, princeps cocorum, templum incendit et Ierusalem totam evertit. Balthasar in convivio manum contra se
25   scribentem aspexit: "Mane, Thechel, Phares," et eadem nocte interfectus est a Chaldeis. "Sedit populus manducare et bibere, et surrexerunt ludere," set "adhuc esce eorum erant in ore ipsorum, et *ira Dei ascendit super eos*." "Qui vescebantur voluptuose interierunt in viis." Dives ille qui "epulabatur cotidie splendide" "sepultus est in inferno."

---

[14] Passages set off by quotation marks are from the Bible; for specific identifications, see Lewis. Reprinted by permission.

[19] Of Drunkenness

[30] What is more unsightly than a drunkard, in whose mouth is a stench, in whose body a trembling; who utters foolish things, betrays secrets; whose reason is taken away, whose face is transformed? "For there is no secret where drunkenness reigneth." "Whom have the well-filled cups not made well spoken?" Then wine does not suffice, nor cider, nor beer, but mead, syrup, spiced wine are eagerly prepared with great labor, with not a little care, with the greatest expense. [35] But after that there are fights and brawls, disputes and quarrels. "For wine drunken with excess," as the wise man says, "raiseth quarrel and wrath and many ruins." And Osee: "Fornication and wine and drunkenness take away the understanding." Therefore the Apostle says: "Avoid wine, wherein is [lust]." And Solomon: "Wine is an inebriating thing and drunkenness riotous." The son of Rechab and the son of Zachary did not drink wine or cider or anything that could inebriate." [40]

[20] Examples against Drunkenness

Drunkenness exposed the private parts, committed incest, killed the son of the king, strangled the head of the army. What Solomon says is therefore true: "They that give themselves to drinking and that [meet] together [for that purpose] shall be consumed." And Isaias: "Woe to you that rise up early in the morning to follow drunkenness and to drink till the evening in order to be inflamed with wine [45]. The harp and the lyre and the timbrel and the pipe and wine are in your feasts." "Woe to you that are mighty at drinking wine and stout men at mixing drunkenness." "Behold joy and gladness, killing calves and slaying rams, eating flesh and drinking wine. Let us eat and drink, for tomorrow we die. And it will be revealed to my ears, says the Lord of Hosts, 'if this iniquity shall be forgiven you [50] till you die.'" "Woe to the crown of pride of Ephraim." "The priests and the prophets have been ignorant of judgment." O shame, when the blessing was asked of a certain father at the reciting of the gospel reading, he is reported to have said in a high voice, belching forth the inebriation of the day before and the drunkenness of the night: "May the King of the Angels bless the drink of his servants." [55]

St. Jerome, *Against Jovinian*

II, 8 (Col. 297): Moreover greed for food, who does not know that it is the mother of avarice and holds the soul weighed down to earth as if by a kind of fetters? On account of the brief pleasure of the palate, lands and seas are traversed; and so that honey-sweetened wine and costly food may pass through our gullet, we sweat over the labors of our whole life. [5]

---

38   **lust** luxury *Lewis.*
43–4   **meet . . . for that purpose** club together *Lewis.*

[19] De Ebrietate

30   Quid turpius ebrioso, cui fetor est in ore, tremor in corpore; qui promit
stulta, prodit occulta; cui mens alienatur, facies transformatur? "Nullum enim
secretum ubi regnat ebrietas." "Fecundi calices quem non fecere disertum?"
Porro non sufficit vinum, non sicera, non cervisia, set studiose conficitur
mulsum, syropus, claretum labore multo, sollicitudine non modica, sumptu
35   maximo. Set inde contenciones et rixe, lites et iurgia. "Vinum enim multum
potatum," ut ait sapiens, "irritacionem et iram et ruinas multas facit." Et Osee:
"Fornicacio et vinum et ebrietas auferunt cor." Propterea dicit Apostolus:
"Fugite vinum, in quo est luxuria." Et Salomon: "Ebriosa res vinum / et
tumultuosa ebrietas." Filius Rechab et filius Zacharie vinum et siceram et
40   omne quod inebriare poterat non biberunt.

[20] Exempla contra Ebrietatem

Ebrietas verenda nudavit, incestum commisit, filium regis occidit, principem exercitus iugulavit. Verum est ergo quod Salomon ait: "Vacantes potibus
et dantes symbolum consumentur." Et Ysaias: "Ve qui consurgitis mane ad
ebrietatem sectandam et potandum usque ad vesperum ut vino estuetis.
45   Cythara et lyra et tympanum et tibia et vinum in conviviis vestris." "Ve qui
potentes estis ad bibendum vinum et viri fortes ad miscendam ebrietatem."
"Ecce gaudium et leticia, occidere vitulos et iugulare arietes, comedere carnes
et bibere vinum. Comedamus et bibamus, cras enim moriemur. Et revelabitur
auribus meis, dicit Dominus Exercituum, 'si dimittetur hec iniquitas vobis
50   donec moriamini'." "Ve corone superbie Effraym." "Sacerdos et propheta
nescierunt pre ebrietate: absorti sunt a vino, nescierunt videntem, ignora-
verunt iudicium." Proh pudor, cum ad pronunciandam evangelicam leccionem
a quodam patre benedictio peteretur, hesternam crapulam et nocturnam
ebrietatem eructuans, fertur alta voce dixisse: "Potum servorum suorum
55   benedicat Rex Angelorum."

S. Eusebii Hieronymi, *Adversus Jovinianum Libri Duo.*[15]
(from J.-P. Migne, ed. *Patrologiae Latina*, Vol. XXIII [Paris, 1845]
cols. 297–305)

II, 8 (Col. 297): Porro ciborum aviditas, quod avaritiae mater sit, et animum
quasi quibusdam compedibus degravatum in terra teneat, quis ignorat?
Propter brevem gulae voluptatem, terrae lustrantur et maria; et ut mulsum
vinum pretiosusque cibus fauces nostras transeat, totius vitae [*MS.* opere]
5   opera desudamus.

---

[15] Vols. II and III of Jerome: the *Epistola Adversus Jovinianum* is Vol. II.

II, 10 (Col. 299): Without flavor and foods, moreover, it is impossible for the human body to subsist. Therefore reason ought to be present, so that we may take such and so many foods with which the body may not be over-burdened, nor the liberty of the spirit weighed down; for which reason one must not only eat, but walk about, and sleep, and digest, and afterwards, with the veins swollen, hold in check the urge of the passions [10]. 'Wine is a lustful thing, and drunkenness dishonorable. Anyone who is associated with these things will not be wise' (Proverbs 20:1). Nor may we approve foods which either are difficult to digest or, once eaten, we regret that they were pro-duced and squandered by great effort. [Food] of vegetables, fruits, and legumes is both more easily prepared and does not need the skill and costs of [15] cooks: and it supports the human body without worry and, taken in mod-eration (for that which does not have any incitement for the palate is not devoured greedily), is digested with greater ease. For no one is overburdened by one or two foods, and these simple, to the point of inflation of the belly, which is brought on by diversity of meats and [20] deliciousness of taste. Pans steam with various smells and attract those whose hunger is satisfied, like captives, to eat again. For which reason diseases are also stirred up by very great repletion; and many remedy the impatience of gluttony by vomiting, and what has entered foully exits more foully still.

II, 12 (Col. 302): But overeating of the simplest foods is also to be avoided. For nothing so overwhelms the soul as a belly full and boiling over, and turning itself this way and that [25], and blowing out its effluvium in belching or breaking of wind. What kind of fasting is it, or indeed what repast after fasting, when we are distended by yesterday's meals and the gullet, our laboratory, is turned into a latrine? And when we contemplate seeking the reputation of a more extended abstinence from food, we devour so much that the night of the second day scarcely will digest it. Therefore it is not to be called fasting so much as hangover and stinking and indigestion [30].

II, 15 (Col. 305): I shall show, first, that Adam in paradise accepted the injunction that, while he might eat other fruits, he was to abstain from one tree. The bliss of paradise without abstinence from food could not be declared. As long as he fasted he was in paradise: he ate, and was ejected. . . .

II. The Folktale

Exemplum I. *Of three companions who found a treasure*

Exemplum of avarice. A certain hermit, wishing to build a garden in a grove, while digging found by chance a treasure; and at once he cried out three times in a loud voice, "Death! death! death!" Three companions, traders who were passing by, came saying, "Where is death, which you cry out on?"

II, 10 (Col. 299): Absque gustu autem et cibis impossibile est humanum corpus subsistere. Adesse ergo debet ratio, ut tales ac tantas sumamus escas, quibus non oneretur corpus, nec libertas animae praegravetur; quia et comedendum est, et deambulandum, et dormiendum, et digerendum, et postea
10   inflatis venis, incentiva libidinum sustinenda. *Luxuriosa res vinum, et contumeliosa ebrietas* (*Prov.* XX, 1). Omnis qui cum his miscetur, non erit sapiens. Nec tales accipiamus cibos, quos aut difficulter digerere, aut comesos, magno partos et perditos labore doleamus. Olerum, [col. 300] pomorum, ac leguminum, et facilior apparatus est, et arte impendiisque
15   cocorum non indiget: et sine cura sustentat humanum corpus, moderateque sumptus (quia nec avide devoratur, quod irritamenta gulae non habet) leviori digestione concoquitur. Nemo enim uno aut duobus cibis, hisque vilibus, usque ad inflationem ventris oneratur, quae diversitate carnium et saporis delectatione concipitur. Cum variis nidoribus fumant patinae, ad esum sui,
20   expleta esurie, quasi captivos trahunt. Und et morbi ex saturitate nimia concitantur; multique impatientiam gulae, vomitu remediantur, et quod turpiter ingesserunt, turpius egerunt.

II, 12 (Col. 302): Sed et ex vilissimis cibis vitanda satietas est. Nihil enim ita obruit animum, ut plenus venter et exaestuans, et huc illucque se vertens, et
25   in ructus vel in crepitus ventorum efflatione respirans. Quale illud jejunium est, aut qualis illa refectio post jejunium, cum pridianis epulis distendimur, et guttur nostrum meditatorium efficitur latrinarum? Dumque volumus pro-lixioris inediae famam quaerere [*Al.* fama carere], tantum voramus, quantum vix alterius diei nox digerat. Itaque non tam jejunium appellandum est, quam
30   crapula, ac fetens, et molesta digestio.

II, 15 (Col. 305): . . . docebo primum Adam in paradiso accepisse praeceptum, ut caetera poma comedens, ab una arbore jejunaret. Beatitudo paradisi absque abstinentia cibi non potuit dedicari. Quamdiu jejunavit, in paradiso fuit: comedit, et ejectus est.

II. The Folktale

Exemplum I. *De tribus sociis, qui thesaurum invenerunt*

(from Josef Klapper, ed., *Exempla aus Handschriften des Mittelalters*, Sammlung mittellateinischer Texte 2 [Heidelburg: Carl Winter, 1911], p. 72, #98).[16]

Exemplum de Avaricia. Quidam heremita volens in nemore ortum edificare, ex casu fodiendo invenit thezaurum, statimque clamavit ter magna voce, "Mors, mors, mors!" Pretereuntes vero tres socii mercatores venerunt,

---

[16] Taken from Breslau, Königlichen und Universitätsbibliothek MS I.F. 551, inside front cover (written in Prague, 1406).

He showed them the treasure [5] and at once they drove him away from there. Retreating, he returned to his cell. But the others, considering what was to be done, arranged that one of them should go to town and fetch provisions. But as he was leaving they thought that they would kill him when he went down into the hole. He himself, as he was leaving, thought also about the destruction of those two, and buying a drug poisoned all the food and, [10] coming to them, said, "Do you want to eat first or to get the treasure out?" They answered, "Let us get the treasure out first." And they made him go down into the hole so that they might kill him. So as he was going down they killed him; and they, eating afterwards, both died. And thus the treasure remained untouched. And so when the hermit came and saw them dead, he said, [15] "Truly treasure is nothing else than danger and death."

Exemplum II. *Of Contempt for the World*

When a certain philosopher was taking a walk through a certain wood with his disciples, they found a very large quantity of gold. And the disciples asked of him, "What is this?" He answered, "Sons, it is an evil thing. Do not touch it, for on its account occur homicides, thefts, perjuries." And when he had said this they departed. But two of them [20], tempted, said to each other, "Let one go to buy bread and the other to fetch a mule." But he who bought bread pondered how he might kill his companion so that he might have all the gold. And having bought two loaves he poisoned one to give to his companion. And when they came to the wood, he who had brought the bread said, "Let us eat"; the other [25] said, "Wait for me and eat, and I will cut a stick to lead the mule." And he went and, having made the stick, killed his companion from hiding. And thinking that he possessed all the gold, he began to eat the poisoned bread. And thus he also died himself.

Exemplum III

One reads in the life of St. Bartholomew that, when our lord Jesus [30] Christ walked with his disciples through a certain wood and empty solitude, they came upon a sack full of gold and silver. At this discovery the disciples said to Jesus, "What is this, Master?" He answered, "My children, do not touch it, because it is the worst of things. For because of this there often arise homicides, perjuries, thefts, and other infinite evils and sins; and because of this [35] many souls descend into the abyss of Hell." The disciples said nevertheless, "Tell us what it is. What is its name?" The Lord said to them, "It is gold, and it is called gold. You ought to beware nevertheless lest you touch it." When this was said, they began to leave. But two of the disciples, tempted,

26   **facto** [MS fc'o]; T secto.
35   **inferni** infernum T; **quid est hoc** *add* et T.

dicentes, "Ubi est mors, quam clamasti?" Ille vero monstravit eis thezaurum,
5   et statim eum abinde repulerunt. Qui recedens venit ad cellam suam. Isti vero,
cogitantes quid essent facturi, ordinaverunt ut unus ex illis in civitatem iret et
expensas aportaret. Eo vero abeunte cogittaverunt ut eum, cum in foveam
descenderet, interficerent. Ipse vero vadens eciam cogitavit de perdicione
istorum duorum, venenumque comparans omnia cibaria intoxicavit; ven-
10   iensque ad illos dixit, "Volumusne prius comedere vel thezaurum excipere?"
Qui responderunt, "Prius thezaurum excipiemus." Feceruntque illum ad
foveam descendere, ut eum occiderent. Descendente vero eo, ipsum occi-
derunt; et ipsi postmodum comedentes ambo mortui sunt. Et sic thezaurum
intactum reliquerunt. Quo cum heremita venisset et eos mortuos vidisset, ait,
15   "Vere non est aliud thezaurus nisi periculum et mors."

Exemplum II. *De Contemptu Mundi*
(from British Library, MS Add. 11872, fol. 82v, no. 12)[17]

Cum quidam philosophus ambularet per quodam nemus cum discipulis
suis, invenerunt maximam quantitatem auri. Et quesierunt discipuli ab eo,
"Quid hoc est?" Respondit, "Filii, mala res est. Nolite tangere, nam propter
illud fiunt homicidia, furta, perjuria." Et hiis dictis abierunt. Duo autem ex
20   ipsis temptati dixerunt ad invicem: "Unus eat ad emendum panem et alius ad
educendum mulum." Ille vero qui panem emerat cogitavit qualiter socium
interficeret, ut totum aurum haberet. Et acceptis duobus panibus, unum
toxicavit ut daret socio. Similiter alter cogitavit qualiter socium occideret. Et
cum venissent ad nemus, dixit ille qui panem portaverat, "Comedamus"; alius
25   dixit, "Expecta me et comede, et ego incidam baculum ad educendum
mulum." Et ivit et, facto baculo, latenter interfecit socium. Et cogitans habere
aurum totum, cepit comedere panem toxicatum. Et sic [fol. 83r] mortuus est et
ipse.

Exemplum III
(from British Library, MS Add. 27336, fol. 40, #187)[18]

Legitur in legenda beati Bartolamei quod, cum dominus noster Yhesus
30   Christus ambularet cum discipulis suis per quoddam nemus et vastam
solitudinem, invenerunt unum saccum auro et argento plenum. Eo invento
dixerunt discipuli ad Yhesum, "Quid est hoc, magister?" Qui respondit,
"Filioli mei, nolite hoc tangere, quia res pessima est. Nam propter hoc sepe
fiunt homicidia, perjuria, furta, alia quoque infinita mala et peccata; et propter
35   hoc multe anime descendunt ad abissum inferni." Dixerunt discipuli tamen,
"Dicas quid est hoc. Quod nomen habet?" Dixit ei[s] dominus, "Aurum est et

---

17 Italian, about A.D. 1400. No. 11, fol. 81v, is headed "De contemptu mundi"; no. 12 is headed "De
   eodem."
18 In margin; #184 in Herbert and in Tupper. Early fifteenth century; "evidently compiled by a Franciscan
   in northern Italy" (Herbert 647). My corrections in this text are for the most part reinterpretations of
   MS abbreviations; T = Tupper's readings.

said to each other, "Let us go and get the gold and possess it; and thus we shall always be rich and satisfied." Then they said to each other that one would go to buy needful provisions; the other would go to acquire a mule that would carry away the sack of gold and silver. And so it was done; but each, already struck by the arrow of the devil through envy or avarice, pondered how he might kill the other. And so he who had bought the bread placed poison in one loaf so that his companion [45] might fall in eating bread. The other said to his companion, after both came to the sack, "Wait for me here while I go and cut a stick to control the mule," thinking and intending to kill the other with his stick. This one, having made the stick and returned to his companion, found him eating the bread that was not poisoned, and killed him from hiding with the raised stick, saying to himself, [50] "Now I shall possess all the gold by myself." And when he hastened to the bread to eat, the bread in which the poison was happened to come to his hand; and upon tasting this at once he fell dead. Therefore it is manifest that Our Lord spoke the truth when he said, "My children, do not touch this, because it is the most evil of things." But Our Lord Jesus Christ, wishing afterwards to show the truth of this thing to his disciples, came with them [55] to the foresaid place and said to them, "Thus I said to you: that for the sake of gold and silver many evils come about. As you see, it has just happened here." When they had seen this they departed.

Novella

Which tells of a hermit who, while going through a wild region, found a very great treasure.[19]

Going one day through a wild region, a hermit found an enormous cave which was well concealed, and withdrawing inside it to rest himself because he was quite tired, as soon as he entered the cave he saw there in a [5] certain part a great shining, for there was a good deal of gold; and as soon as he was aware of it, he left immediately and began to run through the wilderness, as fast as he could go. As he was running thus, this hermit stumbled upon three formidable bandits, who were living in that wilderness to rob anyone who passed through there, never having realized that this gold was there. Now when these men who [10] were staying hidden saw this man fleeing in this way, without having anyone behind who chased him, they were somewhat fearful, but still they confronted him in order to know why he was fleeing,

42   **sed** *om* T.
43   **vel** ultra T.
44   **vero** *om* T.
47   **deducendum** redeundum T. **intendens** intendans T.
48   **socium** sotium T.
49   **latenter** latentem T
52   **Unde** Unum T. **patuit** paruit T. **quando** quum T.
53   **quia** quae T.

[19] I am grateful to Teresa Kennedy for her help in this translation and that of the *Play of St. Anthony*.

aurum vocatur. Cavere tamen debetis ne illud tangatis." Hoc dicto abire
ceperunt. Duo autem ex discipulis temptati ad invicem dicunt, "Eamus et
accipiamus aurum et possidemus illud; et sic semper divites et pleni erimus."
40   Qui cum dixerunt ad invicem ut unus eorum iret ad emendum cibaria
neccessaria; alius iret ad aquirendum unum mullum qui asportaret auri et
argenti saccum. Quod et factum est, sed uterque, iam sagita [fol. 40v] diaboli
per invidiam vel avaritiam percusus, cogitavit qualiter alium posset interficere. Ille vero qui panem emerat in uno pane posuit tosicum ut socium
45   cecideret comendendo panem. Alius vero dixit socio, postquam ambo ad
saccum pervenerunt, "Expecta me hic, donec vadam et incidam unum
baculum ad deducendum mullum," cogitans et intendens alium suo baculo
interficere. Qui, facto baculo, reversus ad socium invenit eum panem non
tosicatum comedentem; qui abrecto baculo latenter occidit eum, dicens intra
50   se, "Modo solus totum aurum possidebo." Et accurens ad panem ut comederet
occurit ei panis in quo tosicum erat; quo gustato et statim cecidit mortuus.
Unde sic patuit quod dominus verum ixit quando dixit, "Filioli mei, nolite hoc
tangere, quia res pessima est." Volens autem dominus postmodum noster
Yhesus Christus hostendere huius rei veritatem discipulis suis, venit cum eis
55   ad locum predictum et dixit eis, "Sic dixi vobis: quod propter aurum et
argentum multa mala fiunt, sic ut videtis; modo accidit hic." Quo viso
abierunt.

Novella

(from the *Libro di Novelle et di Bel Parlar Gentile*, ed. Vincenzo Borghini
[Firenze: Filippo & Iacopo Giunti, 1572]. Novella #82, pp. 86–8.)[20]

Qui conta d'uno romito che andando per un luogo foresto trovo molto
grande tesoro. Andando un giorno un romito per un luogo foresto, si trovò una
grandissima grotta, laquale era molto celata, e ritirandosi verso là per
riposarsi, pero che era assai affaticato; come é giunse alla grotta si la vide in
5   certo luogo molto tralucere, impercio che vi havea molto oro: e si tosto come
il conobbe, incontanente si partio, & comincio a correre per lo diserto, quanto
e' ne potea andare. Correndo cosi questo romito s'intoppo in tre grande
scherani, liquali stavano in quella foresta per rubare chi unque vi passava. Ne
gia mai si erano accorti, che questo oro vi fosse. Hor vedendo costoro, che
10   nascosti si stavano, fuggir cosi questo huomo, non havendo persona dietro
che'l cacciase, alquanto hebbero temenza, ma pur se li pararono dinanzi per
sapere perche fuggiva, che di cio molto si maravigliavano. Ed elli rispose &
disse. Fratelli miei io fuggo la morte, che mi vien dietro cacciando mi. Que'

---

[20] For the identification of Borghini as the compiler of this collection, see Guido Biagi, ed., *Le Novelle antiche dei Codici Panciatichiano-Palatino 138 e Laurenziano-Gaddiano 193* (Firenze, 1880), pp. xxvii–xxviii and clv–ccvi. A similar collection, perhaps Borghini's source for novellas added to the Gualtaruzzi edition, was Panciatichiano-Palatino MS 138, from the early sixteenth century (p. xcvii). Biagi argues that in spite of differences this MS was Borghini's direct source, p. clxxxi; for another view, see D'Ancona, pp. 4–6. See Biagi's edition of the MS text corresponding to Borghini's Novella 82, pp. 181–3.

because they were full of curiosity about it. And he answered and said, "My brothers, I am fleeing death, which is coming behind me, chasing me." But seeing neither man nor beast that was chasing him, they said, "Show us what is chasing you, and lead us there where it is." Then the hermit said to them, "Come with me and I will show it to you," begging them at the same time that they not go to it, because as for himself he would flee from it. And they, wishing to find it in order to see how it was made, did not ask him about anything else. The hermit, seeing that he could [do] no more, and being afraid of them, led them to the cave from which he had departed and said to them, "Here [20] is death, which was chasing me," and showed them the gold that was there; and they recognized it at once and began to be very joyful and to take great pleasure together. Then they sent away this good man, and he went about his own business; and the others began to talk among themselves about how simple-minded a person he was. These bandits, all three together, remained [25] to guard that wealth, and they began to discuss what they wished to do. One of them answered and said, "It seems to me, since God has given us such high fortune, that we must not leave here until we carry away all this wealth." And another said, "Let us not do so. Let one of us take some of it and go to town and sell it and fetch some bread and wine and whatever else [30] we need, managing the task the best he can. Let him do whatever it takes to provide for us." To this all three agreed together. The Devil, who is ingenious and wickedly arranges to do whatever evil he can, put in the heart of the one who was going to town for supplies, "Since I will be in town" (he was saying to himself), "I will eat and drink as much as I need, and then provide for myself [35] certain things of which I have need now at present; and then I will poison what I am taking to my companions; so that, since they will both be dead men, it will be I who am lord of all that wealth and, since it seems to me there is a great deal, then I will be the richest man of all this region from that wealth." And as this came to his mind, so he acted. He took for himself as much food as he needed and then [40] poisoned all the other, and carried it so to his companions. While he went to town, as we have said, if he thought and planned wickedly to kill his companions in order that everything would belong to him, the others thought of him no better than he of them; and they said to each other, "As soon as this companion of ours returns with bread and wine and the other things we need, [45] we will kill him, and then we will eat as much as we wish, and then all that great wealth will be between us two. And since we will need to make fewer shares of it, each of us will have so much the greater share." Now that one is coming who went to town to buy the things that they needed. When he had returned to his companions, as soon as they saw him they fell on him with lances and with a knife and killed him. [50] Seeing that they had killed him, they ate what he had brought; and as soon as they were full, both fell dead. And so they died all three, because each killed the other, as you have heard, and did not get the wealth. And thus the Lord God rewards the traitors, who went in search of death and in this way found it, and as they deserved. And the wise man sagely [55] fled it, and the gold remained free as at first.

non vedendo ne huomo, ne bestia, chi il cacciasse, dissero. Mostraci chi ti
15 caccia: e menaci cola ove ella è. Allhora il romito disse loro: venite meco e
mostrerrollavi, pregandoli tutta via che non andassero ad essa, impercio che
elli per se la fuggia. Ed eglino volendola trovare, per vedere come fosse fatta,
nol domandavano di altro. Il romito vedendo che non potea piu, e havendo
paura di loro, gli condusse alla grotta, onde egli s'era partito, e disse loro. Qui
20 è la morte, che mi cacciava, e mostro loro l'oro che v'era, ed eglino il
conobbero incontanente, e molto si cominciarono a rallegrare & a fare insieme
grande sollazzo. Allhora accommiatarono questo buono huomo: ed egli sen'
ando per i fatti suoi: e quelli cominciarono a dire tra loro, come elli era
semplice persona. Rimasero questi scherani tutti e tre insieme, a guardare
25 questo havere, e incominciarono a ragionare quello che voleano fare. L'uno
rispuose e disse. A me pare, da che Dio ci ha data cosi alta ventura, che noi
non ci partiamo di qui, insino a tanto che noi non ne portiamo tutto questo
havere. Et l'altro disse; non facciamo cosi. L'uno di noi ne tolga alquanto. e
vada alla cittade e vendalo, e rechi del pane & del vino e di quello che ci
30 bisogna e di cio s'ingegni il meglio che puote: faccia egli, pur com'elli ci
fornisca. A questo s'accordarono tutti e tre insieme. Il Demonio ch'è
ingegnoso, e reo d'ordinare di fare quanto mal e puote, mise in cuore a costui
che andava alla citta per lo fornimento, da ch'io sarò nella cittade (dicea fra se
medesimo) io voglio mangiare e bere quanto mi bisogna, e poi fornirmi di
35 certe cose delle quali io ho mestiere hora al presente: e poi avvelenero quello
che io porto a miei compagni: si che, da ch'elli saranno morti amendue, si saro
io poi Signore di tutto quello havere, e secondo che mi pare egli è tanto, che io
saro poi il piu ricco huomo di tutto questo paese da parte d'havere: e come li
venne in pensiero, cosi fece. Prese vivanda per se quanta gli bisogno, e poi
40 tutta l'altra avvelenoe, e cosi la porto a que suoi compagni. Intanto ch'ando
alla cittade secondo che detto havemo: se elli pensoe ed ordinoe male per
uccidere li suoi compagni, accio che ogni cosa li rimanesse: quelli pensaro di
lui non meglio ch'elli di loro, e dissero tra loro. Si tosto come questo nostro
compagno tornera col pane e col vino e con l'altre cose che ci bisognano; si
45 l'uccideremo, e poi mangeremo quanto vorremo, e sara poi tra noi due tutto
questo grande havere. Et come meno parti ne faremo, tanto n'haveremo
maggior parte ciascuno di noi. Hor viene quelli, che era ito alla cittad a
comperare le cose che bisognava loro. Tornato a suoi compagni incontanente
che'l videro: gli furono addosso con le lancie e con le coltella, e l'uccisero. Da
50 che l'hebbero morto, mangia[r]ono di quello che egli havea recato: e si tosto
come furono satolli, amendue caddero morti: e cosi morirono tutti e tre: che
l'uno uccise l'altro si come udito havete, e non hebbe l'havere: e cosi paga
Domenedio li traditori che egli andarono caendo la morte, & in questo modo
la trovarono, et si come ellino n'erano degni. Et il saggio saviamente la
55 fuggio, e l'oro rimase libero come di prima.

The Play of Saint Anthony

[*The play opens with St. Anthony's decision, after discussions with a hermit, three companions, and his sister, to give his patrimony to the poor and become a hermit himself. Observing his activities, Satan sends the Spirits of Lust, Sloth, and Gluttony to tempt him (actually, to argue with him); they are unsuccessful. Anthony then meets two pagan philosophers with their interpreter, who leave after a discussion.*]

Then comes the SPIRIT OF AVARICE, *and places a small silver plate where Anthony has to pass, and says:*

Since my companions have not harmed
Your soul with all their arts,
And [even] if you are defended by your virtue,
5   I hope this will serve to subdue you,
For every wise man is taken by such a snare,
And this will be a good means of separating you
From your way, which is such an annoyance to us.
Now I shall find out if you are so perfect.

ANTHONY *goes through the wilderness and finds the basin and says thus:*
10   O [you who were] chased out of heaven, I know you!
These are your tricks and your traps!
You would like to make me leave the wilderness,
Because you take it ill that men stand alone.
And your food seems sweet and yet is poisonous,
15   And your pleasures are afterwards pains and sorrows.
This was not dropped here by mortal man,
But has fallen from the infernal kingdom.

The SPIRIT, *seeing that he does not take it, places there a heap of gold, and says thus:*

If you have not given in to this,
Perhaps you left it because it seems small to you;
20   But I will set before you such a choice
That you will certainly change the game;
And if with regard to that I am still scorned,
Never again will I return to this place.
For the sound of gold is wont to conquer
25   Everyone – and let him be what you will, bad or good.

ANTHONY *goes through the wilderness and finds the heap of gold and says:*
O evil beast, are you still not tired
Of setting snares for me, still in the usual way?
It is now a long time since I have not gone a step
But that you have tailed me always;
30   Now from henceforth you can go for a walk yourself,
Since you have exhausted yourself in vain.
Really you are inept, and you think you are astute:
Thinking to win, you have lost.

Play: *Rappresentazione di Sant' Antonio*

(from the edition of Alessandro D'Ancona, ed. *Sacre Rappresentazioni dei
secoli XIV, XV, et XVI*, II [Firenze, 1872], pp. 33–63.)

Dipoi viene lo SPIRITO DELL'AVARIZIA, *e pone uno piatello d'ariento dove
ha a passare Antonio, e dice:*
Po' che i compagni mia non hanno offeso
L'anima tua con tutte lor arti,
E se per tua virtù ti se' difeso,
A questo, spero, converrà piegarti,
5   Perchè ogni savio a tal lacciuol è preso,
E questo fia buon mezo a separarti
Dalla tua via, che c'è tanto in dispetto.
Or m'avedrò se se' cosi perfetto.
ANTONIO *va pel diserto, e trova il bacino e dice cosi:*
10   O cacciato dal cielo, i' ti conosco!
Questi son de' tuo inganni e tuo lacciuoli!
Tu mi vorresti far uscir del bosco,
Chè ha' per mal che gli uomini stien soli.
El tuo cibo par dolce, et è pur tosco,
15   E' tuo diletti son poi pene e duoli.
Questo non è caduto a uom martale,
Ma è caduto dal regno infernale.

Lo SPIRITO *veggendo che non lo toglie, vi mette uno monte d'oro, e dice cosi:*
Se tu non hai a questo acconsentito
Forse è rimasto perchè ti par poco,
20   Ma metterotti innanzi un tal partito
Che certamente tu muterai gioco;
E se di ciò io rimarrò schernito,
Mai più vo' ritornare in questo loco,
Perchè dell'oro suol vincere il suono
25   Ogniuno, e sia qual vuol, cattivo o buono.
ANTONIO *va pel diserto e truova il monte dell'oro, e dice:*
O mala bestia, ancor non se' tu lasso
Di farmi insidie, pur al modo usato?
Già è gran tempo non son ito un passo
Che tu non m'abbi sempre codïato:
30   Ma oggimai tu puoi andare a spasso,
Da poi che ti se' invano affaticato;
Ben se' da poco, e pàrti essere astuto:
Credendo guadagnar, tu hai perduto.

Two rascals meet together, one called Scaramuccia and the other
Tagliagambe, and SCARAMUCCIA *says:*
    O Tagliagambe, how are you spending your time?

35   And where did you come from? Have you good news?

TAGLIAGAMBE *answers and says:*
    I want to tell you the truth, [but] I don't understand you,
    But well I know that I have it neither good nor pleasant,
    And am led in such a way that I give up;
    And would return from the stars for a penny,

40   Nor can I give myself peace by any means,
    Because not a groat remains in my purse.

SCARAMUCCIA *answers and says:*
    Now I tell you, we are well paired,
    And we can say: the best reaps the worst,
    For there were robbed from me

45   Enough coins at the fair at Reggio
    That it makes the sum of a thousand ducats;
    For that reason I ask a favor of you:
    That the two of us become robbers
    If we wish to recover our money.

TAGLIAGAMBE *answers and says:*
50   You have said well, and I'm satisfied with it;
    And in short from now on I promise and swear to you
    That if ever I've done well, I repent it;
    And I have a heart that is made so hard
    That if I were to see the one who engendered me

55   Passed from life, I would not care about it;
    And there is no evil that I would not do,
    Provided that I might have money and possessions.

SCARAMUCCIA *answers and says:*
    We don't need to argue about this;
    And death to whichever of us repents first.

60   But let us begin with what we ought to do,
    Because the time passes and we do nothing.
    Look, here comes one of my friends,
    Who will be exactly suitable, if you agree,
    That we should take him into our company,

65   Because he is spirited and full of boldness.
    Welcome, my friend Carapello!
    See whether Fortune has guided you
    Into our lap! If you will have judgment,
    You couldn't be in better luck !

CARAPELLO *answers and says:*
70   If I had been stabbed with a knife,
    I would then certainly be welcome,
    And this would be to me a new gift:

---

71   welcome: pun on *arrivato*, which is also used of blows and wounds; see D'Ancona's note, p. 52.

Dua malandrini si riscontrano insieme, e l'uno si chiama Scaramuccia e
    l'altro Tagliagambe, e SCARAMUCCIA *dice:*
    O Tagliagambe, che va' tu facendo,
35   E d'onde vieni? ha' tu buone novelle?
Risponde TAGLIAGAMBE *e dice:*
    I' ti vo' dire il vero, io non t'intendo,
    Ma ben so ch'i' non l'ho nè buon nè belle;
    E son condotto in modo ch'i' m'arrendo,
    E per danar tornere' dalle stelle,
40   Nè darmi pace in nessun modo posso,
    Perchè non m'è rimasto in borso un grosso.
Risponde lo SCARAMUCCIA *e dice:*
    Or ti dich'io, no' siam ben apaiati,
    E possiam dire: el me' ricolga il peggio,
    Però che a me sono stati rubbati
45   Tanti danari alla fiera di Reggio,
    Che fa la somma di mille ducati;
    Per tanto d'una grazia ti richieggio,
    Che tutta dua diventiam malandrini
    Se racquistar vogliam nostri fiorini.
Risponde il TAGLIAGAMBE *e dice:*
50   Tu hai ben detto, e io ne son contento;
    E infin da ora i' ti prometto e giuro
    Che se mai feci bene, i' me ne pento;
    E ho un cuor che è fatto tanto duro
    Chè s'i' vedessi aver di vita spento
55   Quel che m'ingenerò, non me ne curo,
    E non è mal verun ch'i' non facessi,
    Pur che danari e robba aver potessi.
Risponde lo SCARAMUCCIA *e dice:*
    Cotesto non bisogna ragionare,
    E muoia qual dì noi prima si pente.
60   Diam pur principio a quel che dobbiam fare,
    Chè'l tempo passa e non facciam nïente;
    Ecco di qua venire un mio compare
    Che apunto sarà buon, se vi consente,
    Che noi il pigliamo in nostra compagnia,
65   Che è animoso e pien di gagliardia.
    Ben venga il compar mïo Carapello!
    Vedi se la ventura t'ha guidato
    In grembo a noi! se tu arai cervello,
    Tu non potresti esser me' capitato.
Risponde CARAPELLO *e dice:*
70   S'i' fussi trapassato d'un coltello
    Sare' dicerto allor bene arrivato,
    E questa mi sarebbe nuova mancia:

Everything else would seem to me nonsense.
SCARAMUCCIA *answers and says:*
> To tell you the truth, friend, we are willing

75   That anyone whosoever may restore our money to us;
For this reason I ask you to join up with us,
Because we will make you get over such sorrows.
CARAPELLO *answers and says:*
> Friend, you are certainly in the right,
Because I have not stood worse within ten years:

80   For which reason this seems to me such great news
That it wipes out every sorrow and pain for me.
TAGLIAGAMBE *answers and says:*
> It turns out well, since we are agreed
Each one to do the worst that we can;
But I want to give you first a good reminder,

85   If we are to be together for a long time;
Let none of you be deaf to this speech:
That we divide our booty fairly;
For if one of us cheats the others,
We will come immediately to a fight.
CARAPELLO *answers:*

90   O my Scaramuccia, what are we waiting to do?
Today is a day on which it is good to go on our way;
The fair at Alexandria is beginning, as it happens,
And we shall find someone along the road.

95   We need to gain clothes and money;
You take your lance, and you your sword,
And all three of us will go in company,
And whatever anyone gains, let it be shared.
> My heart tells me today, my companions,
That we shall make some great profit.

100   We shall find merchants and pilgrims
Who are going from Alexandria to Damietta.
Cursed be fours and six,
Because they've emptied my purse.
I wouldn't be able to make a blind man sing;

105   But the first one I find has to pay.
All three go on their way. [*Satan commands devils to go and beat Anthony;
after they do so, Jesus appears and comforts him.*]
ANTHONY *is healed and goes through the wilderness; and he meets the
robbers and says to them:*
> Flee, my brothers! flee quickly,
Turn back for your best interest,
Do not go to that place that is death for you,
Which will kill you with great pain.

110   Your limbs and your ready weapon will not avail you,

---

102   fours and six: a game of dice.
104   make a blind man sing: i.e., I'm flat broke.

Ogni altra cosa mi pare' una ciancia.
Risponde lo SCARAMUCCIA *e dice:*
    A dirti il ver, compar, noi siam disposti
75   Che chi che sia ristori i nostri danni;
    Ond'io ti priego che con noi t'accosti,
    Che ti faremo uscir di tanti affanni.
Risponde CARAPELLO *e dice:*
    Compar, di certo, voi vi siate aposti,
    Chè peggio non istetti è già dieci anni:
80   Onde questa mi par si gran novella
    Ch'ogni dolor e pena mi cancella.
Risponde il TAGLIAGAMBE *e dice:*
    Ella va ben, poi che no' siam d'accordo
    A far ogniun il peggio che possiamo:
    Ma voglio darvi in prima un buon ricordo,
85   Se lungo tempo insieme esser vogliamo,
    Al qual parlar nessun di voi sie sordo:
    Che giustamente le prede partiamo:
    Chè qual di noi facessi agli altri truffa,
    Subitamente verremo alla zuffa.
Risponde CARAPELLO:
90   O Scaramuccia mio, che stiam noi a fare?
    Oggi è un di che è buon ire alla strada,
    La fiera d'Alessandria ha cominciare,
    E qualcun troverrem per la contrada.
    Panni e danar bisogna guadagnare:
95   Toi la tua lancia e tu torrà la spada,
    E tutti a tre n'andiamo in compagnia,
    E ciò che si guadagna, a mezo sia.
    E' mi dice oggi il cuor, compagni miei,
    Che noi farem qualche gran guadagnata.
100   Noi troverem mercatanti e romei
    Che vanno d'Alessandria a Damïata.
    Che maladetto sia quaderno e sei,
    Però che m'hanno la borsa votata.
    Io non potrei un cieco far cantare;
105   Ma il primo ch'i' trüovo gli ha a pagare.
Vanno tutti a tre alla strada . . .
   . . .
Antonio è sanato e va pel diserto: e riscontra e'malandrini e dice loro:
    Fuggite, frate' miei, fuggite forte,
    Tornate a drieto pel vostro migliore,
    Non andate in costà che v'è la morte,
    La qual v'ucciderà con gran dolore.
110   Non vi varrà le membra e l'arme accorte,

Nor your boldness nor great courage;
And if you do not follow my advice,
If you go farther, you will soon die there.

TAGLIAGAMBE *answers and says*:

This one must be out of his senses,

115   And for hunger gone out from his cell.
These hermits experience great hardship;
They have little to eat and [are] badly clothed;
To pay attention to him is a talking to the wind.
Still, let us quickly make up our minds

120   And go to discover this death,
For he will be noble who will escape.

Then they go there and find the heap of gold, and TAGLIAGAMBE *says:*

Look, brothers, what lunacy
Flourishes in that idiot, the old hermit,
Saying that an evil death was here!

125   He calls death that which is life.
If we had not come by this road,
We would have missed our good fortune.
This will be better than prison for stabbing,
And we will not have to fight any other battle.

130   Companions, I have resolved, if it pleases you,
That one of you go as far as Damascus,
And bring back something to eat,
And see that you also get a good bottle of something.
And whoever goes, strive to return quickly,

135   Because I am faint from hunger and thirst;
Let him bring sweets, bread, meat, and wine,
Even though he might have to lay out a florin.
Let us draw straws to see who should go,
And let whoever goes carry with him a piece of gold;

140   He will be able to sell it at some bank,
And have them give change for it.

CARAPELLO *answers and says*:

This pleases me, and it ought to be followed;
There is no need by now to make further delay.
Go on, Scaramuccia, and prepare the straws,

145   And let whoever has the shortest take to his heels at once.

[*Scaramuccia draws the shortest straw.*]

TAGLIAGAMBE *answers and says*:

Go quickly, Scaramuccia, and do not forget
To find the food-seller or some cook,
And buy a capon, squabs, and thrushes;
Get two bottles of wine, because one would be too little.

150   If anyone calls to you, keep your ears deaf,

---

140   sell it at some bank: or "have it assayed"; in the portion omitted below the gold is weighed and assayed and a price set by the cashier of the bank.

Nè vostre gagliardie nè gran valore;
E se il consiglio mio non seguirete,
Andando più costà presto morrete.
Risponde il TAGLIAGAMBE *e dice:*
 Costui debbe esser fuor del sentimento

115 E per la fame della cella uscito;
Questi romiti fanno molto stento,
Han poco da mangiare e mal vestito;
Badar con lui è un parlare a vento;
Però pigliam prestamente partito,

120 E andiam questa morte a ritrovare,
Chè sarà gente ch'e' vorrà campare.
Vanno più là, e truovano il monte dell'oro, e il TAGLIAGAMBE *dice:*
 Guardate, frate' mia, quanta pazia
Regna in quel pazerel, vecchio eremita,
Dicendo che era qua la morte ria!

125 E' chiama morte quello che è vita.
Se noi non venevam per questa via,
Nostra ventura era per noi fallita.
Questo fia meglio che un prigion da taglia,
E non arem a fare altra battaglia.

130 Compagni, i' ho pensato, se vi pare,
Che un di voi vada insino a Damasco,
E rechi qualche cosa da mangiare,
E facci anco d'aver qualche buon fiasco.
E ingegnisi chi va, presto tornare,

135 Perch'io di fame e di sete mi casco;
Rechi confetti, pane, carne, e vino,
Se ben dovessi spendere un fiorino.
 Facciamo alle buschette chi debba ire,
E chi va porti seco un pezo d'oro:

140 A qualche banco lo potrà finire,
E facciasi moneta dar da loro.
Risponde CARAPELLO *e dice:*
 Questo mi piace, e debbasi seguire;
E' non si vuol or mai far più dimoro.
Fa', Scaramuccia, e ordina le sorte,

145 E chi ha la minor, calcagni forte.
Risponde il TAGLIAGAMBE *e dice:*
 Va' presto, Scaramuccia, e non ti scordi
Di trovare il Cibaca o qualche cuoco,
E compera un cappon, pippioni e tordi,
To' duo fiaschi di vin, chè un sare' poco.

150 Se gniun ti chiama, tien gli orecchi sordi,

But take care not to stay on for any gambling;
Bring a pair of scales for weighing,
Because then this gold must be divided in three.
SCARAMUCCIA *leaves, and says along the way*:
     I've heard it said a thousand times already
155   That when Fortune turns to you
Not to be slow, and know how to seize her,
Because she turns rarely and stays a short time.
When she comes, whoever lets her depart,
Let him have the harm of his own misfortune;
160   Whoever believes otherwise, he lives in great error:
Each one has his fortune the hour that he is born.
     When could I have greater luck,
If I have not entirely lost my cunning?
But I have certainly made a great error
165   By leaving that to them so that they possess it.
In order to have possessions, everyone is a betrayer.
Let alone another, people defraud a brother.
I was crazy to put myself on the road,
Expecting to get my full share.
170   And they have the soup-ladle in their hands
And will make the soup in their own way.
But what need to give myself such sorrow,
When the intellect teaches me exactly
What I could do to have it all to myself,
175   And nothing harm me or put me out?
Well, then, if I can do it, I need to do it;
And profit goes before shame.
     I need to find a druggist
Who will sell me poison of the strongest,
180   One with which I can poison the bottles,
For there is no more direct way to give them death.
Those villains believed they could trick me
By contriving that the lot fell to me;
But the trick will return upon them,
185   And the gold will be all mine without other worry.
[*He arrives at a bank and exchanges the gold for spending money.*]
Then he goes to the druggist and says:
     My master, you are well met,
I come to you for help and advice.
The DRUGGIST *answers*:
     You are welcome; I am prepared
To do for you as for my own son.
SCARAMUCCIA *answers*:
190   For a short time lately there has come at home
A great quantity of rats, and no one catches them,

170   soup-ladle: see D'Ancona's note, p. 56.

Ma guarda a non fermarti a qualche giuoco;
Reca un par di bilance da pesare,
Chè poi quest'oro si vuole sterzare.
Lo SCARAMUCCIA *si parte e dice per la via:*
    I' ho già mille volte udito dire
155   Che quando ti si volge la ventura
Non esser lento, e sappila ghermire,
Chè rare volte torna, e poco dura.
Quando ella vien, chi la lascia partire
Abbisi il danno della sua sciagura;
160   Chi credesse altro, in grande error si pasce:
Suo ventura ha ciascun l'ora che nasce.
Quando potrei aver sorte maggiore,
S'i' non ho in tutto perduto il cervello?
Ma io ho fatto bene un grande errore
165   A lasciar a color si che arà quello.
Per aver robba, ogniun c'è traditore;
Non ch'altro, ella si frega a un fratello.
Pazo fu' io, a mettermi per via,
Credendo aver tutta la parte mia.
170   E' gli hanno nelle mani el romaiuolo,
E faranno a lor modo la minestra.
Ma che bisogna darmi tanto duolo,
Che lo 'ntelletto a punto m'amaestra
Ch'i' potre' far d'averlo tutto solo,
175   E niuna cosa mi nuoce o sinestra?
Dunque s'i' 'l posso far, far me 'l bisogna,
E l'util vada innanzi alla vergogna.
    A me bisogna uno spezial trovare
Che mi venda veleno del più forte;
180   Un di que' fiaschi potrò avvelenare,
Chè non c'è via più breve a dar lor morte.
E' m'han creduto e' felloni ingannare
Per far che sie toccato a me la sorte;
Ma sopra lor ritornerà l'inganno,
185   E l'òr fie tutto mio sanz' altro affanno.
    . . .
Dipoi va allo speziale e dice:
    Maestro mio, vo' siate il ben trovato;
I' vengo a voi per aiuto e consiglio.
Risponde lo SPEZIALE:
    Ben sia venuto; i' sono apparecchiato
Di far per te come di proprio figlio.
Risponde SCARAMUCCIA:
190   Da poco in qua e' m'è in casa arrivato
Gran quantità di topi e gniun ne piglio,

So much so that they are so many and so huge
That they even chance to nibble my ears.
    For this reason it is proper, master, that you give me
195   A little poison with which I may exterminate them;
I want you to set the payment in your own way;
Provided the poison is good, if the price comes high, let it come.
The DRUGGIST *answers and says*:
I will give you the perfect thing, in truth,
But take care that scandal does not come of it.
200   Get up and go quickly, Domenico,
Bring me here the little box of arsenic.
    Take here what I give you, give me two groats,
And I can assure you that I have served you well;
And I could not give it to you for a smaller price –
205   Indeed, by right it comes to much more;
And, if they take it, they will be stricken
With convulsions and will die in great pain.
SCARAMUCCIA *answers*:
In my opinion, I never spent
My money better; and farewell to you.
Then he goes to the Innkeeper and says:
210   Host, I would like two bottles of a good wine,
White and red, each of which is sweet.
The INNKEEPER *answers*:
I have some Chianti and wine of San Lorino,
Sweet Trebbiano, Vernaccia and Malmsey.
SCARAMUCCIA *answers*:
Get two bottles of it and take this florin,
215   And keep the change until my return;
Meanwhile I want to go to the cook
To see if he has anything to eat.
Then he goes to the Cook and says:
    Have you anything there, Cook, to enjoy?
I would like something for four companions.
The COOK *answers*:
220   Whatever I have here, companion, is at your pleasure;
I have here capons, pullets, and squabs,
And little sausages that give goodness to drinking,
And today a big bowl of macaroni,
And slices of pork liver, and today some black puddings;
225   Now see whether there is anything here that may please you.
[*The scene shifts.*]
TAGLIAGAMBE *says to Carapello*:
    Brother, I want to tell you my thought,
With this proviso: that you swear to me faithfully,
If it doesn't please you, to bury it in forgetfulness
And say nothing to anyone about it.
CARAPELLO *answers and says*:
230   You go first, and then I'll tell you

Per modo tal che son tanti e si vecchi
Che gli hanno ancora a rodermi gli orecchi.
    Di che convien, maestro, che mi diate
195 Un poco di velen col qual gli spenga;
A vostro modo vò' che vi paghiate;
Pur che sia buon, se viene assai, si venga.
    Risponde lo SPEZIALE *e dice:*
        I' tel darò perfetto in veritate,
Ma guarda poi che scandol non ne venga.
200 Levati su e fa' presto, Domenico,
Recami qua il bossol dell' arsenico.
    Tien qui quel ch'io ti do, dammi duo grossi,
E sotti dir ch'i' t'ho servito bene,
E per men pregio dartelo non puossi
205 Ma di ragion molto più se ne viene:
E, se lo pigliano, e' saran percossi
Di spasimo, e morranno con gran pene.
    Risponde SCARAMUCCIA:
        Io non ispesi mai, al parer mio,
Me' mie danari, e fatevi con Dio.
    Poi va all' oste e dice:
210 Oste, i' vorrei duo fiaschi d'un buon vino
Bianco e vermiglio che ogniun dolce sia.
    *Risponde l'*OSTE:
        I' n'ho di Chianti, e vin da san Lorino,
Trebbian dolci, vernaccia e malvagia.
    Risponde lo SCARAMUCCIA:
        Tône duo fiaschi e te' questo fiorino,
215 E serba il resto alla tornata mia;
Intanto infino al cuoco i' voglio andare,
Per veder se gli ha nulla da mangiare.
    Poi ne va al cuoco e dice:
        Àci tu nulla, o cuoco, da godere?
Io ne vorrei per quattro compagnioni.
    Risponde il CUOCO:
220 Ciò ch'io ci ho, compagnion, è al tuo piacere;
Io ci ho capponi, pollastre e pippioni,
E salsicciuoli che danno buon bere,
E òcci un gran catin di macheroni,
E fegatelli, e òcci de' migliacci;
225 Or guarda se ci è nulla che ti piacci.
    Il TAGLIAGAMBE *dice a Carapello:*
        Fratel, i' ti vò' dire il pensier mio:
Con questo, che mi giuri fedelmente,
Se non ti piace, metterlo in oblio,
E a persona non ne dir nïente.
    Risponde CARAPELLO *e dice:*
230 Di' prima tu, e poi ti dirò io

An idea that came into my mind.
And tell me your thoughts boldly,
For whatever we say will be just between us.
TAGLIAGAMBE *answers and says*:
    I've been thinking that this treasure

235   That Fortune has caused us to find,
That this gold should be only yours and mine
So as not to share the wealth with anyone else.
Envy, to tell you the truth, gives me torment;
Therefore answer me whatever you think about it.

240   That someone else may have the wealth does not seem a joke to me,
And to make three parts of it would be [to make it] little.
CARAPELLO *answers*:
    For certain yes, brother, you are right.
Not keeping the truth more hidden than you,
I was feeling inwardly a great distress

245   Which was on this selfsame thought;
And I am sorry that that greedy slacker,
Whose life is not worth a whole loaf,
Should have had Fortune as a friend,
And profit from our hard work.

250   I am with you for whatever you want to do,
That, when he returns and sits down,
In a flash he may be attacked by us.
And he cannot know our intention himself;
In few strokes we shall have killed him.

255   But his coming matters not at all:
We have already taken the life from a hundred –
One more, one less, what does this one add up to?
Scaramuccia returns, and TAGLIAGAMBE *says*:
    What have you sold that piece of gold for?
And how much have you spent for these things?
SCARAMUCCIA *answers*:

260   What do you want to know about it, you piece of bull?
Point by point just now you learned of it.
TAGLIAGAMBE *answers [striking him]*:
    There! little thief, you will not have the treasure
That you believed you would divide with us together.
You good-for-nothing lout, cry out if you can,

265   Because if you do not fly, you will have it in your beard.
After they have killed him, TAGLIAGAMBE *says to Carapello*:
    Now I tell you, my dear brother,
That we shall be able to eat and drink in peace.
And we do not have to have any fear,
Since this good-for-nothing lies dead.

270   Begin by taking a piece of candy;
Taste the wine first, if you like,
Which we will be able then to judge well
Whether it is good and perfect: what do you think of it?

Un pensier che m'andava per la mente,
E dimmi arditamente i pensier tuoi,
Chè quel che noi direm sarà tra noi.
Risponde il TAGLIAGAMBE *e dice:*
 I' ho pensato che questo tesoro
235 Che la ventura ci ha fatto trovare,
Che sol di te e me fusse quest' oro
Per non l'aver con altri a dimezare.
La invidia, a dirti il ver, mi dà martoro;
Però rispondi quel che te ne pare.
240 Che altri n'abbi aver, non mi par giuoco,
E a farne tre parti, e sare' poco.
Risponde CARAPELLO:
 Per certo si, fratel, tu hai ragione.
Non ti tenendo più celato il vero,
Io sentia drento una gran passïone
245 Ch'era a questo medesimo pensiero;
E sammi mal che quel ghiotto poltrone,
Che non val la sua vita una pane intero,
La ventura abbia avuta per amica,
E che si goda la nostra fatica.
250 A quel che si vuol far, pigliam partito
Che, quando e' torna e postosi a sedere,
Che in un baleno e' sia da noi assalito.
El pensier nostro lui non può sapere;
In pochi colpi noi l'arem finito;
255 Ma non si vuol dir nulla al suo venire:
La vita a cento noi abbiam già tolta:
Un più, un men, che monta questa volta?
Scaramuccia torna, e il TAGLIAGAMBE *dice:*
 Che ha' tu venduto quel pezo dell' oro?
E in queste cose poi quanto spendesti?
Risponde SCARAMUCCIA:
260 Che ne vuo' tu saper, pezo di toro?
A punto a punto testè lo sapesti.
Risponde il TAGLIAGAMBE:
 Dò, ladroncel, tu non arai il tesoro
Che con noi insieme divider credesti.
Poltron gaglioffo, grida se tu sai,
265 Che stu non voli, alla barba l'arai.
Poi che l'hanno morto, il TAGLIAGAMBE *dice a Carapello:*
 Or ti dich'io, fratel mio diletto,
Che noi potrem mangiare e bere in pace.
E non abbiam d'avere alcun sospetto,
Po' che questo gaglioffo morto giace.
270 Comincia a tôrre un pezo di confetto,
Assaggia in prima il vino se ti piace,
Che noi potremo poi ben giudicare
S'egli è buono e perfetto: che ti pare?

CARAPELLO *tastes the wine and says*:
> It is excellent – taste a little;
275 > This man was a drinker indeed, and a connoisseur.

TAGLIAGAMBE *tastes it and says*:
> This is a wine that seems to have the nature of fire,
> It is so full-bodied, subtle and potent.
> Let us see now how the cook has treated us,
> And let us torment something with our teeth.
280 > We have fallen from good to better,
> So with his jawbone let everyone help himself.

When they have eaten, TAGLIAGAMBE *says*:
> Now that we have well satisfied our thirst
> And our bellies are full, that there is nothing to worry about,
> And that this fir tree holds a cool shade here,
285 > I would like to discuss seriously together
> How we may chance to live in quiet,
> Avoiding every thought that weighs upon the soul.

CARAPELLO *answers and says*:
> You are right, but I have little experience:
> You speak first, who know something of grammar.

TAGLIAGAMBE *answers*:
290 >   My Carapello, seeing that Fortune
> Has made us both become rich men,
> So she wishes that we be wise, and take care
> That one nail up her wheel very well,
> And rivet the nail in, so that we
295 > May have no fear that one may ever pull it out.

CARAPELLO *answers and says*:
> Yours is a good memory, without a lapse;
> Let us do whatever seems good to you, which I agree to.

TAGLIAGAMBE *answers*:
>   I feel, my brother, a great heat inside
> And it seems to me to be all full of fire,
300 > And upon my heart a pain is so firmly set
> That altogether it makes me faint.
> I am afraid that this rascal
> Has put poison in this wine.
> Alas, alas, this coward
305 > Like a frog has caught us by the mouthful.

CARAPELLO *answers and says*:
>   I myself felt, brother, a great heat inside
> But believed that it had come from the drink,
> For these wines that are adulterated bring it about
> That I cannot hold my eyes open.
310 > I do not believe that he has played a trick on us,
> Because we had not yet done anything to offend him.
> If it were true, we would quickly have noticed it.
> We shall pay a price for having found the gold.

TAGLIAGAMBE *answers*:

CARAPELLO *assaggia el vino e dice:*
 Egli è vantaggiato; assaggia un poco;
275 Costui era pur ghiotto e intendente.
Il TAGLIAGAMBE *l'assaggia e dice:*
 Questo è un vin che par proprio di fuoco,
 Tanto è gagliardo, sottile e possente.
 Veggiamo or come ci ha trattati il cuoco,
 E trassiniam qualche cosa col dente.
280 Di bene in meglio ci siamo abbattuti,
 Si che con le mascella ogniun s'aiuti.
Quando hanno mangiato, il TAGLIAGAMBE *dice:*
 Or che ci siam cavati ben la sete,
 E il corpo pien, che di nulla si teme,
 E che ci tien l'orezo questo abete,
285 Vuolsi che ragioniam di sodo insieme
 Che modo abbiamo a vivere in quïete,
 Fuggendo ogni pensier che l'alma preme.
Risponde CARAPELLO *e dice:*
 Tu hai ragion, ma io ho poca pratica:
 Di' prima tu, che sai ben di gramatica.
Risponde il TAGLIAGAMBE:
290 Carapel mio, da poi che la ventura
 Ci ha fatto diventar tutt' a dua ricchi,
 Si vuol che noi siam savi, e abbiam cura
 Che molto ben la ruota si conficchi
 E ribadisca il chiodo, onde paura
295 Non abbïam che già mai si sconficchi.
Risponde CARAPELLO *e dice:*
 El tuo è sanza fallo buon ricordo;
 Facciam quel che ti par, ch'i' me n'accordo.
Risponde il TAGLIAGAMBE:
 I' sento, fratel mio, drento un gran caldo
 E parmi esser di fuoco tutto pieno,
300 E sopra al cuore un duol s'è posto saldo
 Che tutto quanto mi fa venir meno.
 I' ho paura che questo ribaldo
 Non abbi in questo vin messo veleno.
 Oimè oimè, questo poltrone
305 Come ranocchi ci ha giunti al boccone.
Risponde CARAPELLO *e dice:*
 I' mi sentia, fratel, drento un gran caldo,
 Ma credetti che venissi dal bere,
 Chè questi vin che son conci, lo fanno,
 Che gli occhi aperti io non posso tenere.
310 I' non credo che ci abbi fatto inganno,
 Chè ancor non gli avàn fatto dispiacere.
 Se sarà ver, noi ce n'avedrem tosto:
 D'aver trovato l'or ci sarà costo.
Risponde il TAGLIAGAMBE:

          What devil do I have inside in my guts?
315   It seems a dog that has devoured me.
          A little good news is enough for me;
          How does it help me to have found so much gold?
     CARAPELLO *answers*:
          Let me say that my body torments me;
          And you see already that I am all blown up:
320   This was for certain something besides opium!
          Oh the devil, when I am bursting in this way.
     TAGLIAGAMBE *answers*:
              Brother, if you would go to the Bisticci
          I would give you my whole share;
          But, if he is not there, go to the barber of the Ricci,
325   Who has the prescription for every illness.
     CARAPELLO *answers and says*:
          You wish me to go, and yet I feel the shudders
          Of cruel death, bitter and evil,
          For all the prescriptions of Hippocrates
          Would not have the power to make me move a step.
     When he sees that they are dead, the SPIRIT OF AVARICE *speaks and says*:
330   Now am I clear that it was not in vain
          That I have spent my labor here,
          And I can return with great rejoicing;
          Nor am I afraid that our leader
          May speak abuse to me, into whose power
335   I have led, with my ancient art,
          In exchange for one, three; so I will go
          Before him, happy and full of courage.
     Then he goes to Satan and says:
              Behold, lord, your faithful servant
          Returned victorious to your presence,
340   For with my deceit and bitter gall
          I have so corrupted three companions
          That with tricks and with cruel means
          They have deprived each other of life.
     SATAN *answers and says*:
          Having done this good work,
345   You are worthy without doubt of a crown.
     The play being over, an ANGEL *gives the epilogue*:
              Oh wretched mortals, open your eyes;
          See what worldly treasure does,
          And the world that feeds you with trifles,
          Not being able to give you other refreshment.
350   Do not wait for death to strike;

---

322   the Bisticci: Iacopo di Filippo da Bisticci (d. 1478) was a physician in Florence in the
       mid-fifteenth century, brother to Vespasiano da Bisticci, the humanist bookseller and biographer;
       see Katharine Park, *Doctors and Medicine in Early Renaissance Florence* (Princeton: Princeton
       UP, 1985), pp. 33, 186.

Che diavol ho io drento alle budella?
315   E' pare un can che m'abbi divorato.
Poco bastommi la buona novella;
Che mi giova tanto oro aver trovato?
Risponde CARAPELLO:
Lascia dir me, che 'l corpo mi martella,
E vedi già ch'i' son tutto gonfiato:
320   Questo è stato per certo altro che l'oppio!
O diavol, po' che in questo modo scoppio.
Risponde il TAGLIAGAMBE:
Fratel, se tu volessi ir pel Bisticci
I' ti darò tutta la parte mia:
E, se non v'è, va' pel barbier de' Ricci
325   Che ha la ricetta a ogni malattia.
Risponde CARAPELLO *e dice:*
Tu vuoi ch'i' vada, e già sento capricci
Della morte crudele acerba e ria,
Che tutte le ricette d'Ipocrasso
Non arien forza farmi andare un passo.
Parla lo SPIRITO DELL' AVARIZIA *quando vede che son morti, e dice:*
330   Or son io chiaro che indarno non resta
Avere speso qui la mia fatica,
E posso ritornar con molta festa,
Nè ho paura che villania mi dica
Il duca nostro, nella cui podesta
335   Condotto ho io, con la mia arte antica,
In iscambio d'un, tre; si ch'io vo' gire
Dinanzi a lui, contento e pien d'ardire.
Poi va a SATANASSO *e dice:*
Ecco, signore, il tuo servo fedele
Vittorïoso innanzi a te tornato,
340   Chè con mie falsità e amar fele
Ho tre compagni si contaminato
Chè con inganni e con modo crudele
Hanno l'un l'altro di vita privato.
Risponde SATANASSO *e dice:*
Avendo fatto quest' opera buona,
345   Se' degno sanza dubio di corona.
Finita la festa UNO ANGIOLO *dà licenzia:*
O miseri mortali, aprite gli occhi
Vedete quel che fa il mondan tesoro,
E 'l mondo che vi pasce di finocchi,
Non vi potendo dare altro ristoro.
350   Non aspettate che la morte scocchi,

Make no further stay among sins;
Raise your eyes to heaven which invites you
To long for that infinite glory.
   See, o good people, how many evils
355   Come from that accursed she-wolf,
Which was born in the infernal realm,
And whose hunger is insatiable.
This is poison that from us blind mortals
Takes our life and uses up our health.
360   Vain humans, now look upon these men:
What good has it done them to find the gold?
   Look at Anthony, who in his youth
Abandoned possessions and took up poverty,
In order to attain those celestial heights
365   Where there is neither quarrel nor contention.
Seek God, who is true riches;
Like the wise, learn by others' costs,
And above all think about death;
And in the name of God may you have your dismissal.

III. The Old Man

Maximianus, *Elegy I*[21]

Envious old age, why do you delay in hastening the end?
   Why too do you come slow in this weary body?
Release, I pray, my wretched life from such a prison:
   Death is now rest, to live is pain for me;
5   I am not who I used to be: the best part of us has perished;
   Faintness and shuddering possess this also that remains.
Life is burdensome in sorrow [though] most pleasing in happy circumstances,
   And what is worse than any death – to want to die.
   . . .

---

369   dismissal: A complex word-play: *licenzia* not only means both "epilogue" and "leave to go," but also refers back to Anthony's acquisition, earlier in the play, of a *licenzia* to go and live in the wilderness as a hermit.

[21] I received help in this translation from Michael Sollenburger. See also the translation of L. R. Lind, *Gabriele Zerbi, Gerontocomia: On the Care of the Aged and Maximianus, Elegies on Old Age and Love* (Philadelphia: American Philosophical Society, 1988).

Non fate più ne' peccati dimoro,
Levate gli occhi al ciel el qual v'invita,
A disiar quella gloria infinita.
   Guardate, o buona gente, quanti mali
355   Vengon da questa maladetta lupa,
La qual è nata ne' regni infernali
E la sua fame sanza fin è cupa.
Questo è velen ch'a noi ciechi mortali
La vita toglie e la salute occupa.
360   Uomini vani, or guardate costoro:
Che utile ha lor fatto il trovar l'oro!
   Guardate Anton, che nella giovinezza
Lasciò la robba e la povertà prese,
Per acquistar quella superna altezza
365   Dove non è nè lite nè contese.
Cercate Idio, qual è vera ricchezza:
Come savi, imparate all' altrui spese,
E sopra tutto alla morte pensate;
E col nome di Dio licenzia abbiate.

III. The Old Man

Maximianus, *Elegy I*

(from Richard Webster, ed. *The Elegies of Maximianus* [Princeton: Princeton UP, 1900], with variants from Aemilius Baehrens, ed. *Poetae Latini Minores*, vol. 5 [Leipzig: Teubner, 1883].)

Aemula quid cessas finem properare senectus?
   cur et in hoc fesso corpore tarda venis?
solve precor miseram tali de carcere vitam:
   mors est iam requies, vivere poena mihi,
5   non sum qui fueram: periit pars maxima nostri;
   hoc quoque quod superest langor et horror habent.
lux gravis in luctu, rebus gratissima laetis,
   quodque omni peius funere, velle mori.
   . . .

10   Now because extended age is burdensome and useless to me,
         Since I cannot live, let it be possible for me to die.
      Oh how the hard condition of life presses on the wretched!
         Nor does death lie under human control.
      To die is sweet to the wretched but, longed-for, death recedes:
15   Yet when it is bitter it comes headlong.
      But I – alas! dead in so many respects – in due time
         Must, living, enter the ways to Tartarus.
      Now hearing is less, taste less; my eyes themselves
         Are dimmed; scarcely can I recognize certain things by touch.
20   No odor is sweet, no pleasure is now enjoyable;
         Without the senses, who may think about surviving?
      See, Lethean oblivion comes into my mind,
         Nor can it, confused, now remember itself.
      It rises to no labor, languishes with the body,
25   And, intent on its own ills, is stupefied.
         . . .
      For white and red before, now there tinges the face
         Pallor, and bloodless and funereal color.
      My dry skin shrivels, my sinews stand stiff all over,
30   And my hooked hands lacerate my itching limbs.
      Once laughing eyes now with a perpetual stream
         Bewail their sufferings night and day;
      And where pleasant garlands of eyebrows sheltered them before,
         A hairy shrubbery, leaning from above, presses down;
35   And they are hidden as if shut in a lightless cave:
         I do not know what grim and savage thing they see.
      Now it is terror to have seen an old man, nor can you believe
         This to be a man, who lacks human reason.
         . . .
40   It is a sin to love jokes, banquets, singing:
         O wretches, whose delights hold guilt.
      What are riches to me? for if you take away the use of them,
         However abundant my wealth, I will always be needy.
      Rather, it is a painful thing to depend on created things
45   Which, when you possess them, it is wrong to profane.
      Not otherwise does thirsting Tantalus catch at the waves
         Around him and abstain from foods placed nearby.
      I am made more the guardian of my own possessions,
         Conserving for others the things that have passed away for me;
50   Just as in golden-leaved gardens, hanging down,
         Many an ever-wakeful dragon guards apples not his own.
      Hence above all, cares torment my anxious self;
         Hence no rest is given to my soul.
      To seek for those things which I cannot, always I labor to keep,

10   **inutilis** *Baehrens*; inutile *Webster*.

46   **profane** "dissipate" Lind.

10   nunc quod longa mihi gravis est et inutilis aetas,
         vivere cum nequeam, sit mihi posse mori.
      o quam dura premit miseros condicio vitae:
         nec mors humano subiacet arbitrio.
      dulce mori miseris, sed mors optata recedit:
15   at cum tristis erit praecipitata venit.
      me vero heu tantis defunctum in partibus olim
         vivum Tartareas constat inire vias.
      iam minor auditus, gustus minor; ipsa caligant
         lumina; vix tactu noscere certa queo
20   nullus dulcis odor, nulla est iam grata voluptas;
         sensibus expertem quis superesse putet?
      en Lethaea meam subeunt oblivia mentem,
         nec confusa sui iam meminisse potest:
      ad nullum consurgit opus, cum corpore languet
25   atque intenta suis astupet illa malis.
            . . .
      pro niveo rutiloque prius nunc inficit ora   [133]
         pallor et exanguis funereusque color.
      aret sicca cutis, rigidi stant undique nervi,
30   et lacerant uncae scabida membra manus.
      quondam ridentes oculi nunc fonte perenni
         deplangunt poenas nocte dieque suas;
      et quos grata prius ciliorum serta tegebant,
         desuper incumbens hispida silva premit,
35   ac velut inclusi caeco conduntur in antro:
         torvum nescio quid heu furiale vident.
      iam pavor est vidisse senem, nec credere possis
         hunc hominem humana qui ratione caret.
            . . .
40   crimen amare iocos, crimen convivia, cantus: [179]
         o miseri, quorum gaudia crimen habent.
      quid mihi divitiae, quarum si dempseris usum,
         quamvis largus opum, semper egenus ero?
      immo etiam poena est partis incumbere rebus,
45   quas cum possideas est violare nefas.
      non aliter sitiens vicinas Tantalus undas
         captat et appositis abstinet ora cibis.
      efficior custos rerum magis ipse mearum
         conservans aliis, quae periere mihi;
50   sicut in auricomis dependens plurimus hortis
         pervigil observat non sua poma draco.
      hinc me sollicitum torquent super omnia curae,
         hinc requies animo non datur ulla meo.
      quaerere quae nequeo, semper retinere laboro,

55   And, keeping, always think I've held nothing.
     The old man stands irresolute and trembling, always believing
        In evils, and, foolish, what he does he himself fears.
     . . .
     These are the first-fruits of death, to these ends a lifetime
60   Flows down, and with reluctant steps seeks the last things.
     Not one's bearing, nor one's color itself, nor one's gait in walking,
        Nor one's very beauty that existed before remains.
     The clothing slips from the shoulders as the body sags;
        Whatever was too short for me is now too long.
65   We contract, and we shrink astonishingly in size;
        You'd think the very bones of our body were diminished.
     Nor is it permitted to look at the sky, but old age, facing downward,
        Sees the earth, from which it was born and to which it is to return,
     And becomes three-legged, then four-legged, like a little baby,
70   And creeps dolefully over the filthy ground.
     All things go back to their origins and search for the mother,
        And what was nothing before returns to nothing.
     Thus leaning on his cane, old age, near toppling,
        Strikes sluggish earth with a constant thump,
75   And, moving in measured footsteps, in steady flaps,
        From his wrinkled mouth are heard such words as these:
     "Take me in, Mother, pity your child's distresses;
        I want to warm my tired limbs in your lap.
     Children shrink from me, I cannot appear as before;
80   Why do you allow your offspring to be horrible?
     I've nothing in common with those aboveground; I've fulfilled life's duties;
        Give back, I pray, dead limbs to the paternal soil.
     What is the benefit of straining wretches with punishments?
        It is not for a motherly breast to bear these things."
85   This said, he supports his tottering joints with the stick,
        As he seeks again the hard straw of his neglected bed,
     Where after he has lain down, how does he differ from a miserable corpse?
        Alas, you see only the bones of a drawn-up body.
     And since always I lie down more and live while lying down
90   Who will consider my bed to be of life?
     Now the punishment is totally that we are alive . . .
     . . .
     This too is hard for an old man to have recalled:
     Quarrels, slighting, and destructive losses follow,
95   Nor does anyone, a friend, offer help on account of such things.
     The very boys and the very girls now think it shameful
        To call me master without disputing it;
     They jeer at my gait, laugh now, in a word, at my face
        And trembling head, which once they feared
100 And although I see nothing, still I'll be allowed to look on this,

96   **ipsi** *Baehrens*; ipse *Webster.*

55 et retinens semper nil tenuisse puto.
stat dubius tremulusque senex semperque malorum
    credulus, et stultus quae fecit ipse timet . . .

. . .

    hae sunt primitiae mortis, his partibus aetas   [209]
60   defluit et pigris gressibus ima petit.
non habitus, non ipse color, non gressus euntis,
    non species eadem quae fuit ante manet.
labitur ex umeris demisso corpore vestis.
    quaeque brevis fuerat iam modo longa mihi est.
65 contrahimur miroque modo decrescimus: ipsa
    diminui nostri corporis ossa putes.
nec caelum spectare licet, sed prona senectus
    terram, qua genita est et reditura, videt
fitque tripes, prorsus quadrupes, ut parvulus infans,
70   et per sordentem (flebile) repit humum.
ortus cuncta suos repetunt matremque requirunt,
    et redit ad nihilum, quod fuit ante nihil.
hinc est quod baculo incumbens ruitura senectus
    assiduo pigram verbere pulsat humum
75 et numerosa movens certo vestigia plausu
    talia rugato creditur ore loqui:
'suscipe me, genetrix, nati miserere laborum:
    membra peto gremio fessa fovere tuo.
horrent me pueri, nequeo velut ante videri:
80   horrendos partus cur sinis esse tuos?
nil mihi cum superis: explevi munera vitae:
    redde precor patrio mortua membra solo.
quid miseros variis prodest extendere poenis?
    non est materni pectoris ista pati.'
85 his dictis trunco titubantes sustinet artus
    neglecti repetens stramina dura tori.
quo postquam iacuit, misero quid funere differt?
    heu tantum adtracti corporis ossa vides.
cumque magis semper iaceam vivamque iacendo,
90   quis sub vitali computet esse loco?
iam poena est totum quod vivimus . . .

. . .

    hoc quoque difficile est commemorasse seni.   [280]
iurgia, contemptus violentaque damna secuntur
95   nec quisquam ex tantis praebet amicus opem.
ipsi me pueri atque ipsae sine lite puellae
    turpe putant dominum iam vocitare suum.
irrident gressum, irrident iam denique vultum
    et tremulum, quondam quod timuere, caput.
100 cumque nihil videam, tamen hoc spectare licebit

So that such pain may be harsher for wretched me.
Fortunate is he who has deserved to lead a quiet life
And to conclude his steady days with a happy end:
Hard enough the past memory of good things for wretches,
105   But more heavily, plunged from the highest pinnacle, it falls.

ut gravior misero poena sit ista mihi.
felix qui meruit tranquillam ducere vitam
   et laeto stabiles claudere fine dies:
dura satis miseris memoratio prisca bonorum,
105   et gravius summo culmine mersa ruit.

The Tale of Melibee

WILLIAM ASKINS

Le Livre de Melibee et Prudence   331
(from Paris, BN, MS Fr. 578, ed. J. Burke Severs, with supplementary
material from *Liber Consolationis et Consilii*, ed. Thor Sundby)

The *Tale of Melibee*, or, as it was called in some manuscripts and the early
prints of the *Canterbury Tales*, the *Tale of Chaucer*, is based on a Latin treatise,
the *Liber consolationis et consilii*, written in 1246 by the Italian jurist,
Albertano of Brescia, one of the earliest medieval authors unaffiliated with the
Church or a university to have written a significant body of discursive prose.
The same author composed two other treatises, the *Liber de amore et dilectione*
in 1238 and the *Liber de doctrina dicendi et tacendi* in 1245, each of them, like
the *Liber consolationis et consilii*, nominally addressed to one of his sons.
Though Chaucer's familiarity with these works is sometimes called into question, the evidence long ago presented by Emil Koeppel, much of it drawn from
the *Merchant's Tale* and the *Manciple's Tale*, has never been refuted.[1] These
three works frequently appear in the same manuscript, sometimes accompanied
by Albertano's "sermons" or speeches. Recently inventoried by Paolo Navone
and Angus Graham, there are more than 320 Latin manuscripts containing
Albertano's treatises, about half of them including the *Liber consolationis et
consilii*.[2] The Latin text circulated in England as early as the thirteenth century
and more than a dozen thirteenth-century and fourteenth-century manuscripts of
English provenance survive.[3] Chaucer's contemporaries, like John Gower, were

---

[1] Emil Koeppel, "Chaucer and Albertanus Brixiensis," *Archiv für das Studium der neuren Sprachen und
   Literaturen* 86 (1891): 29–46.
[2] Paola Navone, ed., Albertano da Brescia, *Liber de doctrina dicendi et tacendi* (Tavarnuzze, 1998), pp.
   xlvii–lxxxviii; Angus Graham, "Albertanus of Brescia: A Supplementary Census of Latin Manuscripts," *Studi Medievali* 41 (2000): 429–45.
[3] Manuscripts of the Latin works which circulated in England during the thirteenth and fourteenth
   centuries are listed separately at the end of this introduction. After each shelfmark, I cross-reference
   this list to the inventories of Paola Navone and Angus Graham mentioned in the previous note and
   supply a brief note in brackets regarding the evidence for the claim that these manuscripts were available in England. For details about contents and related matters, see the inventories and the appropriate
   library catalogues. To this list could be added another 12 fifteenth-century manuscripts as well as

familiar with the *Liber consolationis et consilii* and the scribes who copied the *Canterbury Tales* glossed the *Melibee*, the *Merchant's Tale*, and the *Manciple's Tale* with citations from the Latin texts of several of Albertano's treatises.[4] In the edition of the *Liber consolationis et consilii* which he prepared for the Chaucer Society in 1873, Thor Sundby claimed that students of the source of the *Melibee* would do best to consult the Latin text of Albertano, and the Latin alone.[5] Though Sundby certainly overstated his case, his argument seems to have convinced W. W. Skeat to draw his notes to the *Melibee* in the *Oxford Chaucer* almost exclusively from the Latin text.

However, as Skeat of course knew, while Chaucer may have been familiar with the Latin, it is nonetheless clear that when he composed the *Melibee* he turned to the *Livre de Mellibee*, the French translation of the *Liber consolationis et consilii* prepared in 1337 by a Dominican friar from Poligny, Renaud de Louens. Readers of Chaucer have known about the ties between this French translation and the English text since at least the early eighteenth century, when, as Curt Bühler discovered, the owner of one manuscript of the *Livre de Mellibee*, New York Pierpont Morgan Library MS M39, supplemented his imperfect copy of Renaud's translation with material from Chaucer's tale.[6] In the manuscripts, Renaud's translation is frequently attributed to Jean de Meun, whose French translation of Boethius Chaucer consulted when he produced his own *Boece*. In fifteenth-century manuscripts, including the Pierpont Morgan copy just mentioned, Renaud's work was also attributed to Christine de Pisan. Renaud's translation of the *Liber consolationis et consilii* is but one of a number of translations of Albertano's treatises into virtually every European vernacular, and by far the most widely copied. The 35 surviving manuscripts containing it are listed below. In addition to the 64 additional manuscripts containing Chaucer's version of it, there are more than 140 manuscripts containing Italian, French, German, Spanish, Dutch, and Czech translations of Albertano's work.[7] Chaucer was the first of three translators who relied upon Renaud's translation in the course of preparing his own; the other two, the author of *Le Ménagier de Paris* and the fifteenth-century Dutch author, Dirk Potter.[8]

---

fugitive references to the mention of Albertano's treatises in medieval English library catalogues and wills.

[4] Conrad Mainzer, "Albertano of Brescia's *Liber consolationis et consilii* as a Source for Gower's *Confessio Amantis*," *Medium Aevum* 47 (1978): 88–90.

[5] Thor Sundby, ed., *Albertani Brixiensis*. *"Liber consolationis et consilii" ex quo Hausta est Fabula de Melibeo et Prudentia* (London, 1873), p. xx.

[6] For a recent discussion of Bühler's work and the manuscript itself, see Martha Driver, "Chaucer, Christine, and Melibee: Morgan Library, M39 and its Eighteenth-Century Owner," *The Early Book Society Newsletter* 2 (Spring 1997): 4–9.

[7] Angus Graham, "Albertanus of Brescia: A Preliminary Census of Vernacular Manuscripts," *Studi Medievali* 41 (2000): 891–924.

[8] There has not been a detailed comparative study of the practices of these three translators; for a recent discussion of some general similarities between Chaucer and Dirk Potter, see Sabrina Corbellini, *Italiaanse deugden en ondeugden* (Amsterdam, 2000), pp. 163–78.

Though Thor Sundby considered Renaud's translation beneath notice, any uncertainty about its value was settled by the discovery of the manuscript which most closely resembled Chaucer's text: Paris, BN MS fr. 578. Scholars like Sundby and Skeat had focused on manuscripts of Renaud's translation housed in the British Museum, and as late as 1935 Severs himself was working primarily with Paris, BN MS fr. 1165 which, as he acknowledged, did not provide a "satisfactory" text.[9] The importance of Paris, BN MS fr. 578 was first noticed in the early twentieth century by a member of the team of French scholars and schoolteachers who produced a collaborative translation of the *Canterbury Tales* designed to replace the translation which the Chevalier de Chatelain had published in 1857.[10] Though the Chevalier translated the whole of the *Melibee*, turning it indeed into an astonishing French poem, the committee referred to would have none of this. The scholar responsible for the *Melibee*, Charles Bastide, declared that it was "très ennuyeux et très long," argued that its translation into modern French would prove worthless, and settled for a two page summary of the tale. Nonetheless it was Bastide who first suggested that Chaucer's translation might best be read against the version of Renaud in Paris, BN MS fr. 578. This was echoed by Mario Roques in his very thorough discussion of the French translations of Albertano of Brescia published in 1938.[11] Though he acknowledged the work of neither Bastide nor Roques, J. Burke Severs shifted his attention from Paris, BN MS fr. 1165 to Paris, BN MS 578 and it was the latter manuscript, meticulously transcribed and accompanied with a valuable list of variants, which served as the basis for the edition he published in Bryan and Dempster, and that settled any question about the value of Renaud's work to students of Chaucer.[12]

In the course of preparing his edition, Severs studied six manuscripts of the *Livre de Mellibee* with care and mentioned twenty others but was never clear about how closely he had examined them. Lee Patterson has observed that Severs' work was "unfortunately marred by a number of omissions and inaccuracies" but, on close examination, the inaccuracies at least prove few and far between.[13] Severs was unaware of the existence of another eight manuscripts and he failed to consult seven early prints of the *Livre de Mellibee* published in Paris and Geneva between 1481 and 1517, all of these now listed in the inventory of the vernacular translations of Albertano compiled by Angus Graham. While a full collation of these manuscripts and early prints would certainly alter the list of variants Severs produced, it seems unlikely that it would significantly alter the valuable text he prepared in 1941. The question of variants is of course

9 J. Burke Severs, "The Source of Chaucer's Melibeus," *PMLA* 50 (1935): 99.
10 Emile Legouis et al., trans., *Les Contes de Canterbury a Geoffrey Chaucer: Traductions Française* (Paris, 1908), pp. 190–5; Le Chevalier de Chatelain, trans., *Contes de Cantorbery* (London, 1858), vol. 2, pp. 137–215.
11 Mario Roques, "Traductions Françaises des Traités Moraux d'Albertano de Brescia," in *Histoire Littéraire de la France* (Paris, 1938), vol. 37, pp. 488–506.
12 Severs, "The Tale of Melibeus," in Bryan and Dempster, pp. 560–614.
13 Lee Patterson, " 'What Man Artow?': Authorial Self-Definition in *The Tale of Sir Thopas* and *The Tale of Melibee*," *Studies in the Age of Chaucer* 11 (1989): 150.

further complicated by the thousands of variant readings in the manuscripts of the *Melibee* itself, a list of which consumes more than 250 pages in the edition of John Matthews Manly and Edith Rickert, a work which Severs was unable to consult. Rather than attempt a collation of this magnitude, I have followed the lead of Severs and presented what is essentially his text with the changes described below, augmented in the notes by scholarship published since 1941.

As useful as Severs' edition of the *Livre de Mellibee* has proven to be, questions might nonetheless be raised about his discussion of the practices of the French translator, an issue to which he devoted much of his preface. Severs apparently assumed that Renaud de Louens worked with a text of the *Liber consolationis et consilii* which resembled the edition of Thor Sundby. Severs argued that Renaud "handled his Latin source boldly and freely" in order to produce a "more closely knit" work, and in his notes he identified in detail what Renaud had deleted from, and added to, the Latin. While there are clear indications in the *Livre de Mellibee* that Renaud did some editing, it is, however, difficult to assess its extent. Manuscripts containing the Latin works of Albertano are not infrequently abridged, partially perhaps because the Italian's treatises overlapped considerably, whole sections of the *Liber de amore et dilectione*, for example, reappearing in the *Liber de consolatione et consilii*. In recent years, cataloguers have published careful descriptions of these manuscripts which indicate the tendency of scribes to summarize, paraphrase and gloss the Latin texts, as, for example, in Durham University Library MS Cosin V.iii.22, a manuscript unfamiliar to both Sundby and Severs. Severs did consult the Latin text of Philadelphia Free Library MS Lewis 1, but this too contains evidence of abridgment which he did not acknowledge. This situation is mirrored to a degree by the scribal revision and abridgment which mark fifteenth-century copies of the *Melibee* itself, the subject of recent work by Seth Lerer, Kate Harris and others.[14]

This is not to say that the differences between the Latin original and the French translation are accidental or insignificant. In the Latin, Prudence discusses a wide range of issues related to public policy, such matters as defense spending (chapter 35), the kind of thinking that should inform declarations of war (chapters 46–48), and policy towards the poor (chapter 45). She also discusses the value of scholars and scholarship (chapter 10) and herself offers abstract, scholastic discussions of such matters as prudence (chapter 6–9), the nature of power (chapter 36) and the will of God (chapter 38). In the French translation, these political and intellectual considerations are dropped or muted and the general effect is to domesticate Prudence, to present her as someone concerned primarily with how her husband and his circle of advisors think. Though Severs was not concerned with how Renaud de Louens had reconceptualized Prudence, the redefinition of her character in both Renaud's

---

[14] Seth Lerer, *Chaucer and His Readers* (Princeton, 1993), pp. 93–100; Kate Harris, "Unnoticed Extracts from Chaucer and Hoccleve: Huntington HM 144, Trinity College, Oxford D 29 and the *Canterbury Tales*," *Studies in the Age of Chaucer* 20 (1998): 167–200.

and Chaucer's texts has since been the subject of important articles by Delores Palomo and Carolyn Collette.[15] Furthermore, Severs scrupulously avoided historical or political explanations for the differences between the Latin and the French versions, and between the French and the English. Indeed, his sense that the French translation was driven primarily by an "editorial" mentality was itself a response to an attempt to read the *Melibee* in the light of contemporary political history. In his initial study of Chaucer's source, Severs used the formidable information he had collected about the manuscripts of the French translation to dismiss Leslie Hotson's argument about the political thrust of the Tale.[16] Though Severs also claimed that the manuscripts with which he was working had been "hitherto unexamined," they did not escape the attention of Mario Roques, who was studying the same manuscripts at the same moment in the course of preparing his own study of the French translations of Albertano's treatises; and, while Severs maintained that attempts to reduce this text to what he called "political propaganda" were foolish, Roques carefully situated Renaud's text within the political history of the wars between the Burgundian aristocrats of the early fourteenth century. Chaucer's decision to use the French text may have been driven by similar considerations rather than an attraction to the French translator's editorial abilities. James Powell, for example, has recently argued that the translation of Renaud de Louens "commences the process of adapting the *Liber consolationis* to the political, social and cultural climate" of northern Europe.[17] There are further indications that even Renaud's translation was recontextualized as it was copied and recopied. A miniature in one fourteenth-century manuscript depicts Prudence in an aristocratic setting, attacked by the three enemies of Melibee while she and her daughter are walking on the ramparts of her castle, the architecture of which is conspicuously French.[18] An illuminated initial which opens a fifteenth-century version of the same text recasts Prudence as a merchant's wife engaged in what appears to be an animated conversation with Melibee who, for his part, wears the merchant's purse on his belt.[19] I have tried, therefore, to present the text which follows in such a way that readers will be drawn towards the idea of interpreting it in the light of the historical forces which shaped and reshaped it as it was copied and recopied, translated and retranslated.

This approach finds support I believe in recent Chaucer criticism which has paid close attention to both the French source and the Latin text on which it is based. Since the publication of Severs' work, some scholars have emphasized the French origins of the work and produced studies of the text which range

---

[15] Delores Palomo, "What Chaucer Really Did to *Le Livre de Mellibee*," *Philological Quarterly* 53 (1974): 304–20; Carolyn P. Collette, "Heeding the Counsel of Prudence: A Context for the Melibee," *Chaucer Review* 29 (1995): 416–33.

[16] J. Burke Severs, "The Source of Chaucer's Melibeus," pp. 98–9.

[17] James Powell, *Albertanus of Brescia: The Pursuit of Happiness in the Early Thirteenth Century* (Philadelphia, 1992), p. 124.

[18] Paris, Bibliothèque Nationale, MS fr., 1165, fol. 66r.

[19] London, British Library, MS Reg. 19.C.XI, fol. 52r.

from the discussion of its style by Diane Bornstein to the consideration of larger contextual issues of the kind treated by Lee Patterson.[20] This approach to the text is certainly fitting, for it was in Paris that Brunetto Latini first translated one of Albertano's treatises, the *Liber de doctrina dicendi et tacendi*, into French, and it was in Paris that Andreas Grossetto produced one of the translations of Albertano's treatises into Italian. Paris also seems to have served as a center for the dissemination of the Latin manuscripts of Albertano's work, at least north of the Alps.[21] On the other hand, some scholars have emphasized the Latin text, including J. D. Burnley, whose study of its prose style is a response to the work of Diane Bornstein; and David Wallace, whose extended discussion of Chaucer's debt to Albertano of Brescia also pays close attention to the Latin original and its historical context.[22] The most important study of the Latin text in recent years has been Claudia Villa's work on the manuscripts of the sources Albertano exploited when he composed his treatises, i.e. manuscripts of Seneca and St. Augustine which contain his autograph glosses.[23] This has been followed by a great deal of renewed attention to the historical background of the Latin text, especially within the past ten years, including the aforementioned monograph by the historian James Powell; a study by Oscar Nuccio of the mercantile ideologies which shaped the text; an important collection of essays prepared by an international cast of scholars on the occasion of a conference on Albertano held in Brescia in 1994; a critical edition of one of Albertano's treatises by Paula Navone, the first in more than a century; and finally a web site devoted to the Latin and vernacular versions of Albertano's work and related scholarship.[24]

This renewal of interest in Albertano testifies to the value of consulting the Latin text, a point which can be illustrated in a number of ways. For example, at its opening, the Latin text indicates that the enemies of Melibee wound his daughter in the eyes, nose, mouth, hands and ears. Renaud and Chaucer after him substitute *feet* for *eyes* in this list of wounds. Though Severs speculated that this was an editorial lapse, that the scribes had confused French *yeux* and *piez*, a more likely suggestion is the contextual explanation offered by Richard

---

[20] Diane Bornstein, "Chaucer's Tale of Melibee as an Example of the Style Clergial," *Chaucer Review* 12 (1978): 236–54; Lee Patterson, "What Man Artow?", pp. 117–75.

[21] For the circulation of Albertano's work in humanistic circles in late 14th century Paris, see François Autrand, "Culture et Mentalité: Les Libraires des Gens du Parliament au Temps de Charles VI," *Annales: Economies, Sociétés, Civilisations* 28 (1973): 1219.

[22] J. D. Burnley, "Curial Prose Style in England," *Speculum* 61 (1986): 593–614; David Wallace, *Chaucerian Polity: Absolutist Lineages and Associational Forms in England and Italy* (Stanford, 1997), pp. 212–46. These studies and the articles mentioned in note 19 do not, of course, represent the full range of work on the *Melibee* in recent years. A complete survey of it, including studies which take note of the sources of the *Melibee* and regard the text within one historical context or another, would require a separate essay.

[23] Claudia Villa, "La Tradizione delle *Ad Lucilium* a la Cultura di Brescia dell'Eta Carolingia ad Albertano," *Italia Mediovale e Humanistica* 12 (1969): 9–52.

[24] Oscar Nuccio, *Albertano de Brescis: Razionalismo Economico ed Epistemologia dell'"azione umana" nell '200 Italiano* (Rome, 1997); Franco Spinelli, ed., *Albertano de Brescia: Alle Origini del Razionnalismo Economico, dell'Umanismo Civile, della Grand Europa* (Brescia, 1996); Paola Navone, ed., *Albertano da Brescia, Liber de doctrina dicendi et tacendi* (Tavarnuzze, 1998). The address of the website is: http//:freespace.virgin.net/angus.graham/Albertano.htm.

Hoffman, who argued that Renaud had conflated the five senses and the five wounds of Christ when he described the wounded daughter, a claim that is supported by the Latin.[25] On a more general level, the Latin also points towards the ultimate source of the fictional framework of the *Melibee*. The allegory of the violated house and the wounded daughter is based on a passage from Gregory the Great's *Moralia in Job*, which Thor Sundby was unable to identify, and which is itself a meditation on Jeremiah 8:21–9:24. The passage from Jeremiah is the ultimate source of a number of motifs in the fiction as well as the basis for its central ideas.

Given the value of both the French text and its Latin original, I have attempted to produce a version of Chaucer's source which takes both into consideration and duplicates Severs' edition with a number of modifications. Though other contributors to this volume have provided English translations of Chaucer's sources, in the case of this particular text, such a translation seemed pointless, an exercise which would involve little more than producing a modernized version of Chaucer's English and would furthermore consume a great deal of space. Instead I have translated, first, the prefatory remarks with which Renaud opens his translation and, second, the portions of the Latin text which are not represented in the French. I have inserted the translations from the Latin at the points in the French text where they would have appeared had Renaud translated the full text of the *Liber consolationis*. The result may be somewhat distorted since Renaud's translation of the Latin is frequently paraphrastic. Though the best arrangement might have been to present my own translations together with the complete Latin text, Sundby's edition of it, though long out of print, is currently available at the Albertano web site I have mentioned.

To facilitate comparison with the Latin, I have also divided the text into chapters which correspond with those in Sundby's edition. There is some warrant for this division in the manuscripts of Renaud's translation, several of which are themselves divided into chapters, though these chapters do not correspond with those in the Latin. Within the chapters, I have divided the text into discrete passages rather than modern paragraphs, in keeping with the practice of modern editors of medieval prose texts. These passages, sometimes clausulae, sometimes paragraphs, are frequently rubricated in both the Latin and the French manuscripts and, while this practice varies from manuscript to manuscript, I have divided the text this way in order to provide the reader with at least a rough sense of how these texts look in the manuscripts. Each of the discrete passages has been numbered, an approach which seemed preferable to the practice of arbitrarily numbering lines on the basis of how they appear on the printed page. Passages which are preceded by a bracketed number appear only in the French. The numbers in parentheses at the end of line refer to the corresponding line in Chaucer's text. Though the text of the Melibee in the *Riverside Chaucer* alternates line numbers in keeping with the dispute about whether or not the tale

---

[25] Richard Hoffman, "Chaucer's Melibee and Tales of Sondry Folk," *Classica et Medievalia* 30 (1969): 552–77.

belongs in Fragment B^2 or Fragment VII, I have followed the numbering consistent with Fragment VII since it corresponds with the textual and explanatory notes in the same edition.

The list of manuscripts which follows is indebted to Angus Graham, who has kindly shared his work with me prior to its publication and the sigils are adapted from his inventory for the purposes of cross-reference; thus the base manuscript, Paris, BN fr. 578, – which Severs called P3 – is now identified as P7. His manuscript B is here B7; L is L4; P is P12; P2 is P13; P4 is P24. I have compared Severs' edition with readings in these manuscripts and the changes I have introduced are few and for the most part insignificant. I have also examined the nineteen manuscripts of the French text in the Bibliothèque Nationale and one in the British Library and have discovered no evidence which would conflict with Severs' choice of the base text. The base text has been emended when its readings are erroneous in the light of both the other manuscripts of the French text and Chaucer's translation. For each emendation, the manuscripts with the emended reading are listed first, followed by the reading of the base text and then the readings of the other manuscripts. However, errors which are mirrored in Chaucer's translation have not been changed. The list of variants is by no means complete. Only those variants which are reflected in Chaucer's translation or speak to the choice of the base manuscript have been included. I have however discarded the variants from the nineteenth century edition of *Le Ménagier de Paris* which Severs included; until the early prints of Renaud's work are collated, the value of this particular set of variants is unclear and Severs himself once argued that the text of *Le Ménagier de Paris* would prove "untrustworthy" to Chaucer's readers.[26] I have also disregarded minor differences in spelling, scribal "et" variants, and simple inversions of words within clausulae, but have included a few variants which Severs did not record.

The explanatory notes take both the French and the Latin texts into consideration. Explanatory notes about the French text are indebted to Severs, though I disagree with many of his speculative comments about the manuscript Chaucer might have used. I do not repeat information about the sources of these texts found in the edition of Sundby or the *Riverside Chaucer*, but do offer information about unidentified sources and some corrections to the work of both editors. The text which follows then presents little new information about the text of Renaud's translation. Its essential purpose, for reasons I have explained above, is to prompt further study of the relationship between the Chaucer's English and the French and Latin which preceded it.[27]

[26] J. Burke Severs, "The Source of Chaucer's Melibeus," p. 92.

[27] My gratitude to Angus Graham, Robert Correale and Carolyn Collette for their help with this project and special thanks to Joe Bendig of the Computer Science Department at the Community College of Philadelphia for technical assistance. The errors which remain are, of course, my own.

Manuscripts of the *Livre de Mellibee*

I. *Manuscripts represented in this edition*

P7   Paris, Bibliothèque Nationale, MS fr., 578; fols. 56r–70v. 14c. (base text)
B7   Bruxelles, Bibliothèque Royale Albert Ier, MS 9551–9552; fols. 87r–104v. 15c.
L4   London, British Library, MS Reg. 19.C.VII; fols. 123r–148v. 15c.
P12   Paris, Bibliothèque Nationale, MS fr., 1165; fols. 66r–85r. 15c.
P13   Paris, Bibliothèque Nationale, MS fr., 1468; fols. 1r–35r. 15c.
P24   Paris, Bibliothèque Nationale, MS fr., 20042; fols. 1r–25v. 15c.

II. *Other manuscripts*

B2   Beauvais, Bibliothèque de Beauvais, MS 9 (2807); fols. 53–81. 15c.
B3   Besançon, Bibliothèque Municipale, MS 587; fols. 83–106. 15c.
B5   Bruxelles, Bibliothèque Royale Albert Ier, MS 2082 (10394–10414); fols. 151–207. 15c.
B6   Bruxelles, Bibliothèque Royale Albert Ier, MS 2297 (9235–9237); fols. 226–246. 15c.
F29   Fribourg, Bibliothèque Cantonale et Universitaire, MS L.161; fols. 138r–162r. 15c.
G2   Genève, Bibliothèque Publique et Universitaire, MS suppl. 104 (olim 174.d); fols. 255–281. 15c.
K1   Kortrijk, Stedelijke Openbare Bibliotheek (Collection J. Goethals-Vercruysse), MS 363 (XVI.42); fols. 1r–28v. 16c.
L3   Lille, Bibliothèque Municipale, MS 335; fols. 59r–87r. 15c.
L5   London, British Library, MS Reg. 19.C.XI; fols. 52r–65v. 15c.
M1   Madrid, Biblioteca Nacional MS 12760 (Ee. 138); fols. 1–29. 15c.
N1   New York, Pierpont Morgan Library, MS M39; fols. 1–21. 15c.
P4   Paris, Bibliothèque de l'Arsenal, MS 2691 (46 S.A.F.); fols. 26–43. 15c.
P6   Paris, Bibliothèque de l'Arsenal, MS 3356 (250 B.F.); fols. 105–128. 15c.
P8   Paris, Bibliothèque Nationale, MS fr., 580; fols. 41–52. 15c.
P9   Paris, Bibliothèque Nationale, MS fr., 813; fols. 107r–121v. 15c.
P10   Paris, Bibliothèque Nationale, MS fr., 1090; fols. 29r–95r. 14c.
P14   Paris, Bibliothèque Nationale, MS fr., 1540; fols. 59r–68r. 15c.
P15   Paris, Bibliothèque Nationale, MS fr., 1555; fols. 31–49. 14c.
P16   Paris, Bibliothèque Nationale, MS fr., 1746; fols. 76–125. 15c.
P17   Paris, Bibliothèque Nationale, MS fr., 1972; fols. 43r–76r. 15c.
P18   Paris, Bibliothèque Nationale, MS fr., 2240; fols. 37–60. 15c.
P20   Paris, Bibliothèque Nationale, MS fr., 15105; fols. 1r–39r. 15c.
P22   Paris, Bibliothèque Nationale, MS fr., 17272; fols. 101v–113v. 15c.
P23   Paris, Bibliothèque Nationale, MS fr., 19123; fols. 90–109. 15c.
P26   Paris, Bibliothèque Nationale, MS fr., 25547; fols. 79–108. 15c.
P27   Paris, Bibliothèque Nationale, MS nouv. acq. fr. 6639; fols. 1–35. 15c.
P29   Paris, Bibliothèque Nationale, MS nouv. acq. fr. 10554; fols. 62r–85v. 15c.
W1   Wien, Österreichische Nationalbibliothek, MS 2602; fols. 26r–42v. 15c.

III. *Contemporary English manuscripts containing the Latin texts of the works of Albertano of Brescia*

Cambridge: Corpus Christi College MS 306. 14c. Navone C1 [English hand(?) and owner].

Cambridge: Gonville and Caius College MS 61 (155). 13c. Navone C2 [English library].

Cambridge University Library MS Ee.iv.23. 14c. Navone C4 [English owner and contents].

Cambridge University Library MS Ii.vi.39. 14c. Navone C5 [English contents].

Durham: University Library MS Cosin V.iii.22. 14c. Graham D5 [English scribe].

København: Kongelige Bibliothek MS Thott 110. 14c. Navone K3 [Italian hand but English owner and contents].

London: BL MS Add. 6158. 13–14c. Navone L7 [Italian hand but English owner and contents].

London: BL MS Arundel 248. 14c. Navone L9 [English hand and owners; though Navone claims that this is a 15c. manuscript, the treatises of Albertano are in a 14c. hand].

London: BL Royal MS 12.D.VII. 14c. Navone L12 [English hand and owner].

London: Lambeth Palace MS 375. 14c. Navone L14 [English owner].

Manchester: John Rylands University Library, lat. 454. 13c. Navone M5 [English library; Navone was unaware that this manuscript contains all of Albertano's treatises].

Oxford: Bodleian Library MS Add. C. 12. 14c. Navone O1 [English owner].

Oxford: Jesus College MS 25. 14–15c. Navone O8 [English scribe].

Le Livre de Mellibee et Prudence

(from Paris, BN, MS Fr. 578. 14th c., ed. J. Burke Severs [New York, 1941] with
English text from *Liber Consolationis et Consilii*, ed. Thor Sundby
[London, 1873])

Cy commence le livre de Mellibee et Prudence (fol. 56r)

Aprés ce, ma tres chere dame, que j'ay fait le romment sur Boece de Consolation a vostre service et pour vous conforter en Nostre Seigneur, j'ay fait un petit traittié a l'enseingnement et au profit de mon tres cher seigneur, vostre filz, et de tous autres princes et barons qui le vouldront entendre et garder. Lequel traittié j'ay fundé et extrait d'une fiction ancienne que j'ay trovee en escript. Et se commence en la maniere qui cy aprés s'ensuit.

In addition, my dearest lady, to my having translated the Consolation *of Boethius so that I might serve you and so that you might take comfort in Our Lord, I have translated a little treatise for the instruction and the profit of my dearest lord, your son, and all the other princes and barons who might want to heed it and to study it. I have based this treatise on excerpts I have taken from an ancient tale which I found in a manuscript. It begins in the following manner.*

The beginning of the book of consolation and counsel

In times of adversity and tribulation, there are many who become so dejected, so depressed that their troubled souls are incapable of responding to consolation and counsel, so miserable that they sink from bad to worse. Thus, my son John, practitioner of medicine and inventor of tales, I have through my modest skill at writing, provided you with something which will enable you, God willing, to understand not only physical disorders but to provide as well consolation and counsel for the distressed and the immature. You should regard the images in this text with care and you should consider the authorities in this text with close attention and enthusiasm. Then, by the grace of God, you will arrive at an understanding of these things without any difficulty. Look at this picture.

Chapter 1: The example of Melibee

1.1 Uns jouvenceaulx appellez Mellibee, puissans et riches, ot une femme appellee Prudence de laquelle il ot une fille. Advint un jour qu'il s'ala esbatre et jouer et laissa en un lieu sa femme et sa fille et les portes closes. Trois de ses anciens ennemis appuyerent eschielles aus murs de sa maison et par les fenestres entrerent dedens et batirent sa femme forment et navrerent sa fille de cinq playes en cinq lieux de son corps, c'est assavoir, es piez, es oreilles, ou neiz, en la bouche, et es mains, et la laisserent presque morte. Puis s'en alerent. (967–72)

1.2 Quant Mellibee fut retournez a son hostel et vit cest meschief, si commenca forment a plaindre, a plorer, et soy batre en maniere de forsené et sa robe dessirer. (973)

1.3 Lors Prudence sa femme le prist a admonnester qu'il se souffrist; et il tousjours plus fort crioit. Adonques elle s'appensa de la sentence Ovide ou *Livre des remedes d'amours* qui dit que celui est fol qui s'efforce d'empescher la mere de plorer en la mort de son enfant jusques a tant qu'elle se soit bien remplie de larmes et saoulee de plorer; lors est il temps de la conforter et d'attremper sa doulour par doulces paroles. (974–8)

Chapter 2: On consolation

2.1 Pour ce, Prudence se souffri un pou, et quant elle vit son temps, si lui dist ainsi: "Sire, pourquoy vous faites vouus sembler un fol? Il n'appartient point a sage homme de mener si grant duel. (979–81)

1.1   **un lieu** se maison B7; son hostel P13. **forment** *om* P12. **oreilles . . . mains** mains es oreilles ou nes et en la bouche P13.

1.2   **a son** en son B7 P12 P24. **et soy batre** *om* P13.

1.3   **et il** mais cilz B7. **elle** Prudence B7 L4 P12 P13 P24. **des remedes** de remede B7 P12 P13. **s'efforce d'empescher** empesche B7.

1.1 It has frequently been noted that the daughter's name (967) and the phrase *into the feeldes* (968) appear in neither the Latin nor the French. The reading of the phrase *into the feeldes* is however open to question. The rhymed Dutch translation of this work, composed in 1342 and based on the Latin text, says that Melibee, after he left his home, rode into the fields (*riden opten velde*). The French text indicates that he went out to play.

As different as these translations may be, the Dutch and French translators are both responding to the Latin text, the phrase which indicates that once Melibee left his home, *ivit spatiatum*. While a literal translation of *ivit spatiatum* might simply read *he went for a walk*, *spatiatum* carries with it hints of his destination, *spatium*, a public square, a promenade, a playing field, even a race course.

For *appuyerent* Chaucer offers *han it espyed* (970) which Severs thought might have been drawn from MSS like P12 and P13 which read *vindrent et appuyerent* or from some variety of scribal corruption. Severs also thought that *piez* was an erroneous reading which Chaucer followed (972). Though the Latin indicates that the true reading is *yeux*, the word is found in only one French manuscript, B7. Another possibility is that Chaucer and the French scribes conflated the list of the daughter's wounds with the list of the wounds of the crucified Christ, q.v. note 37.19.

2.1 Prudence's response paraphrases a longer citation from *Pamphilius de amore* in the Latin.

2.2 Vostre fille eschappera se Dieu plaist; et se elle estoit ores morte, vous ne vous devez pas destruire pour elle. Car [Senecques] dit que li sages ne doit prendre grant desconfort de la mort de ses enfans, ains doit souffrir leur mort aussi legierement comme il attend la sienne propre. (982–5)

2.3 *I would prefer that you abandon grief rather than have grief abandon you. Stop your grieving as soon as possible since it is impossible to keep it up for a long time even if you want to."*

2.4 Mellibee respondi: "Cui est cil qui se pourroit tenir de plorer en si grant cause de douleur? Nostre Seigneur Jhesu Crist (fol. 56v) mesmes ploura de la mort du ladre, son amy." (986–7)

2.5 "Certes," dist Prudence, "plour attrempee n'est pas deffendue a cellui qui est tristes, mais lui est ottroyee. Car, selon ce que dit Saint Pol l'Appostre en *L'epistre aux Rommains*: On doit mener joye avec ceulz qui joye mainnent, et doit on mener plour et douulour avec ceulz qui l'ont. (988–9)

2.6 *As Cicero said: The nature of a well-ordered mind is to rejoice when things are good and express pain when they are not, and thus constant weeping and tears are inappropriate.*

2.7 Mais ja soit ce que plourer attrempeement soit ottroyez, toutevoye plourer desmesureement est deffendu. Et pour ce l'on doit garder le mesure que Senecques met. 'Quant tu auras,' dist il, 'perdu ton amy, ton oeil ne soit ne secs ne moistes; car ja soit ce que la lerme viengne a l'ueil, elle n'en doit pas yssir; car quant tu auras perdu ton ami, efforce toy de un autre recouvrer; car il te vault mieux un autre ami recouvrer que l'ami perdu plorer.' (990–3)

2.8 Se tu veulz vivre sagement, oste tristesse de ton cuer. Car selon ce que dit Jhesu Syrac: Le cuer lyé et joyeux maintient la personne en la fleur de son aage, mais l'esperist triste li fait secher les os. Et dit oultre que tristesse occist moult de gens. (994–6)

2.9 Et Salemons dit que tout aussi comme la taingne ou les artuisons nuit a la robe et les vermoissiaulx ou bois, tout aussi greve tristesse au cuer. (997)

2.10 *And again: No harm can come to the just man, but the wicked have their fill of troubles.*

2.11 *And as Seneca said in his letters: Nothing is more foolish than to have a reputation for sadness and tears and this never happens to the wise man who, no matter what faces him, stands tall.*

2.2 **pour elle** pour luy B7 P12 P24; pour ce P13. **Car** *om* L4. **Senecques** B7 L4 P12 P24; *om* P13; li sages P7. **li sages** saiges hons P13.
2.4 **ladre** *corr marg* lazare P24.
2.5 **tristes** triste entre les tristes L4; triste ou entre les tristes P12; triste en cuer ou entre les tristes P13. **mener plour ... l'ont** plourer avec ceulx qui pleurent B7 L4 P12 P24.
2.7 **secs** trop sec P12. **moistes** trop moistes P12 P13 P24. **autre recouver** autre amy recouver L4 P13.
2.8 **veulz** *add* doncques B7 L4 P12 P13 P24. **les os** ses os P24. **oultre** ainsi P12 P13.

2.8 These two citations appear in the Latin but the French inverts the order in the Latin.

2.12 Et pour ce nous nous devons porter paciemment en la perte de noz enfans et de noz autres biens temporelz, ainsi comme Job, lequel quant il ot perdu ses enfans et toute sa substance et ot soustenu moult de tribulations, il dist: Nostre Seigneur le m'a donné, Nostre Seigneur le m'a toulu, ainsi comme il l'a voulu faire, il l'a fait. Benoist soit le nom de lui! (998–1000)

2.13 *Therefore we should not complain about our daughter and whatever else has been lost, since what has happened cannot be changed. We should be happy for what we have rather than sad about what we have lost. Someone once consoled the father of a dead child by saying: Do not cry when a good child has been lost; be happy that you bore such offspring as that.*

2.14 *And Seneca said: Nothing becomes offensive so quickly as grief. When that grief is recent, it attracts consolation, but when it becomes chronic, it attracts ridicule and rightly so, since it is either pretentious or foolish.*

2.15 *You need to drive away the sorrows of the world in the light of the truth expressed by Saint Paul in his second letter to the Corinthians: Worldly sorrow leads to death, but that which is Godly leads to repentance and good health.*

2.16 *And therefore you should push these negative events aside and you need to busy yourself night and day so that eventually your sorrow will turn to joy, as the Lord said to the Evangelist.*

2.17 *Solomon said: Where there is mourning, there is the heart of the wise man; where there is exuberance, there the heart of the fool.*

2.18 *And again: Better to go to the house of mourning than to go to the house of mirth."*

2.19 Mellibee respondi a Prudence sa femme ainsi: "Toutes les choses que tu dis sont vrayes et profitables, mais mon cuer est si troublé que je ne scey que je doye faire." (1001)

2.20 Lors Prudence lui dist, "Appelle tous tes loyaulx amis, affins, et parens, et leur demande conseil de ceste chose, et te gouverne selon le conseil qu'il te donront. Car Salemon dit: Tous tes faiz par conseil feras; ainsi ne t'en repentiras." (1002–3)

2.21 Adonques Mellibee appella moult de gens, c'est assavoir, cysurgiens, phisiciens, vieillars et jeunes, et aucuns de ses anciens ennemis qui estoient

2.12 **tribulations** *add* en son corps B7 L4 P12 P13 P24. **l'a voulu** a voulu B7 L4 P12 P13 P24. **lui** nostre seigneur B7 L4 P12 P24.
2.20 **parens** tes parens B7 P12 P24. **le conseil** leur conseil P12 P24. **Car** *om* L4.
2.21 **et retournez** *om* P13. **et aucuns . . . pour amour** B7 L4 P12 P13 P24; *om* P7. **losengiers** *add* et de flateurs et aussi P13.

2.12 Renaud omits from the Latin a final catch phrase from Psalms 11:22.
2.20 Chaucer does not include *parents* among the list of persons Prudence advises Melibee to consult. If other elements in this text have been altered to accommodate the court of Richard II, this may be among them and might help date Chaucer's translation. Richard's father, the Black Prince, died in 1376 and his mother, Joan of Kent, died on 8 August 1385. Renaud's phrase, *affins et parens*, translates the Latin *agnatos quoque et cognatos*, and therefore it might be argued that *parens* means "ancestors," and that Chaucer translates *affins et parens* with a single word: *lynage*. However, as the MED attests, the primary meaning of ME *parents* is Modern English *parents*. The primary meaning of ME *parents* mirrors contemporary French usage and the use of the word in law French.

reconsiliez par semblance et retournez en sa grace et amour, [et aucuns de ses voisins qui luy portoient reverence plus pour doubtance que pour amour]; et avec ce vindrent moult de losengiers et moult de sages clers et bons advocaz. Quant ilz furent ensemble, il leur recompta et monstra bien par la maniere de son parler qu'il estoit moult courrociez et que il avoit moult grant desir de soy vengier tantost et de faire guerre incontinent; toutevoye il demanda sur ce leur conseil. (1004–10)

2.22 Lors un cysurgien, du conseil des autres, se leva et dist: "Sire, il appartient a cysurgien que il porte a un chascun proffit et a (fol. 57r) nul dommage, dont il advient aucune foiz que, quant deux hommes par malice se navrent ensemble, un mesme cysurgien garist l'un et l'autre. Et pour ce il n'appartient a nous de norrir guerre ne supporter partie. Mais a ta fille garir, ja soit ce qu'elle soit navree malement, nous mettrons toute nostre cure de jour et de nuit; et a l'aide de Nostre Seigneur nous la te rendrons toute sainne." (1011–15)

2.23 Presque en ceste maniere respondirent les phisiciens et adjousterent que tout aussi comme selon l'art de medecine les maladies se doivent garir par contraire, aussi doit on garir guerre par vengence. (1016–17)

2.24 Les voisins jadix ennemis qui en grace estoient retourné, les voisins reconsiliez par semblance, les losengiers firent semblant de plorer et commencerent le fait moult [agrever] en loant moult Mellibee de puissance, d'avoir, et d'amis, en vituperant la puissance de ses adversaires, et dirent que tout oultre il se devoit [tantost vengier] et incontinent commencer la guerre. (1018–20)

2.25 Adonque un sage advocat, de la voulenté des autres, se leva et dist, "Beaulx seigneurs, la besoingne pourquoy nous sommes yci assemblez est moult haute et pesant pour raison de l'injure et du malefice qui est moult grans, et pour raison des grans maulx qui s'en pevent ensuivre ou temps advenir, et pour raison des richesses et de la puissance des parties, pour lesquelles choses il seroit grant peril errer en ceste besoingne. (1021–5)

2.21 **recompta** raconta le cas L4 P12 P13; raconta le fait et le cas P24.
2.22 **des . . . leva** se leva du consentement de tous les autres P13. **sire** *add* dist il L4 P12 P24. **Nostre Seigneur** dieu L4.
2.24 **jadix** envieux B7 L4 P12 P13. **losengiers** *add* et flateurs P13. **agrever** L4 P12 P13 P24; a agrever B7; agreve P7. **tantost vengier** B7 L4 P12 P13 P24; *om* P7.
2.25 **grant** moult grans B7.

2.23 The French abbreviates this advice from the physicians and Chaucer's translation of it has in turn bedeviled editors from William Caxton to John Hurt Fisher. This advice involves Latin wordplay which is discussed at some length by Prudence much later in the text (see 31.2–31.4). The Latin reads: *Dicimus quia, sicut per physicam contraria contrariis curantur, ita et in guerra atque vindicta et in aliis rebus contraria contrariis curari consueverunt.* The ambiguous word, what Prudence later calls *verbum dubium*, is *contraria*. Though the physicians use *contrarium* in the sense of *opposite* or *alternative* and appear to be linking the practice of homeopathic medicine with peacemaking, Melibee believes that they are advising him to be *contrary* or *antagonistic* to his enemies, a point the Latin texts in question make quite clear. Renaud attempted to replicate this ambiguity with the phrase *garir guerre par vengeance*. The homophones (*garir* and *guerre*) and the lexical ambiguity of *par* seem calculated to catch the multiple meanings of *contraria contrariis curari consueverunt*. Chaucer seems to have appreciated this; his own rendering, *warisshe werre by vengeaunce* (1016), duplicates the repetition of the homophones in the French and is only confusing if one assumes its meaning is transparent. *Warisshe* may mean *cure*, but it also sounds like several Middle English verbs which suggest aggressive behavior: *warien* and *werreyen*.

2.26 Pour ce, des maintenant nous te conseillons, Mellibee, que tu sur toutes choses ayes diligence de garder ta personne en tele maniere qu'il ne te faille ne espies ne gaites pour toy garder. Aprés, tu mettras en ta maison bonnes garnisons et fors pour toy et ta maison deffendre. (1026–7)

2.27 Mais de mouvoir guerre ou de toy venger tantost, nous n'en povons pas bien juger en si pou de temps lequel vault mieux. Si demandons espace d'avoir deliberation, car on dit communément: Qui tost juge tost se repent. (1028–30)

2.28 *It is inappropriate to rush to judgment since anything done in haste is ill-advised.*

2.29 *Rash judgments are criminal.*

2.30 *And such judgments are soon regretted.*

2.31 Et dit on aussi que le juges est tres bons qui tost entend et tart juge. (1031)

2.32 Car ja soit ce que toute demeure soit ennuyeuse, toutevoie elle ne fait pas a reprendre en jugement et en vengence quant elle est souffisant et raisonnable. (1032)

2.33 *It is written: Delay is annoying but it leads to wisdom.*

2.34 *Delay is best used for deliberation.*

2.35 *And it is commonly said that a slow judge is better than a speedy trial.*

2.36 Et ce nous monstre par exemple Nostre Seigneur Jhesu [Crist] quant la femme qui estoit prinse en avoultire lui fut admenee pour juger que l'on en devoit faire; car ja soit ce qu'il secust bien qu'il y devoit respondre, toutevoye il ne respondi pas tantost, mais va avoir deliberation et escript deux foiz en terre. Pour ces raisons nous demandons deliberation; laquelle eue, nous te conseillerons, a l'aide de Dieu, chose qui sera a ton profit." (1033–4)

2.37 Lors les jeunes gens et la plus grant partie de tous les autres escharnirent cest sage, et firent grant bruit, et dirent que tout aussi comme l'on (fol. 57v) doit batre le fer tant comme il est chaut, aussi l'on doit venger l'injure tant comme elle est fresche, et escrierent a haute voix, "Guerre! Guerre!" (1035–6)

2.38 Adonques se leva un des anciens, et estendit la main, et commanda que l'on feist scilence, et dist, "Moult de gens crient 'Guerre!' haultement qui ne scevent que guerre se monte. Guerre en son commencement est une chose si large et a si grant entree que un chascun y puet entrer et la puet trouver legierement, mais a tres grant pene puet on savoir a quel fin on en puet venir. Car quant la guerre commence, moult de gens ne sont encores nez qui pour cause de la guerre morront jeunes, ou en vivront en doulour et en misere, et

---

2.27 **deliberation** *add* pour nous en advisier L4.
2.32 **ne fait pas** nest pas B7 P13; nest mie L4. **et en** ne en B7 P12 P24.
2.36 **Crist** B7 L4 P12 P13 P24; crit P7. **admenee** presentee P13. **va** voult B7 L4 P12 P13 P24.
2.37 **escharnirent** se leverent et huerent B7 P13. **bruit** noise et grant bruit B7.
2.38 **Moult de gens** il y a moult de gens qui P13; *add* sont qui L4. **haultement** guerre B7 P12 P24. **est une . . . entree** a si grant entree et si large B7.

2.27 As Skeat once pointed out, the final commonplace (1030) combines elements of the three Latin commonplaces which follow (2.28–2.30).
2.37 The French abbreviates the Latin description of the actions of the young men.

fineront leur vie en misere et en chetiveté. Et pour ce, avant que l'en mueve guerre, on doit avoir grant conseil et deliberation." (1037–42)

2.39 Quant ycellui ancien cuida confermer son dit par raison, ilz se leverent presque touz contre lui et intrerompirent son dit souvent et lui dirent qu'il abregeast ses paroles, car la narration de cellui qui presche a ceulz qui ne le veulent oir est ennuyeuse narration. (1043–4)

2.40 [Et Jhesu Syrac dit que musique em plour est ennuyeuse narracion]: c'est a dire que autant vault parler a cellui a cui il ennuye comme chanter devant celui qui plore. Quant icellui sage ancien vit qu'il ne pourroit avoir audience, [si s'assist car] Salemon dit: La ou tu ne pourras avoir audience, ne t'efforce point de parler. (1045–7)

2.41 *When he saw that his audience would only insult him and he realized that it would not respond decently to what it heard, the old man said this, "Ill-advised fools are unable to take advice and thus, naturally, the advice to change is lost on the thoughtless."*

2.42 Si dist, "Je voy bien maintenant que le proverbe commun est vray: Lors faut le bon conseil quant le grant besoing est." Et ce dit, il s'assist comme tout honteux. (1048)

2.43 Encor avoir ou conseil Mellibee [moult de gens qui lui conseilloient] autre chose en l'oreille et autre chose en appert. (1049)

2.44 Mellibee, quant il ot oÿ tout son conseil, il regarda que la tres plus grant partie s'accordoit que l'on feist guerre, [si] s'arresta a leur sentence et la conferma. (1050)

2.45 Lors Dame Prudence, quant elle vit son mary qui s'appareilloit de soy venger et de faire guerre, si lui vient au devant et lui dist moult doulcement, "Sire, je vous pry que vous ne vous hastez et que vous pour tous dons me donnez espace. (1051–2)

2.38 **que l'en ... guerre** qu'elle commence P24. **deliberation** grant deliberation B7 L4 P12 P13 P24.

2.39 **raison** raisons P12.

2.40 **Et Jhesu ... narration** B7 L4 P12; *om* P7. **a cellui** devant cellui B7 L4 P12 P13 P24. **si ... car** P12 P13; et P7; si sasist et L4; et P7; *om* P24.

2.42 **grant** plus grant B7 L4.

2.43 **moult ... conseilloient** B7 L4 P24; qui lui conseilloient moult de gens P7 P12 P13. **l'oreille** *add* et en secret P13.

2.44 **si** B7 L4 P12 P24; il P7 P13. **sentence** conseil P13.

2.45 **Sire** *add* dist elle B7 L4 P12 P24.

2.40 These two citations are reversed in the Latin.

2.42 Chaucer works the final clause about the old man's discomfort, present in both the French and the Latin, into line 1045.

2.44 Though P7 reads *s'accordoit,* all other manuscripts read *s'accordoit et conseilloit* and Severs took this as a sign that P7 came closest to the French text Chaucer used. An alternative explanation might take into consideration the political and rhetorical circumstances which may have shaped Chaucer's text. If this text were pitched towards the court of Richard II, the sense that that court was thoroughly committed to war might have been regarded as offensive.

2.45 Though somewhat obscured by Chaucer's translation, Prudence opens this speech by echoing Ovid, *Remedia Amoris*, 277, as Sundby indicated.

2.46 Car Pierre Alphons dit: Qui te fera bien ou mal, ne te haste pas du rendre, car ainsi plus long temps te attendra ton amy et plus long temps te doubtera ton ennemi. (1053)

2.47 *So, stop your anger, forget your rage and do not imitate the wicked. It should be clear, my lord, that you should take my advice.*"

Chapter 3: The problems with women

3.1 Mellibee respondit a Prudence sa femme: "Je ne propose point user de ton conseil pour moult de raisons: premierement, car un chascun me tendroit pour fol se je par ton conseil et consentement changeoye ce qui est ordonné par tant de bonnes gens. (1055–6)

3.2 Aprés, car toutes femmes sont mauvaises, et nesune n'est bonne, selon le dit de Salemon: 'De mil hommes,' ce dit il, 'ay trouvé un preudomme, mais (fol. 58r) de toutes les femmes je n'en ay trouvé une bonne.' (1057)

3.3 Aprés, se je me gouvernoye par ton conseil, il sembleroit que je te donasse sur moy seignorie, laquelle chose ne doit pas estre, car Jhesu Sirac dit: Se la femme a la seignorie elle est contraire a son mary. (1058–9)

3.4 Et Salemon dit: A ton fil, a ta femme, a ton frere, a ton amy ne donne puissance sur toy en toute ta vie, car il te vault mieux que tes enfans te requierent ce que mestier leur sera que toy regarder es mains de tes enfans. (1060)

3.5 Aprés, se je vouloye user de ton conseil, il convendroit aucune foiz que le conseil fust secret et celé jusques a tant qu'il fust temps du reveller; et ce ne se porroit faire, car il est escript: La genglerie des femmes ne puet riens celer fors ce qu'elle ne scet. (1061–2)

3.6 [Aprés], le philosophe dit: En mauvais conseil les femmes vainquent les hommes. Pour ces raisons je ne doy point user de ton conseil." (1063)

3.1   **user** ouvrer ne user P24.

3.5   **convendroit** me convendroit P24. **faire** estre L4.

3.6   **Aprés** B7 L4 P12 P13 P24; *om* P7.

2.46 As Severs noted, Chaucer concludes the remarks of Prudence with two proverbs that appear in neither the French nor the Latin (line 1054); Severs compared them to those in *Troilus and Criseyde* 1:956 and the *Pardoner's Tale* 1003; however, versions of these proverbs about hasty thinking also appear at two points in the Latin text (see 2.29–2.34 and 14.2–14.10). Furthermore, since they do not appear in Renaud, Chaucer's citation of them might indicate that he was not unfamiliar with the Latin text.

3.5 The citation which concludes this passage (1062), present in the French and Latin, does not appear in Chaucer but is supplied by most editors since Prudence later responds to it.

3.6 This citation, also present in the French and Latin, is not in *Melibee* but is supplied from the French by most editors for the same reason as in 3.5 above. That Chaucer might have had rhetorical reasons for downplaying Melibee's antifeminism is perhaps worthy of consideration.

Chapter 4: In defense of women

4.1 Aprés ce que Dame Prudence ot oÿ debonnairement et en grant patience toutes les choses que son mary voult avant traire, si demanda licence de parler et puis dist: "Sire, a la premiere raison que vous m'avez avant mise puet on respondre legierement, car je dy qu'il n'est pas folie de changer son conseil quant la chose se change ou quant elle appert autrement que devant aprés. Et dy encores que se tu avoies promis et juré de faire ton emprinse, et tu la laissoyes de faire par juste cause, l'on ne devroit pas dire que tu feusses mensongier ne parjure, car il est escript: Li sages ne ment mie quant il mue son propox en mieux. Et ja soit ce que ton emprise soit establie et ordonnee par grant multitude de gens, pour ce ne la convient pas adcomplir, car la verité des choses et les profiz sont mieux trouvez par pou de gens [sages et parlans par raison] que par grant multitude, ou chascun brait et crie a sa voulenté, et tele multitude de gens n'est pas honneste. (1064–9)

4.2 A la seconde raison, quant vous dittes que toutes femmes sont mauvaises et n'en est nulle bonne, sauve vostre reverence, vous parlez trop generaulment quant vous desprisez ainsi toutes, car il est escript: Qui tout desprise a tout desplait. Et Senecque dit que cellui qui veult acquerre sapience ne doit nul despriser, mais ce qu'il scet il le doit enseignier senz presumption, et ce qu'il ne scet il ne doit pas avoir honte de demander a mendre de lui. (1070–2)

4.3 Et que moult de femmes soient bonnes l'on le puet prouver legierement: premierement, car Nostre Seigneur ne fust onques daingnié descendre en femme se elles fussent toutes mauvaises ainsi comme tu le dis. Aprés, pour la bonte des femmes, Nostre Seigneur Jhesu Crist, quant il resuscita de mort a vie, il apparut premier a femme que a homme, car il apparut premier a Marie Magdelaine (fol. 58v) que aus appostres. (1073–5)

4.4 Et quant Salemon dit que de toutes femmes il n'en a trouvé une bonne, [pour ce ne s'ensuist pas que aucune ne soit bonne], car ja soit ce que il ne l'ait trouvee, moult des autres en ont bien trouvé pluseurs bonnes et loyaulx; ou, par adventure, quant Salemon dit qu'il n'a point trouvé de bonne femme, il entend de la bonté souverainne, de laquelle nul n'est bon fors Dieu seulement, selon ce qu'il mesmes le dit en l'Euvangille, car nulle creature n'est tant bonne a cui ne faille aucune chose senz comparoison a la perfection de son creatour. (1076–80)

4.5 La tierce chose est quant tu dis se tu te gouvernoyes par mon conseil il sembleroit que tu me donasses par dessus toy seignorie. Sauve ta grace, il n'est

4.1 **puis dist** dist ainsi P13. **Sire** add dist elle B7 L4 P12 P13. **elle** la chose B7 L4 P13 P24. **Aprés** om B7 L4. **les profiz** le prouffit B7 L4 P12 P24. **sages . . . raison** B7 L4 P12 P13 P24; om P7. **multitude²** add de gens B7 L4 P12 P13 P24. **de gens n'est** n'est B7 L4 P12.
4.2 **reverence** grace B7. **vous parlez . . . quant** om P24.
4.3 **Seigneur** add Jhesu Crist P13. **a femme . . . premier** om L4 P12.
4.4 **pour ce . . . bonne** B7 L4 P12 P13 P24; om P7. **trouvee** add bonnes L4 P13; add nullez bonnez B7. **senz comparoison** om B7. **son dieu** son L4.
4.5 **chose** raison B7 L4 P13.

pas ainsi; car selon ce, nul ne prendroit conseil fors a celui a cui il vouldroit sur soy puissance, et ce n'est pas voir, car celui qui demande conseil a puissance et franche voulenté de faire ce que on lui conseille ou de laisser. (1081–3)

4.6 Quant a la quarte raison, ou tu dis que la janglerie des femmes ne puet celer fors ce qu'elle ne scet, ceste parole doit estre entendue d'aucunes tres mauvaises femmes genglerresses ou parlerresses desquelles on dit: Trois choses sont qui gettent l'omme hors de sa maison: la fumiere, la goutiere, et la mauvaise femme. Et de telle femme parle Salemon quant il dit: Il vauldroit mieux habiter en terre deserte que avec femme rioteuse et courrouceuse. Or scez tu bien que tu ne m'as pas trouvee telle, ains as souvent esprouvé ma grant silence et ma grant souffrance et comment j'ay gardees les choses que l'on doit garder et tenir secretes. (1084–9)

4.7 Quant a la quinte raison, ou tu dis qu'en mauvais conseil les femmes vainquent les hommes, ceste raison n'a point cy son lieu; car tu ne demandes pas conseil de mal faire, et se tu vouloies ouvrer de mauvais conseil et mal faire, et ta femme t'en retrait et t'en vainquist, ce ne seroit pas a reprendre, mais a loer. Et ainsi doit on entendre le dit du prophete: En mauvais conseil vainquent les femmes les hommes. (1090–4)

4.8 Car aucune foiz quant les hommes veulent ouvrer de mauvais conseil, les femmes les en retraient et les vainquent.

4.9 *As Saint Paul said in his letter to the Romans: Do not let yourself be overcome by evil; rather, overcome evil with good.*

4.10 *Were you to claim that men who want good advice are defeated by women who advise them badly, the response would be that such men can weigh the advice they get and that they can reject bad counsel and choose what is good.*

4.11 *As Paul said towards the end of his first letter to the Thessalonians: Test everything and keep only what is good. You might say that this injunction is only relevant when wicked women tender advice to foolish men, but that is certainly not the case here.*

Chapter 5: In praise of women

5.1 Et quant vous blasmez tant les femmes et leur conseil, je vous monstre par moult de raisons que moult de femmes ont esté bonnes, et sont, et leur conseil bon et profitable. (1095)

5.2 Premierement, car l'on a acoustumé de dire: Conseil de femme, ou il est tres cher, ou il est tres vil. (1096)

4.6   **trois ... qui** que troys choses P13. **maison** *add* cest assavoir P13 P24.
4.7   **prophete** philosophe B7 L4.
5.1   **tant** toutes P13. **monstre** monstreray P13. **leur conseil**[2] leurs conseilz P13.
5.2   **conseil** que conseil B7 L4. **il est** *om* B7.

4.8 Chaucer omits this idea, present in the French and the Latin.

5.3 *I think that* tres cher *means most precious and is not a gratuitous phrase. As was said of those who are close to the Lord: Lord, nothing is more valuable than your friends.*

5.4 Car ja soit ce que moult de femmes soient tres mauvaises et leur conseil tres vil, toutevoye l'on en trouve assez de bonnes et qui tres bon conseil et tres cher ont donné. (1097)

5.5 Jacob, par le bon conseil de Rebeque, sa mere, gaingna (fol. 59r) la beneïçon Ysaac, son pere, et la seignorie sur tous ses freres. (1098)

5.6 Judith, par son bon conseil, delivra la cité de Buthulie, ou elle demouroit, des mains Oloferne, qui l'avoit assigee et la vouloit destruire. (1099)

5.7 Abigal delivra Nabal, son mary, de David le Roy, qui le vouloit occirre, et l'appaisa par son sens et par son conseil. (1100)

5.8 Hester, par son bon conseil, esleva moult son pueple ou royaume de Assuere le Roy. Et ainsi puet on dire de moult d'autres. (1101–2)

5.9 Aprés, quant Nostre Seigneur ot creé Adam, le premier homme, il dist: Il n'est pas bon estre l'omme tout seul; faisons lui adjutoire semblable a lui. S'elles donques n'estoient bonnes et leurs conseilz bons, Nostre Seigneur ne les eust pas appellees a l'omme en adjutoire, mais en dommage et en nuisement. (1103–6)

5.10 Aprés, un maistre fait deux vers es quelz il demande et respont et dit ainsi: Quele chose vault mieux que l'or? Jaspe. Quele chose vault plus que jaspe? Sens. Quele chose vault mieux que sens? Femme. Quelle chose vault mieux que femme? Riens. (1107–8)

5.11 *A fourth reason is voiced by Seneca who commended all caring wives when he said: Nothing is better than a kind wife and nothing is more intolerable than a wife who is a nuisance. The wise woman would lay her life on the line for the*

5.4   **trouve assez** a asses trouve B7 L4 P13.
5.7   **l'appaisa** appaisa le roy P24. **conseil** bon conseil B7 L4 P13.
5.8   **d'autres** add femmez B7.
5.9   **a . . . adjutoire** adjutoires de l'omme L4 P12 P13; ayde del homme B7. **en . . . nuisement** domacges et nuisement P12.

5.9 The account of the creation of Eve is somewhat fuller in the Latin. To *adjutoire* all French manuscripts save P7 add with slight variations *car elles ne fussent pas adjutoire a homme* which Chaucer does not translate. Severs believed that this variant was a warrant for the use of P7 as his base text.

5.10 *The Riverside Chaucer* compares this citation with a distich recorded in Hans Walther, *Proverbia Sententiaeque Latinatis Medii Aevi* (Gottingen, 1963–69), item 25064. The exact parallel is actually item 25072. Citations from Walther's work do not always indicate what sources Albertano might have used, but I have taken note of the proverbs Walther records when the source of one of Albertano's citations is not indicated by Sundby or *The Riverside Chaucer*. In this particular case, the same distich also appears in Raimond de Béziers, *Liber Kalilae et Dimnae*, in Leopold Hervieux, ed., *Les Fabulistes Latins* (Paris, 1896–1899), vol. 5, p. 622. Though Raimond de Béziers is never mentioned in accounts of the transmission of Albertano's work, his *Liber Kalilae et Dimnae* contains extensive borrowings from the *Liber consolationis et consilii* and Albertano's other treatises, an indication of the wide circulation of Albertano's work in Paris at the beginning of the fourteenth century.

5.11 This citation, attributed to Seneca, draws from the opening clausula of "The Fable of Admetus and Alcestis" in Fulgentius, *The Mythologies*, book 1, chap. 22; see Leslie George Whitbread, *Fulgentius the Mythographer* (Ohio State University Press, 1971), p. 62.

sake of her husband; the wicked woman thinks her own life of much more conse-
quence than the death of her husband.

5.12 A fifth argument in support of women was offered by Cato when he said:
Remember to tolerate what your wife says if she speaks honestly.

5.13 Furthermore, you should know that a good wife is a good companion.

5.14 It is widely said that a good wife faithfully looks after a good home.

5.15 Now when a good woman does the right thing and proves obedient to her
husband, he is the only one who is drawn to her. She will not only offer him
advice but also appear to control him.

5.16 As a wise man said: The chaste wife rules her obedient husband and men
who can only praise themselves will soon find someone to make fun of them.

5.17 Par ces raisons et par moult d'autres puez tu veoir que moult de femmes
sont bonnes et leur conseil bon et proffitable. Se tu donques maintenant veulz
croire mon conseil, je te rendray ta fille toute sainne et feray tant que tu auras
honeur en cest fait." (1109–11)

5.18 Quant Mellibee ot oÿ parler Prudence, si dist: "Je voy bien que la parole
Salemon est vraye, qui dit: Bresches de miel sont paroles bien ordenees, car
elles donnent doulceur a l'ame et senté au corps; car par tes paroles tres douces
et que j'ay esprouvé ta grant sapience et ta grant loyaulté, je me vueil du tout
gouverner par ton conseil." (1112–14)

5.19 To which she said, "To live in a prudent way, you will have to possess
prudence."

5.20 Melibee responded, "I possess prudence because I possess you and that
after all is your name."

5.21 Then she said, "It is not that I am Prudence but that my words are
prudent."

5.22 To which he responded, "Then tell me what prudence is and what its quali-
ties are, the effects of prudence and how to become prudent."

Chapter 6: On prudence

6.1 She said to him, "Prudence is the ability to distinguish between good and
evil, to choose what is right and avoid what is wrong.

6.2 Prudence overcomes anything with ease and without letting up. As
Cassiodorus said: Prudence has overcome everything without effort and
without flagging.

5.18 **Prudence** *add* sa femme P13. **bresches ... ordenees** que paroles ordonnees sont breches de miel
P13. **et que** et aussi pour ce que P24; et car P13.

6.1 Sundby was unaware that this brief chapter and its opening citation from Cicero's *De inventione* is
drawn from William of Conches, *Moralium dogma philosophorum*, ed. John Holmberg (Uppsala, 1929),
p. 8.

Chapter 7: On the varieties of prudence

7.1 *There are six aspects of prudence: reason, understanding, foresight, circumspection, caution, and calm.*
7.2 *Reason determines what is right and what is wrong.*
7.3 *Indeed reason follows Nature, that is to say, reason imitates Nature.*
7.4 *It can be defined as follows: Reason is the ability to distinguish between good and evil, between what is licit and what is illicit, between what is honest and what is dishonest and, then to do what is right and avoid what is wrong. This is what is meant by the power of reason, that is the science of inquiry.*
7.5 *Understanding is the ability to explore the truth.*
7.6 *Foresight is the ability to observe how the present influences events in the future.*
7.7 *Circumspection, the ability to be wary of harmful vices.*
7.8 *Caution, the ability to tell virtues from vices and to prefer the idea of virtue.*
7.9 *Calm, the virtue of exhibiting control.*

Chapter 8: The effects of prudence

8.1 *Doubtless the most valuable effect of prudence is happiness. Not only are those who are prudent content, but prudence alone can lay the foundation for a happy life. As Seneca says in his letters: The prudent person is restrained, the restrained person is unwavering, the unwavering person is not anxious, the person who is not anxious is free of sadness, and the person who is free of sadness is happy. The prudent man is thus happy and prudence leads to a happy life.*
8.2 *The man who is prudent has advantages because he is someone who is happy and sees what lies ahead, steady and temperate, undisturbed and without sorrow, and he also has all the advantages which derive from the various types of prudence, a number of things which I will not specify here.*

Chapter 9: How to cultivate prudence

9.1 *Prudence and all forms of wisdom can be cultivated through a familiarity with worthwhile learning, the instruction of a good teacher and persistent study.*
9.2 *I would say that well-trained teachers are like excellent physicians or craftsmen, whether masters or apprentices, and that you would choose from among the most experienced artists or professionals and ask for their advice or help if there were work to be done. Now just as a good physician will perform*

7.1 This chapter is also drawn from the *Moralium dogma philosophorum*, ed. Holmberg, pp. 9–11.

satisfactorily as the result of his good training, so a bad one, poorly trained, will make mistakes and harm others. While a good doctor can heal the sick with medicine, a bad doctor can make invalids incurable with medicine, and, after much work and a great deal of expense, his inexperience can kill many of them. And so it goes with bad teachers, craftsmen and laborers whose inexperience and lack of talent lays waste to much good work, a great deal of effort and a considerable amount of money. It would be decent of such persons to destroy their work once they have completed it and to offer it for free and without charge.

9.3 Now, since, as I have said, prudence and all forms of wisdom can be learned through persistent study, what learning is and why it is both valuable and indispensable should be examined.

Chapter 10: On learning and scholarship and the value and importance of scholars

10.1 Study is the devotion of intellectual power to anything which is possessed of high purpose.

10.2 The primary value of study is learning, as I said above, and much has been written about learning in the book De forma vitae *which I have addressed to your brother Vincent.*

10.3 Second, study is valuable because it turns our natural inclinations towards the deepest forms of reflection, towards high-minded practices, and towards discipline. Discipline overcomes natural inclinations and native tendencies and actual practice is superior to the precepts of all teachers.

10.4 Third, it is useful because it encourages hard work as well as careful thought; as Cato said: Once you have learned something, work at it in a disciplined way. As care is to thought, discipline is to work.

10.5 Work therefore is as valuable as study because it allows life to be shaped as though it were an art. As this verse puts it: Art gives and work takes; if you can combines work with the arts, the difficulties that attend the art of living will be eased.

10.6 Seneca said: In a struggle and in all the arts, nothing is more productive than hard work.

10.7 And Pamphilus said: Prudence is always learned through practice and practice leads to the arts which prove instructive to all men.

10.8 And, should study perhaps turn to the knowledge of texts, you can develop your understanding and your intelligence, your mind and your memory in four ways, that is, through effort, through constant reading, through frequent thought and by sharpening the memory.

10.2 It would appear that the fiction has collapsed here and that the identities of the author and Prudence, his son and Melibee have merged.

10.9 *About effort, Seneca said: The sharp mind leaps forward, the broken retreats.*

10.10 *About constant reading, Cassiodorus said: Talent actually diminishes unless it is restored through constant reading.*

10.11 *And you should restore your talents by steadily reading with humility and with calm. It has been said that the good student should be humble and relaxed, free of vain cares and sensual preoccupations, diligent and willing to learn from everyone, unwilling to assume that his own knowledge is sufficient. He should be willing to avoid the authors of perverse ideas as if they were poison, to consider things thoroughly and at length before coming to a conclusion, to be learned rather than merely to seem learned, to admire wisdom when he understands it, to fix his gaze at the things he studies.*

10.12 *Scholarship requires three forms of humility.*

10.13 *The first of these is that no form of knowledge should be regarded with contempt or dismissed because whatever has been written has been written for our edification. Seneca indicated as much when he said: No one should despise the thoughtless, and so forth.*

10.14 *A second form of humility is the view that you should not be embarrassed to learn from anyone. Compare this statement: I would prefer to quietly learn from another than to flaunt my ignorance shamelessly.*

10.15 *Third, once someone has attained knowledge, he should not look down on others; as Seneca put it: When you know something, you should offer it without the expression of arrogance and, when you are less certain, you should offer it gingerly and without trying to hide your ignorance.*

10.16 *And, though I may have said that no writing is worthless, by no means was I suggesting that texts cannot lead to the study of extremely useless things and the waste of time. It is important that the scholar should be careful not to waste his time on useless studies and that he should also avoid the superficial exploration of studies which are valuable and decent. As bad as it is to examine something that is worthwhile in a casual way, it is even worse to expend a great deal of labor on insignificant vanities.*

10.17 *It is clear that intelligent people engage in not only reading but also writing. It has been said that we should not spend all our time simply reading or simply writing. Continuous writing constrains our spirit and exhausts it; continuous reading makes us flabby and diluted. It is better to do these things in turn, to mix the one with the other.*

10.18 *About thinking clearly and frequently and sharpening the memory, Martial said: The way to learn is to consider what you do not know. Learn, but learn with care. Learn, but learn what you should know. It will cost you less if*

10.15 Sundby attributes this citation to Plato though Plato is never mentioned in the Latin manuscripts, a point Sundby acknowledges. Plato is mentioned in the actual source of this citation, Hugh of St. Victor, *Didascalion* 3:13.

10.18 Unidentified by Sundby, the source of this citation is Godfrey of Winchester, *Liber proverbiorum*, ed. Hartwig Gerhard (Würzburg, 1974), p. 207. Albertano apparently thought that he was

you do not immediately throw up what you eat. The cow, when it goes to pasture, carefully chews the grass.

10.19 *Learning is endless since no one is able to learn everything there is.*

10.20 *Furthermore, the memory of man is prone to slip. As the law says: It is divine, not human, to remember everything and to feel that one can never be mistaken.*

10.21 *Consequently, to know more and to keep the memory fresh, you should set aside hours for reading and for learning, and, should you do so, you should learn new things. As Seneca said: When we learn nothing new, we forget what we knew.*

10.22 *Too, learning is for everyone. It is written: You would be wiser than everyone, if you were willing to learn from everyone; but when everyone will learn, everyone is the better off for it. Furthermore, the most valuable knowledge is that which is carefully considered and that which you can easily put to use. It is more productive to remember a few philosophical precepts which are always available and at your command than to acquire a vast knowledge and not be able to remember it. What you do remember encourages thought and intelligence.*

10.23 *As Cicero said in* De senectute: *In order to keep my memory fresh, I recall in the evening everything I have heard, said or done during the day.*

10.24 *You should study night and day and do what Seneca said: I never spend a day in idleness, set aside even a part of the night for study, do not allow time for sleep save when it overtakes me, keep working even when my eyes are wearied with wakefuless and ready to fall shut. It is a good idea to write.*

10.25 *As the result of the cultivation of work and careful study, you can feed your intelligence, ennoble yourself and win an elegant diadem, a notion consistent with this statement: The intelligence which cultivates work and studies with care is deserving of an elegant crown."*

10.26 *Having heard this and thought about it carefully, Melibee said, "My lady, I have not been prudent and I cannot hope to be. I have reached the end of my youth and passed the time attending to the worldly pursuits and the pleasures that were available to me. Though I may be wealthy, I have wasted my energies and I have wasted time and, it could be said: I weep at the loss of my possessions, but I weep much more at the days I have lost; everyone wants to help with my possessions, but no one will help with the days.*

10.27 *Though not prudent, I am nonetheless capable of understanding other things. Indeed: A man who does not become accustomed to virtue when he is young may not know how to disassociate himself from vice when he grows old.*

reading the Roman poet, Martial, rather than these imitations of his work by Godfrey of Winchester; my references are to the numbers assigned these epigrams by Gerhard.

10.26 Unidentified by Sundby, this citation is recorded by Walther, *Proverbia* 4893 with references to a number of *florilegia*.

10.27 Also unidentified by Sundby, this citation is recorded by Walther, *Proverbia* 24381 and appears in the *Liber Kalilae et Dimnae*, ed. Hervieux, vol. 5, p. 514 (not 314 as Walther indicates).

10.28 *But, since a mind wracked with care cannot distinguish truths from errors in judgment, and, since I know neither myself nor what is wise, I would ask that you counsel me about the difficult negotiations in which I am presently involved."*

10.29 *To this Prudence responded, "Clearly you may not be completely wise, but neither are you a complete fool yet. One cannot be wise when he thinks as do fools, and the issue here is not that you have been foolish yourself but that you have taken fools seriously.*

10.30 *As Solomon said: A fool need only walk down the highway. and, because he is a fool, it is obvious that he is stupid.*

10.31 *He also said: In his eyes, the fool is always moving in the right direction.*

10.32 *And then there is this proverb: Every wise man has the sense that he is something of a fool himself. Indeed, because the counsel you have solicited is dubious, you ought to consider just who the fool might really be.*

10.33 *In* De contemptu mundi, *Pope Innocent said: The more a man understands, the more he doubts, and the more a man pretends he knows, the more foolish he is. You can know but a fraction of the knowledge there is to know. No matter how insignificant or simple something seems, one cannot understand it fully or comprehend it easily. A man can be certain, however, that nothing he knows can be known for certain.*

10.34 *Thus, if you do not know yourself, you might learn something from a wise man and you might believe it, but should he know nothing about himself and not believe anyone else, all of his ideas might fall to pieces."*

Chapter 11: On counsel

[11.1] "Puis," dist Prudence, "que tu te veulz gouverner par mon conseil, je te vueil enseingnier comment tu te dois avoir en conseil prendre et retenir. (1115)

11.2 *And because you do want my counsel, we should consider, first, what counsel might be, by whom it might be voiced, how it should be composed, whose counsel should be impeached, whose counsel should be completely avoided, how it should be scrutinized, when and in what fashion it should be accepted, when and in what fashion it might be kept, and when counsel or promises might be changed.*

11.3 *Counsel is a suggestion or a proposal which one man offers or passes along to another man or men and it is meant to urge them to do something*

11.1 **Prudence** dame Prudence P13. **avoir** gouverner P13.

10.28 Unidentified by Sundby, the source of this citation is Godfrey of Winchester, *Liber proverbiorum*, 95.

10.32 Unidentified by Sundby, this citation is recorded by Walther, *Proverbia* 25505 and appears in the *Liber Kalilae et Dimnae*, ed. Hervieux, vol. 5, p. 412.

11.1 This statement serves not as a translation of the opening of this chapter in the Latin, but as a loose summary of this portion of this text. The passage is much abbreviated. At this point, the Latin also outlines the next nine chapters but does so in a diagrammatic fashion, q.v. 11.2.

which is good or evil. The receiver can accept it or ignore it. It is also said that counsel can be addressed to a crowd of people. It is also said of counsel (and this is a legal opinion) that, when it is given, no one may interrupt the speaker, especially when he knows that this interruption might prompt a violent response, as would be the case if one beheld someone using a tool to break down a door or to do something along those lines.

11.4 *As to by whom counsel can be voiced, by counsel we mean:* consulo consulis. *This phrase has two meanings. First, when someone seeks counsel from another, the accusative construction is used. Second, when someone gives counsel to another, the dative construction is used. Consider this verse: I consult you, I seek counsel; when I am a consultant to you, I give counsel.*

11.5 *As to how counsel might be composed, here the word* consilium *has a double meaning. The first is that the word is composed of the words* con *and* scio *(the last of which means I know) which suggests that, with others, we should understand, that we should agree and express agreement with them when counsel seems reasonable. Another view is that the word* consilium *is composed of the words* con *and* sileo *(which means I am speechless) which suggests that, with another or with others, we should say nothing until a suitable or critical opportunity presents itself.*

11.6 *From whom should counsel be requested? Now we should consider from whom you should solicit counsel. The possibilities are three: first, from almighty God, second, from yourself, third from another or from others. When it comes to God, you must be devout and wise; when it comes to yourself, you must be prudent; when it comes to another or others, you must exhibit caution by scrutinizing the advice discreetly, by avoiding rigidity, by taking it up shrewdly, by exhibiting consistent restraint, and by changing calmly.*

11.7 Premierement, en toutes oeuvres tu dois le conseil de Dieu demander devant tous autres et te dois mettre en tel lieu qu'il te daingne conforter et conseiller. (1116)

[11.8] Pour ce disoit Thobie a son filz: En tout temps beneïz Dieu et lui prie qu'il adresse tes voyes, et tuit tes conseilz soient en lui tout temps. (1117–18)

11.9 Et Saint Jaque dit: Se aucun de vous a mestier de sapience, si la demande a Dieu. (1119)

11.10 *Counsel and everything else you might undertake, in word or in deed, should be done in the name of the Lord; as Saint Paul said in his letter to the Colossians: Whatever you may do, whatever you may say, do it in the name of our Lord Jesus Christ and through him give thanks to God the Father.*

11.11 *Now as Paul also said: Every good gift and every perfect gift is from*

11.7 **toutes** *add* tes B7 L4 P12 P13 P24.

11.8 This citation is not in the Latin; unidentified in *The Riverside Chaucer*, its source is Tobias 4:20 as Skeat pointed out.

11.9 The French abbreviates this citation from the Latin.

above and comes down from the Father of lights without whom there would be neither change nor even the flickering of shadows.

11.12 *So you should be wise and devout when seeking counsel from the Lord and those whom the Lord would counsel should pray with the greatest devotion for what might be just or what seems honest. If you do that, doubtless God will grant you what you want.*

11.13 *As the Lord said: Whatever you ask the Father in my Name will be given to you.*

11.14 *I believe that those who act fairly will be treated fairly and that, furthermore, those who give wicked advice will be repaid in kind. As Jesus Sirach said: The man who offers evil counsel will have evil done to him, and he will not know from whence it comes.*

11.15 *Among friends, the law of the land should be considered sacred and we should neither ask for disgraceful things nor should we do them ourselves. In order to seek what is decent from our friends and to do what is decent for them, we must acknowledge the power of the Lord who is our true friend and safeguards the friends we have.*

11.16 *As the law puts it: we should neither outrage our piety nor our esteem nor our modesty, what is commonly called good morals, nor should we believe that such things can be done.*

11.17 *We should not hold in disdain the great strength of the Lord who rules everyone nor should we tempt His wrath and indignation. As Cato put it: one should only ask for what seems honest and fair; only fools want what most people would consider inappropriate.*

11.18 *The counsel of some men may be inconsequential or ineffective when it lacks divine assistance, without which there is nothing we can do. As much has been said in scripture: Nothing can de done without Me. What we should ask for, first, is for counsel from Him who is Justice Himself, and then every good thing will be given to us.*

11.19 Aprés, tu dois prendre conseil a toy mesmes et entrer en ta pensee et examiner que mieux te vault. Et lors tu dois oster trois choses de toy qui sont contrarieuses a conseil: c'est assavoir, ire, couvoitise, et hastiveté. (1120–2)

Chapter 12: On avoiding anger while taking counsel

12.1 Premierement, donques, cellui qui demande conseil a soy mesmes doit estre senz yre par moult de raisons. (1123)

12.2 La premiere est quar cellui qui est courreciez cuide tousjours plus povoir faire qu'il ne puet, et pour ce (fol. 59v) son conseil surmonte tousjours sa force. (1124)

12.2 Chaucer omits (1124) the phrase *et pour ce son conseil surmonte tousjours sa force* found in all the French manuscripts and the Latin. Such an omission might suggest something about the political considerations at issue when Chaucer composed his text; the implication that Richard II was habitually drawn towards the use of force certainly would have been regarded as offensive.

12.3 *It has been written: Those who serve nature accomplish the most; those who would be like gods do much less.*

12.4 L'autre, car cellui qui est courroucié, selon ce que dit Senecques, ne puet parler fors que choses crimineuses, et par ceste maniere il esmuet les autres a courrouz et a yre. (1127–8)

12.5 *Now the law acknowledges the angry man, but the angry man does not acknowledge the law.*

12.6 L'autre, quar celui qui est courcié ne puet bien juger et par consequant bien conseiller. (1125–6)

12.7 *This third reason is that anger frustrates the intelligence; as Cato said: An angry man should not be involved in unsettled litigation; anger keeps the mind from seeing the truth.*

12.8 *When it comes to counsel and other things as well, it is important to restrain the passions and subordinate these impulses to reason.*

12.9 *As Cicero said: Avoid anger. Nothing good can be done with it. Nothing can be settled. When the passions come into play, nothing can be resolved, nothing can be approved by witnesses.*

12.10 *Who can deal with merciless displays of wrath, angry fits and jealous tantrums?*

12.11 *Because those who are enraged may consider advice a crime, it has been said: He who overcomes his anger has conquered his greatest enemy.*

12.12 *If you want to know more about wrath, the wrathful and wrathfulness, read the chapter on how to avoid the companionship of angry men in the book written for Vincent, De forma vitae.*

Chapter 13: On avoiding cupidity and lust while taking counsel

13.1 Aprés, tu dois oster de toy couvoitise; car, selon ce que dit l'apposture: Couvoitise est racine de tous maulx. Et le couvoiteux ne puet riens juger fors que en la fin sa couvoitise soit acomplie, qui acomplir ne se puet, car tant com plus a li couvoiteux, plus desirre. (1129–32)

12.4 **l'autre** la seconde P24.
12.4–12.6 **selon ... conseiller** ne puet bien jugier par consequent bien consillier la tierche (lautre P12) car cil (*om* P12) qui est (si est P12) courouchiez selon ce que dist Senecques ne puet parler fors choses crimineuses et en telles (telle P12) maniere il esmeut les autres (a parole et P12) a courouchier et a yrer B7 L4 P12 P13 P24.
13.1 **oster de toy** de ton coeur oster P24.

12.3 This citation is recorded by Walther, *Proverbia* 24505 and appears in *Liber Kalilae et Dimnae*, ed. Hervieux, vol. 5, p. 661.
12.4 This idea and the one following it in P7 (12.6) are presented in the opposite order in the other French manuscripts and in Chaucer's translation. See the list of variants.
12.6 This is not a translation of the Latin but a summary of the rest of this chapter. *The Riverside Chaucer* treats this passage as though it were a citation and refers the reader to Walther, *Proverbia* 12913. Walther in turn refers to Cato, *Distichs* 2:4. However, the Latin text actually cites this distich below (12.7) and neither Renaud nor Chaucer bothered to translate it.
13.1 A loose translation designed to summarize the Latin.

13.2 *A second reason is that an obsession with pleasure darkens the soul and leads to every sort of evil and vice. As Cicero says in* De senectute: *the deadliest curse that nature has inflicted upon mankind is this preoccupation with sensual pleasure, this need to gratify our appetites beyond the bounds of prudence and restraint. Such obsessions give rise to treason, revolution, and clandestine communication with our enemies and indeed there is no crime, no evil deed to which we will not be driven as a result of our appetite for sensual pleasure. Fornications, adulteries and every similar abomination are brought about by the enticements of pleasure and by them alone. The mind is the best gift that God and Nature have given to men and there is nothing which is more inimical to this divine gift and endowment than the obsession with pleasure. We lose our self-control when we are controlled by our appetites and virtue cannot hold its ground when pleasure reigns supreme. Nothing can be more loathsome or more noxious than the inordinate pleasure which extinguishes the light of the soul.*

13.3 *And clearly the appetite for sensual pleasure is the worst because it is never stirred without leading to sorrow. Pedro Alfonso said: Inordinate desires are never aroused without leading to sorrow. Thus no one can enjoy drinking without being sad when he is thirsty; no one can enjoy a meal without being sad when he is hungry, no one can relax without being miserable when he is at work. And so it goes with the other forms of lust. So remember that even relatively insignificant forms of lust can be a sign that danger lies ahead. Thus this remark: Whatever the voluptuary may do, he can never steer clear of corruption.*

13.4 *The third reason is that insofar as taking counsel and anything else is concerned, among other things, you should avoid cupidity because it will lead to sin and ultimately death. As Saint James says in his epistle: Everyone is tempted when he is distracted by lust and is seduced by it; lust drives him to sin and sin, when it is done, leads him to death.*

13.5 *But the worst thing about cupidity is that there is never enough to hurry the cupidinous soul along.*

13.6 *Thus it is commonly said: To the cupidinous, laziness is dispatch.*

13.7 *A fourth reason why cupidity should be avoided and completely eliminated from counsel is because the cupidinous, when they die, are all carried to hell.*

13.8 *If there is no other way to rid yourself of such obsessions, then you should pluck out your heart.*

13.9 *The fifth reason is that, when it comes to counsel and indeed virtually everything else, you should both avoid and eschew cupidity for the cupidinous love nothing better than what is forbidden.*

13.10 *As Seneca said: At its most intense, cupidity is like a plague because those it destroys are left destitute and because they never get what they want in the end.*

13.11 *When one desire ends, another one begins.*

13.12 *He also said: It is more courageous to overcome cupidity than it is to conquer an army.*

13.13 *The sixth reason is that in every negotiation and every act every form of*

cupidity should be eliminated and avoided, just as the metalworker withdraws iron that was lowered into the fire in order to avoid a great weakness in the metal. Now since the cupidinous never get what they want in the end, as was said, you would do well to flee from them.

13.14 *It is written in the* Didascalion *of Hugh in the chapter on how scripture is to be studied for the correction of morals: Do not pursue what is out of reach. When there is no end in sight, there can be no peace and where there is no peace, God cannot dwell. In peace, the prophet said, is His place and His dwelling is in Sion.*

Chapter 14: On avoiding haste while taking counsel

14.1 Aprés, tu dois oster de toy hastiveté, car tu ne dois pas juger pour le meilleur ce que tantost te vendra au devant, ains y doiz penser souvent. (1133–4)

14.2 *And thus hasty judgments are criminal.*

14.3 *It has been said: The best sort of judge is one who thinks quickly but arrives at his conclusions slowly.*

14.4 Car, selon ce que tu as oÿ dessus, l'on dit communément: Qui tost juge tost se repent. (1135)

14.5 *About advice, it has been written: Advice which has been considered for some time usually proves quite correct.*

14.6 *And, as has been said too: Hasty advice leads to regret.*

14.7 *Therefore you should not give or receive counsel suddenly or when you are rushed but should do so with deliberation and with suitable delay.*

14.8 *In* De formula honestae vitae, *Seneca said: Nothing should seem sudden to you; rather you should always take the long view. Someone who is cautious is not someone who cannot get anything done. He is not dubious, but expectant, not suspicious, but careful.*

14.9 *In important deliberations and meetings, delay is valued, not held in contempt. It is written: To deliberate skillfully, it is best to take time.*

14.10 *Furthermore: Delay may seem despicable but it leads to wisdom.*

[14.11] Tu n'es pas toutes heures en une disposicion, ains trouveras que ce qui aucune foiz te semblera bon de faire, a l'autre te semblera bon de laisser. (1136–7)

Chapter 15: On the importance and necessity of not making secrets public

15.1 Quant tu auras prins conseil a toy mesmes et auras jugié a grant delibera-tion ce que mieux te vault, tien le secret et le garde de reveller a nulle personne

---

14.11 There is nothing quite like this statement in the Latin.

se tu ne cuides que en revellant certainnement tu feras ta condition meilleur et que le reveller te portera proffit. (1138–40)

15.2 Car Jhesu Sirac dit: A ton ami ne a ton ennemi ne recompte point ton secret et ta folie, car il te orront et te regarderont et deffendront en ta presence, et par darriere se moqueront de toy. (1141–2)

15.3 *It has been said: If you want to keep something a secret, tell it to no one.*

15.4 Et uns autres dit: A painnes trouveras tu un tant seulement qui puisse bien celer secret. (1143)

15.5 Et Pierre Alphons si dit: Tant com ton secret est en ton cuer, tu le tiens en ta prison; quant tu le reveles, il te tient en la sienne. Et pour ce il te vaut mieux taire et ton secret celer que prier cellui a cui tu le revelles qu'il le cele. (1144–6)

15.6 Car Senecques dit: Se tu ne te puez taire et ton secret celer, comment prieras tu un autre qu'il le cele? (1147)

15.7 *Should you believe that the counsel of another will better your situation, then think carefully and privately about with whom and to whom you want to gain counsel and reveal secrets; as Seneca said: You can discuss anything with a friend, but first you must consider what sort of person that friend might be.*

15.8 *And Pedro Alfonso said: Be wary of your enemies but be especially careful of your friends for, some day, a friend may turn against you and be more easily capable of doing you harm.*

Chapter 16: On not revealing one's desires while taking counsel

16.1 Se tu cuides que reveller ton secret a un autre face ta condicion meilleur, lors te gouverneras par tel guise. Premierement, tu ne dois faire semblant a ton conseil quele partie tu veulz tenir ne leur monstrer ta voulenté car communément tous conseilliers sont losengeours et especiaulment ceulz qui sont du conseil des grans seigneurs, car ilz s'efforcent plus de dire choses plaisans que proffitables, et pour ce, riches homs n'aura ja bon conseil se il ne l'a premier de soy mesmes. (1148–52)

16.2 *In the course of seeking counsel for yourself, you must take care, first, that you withdraw from advisors whose counsel is not in your best interests; second, that you keep your secrets to yourself if your circumstances do not allow you to seek better counsel from another; third, that you consider and weigh carefully the counsel to which you are inclined; fourth, that you do not indicate whether or not the counsel you receive is in keeping with the counsel you want.*

15.2 **secret et** secret ne B7 P12 P13. **deffendront** supporteront P24.
15.4 **un tant** une personne P24.
15.5 **le revelles** las revele B7 L4.
15.6 **prieras tu** ose tu prier P24.
16.1 **secret** conseil B7 L4 P13. **tel** ceste P13. **a ton conseil** *om* P24.

15.5 The French text paraphrases two citations from Pedro Alfonso in the Latin and Chaucer follows its lead but does not mention the author.

Chapter 17: On soliciting advice from others

17.1 *Seek counsel by yourself and keep it to yourself, and, when the opportunity arises, you can solicit advice from another or from others. What remains to be seen, therefore, is from whom you should solicit advice.*

17.2. Aprés, tu dois considerer tes amis et tes ennemis. Entre tes amis tu doiz considerer le plus loyal, le plus sage, et plus ancien, et le plus esprouvé en conseil; et a ceulz tu dois conseil demander. Premierement, donques, tu doiz appeller a ton conseil tes bons et tes loyaulx amis. (1154–7)

17.3 Car Salemon dit: Aussi comme le cuer (fol. 60r) se delitte en bonne odeur, conseil de bon amy fait a l'ame doulceur. (1158)

17.4 *Indeed nothing is sweeter than to have a friend with whom you can talk as though you were talking to yourself.*

17.5 Et dit aussi: A l'amy loyal nulle chose ne se compere, car ne or ne argent ne sont tant dignes comme la bonté du loyal amy. (1159–60)

17.6 *Too: A friend who remains steadfast will be like another self and will behave with honor within your household.*

17.7 Et dit encor: Amy loyal est une fort deffense; qui le treuve, il treuve un grant tresor. (1161)

17.8 *And it has been also said: a man without a friend is like a body without a soul; an enduring friendship is like a gift from Fortune; life without friends is hardly pleasant.*

17.9 *As to wisdom and experience, I maintain that it is true, as someone once said: The wise man bears arms against the world whenever he thinks.*

17.10 Aprés, tu dois regarder que les loyaulx amis que tu appelles a ton conseil soient sages, car il est escript: Requier tousjours le conseil du sage. (1162–3)

17.11 *It has been written: The man who can walk by the side of a wise man is a man who cannot not fall from a bridge.*

17.12 *In* De formula honestae vitae, *Seneca said: Skillful advice can make the obscure seem clear, the insignificant consequential, the far near, the parts whole.*

17.13 *I maintain that you must test the truth and that you must consider the question of loyalty because many who are said to be wise are in fact malicious and, because of the malice they bear, will advise that others be treated maliciously. Rather than trust everyone, test them all and determine which ones are indeed trustworthy. As Saint John said in his epistle: Beloved, do not believe in every spirit but try to determine if these spirits are from the Lord.*

17.2 **sage** sages et P12 P24. **conseil demander** tout ton conseil demander B7.

17.3 The French abbreviates this citation.

17.9 This citation does not appear in the Latin; Skeat thought its source Proverbs 22:17 or Ecclesiasticus 9:14.

17.14 *And in his letter* to the Thessalonicans, *Paul said: Test everything, then keep what is good and avoid everything that is evil.*

17.15 *And in* Wisdom*: Those who trust too easily show that their minds are shallow.*

17.16 *Complaisance will lead to foolishness.*

17.17 *And another said: Do not praise a friend until you have tested him.*

17.18 *And Solomon said: If you want to make a friend, first test him; many are friendly only when it suits them and will not stand by you in difficult or troubling times.*

17.19 *Thus the philosopher: Beware advice if the person from whom you have requested it has not proven faithful to you.*

17.20 Par ceste mesme raison tu dois appeller les anciens qui assez ont veu et assez esprouvé. Car il est escript en Job: Es anciens est la sapience et en moult de temps est prudence. (1163–4)

17.21 *Furthermore, Cassiodorus said: The more prudent of men always engage in conversation with groups of men whose knowledge has been proven.*

17.22 *And you can learn much from the elderly which will prove especially satisfying since the elderly will provide you with wisdom.*

17.23 *As Martial said: It is easy to have contempt for the ways of ragged old men and since you, Postume, avoid old men, you will get no advice from them.*

17.24 Et Tulles dit: Les grans besoingnes ne se font pas par force ne par legierete de corps, mais par bon conseil, et par auctorité de personne, et par science, lesquelles trois choses n'affoiblissent pas en vieillesse, mais s'efforcent et croissent tous les jours. (1165)

17.25 Aprés, en ton conseil tu dois garder ceste rigle: car au commencement tu dois appeller pou de gens des plus especiaulx; car Salemon dit: Efforce toy d'avoir pluseurs amis, mais entre mil eslis en un a ton conseillier. (1166–7)

17.26 Quant tu auras eu revelé ton conseil a pou de gens, si le puez reveller a pluseurs se besoing est. Toutevoye, les trois condicions que j'ay dictes si doivent estre es conseilliers tousjours gardees, et ne te souffise un conseil tant seulement, mais en fay pluseurs. Car Salomon dit: Sainement est la ou pluseurs conseilz sont. (1168–71)

17.27 *It is clear that to accomplish anything, many advisors are needed; as Solomon says in* Proverbs*: Plans come to nothing without advisors, but when there are many, they succeed.*

17.25 **a ton** a estre ton P13.
17.26 **un conseil** un conseillier L4 P13. **conseilz** conseillers P12 P24.

17.23 Unidentified by Sundby, the source of this citation is Godfrey of Winchester, *Liber proverbiorum*, 53.
17.25 The French here is much fuller than the Latin.

Chapter 18: On avoiding the counsel of fools

18.1 Aprés ce que je t'ay monstré a cui tu doiz prendre conseil, je te vueil monstrer lequel conseil tu doiz fuir et eschever. (1172)

18.2 Premierement, tu dois le conseil des folz eschiver car Salemon dit: A fol ne prens point de conseil, car il ne te saura conseiller fors ce qu'il aime et qu'il li plaist. (1173)

18.3 Et si est escript: La proprieté du fol est tele car il croit legierement tous maulx d'autrui et tous biens de lui. (1174)

18.4 *And Solomon said: The wise man's heart leads him in the right direction but the fool's heart leads him astray.*

18.5 *Elsewhere he said: Do not waste your words on a fool; he will not appreciate your eloquence.*

18.6 *And again: In the eyes of the fool, his way is always the right way, but the wise man heeds advice.*

18.7 *He also said: You may grind the fool in a mortar but you will never separate him from his folly.*

18.8 *Furthermore: When the wise man argues with the fool, he may be angry or may be congenial, but he will never accomplish a thing.*

Chapter 19: On Avoiding the counsel of flatterers

19.1 Aprés, tu doiz fuir le conseil des faintifs losengeurs, lesquelz se efforcent plus de loer ta personne et a toy plaire que a verité dire. (1175)

19.2 *As Cicero says: The greater our wealth, the greater our need to seek the advice of friends, and the greater the attention which should be paid to their advice. Such circumstances also indicate that we should be wary of listening to sycophants or allowing them to flatter us. If we think that we are entitled to praise, it is easy for us to deceive ourselves, a frame of mind which leads to countless errors, to men puffing themselves up with conceit and exposing themselves to ignominy and the worst sorts of mistakes.*

19.3 Et Tulles dit: Entre toutes les pestilences qui sont en amitié, la plus grant est losengerie. (1176)

19.4 *But however pernicious flattery may be, however obnoxious it might prove, it can harm no one save those who believe it and take pleasure in it. A man who listens to flatterers with rapt attention is the kind of man who would as soon flatter himself and find himself quite pleasing.*

19.5 *Thus Cato said: Though others may praise you, you must remember that you are ultimately the judge, that you must trust yourself rather than believe what others say.*

18.2 This citation (Ecclesiasticus 8:20) is not in the Latin though the Latin offers a similar idea.

19.6 *And Seneca said in his letters: Look to yourself rather than listen to others tell you who you are.*

19.7 *The crowd thinks only of itself and you should think about how you see yourself rather than how others see you. It is wiser to please one's self than it is to please the crowd.*

19.8 *This sort of response to most solicitous kinds of counsel agrees with that expressed by Seneca in* De formula honestæ vitae*: When they wish you good health or that you might enjoy a prosperous life, you will find this kind of deceit engrossing or you may dismiss it or you may be open to serious attack. But you should be wary about what might be happening and how long it might last.*

19.9 Et pour ce tu dois plus fuir et doubter les doulces parolee de celui qui te loera que les aigres paroles de celui qui verité te dira. (1177)

19.10 Car Salemon dit: Homme qui dit paroles de losengerie est un lacet pour prendre les innocens. Et dit aussi autre part: Homme qui parle a son ami paroles [doulces] et souees, il lui met devant les piez le laz pour lui prendre. (1178–9)

19.11 *And Cicero said: No intrigues are more insidious than those which are concealed under the pretense of duty or under the name of some intimate connection.*

[19.12] Pour ce dit Tulles: Garde que tu n'enclines point tes oreilles a losengeurs et ne recoip point en ton conseil paroles de losengerie. (1180)

19.13 *Cicero also said: Bitter enemies sometimes deserve better from some men than do friends who might seem agreeable; the former sometimes speak the truth, but the latter never do.*

19.14 Et Caton dit: Advise toy d'eschever paroles [doulces] et souees. (1181)

19.15 *You should not be moved by innocuous language which is pleasant or artful but by the substance of things; thus Seneca says in his letters: You should be moved by substance rather than style, and speech which deals with the truth should be unadorned and plain.*

19.16 *It is incumbent upon you to put your faith in the wise. Rather than put your trust in your own wisdom, you should investigate the wisdom in the advice of others. As Cassiodorus said: One should seek wisdom from those whose knowledge is the greatest. To doubt that and to refuse to seek the advice of the wise is pointless and shameful.*

19.10 **Car** *om* L4. **doulces** L4 P12 P13 P24; doubles P7.
19.12 **garde que** *om* P13.
19.14 **doulces** L4 P12 P13 P24; doubles P7.

19.12 This citation is out of sequence in the French; it is taken from the passage from Cicero's *De officiis* which opens this chapter in the Latin (19.2).

Chapter 20: On avoiding the counsel of those who were enemies once but have since returned to grace

20.1 Aprés, tu dois fuir le conseil de tes anciens ennemis (fol. 60v) qui sont reconciliez, car il est escript: Nul ne retourne seurement en la grace de son ennemi. (1182–3)

20.2 Et Ysopes dit: Ne vous fiez point en ceulz a cui vous aurez eu guerre et ennemitié anciennement, et ne leur revellez point voz secrez. (1184)

20.3 *And he also said: You should have no faith in enemies who seem like friends and whose worthless advice may be utterly hostile to you.*

20.4 Et la raison conferme Senecques et dit que il ne puet estre que la ou a esté le feu longuement qu'il n'y demeure tousjours aucune vapour. (1185)

20.5 *He also said: Better to die with your friends than live with your enemies.*

20.6 Pour ce dit Salemon: En ton ancien ennemi ne te fie nul temps. (1186)

20.7 Et encores se il est reconciliez et se humilie et encline la teste devant toy, ne le croy, car il le fait plus pour son proffit que pour amour de toy, a la fin qu'il puisse avoir [victoire] de toy en soy humiliant et en toy fuyant, laquelle il n'a pas peu avoir en toy poursuyant. (1187–8)

20.8 *And another said: Your enemy may bring tears to your eyes, but, when he sees his moment, not even your blood will satisfy him.*

20.9 Et Pierre Alphons dit: Ne te compaigne pas a tes anciens ennemis, car ce que tu feras de bien, ilz le pervertiront ou le amenuiseront. (1189)

Chapter 21: On avoiding the counsel of those who are soliticious because of fear rather than love

21.1 Aprés, tu dois fuir le conseil de ceulz qui te servent et te portent reverence plus par doubtance que par amour. (1190)

21.2 *These are not friends but despicable enemies. In* De officiis, *Cicero says: Of all things, the most suitable way to be influential is through love and nothing is more inappropriate to that end than is fear. Men tend to hate those whom they fear and to hope that those they hate will die. No amount of power can withstand the hatred of many, and, if we were unaware of this in the past, we certainly know it by now.*

21.3 Car un philosophe dit: Nul n'est bien loyal a cellui que il trop doubte. (1191)

20.1 **fuir** eschever P13 P24.
20.4 **estre** *add* dist il L4 P12. **longuement** long temps B7 P13.
20.7 **humilie** humilite soit en luy par semblant P24. **victoire** B7 L4 P12 P13 P24; vitoire P7. **de** sur P24. **laquelle** *add* victoire P24.
20.9 **pervertiront** *add* en mal B7 P13. **amenuiseront** augmenteront en mal P24.
21.1 **reverence** reverence car ils le font P24.

21.3 The French abbreviates the Latin.

21.4 Et Tulles dit: Nulle puissance d'empire n'est si grant qu'elle puisse durer longuement se elle n'a plus l'amour du pueple que la paour. (1192)

21.5 *But those in a free society who deliberately put themselves in a position to be feared are absolutely mad.*

21.6 *Furthermore those who wish to be feared must inevitably be afraid of those they wish to intimidate.*

21.7 *Pleasantry rather than arrogance is the way to increase love.*

21.8 *Martial said: It is impossible to love the stern and the menacing. They attract no one; no one likes coercion. It is pleasantry not arrogance which leads to love, draws the cow to the bull, the lioness to the lion. Those who want peace avoid the irritable. Therefore bring everyone together so that you may be loved by them all. When you yield to love, you repel hatred.*

21.9 *Fear and loathing will enable you to attract neither friends nor good advice and they can lead to a loss of power. As Cicero put it: No power is strong enough to last if it labors under the weight of fear.*

21.10 *The man whom many fear must fear many.*

21.11 *And as Seneca said is his letters: No one who trades in terror can be secure.*

Chapter 22: On avoiding the counsel of drunks

22.1 Aprés, tu doiz fuir le conseil de ceulz qui sont souvent yvres, car ilz ne scevent riens celer. Et Salemon dit: Nul secret n'est la ou regne yvresse. (1193–4)

Chapter 23: On avoiding the counsel of those who say one thing in private but another in public

23.1 Aprés, tu dois avoir en suspect le conseil de ceulz qui conseillent une chose en secret et autre dient en appert. Car Cassidoires dit: Une maniere de grever son amy est monstrer en appert ce dont l'on veult le contraire. (1195–6)

Chapter 24: On avoiding the counsel of the wicked

24.1 Aprés, tu dois avoir en suspect le conseil de mauvais homme. Car il est escript: Les conseillz des mauvais hommes sont tousjours plains de fraude. (1197)

21.4 **d'empire** d'empereur P13 P24.
22.1 **Et** pour quoy P24.
23.1 **qui** *add* te L4; *add* toy P13. **dit** *add* que cest B7; *add* quil nest P24. **est** . . . **l'on** quant il P13. **monstrer** quant on lui conseille une chose en secret et monstrer L4.
24.1 **homme** hommes P13. **Les conseilz** le conseil B7 L4 P12 P13 P24.

21.8 Unidentified by Sundby, the source of this citation is Godfrey of Winchester, *Liber proverbiorum*, 229.

24.2 Et David dit: Biencureux est l'homme qui na suy le conseil des mauvais. (1198)

Chapter 25: On avoiding or respecting the counsel of young men

25.1 Aprés, tu dois fuir le conseil des jeunes gens, car le sens des jeunes n'est pas encores meur. (1199)
25.2 Et Salemon dit: Doulente la terre qui a enfant a seigneur, de laquelle le prince se des jusne matin!
25.3 *And Martial said: Should you trust the counsel of the young, Melibee, you can expect ruin because you have not been counseled at all.*

Chapter 26: On the general examination of counsel

26.1 Puis que je t'ay monstré a cui tu dois prendre conseil et lequel tu doiz eschever et fuir, je te vueil monstrer et aprendre comment tu dois conseil examiner. En examinant, donques, ton conseil, selon ce que Tulles enseingne, tu dois considerer pluseurs choses. (1200–2)
26.2 *To be sure, when you consider advice, you should be careful that you look at how things start and how they end. For your consideration of counsel to be valuable and helpful, you should be especially careful.*
26.3 *In the course of examining counsel, you must first cast aside and avoid counselors who, as I said above, prove incompatible with good advice, specifically the angry, the sensual, the cupidinous and the impatient.*
26.4 *Second, when you begin negotiations, you should remind yourself that every aspect of a transaction is important in the beginning.*
26.5 *Thus, when you enter into a contract, you should examine every aspect of that contract at the start. The reason for this, as the law says, is that the failure to examine something at the very start makes no sense at all. Those who are the*

25.1 **le sens ... encores** leur conseil nest encore pas P12.
26.1 **et lequel** et de qui conseil P24.

24.2 Not in the Latin and unidentified in *The Riverside Chaucer*, this, as Skeat pointed out, is the opening line of *The Book of Psalms*.
25.1 The French abbreviates the Latin.
25.2 This text in the French is drawn from the Latin, but Chaucer drops it, it is usually said, in deference to Richard II. As Severs noted, the idea is more fully developed in P24 which offers the following gloss to the Latin: *Et le philosophe dit que nous n'eslisons pas les jeunes en princes car communément ils n'ont point de prudence.*
25.3 Unidentified by Sundby, the source of this citation is Godfrey of Winchester, *Liber proverbiorum*, 154.
26.1 The French expands the opening clausula in the Latin and then abbreviates the rest of the text. Severs plausibly suggested that Chaucer's *folwe* (1200) may have arisen from a confusion of *suir* with *fuir* either through misreading or a scribal error. All the French manuscripts have *fuir*. The reference to Cicero is in the French but not the Latin; Chaucer follows the French.

most diligent are circumspect from the beginning. It is written: If you resist taking medicine in the beginning, you will not get better when, as the result of negligence, the disease gets worse.

26.6 *As Sallust said: Every instance of evil originates in something which at first seemed like a good thing.*

26.7 *And since it is true that for all the good that you have done, you will receive, as Jesus Sirach said, twice the evil, you should worry a great deal about the redoubling of evil which is involved in everything.*

26.8 *Now, since there is the danger that something which starts off well will turn out to be twice as bad, that is all the more reason to consider the danger involved in things which were bad at the start or at least seemed bad. As the decretals say: It is difficult to bring something to a good conclusion when it was wicked from the very beginning.*

26.9 *Thus when you speak and act, you will have to think carefully about not only the beginning but also the end. As Pamphilius said: At the outset and in the final analysis, prudence determines whether the outcome will be good or bad, and you should therefore be careful of what you say and had best think before you speak.*

26.10 *As Seneca said in his letters: It is easier to stop wrongdoing in the beginning than it is when it gathers force. He also said: It is easier to avoid wrongdoing alto-gether than it is to stop doing what is wrong. Though we may have control of things at the outset, as circumstances develop, fortune can decide the issue.*

26.11 *It is prudent therefore to examine counsel with much deliberation. The prudent study counsel with great care, but the credulous are quickly led astray by untruths.*

26.12 Premierement, tu dois considerer que en ce que tu proposes et sur quoy tu veulz avoir conseil, pure verité soit gardee et dicte. Car l'on ne puet bien conseiller a celui qui ne dit verité. (1203–4)

26.13 *We should consider what the truth might be, since the truth is honored above all else, as though it were the only way that men can get close to God. Indeed God Himself is Truth as He indicated Himself when He said: I am the way, the truth and the life.*

26.14 *To what I have said about Cicero's notion of sincerity, I would add that the truth we seek should be both unadulterated and sincere and that I would avoid the cunning lie.*

26.15 *As Cassiodorus said: What is good is a truth in which nothing false is mixed.*

26.16 *And the Lord said: The devil is a liar and the father of lies.*

26.17 *And Solomon said: Even an industrious thief is better than a tireless liar.*

26.18 Aprés, tu dois considerer toutes les choses qui se accordent ad ce que tu proposes faire selon ton conseil: se raison s'i accorde, se ta puissance s'i

---

26.18 **toutes** *om* P13.

26.18–26.21 These four clausulae abbreviate the Latin considerably.

accorde, se pluseurs ou meilleurs s'i accordent (fol. 61r) que discordent, ou non. (1205–6)

26.19 Aprés, tu dois considerer ce qui s'ensuit au conseil: se c'est hayne ou amour, paix ou guerre, profit ou dommage; et ainsi de moult d'autres choses. Et en toutes ces choses tu dois tousjours eslire ce qui est a ton proffit, toutes autres choses refusees et rabatues. (1207–8)

26.20 Aprés, tu dois considerer de quelle racine est engendree la matiere de ton conseil et quel fruit elle puet concevoir et engendrer. (1209)

26.21 Et dois encores considerer toutes causes dont elle est venue. (1210)

26.22 *Seneca said: In order to understand how things happen, you must discover how they began and must think about how they might conclude. Then you will be satisfied, as I have said, at the beginning and in the end. Therefore you should consider why things happen, specifically the efficient cause, the material cause, the formal cause and the final cause, as well as the principal cause and the accidental cause responsible for whatever has happened, and the immediate cause and the remote cause as well.*

26.23 *To this end, in order to explore counsel carefully and to handle negotiations prudently, you should focus on what the future holds and imagine how these contingencies will affect your spirit. Furthermore, you should focus not only on the future but also on the past.*

26.24 *In De formula honestæ vitae, Seneca said this: If you are prudent, your consciousness must manage three kinds of time by controlling the present, providing for the future, and remembering the past. Those who disregard the past may risk their lives and those who fail to take the future into consideration may run into the unexpected. At the least, imagine how your spirit might fare in the face of a bad future as well a good one, and how you would sustain it if it were to be restrained.*

Chapter 27: How counsel should be weighed and approved

27.1 Quant tu auras examiné ton conseil en la maniere devant ditte, et trouvé laquelle partie est meilleur plus profitable, et mieux esprouvee de pluseurs [sages] et anciens, tu dois considerer se tu la pourras mener a fin. Quar nul ne doit commencer chose qu'il n'a povoir de faire, et ne doit prendre charge qu'il ne puisse porter. (1211–14)

27.2 *Indeed Cicero says: Anyone in public life should be certain that he has the ability to achieve his goals and should beware thinking only about the honor that might come his way. At the same time, he should neither lose heart through discouragement nor let ambition make him feel too confident. In everything he does, he should make careful preparations before he undertakes it.*

26.21 **elle est** elles puent estre P12 P13.
27.1 **devant** qua je tay P24. **meilleur** la meilleur et B7 L4 P13. **sages** B7 L4 P12 P13 P24; *om* P7. **de faire** de la parfaire P13 P24; du parfaire L4; de parfaire B7.

27.3 L'on dit un proverbe: Qui trop embrace, pou estraint. (1215)

27.4 Et Cathon dit: Essaye toy de faire ce que tu as povoir de faire, pour ce que la charge ne te presse tant qu'il couviengne laisser ce que tu as commencié a faire. (1216)

27.5 *When you initiate something you must consider how it will end, since, as Seneca said: There is much that you may not understand.*

27.6 *For that reason, ask questions in order to discover answers, learn what you must know, and decide what might be the best decision to make. Do not worry about other things which might reduce you to a terrible state of anxiety.*

27.7 *Someone else said: It is a burden to cooperate with someone who cannot find his way. The man who wants to fly before he has his wings will inevitably fall.*

27.8 *Whenever you contemplate what is good, what is valuable, what is honorable, and not what is opportunistic or simply within the realm of possibility, I would urge you to recall what I said above: Those who serve nature accomplish the most; those who would be like gods do much less.*

27.9 S'il est doubte se tu le pourras mener a fin ou non, esliz plus tost le souffrir que le commencier. Car Pierre Alphons dit: [Se tu as paour de dire chose] dont il te couviengne repentir, [il vault mielx non que si]. (1217–18).

27.10 *Wise men accomplish more by remaining silent when they are enveloped by speech. When few or none are silent, there is more talking than we can consider.*

27.11 *Words are like arrows: easy to shoot off, difficult to retrieve or emend. It is usually said: Once you let them slip, words are beyond recall.*

27.12 [C'est a dire, il te vault mielx taire que parler. Par plus fort raison, doncques, se tu as povoir de faire chose dont il te couvienge repentir], il te vault mieux souffrir que commencier. (1219–20)

27.13 Bien dient ceulz qui deffendent a un chascun chose faire dont il duelt et doubte se elle est de faire ou non en la fin. (1221)

27.14 *And another said: Do nothing when you are in doubt and avoid decisions which may be denied by the soul, since, as Seneca said: A man should habitually doubt rash advice.*

27.15 *In short, given what has been said, you should teach yourself and others to choose always what is decent, true, useful, rational and just and to disregard the alternatives.*

27.3   **L'on** car lon B7 L4 P13.

27.4   **couviengne** te couviengne B7 L4 P12 P13 P24.

27.9   **se ... chose** B7 P12; paour de faire P7; *om* L4; se tu as povoir de faire chose P12 P13 P24. **il vault ... si** B7; *om* L4 P7 P13 P24.

27.12   **c'est ... repentir** B7 P12; *om* P7 L4 P13 P24.

27.13   **en** et a P13.

27.9 The bracketed text which concludes this passage and that which begins 27.12 is translated by Chaucer but omitted from all manuscripts save B7 and P12, a clear instance, as Severs said, of eyeskip.

27.12 The last two clausulae do not translate the Latin but serve as a blanket summary of the citations which follow (27.13–27.15).

Chapter 28: When and how counsel should be kept

28.1 *Having considered and understood when and in what fashion counsel should be taken or weighed, we should consider when and in what fashion counsel might be kept.*

28.2 *Surely counsel should be kept when it seems decent and useful as the result of testing and experimentation.*

28.3 *For, as I mentioned above, Paul said: Test everything and hold onto whatever is good.*

28.4 *And thus we should be as steadfast as we can. As Cato said: Be calm and firm, as the circumstances dictate. A wise man can change his views without recrimination.*

28.5 *Now in the* Formula honestae vitae, *Seneca said: Flexibility is not capriciousness, nor steadiness stubbornness. Counsel will be best served by resolve, not stubbornness.*

[28.6] Quant tu auras examiné ton conseil par la maniere dessus dicte, et auras trouve que tu le pourras mener a fin, adonques le retien et le conferme. (1222)

Chapter 29: When counsel or promises can or should be changed

29.1 Or est raison que je te monstre quant et pourquoy l'on doit changier son conseil senz reprehension. (1223)

29.2 *Surely counsel can be changed for many reasons.*

29.2 L'on puet changer son conseil et son propox quant la cause cesse ou quant nouvelle cause survient. Car la loy dit: Les choses qui de nouvel surviennent ont mestier de conseil nouvel. (1224–5)

29.4 *Thus it is commonly said: You should not believe that it is foolish to change a decision.*

29.5 Et Senecques dit: Se ton conseil est venu a la cognoissance de ton ennemi, change ton conseil. (1226)

29.6 Aprés, l'on puet changer son conseil quant on trouve aprés que, par erreur ou par autre cause, mal ou dommage en puet venir. (1227)

29.7 *Now, as Seneca said: To a degree, there are those who may not understand what it right, but they are, and those who may understand, but they are not.*

29.8 *Many of those who lie hold the truth in reserve and truths are concealed within many kinds of lies, but, once you investigate the disenchanted person who seems like a friend or the person who flatters you, it will become apparent that reality has been colored for the sake of deception or dishonesty.*

29.9 *Thus Ovid said: The taste of honey may conceal poison.*

28.6 **dessus dicte** que je tay dit P24.

28.6 Not a translation of the Latin but a summary of the entire chapter.

29.10 *And, as I have said before, for all the good that you do, you will receive twice the evil.*

29.11 Aprés, quant le conseil est deshonneste ou vient de cause deshenneste, car les loys dient que toutes promesses deshonnestes sont de nulle valeur. (1228–9)

29.12 *And counsel should be changed if it might lead to wrongdoing. This is why it is commonly said: Advice should never be against the Lord.*

29.13 Aprés, quant il est impossible ou ne se puet garder bonnement; et en moult d'autres manieres. (1230)

29.14 *As Cicero put it: Promises should not be kept if keeping them proves harmful to him to whom you have made them or if fulfilling the promise would do more harm to you than good to him to whom you have made it.*

29.15 *As I said before: The wise man will not lie in order to change his case for the better. Thus, as the law has it, it is considered inappropriate to take an oath when it complies with something which is inconsistent with the oath itself.*

29.16 Aprés, tu doiz ce tenir pour rigle general: que tout conseil est mauvais qui est si fermes que l'on ne le puet changier par condition qui surviengne." (1231)

29.17 Mellibee, quant il ot oÿ les enseingnemens Dame Prudence sa femme, si respondi: "Dame Prudence," dist il, "jusques a l'eure de maintenant, vous m'avez assez enseingnié en general comment je me doy porter en conseil prendre (fol. 61v) et retenir. Or vouldroye je moult que vous descendissiez en especial et me deissiez ce qui vous semble du conseil que nous avons eu en nostre propre besoingne." (1232–5)

29.18 Lors Dame Prudence respondi: "Sire," dist elle, "je te pry que tu ne repelles point en ton courage se je dy chose qui te desplaise. Car tout ce que je diray, je l'entens dire a ton honneur et a ton proffit, et ay esperance que tu le porteras en pacience. (1236–8)

29.19 *He who takes another to task will enjoy more favor in the end than will the flatterer.*

29.20 Et pour ce je te fais savoir que ton conseil, a parler proprement, ne doit pas estre dit conseil, mais un fol esmouvement senz discretion, ouquel tu as errey en moult de manieres. (1239–40)

Chapter 30: On fallacious counsel

30.1 Premierement, tu as errey a assembler ton conseil car au commencement tu deusses avoir appellé po de gens, et puis aprés pluseurs se besoing fust; mais

---

29.17 **propre** presente B7 L4.
29.18 **sire** sire sire, *first* sire *canc* P7.

29.10 Here Prudence refers to her previous reference (26.7) to this text (Ecclesiasticus 12:7); neither reference appears in the French text.
29.13 The phrase *et en moult d'autres manieres* is present in all the French manuscripts and designed to summarize the Latin, but it is not translated by Chaucer (1230).
29.15 Prudence refers to the point she has made above: 4.1.

tantost tu as appellé une grant multitude de gent chargeuse et ennuyeuse. (1241–3)

30.2 Aprés, tu as errey car tu deusses avoir appelley tant seulement tes loyaulx amis sages et anciens; mais avec ceulz tu as appellé gens estranges, jouvenceaulx, losengers, ennemis reconciliez, et gens qui te portent reverence senz amour. (1244–5)

30.3 Aprés, tu as erré quant tu es venu au conseil acompagnié de ire, couvoitise, et hastiveté, lesquelles trois choses sont contraires au conseil, et ne les as pas abaissees en toy et en ton conseil, ainsi comme tu deusses. (1246–8)

30.4 Aprés, tu as erré quant tu demonstres a ton conseil la voulenté et la grant affeccion de faire guerre que tu avoies incontinent et de prendre tantost vengence; et pour ce ilz ont plus suy ta voulenté que ton profit. (1249–51)

30.5 Aprés, tu as errey car tu as estey content d'un conseil tant seulement, et toutesvoies en si grans et si hautes besoingnes estoient bien neccessaires pluseurs conseilz. (1252–3)

30.6 Aprés, tu as erré car tu n'as pas examiné ton conseil en la maniere dessus ditte. (1254)

30.7 Aprés, tu as erré car quant tu as faite la division entre ceulz de ton conseil, tu n'as pas suy la voulenté de tes loyaulx amis sages et anciens, mais as regardé tant seulement le plus grant nombre. Et tu scez bien que les folx sont tousjours en plus grant nombre que les sages, et pour ce le conseil des chapitres et des grans multitudes de gens ou l'en regarde plus le nombre que la merite des personnes [erre] souvent, car en tel conseil les folx l'ont tousjours gaingnié." (1255–60)

30.8 Mellibee respondi: "Je confesse bien que j'ay errey, mais tu m'as dit que celui ne fait pas a reprendre qui change son conseil en moult de cas, pour quoy je suy appareillez de changer a ta voulenté, car pechié est oeuvre d'ommne, mais perseverer en pechié est oeuvre d'ennemy." (1261–4)

30.9 *Then Prudence responded, "The advice which you consider appropriate would not be considered appropriate in the eyes of the law. As the law puts it: Something is appropriate only if it does not render some agreement inappropriate. In order to determine what is appropriate, it is necessary to scrutinize it, to rid it of its errors, and to understand and to accept what is valuable about it.*

30.2 **jouvenceaulx** add folz L4 P12 P13 P24. **losengers** faulx losengers B7 P13.
30.3 **quant** car B7 L4 P12 P13. **acompagnié de** ensemble avecques toy P12; et avoies avec toy P13. **contraires** contrarieuses P12. **ne . . . as** lesquellez tu nas B7. **et en** ne en B7 P12.
30.4 **quant** car B7 L4 P12 P13. **demonstres** as demonstre B7 L4 P12 P24. **la grant** ta grant L4 P24.
30.5 **conseilz** consilliers P24.
30.7 **suy** sceu P12. **erre** L4 P12; errent B7 P7 P13 P24.
30.8 **dit** add dessus B7 L4 P12 P24. **d'ennemy** de deable B7 L4 P12 P13 P24.

30.4 Chaucer inserts a remark found in neither the French nor the Latin which describes how Melibee elicited bad advice: *They han espied by youre wordes to what thyng ye been enclyned* (1250).

30.7 Chaucer's translation is quite free here and he adds: *Ye han cast alle hire wordes in an hochepot* (1257).

30.8 At the end of this passage P24 adds a clause present in neither the Latin text nor Chaucer's translation of the French: *et pour ce je ne vueil plus en ce penser.*

Chapter 31: On the particular examination of counsel

31.1 *Therefore let us consider the kind of advice that might be considered useful, God willing. In order to do this correctly, we will begin with the details."*

31.2 Lors dist Prudence: "Examinons tout ton conseil, et veons lesquelz ont parley plus raisonnablement (fol. 62r) et donné meilleur conseil. Et pour ce que l'examination soit mieux faite, commençons aux cysurgiens et aus phisiciens, qui premier parlerent. Je," dist elle, "dy que les cysurgiens et les phisiciens dirent en conseil ce qu'ilz devoient dire, et parlerent sagement, car a leur office appartient a un chascun proffiter et a nul nuire; et selon leur dit, ilz doivent avoir grant diligence de la cure de ceulz qu'ilz ont en gouvernement, ainsi comme il ont dit et respondu sagement. Et pour ce je conseille qu'ilz soient haultement guerdonné en tele maniere qu'ilz entendent plus lieement en la cure de ta fille. Car ja soit ce qu'ilz soient tes amis, tu ne dois pas souffrir qu'il te servent pour neant, mais les dois plus largement reguerdonner. Mais quant a la proposicion que les phisiciens, adjousterent que es maladies un contraire se garist par son contraire, je vouldroye bien savoir comment tu l'entens." (1265–78)

31.3 "Certes," dist Mellibee, "je l'entens ainsi: car comme ilz m'ont fait un contraire, que je leur en face un autre. Et pour ce qu'ilz se sont vengez de moy et m'ont fait injure, je me vengeray d'eulz et leur feray injure, et lors auray curé un contraire par autre contraire." (1279–82)

31.4 "Or veez," dist Prudence, "comment un chascun croit legerement ce qu'il vuelt et ce qu'il desirre. Certes," dist elle, "la parole des phisciens ne doit pas estre ainsi entendue. Car mal n'est pas contraire a mal, ne vengence a vengence, ne injure a injure, mais sont semblables. Et pour ce, vengence ne se garit pas par vengence, ne injure par injure, mais accroist tousjours li uns l'autre. Mais la parole doit estre ainsi entendue: car mal et bien sont contraires, paix et guerre, vengence et souffrance, discord et accord; et ainsi de moult d'autres. Mais mal se doit garir par bien, descort par accord, guerre par paix; et ainsi de tous les autres. (1283–90)

31.5 *Follow St. Paul who said in his letter to the Romans: Do not try to overcome evil unless you conquer it with good.*

31.6 *In the same epistle, he said: Do anything you can that will lead to peace.*

31.2 **tout** *om* L4. **dit** art B7 L4 P12 P13. **ilz doivent avoir** avoir B7 L4 P12. **gouvernement** leur gouvernement P12 P24. **tu ne dois** toutesvoies tu ne dois L4 P12 P24. **reguerdonner** paier et guerdonner P24. **adjousterent** adjoustent cest assavoir P13; monstrent B7 L4. **son** un autre L4 P13; autre P24; son autre P12.

31.3 **contraire³** *om* B7 L4 P12 P13 P14.

31.4 **Prudence** dame Prudence P13. **d'autres** *add* chosez B7.

31.2 This conversation between Prudence and Melibee unpacks the ambiguity of word play described above (2.23). The Latin text is very clear on this point and draws attention to the *verbum dubium* employed by the physicians with specific reference to the phrase: *sicut per physicam contraria contrariis curantur, ita et in guerra atque vindicta et in aliis rebus contraria contrariis curari consueverunt*

31.7 Et ad ce s'accorde Saint Pol l'Apostre en moult de lieux. 'Ne rendez,' dit il, 'mal [pour mal], ne mesdit pour mesdit; mais faites bien a cellui qui mal vous fera, et beneïssez cellui qui vous maudira'; et en moult d'autres lieux il admonneste moult a paix et a accord. (1291–4)

31.8 Or couvient parler du conseil que donnerent les advocas, les sages, les anciens, qui furent tuit d'un accord et dirent que devant toutes choses tu dois mettre diligence en garder ta personne et en garnir ta maison, et dirent aussi qu'en ceste besoingne l'on doit aler adviseement a grant deliberation. (1295–8)

31.9 *To be sure, their advice may prove unquestionably correct and may be supported by wisdom of every kind. However, the reasons why you regarded their advice with approval very much require, in my judgment, further examination and discussion. What they said about safeguarding your person will be carefully laid out.*

Chapter 32: On personal safety before war is declared

32.1 *You had better believe that those who plan to wage war against many people would do best to watch out for themselves.*

32.2 Quant au premier point, qui touche la garde de ta personne, tu dois savoir que cellui qui a guerre doit tousjours humblement et devoltement demander la garde et l'aide de Dieu. Car en cest monde nul ne [se] puet garder souffisamment senz la garde de Nostre Seigneur. (fol. 62v) Pour ce dit David le Prophete: Se Dieu de la cité n'est garde, pour neant veille qui la garde. (1299–1304)

32.3 Aprés, la garde de ta [personne], tu la dois commettre a tes loyaulx amis esprouvez et cogneuz, et a eulx dois demander aide pour toy garder. Car Cathon dit: Se tu as besoing d'aide, demande la a tes amis, car il n'est nul si bon phisicien comme le loyal amy. (1305–7)

32.4 Aprés, tu te dois garder de toutes gens estranges et mescogneuz et de leur compagnie, et avoir leur compagnie suspecte. Car Pierre Alphons dit: Ne t'acompagne en chemin a nulle personne se tu ne la cognois avant. Et s'il s'acompaigne a toy senz ta voulenté et enquiert de ta voye, fains que tu veulz aler plus loing que tu n'as proposé; et se il porte lance, si te tien a sa destre; s'il porte espee, tien toy a sa senestre. (1308–12)

32.5 Aprés, garde toy sagement de touz ceulz [desquelz le conseil] je t'ay dit dessus que tu doiz eschever et fuir. (1313)

31.7 **pour mal** B7 L4 P12 P13 P24; pour bien P7. **a paix … accord** paix et accort L4.

32.2 **humblement** devant toutes choses humblement P12 P24; avant toutes autres choses humblement P13. **se** L4 P12 P13 P24; *om* P7. **personne** personnes *final s canc* P7.

32.4 **mescogneuz** menchongniers B7 L4 P13 P24. **suspecte** en suspect B7. **de ta voye** de ta vie P12. **fains** faing de ta voie et P24.

32.5 **desquelz le conseil** L4; lequel conseil P7 P12; que P13 P24. **doiz** *add* leur conseil P24.

32.6 Aprés, garde toy [en telle maniere] que pour la presumpcion de ta force tu ne desprises point ton adversaire tant que tu l'ayes essayé, car sages homs doit tout doubter, especialment ses ennemis. [Et Salemon dit: Beneureux] est celui qui tousjours se doubte, car a celui qui pour la durté de son cuer et de soy a trop grant presumpcion, mal lui vendra. (1314–18)

32.7 Tu dois donques doubter tous agaiz, toutes espies. (1319)

32.8 Car, selon ce que dit Senecques: Te sage qui doubte escheve tous maulx. (1320–1)

32.9 *And he also said: The man who worries about ruin will never be ruined.*

32.10 Et ja soit ce qu'il te soit semblant que tu soies bien seur et en seur lieu, toutevoye tu doiz tousjours avoir diligence de toy garder. (1322)

32.11 Car Senecques dit: Qui seur se garde n'a doubte de nul peril.

32.12 Aprés, tu te doiz garder non pas tant seulement de ton grant fort ennemi, mais de tout le plus petit. Car Senecques dit: Il appartient a homme bien enseingnié qu'il doubte son petit ennemi. (1323–4)

32.13 Et Ovide ou livre *De remede d'amours* dit: La petite vivre occist le grant thorel; et le chien, qui n'est pas moult grant, retient bien le sanglier. (1325–6)

32.14 *Pamphilius said: Little things can lead to great events; a spark can give rise to a huge fire; results of great consequence can arise from modest beginnings.*

32.15 *And furthermore: If such little things prove harmful, the wise man should avoid them.*

32.16 *And Martial said: Those whom the lion may not seize may be killed by the*

32.6   **en telle maniere** B7 L4 P12 P13 P24; *om* P7. **tu . . . essaye** laisses tes gardes P24; tu laisses tes gardes P12. **Et . . . beneureux** B7 L4 P12 P13 P24; bien ame P7. **car a** car B7 P13 P24.

32.8   **Senecques** Seneque qui toutes choses doubte en nulle ne cherra et encores dit il P24; Senesque qui toutes les (choses P24) doubte en nulle ne cherra et encores dit (*add* il P24) B7 L4 P12 P13 P24. **tous** *om* P12.

32.11   **car . . . peril** *om* P12 P13.

32.12   **aprés . . . garder** *om* P12 P13.

32.13   **vivre** mustelle B7 L4 P13.

32.7 The injunction to be wary of *spies* is not in the Latin.

32.8 Chaucer's citation is longer than that in P7; it yokes together two maxims from Publilius Syrus which appear in the Latin and some of the French manuscripts: B7, L4, P13, and P24. See the list of variants.

32.11 Chaucer omits this citation which appears in the Latin and some of the French texts. Severs suggested that he was following the example of two manuscripts, P12 and P13, which also omit it at this point, this the result of eyeskip.

32.13 Chaucer omits the specific reference to the *Remedia amoris* present in the Latin text and all the French manuscripts. More famously he departs from the French text by altering the Ovidian passage so that it reads: *the litel wesele wol slee the grete bole and the wilde hert. And the book seith: 'A litel thorn may prikke a kyng ful soore* (1325–6). Though Skeat once invented an elaborate account of scribal blundering to explain this passage, in recent years, several Chaucerians have argued that the passage contains coded or symbolic references to personalities within the Ricardian *familia*; see, for example, David Aers and Lynn Staley, *The Powers of the Holy: Religion, Politics and Gender in Late Medieval Culture* (University Park, 1996), pp. 227–9.

32.16 Unidentified by Sundby, the source of this citation is Godfrey of Winchester, *Liber proverbiorum*, 50.

spider after all. Worry about not only the big things, Aemule; be anxious about the small.

32.17 Toutesfoiz, tu ne dois pas estre tant doubteux que tu doubtes la ou riens n'a a doubter. (1327)

32.18 *As Seneca said: The timid see danger where there is none.*

32.19 *And elsewhere he says: A man who is constantly afraid is constantly condemned.*

32.20 Car il est escript: Aucunes gens ont enseingnié eulx decevoir; mais ilz ont trop doubte que on ne les deceust. (1328)

32.21 *And Cato said: The coward and the anxiety-ridden are better off dead.*

32.22 Aprés, tu te dois garder de venin et de compagnie de moqueurs. Car il est escript: Avec le moqueur n'ayes compagnie, mes la fuy et sa parole comme le venin. (1329–30)

32.23 *You will become enmeshed in their society and despise others who are affable.*

32.24 Quant au second point, ouquel dirent les sages que tu dois garnir ta maison a grant diligence, je vouldroye bien savoir comment tu entens ceste garnison." (1331–2)

32.25 "Je," dist Mellibee, "entens ainsi: que je doy garnir ma maison de tours, d'eschaffaulx, d'eschifes, et de autres ediffices, par lesquelz je me puisse garder et deffendre, et pour cause desquelz les ennemis doubtent approucher ma maison." (1333–4)

Chapter 33: On the fortified tower

33.1 Lors respondi Prudence: "La garnison de tours haultes et de grans ediffices appartient aucunes foiz a orgueil. (1335)

33.2 *This is the sort of thing that gives rise to fear and loathing, turns neighbors into enemies as a result of their anxiety and leads to much evil, and I have explained this kind of anxiety to you in the chapter on avoiding the counsel of those whose courtesy is driven by fear rather than love.*

32.17 **n'a** nest B7 L4 P13.
32.22 **le moqueur** les moqueurs B7 L4 P12 P13 P24. **la . . . parole** fuy leurs paroles L4 P24; fuy ces paroles P12. **le venin** venin B7 P13.
32.24 **entens** lentens B7 L4 P12 P13 P24.
32.25 **d'eschaffaulx . . . ediffices** craveaulx deschieres de trait delravons de bombardes et de toutes autres choses P13. **deffendre** *add* ma maison P24. **les** mes B7 L4 P13. **doubtent** doubteront P24.

32.20 As Severs noted, this citation from the letters of Seneca (3.3) is unclear in P7 and as a consequence Chaucer's version does not do justice to Seneca. As Chaucer has it, those who fear deception deceive others, but the Latin indicates that those who fear deception teach others to deceive. Two manuscripts of the French text, L4 and P24, in an attempt to clarify, read *leur decevoir* rather than *decevoir*.
33.2 Prudence refers to her earlier discussion of this issue in chapter 21.

33.3 *As Solomon said: He who makes his house grand can anticipate ruin and he who refuses to learn this will fall into evil.*

33.4 Aprés, l'on (fol. 63r) fait les tours et les grans ediffices a grant travail et a grans despens; et quant elles sont faites, elles ne valent riens se elles ne sont deffendues par sages et par bons amis loyaulx et a grans missions. (1336)

Chapter 34: On pride

34.1 *Concerning pride, Jesus Sirach said: The beginning of human pride is to turn against the Lord, to turn one's heart away from one's maker, this the sin with which all pride begins.*

34.2 *He also said: Pride is hateful to God and to man and injustice is repulsive to both.*

34.3 *He also said: Panic and violence make a havoc of houses and desolation overtakes the house of the proud.*

34.4 *And the wise man said: Where there is pride, disgrace follows, but where there is humility, wisdom and glory follow.*

34.5 *And he also said: A man's pride will bring him humiliation, but he who humbles himself will win glory.*

34.6 *And said too: Pride goes before destruction, an arrogant spirit before a fall.*

34.7 *And Job said: A man may be exalted, his head touching the clouds, but then vanish like a phantom in a trice.*

34.8 *Therefore pride is loathsome and the source of a wide array of evils, an issue that has been discussed in the book* De forma vitae *in the chapter on avoiding the friendship of perverse and arrogant men, and, since the fortified tower does give rise to nothing but trouble, it is my advice that you neither build one nor rely upon weapons which are bound to fail or prove inadequate."*

34.9 *Then Melibee responded. "Then how can I protect my house?"*

33.4 **fait ... ediffices** les fait P13.

33.4 Though he mentions "grete edifices" in 1335, Chaucer omits the phrase *gran ediffices* in 1336, but his editors nonetheless supply it from the French text or from two late manuscripts of the *Canterbury Tales*; q.v. *The Riverside Chaucer*, p. 1131. Severs rightly said that the phrase is also missing in P13, but his remark that it is missing from the Latin is at least misleading since the chapter in the Latin opens with a reference to towers and other *aedificiorum*. At issue in the Latin text is the celebrated controversy surrounding the building of towers in Italian cities. While Chaucer also omits the phrase *grans missions* present in the French and represented in the Latin, he does refer to *grete costages* in the previous line (1336). In short, the sense of the Latin, French, and English texts is essentially the same.

Chapter 35: On weapons

35.1 *[Dit Prudence:]* "Et pour ce sachiez que la plus grant garnison et la plus fort que uns riches homs puisse faire a garder son corps et ses biens, c'est qu'il soit amez de ses subgez et de ses voisins; quar Tulles dit, 'Une garnison que l'on ne puet vaincre ne desconfire est l'amour des citiens.' (1337–40)

35.2 *It is another weapon, namely virtue, which protects both body and soul and can prove invincible; on this point, Aesop said: When you face the enemy, the breastplate may not help you, the sharp dagger prove useless, the spear fail you, but virtue will always protect you.*

35.3 *There are other weapons which are used for defensive purposes: moats, high walls, ramparts and the like.*

35.4 *And there are yet other weapons which might be employed primarily for defense but can also be used for aggression: arrows, catapults and other kinds of arms. Of all the weapons with which you could defend your home and your body (which is the home of your soul), there must be something better than a fortified tower.*

35.5 Quant au tiers point, ou li sage et li ancien dirent que l'on ne doit point aler en ceste besoingne soudainnement ne hastivement, mais se doit l'on pourveoir et appareillier a grant diligence [et a grant deliberacion, je croy qu'ilz parlent bien et saigement]. (1341–2)

35.6 [Car Tulles dit: En toutes besongnes devant l'on les commence, on se doit appareillier a grant diligence]. En vengence, donques, en guerre, en bataille, et en garnison faire, devant ce que on encommence, on doit faire son appareil en grant deliberacion. Car Tulles dit: Long appareillement de bataille fait brief victoire. (1343–7)

35.7 Et Cassidoires dit: La garnison est plus puissant quant elle est de long temps pensee. (1348)

35.8 *Matters of war are best considered in time of peace and weapons always drawn at leisure, since a wrong must be investigated and judged with great care. The strong are those who weigh every truth.*

35.9 Or couvient aler au conseil que te donnerent tes voisins qui te portent reverence senz amour, tes ennemis reconciliez, les losengers, ceulz qui te conseilloient d'une chose en secret et disoient autre en appert, les jeunes gens

---

35.1 **faire** avoir B7 L4 P12 P13 P24.
35.5 **et a grant . . . saigement** B7 L4 P12 P13 P24; *om* P7. **parlent** parlerent B7 P12 P13 P24.
35.6 **Car . . . diligence** B7 L4 P12 P13 P24; *om* P7.

35.1 Because chapter 34 and the question Melibee raises at its end do not appear in the French text, the speech which Prudence began in chapter 33 continues here in Renaud and Chaucer.

35.7 The citation of Cassidorus *Variae* 1:17 in the French abbreviates the parallel citation in the Latin.

35.9–35.10 Chaucer drops the phrase *puis que elles sont dictes en general* (1355), present in the Latin and the French and his translation here takes a paraphrastic turn. Severs speculated that his manuscript "was faulty or incomprehensible at this point." It should be noted, however, that the French also abbreviates the discussion of these issues in the Latin.

qui tuit te conseilloient de toy vengier tantost et faire guerre incontinent. Et certes, ainsi comme je t'ay dit dessus, tu erras moult en appeller ces gens a ton conseil, lequel conseil est assez reprouvé par les choses dessus dictes. Toutevoie, puis que elles sont dictes en general, nous descendrons en especial. (1349–55)

35.10 Or veons donques premierement selon ce que dit Tulles, la verité de cest conseil. Et certes de la verité de ceste besoingne ne couvient pas moult enquerre, quar l'on scet bien cui sont ceulz qui t'ont fait ceste injure, et combien ilz sont, et comment et quant et quelle injure il ont faite. (1355–8)

35.11 Examinons, donques, la seconde condicion que Tulles met, que il appelle 'consentement': c'est a dire, cui sont ceulz, et combien il sont, qui se consentent a ton conseil et a ta voulenté. Et considerons aussi cui sont ceulz, et quans, et quelz, qui se consentent a tes adversaires. Quant au premier, l'on scet bien quelz gens se consentent a ta voulenté, car tous ceulz que je t'ay nommé dessus qui conseillent que tu faces guerre tantost. Or veons, donques, que tu es et cui sont ceux que tu tiens tant a amis. Quant a ta personne, ja soit ce que tu soies riches et puissans, toutevoye tu es tout seul et n'as nulz enfans masles, fors une fille tant seulement. Tu n'as freres ne cousins germains ne nulz autres bien prouchains amis pour paour desquelz tes ennemis cessent de toy poursuivre et destruire. Et ta personne destruite, [tu scez bien] que tes richesses se mesleront et se diviseront en diverses parties; et quant (fol. 63v) chascun aura sa piece, il ne te feront force de vengier ta mort. Mais tes ennemis sont trois et ont moult d'enfans, de freres, et d'autres bien prouchains amis desquelz, quant tu en auras occis deux ou trois, encores en demourront assez qui pourront venger leur mort et te pourront occirre. Et ja soit ce que tes amis soient trop plus que les amis de tes adversaires, toutevoye il t'appartiennent moult de loing, et les amis de tes adversaires leur sont prouchains. Et quant ad ce leur condicion est meilleur que la tienne. (1359–76)

35.9 **ces telles** B7 L4 P13 P24.
35.11 **premier** *add* point B7. **masles** *om* P24. **amis** parens P24; parens ne amis P13. **Et ta ... destruite** *om* L4 P13 P24. **tu ... bien** B7 L4 P13 P24; *om* P7 P12. **se mesleront** appetiseront B7 L4; se appetisseront P13. **piece** partie P13.

35.11 Chaucer translates *car tous ceulz que je t'ay nomme dessus qui conseillent que tu faces guerre tantost* as *for trewely, alle tho that conseilleden yow to maken sodeyn werre* (1364), but then adds at the end of the clause a phrase found in neither the French nor Latin: *ne been nat youre freends*. Severs argued that the addition was determined by the grammatical awkwardness of the French text, but a contextual explanation is worthy of consideration. Again, if other elements in the text have been altered to accommodate the court of Richard II, it should be noted that the advice Richard received from his friends was a frequent target of criticism in the 1380s. In line 1365, Chaucer omits the phrase *quo to es et* appearing in all the French manuscripts and in the Latin text. He concludes the same clause with a translation of the phrase *quant a ta personne* which, as Severs noted and as the French manuscripts and Latin text indicate, properly begins the next clause, Chaucer's 1365. Severs speculated that there might be a warrant for Chaucer's mistranslation in some manuscript other than those he examined. In line 1367, by specifically dropping the word *masles*, present in most of the French texts and paralleled by the Latin, Chaucer omits reference to male children among the relatives unavailable to Melibee. Though only one French manuscript, P24, also omits *masles*, Severs asserted that Chaucer must have had such a manuscript before him. However, again, the context into which Chaucer introduced this text deserves consideration.

35.12 Aprés, veons encores se le conseil que l'on t'a donné de la vengence tantost prendre se consent a raison. Et certes tu scez que non. Car selon droit nul ne doit faire vengence d'autrui fors le juge qui a la juridicion sur lui, ja soit ce que vengence soit ottroyee ou promisse a aucun quant on la fait incontinant et attrempeement selon ce que droit le commende. (1377–80)

Chapter 36: On the meanings of the word *posse*

36.1 Aprés, encor sur ce mot 'consentement,' tu dois regarder se ton povoir se consent a ta voulenté et a ton conseil. Et certes on puet dire que non. (1381–3)

36.2 *The word 'posse' has many possible meanings. It can refer to the ease with which something can be done and it could refer to the easiness itself. It can indicate when to do something, specifically when it is equitable. It is used this way in the following statement to which the law attests: do nothing which violates our sense of piety, charity, or modesty or violates our sense of morality and do not believe that such things can be done.*

36.3 *This is how* posse *was used by Mark when he said of Christ: He was not able* (poterit) *to work many miracles there.*

36.4 *And this is how it was used by the apostle in his second letter to the Corinthians: We are not able* (possumus) *to do anything which is against the truth, only that which is for the truth.*

36.5 Posse *can also mean* power *as it did when the Lord in His passion said to Saint Peter: Do you not think that I am able* (possum) *to pray to my Father and that He would send me twelve legions of angels.*

36.6 Posse *can also mean* possibility *as it did when the Lord said to Moses in* Exodus: *You will not be able* (poteris) *to see my face because a man cannot see me and live.*

36.7 Posse *can also mean* abilities *or* facilities *or even* talents *as it did when the Lord said to the evangelist Matthew: Are you able* (poteris) *to drink the cup that I am drinking?*

36.8 Posse *can also mean* grace *as it did when, in the book of Wisdom, the personification of Wisdom said: I know that I would not be able* (possum) *to know anything were it not for the Lord, etc.*

36.9 *As this is how it was used when the Lord said to the Evangelist: No man is able* (potest) *to come to me unless the Father draws him to me.*

36.9 *Another definition of* posse *takes the law into consideration, raises the issue of what it is to be responsible. This sense of the word* posse *is contained in the verse which reads: Power* (posse) *is conferred by the law, by nature, by*

35.12 **se consent** est accordant P13. **scez** scees bien P13. **faire** prendre B7 L4 P13.
36.1 **on puet** tu pues P13 P24.

36.2 Here begins an elaborate semantic discussion of the Latin word *posse* which the French translator might have found daunting or, at least, impossible to translate.

public authority, by meritorious service and, fifth, by the will of God.

36.11 Car, a parler proprement, nous ne povons a riens fors ce que nous povons faire dehuement et selon droit. Et quar selon droit tu ne doiz prendre vengence de ta propre auctorité, l'on puet dire que ton povoir ne se consent point a ta voulenté. (1381–6)

36.12 *Do not try to do more than you are able. It has been written: Those who serve nature accomplish the most; those who would be like gods do much less.*

36.13 *Furthermore: Without its power, no law can result in justice; a criminal cannot be judged when there is an absence of power.*

36.14 *Your power should not be used to exact revenge. A man who craves revenge and fighting with others is as guilty as his enemies and should be delivered to prison. It is written: The person who does not fight fairly is someone who would strip himself of any sense of superiority.*

36.15 *Furthermore: When you are vulnerable to others, you should not expose yourself to blows. Too: When you extend your arms, be careful that you do not expose your body. Among the ignorant and the impetuous with a taste for fighting, not everyone appears to die; others of them can only take a great fall, and that includes the tyrant.*

36.16 *It is commonly said: A man who is willing to die or be destroyed should kill a tyrant. Also: A man who maliciously seeks to avenge an injury will find that revenge makes the injury worse.*

36.17 *As far as the word* consent *or* agreement *is concerned, you should take note of three brief points. The first is that you should consider both those who agree with your view as well as those who disagree with it. The second, whether or not your reason agrees with your view. The third, whether or not your power is in agreement with what is possible or what is unlikely. And as far as the word* consent *is concerned, that is all that needs to be said.*

36.18 Or couvient examiner le tiers point, que Tulles appelle 'consequent.' Tu dois, donques, savoir que a la vengence que tu veulz faire est consequent et ensuit autre vengence, peril, et guerre, et moult de maulx et de dommages lesquelz on ne voit pas maintenant. (1386–9)

36.19 Quant au quart point, que Tulles appelle 'engendrement,' tu dois savoir que ceste injure est engendree de la hayne de tes ennemis; de la vengeance se engendrera autre vengeance, hayne, contens, guerre, et degastemens de tes biens. (1390–2)

36.20 *Fifth, we should examine the relationship between this word and causation.*

36.18 **a la** la P13. **Moult . . . maulx** dautres maulx sans nombre P13; moult daultres maulz sans nombre B7; dautre mal sans nombre et sans mesure L4.

36.11 A loose translation of the corresponding passage in the Latin.
36.13 Recorded by Walther, *Proverbia* 32103.

Chapter 37: On causation

37.1 Quant aux causes, qui eat la darrenier point que Tulles y met, tu dois savoir que l'injure qui t'a esté faite a deux causes ouvrieres et efficaces: la loingtaingne et la prouchainne. (1393–5)

37.2 La lointaingne est Dieu, qui est cause de toutes causes. (1396)

37.3 La prouchainne sont tes trois ennemis. (1397)

37.4 La cause accidental fu hayne. (1398)

37.5 La cause material sont les cing playes de ta fille. (1399).

37.6 La cause formal fut la maniere de faire l'injure: c'est assavoir car ilz appoyerent eschieles et entrerent par les fenestres. (1400)

37.7 La cause final fut car ilz vouldrent oceirre ta fille, et pour eulz ne demora. (1401)

37.8 La cause final lointaingne, a quel fin ilz vendront de ceste besoingne, nous ne la povons pas bien savoir, fors que par conjectures et presumpcions. (1402)

37.9 Car nous devons presumer qu'il en vendront a male fin, par raison du *Decret* qui dit: A grant pene sont menees a bonne fin les choses qui (fol. 64r) sont mal commencees. (1403–4)

37.10 Qui me demanderoit pourquoy Dieu a voulu et souffert que l'on t'a fait tel injure, je n'en sauroye pas bien respondre pour certain. (1405)

37.11 *It is, as Saint Prosper said, senseless to pass judgment upon the secrets in the heart of another.*

37.12 Quar, selon ce que dit l'appostre: La science et le jugement Nostre Seigneur sont si parfont que nulz ne le puet comprendre ne encercher souffisamment. (1406–7)

37.13 *But based on my beliefs or intuition, I say, as Cassiodorus said, that nothing in this world happens without a cause, that events are never happenstance.*

37.14 Toutevoyes, par aucunes presumpcions je tien et croy que Dieu, qui est

---

37.1   **efficaces** efficiens B7. **loingtaingne** cause lontaine P13. **prouchainne** cause prouchaine P13.

37.2   **lointaingne** cause lontaine P13. **causes** choses P12 P13.

37.6   **appoyerent** apporterent B7 L4 P13.

37.8   **la . . . lointaingne** mais la cause final (*om* P12) loingtaine B7 L4 P12 P13. **presumpcions** par presumptions P12 P13.

37.9   **choses** causes P12.

37.10   **tel** ceste P24.

37.12   **le jugement** les jugemens L4 P13; li jugement B7. **Nostre Seigneur** de Dieu P13. **si parfont que** parfont P12. **le puet** les puet B7 L4 P12 P13 P24.

37.1 Rather than translate the French terminology used to describe causation here, Chaucer introduces Latin terms instead. This Latin terminology is not based on Albertano's text but drawn, as Chaucer specifically indicates, from the language of *clerks* and parallel passages surface, predictably, in a number of contemporary philosophical and scientific works.

37.2 The final thought in this passage paraphrases a citation from John 1:3 in the Latin text.

37.12 Though Skeat claimed that Chaucer modified the Pauline text in the Latin (1 Corinthians 4:5) so that it resembled Romans 11:33, Chaucer simply follows the French text.

justes et droiturier, a souffert que ce t'est advenu par cause juste et raisonnable. (1408–9)

37.15 Car tu, qui as nom *Mellibee*, qui vault autant comme cellui qui [boit le miel as] tant voulu boire [de miel], c'est a dire, de la douceur des biens temporelz, des richesses, des delices, et des honneurs de cest monde, que tu en as esté tout yvre, et as oublié Dieu ton creatour. Ne ne lui as porté honneur ne reverence ainsi comme tu deusses. (1410–13)

37.16 *You should refuse to rely on your considerable wealth, to be awash in your vanity, to have everything your eyes desire. As much is said in the forgotten text which reads: You cannot drink honey without swallowing poison.*

37.17 Tu n'as pas bien retenu en ton memoire la parole [de Ovide], qui dit: Dessoubz le miel de la doulceur des biens du corps est estendu le venin qui occist l'ame. (1414–15)

37.18 Et Salemon dit: Se tu as trouve le miel, si en boy a souffisance; car se tu en menjue oultre mesure, il le te couviendra vomir. (1416–17)

37.19 Pour ce, par adventure Dieu a eu despit de toy, et a tourné sa face et les oreilles de sa misericorde d'autre part, et a souffret que tu as esté prins en la maniere que tu as pechié contre lui. Tu as pechié contre Nostre Seigneur; car les trois ennemis de l'umain linage, qui sont le monde, la char, et les dyables, tu les as laissié entrer en ton cuer tout franchement par les fenestres du corps senz toy deffendre souffisamment contre leurs assaulx et leurs temptations, en tel maniere qu'il ont navré l'ame de toy de cinq playes, c'est a dire, de [tous les] pechiez mortelz, qui entrerent au cuer par les cinq sens du corps. Par ceste semblance Nostre Seigneur a voulu et souffert que ces trois ennemis sont entré en ta maison par les fenestres et ont navré ta fille en la maniere dessus ditte." (1417–27)

37.14 **juste et** juste P12.
37.15 **qui as** as P12. **autant** *add* a dire B7 L4 P13. **boit . . . as** B7 P12 P24; le miel a P7; boit le miel le miel as L4 P13. **de miel** B7 P12 P24; *om* P7.
37.17 **de Ovide** L4 P12 P24; david P7; dOvide P13; Ovide B7. **estendu** esconduz P12; repost L4 P24; repus B7.
37.18 **boy** mengue B7 L4 P12 P13 P24.
37.19 **prins** pugnis B7 L4 P12 P13. **les dyables** le deable B7 L4 P12 P13 P24. **du** de ton P13. **de cinq** en cinq B7 L4. **tous les** B7 L4 P12 P13 P24; tous P7. **ces** tes P13 P24.

37.18 At the conclusion of this citation, Chaucer departs from the French and Latin texts by glossing the word *vomir* with the phrase *and be nedy and povre*, a clarification of the kind commonly found in Biblical glosses.

37.19 The Latin text specifies that the daughter of Melibee is wounded in the eyes, nose, mouth, hands and ears. Most of the manuscripts containing Renaud's text substitute *feet* for *eyes* as does Chaucer. This substitution seems based not on scribal error, as Severs thought, but on the conflation of the five senses and the five wounds of Christ to which this passage refers. For an extended discussion, see Richard Hoffman, "Chaucer's Melibee and Tales of Sondry Folk," *Classica et Medievalia* 30 (1969): 562–6.

The allegory of the three enemies of mankind who climb through the windows and maim the daughter is ultimately based, as indicated in the introduction, on medieval readings of *Jeremiah* 8:21–9:24, the most significant of which might be that found in Gregory, *Moralia in Job*, 21,2,4. The allegory was widely discussed in commonplace glosses to this text; see, for example, Jerome, *Commentariorum in Jeremiam Prophetam*, PL, vol. 24, cols. 741–6 and Rabanus Maurus, *Expositio super Jeremiam*, PL, vol. 111, cols. 871–6.

37.20 *Melibee responded, "I grant that there might be some truth to what you have explained or, at least, the appearance of truth, but I do not believe that the will of God would allow such a crime to be committed. God wills that men should do the right thing, not that they should commit crimes, as, indeed, all the writers of sacred scripture have pointed out."*

Chapter 38: The five-fold will of God

38.1 *Prudence responded, "There are five aspects to the will of God: the prescriptive, the prohibitive, next, the permissive, third, the advisory, fourth, the perfective, fifth.*

38.2 *As this verse puts it: He may prescribe and He may prohibit, He might allow, He may advise, He may do it Himself.*

38.3 *The prescriptive aspect of His will is indicated by this statement: Love the Lord your God with all of your heart and all of your soul and all of your intelligence and love your neighbor as you would yourself. And this is the prescriptive aspect of the will of God.*

38.4 *The prohibitive aspect of His will is demonstrated when He forbids others to act, for example, when He said: You shall not commit adultery nor shall you steal, and so forth.*

38.5 *The permissive aspect of His will is demonstrated when God is angry, when He denies His grace to others, turning away from them because of their sins and withdrawing from them so that His anger at their sins will be clear. Others are allowed to punish them for their sins because He Himself permits it.*

38.6 *The advisory aspect of His will is demonstrated when He tenders advice to others, as He did when He said: Go and sell everything you have and give the proceeds to the poor, if you want to be perfect.*

38.7 *The perfective aspect of His will is demonstrated by His ability to accomplish what He pleases and His ability to do anything."*

38.8 "Certes," dist Mellibee, "je voy bien que vous vous efforciez moult par doulces paroles de moy [encliner] ad ce que je ne me venge point de mes ennemis, et m'avez monstré moult sagement les perilz et les maulx qui pourront avenir de ceste vengence. Mais qui voudroit considerer en toutes vengences touz les perilz et les maulx qui s'en pevent ensuir, l'on ne feroit jamés vengence; et ce seroit moult grant dommage, car par vengence les mauvais sont ostez d'entre les bons, et ceulx qui ont cuer de mal faire se retraient quant ilz voient que l'on punit les malfaiteurs. (1427–32)

38.9 *And since a wrong done to one person is a wrong done to many, in order to keep many from being harmed and to avoid many other evils, it is necessary to punish the evildoers."*

38.8 **encliner** B7 L4 P12 P13 P24; entamer P7.

Chapter 39: The duties of judges with respect to revenge

39.1 Ad ce respont Dame Prudence. "Certes," dist elle, "je vous ottroye que de venge vient moult de biens, mais faire vengence n'appartient pas a un chascun fors seulement aus juges et a ceulz qui ont la juridicion sur les malfaiteurs. (1433–4)

39.2 Et dy plus que aussi comme une personne singuliere (fol. 64v) pecheroit en faisant vengence, aussi pecheroit le juge en laissant faire vengence. (1435–6)

39.3 Car Senecques dit: Celui nuit aus bons qui espargne les mauvais. Et selon ce que dit Cassidoires: L'on doubte faire les oultrages quant on scet qu'il desplait aus juges et aus souverains. (1437–8)

39.4 Et uns autres dit, 'Le juge qui doubte faire les droiz fait les mauvais.' (1439)

39.5 *Furthermore: The judge who does not punish the wrongdoer increases the number of wrongdoers.*

39.6 *And another said: The coddling of criminals increases their audacity.*

39.7 *Therefore, judges should exact revenge by punishing men physically and financially.*

39.8 Et Saint Pol l'Appostre dit en l'epistre [aux] Rommains que le juge ne porte pas le glaive senz cause, mais le porte pour punir les mauvais et pour deffendre les prodommes. (1440–1)

39.9 *Good people need not fear the power of judges; as Paul said: It is only the wicked, not those who do the right thing, who should fear those in a position of power. If you want to live without fear, you must live honestly and such authorities will even praise you.*

39.10 *Only the wicked cringe in the face of authority; as Paul also said: If you are a criminal, you should be afraid.*

39.11 *It is written: The good hate vice because they love virtue but the evil hate vice because they fear punishment.*

39.1 **ad ce . . . malfaiteurs** *om* P12.
39.2 **faire vengence** *add* des delinquens P13.
39.8 **aux** B7 L4 P12 P13 P24; des P7. **prodommes** bons P13.

39.1 Not translated by Chaucer but added by all modern editors; the passage is also omitted in P12, the result of eyeskip. Whether or not Chaucer worked with such a manuscript is of course an entirely different question. This chapter deals with the administration of the law, and Renaud himself only translated about half of it. This may reflect difficulties paralleling ideas rooted in the practice of the law in the Lombard communes with similar practices in feudal France and for Chaucer the text might have been further complicated by differences between English common law, on the one hand, and European civil law on the other.

39.3 These clausulae are reversed in the Latin and tied together with repetitive transitional material which the French translator ignored. As Skeat and Severs noted, Chaucer seems to mistranslate the citation from Seneca. While the French and parallel Latin text might be translated *The good are harmed when the evil are spared*, Chaucer offers *That maister is good that proveth shrewes*. This might be due to a faulty manuscript reading as some have suggested, but for the reasons noted above, larger legal questions might also be at issue.

39.6 Unidentified by Sundby, this citation is recorded by Walther, *Proverbia* 3792 and appears in the *Liber Kalilae et Dimnae*, ed. Hervieux, vol. 5, p. 469.

39.12 *Thus, as the law indicates, a judge can and should treat criminals with severity, execute them, punish them, imprison them, and deprive them of their property so that his authority is not regarded with contempt.*

39.13 *As Cicero said: It is not unnatural to take property from a man who has destroyed someone who is honest.*

39.14 *And Cassiodorus said: The authority who holds the insignificant in contempt abuses the entire social contract.*

39.15 *If you would like to consider this carefully, there is considerable discussion of revenge in the book* De forma vitae, *in the chapter on appropriate forms of revenge. When it comes to exacting revenge, you should think about it carefully and you should realize that revenge is appropriate to God or to a secular judge and not to you or to some other individual.*

39.16 Se tu veulz donques avoir vengence de tes ennemis, tu recourras au juge qui a la juridicion sur eulx, et il les punira selon droit et encores s'il ont desservi en [leur] avoir en telle maniere qu'il demourront pouvre et vivront a honte." (1442–3)

39.17 "He!" dist Mellibee, "ceste vengence ne me plait point. Je regarde que fortune m'a norri des mon enfance et m'a aidié a passer moult de fors pas. Je la vueil maintenant essayer, et croy que a l'aide de Dieu elle m'aidera a vengier ma honte." (1444–6)

Chapter 40: On fortune

40.1 "Certes," dist Prudence, "se tu veulz ouvrer de mon conseil, tu n'essaieras point fortune ne ne t'apuyeras a elle. (1447)

40.2 Car, selon le dit de Senecques: Les choses se font folement qui se font en esperance de fortune. (1448–9)

40.3 Car, selon ce qu'il mesmes dit: Fortune est une verriere qui de tant comme elle est plus belle et plus clere et resplendissant, de tant est elle plus tost brisee. (1450)

40.4 *The third reason is that by doing this, by banking on Fortune, you might disregard Nature or forget about it. This proverb says as much: Men who surrender to Fortune are unaware of Nature.*

39.16 **recourras** retourneras P24. **leur** B7 L4; eulx P7 P12 P13 P24.
40.2 **choses** *add* qui P24.
40.3 **belle et plus** *om* B7 L4 P12 P13 P24.

39.16 The French abridges the Latin here, but the sense of the passage is essentially the same. For his part, at line 1443 Chaucer omits the passage: *et encores s'il ont desservi en leur avoir en telle maniere qu'il demourront pouvre et vivront a honte.* Since this text appears not only in all the French manuscripts but also the Latin, a contextual explanation suggests itself. Assuming that Chaucer's text was addressed to the court of Richard II, the suggestion that his enemies be punished in a specific way might have been regarded as impertinent at best.

40.3 Chaucer does not quite omit this passage (1450) as Severs claimed; his translation nonetheless is loose and the simile which likens Fortune to glass is obscured by his language.

40.5 *The fourth reason is this: Fortune, like an inexperienced doctor, kills many.*

40.6 *The fifth reason is that Fortune cannot save those who are devoted to her.*

40.7 Et pour ce ne te fie point en fortune; car elle n'est point estable, et la ou tu cuideras estre plus seurs de son aide, elle te faudra. (1451–2)

40.8 *It is written: In this constantly changing world, nothing stays the same.*

40.9 *And as Seneca says: A man can have neither good fortune nor his own life forever.*

40.10 Et quar fortune t'a norri de ton enfance, je dy que de tant tu te doiz mains fier en lui et en ton sens. Car Senecque dit que celui que [fortune] nourrit trop, elle le fait fol. (1453–5)

40.11 *You should not have confidence in the foolish idea that fortune has anything to offer you. Indeed few or none would voice such foolishness. You should be wise and virtue will overwhelm fortune. As Seneca said in his letters: For the wise man, virtue is superior to fortune.*

40.12 *Nor should you believe that fortune might benefit you since he also said: it is incorrect to think that Fortune bestows upon us anything that is good or evil.*

40.13 *You must understand this thing which unsophisticated people call fortune. In the second book of the* Consolation, *Boethius said: Despite popular opinion, Fortune means nothing.*

40.14 *Thus Cato said: When you are reckless and out of control, it is foolish to call Fortune blind.*

40.15 *And this might be explained as follows: Do not call Fortune blind, because it is not, that is, because it is nothing.*

40.16 Puis, donques, que tu demandes vengence, [et la vengence] qui se fait selon l'ordre de droit et devant le juge ne te plait, et la vengence qui se fait en esperance de fortune est perilleuse et n'est point certainne, tu n'as remede fors que retourner au souverain et vray Juge qui venge toutes les villenies et injures, et il te vengera selon ce qui'il mesmes tesmoingne: 'A moy,' dit il, 'laisse la vengence, et je la feray.' (1456–60)

40.17 *And as the apostle said in his letter to the Colossians: One who does wrong will be paid back for the wrong he does.*

40.18 *And you will, in turn, not only be vindicated but find that all the rancor and anxiety will be removed from your heart and expelled, since, as the Prophet said: Give your heart to the Lord above, and He will support you and will never permit the just to falter."*

40.7 **te ... fortune** ty fie point P24.

40.10 **et quar** quant tu dis que B7 L4 P24; et quant tu diz P12; et quant diz que P13. **lui** elle B7 P13. **ton** son P13. **fortune** B7 L4 P12 P13 P24; nature P7. **trop** *om* L4 P24. **fol** trop fol L4 P24.

40.16 **et la vengence**[1] B7 L4 P12 P24; *om* P7 P13. **que retourner** de recourir B7; que de recourre P12; que de toy retourner et avoir recours P13.

40.10 Though *The Riverside Chaucer* cites Publilius Syrus, *Sententiae*, 172, the source is proverb 173 in the Teubner edition (Leipzig, 1869) or 203 in the Loeb edition (Cambridge, 1934).

40.19 Mellibee respondit. "Se je," dit il, "ne me venge de la villenie que l'on m'a faite, je semondray ceulz qui la m'ont faite et tous autres a moy faire une autre nouvelle villenie. Car il est escript: Se tu sueffres senz venger la vieille villenie, tu semons a la nouvelle. (1461–3)

40.20 Et ainsi pour mon souffrir l'on me fera tant de villenies de toutes pars que je ne le pourray souffrir ne porter; ains seray au bas du tout en tout. Car il est escript: En moult souffrant, (fol. 65r) t'avendront pou de choses que souffrir ne pourras. (1464–6)

40.21 *Therefore I take a bleak view of tolerance and believe that revenge is best."*

40.22 "Certes," dit Prudence, "je vous ottroye que trop grant souffrance n'est bonne, mais pour ce ne s'ensuit pas que chascune personne a cui l'on fait injure en doye prendre vengence, car ce appartient aus juges tant seulement, qui ne doivent pas souffrir que les villenies et les injures ne soient vengees. Et pour ce les deux auttoritez que tu as mises avant sont entendues tant seulement des juges que, quant ilz souffrent trop faire les injures et les villenies senz punicion, ilz ne semonnent pas tant seulement les nouvelles injures, mais les commandent. Ainsi le dit un sage: 'Le juge,' dit il, 'qui ne corrige le pecheur lui commande a pechier'; et pourroient bien tant souffrir les juges et les souverains de maulx en leur terre que les malfaiteurs les getteroient hors de leur terre et de leurs lieux, et leur couvendroit perdre en la fin leurs seignories. (1467–76)

40.23 *You should believe that the authoritative statements of others take precedence over this notion that patience, as you say, is detestable. Were your thinking better, you would not be inclined towards vengeance which agrees with neither reason nor the possibilities available to you. Reason forbids revenge after a period of time and it is reasonable that the impulse to enact revenge should not prove long lasting. It is written: You can conquer the world if you submit to reason. Thus I think that someone who does something which is unreasonable should submit all of his affairs to the just and to a court of law.*

40.24 Mais or posons que tu ayes licence de toy vengier. Je dy que tu n'as pas la puissance quant a present; car se veulz faire comparoison de ta puissance a la puissance de tes adversaires, tu trouveras en trop de choses, selon ce que je t'ay monstré dessus, leur condicion meilleur que la teue. Et pour ce je dy qu'il est bon quant a maintenant de toy souffrir et avoir patience. (1477–80)

40.20 **ainsi** aussi P12 P24. **fera** feroit P24. **villenies** villenie P24. **pou** moult B7 L4 P13; prou P12.
40.22 **s'ensuit** *add* il B7 P24. **doye prendre** prenge P12. **qui** car ilz B7 L4 P13 P24; car P12. **que quant** car quant B7 L4 P13. **les nouvelles** faire les nouvelles B7 P12 P24; faire les L4; faire lesdits P13.
40.24 **condicion** *add* est P24.

40.20 Chaucer omits (1464) the phrase *de toutes pars* which is found in all the French manuscripts and paralleled in the Latin.
40.21 The citation from the *sage* (Caecilus Balbus, *De nugis philosophorum* 41:4) does not appear in the Latin; it does however appear in a similar discussion of the role of judges in the third book of Albertano's *Liber de amore et dilectione* under the rubric: *De vindicta facienda vel obmittenda vel temperanda et de officio judicis vel cuislibet circa vindictam.*

Chapter 41: On struggle

41.1 Aprés, tu scez que l'on dit communément que contendre a plus fort est enragerie; contendre a egal est peril; contendre a mendre est honte, et pour ce l'on doit fuir tout contens tant comme l'on puet. (1481–4)

41.2 Car Salemon dit qu'il est grant honneur a homme qui se scet getter de brigue et de contemps. (1485)

41.3 Et se plus fort de toy te grieve, estudie toy plus en lui appaisier que en toy vengier. Car Senecque dit que celui se met en grant peril qui se courrouce a plus fort de lui. (1486–8)

41.4 Et Cathon dit: Se plus fort de toy te grieve, sueffre toy, car cellui qui t'a une foiz grevé te pourra une autre foiz aidier. (1489–90)

41.5 *If, therefore, you were outraged or angered, you should turn not towards vengeance but towards the safe haven of patience.*

Chapter 42: On patience

42.1 *Patience is the calm tolerance of others, or, as it is defined in the* Moralium dogma philosophorum, *patience is the virtue of bearing insults and sudden adversity with equanimity and patience is the cure for injury.*

[42.2] Or posons que tu ayes licence et puissance de toy venger; je dy encores que moult de choses sont qui te doivent retraire et te doivent encliner a toy souffrir et avoir pacience en l'injure que l'on t'a faite et es autres tribulations de cest monde. (1491–3)

[42.3] Premierement, se tu veulx considerer les deffaulx qui sont en toy, pour lesquelz Dieu a voulu souffrir que ceste tribulacion te soit advenue, selon ce que je t'ay dit dessus. (1494–5)

41.1 **scez** sces bien B7 P13. **fort** *add* de lui B7; *add* de soy P13; *add* que soy P24. **egal** *add* de soy P24.
41.2 **brigue** noise P12.
41.3 **courrouce** contence P24.
42.2 **licence et puissance** puissance et licence P13. P24. **te doivent encliner** B7 L4 P12 P13 P24; encliner P7. **pacience** B7 L4 P12 P13 P24; *add* en toy souffrir P7. **que . . . faite** qui ta este faicte P24.
42.3 **voulu souffrir** souffert B7 L4 P13.

41.2 The French contains a citation from Solomon not in the Latin and Chaucer follows its lead (1485).
42.1 These two definitions of patience are drawn from the *Moralium dogma philosophorum*, ed. Holmberg, p. 30 and p. 41.
42.2–42.8 This entire passage has been added to the Latin. It has not been drawn from Albertano's other treatises as is the case with the other lengthy additions in the French. Nor is it indebted to the *Moralium dogma philosophorum* as the citations which open the chapter might suggest.
42.2 Chaucer omits the phrase *et es autres tribulations de cest monde,* present in all the French manuscripts.

[42.4] Car li poetes dit que nous devons porter en pacience les tribulations qui nous viennent, quant nous pensons que nous les avons bien desservies. (1496)

[42.5] Et Saint Gregoire dit que quant un chascun considere bien le grant nombre des deffaulx et de ses pechiez, les penes et les tribulations qu'[il sueffre] (fol. 65v) lui apperent plus petites; et de tant comme ses pechiez lui semblent plus pesans, de tant sa pene lui semble plus legiere. (1497–1500)

[42.6] Aprés, moult te doit encliner a pacience, la pacience de Nostre Seigneur Jhesu Crist, selon Saint Pierre en ses epistres. 'Jhesu Crist,' dit il, 'a souffert pour nous et a donné a un chascun exemple de lui ensuivre. Car il ne fist onques pechié ne onques de sa bouche ne yssi une villenie. Quant on le maudisoit, il ne maudisoit point; quant on le batoit, il ne menaçoit point' (1501–3)

[42.7] Aprés, moult te doit encliner a pacience, la grant pacience des sains qui sont en Paradis, qui ont eu si grant pacience es tribulations qu'ilz ont souffert senz leur coulpe. (1504–6)

[42.8] Aprés, moult te doit encliner a pacience ce que les tribulacions de cest monde durent tres petit de temps et sont tantost passees, et la gloire que l'on acquiert pour avoir pacience est pardurable, selon ce que l'appostre en l'epistre seconde dit a ceulz de Corinte. (1507–10)

42.9 *A mind that is patient is possessed of fantastic wealth; patience, together with courage, can make a man happy and patience is a cure for sorrow.*

42.10 *Patience, it has been said, should certainly be valued above all of the other virtues; thus this verse: Of all of the virtues, none is as valuable as patience.*

42.11 *And again: When patience does not support her, virtue is a widow.*

42.12 *And Cato said: The greatest form of wealth is always the virtue of patience.*

42.13 *Socrates said: Patience is a refuge from misery.*

42.14 Aprés, tien fermement que celui n'est pas bien enseingnié qui ne scet avoir pacience, car Salemon dit que la doctrine de l'omme est cogneue par pacience. (1511–12)

42.15 Et autre part il mestnes dit que cellui qui est pacient se gouverne par grant prudence. (1513)

42.4   **bien** *om* P13 P24.
42.5   **grant** *om* P12. **des** de ses P12 P13 P24. **qu'il sueffre** B7 L4 P12 P13; quilz sueffrent P7; quil souffri P24.
42.6   **la pacience** *om* P13. **villenie** *add* parolle P24.
42.8   **avoir pacience** *add* es tribulations P12 P24. **seconde** *om* B7 L4. **dit . . . Corinte** *om* P24.
42.14 **Aprés tien** Le scripture raconte et tesmoingne P24; Apres croy P13.
42.15 **qui est** *om* B7 L4 P12 P13 P24.

42.8 Though the French paraphrases this citation of 2 Corinthians 4:17, Chaucer quotes it directly without naming the specific epistle. This text is not in the Latin.

42.14 The French version of this citation from Solomon (Proverbs 19:11) abbreviates the parallel passage in the Latin and, in P24, the citation from Solomon is followed by another which reads: *Nostre Seigneur dit que patience vaint et encores em patience nous procederons nos ames.* This appears in neither the other French manuscripts nor Chaucer and whether or not this addition is scribal or the work of Renaud de Louens is open to question.

42.15 The French abbreviates this citation in the Latin from Solomon (Proverbs 14:29).

42.16 Et lui mesmes dit: L'homme qui est courreceux fait les noises, et le pacient les attrempe. (1514)

42.17 *And you should note that just as patience is best, impatience is terrible, that it has been said: The impulsive person opens himself to punishment, that if you let him have his way with you, you have to do it again and again.*

42.18 *It is impatience that will lead a man to meddle in affairs which have no bearing on him, an act which is wrong as well as foolish; as the rule of law says: A person is guilty if he interferes in things which have nothing to do with him.*

42.19 *As Solomon says in Proverbs: Interfering in the quarrels of others is like lifting a strange dog by the ears.*

42.20 Aussi dit il que mieux vault estre bien pacient que bien fort, et plus fait a priser celui qui puet avoir la seignorie de son cuer que cellui qui par force prent les grans citez. (1515–16)

42.21 Et pour ce dit Saint Jaques en son epistre que pacience est euvre de perfeccion." (1517)

42.22 "Certes," dit Mellibee, "je vous ottroye que pacience est une tres grant vertu et de grant parfeccion, mais chascun ne puet pas avoir la parfeccion que vous alez querant. Je ne suy pas du nombre des bien parfaiz, et pour ce mon cuer ne puet estre en paix jusques a tant qu'il soit vengez. Et ja soit ce que en ceste vengence eust grant peril, je regarde que aussi avoit il grant peril a faire la villenie qui m'a esté faite, et toutesvoies mes adversaires n'ont pas regardé le peril, mais ont hardiement acomplie leur mauvaise voulenté. Et pour ce il me semble que l'on ne me doit pas reprendre se je me met en un po de peril pour moy venger et se je faiz un grant excés. Car l'on dit que excés ne se corrige que par excés; c'est a dire, que oultrage ne se corrige fors que par oultrage. (1518–25)

42.23 *Furthermore, the law allows us to repulse violence with violence and to use crime to stop crime."*

42.24 "He!" dist Dame Prudence, "Vous dictes vostre voulenté, mais certes en cas du monde l'on ne doit faire oultrage par excés pour soy venger ne autrement. (1526–7)

42.16 **attrempe** apaise et attempre P24.
42.20 **force** sa force B7; sa grant force P13.
42.22 **ottroye** *add* dame Prudence P12 P24. **tres** *om* P12 P24. **en ceste . . . peril** ce soit grans perilz a faire la vengance B7. **je regarde . . . peril** *om* P12. **Car l'on . . . par excés** *om* L4.
42.24 **par** ne B7 L4 P12 P13 P24.

42.17 This citation from Proverbs 19:19 does not appear in the French text as this point, but at the conclusion of another speech by Prudence, 42.31 below.
42.18 See 42.33.
42.19 See 42.34.
42.21 The French summarizes a long citation in the Latin from the Epistle of James 1:2–4.
42.22 Chaucer omits two phrases in his translation of Melibee's speech, first, *je regarde que aussi avoit il grant peril* (also lacking in P12); and second: *Car l'on dit que excés par excés* (also lacking in L4). Severs plausibly suggests that both omissions are the result of eyeskip and thus not found in Chaucer's manuscript.
42.24 The French summarizes the Latin and Chaucer omits the phrase *ne autrement* (1527) found in all the French manuscripts. The omission makes the advice somewhat more pointed.

42.25 *A man who follows reason can decide what is best, but the man who ignores it wallows in error. If you have carefully considered what is reasonable, you have spoken badly and you should know better. Taking one risk might do away with another, but, if you recall what was mentioned before, the danger could be compounded.*

42.26 *Furthermore, though your adversaries have sinned gravely, should you resort to excessive revenge, you too will not be immune from sin.*

42.27 Car Cassidoires dit que aussi mal fait celui qui se venge par oultrage comme celui qui fait l'outrage. (1528)

42.28 Et pour ce vous vous devez venger selon l'ordre de droit, non pas par excés ne par oultrage. Car auxi comme vous savez que voz adversaires (fol. 66r) ont pechié encontre vous par leur oultrage, aussi pechiez vous se vous vous voulez venger d'eulz par oultrage et autrement que droit le commande. (1529–30)

42.29 Et pour ce dit Senecques: L'on ne doit nul temps venger mauvaitié par mauvaistié. (1531)

42.30 Et se vous dictes que droit ottroye que l'on deffende violence par violence et barat par barat, certes c'est verité quant la deffense se fait incontinent senz intervalle et pour soy deffendre, non pas pour soy venger, et se il couvient mettre telle attrempance en deffense que l'on ne puisse reprendre celui qui se deffent d'excés ne d'outrage, car autrement ce seroit contre droit et raison. Or voys tu bien que tu ne fais pas deffense incontinent ne pour toy deffendre, mais pour toy venger; et si n'as pas voulenté de faire ton fait attrempeement. (1532–8)

[42.31] Et pour ce il me semble encores que la pacience est bonne; car Salemon dit que celui qui est impacient y aura dommage." (1539)

[42.32] "Certes," dist Mellibee, "je vous ottroye que quant un homme est impacient et courrouciez de ce qui ne lui touche et qui ne lui appartient, se dommage lui en vient, il n'est pas merveille. Car la rigle de droit dit que celui est coulpables qui s'entremet de ce qui ne li appartient point.

42.28 **auxi comme ... leur oultrage** *om* P12. **d'eulz par** de leur P12.
42.30 **ne pour** pour P24.
42.31 **est impacient** nest patient P12; nest pas patient P24.
42.32 **es Proverbes** P12 P24; ou proverbs P7; *om* B7 L4 P13. **qu'il ne ... mort** Car ainsi comme celui qui tient le chien estrange qui ne congnoit ai est aucune fois mors du chien P24. **j'en ... impacient** se je sui courroucies et impatiens B7 P12.

42.28 The French does not follow the Latin closely here; it summarizes the idea in the Latin that revenge violates the rule of law then introduces the idea that revenge is sinful, this taken from an earlier portion of Prudence's speech in the Latin (42.23). Chaucer appears to modify the sense of sin present in the passage when he omits the phrase: *auxi comme vous savez que vos adversaires ont pechié encontre vous par leur outrage.* However, as Severs noticed, the phrase is also omitted in P12 and might be read as another instance of eyeskip.

42.31 This citation is present in the French but not the Latin. It originates in an earlier speech by Prudence; 42.17 above.

42.32 The French significantly alters this response of Melibee; the ideas and citations here are drawn from an earlier speech in the Latin, 42.17–19 above. In that case, they are voiced by Prudence, but in the French, remarkably, they are put in the mouth of Melibee. At line 1542, Chaucer omits the specific reference to Proverbs 26:17 found in the French.

Et Salemon dit [es *Proverbes*] que celui qui s'entremet de la noise d'autruy est semblables a celui qui prent le chien par les oreilles qu'il ne cognoit: aucune foiz le chien le mort. Aussi est il raison que dommage viengne a cellui qui par impacience et courroux se mesle de la noise d'autrui qui riens ne lui appartient. Mais vous savez bien que ce fait me touche moult de pres. Et pour ce j'en suy courrouciez et impacient, et n'est pas merveille. (1540–6)

42.33 Et si ne voy pas, sauve vostre grace, que grant dommage me puisse venir de moy venger. Car je suy plus riche et plus puissant que ne sont mes adversaires; et vous savez que par argent et par avoir se gouvernent les choses et le fait de cest monde. Et Salemon dit que toutes choses obeïssent a peccune. (1547–50)

42.34 *And since wealth and money do control everything, many people think that it is easy to get their share of the money. These persons who imagine that they can be rich are the same persons who drive themselves to want and to poverty, to beggary and to death."*

Chapter 43: On poverty and wealth

43.1 Prudence, quant elle ot oÿ son mary venter de sa richesse et de sa puissance et despriser la pouvreté de ses adversaires, si dist: "Sire tres cher, je vous ottroye que vous estes riches et puissans et que les richesses sont bonnes a ceulz qui les ont bien acquises et qui bien en scevent user. (1551–3)

43.2 *It is true as you have said that money controls everything.*

43.3 *That is, that the common good (or the sharing of wealth) rules and controls everything. Wealth and material possessions are good in themselves since all that God has created is good.*

43.4 Car aussi comme le corps ne puet vivre senz l'ame, aussi ne puet il vivre senz biens temporelz; et par les richesses l'on puet acquerre les grans lignages et les grans amis. (1554–5)

43.5 Et pour ce dit Pamphiles: Se la fille d'un bovier est riche, elle puet eslire de mil hommes lequel qu'elle veult pour mary; car de mil on ne li en refusera pas un. (1556–7)

[43.6] Et Pamphiles mesmes dit: Se tu es amé (c'est a dire, riches) tu trouveras grant nombre de compagnons (fol. 66v) et d'amis. Et se ta fortune se a change que tu soies pouvres, que tu demourras tout seul! (1558–60)

42.33 **savez** *add* bien P24.
43.1 **Sire . . . cher** certes tres chier sire B7 L4 P12; en ceste maniere P24. **qui bien** bien P24.
43.4 **par les** par B7.
43.5 **fille** *add* dist il P12 P24. **mary** son mary P24.
43.6 **amé** beneureux B7 L4 P12 P24.

42.33 The citation from Solomon (Ecclesiasticus 10:19) is not in the Latin.
43.4 This simile is a bit more elaborate in the Latin and Chaucer omits (1555) the phrase *les gran lignages* which is in the French text and paralleled in the Latin, as perhaps inappropriate for his audience.
43.6 This citation from *Pamphilius* is not in the Latin and indeed not in the *Pamphilius de amore*. Chaucer expands the French at 1559–60 in ways which recall the *Knight's Tale* 2779 and the *Miller's Tale* 3204.

43.7 Et encores dit Pamphiles que richesses font nobles ceulz qui sont villains de lignages. (1561)

43.8 *And Horace said: A good family and beauty are the gift of the Queen, Queen Money.*

43.9 *Sometimes, moreover, goods and wealth are acquired by powerful men, such as kings and princes and those whom men follow and fear. And observe that when it is said that material possessions are good and that they can be pursued relentlessly, it is then that we may lose our possessions and wealth, that we are at risk of poverty and indigence and need as well, that we may suffer every evil imaginable.*

Chapter 44: On want

44.1 Ainsi comme de grans richesses vient moult de biens, aussi de grant povreté vient moult de maulx. Car grant pouvreté contraint la personne a moult de maulx faire. Et pour ce l'appelle Cassidoires 'mere de crimes.' (1562–5)

44.2 *It has been said: Poverty does not admit to moderation.*

44.3 *As Pedro Alfonso said: Great necessity drives even the decent man to go to the latrine. Thus you must ask your adversaries for help. This is a most serious matter.*

44.4 Et dit aussi Pierre Alphons que l'une des grans adversitez de cest siecle si est quant un homme, franc par nature, est contraint par povreté de mengier l'aumosne a son ennemi. (1566–7)

44.5 *And that is why it is extremely important for us to approach these adversaries of long standing when we suspect that they could be decent. Granted, it is necessary to suspect the worst, to test these men, all of whom know how to lie, all of whom could tie things in knots and could lead everyone towards indigence, poverty and death.*

44.6 *As the courts and this proverb point out: The poor do not admit to the law.*

44.7 *And Seneca said that poverty turns beggars into liars, that want can have her way with any man and that everyone is subject to it.*

43.7 **richesses font** par richesses sont B7 L4 P24.
44.1 **Ainsi** et aussi B7 L4 P24. **de grant povreté** de povrete B7 L4 P12.
44.4 **dit aussi** pour ce dist B7 P12 P24. **que l'une** une B7 P12 P24. **a** de P12 P24.

43.7 The *Pamphilius de amore* is not cited in the Latin. Chaucer follows the French.

44.1 *The Riverside Chaucer* suggests that the first clausula in this passage is based on Horace, *Epistles* 1.6.37 but that seems unlikely; see 43.8 above. The citation from Cassiodorus is from *Variae* 9.13 not 2.13 as *The Riverside Chaucer* indicates.

In the clausula at the end of the passage, Chaucer translates *crimes* as *ruyne* though the French and the Latin specify *crimes*. Skeat and Severs speculate that his manuscript of the French text was corrupt at this point; a consideration of the audience for this piece might lead to a different conclusion. Any suggestion that the court of Richard II might engage in criminal activity would have been regarded as offensive.

44.4 Chaucer translates (1567) the reading *mengier* which appears to be a scribal misreading of *demander*, present only in L4 which correctly translates the Latin *postulare*.

44.8 *And Cassiodorus said: We should flee from indigence just as we should avoid excess.*

44.9 *Solomon said: There are five things which oppress people: lawlessness, sorrow, hunger, war and, finally, common ignorance, and it is these things which are responsible for poverty.*

44.10 *And he also said: It is better to be dead than to be poor.*

Chapter 45: On beggary

45.1 Et la raison de ce dit Saint Innocent en un sien livre: Doulente et meschant est la condicion des povres mendians: s'il ne demandent, ilz muerent de fain; s'ilz demandent, ilz muerent de honte; et toutevoie neccessité les contraint a demander. (1568–70)

45.2 Et pour ce dit Salemon que mieux vault morir que avoir tele povreté; car, selon ce qu'il dit autre part: Mieux vault la mort amere que tele vie. (1571–2)

45.3 *In* Proverbs, *Solomon also said: Lord! Deliver me from both poverty and wealth.*

45.4 *When we follow all that is good and avoid all that is evil, then goods, possessions, money and wealth become good in themselves, especially if they are possessed by a good man. However, when an evil man possesses them, they are said to be evil since nothing is good for a man unless he is himself decent.*

45.5 *It is not because of their wealth that the evil are said to be evil, but because they use their wealth for wicked ends. As Seneca said: Wealth may cause evil not because it is intrinsically evil but because it excites men who are that way.*

45.6 *A certain philosopher said: Greed is punished by the loss of honor and murder at the hands of traitors.*

45.7 *You should enjoy your wealth but with moderation, wisdom and virtue and, as Cicero said: Virtue is a thing which we acquire through moderation and wisdom.*

45.8 *And Ovid said: There is a virtue in abstinence which is pleasing.*

45.9 *In the course of acquiring property and wealth, you should keep three friends by your side, namely God, a good conscience and a decent reputation. You may not do this without God or a conscience according to the many observations you can find in the book* De amore et dilectione Dei et proximi et

---

45.1 **Saint** *om* B7 L4 P12 P24. **doulente** *add* dist il B7 L4; *add* dit P12. **des . . . mendians** du povre mendiant B7 L4; de povre mendiant P12. **s'il . . . muerent** sil ne demande il meurt B7 L4 P12 P24. **s'ilz . . . muerent** sil demande il meurt B7 L4 P12. **les** le B7 L4 P12 P24.
45.2 **avoir** porter B7 L4.

44.10 See the note to 45.2.
45.2 The first of these two citations (Ecclesiasticus 40:9) appears in the previous chapter, 44.10, and the second (Ecclesiasticus 30:17) does not appear in the Latin at all, though it is cited in the corresponding section of the *Liber de amore et dilectione* to which the text refers below.
45.9 In response to this prompt in the Latin text, the rest of the French introduces material from the chapters in Albertano's *Liber de amore et dilectione* mentioned in this passage.

aliarum rerum et de forma vitae, *in the chapter on acquiring and conserving wealth and the four chapters which follow it. You should take note of this and carefully consider both wealth and poverty as well as indigence and need and fortune. I cannot advise you to rely on your wealth or let it be consumed by war.*

[45.10] Par ces raisons que je t'ay dictes, et par moult d'autres que dire pourroye, je te ottroye que bonnes sont les richesses a ceulz qui bien les acquierent et qui bien en usent. Et pour ce je te vueil monstrer comment tu te dois avoir en amassant les richesses et en usant d'elles. (1573–5)

[45.11] Premierement, tu les dois acquerre non mie ardamment, mais a loisir et attrempeement par mesure. Car l'omme qui est trop ardans d'acquerre richesses se habandonne legierement a tous vices et a touz autres maulx. (1576–7)

[45.12] Et pour ce dit Salemon, 'Qui trop se haste de soy enrichir, il ne sera pas innocent,' et aussi autre part, que la richesse hastivement venue hastivement s'en va, mais celle qui est venue petit et petit se croist tousjours et se multiplie. (1578–80)

[45.13] Aprés, tu dois acquerir les richesses par ton sens et par ton labour a ton proffit et senz dommage d'autrui [car la loy dit que nulz ne se face riches au dommage d'autruy]. (1581–4)

[45.14] Et Tulles dit que doulour, paour, mort, ne autre chose qui puisse advenir a homme n'est tant contre nature comme accroistre sa richesse ou dommage et prejudice d'autrui. (1585–6)

[45.15] Et Cassidoires dit que vouloir acroistre sa richesse de ce petit que le povre mandiant a surmonte [toute] cruauté.

[45.16] Et pour ce que tu les puisse acquerre plus loyaument, tu ne dois pas estre oiseux ne pareceux de faire ton proffit, mais dois fuir toute oisiveté. (1587–8)

[45.17] Car Salemon dit que oisiveté enseingne faire moult de maulx, et dit autre part que celui qui traveille et cultive sa terre mengera du pain, mais celui qui est oiseux cherra en povreté et mourra de fain. Celui qui est oiseux et pareceux ne treuve nulz temps couvenable a faire son proffit. (1590–2)

45.12 **aussi** dit aussi B7 L4 P12 P24. **autre part** *om* B7 L4. 45.13 **labour** travail B7 L4 P12 P24. **car ...**
d'autruy B7 L4 P12 P13 P24; *om* P7.
45.14 **richesse** prouffit B7 L4 P12 P13. **et prejudice** *om* B7 L4 P12 P13.
45.15 **toute** P12 P24; toute toute P7; toutes B7 L4 P13.

45.13 Chaucer expands (1584) this comment on the law, emphasizing rather than altering its point.

45.15 Chaucer drops this citation from Cassiodorus which is present in all the French manuscripts. Severs noted an instance of eyeskip in one manuscript, P24, which spans 45.14 and 45.15 and which, he suggested, might provide a reason for this omission. However, Chaucer does not omit 45.14 and an alternative explanation, contingent upon Chaucer's sense of his audience, might be appropriate. The citation from Cassiodorus does after all suggest that the wealthy are insensitive to the poor and mouthing such a notion under some circumstances might be regarded as tactless.

45.16 Here (1587) Chaucer's text reads: *And though the grete men and the myghty men geten richesses moore lightly than thou.* This is hardly a translation of the French: *Et pour ce que tu puisse acquerre plus loyaument.* Severs offered a speculative account of how the French text might have been corrupted to produce Chaucer's reading, but the context of Chaucer's translation again warrants consideration. There were a number of attempts to curb the spending of Richard II during his minority, q.v. Nigel Saul, *Ricard II* (New Haven, 1997), pp. 164–6.

[45.18] Car selon ce que dit un versifieur: Il se excuse en l'iver de ce qu'il fait trop froit, et en l'este de ce qu'il fait trop chaut. (1593)

[45.19] Pour ces causes dit Cathon. (fol. 67r) 'Veille,' dit il, 'souvent, ne t'abandonne a trop dormir, car li trop grans repox norrist les vices.' (1594)

[45.20] Et pour ce dit Saint Innocent: Fay tousjours aucunes bonnes euvres pour ce que l'ennemi [te] trueuve occuppé. (1595)

[45.21] Car li ennemis ne prent pas legierement [en son euvre ceulx qu'il treuve occupez] en bonnes euvres. (1596)

[45.22] En acquerant, donques, les richesses, tu dois fuir oisiveté. (1597)

[45.23] Aprés, des richesses que tu auras acquises par ton sens et par ton travail et deuement, tu dois user en tele maniere que tu ne soies tenuz pour trop eschars ne pour trop larges. (1598–9)

[45.24] Car aussi comme fait a blasmer avarice, aussi fait a reprendre fole largesse. (1600–1)

[45.25] Et pour ce dit Cathon: Use des richesses que tu auras acquises en tele maniere que l'on ne t'appelle point aver ne chetif. (1602–3)

[45.26] Car il est escript: Grant honte est a l'omme qui a le cuer pouvre et la bourse riche. (1604)

[45.27] Aussi dit il: Use des biens que tu auras acquis sagement, senz mesuser. Car ceulz qui folement degastent ce qu'il ont, quant ilz n'ont plus riens ilz s'abandonnent legerement a prendre l'autrui. (1605–8)

[45.28] Je dy, donques, que tu dois fuir avarice en usant des richesses acquises en tele maniere que l'on ne die pas que tes richesses soient ensevelies, mais que tu les as en ta puissance. (1609–10)

[45.29] Car un sage reprent l'omme aver, et dit ainsi en deux vers: Pourquoy homme qui est cendre et que morir couvient, sevelit son avoir par sa grant avarice, et pourquoy se joint il tant a son avoir que l'on ne l'en puet dessevrer? (1611–13)

[45.30] Car quant il mourra il ne l'emportera pas avec soy. (1614–16)

45.18 **trop froit** en trop froit, en *canc* P7.
45.20 **Innocent** Jerosme B7 L4 P12 P13 P24. **te** B7 L4 P12 P13; ne te P7 P24.
45.21 **son euvre ceulx qu'il treuve occupez** P12; semences quil trueuve occupees P7; son euvre celui qui est occupe L4 P13; son euvre celui qui trouve occupes P24.
45.23 **auras** as P24. **trop larges** fol larges B7 L4 P12 P13 P24.
45.24 **reprendre** blasmer et reprendre P24.
45.25 **Use** *add* dist il B7 P12 P24. **auras** as P13 P24.
45.26 **il ... honte est** il est grant honte P12 P24; cest grant honte B7 L4 P13.
45.27 **auras** as P24. **senz mesurer** par mesure B7; a mesure P12; et par mesure P24. **degastent** despendent B7.
45.29 **aver** avaricieux P13.
45.30 **ne ... pas** nemportera riens B7.

45.20 Following the lead of a number of the French manuscripts, Chaucer attributes this statement to Jerome rather than Innocent.

45.29 Chaucer modifies this passage and adds: *For deeth is the ende of every man as in this present lyf* (1613).

45.30 Chaucer expands this passage considerably but its sense is essentially that of the French.

[45.31] Et pour ce dit Saint Augustin que l'omme aver est semblables a enfer: quant plus devours, et plus vuelt devorer. (1617–18)

[45.32] Et aussi comment tu te dois avoir en maniere que l'on ne te nomme ne aver ne chetif, aussi tu te dois garder que l'on ne te clame pour un fol large. (1619–20)

[45.33] Pour ce dit Tulles: Les biens de ton hostel ne doivent pas estre tant enclox que pitié et debonnaireté ne les puissent ouvrir, et ne doivent pas estre tant ouvert qu'ilz soient abandonnees a un chascun. (1621–3)

[45.34] Aprés, en acquerant les richesses et en usant d'elles, tu dois tousjours avoir trois choses en ton cuer: c'est assavoir, Dieu, conscience, et bonne fame. (1624–5)

[45.35] Tu dois, donques, avoir Dieu en ton cuer; quar pour nulle richesse tu ne dois faire chose qui desplaise a Dieu ton creatour. (1626–7)

[45.36] Car selon le dit Salemon: Mieux vault petit avoir et de Dieu la paour, que grant tresor acquerre et perdre son Seigneur. (1628–9)

[45.37] Et le prophete dit que mieux vault estre preudomme et petit avoir, que estre mauvais et grans richesses avoir. (1630–1)

[45.38] Et aprés, je dy que tu dois acquerre et user des richesses sauve tousiours ta conscience. (1632–3)

[45.39] Car l'appostre dit que la chose dont nous devons avoir plus grant gloire si est quant nostre (fol. 67v) conscience nous porte bon tesmoingnage. (1634)

[45.40] Et le sage dit: Bonne est la conscience quant le pechié n'est en la conscience. (1635)

[45.41] Aprés, en acquerant les richesses et en usant d'elles, tu dois avoir grant cure et grant diligence comment ta bonne fame soit tonsjours gardee. (1636–7)

[45.42] Quar il est escript: Le gaaing doit estre nommé perde qui sa bonne fame ne garde.

[45.43] Et Salemon dit: Mieux vault la bonne renommee que les grans richesses. (1638)

[45.44] Et pour ce il dit autre part: Aies grant diligence de garder ton bon nom et ta bonne fame, car ce te demourra plus que nul tresor grant et precieux. (1639–40)

45.31 **quant ... et** car tant plus devore et tant L4.
45.37 **mauvais** *add* tenus P12.
45.38 **et user** *om* B7.
45.42 **Quar ... garde** *om* L4.
45.44 **pour ce** certes B7 L4 P12 P24.

45.36 Chaucer's modifies this citation by replacing the word *pauor* with *love*. Indeed, he twice repeats the word *love* which is present in neither the French nor the parallel passage in Albertano's *Liber de amore* nor in the *Vulgate*, Proverbs 15:16. Severs speculated that the manuscript Chaucer used read *amour* rather than *pauor* and this notion is repeated in *The Riverside Chaucer*. There is no warrant for this claim, however, and no reason to doubt the possibility that Chaucer, like the Wife of Bath, was not above altering a scriptural citation if it fit his purposes.

45.38–45.48 These ideas about keeping a good name and maintaining a good reputation do not belong in this chapter and are dealt with elsewhere in the Latin; they merely appear at this point in the French text because of the reason explained above (45.9).

45.42 Chaucer omits this citation as does one manuscript, L4, another instance of eyeskip.

[45.45] Et pour ce il ne doit pas estre dit gentilz homs qui, toute autres choses arrieres mises aprés Dieu et conscience, n'a grant diligence de garder sa bonne fame.

[45.46] Et pour ce dit Cassidoires: Il est signe de gentil cuer quant il ayme et desirre bon nom et bonne fame. (1641)

[45.47] Et pour ce dit Saint Augustin: Deux choses te sont neccessaires: bonne conscience et bonne renomee; bonne conscience pour toy, bonne fame pour ton voisin. (1643–5)

[45.48] Et celui qui tant se fie en sa bonne conscience qu'il neglige sa bonne renommee et ne fait force de lui garder, il est cruel et vilain. (1646–7)

Chapter 46: The evils of war

46.1 Or t'ay je monstré comment tu te dois porter en acquerant les richesses et usant d'elles. Et pour ce que vous fiez tant en voz richesces que pour la fiance que vous y avez vous voulez mouvoir guerre et faire bataille, je vous conseille que vous ne commencer point guerre, car la grant fiance de voz richesses ne souffit point a guerre maintenir. (1648–50)

46.2 Pour ce dit un philosophe: L'omme qui guerre vuelt avoir n'aura ja a souffisance d'avoir, car de tant comme l'omme est plus riche, de tant lui'couvient il faire plus grans missions se il veult avoir honneur et victoire. (1651–2)

[46.3] Car Salemon dit: Plus as de richesses, plus as de despendeurs. (1653)

46.4 *The poor cannot sustain a war and, the wealthier a man is, the more considerable will be his losses.*

46.5 *Every man commits a grave sin when he becomes implicated in notorious crimes; according to Martial: Every man who is involved in the most notorious misdeeds has committed a considerable sin. The more a man is involved in war, the greater will be his losses, and the more that war saps his strength, the more will he be subjected to misfortune.*

46.6 *It has been said: The high and mighty are the most easily destroyed by misfortune.*

46.7 *And Lucan said: The envy of fate will annihilate the greatest among us and the day will come when the great will suffer a great fall.*

45.45 **dit** appelles B7. **conscience** bonne conscience L4.
45.47 **Deux . . . neccessaires** il sont a toy necessaires deux choses cest assavoir L4. **neccessaires** *add* cest assavoir B7.
46.1 **les** *om* L4. **car . . . fiance** en la fiance dicelles B7 L4; en la fiance P12 P13 P24. **de voz** car nulles B7 L4 P13.
46.2 **a . . . d'avoir** souffissance P12. **l'omme est** il est P12.
46.3 **Plus** qui plus B7 L4 P13. **as¹** a B7 L4 P12 P13 P24. **as²** a B7 L4 P12 P13 P24.

46.5 Unidentified by Sundby, the source of this citation is Godfrey of Winchester, *Liber proverbiorum*, 218.

46.8 And Martial said: The higher we climb, the farther we fall.

46.9 War leads not only to the loss of wealth but also to the loss of the love of God and heaven and life itself, not to mention friends and acquaintances. In place of these, evil arises and it is as though the souls of men were in hell, their bodies in continual pain.

46.10 For the love and fear of God, you should avoid all of the evils of war as much as you can.

Chapter 47: On avoiding war

[47.1] Aprés, tres cher sire, ja soit ce que par voz richesses vous puissiez avoir moult de gens, toutevoye pour ce ne vous covient pas commencer guerre la ou vous povez autrement avoir paix a vostre honneur et a vostre proffit. (1654–5)

47.2 Battle and occasions which lead to war should be avoided for many reasons.

47.3 The first reason is that war displeases God, for, as the Prophet said: Those who cry for war will be scattered!

47.4 The second reason is that war oppresses not only the individual but also people in general; we have this on the authority of Solomon who said: There are five things which oppress people: lawlessness, sorrow, famine, war, and so forth.

47.5 The third reason to fear war has been expressed as follows: Blessed is the city that fears war in a time of peace.

47.6 We should not only be afraid of war but we should try not even to mention it; it is written: If you want peace, never discuss war.

47.7 A fourth reason for avoiding war is that its outcome is unpredictable and uncertain, not only for mankind in general, but also for other reasons which could be debated.

[47.8] Car la victoire des batailles de cest monde ne gist pas en grant nombre de gens ne en la vertu des hommes, mais en la main et en la voulenté de Dieu. (1656–7)

[47.9] Et pour ce Judas le Macabee, qui estoit chevalier de Dieu, quant il voult combatre contre son adversaire qui avoit plus grant nombre de gens et plus fort qu'il n'avoit, il reconforta sa petite compagnie et dit: Aussi legierement puet donner Dieu victoire a pou de gens comme a moult; car la victoire des batailles ne vient pas du grant nombre des gens, mais vient du ciel. (1658–63)

47.1 **pour ce** *om* B7 L4 P12 P13. **a . . . proffit** prouffit P13.

47.8 **nombre** multitude P13.

47.9 **le Macabee** Machabeus B7 P24. **dit** *add* ainsi L4. **legierement** *add* dit il L4 P12 P24. **moult** *add* de gens L4 P12 P24. **des batailles** de la bataille P12.

46.8 Unidentified by Sundby, the source of this citation is Godfrey of Winchester, *Liber proverbiorum*, 111.

[47.10] Et pour ce, tres cher sire, que nul homme n'est certain s'il est digne que Dieu lui doint victoire, ne plus qu'il est certain s'il est digne de l'amour de Dieu ou non, selon ce que dit Salemon, un chascun doit avoir grant paour (fol. 68r) de guerre commencier. (1664–5)

47.11 *When he killed him with a stone, David said to the Philistine: The universal church will know this, that God enabled us to gain this victory without a sword or spear.*

47.12 *A fifth reason to avoid war is that there is a great risk of danger from which many of the wise will flee.*

47.13 *As Cicero said: We must beware of exposing ourselves to danger needlessly. Nothing is as foolish as that. When we do encounter danger, we should do what doctors do: when the illness is light, prescribe mild remedies and save hazardous or dangerous remedies for the grave illness. Only a lunatic would pray for a storm when it is a calm, but a wise man, when the storm comes, will resist it with every means at his disposal.*

[47.14] Et pour ce que es batailles a moult de perilz, et avient aucune foiz que aussi tost occist on le grant comme le plus petit. (1666–7)

[47.15] Car selon ce qu'il est escript on second *Livre des Roys*, les faiz des batailles sont aventureux et ne sont pas certains: assez legierement fiert li glaives maintenant l'un, ja tantost l'autre. (1668–9)

[47.16] Et pour ce que peril y a et tout sage homme doit fuir peril, l'on doit fuir guerre tant comme l'on puet bonnement. Car Salemon dit: Qui ayme le peril, il cherra ou peril. (1670–1)

47.17 *A sixth reason for avoiding war is that everyone who participates in it can anticipate death. It has been said: Exactly where you can anticipate your death is unclear, but you can and should anticipate that it could happen anywhere, and this is especially true in time of war. There are many other reasons why conflict and war should be avoided, but taking note of all of them at the moment is inappropriate.*"

47.18 Aprés ce que Dame Prudence ot parlé, Mellibee respondit: "Je voy bien," dist il, "dame, que par voz belles paroles et par les raisons que vous mettez avant, que la guerre ne vous plait point; mais je n'ay pas encor oÿ vostre conseil comment je me doy porter en ceste besoingne." (1672–4)

47.14 **plus** *om* B7 L4 P12 P13 P24.

47.15 **assez** car assez B7 P13.

47.16 **que peril y a** quil y a tres grant peril P13. **et tout . . . guerre** tous sages homs doit fuir guerre B7 P13.

47.18 **ot** *add* ainsi B7 L4. **dame** *add* Prudence P12. **les** vos L4. **mettez** me mettez P12; moy mettes P13.

47.10 As *The Riverside Chaucer* indicates, the poet omits (1664) the phrase: *ne plus que il est certain se il est digne de l'amour de Dieu.* Since this passage is present in all the French texts and is not in Latin, it is not improbable that Chaucer could have deliberately altered it, especially if his text was addressed to someone who might have taken the remark as an affront. The emendation in *The Riverside Chaucer* seems wholly unnecessary.

Chapter 48: On avoiding war through negotiation

48.1 "Certes," dist elle, "je vous conseille que vous accordez a voz ennemis, et que vous ayez paix avec eulx. (1675)

48.2 *It is written: When an agreement can be reached, there is always victory.*

48.3 *And we should be joyful because, when we avoid war, our goods increase and multiply. As Solomon said in* Proverbs: *Joy follows those who take counsels of peace.*

48.4 Car Senecques dit en ses epistres que par concorde les petites richesses deviennent grans, et par discorde les grant richesses vont a declin et se fondent tousjours. (1676–7)

[48.5] Et vous savez que uns des souverains biens de cest monde si est paix. Et pour ce dit Jhesu Crist a ses appostres: Bieneurez sont ceulz qui ayment et pourchacent paix, car ilz sont appellez enfans de Dieu. (1678–80)

48.6 *And Cicero said: My opinion is that we should always strive to achieve peace and do it without duplicity."*

48.7 *Melibee said, "How can I be reconciled with my enemies? They are the ones who initiated this discord and they have not sought reconciliation."*

48.8 *Prudence responded, "If your adversaries believe that you want reconciliation, they will ask you for it with great devotion. If they hear this, they will be sorry for their sins and their stupidity and they will want to obey all of your mandates and whatever the courts and the judges require. They prefer their honor to risk and war because they are afraid of the danger that body, soul and possessions will be destroyed.*

48.9 *Furthermore I must tell you that the fact that your enemies have not begun the process of reconciliation does not mean that you cannot do it. It has been written: When another initiates dissension, you can initiate peacemaking.*

48.10 *The prophet indicated that reconciliation and peace should not only be expected from others but that it should prompt inquiry and that it should be pursued; he said: Rather than yield to evil, do good, ask about peace, and pursue it.*

48.11 *And the apostle said in his letter to the Romans: Never repay evil with evil but show all men not only that your heart is good but also that you will do all you can to live in peace with everyone.*

48.12 *And in* Isaiah *it is written: How lovely are the feet of those who preach*

48.1 **ennemis** adversaires B7 P12 P13 P24.
48.4 **Senecques** Saint Jaques P12.
48.5 **souverains biens** grans et souverains biens B7 P13; grans biens et des souverains L4; grans et des souverains biens P12; souverains grans biens P24.

48.5 This remark and the citation (Matthew 5:9) are not in the Latin. Also, as *The Riverside Chaucer* points out and as Manly and Rickert first observed, where the French text has *paix*, Chaucer writes *unytee and pees* (1678), perhaps another sign of the political circumstances into which this work was introduced. The lack of unity at the court of Richard II, especially in the late 1380s, has been frequently described.

peace. Therefore you must seek peace and forget the wrongs that have been done to you.

48.13 *As Seneca said in his letters: We should forget injuries and remember the good things that have happened to us. The cure for injuries is forgetfulness.*

48.14 *As Jesus Sirach said: You should neither remember your neighbor's every offense nor respond in an injured way."*

48.15 *Melibee said, "Whatever you may say to me, I cannot forget these wrongs, wrongs which, in some cases, would allow others to make war or fight."*

48.16 *Prudence responded, "Every man who is obsessed with war and fighting is vicious and sinful, and it is written: one cannot win the crown unless one does so in a legitimate way.*

48.17 *Combat may keep every combatant from deserving eternal life and the crown of perpetual victory. Rather, you should be at peace with everyone for it is written: When you are at peace with men, you have won the war."*

48.18 *Melibee said, "I did not say that I wanted to wage war against the living only that I wished to do so against the men who have wronged me."*

[48.19] "He!" dist Mellibee, "or voy je bien que vous n'amez pas mon honneur. Vous savez que mes adversaires ont commencié le riot et la brigue par leur oultrage, et veez qu'il ne requierent point la paix et ne demandent pas la reconciliacion. Voulez donques que je me aille humilier et crier merci? Certes ce ne seroit pas mon honneur. Car aussi comme l'on dit que trop grant familiarité engendre mesprisement, aussi fait trop grant humilité." (1681–6)

Chapter 49: When it is legitimate to go to battle

49.1 *Prudence replied, "There are eight legitimate reasons to fight: to protect the Faith and keep it from harm, to abet justice, to secure peace, to preserve freedom, to avoid slavery, to thwart violence, to avoid physical harm, and finally when it is absolutely necessary. We should look at these individually.*

49.2 *It is legitimate to go to war and to fight for the faith. Faith, supported by all of the virtues, should be our shield and we should fight with the aid of this shield, a point made by the apostle in his letters to the Ephesians: Always carry the shield of faith so that you can use it to put out the burning arrows of the wicked one.*

49.3 *About this, this has been said: When challenged, Faith is the first of the warriors on the field to face the uncertainties of conflict. Thus it is appropriate to go to war and to fight for the faith.*

49.4 *Indeed, rather than be forced to abandon the Catholic faith, it is better to die, as did Judas Maccabaeus, Moses, David, Charlemagne and other warriors. An infinite number of saints have died while fighting for the faith.*

49.5 *In the same way you should fight for justice and fight to the death; as Jesus*

48.19 **humilier et** humilier pardevers eulx et leur B7 L4 P13.

Sirach said: When your soul cries out for justice and when you fight to the death for it, God will defeat your enemies for you.

49.6 *When it is believed that war will lead to peace, then hands can turn to battle. As Cicero said: The only reason for going to war is that we may live unharmed in peace.*

49.7 *He also said: War should be undertaken for no other reason than to secure peace.*

49.8 *We can struggle to the death to conserve liberty and resist indentured servitude; as Cicero said: When the circumstances dictate, we must lift our swords and prefer death to dishonor and slavery.*

49.9 *As Seneca said: It is noble to be slain when your servitude is shameful.*

49.10 *Insofar as indentured servitude is concerned, I would add that if the debts which lead to servitude are legitimate, then one should not be distressed. As Saint Paul said in his epistle to the Corinthians: Each of you should accept the station to which he was called, and, if you were called to be a servant, you should not be anxious.*

49.11 *But, as Saint Peter said in his first epistle: Servants, fear your master always, the good and the gentle as well as those who are cross.*

49.12 *It is similarly appropriate to resist violence, to prefer violence to death; as the authority mentioned above said: When the circumstances dictate, and so forth.*

49.13 *It is permissible to resist violence through fighting and going to battle; as the laws and the decretals say: Every law and every court will allow force to be repelled with force.*

49.14 *Force is appropriate not only when men are vulnerable, but also when, through no fault of their own, they cannot take their case to the courts, as the law indicates.*

49.15 *It is permissible to fight and to go to battle to protect one's person; as the law says: It is appropriate to do whatever it takes for the sake of protecting one's person. Reason naturally permits a man to defend himself against danger.*

49.16 *Not only is self-defense permissible, but it is legitimate to respond to violence the moment it happens. As the law indicates, it is better to take care of such things when they happen than it is to be vindicated when the violence has come to an end.*

49.17 *You are not only permitted to defend yourself, but, if you cannot avoid danger and a man is killed, the laws and the courts will not punish you. Indeed, as the law says: when rams and cows are mixed together, and one threatens the other with death, the others should be defended rather than allowed to die.*

49.18 *Resistance to injuries and bodily harm is permitted and it can be said that someone who does not resist injury if he can is in fact vicious and culpable. As Cicero said: Someone who does not oppose a wrong is as guilty as someone who has deserted his parents, his friends or his country.*

49.19 *You should defend yourself against bodily harm with self-control and with moderation in order to remain blameless. That is to say, if someone beats you,*

49.12 This is a reference to the previous citation from Cicero (49.8).

you should beat him only to protect yourself and not out of a desire to exact revenge.

49.20 *When it is necessary to fight or go to battle, you are required to give warning and formally declare your intentions.*

49.21 *Cicero said: No war is just unless it follows a formal demand for satisfaction, unless warning has been given, and unless there is an official declaration of war.*

49.22 *Then, as Cato said: Fight for your fatherland.*

49.23 *What has been said about fighting and going to war is relevant only to those who are not members of religious orders. The clergy should strive for perfection and cannot take up arms. Thus the words of the Lord: Vengeance is mine and I will be revenged.*

49.24 *He also said: If someone slaps you on the one cheek, you should offer him the other and, should someone steal your shirt, you should offer him your coat. Thus the clergy cannot go to war and should instead risk death rather than resorting to violence or committing mortal sin."*

49.25 *Melibee responded, "If I heard you correctly and I can raise my hands and fight for peace, then why is it that I cannot fight my enemies for the sake of having peace."*

[49.26] Lors Dame Prudence fist semblant d'estre courroucee, et dist: "Certes, sire, sauve vostre grace, j'aime vostre honneur et vostre profit comme le mien propre et l'ay tousjours aymé, et vous ne autres ne veistes onques le contraire. (1687–9)

[49.27] Et se je vous avoye dit que vous devez pourchacer la paix et la reconciliacion, je n'auroye pas tant mespris comme il vous semble. Car un sage dit: La discencion commence par autre, la reconciliacion tousjours par toy. (1690–1)

[49.28] Et le prophete dit: Fuy le mal et fay le bien; quier paix et la pourchace tant comme tu pourras. (1692–3)

[49.29] Toutevoye, je ne vous ay pas dit que vous requerez la paix premier que voz adversaires car je vous scey bien de si dur cuer que vous ne feriez a piece tant pour moy. Toutevoye, Salemon dit que mal vendra a la fin a cellui qui a le cuer trop dur. (1694–6)

49.30 *Only the fool swims against the current when he could have tacked downstream.*

49.31 *It is simply foolish of you to risk danger and war and a conflict which might prove destructive in the end when you could have the guarantee of peace and the peace of the sacraments at your disposal. A man who has the good sense to see what is right but the bad sense to choose what is wrong is a man who turns wisdom into foolishness."*

[49.32] Quant Mellibee oÿ Dame Prudence faire semblant de courroux, si dist, "Dame, je vous prie qu'il ne vous desplaise chose que je die, (fol. 68v) quar

49.29 **a . . . tant** riens L4.
49.32 **oÿ** ot oy P12. **dist** *add* ainsi P13. **chose** de chose B7 L4 P12 P13.

vous savez que je suis courreciez, et n'est pas merveille; et ceulz qui sont courrouciez ne scevent pas bien qu'ilz font ne qu'il dient. Pour ce dit le philosophe que [les troublés] ne sont pas bien cler voyant. (1697–1701)

49.33 Mais dittes et conseilliez ce qu'il vous plaira, et je suis appareilliez du faire. Et se vous me reprenez de ma folie, je vous en doy plus priser et amer. Car Salemon dit que celui qui reprent durement cellui qui foloye, il doit trouver plus grant grace envers lui que cellui qui le deçoipt par douces paroles." (1702–5)

49.34 "Je," dist Dame Prudence, "ne fais semblant d'estre yree ne courroucee fors que pour vostre grant profit. Car Salemon dit: Mieux vault cil qui le fol reprent et qui lui monstre semblant d'ire, que lui loer quant il mesprent et de ses grans folies rire. (1706–8)

[49.35] Et dit aprés: Par la tritesse du visage corrige le fol son courage." (1709–10)

49.36 Adonques dist Mellibee, "Dame, je ne sauroye responde a tant de belles raisons comme vous mettez avant. Dictes briefment vostre voulenté et vostre conseil et je suy prest de l'acomplir." (1711–12)

[49.37] Lors Dame Prudence lui descouvri toute sa volenté et lui dist ainsi: "Je conseille que vous, devant toutes [choses], faites paix a Dieu et vous reconciliez a lui. Car selon ce que je vous ay dit autresfoiz, il vous a souffert avenir ceste tribulacion pour voz pechiez. Et se vous faites ce, je vous promet de par lui que il amenera voz adversaires a voz piez et appareillez de faire toute vostre voulenté. Car Salemon dit: Quant les voyes de l'omme plaisent a Dieu, il lui convertist ses ennemis et les contraint de requerre et de demander la paix. (1713–20)

49.38 Aprés, je vous prie qu'il vous plaise que je parle a secret a voz adversaires senz faire semblant que ce viengne de vostre consentement; et lors quant je verray et sauray leur voulenté, je vous pourray conseiller plus seurement." (1721–3)

[49.39] "Faites, dame," dist Mellibee, "vostre voulenté, quar je met tout mon fait en vostre disposicion." (1724–5)

49.40 Lors Dame Prudence, quant elle vit la bonne voulenté de son mary, si ot deliberation en soy mesmes et pensa comment elle pourroit mener ceste besoingne a bonne fin. Et quant elle vit qu'il fu temps, elle manda les

49.32 **philosophe** prophete B7 L4 P13. **les troublés** B7 L4 P13 P24; li tromble P7; oeil troubles P12. **ne sont** nest P12.
49.33 **dittes** dittez moi B7 P13. **envers lui** *om* P12.
49.36 **Dame** *om* B7 L4. **mettez** moy mettes P13.
49.37 **choses** P12 P24; *om* P7; choses que B7 L4 P13. **ce je . . . lui que** ce que je vous promet de par luy P12. **amenera** vous amenera B7 L4 P12 P13 P24. **toute** *om* B7 L4 P13.
49.38 **a secret . . . adversaires** a voz adversaires en secret P12. **verray et** *om* B7 L4 P12 P13 P24.
49.39 **Faites . . . Mellibee** Dame dist il faites P12 P13.
49.40 **qu'il fu** son P24.

49.35 Not in the Latin. The exchange between Melibee and Prudence is more elaborate in the French than it is in the Latin.
49.37 Not in the Latin.
49.39 Not in the Latin.

adversaires en lieu secret, et leur proposa sagement les grans biens qui sont en paix et les grans perilz qui sont en guerre, et leur enseigna moult doulcement comment, ilz se devoient repentir de l'injure qu'ilz avoient faite a Mellibee son seigneur, et a elle, et a sa fille. (1726–32)

49.41 Quant ceulz oïrent les doulces paroles de Dame Prudence, ilz furent si surprins et orent si grant joye que nul ne le pourroit extimer. "He! Dame Prudence," dirent il, "vous nous avez denoncié en la beneÿson de doulceur, selon ce que dit David le Prophete; car la reconciliacion (fol. 69r) dont nous ne sommes pas digne et que nous deussions requerre a grant devocion et a grant humilité, vous par vostre doulceur la nous avez presentee. (1733–8)

[49.42] Or veons nous bien que la sentence Salemon est vraye, qui dit que la douce parole multiplie les amis et fait debonnaire les ennemis." (1739–40)

49.43 "Certes," dirent il, "nous mettons nostre fait en vostre voulenté et sommes appareillié en tout et par tout obeïr au dit et commandement de Monseigneur Mellibee. Et pour ce, tres chere dame et benigne, nous vous requerons et prions tant humblement comme nous povons plus qu'il vous plaise acomplir par fait voz doulces paroles. Toutevoye, tres chiere dame, nous considerons et cognoissons que nous avons offendu Messire Mellibee oultre mesure et plus que nous ne pourrions amender. Et pour ce, se nous obligons nous et noz amis a faire sa voulenté et son commandement, par adventure il, comme courrouciez, nous donra tele painne que nous ne la pourrons porter ne acomplir. Et pour ce, plaise vous en ce fait avoir tel advisement que nous et noz amis ne soyons desheritez et perduz par nostre folie." (1741–51)

49.44 "Certes," dist Prudence, "il est dure chose et perilleuse que uns homs se commette du tout en l'arbitrage et en la puissance de ses ennemis. Car Salemon dit, 'Oyez moy,' dit il, 'tuit pueple et toutes gens et gouverneurs d'Eglise: a ton fil, a ta femme, a ton frere, a ton cousin, et a ton amy, ne donne puissance sur toy en toute ta vie.' [Se il a donques] deffendu que l'on ne doint point puissance sur soy a son ami, par plus fort raison il deffent qu'il l'on ne la donne pas a son ennemi. Toutevoye, je vous donne conseil que vous ne vous deffiez point de mon seigneur, car je le cognois et scey qu'il est debonnaires, larges, et courtois, et n'est point couvoiteux d'avoir. Il ne desirre en ce monde fors que honneur tant seulement. Aprés, je scey que en ceste besoingne il ne fera riens senz mon

---

49.41 **Prudence** *om* P24. **denoncié en** avance P13. **vostre** *add* grant B7 L4 P13 P24.

49.43 **voulenté** bonne voulente B7 P12. **se** *om* L4 P12 P13 P24. **sa** toute sa B7 P12 P13 P24. **par** mais par P13. **courrouciez** ire contre noz P13. **plaise** dame plaise P13. **nous et** nous ne B7 P12 P13.

49.44 **Oyez** croy P12. **Se ... donques** B7 L4 P13 P24; sil deffent dont P7; sil a P12. **a son ami** a frere ne a ami B7 P12 P24; a frere ne ami L4 P13. **donné** *om* B7 L4 P13.

49.42 In the Latin, the three foes do not buttress their response with this citation from Ecclesiasticus 6:5. It appears below in a speech voiced by Melibee (51.14).

49.44 The French is especially paraphrastic at this point, omitting from the Latin such things as a reference to an earlier chapter (Chapter 20) in what Prudence calls *hoc libro*. Chaucer, in turn, is also somewhat paraphrastic, especially his rendering of 1760–4 where the French text introduces ideas that are not in the Latin.

conseil; et je feray, se Dieu plait, que ceste besoingne venra a bonne fin en telle maniere que vous vous devrez loer de moy." (1752–64)

49.45 "Nous," dirent il, "mettons nous et noz biens en tout et par tout en vostre ordonnance et disposicion, et sommes appareillez [de venir] au jour que [vous nous] vouldrez donner, et faire obligations si fors comme vous plaira que nous acomplirons la voulenté de Messire Mellibee et la vostre." (1765–8)

49.46 Dame Prudence, quant ot oÿe la response d'eulz, si leur commande aler en leurs lieux secretement, et elle d'autre part retourna vers Mellibee son seigneur et lui reconta comment elle les avoit trovez repentans et recognoissans leurs pechiez et appareilliez de souffrir toute pene, requerans sa pitié et sa misericorde. (1769–73)

49.47 Lors Mellibee respondi, "Cellui eat dignes de pardon qui ne excuse (fol. 69v) point son pechié, mais le cognoist et s'en repent et demande indulgence. Car Senecques dit: La est remission ou est confession; car confession est prouchainne a [innocence]. Et dit autre part: Celui eat presque ignocent qui a honte de son pechié et le recognoit. Et pour ce je m'accorde a paix, mais il est bon que nous le facions de la voulenté et consentement de noz amis." (1773–8)

49.48 Lors Prudence fist une chiere liee et joyant et dist: "Certes," dist elle, "Vous avez trop bien respondu; car tout aussi comme par le conseil et par l'ayde de voz amis vous avez eu en propox de vous vengier et de faire guerre, aussi senz demander leur conseil vous ne devez accorder ne paix faire. Car la loy dit que nulle chose n'est tant selon nature comme la chose deslier pour ce dont elle a esté liee." (1779–83)

49.49 Et lors incontinent Dame Prudence envoya messagiers, et manda querre leurs parens et leurs anciens amis loyaulx et sages, et leur recompta le fait en la presence de Mellibee tout par ordre par la maniere qu'il eat devisié dessus, et leur demanda quel conseil il donnoient sur ce. Lors les amis Mellibee, toutes les choses dessus dictes deliberees et examinees a grant diligence, donnerent conseil de paix faire et que l'on les receust a misericorde. (1784–90)

49.50 Quant Dame Prudence ot le consentement de son seigneur et le conseil de ses amis a son entencion et pour soy, si fut moult liee de cuer. "L'on dit," dist

---

49.45 **nous dirent il** et lors ilz respondirent dame P13. **de venir** B7 L4 P12 P13 P24; *om* P7. **vous nous** B7 L4 P12 P13; vous P7 P24. **la vostre** de vous P13.

49.46 **les . . . trovez** avoit retourne sea adversaires P24.

49.47 **respondi** dist aussi P13. **remission** la remission B7 L4 P12 P13. **est confession** est la confession B7 L4. **innocence** B7 L4 P12 P13 P24; ygnorance P7.

49.48 **elle¹** *add* sire P12. **tant** *add* bonne P24. **pour** par B7 L4 P12 P13 P24.

49.49 **messagiers** messages P12 P13. **par . . . maniere** ainsi L4. **misericorde** *add* et a mercy B7; mercy et a misericorde P13.

49.50 **ot** *add* oy P24. **L'on . . . elle** et dist on dist B7.

49.50 There are a number of elements in this passage which might suggest that Chaucer consulted the Latin text while translating the French. First, he departs from all the French texts by omitting the phrase *si comme ilz se sont presentez*, a phrase not found in the Latin. Second, he departs from P7 by including the phrase *et incontinant* in clausula 1799 rather than the one which follows it (1800); this a correct reading which also squares with the Latin text. On the other hand, he follows P7 by not including a phrase found, with some variation, in the other French manuscripts: *et sans dilacion ensemble leurs*

elle, "ou proverbe: Du bien que puez faire le main, ne attend soir ne l'andemain. Et pour ce je conseille que l'on envoye tantost messagiers sages et advisez a ces gens pour leur dire que, se ilz veulent [traittier] de paix et d'accord si comme ilz se sont presentez que ilz se traient vers nous et incontinant." Ainsi comme Dame Prudence le conseilla, il fu fait. (1791–1800)

49.51 Quant ces trois malfaiteurs et repentans de leurs folies oÿrent les messagiers, si furent liez et joyeux, et respondirent benignement, en rendant graces a Messire Mellibee et toute sa compagnie, qu'il estoient prests et appareilliez d'aler vers eulz senz dilation et d'obeir en tout et par tout a leur commandement. (1801–5)

49.52 *When they were about to go there, one of them said, "We should take a great entourage with us and they will greet us with honor." Then another one said, "Doing this would delay our progress. Whatever the dangers at sea or on land, delay arouses suspicion. I would advise that it might please these others if we go without delay."*

49.53 Et assez tost aprés, ilz se misdrent a la voye d'aler a la court de Messire Mellibee, ensemble leurs fiances et aucuns de leurs loyaulx amis. Quant Mellibee les vit en sa presence, si dit: "Il est verité que vous, senz cause et senz raison, avez fait grant injure a moy, a Dame Prudence ma femme, et a ma fille, en entrant en ma maison en violence [et en faisant] tel oultrage comme chascun scet, par laquelle vous avez mort desservie. Et pour ce je vueil savoir de vous se vous voulez mettre du tout la punicion et la vengence de cest oultrage a ma voulenté et de Dame Prudence ma femme." (1806–15)

49.54 Lors l'ainsnel et le plus (fol. 70r) sage des trois respondit pour tous et dist, "Nous ne sommes pas dignes de venir a la court de tel homme comme vous estes. Car nous avons tant meffait que voirement nous sommes digne de mort,

---

49.50 **le main** huy P24. **ne attend . . . l'andemain** natendes pas demain P24; natens mie jusques a landemain L4; natens pas jusquea a lendemain B7; natens pas a lendemain P12. **traittier** B7 L4 P12 P13 P24; traittie P7. **nous et incontinant** vous incontinent et sans dilation B7 L4 P13.

49.51 **trois** om P12. **liez** moult liez B7 L4 P13. **benignement** moult benignement P12. **leur** son B7 L4 P13.

49.53 **d'aler** om L4. **ensemble . . . amis** ensemble avec aucuns de leur loyaux amis faire leur fiance P12. **dame prudence ma femme**[1] ma femme prudence B7 P13 P24. **fille** *add* aussi B7. **en violence** par violence B7 L4 P13 P24; a violence P12. **et en faisant** B7 L4 P24; faisant et P7; et faisant P12 P13.

49.54 **dist** sire dit il B7 P12 P13 P24; sires dirent ilz L4.

---

pleges loyaulx et convenable, this an accurate translation of the Latin. Then again he drops the introductory phrase *ainsi comme Dame Prudence le conseilla* at 1800, a phrase which appears in most of the French texts but not the Latin.

49.54 In Chaucer, the spokesman for the three enemies, engages in rhetoric somewhat more theatrical than that in the French and the French in turn exaggerates the parallel passage in the Latin. In both Renaud and Chaucer, the spokesman alludes to Melibee's reputation in the eyes of the world, a point not made within the more parochial confines of the Latin. Chaucer tends to emphasize the flattery the spokesman heaps upon Melibee rather than his contrite demeanor. He does drop the phrase *non pas de vie* (1819) which appears in all the French texts but not the Latin. He also omits the phrase *a genoulz et en lermes* which appears in the French text and is paralleled in the Latin. While Chaucer indirectly alludes to the fact that the three enemies have got down on their knees (1827), the French text explicitly refers to their willingness to do so and the Latin describes that gesture.

non pas de vie. Toutevoye, nous nous fyons en vostre douceur et debonnaireté, dont vous estes renommez par tout le monde. Et pour ce nous nous offrons a vous, appareilliez d'obeir a tous voz commandemens, et vous prions a genoulz et en lermes que vous ayez de nous pitié et misericorde." (1816–26)

49.55 *Then they fell prostrate at the feet of Melibee and Lady Prudence and fervently begged them for their forgiveness.*

49.56 Lors Mellibee les releva benignement, et reçupt leur obligation par leur serement et sur leurs pleges, et leur assigna journee de retourner a sa court et de eulz offrir a sa presence pour oïr sentence et sa voulenté. Ces choses ainsi ordonnees, un chascun d'une part et d'autre se departy d'ensemble. (1827–31)

49.57 *Later Melibee called on the physicians and inquired about the convalescence of his daughter. The doctors said, "Behold, you daughter can be discharged and her convalescence can be assured without a doubt." Then Melibee rewarded them handsomely, as they requested, and his daughter steadily regained her health.*

49.58 Dame Prudence parla premierement a son seigneur Mellibee et lui demanda quelle vengence il entendoit prendre de see adversaires. (1832–3)

49.59 "Certes," dist Mellibee, "je les entend a desheriter de tout ce qu'ilz ont et les envoyer oultre mer senz retour." (1834–5)

49.60 "Certes," dist Dame Prudence, "ceste sentence seroit trop felonnesse et contre raison. Car tu es trop riches n'as pas besoing de l'autrui richesse ne de l'autrui argent, et pourroyes estre par raison notez et reprins de couvoitise qui est un tres grant vice et racine de tous maulx selon ce que dit l'appostre. (1836–40)

Chapter 50: Honor

50.1 Il te vauldroit mieux tant perdre du tien que prendre le leur par ceste maniere; mieulx vault perdre a honneur que gaingnier a honte; et autre part aussi: Le gaing doit estre appellez perte qui la bonne fame ne garde. (1841–2)

49.56 **leur obligation** leurs obligations B7 L4. **leur serement** leurs seremens B7 L4 P13 P24. **d'ensemble** dillec et sen alerent a leurs maisons P13.
49.59 **oultre mer** en exil B7 P13. **senz retour** sans jamais retourner P13 P24.
49.60 **richesse . . . l'autrui** *om* L4.
50.1 **Il te** et te L4; et vous P13. **maniere** *add* car il est escript B7 L4 P13.

49.55 This gesture is not described in the texts of Renaud and Chaucer.
49.56 Though the French follows the Latin at this point, the Latin is marked by a sense of celebration which has been stripped from the French. Chaucer's translation of the French is somewhat loose, but its sense is essentially the same.
49.57 The French drops Melibee's discussion of the state of his daughter's health with the physicians.
49.60 The phrase concluding this passage, *selon ce que dit l'appostre*, appeared to Severs to be pointed in such a way that it was meant to introduce the next clausula in P7 (50.1). However, as Severs acknowledged, such is not the case in L4 nor does it appear to be the case in P12, P13 or P24, manuscripts which he did not mention. While a similar phrase is not used in the Latin, Chaucer was certainly familiar with the citation of 1 Timothy 6:10 which precedes this phrase; it is the Pardoner's favorite text and it is not surprising that Chaucer read it correctly.

50.2 *It is commonly said: honesty surpasses all of the riches that can be imagined.*

50.3 *Honesty and a good reputation are superior to all the money in the world; as Jesus Sirach said: Be careful of your good name; it will last you longer than a thousand great hoards of treasure.*

50.4 *And it has also been said: A bright glance gives joy to the soul and a good name gives strength to the bones.*

50.5 *Therefore you should spurn all ill-gotten gain; it is written: Ill-gotten gain should be considered a loss.*

50.6 *Cassiodorus said: The pursuit of fame is augmented by the neglect of riches.*

50.7 *The intelligent soul regards a good reputation as its own reward because a man will be remembered for his goodness and his good name. The same author said: Those who will be remembered best are those whose reputation has been praised.*

50.8 *Solomon said: Better a good name than great riches; and he also said: Better a good name than precious oils.*

50.9 *Seneca said: There is more safety in the good opinion of men than there is in money; since, as he also said: When the days are dark, a good name will shine brightly.*

50.10 *You should despise money in keeping with the words of the apostle who said in the letter to Timothy: Dwell upon whatever is honorable.*

50.11 *A certain philosopher said: A man must be silent about every virtue unless his reputation is widely acknowledged.*

50.12 Et dit plus que l'on ne se doit pas tant seulement garder de faire chose par quoy l'on perde sa bonne renommee, mais se doit on tous les jours efforcier de faire aucune chose pour acquerre nouvelle fame. Car il est escript: La vieille renommee est tost alee quant elle n'est renouvellee. (1843–6)

50.13 Aprés, quant ad ce que tu dis que tu les veulz envoier oultre mer senz jamés retourner, il me semble que ce seroit mal use de la puissance qu'il t'ont donnee [sur eulx] pour faire a toy honneur et reverence. Et le droit dit que celui est digne de perdre son privilege qui mal use de la puissance qui lui a esté donnee. (1847–50)

50.14 Et dy plus car supposé que tu leur puisses engendrer tele painne selon droit, laquelle chose je ne te ottroye point, je dy que tu ne la pourroies pas mener de fait a execucion, ains par aventure couvendroit retourner a la guerre comme devant. (1851–4)

50.13 **oultre mer** en exil B7 P13. **seroit mal use** seroit mesuse P24. **sur eulx** B7 L4 P12 P13 P24; *om* P7. **qui mal use** qui mesuse B7 P12 P13.
50.14 **engendrer** enjoindre B7 L4 P12 P13. **laquelle chose** que L4 P12 P13 P24; ce que B7.

50.13 Chaucer omits the phrase *senz jamés retourner* present both in the Latin text and in the French, perhaps because of contemporary political circumstances in which exile may have been at issue. Chaucer also omits the phrase *pour faire a toy honneur et reverence* (1149), also present in the French and the Latin, and here too similar considerations might prove relevant.

50.15 Et pour ce, se tu veulz que l'on obeïsse a toy, il te couvient sentencier plus courtoisement. Car il est escript: A cellui qui plus courtoisement com ande, obeÿst on mieulx." (1855–7)

50.16 *Melibee responded, "It is not clear to me how that idea will discomfit my enemies. A criminal who deserves no mercy should experience sustained corporal punishment in keeping with the practices of the court. The less they are punished, the more tolerant they will be of physical abuse. The issue is not that they should be punished less, but exactly where they should suffer physical torment. As the law says: it is the opinion of the courts that corporal punishment is more effective that a fine.*

50.17 *Furthermore, as Jesus Sirach has said: Kingdoms pass from clan to clan because of injustice, lawlessness and violence. It would not be inconsistent with the injustice, injury and violence enacted against us if they were exiled and forced to wander from place to place with all of their possessions lost."*

50.18 *Prudence responded: "Jesus Sirach was talking about divine law, and you are talking about laws of the most severe sort. It is inappropriate to compare divine law with these severe laws, unless the issue is peace and friendly agreements.*

50.19 *I would advise you not to harm them in such a way and to ignore these wicked notions. As the emperor Constantine said: Those who are known to have done what is evil should be forced to understand what is good. A man who has distanced himself from struggle is a man whose life proves victorious.*

50.20 Et pour ce je te prie que en ceste besoingne te plaise vaincre ton cuer. Car (fol. 70 v) Senecques dit: Deux foiz vaint qui son cuer vaint. (1858–9)

50.21 *Furthermore: the best victory is one which lasts forever.*

50.22 Et Tulles dit: Riens ne fait tant a loer en grant seigneur comme quant il est debonnaire et se appaise legierement. (1860–1)

Chapter 51: On clemency and piety and mercy

51.1 *And someone else said: He is forever a victor who resorts to clemency.*

51.2 *Furthermore I tell you that piety and clemency should not only be treasured and valued by the poor and the average man, but that they should grace as well the princes and the kings who safeguard and preserve their realms. For Saint Paul said in the first letter to Timothy: Piety is forever rewarding since it holds out the promise of life here and now as well life in the future.*

51.3 *Cassiodorus said: The piety of every leader is in fact what safeguards the realm.*

51.4 *And Solomon said in Proverbs: Mercy and truth guard the king and clemency serves as his throne.*

50.22 The reading *seigneur* is found only in P7; the other French manuscripts read *homme* and the Latin *viro*. Chaucer does follow P7 when he translates (1860) and Severs thought that this spoke to his choice of manuscript. The rhetorical circumstances into which Chaucer introduced his text might also come into play here; *seigneur* seems more appropriate to a courtly audience.

51.5 *And the emperor Constantine said: The only truth that a lord need prove is that the truth is at his service when he exhibits piety.*

51.6 *And, in* De clemencia imperatoris, *Seneca said: No one should have more mercy than a king and, though bees are easily provoked because they have such tiny bodies, a king should have no sting.*

51.7 Et pour ce je te prie qu'il te plaise toy porter en telle maniere en ceste vengence que ta bonne renommee soit gardee, et que tu soies loez de pitié et de doulceur, et qu'il ne te couviengne pas repentir de chose que tu faces. Car Senecques dit: Mal vaint qui se repent de sa vittoire. (1862–6)

51.8 *I would advise you to follow the idea of Seneca who said: If you happen to discover that you have your enemies in your power, you may think that you will be satisfied with revenge. However, I know that the most decent and effective form of revenge is to ignore them.*

51.9 Pour ces choses je te prie que tu adjoustes a ton jugement misericorde, a celle fin que Dieu ait de toy misericorde en son darrenier jugement. Car Saint Jaques dit en son epistre: Jugement senz misericorde sera fait a cellui qui ne fera misericorde." (1867–9)

51.10 Quant Mellibee ot oÿ toutes les paroles Dame Prudence et ses sages enseignemens, si fut en grant paix de cuer et loa Dieu, qui lui avoit donné si sage compagnie. (1870–3)

51.11 *And having heard these things and thought about them carefully, Melibee said, "Fragrant oil and perfumes warm the heart and the advice of a good friend sweetens the soul; that is to say, I have changed my position as the result of your sweet and agreeable advice, subscribe to your kindness, and will follow your will in every way in these negotiations."*

51.12 *When that was done, the aforementioned adversaries and their witnesses went to the court of Lord Melibee, then got down on their knees and cried while they were prostrate at the feet of the lord and Lady Prudence. They said, "Behold, we have come to you prepared for anything and ready to obey your every command. Nonetheless, however unworthy, we would beg that your power over us extend not to revenge but to peace, clemency and piety and that you bless us with your forgiveness. The result will be that you will be more powerful since it is written: By forgiving much, power becomes more powerful."*

51.13 Et quant la journee vint que ses adversaires comparurent en sa presence, il parla a eulz moult doulcement. "Ja soit ce," dist il, "que vous vous soyez portez envers nous moult orguilleusement, et de grant presumpcion vous soit advenu,

---

51.9 **fera** aura eu L4 P13.
51.10 **toutes** *om* P12. **paroles** *add* et raisons de L4. **loa** *add* et regratia L4.

51.10 As Severs noted, Chaucer's version of this passage resembles the parallel passage in the Latin somewhat more than it does the French text. In any case, it is not a "translation" at all and its language seems purely Chaucerian.

51.12 In Renaud and Chaucer, the tale concludes with Melibee's addressing his three enemies and forgiving them, but the Latin concludes with a more elaborate speech and the kiss of peace which concluded medieval arbitration ceremonies.

toutevoie la grant humilité que je voy en vous me contraint a vous faire grace. Et pour ce nous vous recevons en nostre amitié et en nostre bonne grace, et vous pardonnons toutes injures et tous voz meffaiz encontre nous, a celle fin que Dieu, ou point de la mort, nous vueille parclormer les nostres. (1874–83)

51.14 *Furthermore, kind words and gentle responses soothe our anger and indignation; as Solomon said: Sweet talk multiplies our friends and lessens our enemies.*

51.15 *Too: While sharp words encourage anger, a gentle reply deflects wrath.*

51.16 *And, according to another authority: While harsh words initiate enmity, decent speech leads to friendship.*

51.17 *Your devout hearts, contrition and penance, as well as the confession of sin will lead us toward peace, clemency and piety. And thus you will be regarded as a neighbor, since, as Solomon says: Better a friend nearby than a brother far away.*

51.18 *As Cato said: One who could have harmed you can help you now. We hope therefore that you will do what you have said, love our Lord and honor us and, for our part, we will forgive all of the injuries, the wrath and the indignation and all of the contempt which you have heaped upon us and we will accord you our grace and good will."*

51.19 *And then, their hands raised, they received the kiss of peace.*

51.19 *Then Melibee, following in the footsteps of the Lord, said, "Go in peace and sin no more."*

51.20 *Whereupon they exited with happiness and joy.*

And thus ends the Liber consolationis et consilii *which Albertano, the jurist from Brescia, from the quarter of Saint Agatha, composed and compiled in the year of Our Lord 1246 in the months of April and May.*

51.13 **doulcement** *add* en ceste maniere L4. **nous**[1] moy B7 L4 P12 P24. **amitie . . . grace** grace et amittie P24. **meffaiz** *add* que avez faiz P13.

51.13 Chaucer's opens Melibee's final speech (1878–80) with language which parallels not the French but the Latin: *Insuper etiam vestra devotio cordisque contritio et poenitentia atque peccati confessio nos induxerunt ad placabilitatem, clementiam et pietatem.* The language concluding the speech In Chaucer (1885–7) is found in neither the Latin nor the French, but echoes I John 1:9.

51.18 The last four lines in Chaucer's translation (1885–8) do not follow the French but do resemble the Latin text.

51.19 In the Latin, the final words of Melibee imitate the words of Christ to the woman taken in adultery (John 8:11)

The Monk's Tale

THOMAS H. BESTUL

The *Monk's Tale* is a collection of seventeen stories describing the fall of great men or women (or in one case, an angel) from good fortune into permanent misery. The individual narratives vary in length from a single stanza of eight lines to sixteen stanzas for the longest story (Zenobia). In the Prologue of the Tale, the Monk calls such stories tragedies, a term that is elaborated upon in the first stanza of the Tale and again in the last. Tragedy is a type of narrative describing the fall of those in high rank through trust in Fortune (derived from the Roman goddess Fortuna), who is capricious and inevitably withdraws her gifts. The stories are told as a warning to others not to trust in the "blynd prosperitee" offered by Fortune (VII 1997). The theory of tragedy embodied in the Tale, particularly its connection with Fortune and its emphasis on moral instruction, seems to reflect late medieval definitions of tragedy as a narrative form.[1] The philosophical conception of Fortune that lies behind this theory of tragedy, together with the association of Fortune with the fall of the great, was well known in the Middle Ages, authoritatively expressed in the *De consolatione philosophiae* of Boethius, a work Chaucer translated.[2]

The general conception of a collection of tales on the downfall of the great Chaucer seems to have been taken from the *De casibus virorum illustrium* ("On the Falls of Illustrious Men") of Giovanni Boccaccio. This indebtedness appears to be indirectly acknowledged in several of the manuscripts, which include the title *De casibus virorum* at either the beginning or the end of the Tale. The epigraph to the Tale in the *Riverside Chaucer* is: "Heere bigynneth the Monkes Tale De Casibus Virorum Illustrium." On the basis of the manuscript evidence, it is likely, but not certain, that Chaucer himself was responsible for this apparent confirmation of an obligation to Boccaccio. Within the Prologue and the Tale themselves, however, Chaucer never names Boccaccio, and at line 2325, the Monk-narrator inexplicably suggests that Petrarch was his source, even though the story of Zenobia that is being told closely follows Boccaccio in

---

[1] See D. W. Robertson, Jr., "Chaucerian Tragedy," *English Literary History* 19 (1952): 1–37; reprinted in *Chaucer Criticism*, vol. 2, ed. Richard J. Schoeck and Jerome Taylor (Notre Dame, Ind.: Notre Dame University Press, 1961), pp. 86–121; Piero Boitani, "Two Versions of Tragedy: Ugolino," in Piero Boitani, *The Tragic and Sublime in Medieval Literature* (Cambridge: Cambridge University Press, 1989), pp. 20–55; Henry Ansgar Kelly, *Ideas and Forms of Tragedy from Aristotle to the Middle Ages* (Cambridge: Cambridge University Press, 1993); Henry Ansgar Kelly, *Chaucerian Tragedy* (Cambridge: D. S. Brewer, 1997), esp. pp. 65–79.

[2] Boethius, *De consolatione philosophiae* 2.pr2; 3.pr5.

certain of its details. It is worth noting that in other instances where Chaucer borrows from Boccaccio he never acknowledges him as a source, perhaps "in keeping with a medieval preference for antique and Latin over 'modern' and vernacular sources of historical information," as Stephen Barney puts it in the case of *Troilus*.[3]

Boccaccio's *De casibus* is a lengthy collection, in Latin prose, of "tragedies" in the medieval sense described above, although it important to note, as Henry Ansgar Kelly has argued, that Boccaccio did not conceive of his narratives explicitly as "tragedies" but as cautionary tales. The great and powerful are brought low through the workings of Fortune, to the accompaniment of many moralizing reflections. To designate such narratives as tragedies appears to be Chaucer's innovation.[4] Boccaccio's *De casibus* was widely popular in the Middle Ages and often imitated, for example by Lydgate in his *Fall of Princes*, and later in the *Mirror for Magistrates* (1559). Even though Boccaccio may have contributed the general idea of a series of tragic narratives, it is significant that Chaucer's individual stories are not based closely or directly on Boccaccio's versions, as Robert K. Root reminds us.[5] Of Chaucer's seventeen tragedies, six are found in the *De casibus*: Adam, Samson, Croesus, Zenobia, Nero, and the story of Pompey included in Julius Caesar. Yet for none of these, according to Root, is Boccaccio the primary source, although he contributed a phrase or two or a stanza to several of them.[6] It is also important to observe that the stories of Lucifer, Holofernes, and Antiochus appear to have no known precedents as subjects of *De casibus* tragedies, either in Boccaccio or elsewhere.

Another possible source for the general conception of the Tale is the *Roman de la Rose*, a work well known to Chaucer, and of which he made at least a partial translation. The *Roman* includes a long discussion of the goddess Fortune with stories of those who fall victim to her arbitrary operations.[7] It is sometimes suggested that the example of the *Roman* also inspired Chaucer to include tragedies based on the lives of his near contemporaries. As well as referring to men of old, the *Roman* records the very recent tragic fates of Manfred of Sicily and his nephew Conradin.[8] Such a strategy is by no means unique to the *Roman de la Rose*, however. In a disquisition on the transitory nature of worldly happiness in his *Commentary on Proverbs*, Alexander Nequam (d. 1217) refers to the bad fortunes of William II of England, Richard the Lion-Hearted, and Frederick Barbarossa along with such personalities as Semiramis, Priam, Agamemnon, Osiris, Nebuchadnezzar, Belshazzar, Alexander the Great, Julius Caesar, and Nero.[9] While the contribution of the *Roman de la Rose* to the

---

[3] Stephen A. Barney, in *The Riverside Chaucer*, p. 1022; see also N. R. Havely, *Chaucer's Boccaccio: Sources of Troilus and The Knight's and Franklin's Tales* (Cambridge: D. S. Brewer, 1980).

[4] H. A. Kelly, *Chaucerian Tragedy*, pp. 11–12.

[5] Robert K. Root, in Bryan and Dempster, p. 616. Root is the author of the chapter on the *Monk's Tale* in Bryan and Dempster, pp. 615–44.

[6] Bryan and Dempster, p. 616; Root describes the likely borrowings from Boccaccio.

[7] See *Roman de la Rose*, lines 5829–6901.

[8] See Bryan and Dempster, p. 617.

[9] Oxford, Jesus College, MS 94, fols. 57v–58r (there is no edition).

general plan of the *Monk's Tale* must remain difficult to determine, it is quite certain, as noted below, that the section of the *Roman* on Fortune written by Jean de Meun was the primary source for Chaucer's tragedies of Nero and Croesus.

Turning to the individual tragedies that make up the *Monk's Tale*, it should be remembered that individually and collectively they are fashioned from a wide array of sources, including the Bible and Dante as well as Boccaccio. As many scholars have pointed out, it is often impossible to identify specific sources and fruitless to try, since Chaucer seems to have based many of his stories on several possible literary sources and frequently depended upon what is best termed general knowledge.[10] What went into making up Chaucer's general knowledge as it relates to these specific stories, cannot, of course, be known with any certainty.

He would have read the Vulgate Bible directly, which is the primary source of the tragedies of Lucifer, Adam, Samson, Nebuchadnezzar, Belshazzar, Holofernes, and Antiochus.[11] Knowledge of biblical stories as well as of elaborations on the biblical narrative could have come to him by other means as well, such as from sermons or homilies he may have heard, or from reading in such standard Latin compendia as the *Glossa ordinaria* (c. 1200), the *Historia scholastica* of Peter Comestor (d. 1179), or the *Legenda aurea* of Jacobus de Voragine (d. 1298). It has been suggested that he used a French biblical compilation, the *Bible historiale* (c. 1294) of Guyart Desmoulins as an intermediate source.[12] The situation is further complicated because such popular Latin and vernacular compilations were used again and again as sources for many subsequent didactic, historical, and literary works. The amplifications and renarrations they contain are likely to have contributed some of the details to Chaucer's biblical tragedies, but in most cases, the similarities that have been pointed out by scholars are general and inconclusive.[13]

A widely circulated repository of historical information that Chaucer is likely to have known is the *Speculum historiale* of Vincent of Beauvais (d. c. 1264), which relates the histories of many figures of the antique world treated in the *Monk's Tale*, including Alexander the Great, Nero, and Julius Caesar. Yet Vincent's *Speculum* does not appear to have contributed directly to Chaucer's Alexander, although it has been credibly proposed as a source for certain details in the tragedies of Nero and perhaps Caesar.[14] As in the case of the biblical

---

[10] *The Riverside Chaucer*, p. 929.

[11] For specific biblical references, see the Sources and Texts section below.

[12] See Dudley R. Johnson, "The Biblical Characters of Chaucer's Monk," *PMLA* 66 (1951): 827–43; Johnson suggests the *Bible historiale* as the primary source for the biblical portions of the Tale, except for the tragedy of Antiochus. The most convincing evidence is a detail about Daniel in the tragedy of Nebuchadnezzar; see *The Riverside Chaucer*, p. 931 (note on line 2152).

[13] See the excellent notes on the individual tragedies in *The Riverside Chaucer*, pp. 929–35.

[14] See the studies of Aiken and Waller cited in the Sources and Texts section on Nero. For the possibility that Chaucer may have known the *Speculum* in a fourteenth-century French translation, see Kelly, *Chaucerian Tragedy*, p. 67. In the case of Alexander, Root finds no evidence that Chaucer used Vincent as his immediate source; Bryan and Dempster, p. 641.

stories, information and details are likely to have been available in intermediate sources.

In constructing tragedies of biblical and historical figures whose stories were common knowledge in the later Middle Ages, Chaucer undoubtedly relied on his memory of any number of written or oral versions of the stories. Memory was an important part of literary invention for Chaucer, as it was for many medieval authors. The Monk in the Prologue to the Tale states that he has some hundred tragedies in his "celle" (line 1972), which may be a reference to the cell of his memory rather than to his quarters in the monastery, as it is usually taken to be.[15] A composing process on Chaucer's part that relied more on memory than on written sources lying at his elbow would account for the occasional close resemblance of certain phrases, lines, and paragraphs to particular written works, while other parts of the tragedy are quite different, remembered from other prototypes.

The Monk's tragedies from the antique world are generally based on stories familiar in the Middle Ages, but a few specific sources, or partial sources, have been identified. The story of Hercules, for example, was found in Ovid's *Metamorphoses* and *Heroides*, as well as in Boethius, *De consolatione philosophiae*, which seems to have been Chaucer's immediate source.[16]

The tragedy of Zenobia, Queen of Palmyra, is taken from Boccaccio's *De mulieribus claris*, with some details from his *De casibus*.[17]

Nero, Alexander the Great, Julius Caesar, and Croesus were all figures from antiquity whose stories were broadly disseminated in the Middle Ages. As noted above, the immediate source of the tragedy of Nero appears to be the *Roman de la Rose*, which in turn draws upon Boethius's *De consolatione philosophiae*. Chaucer refers explicitly to Suetonius (line 2465), whose *Vitae caesarum* contains the standard classical account of Nero's life, but it is not certain that Chaucer used Suetonius directly. It has recently been suggested that some details on Nero's new clothing and his fishing with golden nets (lines 2471–8) may be based on the fourteenth-century *Alphabetum narrationum*.[18]

The tragedy of Croesus is also quite clearly drawn from the *Roman de la Rose*. It is based on the account of his life in the section on Fortune, although scholars have suggested that minor details may have been contributed by other works.[19]

The story of Alexander the Great was among the most popular in the Middle Ages, and no particular source for Chaucer's very brief account of his life has been or is likely to be identified. Indeed the Monk tells us at the beginning of his

---

[15] See Mary Carruthers, *The Book of Memory: A Study of Memory in Medieval Culture* (Cambridge: Cambridge University Press, 1990), p. 35. This reference, as well as the ideas in this paragraph, I owe to a suggestion of Edward Wheatley.

[16] See *The Riverside Chaucer*, note on line 2095; Bryan and Dempster, pp. 629–30; and see the discussion of this tragedy in the Sources and Texts section for minor sources.

[17] See *The Riverside Chaucer*, note on line 2247; Bryan and Dempster, p. 632.

[18] See the study by Vincent DiMarco cited below in the Sources and Texts section on Nero.

[19] *The Riverside Chaucer*, p. 934.

tragedy that "The storie of Alisaundre is so commune" that everyone knows something of it (lines 2631-3). Alexander was treated in such standard historical compendia as the *Speculum historiale*, as noted above, and he was also the subject of popular romances in the vernacular. Middle English examples are *King Alisaunder* and the *Wars of Alexander*.[20]

The tragedy of Julius Caesar similarly seems based principally upon general knowledge, derived ultimately from the accounts in Lucan, Suetonius, and Valerius Maximus, ancient authors whom Chaucer names in the tragedy (lines 2719-20), although it is not necessary to assume that he knew them at first hand.

The tragedies of Pedro, King of Castile and Leon (d. 1369); Pierre de Lusignan, King of Cyprus (d. 1369); Bernabò Visconti of Milan (d. 1385); and Ugolino, Count of Pisa (d. 1289) are collectively known to present-day scholarship as the "modern instances" since they recount the stories of historical Europeans who died in Chaucer's own lifetime or in recent memory. They are of special interest because they are often thought to have been written later than the rest of the tragedies and interpolated into the body of the Tale.[21] While the most recent tragedies seem to have been based on Chaucer's personal knowledge or word of mouth information, the tragedy of Ugolino is taken from Dante's *Inferno*, and the account of the death of the King of Cyprus, which does not correspond to historical fact, may be derived from Guillaume de Machaut's poem *La Prise d'Alexandrie*.[22] As noted above, Chaucer may have adopted the idea of writing tragedies based upon recent examples from the precedent of the *Roman de la Rose*.

Aside from DiMarco's identification of a possible source for some details of the tragedy of Nero, mentioned above, no new sources for the *Monk's Tale* have been recently discovered or proposed. A minor, late analogue to the story of Ugolino has been suggested, but in the last fifty years or so, very little scholarship has appeared to unsettle the consensus on sources established by R. K. Root in Bryan and Dempster.[23]

[20] For Alexander in the Middle Ages, see George Cary, *The Medieval Alexander* (Cambridge: Cambridge University Press, 1956); D[avid]. J. A. Ross, *Alexander Historiatus: A Guide to Medieval Illustrated Alexander Literature* (London: Warburg Institute, 1963); *The Medieval Alexander Legend and Romance Epic: Essays in Honour of David J. A. Ross*, ed. Peter Noble, Lucie Polak, and Claire Isoz (Millwood, NY: Kraus International, 1982).

[21] The "modern instances" are placed differently in different manuscripts; for a discussion of the textual problem and the date of composition, see the notes in *The Riverside Chaucer*, pp. 929-30.

[22] In the case of Ugolino, it has been suggested that Chaucer may have used other literary sources in addition to Dante; see the Sources and Texts section below; for Pierre de Lusignan, see Bryan and Dempster, pp. 636-7.

[23] See the study by Rossell H. Robbins cited in the Sources and Texts section on Ugolino.

Sources and Texts

1. Lucifer

The fall of the wicked angels was a part of standard Christian belief in the Middle Ages; see Augustine, *City of God*, book 11. On Lucifer, see Isaiah 14:12. Boccaccio's *De casibus* begins with Adam and Eve, not Lucifer.

2. Adam

The story of Adam is found in Genesis 2–3. It was a commonplace that Adam was created in a field where Damascus later stood (the "feeld of Damyssene," line 2007).[24]

3. Samson

The ultimate source of the story of Samson is the biblical account in Judges 13–16. The story of Samson is also treated in Boccaccio's *De casibus* 1.17, but it does not appear to have influenced Chaucer's version in any notable way. Joseph Grennen considers some of the details of Chaucer's adaptation.[25] For possible intermediate sources for this and the other biblical tragedies, see the studies of Aiken and Johnson.[26]

4. Hercules

For the widely known story of Hercules, Chaucer seems to have followed the account in Boethius, *De consolatione philosophiae* 4.m7.13–31, and he may have used elements from the version in Ovid's *Metamorphoses* 9 or *Heroides* 9. Texts of the versions in Boethius and the *Metamorphoses* are given here. Deianara (lines 2119–26) is treated briefly in Boccaccio's *De claris mulieribus* 23. Hercules is not a major figure in the *De casibus*. Robert A. Pratt discusses possible sources for Chaucer's knowledge of the Pillars of Hercules and the mysterious reference to "Trophee" (lines 2117–18); the latter problem has been re-examined by Vincent DiMarco.[27]

---

[24] See *The Riverside Chaucer*, p. 930.
[25] Joseph E. Grennen, " 'Sampsoun' in the *Canterbury Tales*: Chaucer Adapting a Source," *Neuphilologische Mitteilungen* 67 (1966): 117–22.
[26] Cited at note 12 and note 38, respectively.
[27] Robert A. Pratt, "Chaucer and the Pillars of Hercules," in *Studies in Honor of Ullman*, ed. Lillian B. Lawler, et al. (St. Louis, MO: The Classical Bulletin, 1960), pp. 118–25; Vincent DiMarco, "Another Look at Chaucer's 'Trophee,' " *Names* 34 (1986): 275–83.

A. Boethius, *De consolatione philosophiae* 4.m7.13–31

(Text and translation from *De consolatione philosophiae*, ed. H. F. Stewart and
E. K. Rand, trans. S. J. Tester [Cambridge, Mass.: Harvard University Press,
1973], p. 380)

	Herculem duri celebrant labores.
	Ille Centauros domuit superbos,
15	Abstulit saevo spolium leoni
	Fixit et certis volucres sagittis,
	Poma cernenti rapuit draconi
	Aureo laevam gravior metallo,
	Cerberum traxit triplici catena.
20	Victor immitem posuisse fertur
	Pabulum saevis dominum quadrigis.
	Hydra combusto periit veneno,
	Fronte turpatus Achelous amnis
	Ora demersit pudibunda ripis.
25	Stravit Antaeum Libycis harenis,
	Cacus Evandri satiavit iras
	Quosque pressurus foret altus orbis
	Saetiger spumis umeros notavit.
	Ultimus caelum labor inreflexo
30	Sustulit collo pretiumque rursus
	Ultimi caelum meruit laboris.

[Harsh labors make the fame of Hercules:
He tamed the arrogant Centaurs,
Stole the spoil from the savage lion,
Pierced the Stymphalian birds with arrows sure;
He seized the fruits from the watching dragon,
His hand the heavier for the golden ball,
[13–19] And with triple chain led Cerberus.
The tale is told how he beat and gave as fodder
That cruel master to his own savage steeds.
Its poison burnt, the Hydra died;
The river Achelous, in shame for his hornless brow,
Disgraced, did bury in his banks his face.
[20–25] Hercules stretched Antaeus's length on Libyan sands,
And Cacus dead sated Evander's wrath.
Those shoulders which the high sphere of heaven was to press
The bristled boar did fleck with foam.
As his last labor he with unbended neck
Bore up the heavens, and as his reward
[26–31] For that last labor, heaven deserved.]

B. Ovid, *Metamorphoses* 9.134–241

(Text and translation from Ovid, *Metamorphoses*, ed. Frank Justus Miller, 2nd ed., rev. G. P. Goold [Cambridge, Mass.: Harvard University Press, 1984], pp. 12–21)

Longa fuit medii mora temporis, aetaque magni
135 Herculis inplerant terras odiumque novercae.
victor ab Oechalia Cenaco sacra parabat
vota Iovi, cum Fama loquax praecessit ad aures,
Deianira, tuas, quae veris addere falsa
gaudet, et e minimo sua per mendacia crescit,
140 Amphitryoniaden Ioles ardore teneri.
credit amans, venerisque novae perterrita fama
indulsit primo lacrimis, flendoque dolorem
diffudit miseranda suum. mox deinde "quid autem
flemus?" ait "paelex lacrimis laetabitur istis.
145 quae quoniam adveniet, properandum aliquidque novandum est,
dum licet, et nondum thalamos tenet altera nostros.
conquerar, an sileam? repetam Calydona, morerne?
excedam tectis? an, si nihil amplius, obstem?
quid si me, Meleagre, tuam memor esse sororem
150 forte paro facinus, quantumque iniuria possit
femineusque dolor, iugulata paelice testor?"
in cursus animus varios abit. omnibus illis
praetulit inbutam Nesseo sanguine vestem
mittere, quae vires defecto reddat amori,
155 ignaroque Lichae, quid tradat, nescia, luctus
ipsa suos tradit blandisque miserrima verbis,
dona det illa viro, mandat. capit inscius heros,
induiturque umeris Lernaeae virus echidnae.
    Tura dabat primis et verba precantia flammis,
160 vinaque marmoreas patera fundebat in aras:
incaluit vis illa mali, resolutaque flammis
Herculeos abiit late dilapsa per artus.
dum potuit, solita gemitum virtute repressit.
victa malis postquam est patientia, reppulit aras,
165 inplevitque suis nemorosam vocibus Oeten.
nec mora, letiferam conatur scindere vestem:
qua trahitur, trahit illa cutem, foedumque relatu,
aut haeret membris frustra temptata revelli,
aut laceros artus et grandia detegit ossa.
170 ipse cruor, gelido ceu quondam lammina candens
tincta lacu, stridit coquiturque ardente veneno.
nec modus est, sorbent avidae praecordia flammae,
caeruleusque fluit toto de corpore sudor,
ambustique sonant nervi, caecaque medullis
175 tabe liquefactis tollens ad sidera palmas

"cladibus," exclamat "Saturnia, pascere nostris:
pascere, et hanc pestem specta, crudelis, ab alto,
corque ferum satia. vel si miserandus et hosti,
hoc est, si tibi sum, diris cruciatibus aegram
180   invisamque animam natamque laboribus aufer.
mors mihi munus erit; decet haec dare dona novercam.
ergo ego foedantem peregrino templa cruore
Busirin domui? saevoque alimenta parentis
Antaeo eripui? nec me pastoris Hiberi
185   forma triplex, nec forma triplex tua, Cerbere, movit?
vosne, manus, validi pressistis cornua tauri?
vestrum opus Elis habet, vestrum Stymphalides undae,
Partheniumque nemus? vestra virtute relatus
Thermodontiaco caelatus balteus auro,
190   pomaque ab insomni concustodita dracone?
nec mihi centauri potuere resistere, nec mi
Arcadiae vastator aper? nec profuit hydrae
crescere per damnum geminasque resumere vires?
quid, cum Thracis equos humano sanguine pingues
195   plenaque corporibus laceris praesepia vidi,
visaque deieci, dominumque ipsosque peremi?
his elisa iacet moles Nemeaea lacertis:
hac caelum cervice tuli. defessa iubendo est
saeva Iovis coniunx: ego sum indefessus agendo.
200   sed nova pestis adest, cui nec virtute resisti
nec telis armisque potest. pulmonibus errat
ignis edax imis, perque omnes pascitur artus.
at valet Eurystheus! et sunt, qui credere possint
esse deos?" dixit, perque altam saucius Oeten
205   haud aliter graditur, quam si venabula taurus
corpore fixa gerat, factique refugerit auctor.
saepe illum gemitus edentem, saepe frementem,
saepe retemptantem totas infringere vestes
sternentemque trabes irascentemque videres
210   montibus aut patrio tendentem bracchia caelo.
       Ecce Lichan trepidum latitantem rupe cavata
aspicit, utque dolor rabiem conlegerat omnem,
"tune, Licha," dixit "feralia dona dedisti?
tune meae necis auctor eris?" tremit ille, pavetque
215   pallidus, et timide verba excusantia dicit.
dicentem genibusque manus adhibere parantem
corripit Alcides, et terque quaterque rotatum
mittit in Euboicas tormento fortius undas.
ille per aërias pendens induruit auras:
220   utque ferunt imbres gelidis concrescere ventis,
inde nives fieri, nivibus quoque molle rotatis
astringi et spissa glomerari grandine corpus,
sic illum validis iactum per inane lacertis
exsanguemque metu nec quicquam umoris habentem

225   in rigidos versum silices prior edidit aetas.
nunc quoque in Euboico scopulus brevis eminet alto
gurgite et humanae servat vestigia formae,
quem, quasi sensurum, nautae calcare verentur,
appellantque Lichan. at tu, Iovis inclita proles,
230   arboribus caesis, quas ardua gesserat Oete,
inque pyram structis arcum pharetramque capacem
regnaque visuras iterum Troiana sagittas
ferre iubes Poeante satum, quo flamma ministro
subdita. dumque avidis comprenditur ignibus agger,
235   congeriem silvae Nemeaeo vellere summam
sternis, et inposita clavae cervice recumbis,
haud alio vultu, quam si conviva iaceres
inter plena meri redimitus pocula sertis.
      Iamque valens et in omne latus diffusa sonabat,
240   securosque artus contemptoremque petebat
flamma suum. timuere dei pro vindice terrae.

[Meanwhile, long years had passed; the deeds of the mighty Hercules had
filled the earth and had sated his stepmother's hate. Returning victorious from
Oechalia, he was preparing to pay his vows to Jove at Cenaeum, when tattling
Rumor came on ahead to your ears, Deianira, Rumor, who loves to mingle
false and true and, though very small at first, grows huge through lying, and
she reported that the son of Amphitryon was enthralled by love of Iole.
[131–40] The loving wife believes the tale and completely overcome by the
report of this new love, she indulges her tears at first and, poor creature, pours
out her grief in a flood of weeping. But soon she says: "Why do I weep? My
rival will rejoice at my tears. But since she is on her way hither I must make
haste and devise some plan while I may, and while as yet another woman has
not usurped my couch. [141–6] Shall I complain or shall I grieve in silence?
Shall I go back to Calydon or tarry here? Shall I leave my house or, if I can
nothing more, stay and oppose her? What if, O Meleager, remembering that I
am your sister, I make bold to plan some dreadful deed, and by killing my
rival prove how much a woman's humiliation and grief can do?" Her mind is
divided between various courses; but to all other plans she prefers to send to
her husband the tunic soaked in Nessus' blood, in the hope that this may
revive her husband's failing love; and to Lichas, ignorant of what he bears,
with her own hands she all unwittingly commits the cause of her future woe,
and with honeyed words the unhappy woman bids him take this present to her
lord. The hero innocently received the gift and put on his shoulders the tunic
soaked in the Lernaean hydra's poison. [147–58]

He was offering incense and prayers amid the kindling flames and pouring
wine from the libation bowl upon the marble altar: then was the virulence of
that pest aroused and, freed by the heat, went stealing throughout the frame of
Hercules. While he could, with his habitual manly courage he held back his
groans. But when his endurance was conquered by his pain, he overthrew the
altar and filled woody Oeta with his cries. At once he tries to tear off the
deadly tunic; but where it is torn away, it tears the skin with it and, ghastly to
relate, it either sticks to his limbs, from which he vainly tries to tear it, or else

lays bare his torn muscles and huge bones. [159–69] His very blood hisses and boils with the burning poison, as when a piece of red-hot metal is plunged into a pool. Without limit the greedy flames devour his vitals; the dark sweat pours from his whole body; his burnt sinews crackle and, while his very marrow melts with the hidden, deadly fire, he stretches suppliant hands to heaven and cries: "Come, feast, Saturnia, upon my destruction; feast, I say; look down, thou cruel one, from thy lofty seat, behold my miserable end, and glut thy savage heart! Or, if I merit pity even from my enemy – that is, from thee – take hence this hateful life, sick with its cruel sufferings and born for toil. [170–80] Death will be a boon to me, surely a fitting boon for a stepmother to bestow! Was it for this I slew Busiris, who defiled his temples with strangers' blood? that I deprived the dread Antaeus of his mother's strength? that I did not fear the Spanish shepherd's triple form, nor thy triple form, O Cerberus? Was it for this, O hands, that you broke the strong bull's horns? that Elis knows your toil, the waves of Stymphalus, the Parthenian woods? that by your prowess the gold-wrought girdle of Thermodon was secured, and that fruit guarded by the dragon's sleepless eyes? [190–1] Was it for this that the centaurs could not prevail against me, nor the boar that wasted Arcady? that it did not avail the hydra to grow by loss and gain redoubled strength? What, when I saw the Thracian's horses fat with human blood and those mangers full of mangled corpses and, seeing, threw them down and slew the master and the steeds themselves? By these arms the monster of Nemea lies crushed; upon this neck I upheld the sky! The cruel wife of Jove is weary of imposing toils; but I am not yet weary of performing them. But now a strange and deadly thing is at me, which neither by strength can I resist, nor yet by weapons nor by arms. Deep through my lungs steals the devouring fire, and feeds through all my frame. [191–202] But Eurystheus is alive and well! And are there those who can believe that there are gods?" He spoke and in sore distress went ranging along high Oeta; just as a bull carries about the shaft that has pierced his body, though the giver of the wound has fled. See him there on the mountains oft uttering heart-rending groans, oft roaring in agony, oft struggling to tear off his garments, uprooting great trunks of trees, stretching out his arms to his native skies. [202–10]

Of a sudden he caught sight of Lichas cowering with fear in hiding beneath a hollow rock, and with all the accumulated rage of suffering he cried: "Was it you, Lichas, who brought this fatal gift? And shall you be called the author of my death?" The young man trembled, grew pale with fear, and timidly attempted to excuse his act. But while he was yet speaking and striving to clasp the hero's knees, Alcides caught him up and, whirling him thrice and again about his head, he hurled him far out into the Euboean sea, like a missile from a catapult. [211–18] The youth stiffened as he yet hung in air; and as drops of rain are said to congeal beneath the chilling blast and change to snow, then whirling snowflakes condense to a soft mass and finally are packed in frozen hail: so, hurled by strong arms through the empty air, bloodless with fear, his vital moisture dried, he changed, old tradition says, to flinty rock. Even to this day in the Euboean sea a low rock rises from the waves, keeping the semblance of a human form; [219–27] this rock, as if it were sentient, the sailors fear to tread on, and they call it Lichas. But you, illustrious son of Jove, cut down the trees which grew on lofty Oeta, built a

huge funeral pyre, and bade the son of Poeas, who set the torch beneath, to take in recompense your bow, capacious quiver and arrows, destined once again to see the realm of Troy. And as the pyre began to kindle with the greedy flames, you spread the Nemean lion's skin on the top and, with your club for pillow, laid you down with peaceful countenance, as if, amid cups of generous wine and crowned with garlands, you were reclining on a banquet-couch.

And now on all sides the spreading flames were crackling fiercely, and licking at the careless limbs that scorned their power. The gods felt fear for the earth's defender. [228–41]]

5. Nebuchadnezzar (Nabugodonosor)

The tragedy is based on the biblical account in Daniel 1–4. Root notes that there are several errors in Chaucer's version, which may point to an intermediate source.[28] Dudley R. Johnson has proposed the *Bible historiale* of Guyart Desmoulins (c. 1294), which would explain several of these discrepancies.[29]

6. Belshazzar (Balthasar)

The tragedy of Balshazzar, the son of Nebuchadnezzar, is based on the account in Daniel 5.

7. Zenobia (Cenobia)

The tragedy is based on Boccaccio's *De mulieribus claris*; the relevant sections are given here. Chaucer also may have used Boccaccio's *De casibus* 8.6, especially in the final stanza.[30] Vincent DiMarco suggests some possible sources for the enigmatic 'vitremyte' worn by Zenobia (line 2372) and discusses its use in Boccaccio.[31]

---

[28] See Bryan and Dempster, p. 632.
[29] See Dudley R. Johnson, "The Biblical Characters of Chaucer's Monk," cited above (note 12). The *Bible historiale* could have provided the source for the non-biblical detail that Daniel was castrated at the order of Nebuchadnezzar; see *The Riverside Chaucer*, p. 931 (note on line 2152).
[30] Bryan and Dempster, pp. 632–3; *The Riverside Chaucer*, p. 932.
[31] Vincent DiMarco, "Wearing the 'Vitremyte': A Note on Chaucer and Boccaccio," *English Language Notes* 25 (1988): 15–19.

Boccaccio, *De mulieribus claris* 100 [98]

(Text from *Tutte le opere di Giovanni Boccaccio*, ed. Vittore Branca, vol. 10,
ed. Vittorio Zaccaria [n.p.: Mondadori, 1967]; trans. Thomas H. Bestul)

De Zenobia Palmirenorum regina

Zenobia Palmirenorum fuit regina, tam eximie virtutis femina, priscis
testantibus literis, ut ceteris gentilibus inclita fama preponenda sit. Hec ante
alia genere fuit insignis. Nam a Ptholomeis Egyptiorum regibus claram volunt
originem habuisse, parentibus tamen memorie non concessis. Dicunt autem
hanc a pueritia sua, spretis omnino muliebribus offitiis, cum iam corpusculum
eduxisset in robur, silvas et nemora coluisse plurimum et accinctam pharetra,
cervis capriisque cursu atque sagittis fuisse infestam. Inde cum in acriores
devenisset vires, ursos amplecti ausam, pardos leonesque insequi, obvios
expectare, capere et occidere ac in predam trahere; et impavidam, nunc hos
nunc illos saltus et prerupta montium discurrere, lustra perscrutari ferarum et
sub divo somnos etiam per noctem capere, imbres, estus et frigora mira
tolerantia superare, <amores hominum et contubernia spernere>[32] assuetam et
virginitatem summopere colere. Quibus fugata muliebri mollicie adeo eam in
virile robur duratam aiunt ut coetaneos iuvenes luctis palestricisque ludis
omnibus viribus superaret.

   Tandem, instante etate nubili, amicorum consilio, Odenato, iuveni equis
studiis durato et longe Palmirenorum nobiliori principi, nuptam volunt. Erat
hec speciosa corpore, esto paululum fusca colore; sic enim, urente sole,
regionis illius omnes sunt incole; preterea nigris oculis niveisque dentibus
decora. Que cum cerneret Odenatum, capto a Sapore rege Persarum Valeriano
Augusto turpique servitio damnato et Galieno filio effeminate torpescente, ad
orientale occupandum imperium intentum, non immemor duriciei pristine
armis formositatem tegere et sub viro militare disposuit; et cum eo, sumpto
regio nomine et ornatu, atque cum Herode privigno, collectis copiis, in
Saporem, late iam Mesopotamiam occupantem, animose progressa est; et,
nullis parcens laboribus, nunc ducis, nunc militis officia peragens, non solum
acerrimum virum et bellorum expertum virtute armorum superavit, sed
creditum eius opere Mesopotamiam in iurisdictionem venisse et Saporem,
castris eius cum concubinis et ingenti preda captis, usque Thesiphontem
pulsum atque secutum. Nec multo post Quietum, Macriani filium, qui patrio
sub nomine orientis imperium intraverat, ut opprimeretur curavit vigilanti
studio. Et cum iam omnem orientem ad Romanos spectantem una cum viro
pacatum obtineret, et ecce a Meonio consobrino suo Odenatus una cum
Herode filio occisus est; et, ut quidam asserunt, ob invidiam, existimantibus
aliis, Zenobiam in mortem Herodis prestitisse consensum, eo quod sepius eius
damnasset molliciem et ut filiis Herenniano et Thimolao, quos ex Odenato
susceperat, successio cederet regni. Et imperante Meonio aliquandiu quievit.
Verum Meonio brevi a militibus suis trucidato, quasi possessione vacua

---

[32] Missing in the base MS, but found in most MSS and early prints; see Zaccaria, p. 549.

derelicta, generosi animi mulier in predesideratum imperium intravit continuo et, filiis eius adhuc parvulis, imperiali sagulo humeris perfusa et regiis ornata comparuit, filiorumque nomine, longe magis quam sexui conveniret, gubernavit imperium. Nec segniter; nam in eam nec Galienus, nec post illum Claudius imperator aliquid attemptare ausi sunt. Similiter nec orientales Egyptii neque Arabes aut Saraceni, vel etiam Armeni populi, quin imo eius timentes potentiam suos posse servare terminos fuere contenti.

Fuit enim illi tanta bellorum industria et adeo acris militie disciplina, ut eque illam magni penderent sui exercitus et timerent. Apud quos nunquam concionata est nisi galeata; et in expeditionibus vehiculo carpentario perrarissime utebatur, equo sepius incedebat et non nunquam tribus vel quattuor milibus passuum cum militibus pedes signa precedebat: nec fastidivit cum ducibus suis quandoque bibisse, cum esset alias sobria; sic cum persis et armenis principibus ut illos urbanitate et facetia superaret. Fuit tamen adeo pudicitie severa servatrix ut nedum ab aliis abstineret omnino, sed etiam Odenato viro suo, dum viveret, se nunquam exhibere, preter ad filios procreandos, voluisse legimus; hac in hoc semper habita diligentia, ut post concubitum unum, tam diu abstineret ab altero, donec adverteret utrum concepisset ex illo; quod si contigerat, nunquam preter post partus purgationes a viro tangi patiebatur ulterius; si autem non concepisse perceperat, se ultro poscenti viro consentiebat.

O laudabile iudicium mulieris! Satis quidem apparet arbitratam nil ob aliud a natura mortalibus immissam libidinem quam ut prolis innovatione continua conservetur posteritas et reliquum, tanquam supervacaneum, viciosum.

Perrarissimas quidem huiuscemodi moris comperies mulieres. Hec tamen ne a mente differrent ministeria, ad oportuna domestica preter eunuchos, etate atque moribus graves, neminem unquam, vel perraro, admicti voluit. Vixit preterea ritu regio et magnifico sumptu usa, ea qua reges utuntur pompa; persicoque more voluit adorari et ad instar romanorum imperatorum convivia celebravit, in eis vasis usa aureis gemmatisque quibus olim usam Cleopatram acceperat; et quanquam servatrix thesaurorum permaxima esset, nemo, ubi oportunum visum est, ea magnificentior aut profusior visus est. Et si plurimum venationibus armisque vacasset, non obstitere hec quin literas egyptias nosceret et sub Longino philosopho preceptore grecas etiam disceret. Quarum suffragio hystorias omnes latinas grecas et barbaras summo cum studio vidit et memorie commendavit. Nec hoc tantum quin imo creditum est illas etiam sub epythomatis brevitate traxisse et preter suum ydioma novit egyptium eoque, cum syriacum sciret, usa est.

Quid multa? Tanti profecto fuit hec ut, Gallieno atque Aureolo et Claudio Augusto sublatis, et Aureliano, integre virtutis homine, in principatu suffecto, ad ignominiam romani nominis expiandam et ad ingentem gloriam consequendam, in se traxerit. Nam, marcomannico bello peracto, et Rome rebus compositis, Aurelianus cum omni cura zenobianam expeditionem assumpsit, et multis egregie, adversus barbaras nationes eundo, confectis, cum legionibus tandem haud longe Emessam civitatem devenit, quam penes Zenobia, in nullo perterrita, una cum Zaba quodam, quem belli susceperat sotium, cum exercitu suo consederat. Ibi inter Aureli\<an\>um[33] et Zenobiam

---

[33] MS *Aurelium* is evidently an error for *Aurelianum*; see Zaccaria, p. 550.

de summa rerum acriter et diu pugnatum est. Ad ultimum, cum romana virtus videretur superior, Zenobia cum suis in fugam versa Palmira sese recepit. In qua evestigio a victore obsessa est. Quam cum aliquandiu, nullas volens conditiones deditionis audire, mira solertia defendisset, in penuriam oportunarum rerum deducta est. Hinc nequeuntibus Palmirenis Aurelianorum obsistere viribus, interceptis etiam ab eodem Persis Armenisque et Saracenis auxilio Zenobie venientibus, armorum vi civitas a Romanis capta est. Ex qua cum Zenobia vecta dromonibus[34] cum filiis in Persas aufugeret, ab aurelianis militibus secuta et capta cum filiis, Aureliano viva presentata est. Ex quo non aliter quam si maximum superasset ducem et acerrimum reipublice hostem, Aurelianus gloriatus est eamque triunpho servavit et adduxit cum filiis Romam. Inde ab Aureliano celebratus <triunphus>,[35] spectaculo Zenobie admirandus, in quo, inter alia egregia et memoratu dignissima, currum duxit, quem sibi ex auro gemmisque preciosissimum Zenobia fabricari fecerat, sperans se Romam venturam, non quidem captivam, sed rerum dominam atque triunphaturam et romanum possessuram imperium; quem et ipsa cum filiis precessit. Verum ipsa catenis aureis collo manibus pedibusque iniectis corona et vestimentis regiis ac margaritis et lapidibus pretiosis honusta, adeo ut, cum roboris inexhausti esset, pondere fessa persepe subsisteret. Sane consumato triunpho thesauro et virtute spectabili, aiunt illam privato in habitu inter romanas matronas cum filiis senuisse, concessa sibi a senatu possessione apud Tiburtum, que zenobiana diu postmodum ab ea denominata est, haud longe a divi Adriani palatio, quod eo in loco est cui Conche ab incolis dicebatur.

[*Zenobia, Queen of Palmyra*

Zenobia was queen of Palmyra and of such exceptional virtue, as ancient writings bear witness, that she must be placed above all other pagans in her glorious fame. First of all, she was eminent in birth. Indeed they were of the opinion that she had an illustrious origin from the Ptolomies who were kings of Egypt, yet her ancestors had disappeared from memory. They say that from her youth she completely rejected womanly offices, and when her small body had grown in strength, she especially sought out forests and groves, and girded with a quiver was dangerous to stags and roe through arrows and the chase. Then, when she had attained greater strengths, they say that she dared to embrace bears, to pursue leopards and lions, to lie in wait for them, to take and kill them and to drag them as booty; and to traverse fearlessly now these, now those mountain passes and rugged places, to search out the haunts of wild beasts, and to sleep the entire night in the open air, to overcome rain, heat, and cold with marvelous endurance; and she was accustomed to scorn the love and companionship of men and above all to cherish virginity. Since womanly softness had been put to flight by these things, she was so hardened in manly strength that she surpassed in all strength boys of her own age in wrestling and gymnastic games. Finally, when she was of marriageable age, on the counsel

---

[34] Apparently some confusion between the forms *dromas/dromadis* and *dromo-onis*; see Zaccaria, p. 550; the edition in Bryan and Dempster has *dromedariis*.

[35] Supplied from other MSS; see Zaccaria, p. 550.

of friends they resolved to marry her to Odenatus, a youth made hardy by equal endeavors and by far the most noble prince of the Palmyrans.

She was beautiful of body, somewhat swarthy in color – as indeed all the inhabitants of that region are from the burning sun. Moreover, she was becoming in her dark eyes and snow-white teeth. When she saw that Odenatus was intent on seizing the eastern empire, Augustus Valerianus having been captured by Sapor, king of the Persians, and condemned to shameful service, and his son Galienus being effeminately indolent, she was not unmindful of her pristine toughness and arranged to cover her beauty with arms and to perform military service under her husband. With her husband, who had assumed the royal name and trappings, and with her stepson Herod, once the troops had been gathered, she boldly advanced against Sapor, who now had extensively occupied Mesopotamia. Sparing no pains, performing the duties now of a general, now of a soldier, she not only surpassed in strength of arms a man fiercest and skilled in arms, but also, it must be believed, by her effort Mesopotamia came under control, and she routed and pursued Sapor as far as Thesiphontem, after his camps with his concubines and vast booty had been taken.

Not long after she took care, with watchful zeal, to overpower Quietus, son of Macrianus, who, under his father's name, had entered the empire of the east. And now after she, together with her husband, had taken possession of and pacified the entire east which faced the Romans – behold Odenatus, together with his son Herod, was killed by his cousin Meonius. As some assert, this was done on account of envy, while others thought that Zenobia had agreed to the death of Herod, whose softness she had often condemned, so that the succession of the kingdom might fall to her sons Herennianus and Thimolaus, whom she had had by Odenatus. And while Meonius ruled, she remained quiet for some time. Yet when Meonius was struck down by his soldiers after a short time, this woman of noble spirit immediately entered into the long-desired empire, as if it were abandoned property for the taking. Since her sons were still young, she appeared with the imperial cloak on her shoulders and adorned with the regalia governed the empire in the name of her sons, far distant from what was suited to her sex. Nor did she govern indifferently: for neither Galienus, nor after him the emperor Claudius, dared to attempt anything against her. Likewise, neither the Egyptians of the east, nor the Arabs or Saracens, nor even the people of Armenia dared anything; on the contrary, fearing her power, they were content to keep within their boundaries.

Indeed she had such great diligence for war, and was so keen for military discipline, that her great armies equally esteemed her and feared her. In their presence she never delivered a speech unless she was helmeted; and on her expeditions she very rarely used a carriage; more often she went forth on a horse and always, together with her infantry, preceded the insignia by three or four thousand paces. She did not flinch at any time from drinking with her generals, although she was otherwise sober; and she did likewise with the Persian and Armenian princes so that she might surpass them in urbanity and drollery. Yet she was such a strict observer of chastity that not only would she abstain entirely from others, but also we read that she never wished to give herself to her husband, Odenatus, while he lived, except for begetting

children. In this she always observed this precaution, that after one sexual encounter, she abstained so long from a second until she knew whether she had conceived from the former; if this happened, she never allowed herself to be touched any further by her husband except for the purgations after birth; if, however, she perceived that she had not conceived, she consented again to her importunate husband.

O commendable judgment of a woman! Indeed it is apparent enough that she thought that sexual desire was placed in mortal men for nothing other than to maintain posterity by the continual renewing of offspring; and the rest of it she thought depraved and superfluous. Indeed you will find women of this kind of morals to be very rare. Yet, lest her servants be of a different mind, she wished in household services to be involved with no one, or very rarely, except eunuchs weighty in age and morals.

Furthermore, she lived according to the royal manner and enjoyed at sumptuous expense the ostentation belonging to kings; and in the Persian custom she wished to be adored. She celebrated banquets after the manner of the Roman emperors, in which she used gold and bejeweled vessels which Cleopatra had once had the use of; and although she was a great guardian of the treasury, no one was seen to be more magnificent or lavish than she when it seemed opportune.

And if she devoted herself mostly to hunting and feats of arms, that did not prevent her from learning Egyptian letters and also Greek, under the instruction of the philosopher Longinus. With the aid of these she understood with the greatest application all the Latin, Greek, and barbarian histories and committed them to memory. Nor is this all: on the contrary, it is believed that she drew them together under the concise form of an epitome. Besides her own idiom, she came to know Egyptian, and used it although she knew Syriac very well.

What more? She was truly a person of such consequence that after Galienus and Aureolus and Claudius Augustus had been removed and Aurelianus, a man of complete virtue, had been chosen for the chief place to atone for the shame of the Roman name and to pursue great glory, she drew an attack on herself. For, after the Marcomannian war had been completed and when matters were set right at Rome, Aurelianus with all carefulness undertook a Zenobian expedition; and many things having been accomplished uncommonly well in going against the barbarian nations, he finally arrived with his legions not far from the city of Emessa, in which Zenobia, not at all terrified, had established herself with her army, together with a certain Zaba, whom she had taken as an ally in war. There Aurelianus and Zenobia fought long and vehemently for supreme power. Finally, when Roman strength was seen to be superior, Zenobia retreated toward Palmyra with her forces, where she was immediately besieged by the victor. Although she defended it for some time with marvelous skill, wishing to hear no terms of surrender, she was brought into scarcity of necessary things. Hence, since the Palmyrans were unable to resist the forces of Aurelianus, and since the Persians, Armenians, and Saracens who were coming to the aid of Zenobia had been intercepted by Aurelianus, the city was captured by the Romans through force of arms. Although Zenobia would have fled from it into Persia with her sons, carried by many oared vessels [or camels? see note 34], she was followed by

the soldiers of Aurelianus and captured along with her sons, and presented alive to Aurelianus. Aurelianus gloried in this not otherwise than if he had conquered the greatest general and most bitter enemy of the republic, and he kept her for a triumph and led her with her sons to Rome. Thereupon a triumph was celebrated by Aurelianus, made wonderful by the public display of Zenobia; in which, among other things excellent and most worthy of mention, he drove a chariot, which Zenobia had had made for herself, most precious with gold and gems, hoping to have come to Rome not as a captive, but as the mistress of events, and to triumph and possess the Roman empire. She went before this chariot with her sons. Indeed she was loaded with golden chains cast upon her neck, hands, and feet, and with a crown and royal vestments and pearls and precious stones, so much so that, although she was of inexhaustible strength, she very often halted, feeble from the weight.

After the triumph had been well completed, notable in expense and in virtue, they say that she with her sons grew old among the Roman matrons as a private person. An estate near Tivoli was granted to her by the Senate, a place which long afterwards was named Zenobiana after her, not far from the palace of the divine Hadrian, which is in that place called Conche by the inhabitants.]

8. Peter of Spain

The first of the so-called "modern instances," the story describes the assassination of King Pedro of Castile in 1369. No written source has been identified, and Chaucer is thought to have relied on contemporary reports.[36]

9. Peter of Cyprus (Pierre de Lusignan)

Peter, King of Cyprus, was assassinated in 1369. Although the event occurred in Chaucer's lifetime, the account of the assassination differs in detail from historical fact and may depend on the version in Guillaume de Machaut's *La Prise d'Alexandrie*, given here.

---

[36] Means by which Chaucer could have acquired knowledge of the episode are examined by Henry Savage, "Chaucer and the 'Pitous Deeth' of 'Petro, Glorie of Spayne,'" *Speculum* 24 (1949): 357–75. On the possibility of Chaucer's direct contact with Spain, see Fernando Galvan Reula, "Medieval English Literature: A Spanish Approach," in *Actas del Primer Congreso Internacional de S.E.L.I.M.* (Oviedo: Universidad de Oviedo, 1989), pp. 98–111.

Guillaume de Machaut, *La Prise d'Alexandrie, ou, Chronique du Roi Pierre Ier de Lusignan,* lines 8631–5; 8686–703

(Text from *La Prise d'Alexandrie,* ed. Louis de Mas Latrie [Geneva: Flick, 1877]; trans. Thomas H. Bestul)

The barons go to the king's palace.

8631 Au matinet, à grans eslais,
   S'en alerent vers le palais,
   Droit à l'eure que la corneille
   Les paresseus huche & esveille,
   C'est à dire à l'aube crevant.

8686 Devant son lit sont aresté
   De mal faire tuit apresté.
   Li sires d'Absur la courtine,
   Qui de soie estoit riche & fine,
   Tira, pour le roy mieux veoir,
8691 Et pour son cop mieux asseoir.
   Et si tost com li roys le vit,
   De son lit en gisant li dist:
   "Estes vous là, sires d'Absur,
   Faus garson, traïtre, parjur.
8696 Qui vous fait entrer en ma chambre?"
   Et il respondi sans attendre:
   "Je ne sui mauvais ne traïtes,
   Mais tel estes vous, com vous dites;
   Dont vous morrez, sans nul respit,
8701 De mes mains." Et en ce despit
   Lors en son lit sus li coury
   Et ij. cos ou iij. le fery.

[In the morning they went toward the palace with great eagerness just at the hour when the crow cried and roused the sluggish: that is to say, they started with the dawn. [8631–5]

They stopped before his bed, all of them ready to do evil. The Lord of Absur drew the curtain, which was of silk, rich and fine, in order to see the king better and better to place his blow. And as soon as the king saw him he said to him while lying in his bed, "Is that you, Lord of Absur, false fellow, traitor, perjurer – who let you into my chamber?" And he responded without hesitation: "I am neither wicked nor treacherous, but you are such as you have said, for which you will die at my hands, with no respite." And with such contempt he then rushed into his bed over him and struck him two or three blows. [8686–703]]

10. Bernabò Visconti (Barnabo de Lumbardia)

Bernabò died in prison in 1385. It is thought that Chaucer's account is based on oral information and personal knowledge rather than an identifiable written source.

11. Ugolino

Ugolino of Pisa died in prison in 1289. Chaucer's tragedy is based on the version of his story in Dante's *Inferno*, given here. Scholars have suggested that Chaucer used other sources for certain details. A late fifteenth-century analogue of the Ugolino story has been identified by Robbins.[37]

Dante, *La commedia*, *Inferno* 33.1–75

(Text from *La divina commedia*, ed. C. H. Grandgent, rev. Charles Singleton
[Cambridge, Mass.: Harvard University Press, 1972], pp. 291–4; trans. from
The Divine Comedy, vol. 1, trans. Charles Singleton
[Princeton, NJ: Princeton University Press, 1970])

Dante and Virgil come upon Ugolino in the ninth circle of hell, where traitors are found. He leaves off gnawing the head of his enemy, Archbishop Ruggieri, to tell his story.

    La bocca sollevò dal fiero pasto
quel peccator, forbendola a'capelli
3   del capo ch' elli avea di retro guasto.
    Poi cominciò: "Tu vuo' ch'io rinovelli
disperato dolor che'l cor mi preme
6   già pur pensando, pria ch'io ne favelli.
    Ma se le mie parole esser dien seme
che frutti infamia al traditor ch'i' rodo,
9   parlare e lagrimar vedrai insieme.
    Io non so chi tu se' né per che modo
venuto se' qua giù; ma fiorentino
12 mi sembri veramente quand' io t'odo.
    Tu dei saper ch'i' fui conte Ugolino,
e questi è l'arcivescovo Ruggieri:
15 or ti dirò perché i son tal vicino.
    Che per l'effetto de' suo' mai pensieri,
fidandomi di lui, io fossi preso
18 e poscia morto, dir non è mestieri;
     però quel che non puoi avere inteso,

[37] Rossell H. Robbins, "A New Chaucer Analogue: The Legend of Ugolino," *Trivium* 2 (1967): 1–15; for the additional sources, see *The Riverside Chaucer*, p. 933.

cioè come la morte mia fu cruda,
21   udirai, e saprai s'e' m'ha offeso.
      Breve pertugio dentro da la Muda,
la qual per me ha 'l titol de la fame,
24   e'n che conviene ancor ch'altrui si chiuda,
      m'avea mostrato per lo suo forame
più lune già, quand' io feci'l mal sonno
27   che del futuro mi squarciò'l velame.
      Questi pareva a me maestro e donno,
cacciando il lupo e' lupicini al monte
30   per che i Pisan veder Lucca non ponno.
      Con cagne magre, studiose e conte
Gualandi con Sismondi e con Lanfranchi
33   s'avea messi dinanzi da la fronte.
      In picciol corso mi parieno stanchi
lo padre e' figli, e con l'agute scane
36   mi parea lor veder fender li fianchi.
      Quando fui desto innanzi la dimane,
pianger senti' fra'l sonno i miei figliuoli
39   ch'eran con meco, e dimandar del pane.
      Ben se' crudel, se tu già non ti duoli
pensando ciò che 'l mio cor s'annunziava;
42   e se non piangi, di che pianger suoli?
      Già eran desti, e l'ora s'appressava
che'l cibo ne solea essere addotto,
45   e per suo sogno ciascun dubitava;
      e io senti' chiavar l'uscio di sotto
a l'orribile torre; ond' io guardai
48   nel viso a' mie' figliuoi sanza far motto.
      Io non piangëa, sì dentro impetrai:
piangevan elli; e Anselmuccio mio
51   disse: 'Tu guardi sì, padre! che hai?'
      Perciò non lagrimai né rispuos' io
tutto quel giorno né la notte appresso,
54   infin che l'altro sol nel mondo uscìo.
      Come un poco di raggio si fu messo
nel doloroso carcere, e io scorsi
57   per quattro visi il mio aspetto stesso,
      ambo le man per lo dolor mi morsi;
ed ei, pensando ch'io'l fessi per voglia
60   di manicar, di sùbito levorsi
      e disser: 'Padre, assai ci fia men doglia
se tu mangi di noi: tu ne vestisti
63   queste misere carni, e tu le spoglia.'
      Queta'mi allor per non farli più tristi;
lo dì e l'altro stemmo tutti muti;
66   ahi dura terra, perché non t'apristi?
      Poscia che fummo al quarto dì venuti,
Gaddo mi si gittò disteso a' piedi,

69   dicendo: 'Padre mio, ché non m'aiuti?'
       Quivi morì; e come tu mi vedi,
     vid' io cascar li tre ad uno ad uno
72   tra' l quinto dì e 'l sesto; ond' io mi diedi,'
       già cieco, a brancolar sovra ciascuno,
     e due dì li chiamai, poi che fur morti.
75   Poscia, più che'l dolor, poté'l digiuno."

[*Ugolino*

From his savage repast the sinner raised his mouth, wiping it on the hair of the head he had spoiled behind, then began, "You will have me renew desperate grief, which even to think of wrings my heart before I speak of it. But if my words are to be seed that may bear fruit of infamy to the traitor whom I gnaw, you shall see me speak and weep together. [1–9] I do not know who you are, nor by what means you have come down here; but truly you do seem to me Florentine when I hear you. You have to know that I was Count Ugolino, and this is the Archbishop Ruggieri. Now I will tell you why I am such a neighbor to him. How, by effect of his ill devising, I, trusting in him, was taken and thereafter put to death, there is no need to tell; but what you cannot have heard, that is, how cruel my death was, you shall hear and you shall know if he has wronged me. [10–21]

"A narrow hole in the Mew which because of me has the title of Hunger, and in which others are yet to be shut up, had, through its opening, already shown me several moons, when I had the bad dream that rent for me the veil of the future. This man appeared to me as master and lord, chasing the wolf and the whelps upon the mountain for which the Pisans cannot see Lucca. With trained hounds, lean and eager, he had put in front of him Gualandi with Sismondi and with Lanfranchi, and after a short run the father and the sons seemed to me weary, and it seemed to me I saw their flanks ripped by the sharp fangs. [22–36]

"When I awoke before the dawn I heard my children, who were with me, crying in their sleep and asking for bread. You are cruel indeed if you do not grieve already, to think what my heart was foreboding; and if you weep not, at what do you ever weep?

"They were awake now, and the hour approached when our food was usually brought to us, and each was apprehensive because of his dream. And below I heard them nailing up the door of the horrible tower; whereat I looked in the faces of my children without a word. [37–48]

"I did not weep, so was I turned to stone within me. They wept, and my poor little Anselm said, 'You look so, father, what ails you?' I shed no tear for that, nor did answer all that day, nor the night after, until the next sun came forth on the world. As soon as a little ray made its way into the woeful prison, and I discerned by their four faces the aspect of my own, I bit both my hands for grief. And they, thinking I did it for hunger, suddenly rose up and said, 'Father, it will be far less painful to us if you eat of us; you did clothe us with this wretched flesh, and do you strip us of it!' [59–63]

"Then I calmed myself in order not to make them sadder. That day and the

next we stayed all silent: Ah, hard earth! why did you not open? When we had
come to the fourth day Gaddo threw himself outstretched at my feet, saying,
'Father, why do you not help me?' There he died; and even as you see me, I
saw the three fall, one by one, between the fifth day and the sixth; whence I
betook me, already blind, to groping over each, and for two days I called them
after they were dead. Then fasting did more than grief had done." [64–75]]

12. Nero

The major source for the story of Nero is the section on Fortune in Jean de
Meun's portion of the *Roman de la Rose*, given here. The second stanza of
Chaucer's tragedy (lines 2471–8), however, seems to be dependent on other
sources. Root suggests Boccaccio, *De casibus* 7.3; Suetonius, *Vitae caesarum*,
Nero 30.3; or Boethius, *De consolatione philosophiae* 3.m4.1–4, as possibilities. Aiken proposes Vincent of Beauvais, *Speculum historiale* 8.7.[38] Waller
shows that the detail of the golden nets in that stanza is found in many historical
accounts known in the Middle Ages.[39] Vincent DiMarco suggests that the particular arrangement of the details of Nero's fishing with golden nets and the
arrangement of his new clothing may be based on the *Alphabetum narrationum*,
a popular work written in the early fourteenth century.[40]

Roman de la Rose, lines 6184–488

(Text from *Le Roman de la Rose*, ed. Ernest Langlois, vols. 2–3 [Paris: Champion,
1920–1]; trans. from *The Romance of the Rose*, trans. Charles Dahlberg, 3rd ed.
[Princeton, NJ: Princeton University Press, 1995], pp. 122–6)

Reason speaks to the lover on the nature of Fortune, relating the story of
Nero.

6184   E ce peut l'en tantost prouver
         E par Seneque e par Neron,
         Don la parole tost lairon,
         Pour la longueur de la matire,
6188   Car je metraie trop a dire
         Les faiz Neron, le cruel ome,
         Coment il mist les feus a Rome,
         E fist les senateurs ocierre;

---

[38] See Bryan and Dempster, p. 640; Pauline Aiken, "Vincent of Beauvais and Chaucer's Monk,"
Speculum 17 (1942): 60–2.

[39] Martha S. Waller, "The Monk's Tale: Nero's Nets and Caesar's Father – an Inquiry into the Transformation of Classical Roman History in Medieval Tradition," *Indiana Social Studies Quarterly* 31
(1978): 46–55.

[40] Vincent DiMarco, "Nero's Nets and Seneca's Veins: A New Source for the *Monk's Tale*?," *Chaucer
Review* 28 (1994): 384–92.

6192 Si rot bien cueur plus dur que pierre
     Quant il fist ocierre son frere,
     Quant il fist desmembrer sa mere,
     Pour ce que par lui fust veüz
6196 Li leus ou il fu conceüz;
     E puis qu'il la vit desmembree,
     Selonc l'estoire remembree,
     La beauté des membres juija.
6200 He! Deus! Con ci felon juige a!
     N'onc de l'ueil lerme n'en issi,
     Car l'estoire le dit issi;
     Mais, si come il juijait des membres,
6204 Comanda il que de ses chambres
     Li feïst l'en vin aporter,
     E but pour son cors deporter.
     Mais il l'ot anceis queneüe;
6208 Sa sereur ravait il eüe;
     E bailla sei meïsme a ome
     Cil desleiaus que je ci nome.
     Seneque mist il a martire,
6212 Son bon maistre, e li fist eslire
     De quel mort mourir il vourrait;
     Cil vit qu'eschaper ne pourrait,
     Tant iere poissanz li maufez:
6216 "Donc seit," dist il, "uns bainz chaufez,
     Puis que d'eschaper est neienz,
     E me faites saignier laienz
     Tant que je muire en l'eve chaude,
6220 E que m'ame joieuse e baude
     A Deu qui la fourma se rende,
     Qui d'autres tormenz la defende."
     Emprès ce mot, senz arester,
6224 Fist Nerons le baing aprester,
     E fist enz le preudome metre,
     E puis saignier, ce dit la letre,
     Tant qu'il li couvint l'ame rendre,
6228 Tant li fist cil dou sanc espandre;
     Ne nule achaison ni savait
     Fors tant que de coustume avait
     Nerons que toujourz des s'enfance
6232 Li soulait porter reverence,
     Si con deciples a son maistre:
     "Mais ce ne deit," dist il, "pas estre,
     Ne n'est pas bel en nule place
6236 Que reverence a ome face
     Nus on, puis qu'il est empereres,
     Tant seit ses maistres ne ses peres."
     E pour ce que trop li grevait
6240 Quant encontre lui se levait,

Quant son maistre voait venir,
N'il ne se poait pas tenir
Qu'il ne li portast reverence
6244 Par la force d'acoustumance,
Fist il destruire le preudome.
Si tint il l'empire de Rome,
Cil desleiaus que je ci di,
6248 E d'orient e de midi,
D'occident, de septentrion
Tint il la juridicion.
E se tu me sez bien entendre,
6252 Par ces paroles peuz aprendre
Que richeces e reverences,
Dignetez, eneurs e poissances,
Ne nules graces de Fortune,
6256 Car je n'en excete nes une,
De si grant force pas ne sont
Qu'eus facent bons ceus qui les ont,
Ne dignes d'aveir les richeces,
6260 Ne les eneurs ne les hauteces.
Mais s'il ont en aus engrestiez,
Orgueil, ou queusque mauvaistiez,
Li grant estat ou il s'encroent
6264 Plus tost les montrent e descloent
Que se petiz estaz eüssent,
Par quei si nuire ne peüssent;
Car, quant de leur poissances usent,
6268 Li fait les volentez encusent,
Qui demontrance font e signe
Qu'il ne sont pas ne bon ne digne
Des richeces, des dignetez,
6272 Des eneurs e des poetez.
E si dit l'en une parole
Comunement, qui mout est fole,
Si la tienent tuit pour veraie,
6276 Par leur fol sen qui les desveie,
Que les eneurs les meurs remuent;
Mais cist mauvaisement argüent,
Car eneurs n'i font pas muance,
6280 Mais eus font signe e demontrance
Queus meurs en aus avant avaient,
Quant es petiz estaz estaient,
Cil qui les chemins ont tenu
6284 Par quei sont aus eneurs venu;
Car, s'il sont fel e orguilleus,
Despiteus e mal semilleus
Puis qu'il vont eneurs recevant,
6288 Saches tel ierent il devant
Con tu les peuz après voeir,

S'il en eüssent lors poeir.
Si n'apele je pas poissance
6292 Poeir mal ne desordenance,
Car l'escriture dit e bien
Que toute poissance est de bien,
Ne nus a bien faire ne faut
6296 Fors par feiblece e par defaut;
E, qui serait bien cler veianz,
Il verrait que maus est neienz,
Car ainsinc le dit l'escriture.
6300 E se d'auctorité n'as cure,
Car tu ne veauz, espeir, pas creire
Que toute auctoritez seit veire,
Preste sui que raison i truisse,
6304 Car il n'est riens que Deus ne puisse.
Mais, qui le veir en veaut retraire,
Deus n'a poissance de mal faire;
E se tu iés bien conoissanz,
6308 E veiz que Deus est touz poissanz
Qui de mal faire n'a poeir,
Donc peuz tu clerement voeir
Que, qui l'estre des choses nombre,
6312 Maus ne met nule chose en nombre;
Mais si con li ombres ne pose
En l'air ocurci nule chose
Fors defaillance de lumiere,
6316 Trestout en autele maniere,
En creature ou biens defaut
Maus n'i met riens fors pur defaut
De bonté, riens plus n'i peut metre.
6320 E dit encore plus la letre,
Qui des mauvais comprent la some:
Que li mauvais ne sont pas ome,
E vives raisons i ameine;
6324 Mais ne vueil or pas metre peine
A tout quanque je di prouver,
Quant en escrit le peuz trouver.
E nepourquant, s'il ne te grieve,
6328 Bien te puis par parole brieve
De raisons amener aucune:
C'est qu'il laissent la fin comune
A quei tendent e tendre deivent
6332 Les choses qui estre receivent:
C'est de touz biens le souverain
Que nous apelons prumerain.
Autre raison i ra, beau maistre,
6336 Pour quei li mauvais n'ont pas estre,
Qui bien entent la consequence:
Qu'il ne sont pas en ordenance

En quei tout leur estre mis ont
6340 Trestoutes les choses qui sont;
Don il s'ensuit a cler veiant
Que li mauvais sont pour neient.
    Or veiz coment Fortune sert
6344 Ça jus en cet mondain desert,
E coment el fait a despire,
Qui des mauvais eslut le pire
E seur touz omes le fist estre
6348 De cet monde seigneur e maistre,
E fist Seneque ainsinc destruire.
Fait bien donques sa grace a fuire,
Quant nus, tant seit de bon eür,
6352 Ne la peut tenir asseür.
Pour ce vueil que tu la despises,
E que ses graces riens ne prises.
Claudiens neïs s'en soulait
6356 Merveillier, e blasmer voulait
Les deus de ce qu'il consentaient
Que li mauvais ainsinc montaient
Es granz eneurs, es granz hauteces,
6360 Es granz poeirs, es granz richeces;
Mais il meïsmes i respont,
E la cause nous en espont,
Con cil qui bien de raison use;
6364 E les deus assout e escuse,
E dit que pour ce le consentent
Que plus emprès les en tormentent,
Pour estre plus forment grevé;
6368 Car pour ce sont en haut levé
Que l'en les puisse après voeir
De plus haut trebuichier choeir.
E se tu me faiz cet servise
6372 Que je ci t'enjoing e devise,
Jamais nul jour ne trouveras
Plus riche ome que tu seras;
Ne jamais ne seras irez,
6376 Tant seit tes estaz empirez
De cors ne d'amis ne d'aveir,
Ainz voudras pacience aveir;
E tantost aveir la pourras
6380 Com mes amis estre vourras.
Pour quei donc en tristeur demeures?
Je vei maintes feiz que tu pleures
Come alambic seur alutel:
6384 L'en te devrait en un putel
Tooillier come un viez panufle.
Certes je tendraie a grant trufle,
Qui dirait que tu fusses on

6388 Qu'onques on en nule saison,
Pour qu'il usast d'entendement,
Ne mena deul ne marement.
Li vif deable, li maufé
6392 T'ont ton athanor eschaufé,
Qui si fait tes eaus lermeier,
Qui de nule rien esmaier
Qui t'avenist ne te deüsses,
6396 Se point d'entendement eüsses.
Ce fait li deus qui ci t'a mis,
Tes bons maistres, tes bons amis,
C'est Amours, qui soufle e atise
6400 La brese qu'il t'a ou cueur mise,
Qui fait aus eauz les lermes rendre.
Chier te veaut s'acointance vendre,
Car ce n'aferist pas a ome
6404 Que sens e proece renome.
Certes malement t'en diffames.
Laisse plourer enfanz e fames,
Bestes feibles e variables;
6408 E tu seies forz e estables,
Quant Fortune verras venir.
Veauz tu sa roe retenir,
Qui ne peut estre retenue
6412 Ne par grant gent ne par menue?
Cil granz empereres meïsmes,
Nerons, dont l'essemple meïsmes,
Qui fu de tout le monde sires,
6416 Tant s'estendait loing ses empires,
Ne la pot onques arester,
Tant peüst eneurs conquester;
Car il, se l'estoire ne ment,
6420 Reçut puis mort mauvaisement,
De tout son peuple anceis haïz,
Don il cremait estre envaïz;
Si manda ses privez amis,
6424 Mais onc li message tramis
Ne trouverent, que qu'il deïssent,
Nus d'aus qui leur uis leur ouvrissent.
Adonc i vint priveement
6428 Nerons mout poereusement,
E hurta de ses propres mains,
N'onc ne l'en firent plus, mais meins,
Car, quant plus chascuns apela,
6432 Chascuns plus s'enclost e cela,
Ne nus ne li vost mot respondre.
Lors le couvint aler repondre,
Si se mist, pour sei herbergier,
6436 O deus siens sers, en un vergier,

Car ja pluseur par tout couraient
Qui pour ocierre le queraient,
E criaient: "Neron! Neron!
6440 Qui le vit? Ou le trouveron?"
Si qu'il neïs bien les oait,
Mais conseil metre n'i poait.
Si s'est si forment esbaïz
6444 Qu'il meïsmes s'est enhaïz;
E quant il se vit en ce point
Qu'il n'ot mais d'esperance point,
Aus sers pria qu'il le tuassent,
6448 Ou qu'a sei tuer li aidassent.
Si s'ocist, mais ainz fist requeste
Que ja nus ne trouvast sa teste,
Pour ce qu'il ne fust queneüz
6452 Se ses cors fust emprès veüz;
E pria que le cors ardissent
Si tost come ardeir le poïssent.
E dit li livres anciens,
6456 Diz *des Doze Cesariens*,
Ou sa mort trouvons en escrit,
Si con Sutonius l'escrit,
Qui la lei crestiene apele
6460 Fausse religion nouvele
E maufaisant, ainsinc la nome,
Veiz ci mot de desleial ome,
Que en Neron fu defenie
6464 Des Cesariens la lignie.
Cist par ses faiz tant pourchaça
Que tout son lignage effaça,
Nepourquant tant fu coustumiers
6468 De bien faire es cinc anz prumiers
Qu'onc si bien ne gouverna terre
Nus princes que l'en seüst querre,
Tant sembla vaillanz e piteus,
6472 Li desleiaus, li despiteus;
E dist en audience a Rome,
Quant il, pour condanner un ome,
Fu requis de la mort escrire,
6476 Ne n'ot pas honte de ce dire,
Qu'il vousist meauz non saveir letre
Que sa main pour escrire i metre,
Si tint, ce veaut li livres dire,
6480 Entour dis e set anz l'empire,
E trente e deus dura sa vie;
Mais ses orgueauz, sa felonie
Si forment l'orent envaï
6484 Que de si haut si bas chaï,
Con tu m'as oï raconter,

Tant l'ot fait Fortune monter,
Qui tant le fist emprès descendre,
6488 Con tu peuz oïr e entendre.

[*Nero*

[6184] One can prove the nature of Fortune immediately by both Seneca and Nero, of whom we will speak quickly because of the length of our matter. I would use up too much time in telling the deeds of Nero, that cruel man, and about how he set fire to Rome and had the senators killed. Indeed, he had a heart harder than stone when he had his brother killed, when he had his mother dismembered so that he might see the place where he was conceived. After he saw her dismembered, according to the story that men remember, he judged the beauty of her limbs. Ah, God! What a criminal judge she had! According to the story no tear issued from his eyes, but, as he was judging the limbs he commanded that wine be brought from his rooms, and he drank for his body's pleasure. But he had known her before, and he had also possessed his sister. And he gave himself to other men, this disloyal one that I speak of.

[6211] He made a martyr of Seneca, his good master, and he made him choose the death by which he wanted to die. Seneca saw that the devil was so powerful that he could not escape. "Then," he said, "since it is impossible to escape, let a bath be heated and have me bled therein so that I may die in warm water and that my joyous, happy soul may return to God, who formed it and who forbids it any further torments."

[6223] After these words, without delay, Nero had the bath brought and the good man put into it. Then, the text says, he had him bled until he was forced to give up his soul, so much blood was he made to pour out. Nero knew no other cause for this deed than that, by custom, he had from his infancy practiced showing respect to him, as a disciple does to his master.

[6234] "But this should not be," said Nero. "It is not fitting that any man, after he is emperor, should show reverence to another man, whether he be his master or his father."

[6239] Therefore it troubled him greatly when he saw his master coming and he arose in his presence, but he could not refrain from showing reverence from the force of habit, and he therefore had the worthy man destroyed. And it was this unlawful creature of whom I speak who held the empire of Rome; the east, the south, the west and north he held in his jurisdiction.

[6251] And if you know how to listen well to me, I can teach you, in our talks, that riches and reverences, dignities, honors, and powers, and all other gifts of Fortune – for I do not except even one – are not powerful enough to make good men of those who possess them or to make them worthy of having wealth, honors, or high station. But if they have inner qualities of harshness, pride, or some other evil, they show and reveal these qualities sooner in the grand estate to which they raise themselves than if they had occupied low stations, in which they could do no such harm; for, when they use their powers, their deeds reveal their wills and give a demonstration, an outward sign, that they are neither good nor worthy of riches, dignities, honors, or powers.

[6273] In this connection, men have a common saying that is very foolish, if their silly reasoning gets them off the track and they take it as entirely true. Honors, they say, change manners. But they reason badly, for honors work no change, but give a demonstration, an outward sign that those who have taken the roads by which they came to these honors had just such manners in themselves before, when they were in low estate. If they are cruel and proud, spiteful and malicious after they have come to receive honors, you may know that, if they had then had the power, they would formerly have been such as you can see them afterward.

[6291] However, I do not give the name of power to evil or unregulated power, for our text says, and says well, that all power comes from the good and that no man fails to do good except through weakness and omission; and he who understood clearly would see that evil is nothing, for so the text says. If you do not care for authority, for perhaps you do not believe that all authorities are true, I am ready to find reasons, for there is nothing that God cannot do. But if you want to extract the truth from this observation, it is that God cannot do evil; and if you understand well, and see that God, who has not the power to do evil, is all-powerful, then you can see clearly that no matter who numbers the being of things, evil contributes nothing to their number. Just as the shadow places nothing in the air that is darkened except a lack of light, so in an exactly similar way, in a creature in whom good is lacking, evil puts nothing except a simple lack of goodness and can put there nothing more. [6320] The text, which embraces the whole range of evil things, goes on to say that the wicked are not men, and it brings lively reasons to this conclusion; but I do not want to take the trouble now to prove all that I say when you can find it in writing. Nevertheless, if it does not disturb you, I can very well bring out some of the reasons in a short talk. The wicked are not men because they abandon the common goal toward which things that receive being aspire and must aspire. That goal, which we call the first, is the sovereign of all good things. I have another reason, fair master, why the evil have no existence, if you will listen carefully to the conclusion: since they are not in the order in which all things existing have placed their being, then it follows, for him who sees clearly, that the evil are nothing.

[6343] You see now how Fortune serves, here below in the desert of this world, how spitefully she works; she chose the worst among evil men and made him lord and master over all men of this world and thus brought about Seneca's destruction. One does well then to flee her favor when no one, however happy, can consider it secure. Therefore I want you to despise her and to give no value to her favors. Even Claudian used to be amazed at them and used to wish to blame the gods for allowing the wicked to rise to great honors, high stations, powers, and riches. But he himself gives the answer and explains the cause to us like a man who uses his reason well. He absolves and excuses the gods and says that they agree to this situation so that afterward they may torment the wicked to the same extent that they have grieved the gods. For they are raised on high in order that afterward men may see them fall from a greater height.

[6371] And if you do me the service that I here enjoin and describe to you, you will never, at any time, find a man richer than you, nor will you ever be angered, no matter how much the condition of your body, your friends, or

your possessions may decline, but instead you will want to have patience. And you will want to have it as soon as you wish to be my friend. Why then do you dwell in sorrow? Many times I see you crying as an alembic does into an aludel. You should be stirred into a mud-puddle like an old rag. Certainly I would consider anyone a big joke who said that you were a man, for no man at any time, provided that he used his understanding, ever encouraged sorrow or sadness. The living devils, the evil ones, have heated your furnace, which makes your eyes thus flow with tears; but if you had used your understanding you should never have been downcast by anything that happened to you. This is the work of the god who put you here, your good master, your good friend; it is Love who fans and inflames the coals that he has put in your heart, who makes the tears come back to your eyes. He wants to sell his company at a high price, for it might not be suitable for a man to make his intelligence and prowess widely known. Certainly you are badly defamed. Leave weeping to children and women, weak and inconstant animals; be strong and firm when you see Fortune coming. Do you want to hold back her wheel that cannot be held back by the great or the small?

[6414] Nero, the great emperor himself, whose example we have brought up and whose empire stretched so far that he was lord of the world, could not stop her wheel, however many honors he might conquer. For, if history does not lie, he afterward received an evil death, hated by all his people and fearing that they would attack him. He sent for his close friends, but the messengers sent to them never found any of them, whatever they might say, who would open their doors to them. Then Nero came secretly, in great fear, and pounded with his own hands; they did no more, but less, for the more he called to each of them, the more each one shut himself up and hid, and no one wanted to reply a word to him. Then he had to go and hide, and for protection he installed himself, with two of his servants, in a garden, for already several people who sought him out to kill him were running about everywhere, crying "Nero! Nero! Who has seen him? Where can we find him?" Even though Nero heard them clearly, he could give no advice. He was quite dumbfounded that he himself was hated; and when he saw himself in such a situation, with no hope whatever, he begged his servants to kill him or to help him kill himself. He then killed himself, but first he requested that no one should ever find his head so that if afterward his body were seen it would not be recognized. And he begged that they burn his body as soon as they could.

[6455] The old book called *The Twelve Caesars*, where we find the account of his death, as Suetonius wrote it – Suetonius, who calls the Christian law a false and wicked religion (he so names it; look up the words of the unlawful man) – the old book says that the line of the Caesars finished with Nero. By his deeds he secured the obliteration of his whole lineage. Nevertheless, he was so accustomed to doing good in the first five years that no prince that one could have sought ever governed the land so well, so valiant and merciful did this lawless and merciless man seem. In audience at Rome, when, to condemn a man, he was required to write out the death order, he said without shame at his words that he would rather not know how to write than put his hand to write such an order. According to the book, he held the empire about seventeen years, and his life lasted for thirty-two. But pride and his criminality had attacked him so powerfully that he fell from high to

low degree, as you have heard me tell. It was Fortune who caused him to mount up so high and afterward to descend, as you may hear and understand.]

13. Holofernes

The story of Holofernes is taken from the Vulgate Book of Judith. See Judith 2:1–18; 3:13; 4:5–7; 5:29; 12:20; 23:1–12.

14. Antiochus

The tragedy of Antiochus IV, King of Syria (175–163 B.C.) is based on the biblical account in 2 Maccabees 9.

15. Alexander the Great

The details of the tragedy of Alexander the Great were commonplace in the Middle Ages, and no specific source for Chaucer's account has been identified.

16. Julius Caesar

Chaucer correctly names Lucan, Suetonius, and Valerius Maximus as sources for the tragedy of Julius Caesar (lines 2719–20), but there is no conclusive evidence that he used any of them directly.[41] The details of Caesar's life and death were well known in the Middle Ages, available in numerous sources. Aiken finds some parallels with the account in Vincent of Beauvais, *Speculum historiale* 6.35–42.[42]

17. Croesus

The tragedy of Croesus is based on Reason's explanation of Fortune in Jean de Meun's part of the *Roman de la Rose*, given here. Aiken notes similarities to the account in Vincent of Beauvais's *Speculum historiale*.[43] The first stanza of the Monk's tragedy (lines 2727–34) may follow Boethius, *De consolatione philosophiae* 2.pr2.34–6.[44]

---

[41] See F. P. Lock, "Chaucer's Monk's Use of Lucan, Suetonius, and 'Valerie,' " *English Language Notes* 12 (1975): 251–5, a comparative study which does not demonstrate Chaucer's direct knowledge of these authorities.

[42] Aiken, "Vincent of Beauvais," p. 67; see also Root's detailed discussion in Bryan and Dempster, pp. 642–4.

[43] Aiken, "Vincent of Beauvais," pp. 67–8.

[44] See Bryan and Dempster, p. 644; *The Riverside Chaucer*, p. 935.

Roman de la Rose, lines 6489–630

(Text from *Le Roman de la Rose*, ed. Ernest Langlois, vol. 3 [Paris: Champion, 1921], pp. 7–12; trans. from *The Romance of the Rose*, trans. Charles Dahlberg, 3rd ed. [Princeton, NJ: Princeton University Press, 1995], pp. 126–8)

Reason speaks to the lover on the nature of Fortune, relating the story of Croesus.

N'onc ne la pot tenir Cresus
Qu'el nou tournast e jus e sus,
Qui refu reis de toute Lide,
6492 Puis li mist l'en au col la bride,
E fu pour ardre au feu livrez,
Quant par pluie fu delivrez,
Qui le grant feu fist tout esteindre,
6496 N'onques nus n'osa la remaindre;
Tuit s'en foïrent pour la pluie:
Cresus se mist tantost en fuie,
Quant il se vit seul en la place,
6500 Senz encombrement e senz chace
Puis refu sires de sa terre,
E puis resmut nouvele guerre,
Puis refu pris, e puis penduz,
6504 Quant li songes li fu renduz
Des deus deus qui li aparaient,
Qui seur l'arbre en haut le servaient:
Jupiter, ce dist, le lavait,
6508 E Phebus la toaille avait,
E se penait de l'essuier.
Mar se vost ou songe apuier,
Don si grant fiance acuilli
6512 Qu'il come fos s'enorguilli.
Bien li dist Phanie, sa fille,
Qui tant estait sage e soutille
Qu'el savait les songes espondre,
6516 E senz flater li vost respondre:
"Beaus pere," dist la dameisele,
"Ci a doulereuse nouvele.
Vostre orgueauz ne vaut une coque;
6520 Sachiez que Fortune vous moque.
Par cet songe poez entendre
Qu'el vous veaut faire au gibet pendre;
E quant sereiz penduz au vent,
6524 Senz couverture e senz auvent,
Seur vous plouvra, beaus sires reis,
E li beaus solauz de ses rais

Vous essuiera cors e face.
6528 Fortune a cete fin vous chace,
Qui tost e done les eneurs,
E fait souvent des granz meneurs,
E des meneurs refait graigneurs,
6532 E seignourir seur les seigneurs.
Que vous iraie je flatant?
Fortune au gibet vous atent,
E quant au gibet vous tendra,
6536 La hart ou col, el reprendra
La bele courone doree
Don vostre teste a couronee;
S'en iert uns autres couronez,
6540 De cui garde ne vous donez.
     E pour ce que je vous espoigne
Plus apertement la besoigne,
Jupiter, qui l'eve vous done,
6544 Cist est li airs qui pleut e tone,
E Phebus, qui tient la toaille,
C'est li solauz, senz nule faille;
L'arbre par le gibet vous glose,
6548 Je n'i puis entendre autre chose.
Passer vous couvient cete planche,
Fortune ainsinc le peuple venche
Dou bobant que vous demenez,
6552 Come orguilleus e forsenez.
Si destruit ele maint preudome,
Qu'el ne prise pas une pome
Tricherie ne leiauté,
6556 Ne vil estat, ne reiauté;
Anceis s'en jeue a la pelote,
Come pucele nice e sote,
E giete a grant desordenance
6560 Richece, eneur e reverence;
Dignetez e poissances done,
Ne ne prent garde a quel persone;
Car ses graces, quant les despent,
6564 En despendant si les espant
Qu'el les giete en leu de pouties
Par puteaus e par praeries;
Qu'el ne prise tout une bille
6568 Fors que Gentillece, sa fille,
Cousine e prouchaine Cheance,
Tant ia tient Fortune en balance.
Mais de cele est il veirs, senz faille,
6572 Que Fortune a nul ne la baille,
Coment qu'il aut dou retolir,
S'il ne set si son cueur polir
Qu'il seit courteis, preuz e vaillanz.

6576 Car nus n'est si bien bataillanz,
Se de vilenie s'apresse,
Que Gentillece ne le laisse.
Gentillece est noble e si l'ain,
6580 Qu'el n'entre pas en cueur vilain,
Pour ce vous pri, mon trés chier pere,
Que vilenie en vous n'apere;
Ne seiez orguilleus ne chiches,
6584 Aiez, pour enseignier les riches,
Large cueur e courteis e gent,
E piteus a la povre gent;
Ainsinc le deit chascuns reis faire.
6588 Large, courteis e debonaire
Ait le cueur, e plein de pitié,
S'il quiert dou peuple l'amitié,
Senz cui reis en nule saison
6592 Ne peut ne que uns simples on."
Ainsinc le chastiait Phanie.
Mais fos ne veit en sa folie
Fors que sen e raison ensemble,
6596 Si come en son fol cueur li semble
Cresus, qui point ne s'umelie,
Touz pleins d'orgueil e de folie,
En touz ses faiz cuide estre sages,
6600 Combien qu'il feïst granz outrages.
"Fille," fait il, "de courteisie
Ne de sen ne m'aprenez mie;
Plus en sai que vous ne savez,
6604 Qui si chastié m'en avez.
E quant par vostre fol respons
M'avez mon songe ainsinc espons,
Servi m'avez de granz mençonges;
6608 Car sachiez que cist nobles songes,
Ou fausse glose voulez metre,
Deit estre entenduz a la letre;
E je meïsmes l'i entens,
6612 Si con nous le verrons en tens.
Onc ausinc noble vision
N'ot si vil esposicion.
Li deu, sachiez, a mei vendront,
6616 E le servise me rendront
Qu'il m'ont par cet songe tramis,
Tant est chascuns d'aus mes amis,
Car bien l'ai pieç'a deservi."
6620 Veiz con Fortune le servi;
Qu'il ne se pot onques defendre
Qu'el nou feïst au gibet pendre.
N'est ce donc bien chose prouvable
6624 Que sa roe n'est pas tenable,

Quant nus ne la peut retenir,
Tant sache a grant estat venir?
E se tu sez riens de logique,
6628   Qui bien est science autentique,
Puis que li grant seigneur i faillent
Li petit en vain s'i travaillent.

[*Croesus*

[6489] Croesus could in no way hold back her wheel from turning both below and above. He was a king, of all Lydia. Afterward men put a bridle on his neck, and he was given over to the fire to be burned but was freed by a rain that extinguished the great fire. No man whatever dared remain there; all fled on account of the rain, and when Croesus saw that he was alone in that place, he immediately took flight without hindrance or pursuit. Afterward he again became lord of his land, stirred up a new war, was captured again, and then was hanged. Thus was fulfilled the dream about the two gods who belonged to him and who served him at the top of a tree. Jupiter, it was said, washed him, and Phoebus had the towel and took pains to wipe him. It was an evil hour when he wanted to depend on the dream; his trust in it grew so great that he became foolishly proud. His daughter Phania, who was very wise and subtle, told him indeed that she knew how to explain the dreams, and she wanted to reply to him without flattery:

[6517] "Fair father," said the girl, "there is sad news here. Your pride is not worth a shell. Understand that Fortune mocks you. By this dream you may understand that she wants you hanged on the gibbet. And when you are hanging in the wind, without cover or roof, then, fair lord king, it will rain on you and the fair sun will wipe your body and face with his rays. Fortune pursues you to this end. She steals honors and gives them; she often makes great men lowly and again elevates the lowly to greatness and exercises her lordship over lords. Why should I go about to flatter you? Fortune awaits you at the gibbet, and when you make your way there with the halter on your neck, she will take back the beautiful golden crown with which she has crowned your head. Then with it will be crowned another to whom you give no thought or care.

[6541] "To explain the matter more openly to you: Jupiter, who gives you water, is the atmosphere that rains and thunders, and Phoebus, who holds the towel, is, without fail, the sun. I gloss the tree to you as the gibbet; I can understand nothing else by it. You will have to walk that plank. Thus Fortune avenges the people for the haughty way in which, like one beside himself with pride, you have conducted yourself. Thus she destroys many a valiant man, since she considers neither treachery nor loyalty, low estate nor royalty worth an apple. Instead, she plays pelote with them, like a silly, stupid girl, and in a completely disordered way throws out wealth, honor, and reverence; she gives dignities and powers without regard for which person receives them, for when she spends her graces she so spreads them about that she throws them over dirty pools and prairies as though they were dust. She counts nothing worth a ball except her daughter Nobility, cousin and

neighbor to Fall, and Fortune keeps her very much in suspense. But it is true without fail that Fortune gives Nobility to no one, however he may go about to capture her, if he does not know how to polish his heart so that he may be courteous, valiant, and brave. For no man is so valiant in combat that Nobility does not desert him if he is beset by base cowardice.

[6579] "I love Nobility because she is noble, for she never enters a base heart. Therefore I beg you, my dear father, that you show no such base feelings. Be neither proud nor miserly; in order to teach the wealthy, have a heart that is generous, courteous, noble, and compassionate toward the poor. Every king should act thus. If he seeks the people's friendship, let him keep a heart that is generous, courteous, sweet-tempered, and full of compassion, for without the love of his subjects, no king, at any time, can be anything more than a common man."

[6593] Thus Phania scolded him. But a fool sees nothing in his folly, as it seems to him in his foolish heart, except sense and reason together. Croesus did not humble himself in any way; full of pride and folly, he thought all his deeds wise, no matter what great outrages he might commit.

[6601] "Daughter," he said, "don't teach me about courtesy or good sense. I know more about them than do you, who have thus scolded me about them. In your foolish response, when you explain my dream to me in this way, you have served me with great lies; for know that this noble dream, to which you want to put a false gloss, should be understood according to the letter. I myself understand it in this way, just as we shall see it in time. No such noble dream ever had so base an explanation. You may know that each of the gods is so much my friend that together they will come to me and do me the service that they have indicated through this dream, for I have well deserved it for a long time."

[6620] Now see how Fortune served him. He could in no way prevent her having him hanged on the gibbet. Is it not then a matter open to proof that her wheel cannot be delayed, since no man, no matter how exalted a station he may know how to reach, can hold it back. And if you know any logic, an authentic science indeed, you will know that after the great lords fail to stop it, the little ones will exert themselves in vain to the same end.]

The Nun's Priest's Tale

EDWARD WHEATLEY

Central to the Chaucer canon, the *Nun's Priest's Tale* in its broadest outlines represents a genre as familiar to modern audiences as to Chaucer's, the beast fable. However, the simple skeleton of a fable plot is here fleshed out with material from a largely medieval genre, the beast epic, and this hybrid creation is adorned with exempla and rhetorical flourishes drawn from biblical and scholastic commentary, notably in Chauntecleer's and Pertelote's debate on the significance of dreams. In the later Middle Ages beast fables not only comprised an important part of the Latin grammar-school curriculum but also had a lively history in sermons, visual arts, and popular literature.[1] The best known beast epic, the Old French *Roman de Renart*, was compiled by Pierre de St. Cloud in the late twelfth and early thirteenth centuries.[2] It exists in fourteen full-length manuscripts, and numerous others reproducing only one of the compilation's two branches;[3] the poem also spawned many imitations.

---

[1] For the history and uses of fable in the Middle Ages, see Jan M. Ziolkowski, *Talking Animals: Medieval Latin Beast Poetry, 750–1150* (Philadelphia: University of Pennsylvania Press, 1993), pp. 15–32; R. T. Lenaghan, *Caxton's Aesop* (Cambridge, Mass.: Harvard University Press, 1967), pp. 9–18; and Edward Wheatley, *Mastering Aesop: Medieval Education, Chaucer, and His Followers* (Gainesville: University Press of Florida, 2000).

[2] Ernest Martin, ed., *Le Roman de Renart* (Strasbourg, 1882).

[3] See Anthony Lodge and Kenneth Varty, *The Earliest Branches of the 'Roman de Renart'* (New Alyth, Perthshire, 1989), pp. 13–15.

The major questions about the sources and analogues of this tale, many of which were raised but not authoritatively answered by Kate Oelzner Petersen in her 1898 monograph *On the Sources of the Nonne Prestes Tale*,[4] have in the past thirty years found some resolution, primarily in the work of Robert A. Pratt. Petersen discussed and reproduced a number of texts showing a variety of degrees of similarity to Chaucer's tale, but she sketched the tale's fabulistic pedigree only within a very broad folkloric context (pp. 1–9), and then asserted that in spite of the tale's debt to the French *Renart* literature, its closest surviving relative is *Reinhart Fuchs*, a German beast epic extant in only three manuscripts.[5] Having examined possible sources for Chauntecleer's longest exempla on the reliability of dreams, Petersen concluded that while both were available in the works of Cicero and Valerius Maximus, Chaucer probably borrowed them from two sections of a book which he (like his contemporaries Thomas Hoccleve and John Lydgate) certainly knew, Dominican Robert Holkot's *Super Libros Sapientiae*, a commentary on the biblical Books of Wisdom (pp. 98–111).

As early as 1913 the influence of *Reinhart Fuchs* upon Chaucer's tale was challenged by Lucien Foulet,[6] and in the following year Lilian Winstanley began to shift attention from the German beast epic to *Renart le Contrefait*, a 40,000-line opus by a certain "clerc de Troyes" who wrote and then substantially revised the work between 1319 and 1342.[7] Winstanley, however, avoided the thorny issue of how Chaucer might have known a poem which survives in only two manuscripts, one of each of the poet's redactions. In 1917, I. C. Lecompte demonstrated that the German *Reinhart* and Chaucer's tale are both redactions of Pierre de Saint Cloud's version of the *Renart* cycle.[8] In Bryan and Dempster, James R. Hulbert judged that the status of *Reinhart Fuchs* as a source remained uncertain, but nevertheless he reproduced a lengthy section of the German beast epic in his chapter on the *Nun's Priest's Tale*.[9] But because Petersen's hypothesis has had no serious defenders since 1941, the German text is not included here.

During the past fifty years, the lion's share of scholarship on the sources and analogues of this tale can be claimed by Robert A. Pratt. He defined Chaucer's debt not only to the *Roman de Renart* but also to *Renart le Contrefait*, listing the

---

[4] Boston, 1898.

[5] Petersen's hypothesis about Chaucer's main source, discussed on pp. 47–90, was drawn from Carl Voretzsch, "Der Reinhart Fuchs Heinrichs des Glîchezâre und der Roman de Renart," *Zeitschrift für Romanische Philologie* 15 (1891): 124–92, 344–74; 16 (1892): 1–39. For a description of the German work, see the introduction (pp. ix–xxi) to *Der Reinhart Fuchs des Elsässers Heinrich*, ed. Katharina von Goetz, Frank Hainrichvark, and Sigrid Krause, with Klaus Düwel (Tübingen, 1984).

[6] *Le Roman de Renard* (Bibliothèque de l'Ecole des Hautes Etudes, fasc. 211, 2nd ed.; Paris, 1968), pp. 393–432.

[7] *Chaucer: The Nonne Prestes Tale*, Pitt Press Series (Cambridge: Cambridge University Press, 1914), pp. lviii–lxiii. *Le Roman de Renart le Contrefait*, Gaston Raynaud and Henri Lemaître, eds. (1914; rpt. Geneva, 1975).

[8] "Chaucer's *Nonne Prestes Tale* and the *Roman de Renard*," *Modern Philology* 14 (1917): 737–49.

[9] Bryan and Dempster, pp. 658–62.

verbal parallels between the Old French and Middle English texts.[10] In addition, he examined Marie de France's "Del cok e del gupil," the twelfth-century fable upon which Chaucer drew most heavily. Pratt summarized his conclusions as follows:

> Although his plot was based directly on Marie's, Chaucer developed and enriched it with a number of verbal expressions, motifs, and bits of action suggested by the *Roman de Renart* and *Renart le Contrefait*. . . . Guided by these two poems, Chaucer prefaced the fable section with the cock's dream and the discussion of it. In *Renart le Contrefait* he found a dream worthy of Marie's style – simple, direct, and clear; for he recognized the qualities of the structure of her fable and allowed them to condition the neat, logical form of his basic narrative. The debate was inspired chiefly by the *clerc de Troyes* and Robert Holcot. But only the *Roman* offers the complete sequence of farmyard, dream, discussion, enticement to sing with eyes closed, capture, chase, escape, and *moralite*; . . . Pierre de Saint Cloud must be credited for the over-all design of Chaucer's narrative. (pp. 443–4)

In a later article on Latin sources, Pratt discussed the centrality of two *lectiones* from Robert Holcot's commentary on the Book of Wisdom, *Super Sapientiam Salomonis*, to Chauntecleer's two longest exempla about dreams (VII, 2984–3104).[11] Glancing back at an issue raised by his earlier articles, Pratt also explained that the evidently little-known *Renart le Contrefait* could have come to Chaucer's attention by way of his friend Eustache Deschamps, a French poet whose work shows his familiarity with the beast epic (p. 546, n. 27).

The provenance of Chauntecleer's briefer exempla of St. Kenelm (VII, 3110–21) and Andromache's prophecy to Hector (VII, 3141–50) remains unclear, largely because their brevity and consequent generality make them resemble a number of earlier texts. Pratt asserted that Chaucer altered the legend from the *Passio Sancti Kenelmi Martiris*, making the nurse's advice stronger.[12] Derek Pearsall has suggested that the story of St Kenelm in *The Early South English Legendary*,[13] though not entirely identical to Chaucer's story, is an equally likely source of it.[14] In either event, both of these possible sources are far longer than the ten lines to which Chaucer reduced the exemplum.

Pratt's view that the Andromache exemplum came from lines 31323–40 of *Le Roman de Renart le Contrefait* seems plausible, given the similar length of both exempla and a substantial number of verbal echoes in Chaucer's,[15] but Pearsall has pointed out that the story was also available to Chaucer in a trio of Troy

---

[10] "Three Old French Sources of the Nonnes Preestes Tale," *Speculum* 47 (1972): 422–44, 646–68.

[11] "Some Latin Sources of the Nonnes Preest on Dreams," *Speculum* 52 (1977): 538–70, 549–50, 556–7.

[12] Pratt directs his readers to Rurik von Antropoff, *Die Entwicklung der Kenelm-Legende* (Inaugural Diss., Bonn, 1965), pp. vii, xxxv–xxxvi.

[13] Carl Horstmann, ed. EETS OS 87, 1887, pp. 348–9.

[14] See *The Nun's Priest's Tale. A Variorum Edition of the Works of Geoffrey Chaucer*, vol. 2, pt. 9 (Norman: University of Oklahoma Press, 1984), p. 192.

[15] *Speculum* 47 (1972): 648; 52 (1977): 561.

books which he knew, those by Dares Phrygius, Benoit de Sainte Maure, and Guido della Colonna.[16]

Pratt (pp. 546–7) concurred with Pauline Aiken's assertion that Chaucer borrowed Pertelote's knowledge of laxatives and medical lore from Vincent of Beauvais's *Speculum doctrinale*, chapters 14.87 and 13.10016.

Aside from numerous references by both the Nun's Priest and his animal characters to textual authorities ranging from Boethius to Bishop Bradwardyne, the tale includes a number of fairly lengthy allusions that reinforce the mock-heroic nature of the conflict between the cock and fox. In VII 3355–61, the lamenting hens are compared to the women of the defeated Ilion mourning Pyrrhus's murder of Priam; although Chaucer states that the killer grabbed Priam by the beard instead of by the hair as Virgil asserts, it is nevertheless likely that he took the allusion from Book 2 of the *Aeneid*. In the next lines (VII, 3362–8), Pertelote's shrieks are compared to those of Hasdrubal's wife upon the death of her husband and the conflagration of Carthage at the hands of the invading Romans. While this story was available to Chaucer through Valerius Maximus, it is also found in Jerome's anti-feminist *Epistola adversus Jovinianum* 1.43, a text mentioned in the Wife of Bath's Prologue (III, 674 ff.) and summarized in Dorigen's complaint in the *Franklin's Tale* (V, 1355 ff.) Finally the Nun's Priest likens the hens' anguish to that of the Roman senators' wives who watched Nero burning the city, a reference readily available to Chaucer in Boethius's *De Consolatione Philosophiae* 1, m. 6.

In the *Variorum* edition of the tale (pp. 14–29), Pearsall has summarized its critical history to 1980, outlining the major issues in the debates on its sources and analogues in greater detail than space will permit here. Finally, as if tacitly acknowledging the force of Pratt's arguments about the sources of the tale, few scholars have contributed to the debate since his work was published, and those who have entered it have preferred to examine only peripheral influences.[17]

---

[16] Pearsall, *Variorum*, p. 197.

[17] See, for example, David G. Hale, "Another Latin Source for the Nun's Priest on Dreams," *Notes and Queries* 36 (1989): 10–11; and Donald N. Yates, "Chanticleer's Latin Ancestors," *Chaucer Review* 18 (1983): 116–26.

I

Marie de France: Fable 60: The Cock and the Fox

It is recounted that a cock stood on a dungheap and sang; a fox came to his side and addressed him with very beautiful words. (5) "Sir," he said, "I see that you are very beautiful; never have I seen so fine a bird. You have a voice clearer than anything: other than your father, whom I knew well, never has a bird sung better: but he did do it better, because he closed his eyes." (11) "So can I," said the cock. He flapped his wings, and he closed his eyes, thinking to sing more clearly. The fox sprang and took him; toward the forest with him he went. In a field through which he passed, all the shepherds ran after him, and (19) the dogs barked at him from all around. Thus the fox who holds the cock; he will fare badly if he comes near them! "Go on," said the cock, "Shout to them that I belong to you and you will never let me go." The fox wanted to speak loudly, but then the rooster leapt out of his mouth (25) and mounted a tall tree trunk. When the fox saw this, he thought himself thoroughly immature in that the cock had tricked him so. With irritation and outright anger, he began to curse his mouth which spoke when it should have been quiet. (32) The cock responded, "Thus I ought to do: to curse the eye that wanted to close when it should have guarded and watched lest evil come to its lord." (36) This is what fools do: they all speak when they ought to be quiet, and are quiet when they ought to speak.

I

Marie de France: Fable 60: Le Coq et le renard

(from *Marie de France: Les Fables*, ed. Charles Brucker [Louvain: Peeters, 1991])

D'un cok recunte ki estot
sur un femer e si chantot;
par delez li vient un gupilz
si l'apela par muz beaus diz.
5   "Sire," fet il, "mut te vei bel,
unc[es] ne vi si gent oisel;
clere voiz as sur tute rien:
fors tun pere, que jo vi bien,
unc[es] oisel meuz ne chanta;
10   mes il le fist meuz, kar il cluna."
"Si puis jeo fere," dist li cocs.
Les eles bat, les oilz ad clos,
chanter quida plus clerement.
Li gupil saut e si l[e] prent;
15   vers la forest od lui s'en va.
Par mi un champ, u il passa,
curent aprés tut li pastur,
li chiens le hüent tut entur.
Veit le gupil, ki le cok tient;
20   mar le guaina si par eus vient!
"Va," fet li cocs, "si lur escrie
que sui tuens, ne me larras mie."
Li gupil volt parler en haut,
e li cocs de sa buche saut,
25   sur un haut fust s'[en] est muntez.
Quant li gupilz s'est reguardez,
mut par se tient enfantillé,
que li cocs l'ad si enginné;
de maltalent e de dreit' ire
30   la buche cumence a maudire
ke parole quant devereit taire.
Li cocs respunt: "Si dei jeo faire:
maudire l'oil ki volt cluiner
quant it deit guarder e guaiter
35   que mal ne vienge a sun seignur."
Ceo funt li fol: tut li plusur
parolent quant deivent taiser,
teisent quant il deivent parler.

II

The Romance of Reynard the Fox

(trans. D. D. R. Owen (Oxford University Press, 1994), pp. 53–9)

It so happened that Reynard, that utter rascal who was always up to his tricks, made his way to a farmstead situated in a wood and well supplied with hens and cocks, ducks and drakes, ganders and geese. Its owner, Constant de Noues, an extremely wealthy peasant, lived just by the farmyard in a very well-stocked house with a rich supply of hens and capons. There was a great deal of this and that: salted meat, hams and bacon, and he had an abundance of corn. He was in a splendid situation; for his orchard was very productive, with many fine cherries and all kinds of fruit, apples and so forth.

[44] Reynard goes there to amuse himself. The property was securely enclosed with stout, pointed oak stakes reinforced with hawthorn bushes. Master Constant had put his chickens inside for protection. Reynard slinks towards it head down until he has come right up to the enclosure. Very enterprising though he was, the strength of the thorn hedge is such an impediment that he cannot get past it either by burrowing or with a leap; but he is unwilling to miss out on the chickens. He crouches in the middle of the road, restlessly turning his head this way and that. He supposes that if he jumps and so comes down from some height, he will be seen by the hens, who will take cover under the thorns; and he might well be spotted before catching anything worth while.

II

Le Roman de Renart

(ed. Jean Dufournet and Andrée Méline [Paris: Flammarion, 1985], Branch II,
lines 23–468, vol. 1, pp. 208–32). The editors include a modern French translation
but no textual variants, and use as their base text the complete edition by
Ernst Martin (Paris and Strasbourg: Trübner, 1882–87)

    Il avint chose que Renars,
    Qui tant par fu de males ars
25   Et qui tant sot toz jors de guile
    S'en vint traiant a une vile.
    La vile seoit en un bos.
    Molt i ot gelines et cos,
    Anes et malarz, jars et oës.
30   Et li sires Constans des Noës,
    Un vilain qui moult ert garnis,
    Manoit moult pres du plesseïs.
    Plenteïve estoit sa maisons.
    De gelines et de chapons
35   Bien avoit garni son hostel.
    Assez i ot et un et el:
    Char salee, bacons et fliches.
    De blé estoit li vilains riches.
    Molt par estoit bien herbergiez,
40   Que moult iert riches ses vergiers.
    Assez i ot bonnes cerises
    Et pluseurs fruis de maintes guises.
    Pommes i ot et autre fruit.
    La vait Renart pour son deduit.
45   Li courtilz estoit bien enclos
    De piex de chesne agus et gros.
    Hourdés estoit d'aubes espines.
    Laiens avoit mis ses gelines
    Dant Constant pour la forteresce.
50   Et Renart celle part s'adresce,
    Tout coiement, le col bessié,
    S'en vint tout droit vers le plessié.
    Moult fu Renart de grant pourchaz.
    Mais la force des espinars
55   Li destourne si son affaire
    Que il n'en puet a bon chief traire,
    Ne pour mucier ne pour saillir;
    N'aus gelines ne veult faillir.
    Acroupiz s'est enmi la voie.
60   Moult se defripe, moult coloie.

He was much concerned, anxious to get his hands on the hens he sees pecking away in front of him. Reynard keeps starting up, then flattening himself. At the corner of the fence he spied a broken stake and made his way inside. By the gap in the enclosure the peasant had planted some cabbages. Reynard came to these and went through them, crouching low so as not to be seen by anyone. But the chickens craned their necks, having noticed him when he dropped down; and every one of them scurried away.

[81] The cock, Sir Chantecler, had made his way by a ditch between two stakes to perch on a dunghill beside a path next to the wood. With his feathered feet and full of pride, he confronts the chickens, sticking out his neck and asking them why they are fleeing towards the house. Pinte, the wisest of them and the layer of those great eggs, answered from her perch to the cock's right. She told him how things stood, saying: "We've had a fright."

"Why? What did you see?"

"Some savage beast or other that can very soon do us some harm if we don't get out of this garden."

"That's sheer nonsense, I assure you," says the cock. Don't be afraid: you're quite safe here."

"But I swear I saw it," said Pinte. "I definitely saw it, on my word of honor."

"How did you manage that?"

"How? I saw the fence shake and the cabbage leaves quiver where whatever's hiding is lying down."

"That'll do, Pinte," the cock replies. "I can assure you you've nothing to worry about, because I promise you

Il se pourpense que s'il saut,
Pour quoi il chiece auques de haut,
Il iert veüz et les gelines
Se ficheront souz les espines,
65   Si pourroit tost estre seurpris
Ainz qu'il eüst gaires acquis.
Moult par estoit en grant esfroi:
Les gelines veult traire a soi
Que devant lui voit pasturant.
70   Et Renart vait cheant levant.
Ou retour de la soif choisist
Un pel froissié, dedenz se mist.
La ou li paliz iert desclos,
Avoit li vilains planté chos:
75   Renart y vint, oultre s'em passe,
Cheoir se laist en une masse
Pour ce que la gent ne le voient;
Mais les gelines en coloient,
Qui l'ont choisi a sa cheoite.
80   Chascune de fuïr s'esploite.
     Mesire Chantecler li cos,
En une sente, les le bos,
Entre deus piex souz la raiere
S'estoit traiz en une poudriere.
85   Moult fierement leur vient devant,
La plume ou pié, le col tendant,
Si demande par quel raison
Elles s'en fuient vers maison.
Pinte parla qui plus savoit,
90   Celle qui les gros hués ponnoit,
Qui pres du coc jucoit a destre;
Si li a raconté son estre
Et dit, "Paour avons eüe."
"Pourquoi? Quel chose avez veüe?"
95   "Je ne sai quel beste sauvage
Qui tost nous puet faire damage,
Se nous ne vuidons ce pourpris."
"C'est tout noient, ce vous plevis,"
Ce dit li cos: "N'aies peür,
100 Mais estes ci tout asseür."
Dist Pinte, "Par ma foi, jel vi:
Et loiaument le vous affi,
Que je le vi tout a estrouz."
"Et comment le veïstes vous?"
105 "Comment? je vi la soif branler
Et la fuelle du chou trembler
Ou cilz se gist qui est repus."
"Pinte," fait il, "or n'i a plus.
Trives avez, jel vous ottroi:

faithfully that I know of no polecat or fox that would dare come into this garden. Some joke, that is! So back you go!"

Chantecler mounted his dunghill again; for he was not afraid of anything a fox or dog might do to him – he had no cause for alarm, believing himself to be quite safe. He had a totally confident air, not knowing the threat he was under. Fool that he was, he feared nothing. With one eye open and the other shut, one claw extended and the other clenched, he perched up there beside a shed.

[125] Having thus taken his stance, the cock gave the impression of being tired of crowing and keeping on the alert; and he fell into a doze. Having dropped off into his welcome sleep, he started to dream. Don't think I am lying when I say that he dreamed (yes, truly – it's all in the story) that there was some creature or other in that well-fenced enclosure which, so it seemed, came straight at him and gave him a terrible fright. It was carrying a rust-red cloak with a collar of bones, which it forced him to put on. Chantecler was very troubled by this dream that so disturbed his sleep; and he was puzzled by the cloak, for its neck-opening was all awry and he was wearing it the wrong way round. The neck was so tight on him and hurt him so much that he woke in great distress. What amazed him even more was that its front was white and he got into it so that his head went into its cap, while his tail stayed in the neck-opening. That dream made him shudder and convinced him he was in a sorry plight, judging by the terrifying nature of the vision.

110 Que, par la foi que je vous doi,
    Je ne sai putoiz ne gourpil
    Que osast entrer ou courtil.
    Ce est gas, retournez arriere."
    Cilz se radresce en sa poudriere,
115 [Qu'il na paour de nulle riens
    Que li face gourpilz ne chiens;
    De nulle riens n'avoit peür,
    Que moult cuidoit estre aseür.]
    Moult se contint seürement,
120 Ne set gaires q'a l'eil li pent.
    Rien ne douta, si fist que fox.
    L'un oeil ouvert et l'autre clos,
    L'un pié crampi et l'autre droit
    S'est apuiez delez un toit.
125   La ou li cos est apoiez
    Conme cilz qui iert anuiez
    Et de chanter et de veiller,
    Si conmença a someillier.
    Ou someillier que il fasoit
130 Et ou dormir qui li plaisoit,
    Conmença li cos a songier;
    Ne m'en tenés a mençonger.
    Car il sonja (ce est la voire,
    Trover le poëz en l'estoire)
135 Que il avoit ne sai quel cose
    Dedenz la cort, que bien ert close,
    Qui li venoit enmi le vis,
    Ensi con il li ert avis,
    (Si en avoit molt grant friçon)
140 Et tenoit un ros peliçon
    Dont les goles estoient d'os,
    Si li metoit par force el dos.
    Molt ert Chantecler en grant peine
    Del songe qui si le demeine,
145 Endementiers que il somelle;
    Et del peliçon se mervelle,
    Que la chevece ert en travers,
    Et si l'avoit vestu envers.
    Estrois estoit en la chevece
150 Si qu'il en a si grant destrece
    Qu'a peines s'en est esveilliez.
    Mes de ce s'est plus merveilliez
    Que blans estoit desos le ventre
    Et que par la chevece i entre,
155 Si que la teste est en la faille
    Et la coue en la cheveçaille.
    Por le songe s'est tresailliz,
    Que bien cuide estre malbailliz

[161] Wide awake now, the cock said, "Holy Spirit, save me from capture today and let me come to no harm!" With that he dashes off at top speed, clearly far from being reassured, heading for where the hens were under the hawthorn bushes and not stopping until he has reached them. He called to Pinte, in whom he had complete trust, and drew her aside: "Pinte, there's no point hiding it: I'm extremely upset and alarmed and very much afraid of being caught out by some bird or wild animal who can soon do us some harm."

"Come now, my dear husband!" says Pinte, "you shouldn't say that. It's wrong to give us a fright. Come here and I'll tell you something: by all the saints we pray to, you're like the dog that yelps before it's been hit by the stone. What's frightened you? Just tell me what the matter is."

[186] "What?" said the cock. "Don't you know I've had a strange dream by the hole over there next to the barn? It was a terrible vision, and that's why I'm looking so pale. I'll tell you the whole dream, without leaving anything out. Will you be able to give me some advice about it? While I was asleep, it seemed to me that some beast or other arrived wearing a reddish cloak. It was a good fit – no need for scissors to be used on it; and he forced me to put it on. The collar was trimmed with bone and was quite white, but very hard; and it was made askew and extremely tight, which was very distressing for me. Its fur was turned to the outside. That's how the cloak was rigged out, and I got into it by the neck opening, but didn't stay in it long at all. That's how I put it on,

Por la vision que a veüe
160 Dont il a grant peor eüe.
Esveillies s'est et esperiz
Li cos et dist, "Seint esperiz,
Garis hui mon cors de prison
Et met a sauve garison!"
165 Lors s'en torne grant aleüre
Con cil qui point ne s'aseüre
Et vint traiant vers les gelines,
Qui estoient soz les espines.
Tres q'a eles ne se recroit.
170 Pinte apela ou molt se croit,
A une part l'a asenee:
"Pinte, n'i a mester celee:
Molt sui dolanz et esbahiz;
Grant poor ai d'estre traïz
175 D'oisel ou de beste sauvage.
Qui tost nos puet fere damage."
"Avoi!" fait Pinte, "baus dos sire,
Icee ne devés vos pas dire;
Mau fetes qui nos esmaiés.
180 Si vos dirai, ca vos traiés!
Par trestoz les seinz que l'en prie,
Vos resemblés le chen qui crie
Ains que la pierre soit coüe.
Por qu'avés tel poor oüe?
185 Car me dites que vos avés."
"Qoi?" dist li cos, "Vos ne savés
Que j'ai songié un songe estrange,
Deles cel trou les cele granche,
Et une avisïon molt male,
190 Por qoi vos me veés si pale.
Tot le songe vos conterai,
Ja riens ne vos en celerai.
Saureés m'en vos conseillier?
Avis me fu el somellier
195 Que ne sai quel beste veneit
Qui un ros peliçon vestoit,
Bien fet sanz cisel et sanz force,
S'il me fesoit vestir a force.
D'os estoit fete l'orleüre,
200 Tote blance, mes molt ert dure;
La chavesce de travers fete,
Estroite, qui molt me dehaite.
Le poil avoit dehors torné.
Le peliçon si atorné
205 Par la chevece le vestoie,
Mais molt petit i arestoie.
Le peliçon vesti ensi:

but I got out of it backwards. When I did so, I was amazed to find the tail on the top. I've come here quite bewildered. Don't be surprised, Pinte, if my heart's in palpitations, but give me your opinion. I've been quite upset by the dream. By the faith you owe me, do you know what it means?"

Pinte, who has his full confidence, replies, "You've told me the dream, but, please God, it's a false one. Still, I'll interpret it for you, because I really will be able to answer your questions about it."

[223] "The creature you saw in your sleep that was wearing the reddish cloak and caused you such trouble is, I'm sure, the fox. You can tell that easily by the cloak's reddish color and by its being forced onto you. The bone border is the teeth he'll use to get you inside. The crooked collar that hurt you because it was so narrow is the animal's mouth that will squeeze your head: that's your way in, and you'll certainly get it round you. As for the tail being uppermost, by all the world's saints, it's because the fox when he comes will take you by the neck, so the tail will be sticking up. That's how it will be, as God's my savior. No silver or gold will protect you. And the fur turned to the outside? That's true, because the fox always wears his coat inside out, however much it may pour with rain. Now you've heard the full meaning of your dream. I give you my firm assurance: before you've got past midday, that's truly what will happen to you.

But if you'll take my word for it, you'll go back where you came from, because I know for a fact that he's hiding behind here

Mes a reculons m'en issi.
Lors m'en merveillai a cele ore
210 Por la coue qui ert desoure.
Ça sui venus desconseilliez.
Pinte, ne vos en merveilliez,
Se li cuers me fremist et tramble,
Mes dites moi que vos en semble.
215 Molt sui por le songe grevez.
Par cele foi que me devez,
Savez vos que ce senefie?"
Pinte respont, ou molt se fie,
"Dit m'avez," fait ele, "le songe.
220 Mes, se Dex plest, ce est mençoigne.
Ne porquant si vos voil espondre,
Car bien vos en saurai respondre.
   Icele chose que veïstes,
El someller que vos feïstes,
225 Qui le ros peliçon vestoit
Et issi vos desconfortoit,
C'est li gorpils, jel sai de voir.
Bien le poés apercevoir
Au peliçon qui ros estoit
230 Et qui par force vos vestoit.
Les goles d'os, ce sont les denz
A qoi il vos metra dedenz.
La chevece qui n'iert pas droite,
Qui si vos iert male et estroite,
235 Ce est la boce de la beste,
Dont il vos estreindra la teste.
Par iloques i enterois,
Sanz faille vos le vestirois.
Ce que la coue est contremont,
240 Par les seinz de trestot le mont,
C'est li gorpils qui vos prendra
Parmi le col, quant il vendra,
Dont sera la coue desore.
Einsi ert, se Dex me secore.
245 Ne vos gara argent ne ors.
Li peus qui ert torné defors,
C'est voirs, que tot jors porte enverse
Sa pel, quant il mels plot et verse.
Or avez oï sanz faillance
250 De vostre songe la senblance.
Tot soürement le vos di:
Ainz que voiez passé midi,
Vos avandra, ce est la voire.
Mes se vos me volieez croire,
255 Vos retornerïez ariere.
Car il est repos ci derere

in this bush to trick you and take you unawares." [259] When Chantecler had heard her give her interpretation of the dream, "Pinte," he said, "you're quite crazy. You've spoken utter rubbish, saying that I'll be caught out and that the beast that will take me by force is in this enclosure. A curse on anyone who ever believes that! You've told me nothing I can take seriously; and may I never prosper if I believe I'll be any the worse for this dream!"

"Sir," said she, "may God grant it so! But if it doesn't turn out the way I've told you, I give you my firm pledge that I'll not be your loving wife any more."

"Pinte," he replied, "there's no risk of that."

Having made light of the dream, he immediately went back on to his dunghill to bask in the sun and dozed off once more. Then, when Reynard, who was extremely prudent and amazingly crafty, felt sure of things and saw Chantecler asleep, he at once moved towards him, universal plague that he was and master of so many low tricks. Step by step, without hurrying, and head lowered, he moves forward. If Chantecler waits long enough for Reynard to get him between his teeth, then he will have cause to feel sorry for himself!

[291] The instant Reynard saw Chantecler, he wanted to plunge his teeth into him. But in his eagerness he missed him, because Chantecler jumped to one side. He eyed Reynard and easily recognized him, but stayed on the dungheap. When Reynard realized he had missed him, he felt very aggrieved. So now he begins to plan how to trick Chantecler, for if he fails to eat him he will have been wasting his time. "Chantecler," he called, "don't run away; you've nothing to worry about! I'm delighted to find you in good health,

En cest boisson, jel sai de voir,
Por vos traïr et decevoir."
    Quant cil ot oï le respons
260 Del songe, que cele ot espons,
"Pinte," fait il, "molt par es fole.
Molt as dit vileine parole,
Qui diz que je serai sorpris,
Et que la beste est el porpris
265 Qui par force me conquerra.
Dahez ait qui ja le crera!
Ne m'as dit rien ou ge me tiegne.
Ja nel crerai, se biens m'aviegne,
Que j'aie mal por icest songe."
270 "Sire," fait ele, "Dex le donge!
Mais s'il n'est si con vos ai dit,
Je vos otroi senz contredit
Je ne soie mes vostre amie."
"Pinte," fait il, "Ce n'i a mie."
275 A fable est li songe tornez.
A itant s'en est retornez
En la poudrere a solaller,
Si reconmance a someller.
Et quant il fu aseürez,
280 (Molt fu Renars amesurez
Et voisiez a grant merveille)
Quant il voit que celui somelle,
Vers lui aprime sanz demore
Renars, qui tot le mont acore
285 Et qui tant set de maveis tors.
Pas avant autre, tot sanz cors,
S'en vet Renars le col baissant.
Se Chantecler le paratent
Que cil le puisse as denz tenir,
290 Il li fera son jou poïr.
    Quant Renars choisi Chantecler,
Senpres le volst as denz haper.
Renars failli, qui fu engrés,
Et Chantecler saut en travers.
295 Renart choisi, bien le conut,
Desor le fumier s'arestut.
Quant Renars voit qu'il a failli,
Forment se tint a malbailli,
Or se conmence a porpenser,
300 Conment il porroit Chantecler
Engignier, car s'il nel manjue,
Dont a il sa voie perdue.
"Chantecler," ce li dist Renart,
Ne fuïr pas, n'aiés regart!
305 Molt par sui liez, quant tu es seinz,

because you're my first cousin."

That reassured Chantecler, and he was so happy he crowed a little song. Then Reynard said to his cousin, "You remember Chanteclin, the fine father who sired you? There never was a cock who sang like him: he could be heard over a league away. He was very good at singing a high note and could hold it for an extremely long time with both eyes closed: his was a powerful voice. He didn't gaze into the distance when he was singing songs and ditties."

[319] "Cousin Reynard," said Chantecler, "you're not trying to play a trick on me?"

"No, never!" said Reynard. "But now just close your eyes and sing! We're each other's flesh and blood, and I'd rather lose one of my paws than see you in any distress, because you're a very close relative of mine."

Chantecler replied, "I don't believe you. Get a little way back from me, and I'll give you a song. There won't be anyone in the neighborhood who won't hear my top notes."

That made old Reynard smile. "Come on then, cousin, sing up! I'll be able to tell all right if my uncle Chanteclin ever disowned you."

At that Chantecler began at the top of his voice, and then gave a crow with one eye closed and the other open, as he was desperately afraid of Reynard and kept glancing at him. Reynard said, "That's nothing. Chanteclin used to sing differently, keeping it up for a long time and with his eyes shut: he could be heard clearly in twenty farms around." Chantecler believes what he says. So then he gives full vent to his melody, eyes tightly closed.

[348] Reynard could wait no longer. Leaping from under a red cabbage, he seizes Chantecler by the neck and runs away, highly delighted to have found some prey.

Car tu es mes cosins germeins."
Chantecler lors s'asoüra,
Por la joie un sonet chanta.
Ce dist Renars a son cosin
310 "Membre te mes de Chanteclin,
Ton bon pere qui t'engendra?
Onques nus cos si ne chanta:
D'une grant liue l'ooit on,
Molt bien chantoit en haut un son
315 Et molt par avoit longe aleine
Les deus els clos, la vois ot seine.
D'une leüe ne veoit,
Quant il chantoit et refregnoit."
   Dist Chantecler, "Renart cosin,
320 Volés me vos trere a engin?
"Certes," ce dist Renars, "non voil.
Mes or chantez, si clinniés l'oeil!
D'une char somes et d'un sanc.
Meus voudroie estre d'un pié manc
325 Que tu eüsses maremenz,
Car tu es trop pres mi parenz."
Dist Chantecler, "Pas ne t'en croi.
Un poi te trai en sus de moi
Et je dirai une chançon.
330 N'aura voisin ci environ
Qui bien n'entende mon fauset."
Lores s'en sozrist Renardet:
"Or dont en haut: chantez, cosin!
Je saurai bien, se Chanteclin,
335 Mis oncles, vos fu onc neant."
Lors comenca cil hautement;
Puis jeta Chantecler un bret.
L'un oil ot clos et l'autre overt,
Car molt forment dotoit Renart.
340 Sovent regarde cele part.
Ce dist Renars, "N'as fet neent.
Chanteclins chantoit autrement
A uns lons trez les eilz cligniez:
L'en l'ooit bien par vint plaissiez."
345 Chantecler quide que voir die.
Lors let aler sa meloudie,
Les oilz cligniez, par grant aïr.
Lors ne volt plus Renars soffrir.
Par de desoz un roge chol
350 Le prent Renars parmi le col;
Fuiant s'ent va et fait grant joie
De ce qu'il a encontré proie.
Pinte voit que Renars l'enporte,
Dolente est, molt se deconforte,

Seeing Reynard make off with the cock, Pinte is very distressed and grief-stricken. As she watched Chantecler being carried away, she called, "That's just what I told you, husband; and yet you made fun of me and thought I was stupid. But now the warning I gave you has come true. Your wits have let you down. It was silly of me to explain it to you, for no fool knows fear until he's got caught. Poor wretch that I am, this is the end of me, because if I lose my husband now, I've lost all my dignity forever!"

[369] The good farmer's wife had opened the door on to her yard because, as it was evening, she wanted to bring her hens under cover. She calls to Pinte, Bise, and Rosette, but none of them comes in. Seeing that they have not come, she wonders what they can be doing. She yells long and loud for her cock, then spots Reynard making off with him. At that she sets out to the rescue, and the fox starts to run. Finding that she cannot catch him, she decides to give a shout. "Help!" she bellows. The countryfolk were playing at boules; and, on hearing her shriek, they all came over and asked what the matter was. She sighed as she told them: "Ah, me, what a disaster!"

"How's that?" they ask.

"Because I've lost my cock that the fox is carrying off."

Constant said, "You filthy old slut, what were you doing not to catch him?"

"It's wrong of you to say that, sir," she said. "By God's holy saints, I couldn't catch him."

"Why not?"

"He wouldn't wait for me."

"And what if you'd hit him?"

"I didn't have anything to do it with."

"With this stick."

"By God, I couldn't, because he goes at such a gallop that even two Breton dogs wouldn't get him."

"Which way's he going?"

"Straight over there."

The rustics run helter-skelter, all yelling, "There, over there!"

355 Si se conmence a dementer,
    Quant Chantecler vit enporter,
    Et dit, "Sire, bien le vos dis
    Et vos me gabïez todis
    Et si me tenieez por fole.
360 Mes ore est voire la parole
    Dont je vos avoie garni.
    Vostre senz vos a escharni.
    Fole fui, quant jel vos apris,
    Et fox ne crient tant qu'il est pris.
365 Renars vos tient qui vos enporte.
    Lasse dolente, con sui morte!
    Car, se je ci pert mon seignor,
    A toz jors ai perdu m'onor."
       La bone feme del mainil
370 A overt l'uis de son cortil.
    Car vespres ert, por ce voloit
    Ses jelines remetre en toit.
    Pinte apela, Bise et Rosete:
    L'une ne l'autre ne recete.
375 Quant voit que venues ne sont,
    Molt se merveille qu'elles font.
    Son coc rehuce a grant aleine.
    Renart regarde qui l'enmeine;
    Lors passe avant por le rescore
380 Et li gorpils conmence a core.
    Quant voit que prendre nel porra,
    Porpense soi qu'el crïera.
    "Harou!" escrie a pleine gole.
    Li vilein qui sont a la çoule,
385 Quant il oënt que cele bret,
    Trestuit se sont cele part tret,
    Si li demandent que ele a.
    En sospirant lor reconta,
    "Lasse, con m'est mal avenu!"
390 "Coment?" font il. "Car j'ai perdu
    Mon coc que li gorpil enporte."
    Ce dist Costans, "Pute vielle orde,
    Qu'avés dont fet que nel preïstes?"
    "Sire," fait ele, "mar le dites.
395 Par les seinz Deu, je nel poi prendre.
    "Por quoi?" "Il ne me volt atendre."
    "Sel ferissiez?" "Je n'oi de quoi."
    "De cest baston." "Par Deu, ne poi:
    Car il s'en vet si grant troton
400 Nel prendroient deus chen breton."
    "Par ou s'en vet?" "Par ci tot droit."
    Li vilein corent a esploit.
    Tuit s'escrïent, "Or ça, or ça!"

[404] Up ahead Reynard heard them. He came to the gap and gave such a bound that he landed on his backside. They heard the sound of his jump and all shouted, "This way, this way!"

"Quick, after him!" said Constant; and the peasants run as hard as they can. Constant calls up his mastiff, commonly known as Malvoisin. "Bardol, Travers, Humbaut, Rebours, keep chasing that rusty Reynard!"

As they ran on, they caught sight of Reynard and yelled together, "Look, there's the fox!"

Now Chantecler is in deadly peril unless he can think of some cunning ruse. "Hey, Sir Reynard," he says, "can't you hear all the insults those bumpkins are shouting at you? Constant's hard on your heels; so just you let him have one of your gibes when we're out of that gate. When he says, 'Reynard's carrying him off,' you can say, 'And there's nothing you can do about it.' That's the best way to upset him."

[429] There is none so wise as to commit no folly. Reynard, the arch-deceiver, was himself tricked on this occasion. At the top of his voice he shouted, "I'm taking away my share of this one, and there's nothing you can do about it." When Chantecler felt his mouth slacken, he beat his wings, gave him the slip, and flew up into an apple tree. Reynard stayed down on a dunghill, furious and miserable as he brooded on how the cock had escaped from him.

Chantecler laughed at him. "Reynard," he said, "how do things seem to you? What's your feeling about this world?"

The scoundrel trembled and shook, then railed at him. "A curse," says he, "on the mouth that goes chattering at the moment when it should keep silent."

"Let's have things my way," says the cock: "A plague on the eye that dozes off at the moment when it should be on watch!

Renars l'oï qui devant va.
405 Au pertuis vint, si sailli jus
Qu'a la terre feri li cus.
Le saut qu'il fist ont cil oï.
Tuit s'escrïent, "Or ça, or ci!"
Costans lor dist, "Or tost après!"
410 Li vilein corent a esles.
Costans apele son mastin,
Que tuit apelent Mauvoisin,
["Bardol, Travers, Humbaut, Rebors,
Corés après Renart le ros!"]
415 Au corre qu'il font l'ont veü
Et Renart ont aperceü.
Tuit s'escrïent, "Vez le gorpil!"
Or est Chanteclers en peril,
S'il ne reseit engin et art.
420 "Conment," fait il, "sire Renart,
Dont n'oëz quel honte vos dïent,
Cil vilein qui si vos escrïent?
Costans vos seut plus que le pas:
Car li lanciez un de vos gas
425 A l'issue de cele porte.
Quant il dira, 'Renars l'enporte,'
'Maugrez vostre,' ce poés dire.
Ja nel porrés mels desconfire."
    N'i a si sage ne foloit.
430 Renars qui tot le mont deçoit,
Fu deçoüs a cele foiz.
Il s'escria a haute vois:
"Maugre vostre," ce dist Renart,
"De cestui enpor je ma part."
435 Quant cil senti lache la boce,
Bati les eles, si s'en toche,
Si vint volant sor un pomer.
Renars fu bas sor un fomier,
Greinz et maris et trespensés
440 Del coc qui li est escapez.
Chantecler li jeta un ris.
"Renart," fait il, "que vos est vis?
De cest siegle que vos en semble?"
Li lecheres fremist et tramle.
445 Si li a dit par felonie:
"La boce," fait il, "soit honie,
Qui s'entremet de noise fere
A l'ore qu'ele se doit tere!"
"Si soit," fet li cos, "con je voil:
450 La male gote li cret l'oil
Qui s'entremet de someller
A l'ore que il doit veillier!

Cousin Reynard," Chantecler went on, "no one can trust you. A curse on your cousinship! It almost did for me. Off you go, Reynard you perjurer! If you're here much longer, you'll leave your coat behind!"

Reynard has no time for his prattle and, having nothing more to say himself, goes away at once. He does not rest or linger, faint as he is for lack of sustenance. He takes flight along a path beside an open field and through a thicket. He is very miserable and distressed about the cock escaping him without his eating his fill of it.

III

Le Roman de Renart le Contrefait

(Gaston Raynaud and Henri Lemaître, eds., vol. 2 [Paris: Champion, 1914])

([30819–31088] Renard bemoans his bad luck and mistreatment at the hands of Fortune; he compares himself to Hecuba, Hercules, and ten other legendary and historical figures.)

[31089] Thus Renard tormented himself with the pain that he felt and the misfortune that held him, until he approached a farm. A peasant was on this farm; as much by luck as by guile, he had acquired enough to have it, and this gave him the reputation of being wise, although he was foolish and tough. His residence was well enclosed by walls, with hedges and palings around it; because he feared for himself a great deal, lest someone should take his possessions or do him grief, he kept his residence enclosed and fortified. Just as Renard arrived there, he met a man.

([31105–264] Renard learns from the man that the inhabitant of the walled compound is renowned for his wisdom because he is rich. Renard says that he will try to find a way into the compound to talk to the rich man. He sees hens in the compound, but fearing his bad luck, he does not dare attack them. Renard again bemoans his poverty as well as his cowardice, but he comforts himself with the knowledge that he still has his strength and his wits. He also tells himself that he would rather die while attempting a conquest than to end in despair over his poverty.)

[31265] So Renard took heart and pushed himself into the enclosure. He saw the hens who kept themselves in the garden;

Cosins Renart," dist Chantecler,
"Nus ne se puet en vos fier.
455 Dahez ait vostre cosinage!
Il me dut torner a damage.
Renart parjure, alés vos ent!
Se vos estes ci longement,
Vos i lairois vostre gonele."
460 Renars n'a soing de sa favele.
Ne volt plus dire, atant s'en torne,
Ne repose ne ne sejorne;
Besongnieus est, le cuer a vein.
Par une broce lez un plein
465 S'en vait fuiant tot une sente.
Molt est dolans, molt se demente
Del coc qui li est escapés,
Quant il n'en est bien saolés.

III

Le Roman de Renart le Contrefait

(Gaston Raynaud and Henri Lemaître, eds., vol. 2 [Paris: Champion, 1914])

Ainsi Regnart se dementoit
31090 De la dolleur que il sentoit
Et de mal heür qui le tient,
Tant que vers une ville vient.
Ung vilain ot en celle ville;
Tant par bonheur come par guille
31095 Ot assez acquis de l'avoir,
Pour ce ot renom de sçavoir,
Et il fu entules et durs;
Son pourprins ot bien clos de murs,
De hayes et de palis fors;
31040 Car il doubtoit fort de son corps,
Que son avoir on ne presist,
Ou que grief on ne lui fesist;
Pour ce clos et fort se tenoit.
Ainsi com Regnart la venoit,
31045 Si a rencontré ung bon homme.
. . .

31265 Adont Regnart confort a prins,
Et s'est bouté ens ou pourprins.
Si a les gelines veües
Qui ou gardin se sont tenues;

and as soon as they saw him, immediately they made plenty of room for him, and quickly they ran away without greeting him. Chantecler, who was in the habit of guarding them, asked them why they went fleeing into the house. They said, "We were afraid, because we saw a terrible beast."

[31277] "Watch out," said he, "Don't be afraid, and all of you be assured, our lord is a rich man, and there is neither man nor beast – this we know – who would dare do wrong to our lord nor who would oppose him, nor anyone who would dare do us an injury for fear of him. And if anyone comes who promises you harm, say, 'We belong to a rich man!' If you have power over death, you will not be mistreated."

[31289] Then, one claw clenched, the other straight, he perched under a shed. Here he began to sleep and to dream a very fearsome dream. For it seemed to him that a beast was playing with him; the beast held him around the head and forcibly led him at his will. The cock took such fright that he was completely shaken because of it, and he awoke in great fear; he would not be reassured from that moment on.

[31301] He called Pinte in whom he confided, and he desired to tell her his dream, and to have her expound it and give him very good counsel. Pinte responded, "Now I hear a wondrous thing, when a man asks counsel of woman; really it is very great shame that, when the counsel of a woman is required, one can hardly find reliable advice. If any good should come from it, it is by chance: therefore a man should pay it no heed. But notwithstanding, it happens that many of them have had good advice – those who have wanted to believe [women] truly; but certainly it's the truth that even if women quote the gospels,

Et si tost com elles le virrent,
31270 Tantost belle place lui firent,
Et tost s'en vont sans acorder.
Chantecler qui les soeult garder,
Leur demanda pour quel raison
Elles vont fuiant en maison.
31275 Dient, "Paour avons eü,
Car male beste avons veü."
"Gardez," dist il, "n'ayez peür,
Et soyez toutes asseür,
Monseigneur est ung riches homs,
31280 Il n'est homs, beste, ce sçavons,
Cui Monseigneur meffaire osast
Ne qui contre lui s'opposast;
Ne nul pour doubtance de lui
Ne nous oseroit faire anuy,
31285 Et s'aucun vient qui mal vous nomme,
Dites, 'Nous sommes a riche homme!'
Se vous aviez mort le bailli,
Ne seriez vous pas mal balli."
Lors, ung piet cranpy, l'autre droit,
31290 S'est acroupy dessoubx ung toit.
Illec se print a sommeillier,
Et ung monlt fier songe a songier;
Et lui sembloit que une beste
Faisoit de lui une grant feste;
31295 Par my la teste le tenoit,
A son voloir le demenoit.
Tel paour a le coq eü
Que trestout en est esmeü,
Et s'esveilla a grant peür;
31300 Huy mais ne sera asseür.
    Pinte apelle il ou il se fye,
Et a talent que il lui dye
Le songe, et qu'elle lui esponne,
Et que tresbon conseil lui donne.
31305 Pinte respond, "Or oy merveille,
Quant homs a feme se conseille;
Certes ce est trop grant deffault,
Quant a femme consseillier fault,
Que a paine y poeut on trouver
31310 Conseil qui se puist bien prouver;
Se bien en vient, c'est aventure:
Pour ce, homs n'en doit avoit cure.
Et non pour quant est advenu,
Maint en ont bon conseil eü,
31315 Ceulx qui les ont volu bien croire;
Mais certes ce est chose voire,
S'elles disoient Euvangilles,

it seems to many people that these sayings are ruses, and for this people don't want to believe women, however many good things they are accustomed to saying. And many great things would happen to them, if some men believed women better.

[31323] "Andromache, the wife of Hector, strong as a lion, cruel as a bull – he would definitely not have been put to death so soon, if her lord had believed her when for love and for honor she said to Hector, her lord, 'Sir, do not go on this day into battle nor into fighting. If on this day you go there, just as it has been revealed by the gods, you will be killed without fail; I advise and give you this counsel for your good. I beg you, in order to put off death, that you be willing to protect yourself from this.' However true her words may have been, Hector refused to believe her. He went to battle and died there because of Achilles, who slew him.

[31341] The Duke of Bar, if he had believed a woman, would certainly not have met his death when he wanted to go to Athens, to that land so far away, where many men were killed in the year 1336; there they had bad luck with the Count of Braine. With good intentions his lover had spoken to him: 'Sir, for God's sake, don't go there at all; it's an unlucky place where no one at all is safe. Many a good man has perished there. For our great love I beg that you grant me this gift: that you not go on this voyage at all, because later you will regret it." That man was unwillling to assent to her counsel; he went there, he didn't come back. It would have been better if he had believed her counsel.

[31361] "Because of this I say to you: no matter how little one believes women in something that one hears from them, anytime anyone believes them, it does him profit and honor. You ought to have my counsel, inasmuch as you asked me for it,

Semble a pluseurs que ce sont guiles,
Et pour ce croire ne les voeullent,
31320 Combien que maint bien dire soeulent
Et monlt grans biens en advenissent,
Se les pluseurs mieulx les creïssent.
    Andromada, la femme Hector,
Fort com lion, cruel com tor,
31325 Se son seigneur creü l'eüst,
Si tost a mort point mis ne fust,
Quant par amour et par honneur
El dit a Hector, son seigneur:
'Sire, n'alez pas ad ce jour
31330 En bataille ny en estour!
Se ad ce jour vous y allez,
Si com des dieux est revellez,
Ochis serez sans nulle faille,
Pour bien le vous conseille et baille;
31335 Si vous pri, pour mort retarder,
Que vous en voeulliez bien garder.'
Combien que desist chose voire,
Oncquez Hector ne le vaut croire;
Il y ala, et la morut
31340 Par Achilès qui le ferut.
Le duc de Bar, s'il eust creü
Femme, la mort n'eust point eü,
Quant il vault aler a Athenes,
En celle terre tant lointainez
31345 Ou maint homme ont esté ochis,
L'an mil trois cens et trente et sis;
La se sont il a male estraine
Avecquez le conte de Braine.
De bon coeur bien lui dist s'amie:
31350 'Sire, pour Dieu, n'y alez mie;
Ce est ung lieu mal eürés,
Ou nul n'est point asseürés;
Maint bon preudom y est pery.
Sique par grant amour vous pry
31355 Que ce don donner me voeulliez
Qu'en ce voiage point n'allez,
Car tart seriez au repentir.'
Cil ne s'i vault point assentir;
Alez y est, n'est revenu.
31360 Mieulx vaulsist eust conseil creü.
Pour ce vous dis: "Comment qu'on croye
Peu femme de chose qu'on oye,
Aucuneffois qui les creroit,
S'honneur et son proffit feroit.
31365 De moy conseil avoir devez
Pour tant que requis m'en avez,

and because of this I will teach it to you. Now listen to what I will tell you."

[31369] Pinte continued, "Lord Chantecler, in spite of himself a coward can see clearly. Cowardice comes from a sluggish spirit. In spite of himself a coward can be wise. No one ought to be afraid of that about which he doesn't know, either in opinion or in belief, unless it is for a real reason. Do you plan to be held by your fear in the time to come? I have never seen any fearful people who were happy for long. All bad people are in poverty, and all good ones are in security. No man yet has been able to have so much or to acquire sense or knowledge if he has so fearful a heart that he is unhappy. He has never gone into any company without his whole heart trembling within him so that he can have no joy. Solomon, who knew so much, says, 'No one holds so great a joy as that which comes from the heart, but for the one who has a fearful heart, all his limbs are on fire.' A fearful man doesn't know how to love anyone, nor how to keep himself properly. A fearful man doesn't know how to speak or remain quiet . . .

([31398–468] For seventy verses Pertelote continues her amplification of the general character of a cowardly man, including in it some examples of self-preservatory fear which she considers normal.)

[31469] A dream has moved you, without fail; be peaceful, and do not be bothered. Take the future as it comes; it will not hold itself back for you alone. He who takes all annoyances willingly is established in a good position."

[31475] Thus Pinte supported him, counseling him of the good that she knew. "Now come what will," said he, "but may bad luck not take me." At that point he left to amuse himself.

[31480] He who is always plying his trade stops neither day nor night. Such was Renard, who was enjoying himself under the eaves in a nook. When he heard the sound of the cock,

Et pour ce je le vous liray.
Or entendez que je diray."
Pinte respond: "Damp Chantecler,
31370 Envis poeut couart vëoir cler.
Couardie vient de lent corage;
Envis poeult couart estre sage,
Nul ne doit trop paour avoir
De ce dont il ne scet le voir,
31375 Ne par cuidance ne par croire,
S'ilz ne font la cause auquez voire.
Cuidiez vous le temps advenir
Par vostre paour retenir?
Je ne vis oncquez nulz peureux
31380 Qui fussent gaires bien eureux.
Tous malvais sont en povreté,
Et tous bons sont en sceureté.
Ja nulz homs ne poeult tant avoir
Ne acquerre sens ne sçavoir,
31385 S'il a le coeur trop peüreux
Que il ne soit malheüreux;
Ja n'yert en nulle compagnie,
Que tout le coeur ne lui fremie,
Ne que il puisse joye avoir.
31390 Salomon qui tant ot sçavoir,
Dit, "Nul si grant delit ne tient
Comme cellui qui du coeur vient,
Tous ses menbres le sont au foeur,
Cellui qui a paoureux coeur.
31395 Paoureux ne scet nullui aimer,
Ne lui proprement bien garder;
Paoureux ne scet parler ne taire . . .
. . .

Songe t'a esmeü, sans faille;
31470 Soies en paix, et ne t'en chaille.
Preng le temps ainsi qu'il venra,
Qui pour toy quoy ne se tenrra.
Cil est assis en bon degré
Qui trestous anuis prent en gré."
31475   Ainsi Pinte le conforta
Le bien qu'il scet lui ennorta;
"Or adviengne," dist il, "qu'aviengne,
Mais que mal eür ne me tiengne!"
Atant s'en va esbanïer.
31480   Cil qui toudis fait son mestier,
Ne se cesse ne jour ne nuit.
C'est Regnart qui fut en deduit
Soubz ung toit en ung angleçon.
Quant il ouÿ du cocq le son,

he raised himself a little to see if he could have the cock. Chantecler saw him clearly, and his heart leapt at the sight. So he cried out immediately: "Unworthy thief, don't delay. Here, thief, out of this enclosure, or you will be bound and taken at once."

[31493] Renard, who feared bad luck, was hungry and thoroughly beaten, said, "Don't be afraid, for I come to calm you and to tell you good news, and please, call me to your side, because from God I have brought here that by which you will be comforted. I took great pains in order to have it. Nothing else has led me here; I don't want to annoy you in the least, but now may it please you to linger until I have instructed you about peace and love and charity, because as long as Christianity lasts, I will go about preaching the Scripture, as God said at the Ascension: *Predicate Euvangelium!*"[1]

([31511–33181] Here begins Renard's lengthy attempt to persuade Chantecler that he is in fact a preacher. Renard tells the exemplum of the peasant, the ass, and two panniers [31617–723], meant to teach Chantecler not to disdain good counsel. The cock responds with two other exempla, the two blind men of Rome [31787–862], and the two clerics and their lord [31867–32096]. Beyond the general similarity between Chaucer's Chauntecleer and the beast-epic's rooster as tellers of exempla, this section of *Renart le Contrefait* has few points in common with Chaucer's tale. Renard twice mentions Chantecler's father [31557 ff. and 32490 ff.]; while in the later passage the fox says that Chantecler resembles his father, that resemblance is based upon religious bearing, not vocal talent as in the *Nun's Priest's Tale*. A further isolated similarity appears in line 31867, as Chantecler is beginning his second exemplum. He introduces it by saying that the story comes from an "authority," but he does not give that authority's name. ["Je truis en une Auctorite/ Que il advint en verite/ Qu'ung riche homme deux clercz avoit . . ."; ("I find in an Authority that it once truly happened that a rich man had two clerics . . .")]

In *Renart le Contrefait* Renard tricks Chantecler into closing his eyes by telling him that if he lays his head on the ground, he will be able to see hell; however, because the light from heaven is too bright to allow him a view of such a dim place, the cock must close the eye pointing skyward. Renard tells the story of Lot's wife to teach Chantecler that he must not look where God has forbidden [33019–180].)

[33181] Chantecler put his head on the ground, like one who intends to look for hell. The Author who has written this book agrees strongly with this fact: whoever seeks evil, evil finds; he who wants hell gets it. Equally correct is that what you seek, at last you will find – as much evil as good. I hold to this dictum by the Author. And when Renard saw him sitting, he said to him, "Do you see nothing?"

"No," said he, "other than the clouds."

[33194] "Oh, friend," said he, "you are killing yourself. I'm telling you in short, you will become like Lot's wife – I can't protect you any longer from that. Chantecler, I don't know how to lie. If you do not close [your eye] right away, you will surely die soon." Chantecler was greatly surprised by this,

---

[1] "Preach the Gospel," a phrase from Mark 16:15.

31485 Ung peu se lieve pour sçavoir
　　　Se il porroit le cocq avoir.
　　　Chantecler l'a bien perceü,
　　　Le coeur en ot tout esmeü.
　　　Adont s'escria tout esrant:
31490 "Malvais lerres, ne te demant.
　　　Ych, lerres, hors de ce pourpris,
　　　Ou tost seras lÿez et pris!"
　　　Regnart qui mal eür doubtoit,
　　　Fain eut et bien batu estoit,
31495 Dist, "Ne te voeulles esmaier!
　　　Car cy vieng pour toy apaier
　　　Et pour dire bonnes nouvelles,
　　　Et, si te plest, lez toy m'apelles,
　　　Car j'ay de Dieu cy aporté
31500 Dont tu seras reconforté.
　　　J'ay a le avoir mis grant paine
　　　Aultre chose cy ne m'amaine;
　　　Ne te voeulle mie ennuier,
　　　Mais or te plaise a detrïer
31505 Jusques je t'aye recité
　　　Paix et amour et charité,
　　　Car tant que Crestïenté dure,
　　　Je m'en voy preschant l'Escripture,
　　　Com Dieu dit a l'Ascencion:
31510 'Predicate Euvangelium!' "
　　　. . .

　　　Chantecler mist son chief sur terre,
　　　Com cil qui voulloit enffer querre.
　　　L'Acteur qui cestui livre a fait
　　　S'acorde bien a cestui fait
33185 Que qui mal quiert que mal luy viengne;
　　　Qui enffer voeult, qui le retiengne.
　　　A l'acord est ce que querras
　　　Que au derrain le trouveras;
　　　Autant du mal comme du bien.
33190 Ceste raison de l'Acteur tien.
　　　Et quant Regnart le vit seant,
　　　Si lui a dit, "Vois tu neant?"
　　　"Nennil," dist il, "fors que les nues."
　　　"O amis," dist il, "tu te tues.
33195 Je le te dy a ung court mot,
　　　Tu devenras la femme Loth,
　　　Je ne t'en puis plus garantir.
　　　Chantecler, je ne sçay mentir.
　　　Se ne le clos appertement,
33200 Tantost morras sceürement."
　　　Chantecler s'en esbahist monlt,

and because of it he closed the eye pointing upward.

When Renard saw that he couldn't see a thing, he dug his teeth into his spine. Then Chantecler shuddered. Renard said, "I haven't failed. My prayer is truly fortuitous; you will see hell without delay." Then he seized him by the neck with his teeth, at which Chantecler became frantic, and he said, "I'm looking for hell now, alas!"

[33212] Chantecler then declared himself unfortunate; he said that no one could traffic with an evil person but that he would come to lament it. Renard had nothing but a heart full of ire, regardless of whatever words Chauntecler knew how to say. He carried the cock off happily; now he no longer went along complaining. With great leaps he left the garden, and as soon as he could he got himself to the countryside; but the hens were greatly frightened when they saw Renard and Chantecler. Quickly they took to howling.

[33224] Then Chantecler could not stay silent: "Renard, you who have such a happy heart, give them and the people who are coming after you a good howl in return, because it seems to them that they already have you; the hens have roused them, they are foolish and stupid. Now tell them that you will return as soon as you will have eaten me."

[33233] Renard was full of such great joy that there was not a bit of this that he examined. Because of this joy, without delay he began to howl loudly, and said, "I will come back by here; I will have all of these hens."

[33239] As the Author has told it to us – and what he says is true – too much joy makes a man go mad so that he knows neither how to protect himself nor to conduct himself. In great joy he has less security than he has in great poverty. Through too much joy a man wrongs himself, because he does not know what he says and what he does. An overly joyous man sees nothing, knows neither whom he loves nor whom he fears, nor knows whether someone is telling him evil or good.

Et pour ce clot il l'oeul amont.
Quant Regnart voit qu'il ne voit goute,
Les dens en l'eschine lui boute.
33205 Adonc Chantecler tressailli.
Dist Regnart: "Je n'ay pas failli.
Mon orison est bien eurée.
Enffer verras sans demourée."
Lors l'aert aulx dens par le col
33210 Dont Chantecler se tint pour fol,
Et dit, "Enffer querois, or las!"
Chantecler lors se claime las;
Dist nul ne poeut malvais hanter
Que il n'en viengne au gramenter.
33215 Regnart n'ot mais le coeur plain d'ire,
Quelque parole que sceust dire;
Le Cocq emporte lyement;
Or ne s'en va mais complaignant.
Par les grans saultz du jardin ist;
33220 Plus tost que pot au plain se mist;
Mais les gelines monlt s'effroient,
Quant Regnart et Chantecler voient;
Trestoutes se prindrent a braire.
Lors ne se pot Chantecler taire:
33225 "Regnart, qui tant as le coeur gay,
Encor leur fay ung bel abay
Et aulx gens qui aprez toy viennent,
Car leur semble ja qu'ilz te tiennent;
Gelines les ont esmeüs;
33230 Ilz sont sotz et despourveüs:
Or leur dis que tu revenras
Si tost que tu mengié m'aras."
Regnart fu plain de si grant joye
Qu'il n'est nule goute qu'il voye.
33235 Pour ce de joye sans delayer
Commença fort a abbayer,
Et dist, "Par cy je revenray;
Toutes ces gelines aray."
L'Acteur si le nous a descript,
33240 Et il est bien voir qu'il le dit,
Trop joye fait l'homs foloyer
Ne se scet garder n'avoyer;
En grant joye a moins sceureté
Que il n'a en grant povreté.
33245 Par trop grant joye homs se meffait,
Qu'il ne scet qu'il dit ne qu'il fait.
Homs trop joieulx si ne voit goute,
Ne scet qu'il ayme ne qu'il doubte,
Ne scet s'on lui dit mal ou bien.

[33250] To Lord Renard it appeared good there, because his joy was due to his prey, so that he felt unaware of either vale or road. At these peasants he howled, and for his great joy he cried to them, "Peasants, peasants, I will come back here; I will have all of your hens!"

[33257] When the cock felt the mouth open, he beat his wings and fell out. Now he was no longer in evil bonds, and he said, "Good is the experienced person who practises so that by thinking and by speaking he can free himself from evil hands. Hell I have looked for, hell I have found, and then I tricked hell."

[33265] And quickly and without delay, the dogs began to bark; they went their way after Renard, who had a lot of unhappiness in his heart. When he heard the dogs coming, he wanted to keep running hard, but he could never flee from them so well that the dogs did not reach him. They tore his pelt to pieces – no word that he said did him any good, complaining or shouting or crying. They drove him along without slowing down, so that from several spots the blood leapt from him. Renard escaped with a leap, for they didn't succeed in their pursuit, but they knew very well how to abuse him.

IV

Robert Holkot, *On the Wisdom of Salomon*

(A) Lectio 103

Two Arcadian friends making a journey together came to Megara; one went to stay with a friend, the other lodged at an inn. He who was a guest saw in dreams his comrade . . . praying him to help him; for by running to him quickly he might free him from imminent danger. Awakened by the sight, the dreamer leaped up and undertook to go to the inn in which his friend was lodged. Then through disastrous fate he condemned his friend's most human proposal as needless and again sought bed and sleep. Then the same man, appearing to him wounded, implored him – even though he had neglected to

33250 A dampt Regnart y parut bien,
Car sa joye fu de sa proye
Que il ne sent ne val ne voye.
Pour ces les vilains abbaya
Et par trop grant joye leur crya:
33255 "Vilain, vilain, ça je venray;
Toutes vos gelines aray."
Quant le Coq sent que la bouce oeuvre
Les aelles bat, si se dechoivre.
Or n'est il mais en maulx lÿens,
33260 Et dit, "Bon est praticïens
Que par penser et par diter
Se poeut de males mains jetter.
Enffer ay quis, enffer ay eu
Et puis enffer ay deceü."
33265 Et tantost et sans delayer,
Les chiens prindrent a abbayer;
Aprez Regnart le cours en vont
Qui au coeur avoit meschief monlt.
Quant il oÿt les chiens venir,
33270 A bien fuÿr se vault tenir;
Mais oncquez si bien n'y fuÿ
Que chiens ne l'ayent consieuÿ,
Si lui despecherent la plice;
Ne lui vault parole qu'il dice,
33275 Plaindre ne braire ne crïer.
Si le mainent sans detrïer
Qu'en pluseurs lieux le sang lui sault.
Regnart eschappa par ung sault,
Pour ce que point de sieute n'eurent,
33280 Mais trop bien lapider le sceurent.

IV

Robert Holkot, *Super Sapientiam Salomonis*

(Oxford, Balliol College MS 27, ed. and trans. R. A. Pratt *Speculum* 52
[1977]: 549, 556–7)

(A) Lectio 103 (fol. 157va, lines 13–37)

Duo familiares Archades iter una facientes Megaram venerunt. Quorum alter
se ad hospitem contulit, alter in tabernam meritoriam divertit. Is qui in
hospicio erat vidit in sompnis comitem suum orantem ut sibi cauponis insidiis
circumvento opem ferret; posse enim celeri eius accursu se inminenti periculo
liberari. Quo viso excitatus prosiliit tabernamque in qua is diversabatur petere
conatus est. Pestifero deinde fato eius humanissimum propositum tamquam
supervacuum dampnavit et lectum ac sompnum repetiit. Tunc idem ei saucius
oblatus obsecravit ut etsi vite sue auxilium ferre necglexisset neci saltem

save the man's life – that at least he would not deny vengeance for his murder; for his body, slaughtered by the innkeeper, was being carried, covered with dung, in a very large cart to the gate. Moved by the so steadfast entreaties of his comrade, he immediately ran to the gate, seized the cart which had been mentioned to him in his sleep, and brought the inkeeper to capital punishment.

(B) Lectio 202

Fourth, dreams originate in us sometimes from good spirits . . . and such appears to be the dream of Simonides, of whom Valerius tells in 1 [.7]: Simonides, when he brought his ship to shore and found a body lying unburied and comitted it to burial, being warned by it through a dream not to sail the next day, remained ashore. Those who had set sail from that place were sunk by waves and storms within his sight. He was joyful that he had preferred to entrust his life to a dream rather than to a ship. . . ."

ulcionem non negaret. Corpus enim suum a caupone trucidatum cum maximo plaustro ferri ad portam stercore coopertum. Tam constantibus familiaris precibus compulsus protinus ad portam cucurrit et plaustrum quod in quiete demonstratum erat comprehendit. Cauponemque ad capitale supplicium produxit.

(B) Lectio 202 (fol. 299va, lines 22–39)

Quarto, originantur non numquam in nobis sompnia a spiritibus bonis . . . et tale videtur sompnium Simonidis de quo narrat Valerius libro 1, capitulo 5: Simonides cum ad litus navem appulisset inhumatumque corpus iacens repperisset et illud sepulture mandasset, admonitus ab eo per sompnium ne proximo die navigaret in terra remansit. Qui inde solverant fluctibus et procellis in eius conspectu obruti sunt. Ipse letatus est quod vitam suam sompnio quam navi credere maluisset.

The Second Nun's Prologue and Tale

SHERRY L. REAMES

With regard to the sources of the Prologue, the basic research was all done before 1920. Most obvious and first to be recognized was the indebtedness of the "Invocacio ad Mariam," or at least three stanzas of it (lines 36–56), to the prayer to the Virgin spoken by St. Bernard in Dante's *Paradiso*, canto XXXIII.[1] In 1891 Ferdinand Holthausen identified the Marian antiphon "Salve Regina" as the main source behind the next stanza and a half (lines 57–66, and perhaps 68).[2] In 1911 Carleton Brown filled in most of the remaining gaps when he reviewed the evidence for the Prologue's direct dependence on these and several other possible sources.[3] Brown admitted two additional texts to the list of actual sources, pointing out the clear echoes from the opening of Fortunatus'

---

[1] This discovery was made so early that F. J. Furnivall referred to it in the 1880s as knowledge that had become part of the common domain (*Originals and Analogues of Some of Chaucer's Canterbury Tales*, ed. Furnivall et al., Chaucer Society Publications, 2nd ser., nos. 7, 10, 15, 20, and 22 [London, 1872–87], p. 191).

[2] "Zu Chaucers Cäcilien-Legende," *Archiv für das Studium der neueren Sprachen und Literaturen* 87 (1891): 265.

[3] "The Prologue of Chaucer's 'Lyf of Seint Cecile,' " *Modern Philology* 9 (1911–12): 1–16.

hymn "Quem Terra" in Chaucer's lines 43–7 and the somewhat more tenuous parallels between Chaucer's lines 68–70 and a passage in *Paradiso* XXXII. Brown plausibly contended, however, that some images and phrases in the "Invocacio" were simply drawn from the common currency of medieval hymns to the Virgin, and he also concluded that Chaucer was drawing on a long tradition, rather than imitating any particular source, when he opened the Prologue with a discussion of idleness.[4]

In 1915 Frederick Tupper provided a useful addendum to Brown's article when he pointed out that Chaucer could have found both the "Salve Regina" and the "Quem Terra" in the Hours (or Little Office) of the Virgin Mary, a liturgical office that was made widely accessible to members of the laity through its inclusion both in Latin Books of Hours and in the Middle English *Prymer* or *Lay Folks' Prayer Book*.[5] Two years later John Livingston Lowes proposed several additional sources for the Prologue, most notably a passage in praise of the Virgin in Alan de Lille's *Anticlaudianus*, which contains parallels to several of Chaucer's small additions to Dante in lines 37–8, 42, and 56, and a passage in Macrobius's commentary on the *Somnium Scipionis* which contains parallels to Chaucer's language in lines 71–4 about the plight of the human soul as imprisoned, troubled by the contagion of the body, and weighted down by earthly lusts.[6] Unfortunately for Lowes' argument, however, the parallels he cites were all commonplaces either in the hymn tradition, as Brown had suggested, or in late-medieval religious culture more generally.[7]

G. H. Gerould included Macrobius and Alan among the sources for the Prologue when he compiled his chapter for Bryan and Dempster, but his wording suggests a certain skepticism about their pertinence,[8] and I believe

---

[4] Chaucerians long repeated the hypothesis that Chaucer had derived at least the general idea of these stanzas from the prologue to Jean de Vignay's French translation of the *Legenda aurea*; but the likelihood of this debt melted away a century ago, when it was established that Chaucer based the tale that follows on the Latin text of the *Legenda* rather than on Jean's version.

    The only source Brown found worth quoting for this part of the prologue was a distich attributed to Cato: "Plus vigila semper, ne somno deditus esto./ Nam diuturna quies vitiis alimenta ministrat" [Be very sure to stay alert and not sleep all the time, for too much rest supplies the nourishment for vices] (Lib. I, no. 2). Richard Hazleton links the prologue's opening stanza more specifically and helpfully with the glossula tradition on Cato; see "Chaucer and Cato," *Speculum* 35 (1960): 365–7.

[5] "Chaucer's Bed's Head," *Modern Language Notes* 30 (1915): 9–11. This information solves a real problem because the "Salve Regina," which became popular relatively late in the Middle Ages, was not ordinarily included in breviaries alongside the "Quem Terra" and other Marian hymns.

    Brown's response to Tupper, a few months later, included the text of a Middle English translation of the "Salve Regina" that parallels the wording in Chaucer's prologue even more closely than does the translation Tupper had found in Littlehales' edition of the *Prymer*. See "Chaucer and the Hours of the Blessed Virgin," *Modern Language Notes* 30 (Nov. 1915): 231.

[6] "The Second Nun's Prologue, Alanus, and Macrobius," *Modern Philology* 15 (1917–18): 193–202.

[7] Thus, for example, a later scholar explains that Alan's passage on the Virgin borrows from the Canticle of Canticles, Old Testament Book of Wisdom, a standard litany of the Blessed Virgin, and the famous Marian hymn "Ave Maris Stella," again by Fortunatus. See James J. Sheridan, trans. and commentary on *Anticlaudianus, or The Good and Perfect Man*, by Alan of Lille (Toronto, 1973), p. 153n.

[8] For example, he introduces the excerpts from Macrobius with the following cautious wording: "Similarly there may be in the *Invocacio* (lines 71–4) echoes, directly or indirectly received, of the following passages" (p. 666).

there is no justification for reprinting these texts in the present chapter. With regard to the other sources for the Prologue, I have updated the material in Bryan and Dempster only by using a better edition of Dante, supplying translations of all the texts, and adding a reference to a seminal article by Erich Auerbach on Dante's prayer to the Virgin and the rich Latin traditions that inform both it and Chaucer's "Invocacio ad Mariam."[9]

Although little has been added to our knowledge of the *Second Nun's Prologue* since the time of Bryan and Dempster, the picture has changed rather enormously with regard to her Tale. The Tale's genre, the saint's legend, has received a great deal of serious attention in the past thirty years from historians and literary scholars alike; there is room here to cite only a few outstanding examples of the new ways of looking at medieval saints and the ways in which they were represented.[10] In addition, several studies have appeared which shed valuable light on the particular Latin saint's legend from which Chaucer's tale derives, the *Passio S. Caeciliae*. Hippolyte Delehaye has established beyond much doubt that the *Passio* must have been composed between about 486 and 545, that much of its plot was borrowed from a story in Victor of Vita's *History of the Persecution of the Vandals* and some of Cecilia's speeches from other well-known sources, and that it contains just a few vestiges of historical truth – some names of martyrs, some places in Rome, and the likelihood that the basilica of S. Cecilia in Trastevere was founded on property donated by a historical person named Cecilia.[11] More recently, Thomas H. Connolly has exhaustively studied the legend's development from its origins to the Renaissance, illuminating many more aspects of its symbolism and iconography than his explicit focus on Cecilia and music might suggest.[12]

Much has also been learned in the past few decades about the multiplicity of abridged forms in which saints' legends circulated in the later Middle Ages and the variety of purposes, both religious and socio-political, that were served by

---

[9] "Dante's Prayer to the Virgin (Paradiso, XXXIII) and Earlier Eulogies," *Romance Philology* 3 (1949–50): 1–26. Some of this material has become familiar to Chaucerians through Paul M. Clogan's "Figural Style and Meaning of the Second Nun's Prologue and Tale," *Medievalia et Humanistica*, n.s. 3 (1972): 213–40, which borrows extensively from Auerbach's article but unfortunately fails to cite it.

[10] Two fine and pertinent examples of recent work in the field are Karen A. Winstead, *Virgin Martyrs: Legends of Sainthood in Late Medieval England* (Ithaca, NY, 1997) and the interdisciplinary collection entitled *Interpreting Cultural Symbols: Saint Anne in Late Medieval Society*, ed. Kathleen Ashley and Pamela Sheingorn (Athens, Georgia, 1990). More purely historical, but essential for anyone studying the cult of the saints in the later Middle Ages, is André Vauchez's massive study, *La sainteté en Occident aux derniers siècles du Moyen Age, d'après les procès de canonisation et les documents hagiographiques* (Rome, 1981), now available in English as *Sainthood in the Later Middle Ages*, trans. Jean Birrell (Cambridge, Engl., 1997). Also essential is *Saints and Their Cults: Studies in Religious Sociology, Folklore and History*, ed. Stephen Wilson (Cambridge, Engl., 1983), which includes a number of excellent essays and the best annotated bibliography published to date.

[11] *Étude sur le légendier romain: les saints de Novembre et de Décembre* (Brussels, 1936), pp. 73–96. Although this book was published before Bryan and Dempster, Gerould seems to have been unaware of it when he prepared his chapter on the *Second Nun's Tale*.

[12] Especially informative are his two-part article, "The Legend of St. Cecilia: I, The Origins of the Cult," *Studi musicali* 7 (1978): 3–37, and "The Legend of St. Cecilia: II, Music and the Symbols of Virginity," *Studi musicali* 9 (1980): 3–44, and his book, *Mourning into Joy: Music, Raphael, and Saint Cecilia* (New Haven, 1994).

some of these forms. It now seems clear that Chaucer based his retelling of the Cecilia legend on two different Latin abridgements of the *Passio S. Caeciliae*. The first of these, which Chaucer closely followed for the etymology of Cecilia's name and approximately the first half of the narrative (lines 85–348), and may have consulted occasionally thereafter,[13] comes from the *Legenda aurea* of the Dominican friar Jacobus de Voragine. This famous collection, surviving in hundreds of manuscripts and dozens of early printed editions, was evidently designed for the use of Dominican and other preachers and has a marked predilection for certain kinds of material rather than others.[14] As is typical of this work, the *Legenda* account of St. Cecilia plays up the element of conflict in the legend, drastically cutting the scenes in which converts are instructed but retaining a substantial amount of confrontational dialogue from Cecilia's trial and even more from the debate between the persecutor and Cecilia's principal converts, Valerian and Tiburce. The *Legenda* account also makes a number of subtler alterations in the legend; among these are increasing the role of Pope Urban, making the saints a bit more intrepid and impervious to pain, and having Cecilia give her property to the poor, as the mendicants would have recommended, instead of dividing it among her own followers.

The second abridgement, from which Chaucer derived almost everything from line 349 to the end of the tale, has been studied relatively little thus far.[15] It was not even recognized as a Chaucerian source until the 1980s because it is just a liturgical version, ordinarily copied and circulated specifically for use in the liturgy at Matins on St. Cecilia's feast day, and has neither a known author nor a distinctive *incipit*.[16] More surprisingly, this anonymous liturgical text is not found in the surviving breviaries of Sarum or any other British rite, which

---

[13] I refer in particular to Chaucer's lines 398 (the beheading of Tiburce and Valerian), 410–13 (Almachius's first summons to Cecilia), 437 (her first response to his boast about his power), and 521 (the claim that she "felede no wo" in the bath that is supposed to kill her).

[14] On the selectivity with which Jacobus abridged his sources, see especially Sherry L. Reames, *The Legenda aurea: A Reexamination of Its Paradoxical History* (Madison, Wisconsin, 1985). Alain Boureau studies the work from a more purely literary-critical perspective in *La Légende dorée: Le système narratif de Jacques de Voragine (†1298)* (Paris, 1984). More than twenty other scholars, many of them studying the vernacular translations and adaptations of Jacobus's work, described their projects in *Legenda aurea: Sept siècles de diffusion*, ed. Brenda Dunn-Lardeau, Actes du Colloque International sur la *Legenda aurea*, texte latin et branches vernaculaires, Cahiers d'études médiévales, Cahier spécial 2 (Montreal and Paris, 1986). Two major recent studies not signaled in that collection are Giovanni Paolo Maggioni, *Ricerche sulla composizione e sulla trasmissione della "Legenda aurea"* (Spoleto, 1995) and Reglinde Rhein, *Die Legenda aurea des Jacobus de Voragine: Die Entfaltung von Heiligkeit in "Historia" und "Doctrina"* (Cologne, 1995).

[15] I give detailed comparisons, demonstrating the closeness of the relationship between this source and Chaucer's tale, in the first ten pages of "A Recent Discovery concerning the Sources of Chaucer's 'Second Nun's Tale,' " *Modern Philology* 87 (1989–90): 337–61 (cited below as "A Recent Discovery"). This article supersedes my earlier study of the tale's relationship with the Latin versions of the *Passio* in "The Sources of Chaucer's 'Second Nun's Tale,' " *Modern Philology* 76 (1978–79): 111–35.

[16] Recensions of saints' legends in liturgical manuscripts have received virtually no attention from modern scholars because they fall into the grey area between liturgy and hagiography. In fact, the Bollandists' great indexes and catalogs of hagiographical texts have nearly always excluded liturgical manuscripts, and few liturgical scholars have taken an interest in the non-Biblical lessons that were read at Matins.

one would think most likely to have been familiar to Chaucer.[17] So far, in fact, it has turned up exclusively in breviaries and office lectionaries written for the Vatican, the Franciscans, or other communities that followed their lead in adopting the "use of the Roman curia" [*consuetudinem curie romane*]. Since the majority of the identifiable manuscripts seem to be Franciscan, I originally called it the Franciscan abridgement; but a more adequate designation would be "Roman curia/ Franciscan."

Unlike the *Legenda aurea* version of the Cecilia legend, the Roman curia/ Franciscan version does not look like an abridgement at the start. In fact, it follows the *Passio S. Caeciliae* quite faithfully for the initial episodes in the legend, omitting nothing except the prologue until it reaches the long, didactic scene in which Cecilia instructs Tiburce and persuades him to accept baptism. From this point to the beginning of Cecilia's trial, the Roman curia/ Franciscan version abridges the narrative more drastically than the *Legenda* does, retaining just a few details from the *Passio* to supplement its own brief summaries of the intervening events – Tiburce's conversion, the arrest and trial of the two brothers, their conversion of Maximus, his vision, and Cecilia's conversion of Almachius's officers.[18] For Cecilia's trial itself, on the other hand, this version retains a larger proportion of the original dialogue than the *Legenda* does and seems to have made its selections by a different set of criteria. And for the remainder of the legend, including Cecilia's execution, burial, and final legacies, this version returns to its original pattern, reproducing the readings of the *Passio* verbatim, or nearly so.

The conclusion that Chaucer actually worked from two separate abridgements of the *Passio*, faithfully translating first one and then the other, is based on probabilities rather than certainties, of course, but the probabilities are very strong. There is no doubt about his use of the *Legenda aurea* abridgement, for its distinctive opening sentence and its two unique additions, the etymological account of Cecilia's name and the excerpt from the Ambrosian liturgy, are all reproduced in the first half of his tale. And the second half of his tale so closely reproduces the distinctive features of the Roman curia/ Franciscan abridgement – including many lines which the *Legenda* omits and some rewriting of the *Passio* that does not occur in any other version – as to defy any explanation other than direct dependence. One can never entirely rule out the possibility that Chaucer worked from a lost Latin source in which these two abridgements had already been combined. However, I can say with some confidence that this possibility is remote. Since the time of Bryan and Dempster there have been at least

---

17 In this context, the abridged versions of the Cecilia legend in British breviaries are noteworthy because their characteristic emphases differ quite significantly from those of both the abridgements that Chaucer chose to use for the *Second Nun's Tale*. For specifics see Sherry L. Reames, "*Mouvance* and Interpretation in Late-Medieval Latin: The Legend of St. Cecilia in British Breviaries," in *Medieval Literature: Texts and Interpretation*, ed. Tim W. Machan (Binghamton, NY, 1991), pp. 159–89.

18 However, the Roman curia/ Franciscan version preserves a fuller narrative than the *Legenda* does at a few points – most notably, Tiburce's baptism and Cecilia's exhortation to the brothers before their martyrdom.

two comprehensive attempts to identify all the extant manuscripts of the *Legenda aurea*.[19] I have personally examined the chapter on Cecilia in more than 225 of them, including all the known copies in British libraries and most of those in France, and have found far less textual variation among them than Gerould supposed there might be (pp. 669–70). Omissions are common, but rewriting is rare and substantive additions from other sources are practically nonexistent.[20]

When one looks closely at the text of the *Second Nun's Tale*, one finds additional support for the hypothesis that Chaucer himself joined the two sources together instead of finding the combination ready-made. There is a change in versification and style which coincides almost exactly with the change from one source to the other. In the part of the tale based on the *Legenda*, Chaucer treats each rime royal stanza as a separate unit, often resorting in the final lines to conspicuous repetitions and other fillers so that the beginning of the next speech or event can be deferred to the next stanza.[21] As he begins the transition to the second source in lines 342–4, however, he starts to let the narrative run freely from one stanza to the next and immediately reduces his use of fillers. From this point on, he handles the rime royal stanza with noticeably more fluency, efficiency, and effectiveness than he did from the beginning of the tale through line 341. This sudden leap in mastery of the stanza form suggests that the second half of the tale must have been written a good deal later than the first half – i.e., that it either completes a work originally left unfinished or replaces the original ending with a revised version. In either case, the implication is that Chaucer came back to this part of the tale with a new source and a new sense of purpose.

Since all the differences between the *Legenda aurea* and Roman curia/ Franciscan abridgements of the legend are potentially important for understanding the implications of Chaucer's decisions to begin with one and then switch to the other, both of these texts are reproduced and translated below in their entirety. For the *Legenda* I have selected a copy text from the group of English manuscripts that comes closest to approximating the readings Chaucer gives in the tale. The readings within this group vary so little that my chosen copy text – Cambridge, Trinity College MS B.15.1 – could easily be replaced by eight or ten other manuscripts, including British Library MSS Stowe 49 and Harley 3657; Bodleian Library MSS Barlow 12, Can. Misc. 142, and Lyell 13; Westminster Abbey MS 12; Winchester College MS 9; and Worcester Cathedral MS F.45. But all the manuscripts in this group are at least slightly preferable to

---

[19] See Thomas Kaeppeli, *Scriptores Ordinis Praedicatorum medii aevi*, vol. 2 (Rome, 1975), pp. 350–9, and Barbara Fleith, *Studien zur Überlieferungsgeschichte der lateinischen Legenda aurea* (Brussels, 1991), a much more ambitious study of the *Legenda*'s textual tradition which attempts to categorize the manuscripts and list their contents.

[20] Among all the copies of the *Legenda* I have examined, only Glasgow University Library MS Gen. 1111 – a deluxe illuminated manuscript that was apparently produced in 15th-century Flanders – makes any significant additions to the usual text of the chapter on Cecilia. Unlike the combination of sources in Chaucer's tale, the additions here occur throughout the narrative and evidently come from the *Passio* itself.

[21] See e.g. lines 175, 210, 222–4, 245, 265–6, 270–3, 293–4, and 306–8.

Bodleian Library MS Bodley 336, a manuscript with some eccentric readings which Gerould used as his copy text in Bryan and Dempster. The other manuscripts listed below were chosen for my corpus of variants because they have one or more unusual readings that might conceivably have been present in Chaucer's source.

B	Oxford, Bodleian Library MS Bodley 336 (used by Gerould) – early 14th c., Canterbury
C1	Cambridge University Library MS Dd.4.26 – ca. 1400
C2	Cambridge University Library MS Gg.2.18 – 14th c., Norwich
C3	Cambridge University Library MS Add. 6452 – mid 14th c., German
D	Durham Cathedral MS B.iv.39 – early 14th c.
F	Cambridge, Fitzwilliam Museum MS CFM 11 – 1342, French
H	London, British Library MS Harley 5210 – 15th c., probably Italian
L	Oxford, Bodleian Library MS Laud Misc. 183 – late 14th c., German
P	Cambridge, Peterhouse College MS 132 – 13th or early 14th c., Lincoln diocese
R	Oxford, Bodleian Library MS Rawlinson C.168 – 14th c., probably English
S	Salisbury Cathedral MS 40 – early 14th c., Italian
T1	Cambridge, Trinity College MS B.15.1 – 14th c., Winchester
T2	Cambridge, Trinity College MS O.8.20 – early 14th c., Cambridge
V	Vatican Library MS Ottob. lat. 331 – 14th c., Cambridge

Editing the Roman curia/ Franciscan abridgement of the Cecilia legend is a less formidable task than editing the *Legenda aurea* abridgement because the number of usable manuscripts is much smaller. It was standard practice in the late Middle Ages for copyists of breviaries to give the lessons only in severely truncated form, to save space and expense. Hence, despite the enormous number of surviving breviaries that supposedly follow the lectionary of the Roman curia, in half a dozen years of assiduous searching I have found only five manuscripts that give the complete account of Cecilia that Chaucer translated, and another 35 that include at least one excerpt from the distinctive, abridged part of this text.[22] The earliest manuscript with the complete account, which I have chosen as my copy text, is Paris, Bibliothèque Nationale MS latin 3278. My corpus of variants also includes readings from the other four complete copies, the three manuscripts that seem to be of English provenance (one of them only a small fragment), and eight additional manuscripts with relatively unusual readings that may shed some light on details in Chaucer's version. Unfortunately, large segments of the narrative Chaucer translated are missing from most of the manuscripts. For example, only the five complete copies and the English manuscript from University College, London, give more than a few lines from Cecilia's trial, and many of the manuscripts omit it altogether.

---

[22] I am referring here to the portion of the text after line 118, where the abbreviation and rewriting of the *Passio* begin.

A   Paris, Bibliothèque de l'Arsenal ms. 596 – Franciscan breviary, later 15th c., Paris (complete account)

As   Assisi, Biblioteca Communale MS 694 – Franciscan breviary, ca. 1230–50, Italian

B   Oxford, Bodleian MS Latin liturgies d.3, items 15–16 – fragment from a lectionary, 13th c., English[23]

Ca1   Rome, Biblioteca Casanatense MS 1410 – Franciscan lectionary, 13th/14th c., probably Italian (complete account)

Ca2   Rome, Biblioteca Casanatense MS 457 – local lectionary of saints, 14th c., Benevento

Ch   Chambéry, Bibliothèque Municipale ms. 4 – Franciscan breviary, 1428–47, Italian workmanship for Marie of Savoie

Co   Ithaca, Cornell University Library MS Bd.Rare BX C36 B845 – Franciscan breviary, late 15th c., prob. Netherlands (essentially complete account)[24]

CU   Cambridge University Library MS Add. 7622 – Franciscan breviary, late 13th c., apparently English

M   New York, Pierpont Morgan Library MS M.200 – Franciscan breviary, late 14th c., Italian

N   Paris, Bibliothèque Nationale ms. latin 3278 – Roman lectionary, later 13th c., probably for St. Peter's in the Vatican[25] (complete account)

P   Paris, Palais des Beaux Arts ms. 42 – Franciscan breviary, late 15th c., for René II of Lorraine

U   London, University College MS Latin 6 – part of a Franciscan breviary, 13th c., probably English

V1   Vatican, MS Vat. lat. 14701 – Roman curia breviary, 15th c., Notre-Dame des Doms, Avignon (complete account)

V2   Vatican, MS Regin. lat. 2051 – Franciscan breviary, 13th–14th c., Ascoli Piceno [Italy]

V3   Vatican, MS Urbin. lat. 112 – Roman curia breviary, 1487, written in Florence for Matthew Corvinus, king of Hungary

V4   Vatican, MS Vat. lat. 7692 – Franciscan breviary, 1462, Tuscany

Besides the two main sources on which Chaucer's retelling is based, the chant texts in the liturgical office for St. Cecilia's feast day may have contributed to the way Chaucer and his contemporaries understood certain details in the legend. For example, it is possible that everyone remembered the angel as standing beside Cecilia, a detail from the *Passio* which the *Legenda* had omitted, because the traditional iconography of this scene had been reinforced over and over by use of the responsory which begins, "Ceciliam intra cubiculum

---

[23] The term *lectionary*, as used in this list, refers to a lectionary for the Daily Office – i.e., a book containing only the lessons to be read at Matins. Since lectionaries did not have to make room for all the antiphons, responsories, prayers, and other texts that were used in the daily round of services, they typically (though not always) give fuller versions of the lessons than breviaries do.

[24] This manuscript omits the account of the old man who appears at Valerian's baptism (lines 58 to 71), but it is complete for our purposes because it includes the entire portion of the text that Chaucer translated.

[25] See "A Recent Discovery," pp. 349–50, for further information on this important manuscript and the research that has been done to identify its provenance.

orantem invenit, and juxta eam stantem angelum Domini" ([Valerian] found Cecilia praying in the chamber and standing beside her an angel of the Lord).[26] More surprisingly, there are chant texts which suggest that the mysterious old man in the preceding scene was sometimes interpreted as a second, angelic manifestation of Pope Urban.[27] Although the chant texts in the liturgical office are too minor and tangential a Chaucerian source to merit reprinting in this volume, students seriously interested in Cecilia's cult and legend will want to become familiar with them.

[26] In the Sarum office for Cecilia, from which I quote, this is the seventh responsory at Matins. The same chant text is found, with minor variants and at different points in the service, in most other medieval versions of the office for Cecilia's feast day. Since there is no mention of standing at the corresponding point in the *Legenda*, both Kölbing and Holthausen cite Chaucer's line 219 as a borrowing from the *Passio*.

[27] Even the Sarum version of the office, which retains relatively few of the figurative connections made in the standard version used on the Continent, includes a responsory which reads, "O beata Cecilia, que duos fratres convertisti, Almachium judicem superasti, Urbanum episcopum in vultu angelico demonstrasti" [O blessed Cecilia, who converted two brothers, overcame the judge Almachius, (and) revealed Bishop Urban with the face of an angel]. For a fuller discussion of this issue which includes Continental chant texts referring to the old man, see my recent article, "The Office for St. Cecilia," in *The Liturgy of the Medieval Church*, ed. Thomas Heffernan and E. Ann Matter (Kalamazoo, MI: Medieval Institute Publications, 2001), pp. 246–59.

My research was supported by grants from the American Council of Learned Societies, the American Philosophical Society and the Graduate School Research Committee of the University of Wisconsin, Madison. I am also indebted to Matthew Hogan for help with translations and Robert E. Lewis and Robert M. Correale for editorial suggestions that improved the final draft.

I

Dante's *Paradiso*

(from Dante's *Paradiso*, trans. John D. Sinclair
[Oxford University Press, 1961])

A. "Virgin Mother, daughter of thy Son, lowly and exalted more than any creature, fixed goal of the eternal counsel, thou art she who didst so ennoble human nature that its Maker did not disdain to be made its making. In thy womb was rekindled the love by whose warmth this flower [the Rose of the blessed souls in heaven] has bloomed thus in the eternal peace; here thou art for us the noonday torch of charity, and below among mortals thou art a living spring of hope. Thou, Lady, art so great and so prevailing that whoso would have grace and does not turn to thee, his desire would fly without wings. Thy loving-kindness not only succours him that asks, but many times it freely anticipates the asking; in thee is mercy, in thee pity, in thee great bounty, in thee is joined all goodness that is in any creature. This man [Dante], who from the nethermost pit of the universe to here has seen one by one the lives of the spirits, now begs of thee by thy grace for such power that with his eyes he may rise still higher towards the last salvation; and I, who never burned for my own vision more than I do for his, offer to thee all my prayers, and pray that they come not short, that by thy prayers thou wilt disperse for him every cloud of his mortality so that the supreme joy may be disclosed to him. This too I pray of thee, Queen, who canst do what thou wilt, that thou keep his affections pure after so great a vision. Let thy guardianship control his human impulses. See Beatrice and so many of the blest who clasp their hands for my prayers."

I

Dante's *Paradiso*

(*La Divina Commedia*, ed. and annot. C. H. Grandgent, rev.
Charles S. Singleton [Harvard University Press, 1972])

A. St. Bernard's Prayer, Canto XXXIII, 1–39

"Vergine Madre, figlia del tuo figlio,
umile e alta più che creatura,
termine fisso d'etterno consiglio,
   tu se' colei che l'umana natura
5 nobilitasti sì, che 'l suo fattore
non disdegnò di farsi sua fattura.
   Nel ventre tuo si raccese l'amore,
per lo cui caldo ne l'etterna pace
così è germinato questo fiore.
10   Qui se' a noi meridïana face
di caritate, e giuso, intra' mortali,
se' di speranza fontana vivace.
   Donna, se' tanto grande e tanto vali,
che qual vuol grazia e a te non ricorre,
15 sua disïanza vuol volar sanz' ali.
   La tua benignità non pur soccorre
a chi domanda, ma molte fïate
liberamente al dimandar precorre.
   In te misericordia, in te pietate,
20 in te magnificenza, in te s'aduna
quantunque in creatura è di bontate.
   Or questi, che da l'infima lacuna
de l'universo infin qui ha vedute
le vite spiritali ad una ad una,
25 supplica a te, per grazia, di virtute
tanto, che possa con li occhi levarsi
più alto verso l'ultima salute.
   E io, che mai per mio veder non arsi
più ch'i' fo per lo suo, tutti miei prieghi
30 ti porgo, e priego che non sieno scarsi,
   perchè tu ogne nube li disleghi
di sua mortalità co' prieghi tuoi,
sì che 'l sommo piacer li si dispieghi.
   Ancor ti priego, Regina, che puoi
35 ciò che tu vuoli, che conservi sani,
dopo tanto veder, li affetti suoi.
   Vinca tua guardia i movimenti umani:
vedi Beatrice con quanti beati
per li miei prieghi ti chiudon le mani!"

B. "Opposite Peter see Anna sitting, so well content to gaze on her daughter that she does not move her eyes while singing hosanna."

II

"Quem Terra"

(from *The Prymer, or Lay Folks' Prayer Book*, ed. Henry Littlehales, EETS os 105 [London, 1895], p. 2)

The cloistre of Marie beriþ him
whom þe erþe, watris and hevenes
worschipen, louten, and prechen,
þe which governeþ þe þre maner schap of þe world.

III

"Salve Regina"

(from *Mateyns of Our Lady* in Bodleian MS Ashmole 1288, as printed by Carleton Brown in *Modern Language Notes* 30 [1915]: 231)

Heil, qweene, modir of merci,
Heil, liif, swetnesse and oure hope.
To þee we crien, outlawid sones of Eve,
To þe we siȝen, weymentynge and wepinge in þis valey of teeris.
5   Hiȝe þou þerfore, oure advocat,
Turne to us þou þi merciful iȝen,
And shewe þou to us Jhesu, þe blessid fruyt of þi wombe, after þis exilyng.

B. from Bernard's account of the saints in the Rose, Canto XXXII, 133–5

Di contr' a Pietro vedi sedere Anna,
tanta contenta di mirar sua figlia,
che non move occhio per cantare osanna.

II

Opening of Fortunatus' hymn "Quem Terra"

(from Mone, *Lat. Hymn. des Mittelalt.*, II, 128)

Quem terra, pontus, aethera
colunt, adorant, praedicant,
trinam regentem machinam,
claustrum Mariae bajulat.

III

"Salve Regina"

(from Daniel, *Thesaurus hymnologicus* [1855–6], II, 321)

Salve regina, mater misericordiae,
  Vita, dulcedo et spes nostra, salve.
  Ad te clamamus exules filii Hevae,
Ad te suspiramus gementes et flentes in hac lacrimarum valle.
5   Eia ergo advocata nostra,
  Illos tuos misericordes oculos ad nos converte,
Et Jesum benedictum fructum ventris tui nobis post hoc exilium ostende.
    O clemens, o pia, o dulcis virgo Maria.

---

8   This final line was often omitted in medieval versions of the antiphon, but Littlehales found it in
    Cambridge University Library MS Dd.11.82, the early 15th-century manuscript of the *Primer* on
    which he based his edition: "O þou deboner, O þou meke, O þou swete maide marie, hail!" (*Prymer
    or Lay Folks' Prayer Book*, EETS os 105 [London, 1895], p. 34).

IV

Golden Legend

[Etymology of her name] "Cecilia" is derived from *celi lilia*, "lily of heaven," or from *cecis via*, "a path for the blind," or from *celum*, "heaven," and "Leah." Or "Cecilia" means *cecitate carens*, "lacking blindness," or is derived from *celum*, "heaven," and *leos*, which means "people." She was indeed a heavenly lily through the modesty of virginity, or she is called a lily because she had the white color of purity, the fresh green strength of conscience, and the fragrance of good reputation. She was also a path for the blind through the guidance of her example, a heaven through her perpetual contemplation, "Leah" through her tireless activity. Or she is called a heaven because, as Isidore explains, the philosophers said that heaven is revolving, round, and burning. And she likewise was revolving in diligent activity, round in perseverance, and burning in fiery charity. She lacked blindness because of the brightness of her wisdom, and she was a heaven of the people because in her, as in a spiritual heaven, the people gaze for inspiration at the heaven, the sun and moon and stars – that is, at the brightness of her wisdom, the magnanimity of her faith, and the diversity of her virtues.

[About Saint Cecilia] The illustrious virgin Cecilia, who came from a noble Roman lineage and was nourished from the cradle in the Christian faith, always carried the gospel of Christ hidden in her breast. She was always occupied with divine conversations and prayer, both by day and by night, and entreated God to preserve her virginity. When she was betrothed to a young man named Valerian and the wedding date was set, she wore a hair shirt next to her flesh, beneath her clothes of gold. And while the musical instruments played, she sang in her heart to God alone, saying, "O Lord, keep my heart and my body undefiled, lest I be overcome." And she fasted for two or three days at a time, always praying, and entrusted to God what she feared.

The night came when she had to confront the secret silence of the bedroom, alone with her husband, and this is what she said to him: "O dearest and most loving young man, I have a secret to tell you if you will swear to do everything in your power to keep it hidden." After Valerian swore not to reveal it under any circumstances or for any consideration, she said, "I have an angel of God as my lover, who guards my body with extreme jealousy. If he should see any indication that you touch me with unclean love, he will kill you on the spot, and you will lose the best part of your wonderful youth. But if he knows that your love for me is pure, he will love you just as he loves me and will show you his glory."

---

9   **Fuit** *om* T1 *and many other mss.*
11   *second* **celum** *om* B C2 C3 *and many other mss; add marg* C1.
15   **exorta** exhorta, *with* h *canc* T1.
23   **Domino quod** se Domino quem C2; se *add between lines* B C1.
24   **cubiculi** cubili C1 C3 S T2; cubili *corr to* cubiculi B P.
25   **alloquitur** *corr from* aloquitur T1.

IV

Legenda aurea

(from Cambridge, Trinity College MS B.15.1, 14th century)

(fol. 319v) DE ETHIMOLOGIA NOMINIS. Cecilia quasi celi lilia vel cecis via vel a celo et Lia. Vel Cecilia quasi cecitate carens, vel dicitur a celo et leos, quod est populus. Fuit enim celeste lilium per virginitatis pudorem. Vel dicitur lilium quia habuit candorem mundicie, virorem consciencie, odorem
5   bone fame. Fuit etiam cecis via per exempli informacionem, celum per jugem contemplacionem, Lia per assiduam operacionem. Vel dicitur celum quia, sicut dicit Ysidorus, celum philosophi volubile, rotundum, et ardens esse dixerunt. Sic ipsa fuit volubilis per operacionem solicitam, rotunda per perseveranciam, ardens per caritatem succensam. Fuit cecitate carens per
10 sapiencie splendorem. Fuit etiam celum populi quia in ipsam tanquam in celum spirituale populus ad imitandum intuetur celum, solem et lunam et stellas, id est sapiencie perspicacitatem, fidei magnanimitatem, et virtutum varietatem.
     DE SANCTA CECILIA. Cecilia virgo clarissima ex nobili Romanorum
15 genere exorta, et ab ipsis cunabulis in fide Christi nutrita, absconditum semper evangelium Christi gerebat in pectore et non diebus neque noctibus a colloquiis divinis et oracione cessabat, suamque virginitatem conservari a Domino exorabat. Cum autem cuidam juveni, nomine Valeriano, desponsata fuisset et dies nuptiarum instituta esset, illa subtus ad carnem cilicio erat
20 induta et desuper deauratis vestibus tegebatur. Et cantantibus organis, illa in corde suo soli Domino decantabat, dicens, "Fiat, Domine, cor meum et corpus meum immaculatum, ut non confundar." Et biduanis ac triduanis jejuniis orans commendabat Domino quod timebat.
     Venit autem nox in qua suscepit una cum sponso suo cubiculi secreta
25 silencia, et ita eum alloquitur, "O dulcissime atque amantissime juvenis, est (fol. 320) misterium quod tibi confitear si modo tu juratus asseras tota te illud observancia custodire." Jurat Valerianus se illud nulla necessitate detegere, nulla prodere racione. Tunc illa ait, "Angelum Dei habeo amatorem, qui nimio zelo custodit corpus meum. Hic si vel leviter senserit quod tu me
30 polluto amore contingas, statim feriet te, et amittes florem tue gratissime juventutis. Si autem cognoverit quod me sincero amore diligas, ita quoque diliget te sicut et me, et ostendet tibi gloriam suam."

---

4   The noun *viror* means "greenness" in the literal sense but in post-classical Latin also "youthful liveliness, freshness, vigor."

6   In the most general sense, *operacio* means "devotion of effort to a task," but in Christian authors refers more specifically to meritorious or charitable acts. Leah, the older sister of Rachel and first, less beloved wife of Jacob (Genesis 29:16 et seq.), was associated in medieval commentaries with the Active Life; Rachel, with the Contemplative.

Then, chastised by the will of God, Valerian said, "If you want me to believe you, show me this angel; and if I determine that he is truly an angel, then I will do as you say. But if you love another man, I will run you both through with my sword."

Cecilia answered, "If you will believe in the true God and permit yourself to be baptized, you will have the power to see him. Therefore, go to the third milepost from the city on the road called the Appian Way, and say this to the destitute people whom you will find there: 'Cecilia has sent me to you so that you will show me the holy old man Urban, since I have secret messages to give him.' Once you have found him, tell him everything I have said, and when you have been purified by him and return, you will see the angel."

Then Valerian went out and, following the directions he had been given, found the holy bishop Urban hiding among the martyrs' tombs. And when he had told him all of Cecilia's words, Urban raised his hands toward heaven with tears and said, "Lord Jesus Christ, sower of chaste purposes, receive the fruit of the seeds which you sowed in Cecilia. Lord Jesus Christ, good shepherd, your handmaid Cecilia zealously serves you like an ingenious bee. For her spouse, whom she received as a fierce lion, she has sent to you as a very gentle lamb."

And lo, suddenly there appeared an old man dressed in snow-white garments, holding a book written with golden letters. Seeing him, Valerian was so afraid that he fell down as if dead; but when the old man lifted him up, he read these words, "One Lord, one faith, one baptism, one God and Father of all, who is above all and through all and in us all."

When Valerian had read this, the old man asked him, "Do you believe this to be true, or do you still have doubts?"

Then Valerian cried out, "There is nothing under the sky that can more truly be believed."

At once the old man vanished. Then Valerian received baptism from Saint Urban, and on his return found Cecilia in their bedroom, talking with the angel. The angel had two crowns in his hands, made of roses and lilies, and he gave one to Cecilia and the other to Valerian, saying, "Preserve these crowns with a pure heart and a clean body, for I have brought them to you from God's Paradise. They will never wither or lose their fragrance, nor will they be visible except to those who value chastity. As for you, Valerian, since you have trusted good advice, ask whatever you wish."

Valerian answered, "Nothing in this life has been dearer to me than the unparalleled affection of my brother. Therefore I ask that he may know the truth along with me."

The angel replied, "Your request pleases the Lord, and you both will come to Him with the palm [or glory] of martyrdom."

When Tiburce, Valerian's brother, came in after this, he smelled the great fragrance of the roses and said, "I wonder where this fragrance of roses and lilies is

33   **correctus** corectus T1; correptus B C1 C2 D L; correctus *corr to* correptus P.
37   **miliarium** miliare F L.
41   **et redieris** *om* S; et credideris L; rediens B.
47   **apis** apes T1 C2.
61   **ad vos** *om* B.
63   **volueris** *add* et impetrabis C2; *add* ut accipies D; *add* et optinebis R.

Tunc Valerianus nutu Dei cor[r]ectus ait, "Si vis ut credam tibi, ipsum angelum mihi ostende; et si vere probavero quod angelus sit, faciam quod
35 hortaris. Si autem virum alium diligis, te et illum gladio feriam."

Cui Cecilia dixit, "Si in Deum verum credideris et baptizari te permiseris, ipsum videre valebis. Vade igitur in tercium miliarium ab urbe, via que Appia nuncupatur, et pauperibus quos illic invenies dices, 'Cecilia me misit ad vos, ut ostendatis mihi sanctum senem Urbanum, quoniam ad ipsum habeo secreta
40 mandata que perferam.' Hunc dum tu videris, indica ei omnia verba mea, et postquam ab eo purificatus fueris et redieris, ipsum angelum videbis."

Tunc Valerianus perrexit, et secundum signa que acceperat, sanctum Urbanum episcopum intra sepulcra martirum latitantem invenit. Cumque ei omnia verba Cecilie dixisset, ille manus ad celum expandens cum lacrimis ait,
45 "Domine Jhesu Christe, seminator casti consilii, suscipe seminum fructus quos in Cecilia seminasti. Domine Jhesu Christe, pastor bone, Cecilia famula tua quasi ap[i]s tibi argumentosa deservit. Nam sponsum, quem quasi leonem ferocem accepit, ad te quasi agnum mansuetissimum destinavit."

Et ecce subito apparuit senex quidam niveis vestibus indutus, tenens librum
50 aureis litteris scriptum. Quem videns Valerianus pre nimio timore quasi mortuus cecidit, et a sene levatus sic legit, "Unus dominus, una fides, unum baptisma; unus deus et pater omnium, qui super omnes et per omnia et in omnibus nobis."

Cumque hoc legisset, dixit ei senior, "Credis ita esse an adhuc dubitas?"
55 Tunc ille exclamavit dicens, "Non est aliud quod verius credi possit sub celo."

Statimque illo disparente, Valerianus a sancto Urbano baptisma suscepit, et rediens Ceciliam cum angelo loquentem in cubiculo invenit. Angelus autem duas coronas ex rosis et liliis in manu habebat, et unam Cecilie et alteram
60 Valeriano tradidit, dicens, "Istas coronas immaculato corde et mundo corpore custodite, quia de paradyso Dei eas ad vos attuli; nec unquam marcescent, nec odorem amittent, nec ab aliis nisi quibus castitas placuerit videri poterunt. Tu autem, Valeriane, quia utili consilio credidisti, pete quodcumque volueris."

Cui Valerianus, "Nichil mihi in hac vita extitit dulcius quam unicus fratris
65 mei affectus. Peto igitur ut et ipse mecum veritatem agnoscat."

Cui angelus, "Placet Domino peticio tua, et ambo cum palma martirii ad Dominum venietis."

Post hec ingressus Tyburcius, frater Valeriani, cum nimium rosarum sensisset odorem dixit, "Miror, hoc tempore, roseus hic odor et liliorum unde

47 Most medieval Latin dictionaries define *argumentosa* in relation to *argumentum* – hence, "capable in argument," "well-stocked with material," "ingenious," "persuasive," "eloquent." Discussing the significance of the combination *apis argumentosa* as applied to Cecilia, Thomas H. Connolly points out the bee's traditional associations with virginity (because it was believed to reproduce asexually), the bringing of light (because it produced the wax for candles), and prophecy, wisdom, and eloquence (because honey was thought to be related to manna, the "food of angels" provided by God); see part I of Connolly's long article, *Studi musicali* 7 (1978), esp. note 48.

49–53 Modern commentators have generally assumed that the mysterious old man is St. Paul, since the quotation comes from one of his epistles (Ephesians 4:5–6). However, some of the chant texts in the medieval office for Cecilia raise the possibility of a more figurative reading which links him with Cecilia's angelic visitors and even takes him as a manifestation of Urban's own kinship with angels. See above p. 499, note 27.

coming from, at this time. Even if I were holding those roses or lilies in my hands, their perfumes could not fill me with such sweetness. I confess to you, I am so refreshed that I think I have suddenly been changed altogether."

Valerian said to him, "We have crowns which your eyes are powerless to see, blooming with rosy color and snowy whiteness. And just as you have perceived their fragrance through my intercession, so you will be able to see them if you will believe."

Tiburce answered, "Am I hearing this in dreams or are you actually saying these things, Valerian?"

Valerian said, "We have been in dreams until now, but now indeed we abide in reality."

Tiburce asked him, "Where did you learn this?"

Valerian said, "An angel of God taught me, whom you will not be able to see unless you are purified and repudiate all idols."

Ambrose confirms this miracle concerning the crowns of roses in his preface, saying this: "Saint Cecilia was so filled with the heavenly gift that she claimed the palm of martyrdom. She scorned this world, together with the marriage chamber. One proof is the confession called forth from Valerian, her husband, and Tiburce, whom you crowned with sweet-smelling flowers, Lord, by the hand of an angel. The virgin led the men to glory; the world recognized how powerful devotion to chastity is." Thus Ambrose.

Then Cecilia clearly showed him that all idols are incapable of sensation and speech, so that Tiburce answered and said, "Anyone who doesn't believe this is a beast."

Then Cecilia kissed his breast and said, "Today I take you as my kinsman; for just as the love of God made your brother my spouse, so your repudiation of idols will make you a member of my family. Go with your brother, then, so that you may receive purification and become able to see the faces of angels."

Tiburce said to his brother, "Brother, I beseech you to tell me to whom you are going to take me."

Valerian said, "To the bishop Urban."

Tiburce responded, "Do you mean that Urban who has so often been condemned and now remains in hiding? If he were found, he would be burned, and we too would be enveloped in those flames. Thus while we seek a divinity hidden in the heavens, we will bring on ourselves the consuming rage of fire on earth."

Cecilia answered him, "If only this life existed, justly would we fear to lose it. However, there is another, better life that is never lost, which the Son of God described to us. The Son, begotten of the Father, is the creator of all things that have been made, and all things made have been endowed with life by the Spirit, proceed-

---

70   **respirat** respiret D H L S. **poterant** poterunt B; possent D F.
72   **totum** *om* B R; *add marg* P.
74   **roseo** floreo B C2 C3 *and many other mss*; flore D; floreo colore roseo C1. **niveo** nivio T1; nimio R.
81   **non** *om* B C1 C2 *and most other mss*. **nisi** si B C1 C2 *and most other mss*.
85   **talamis** calamis T1 L; thalamis C2 C3 T2; thalamus R.
89   **omnia** *om* B D; *add marg* C1. **insensibilia** surda V.
90   **credit** *corr from* credidit T1. **pecus** *corr from* cecus T1; cecus D T2.
94   **angelicos vultus** angelos B.
102 **juste hanc** *add* solam B C1 C2 F.

70   respirat. Nam si ipsas rosas vel lilia in manibus meis tenerem, nec sic poterant odoramenta tante mihi suavitatis infundere. Confiteor vobis, ita sum refectus ut putem me totum subito immutatum."

    Cui Valerianus, "Coronas habemus, quas tui oculi videre non prevalent, roseo colore et niv[e]o candore vernantes. Et sicut me interpellante odorem

75   sensisti, sic et, si credideris, videre valebis."

    Cui Tyburcius, "In sompnis hoc audio an in veritate ista tu loqueris, Valeriane?"

    Cui Valerianus, "In sompnis usque modo fuimus, sed jam nunc in veritate manemus."

80   Ad quem Tyburcius, "Unde hoc nosti?"

    Cui Valerianus, "Angelus Dei me docuit, quem tu videre non poteris nisi purificatus fueris, et omnibus ydolis abrenunciaveris."

    Huic miraculo de coronis rosarum Ambrosius attestatur in prefacione, sic dicens, "Sancta Cecilia sic celesti est dono repleta ut martirii palmam

85   assumeret. Ipsum mundum est cum [t]alamis (fol. 320v) execrata. Testis est Valeriani conjugis et Tyburcii provocata confessio, quos, Domine, angelica manu odoriferis floribus coronasti. Viros virgo duxit ad gloriam; mundus agnovit quantum valeat devocio castitatis." Hec Ambrosius.

    Tunc Cecilia evidenter ostendit ei omnia ydola esse insensibilia et muta, ita

90   ut Tyburcius responderet ac diceret, "Qui ita non credit pecus est."

    Tunc Cecilia osculans pectus eius dixit, "Hodie te fateor meum esse cognatum. Sicut enim amor Dei fratrem tuum mihi conjugem fecit, ita te mihi cognatum contemptus faciet ydolorum. Vade igitur cum fratre tuo ut purificacionem recipias et angelicos vultus videre valeas."

95   Dixitque Tyburcius fratri suo, "Obsecro te, frater, ut mihi dicas ad quem me ducturus es."

    Cui Valerianus, "Ad Urbanum episcopum."

    Cui Tiburcius, "De illo Urbano dicis qui tociens dampnatus est et adhuc in latebris commoratur? Hic si inventus fuerit cremabitur, et nos in illius

100   flammis pariter involvemur. Et dum querimus divinitatem latentem in celis, incurremus furorem exurentem in terris."

    Cui Cecilia, "Si hec sola esset vita, juste hanc perdere timeremus. Est autem alia melior, que nunquam amittitur, quam nobis Dei filius enarravit. Omnia enim, que facta sunt, filius ex patre genitus condidit; universa autem,

---

83   The "preface" in question is the preface to the mass for St. Cecilia's feast day (Nov. 22) in the liturgy of Milan, which was named after Ambrose. Millett Henshaw quotes the full text in "The Preface of St. Ambrose and Chaucer's 'Second Nun's Tale,'" *Modern Philology* 26 (1928): 15–16.

88   The phrase *devocio castitatis* has a wide range of possible translations, since *devocio* can mean an offering to God, devotion or devoutness more generally, obedience, loyalty, or affection, and the genitive *castitatis* can be either the possessor or the object of this devotion. Florence Ridley discusses a few of the possibilities in her notes to Chaucer's line 283 (*The Riverside Chaucer*, p. 945).

ing from the Father. Therefore, this Son of God, coming into the world, showed us by His words and wondrous deeds that there is another life."

Tiburce said, "Surely you claim that there is one God; why do you now say there are three?"

Cecilia answered, "Just as there are three things in the one wisdom of a human being – namely invention, memory, and understanding – so there can be three persons in one essence of divinity." Then she began to preach to him about the advent and passion of the Son of God, and to point out many correspondences of His passion. "For," she said, "the Son of God was bound so that the human race might be freed from the bonds of sin. The blessed one was cursed so that cursed humanity might obtain blessing. He allowed Himself to be mocked so that humanity might be freed from the mockery of demons. He received a crown of thorns on His head so that He might remove the death sentence from our heads. He accepted bitter gall so that He might restore humanity's sweet taste. He was stripped so that He might cover the nakedness of our parents. He was hanged from a tree so that He might take away the collusion of the [earlier] tree."

Then Tiburce said to his brother, "Have mercy on me and lead me to the man of God so that I may receive purification."

After he had been taken and baptized, he often saw angels of God, and he immediately obtained everything he requested.

Thus Valerian and Tiburce occupied themselves with works of mercy and buried the bodies of saints whom Almachius the prefect had killed. Summoning them to him, Almachius demanded to know why they were burying people who had been executed for their crimes.

Tiburcius replied, "If only we were the servants of those whom you call criminals! They despised what seems to be and is not, and found what seems not to be and is."

The prefect asked, "Whatever is that?"

Tiburce replied, "What seems to be, and is not, is all that exists in this world, which leads human beings to nothingness. And what seems not to be, and is, is the life of the just and the punishment of the wicked."

The prefect said, "I do not think you are talking rationally." Then he ordered Valerian to step forward, saying to him, "Since your brother is not of sound mind, you at least will be able to give a sensible answer. It is certain that you are seriously mistaken, you who despise pleasures and aspire to everything injurious to happiness."

Then Valerian said that he had seen idle men in the winter joking and ridiculing hard-working farmers; but in the summer, when the splendid fruits of their labors arrived, those who had been thought foolish were rejoicing, while those who had seemed clever began to weep. "Similarly, now indeed we endure dishonor and hardship, but in the future we will receive glory and an eternal reward. You, on the other hand, who now enjoy transitory pleasures, in the future will have eternal death."

---

110   **divinitatis** deitatis B C3 L.
113   **tentus** peremptus B; temptus H.
137   **tempore** tempori T1.

105 que condita sunt, ex patre procedens spiritus animavit. Hic igitur filius Dei in
mundum veniens verbis et miraculis aliam vitam esse nobis monstravit."

Cui Tyburcius, "Certe unum Deum esse asseris, et quomodo nunc tres esse
testaris?"

Respondit Cecilia, "Sicut in una hominis sapientia sunt tria, scilicet
110 ingenium, memoria, et intellectus, sic et in una divinitatis essencia tres
persone esse possunt." Tunc cepit ei de adventu filii Dei et passione predicare,
et multas congruitates ipsius passionis ostendere. "Nam ideo," inquit, "filius
Dei est tentus, ut genus humanum dimittatur peccato detentum. Benedictus
maledicitur, ut homo maledictus benedictionem consequatur. Illudi se patitur,
115 ut homo ab illusione demonum liberetur. Spineam coronam accepit in capite,
ut a nobis sentenciam auferat capitalem. Fel suscepit amarum, ut sanaret
hominis dulcem gustum. Expoliatur, ut parentum nostrorum nuditatem
operiat. In ligno suspenditur, ut ligni prevaricacionem tollat."

Tunc Tyburcius fratri suo dixit, "Miserere mei et perduc me ad hominem
120 Dei ut purificacionem accipiam."

Ductus igitur et purificatus, angelos Dei sepe videbat, et omnia que
postulabat protinus optinebat.

Valerianus igitur et Tyburcius elemosinis insistebant et sanctorum corpora
quos Almachius prefectus occidebat sepulture tradebant. Quos Almachius ad
125 se vocans, cur pro suis sceleribus dampnatos sepeliebant, inquisivit.

Cui Tyburcius, "Utinam illorum servi essemus quos tu dampnatos appellas!
Qui contempserunt quod videtur esse et non est, et invenerunt hoc quod non
videtur esse et est."

Cui prefectus, "Quid nam est illud?"

130 Et Tyburcius, "Quod videtur esse et non est, est omne quod in hoc mundo
est, quod hominem ad non esse perducit. Quod vero non videtur esse et est, est
vita justorum et pena malorum."

Cui prefectus, "Non puto quod mente tua loquaris." Tunc jubet astare
Valerianum, dicens ei, "Quoniam non est sani capitis frater tuus, tu saltem
135 poteris sapienter responsum dare. Constat plurimum vos errare, qui gaudia
respuitis et omnia inimica gaudiis affectatis."

Tunc Valerianus se vidisse ait glaciali tempor[e] ociosos jocantes et
operarios agricolas deridentes, sed estivo tempore, dum advenissent gloriosi
fructus laborum, gaudentibus illis qui putabantur vani, ceperunt flere qui
140 videbantur urbani. Sic et nos nunc quidem sustinemus ignominiam et
laborem. In futuro autem recipiemus gloriam et eternam mercedem. Vos
autem qui nunc transitorium habetis gaudium, in futuro autem eternum
invenietis interitum."

The prefect asked, "Are you saying that we who are the most powerful princes will have eternal sorrow while you, the most worthless persons, will possess perpetual joy?"

Valerian replied, "You are little men, not princes, born in your own time, destined quickly to die and to render an account to God more than all others."

But the ruler said, "Why do we waste time in a roundabout course of words? Offer libations to the gods and depart unharmed."

The saints replied, "We offer sacrifices every day to the true God."

The prefect asked, "What is His name?"

Valerian replied, "You will not be able to find out His name even if you fly with wings."

The prefect asked, "Then the name of God is not Jupiter?"

Valerian said, "That is the name of a murderer and a defiler."

Almachius said to him, "Therefore the whole world is wrong, while you and your brother know the true God?"

Valerian replied, "We are not alone, but an innumerable multitude accepts this holy way of life."

Then the saints were handed over into the custody of Maximus, who said to them, "O bright flower of youth, o genuine affection of brotherhood, why do you hasten toward death as if going to a feast?"

Valerian told him that if he would promise to believe, he would see the glory of their souls after death.

And Maximus replied, "May I be consumed by burning thunderbolts if I do not acknowledge the one you worship to be the only God, if what you say happens."

Therefore, this Maximus and his whole household and all the executioners believed and received baptism from Saint Urban, who came there secretly. And when dawn brought the end, Cecilia cried out, saying, "Come on, soldiers of Christ, cast away the works of darkness and put on the armor of light."

Then the saints were led four miles from the city, to the statue of Jove, and when they refused to sacrifice they were beheaded together. Then Maximus claimed with sworn oaths that in the hour of their passion he had seen shining angels and the martyrs' souls, departing like virgins from the marriage chamber, being carried to heaven in the bosoms of the angels. When Almachius heard that Maximus had become a Christian, he had him beaten so long with leaded whips that he drove out his spirit. Saint Cecilia buried his body next to Valerian and Tiburce.

Then Almachius began to investigate the resources of both brothers and had Cecilia, as the wife of Valerian, appear before him, ordering that she should either sacrifice to the idols or receive the sentence of death. When she was subjected to pressure on this account by the officers [Almachius's subordinates], they wept bitterly because such a beautiful young woman, and noble besides, was delivering herself to death. But she said to them, "Good young men, this is not to lose one's youth but to change it, to give up mud and receive gold, to give up a poor little dwelling and receive a precious one, to give up a small corner and receive a bright open space. Wouldn't you hasten quickly if someone were giving gold coins for a penny? When God receives a simple sum, he repays it a hundredfold. Do you believe what I am saying?"

---

169 **aurora** *add* nocti L.
170 **induamini** induimini B C2 C3 *and most other mss.*

Cui prefectus, "Ergo nos invictissimi principes eternum habebimus luctum,
145 et vos persone vilissime perpetuum possidebitis gaudium?"

Cui Valerianus, "Homunciones estis, non principes, tempore vestro nati,
cicius morituri et Deo racionem plus omnibus reddituri."

(fol. 321) Dixit autem preses, "Quid verborum circuitu immoramur?
Offerte diis libamina et illesi abscedite."

150 Sancti responderunt, "Nos Deo vero cotidie sacrificia exhibemus."

Quibus prefectus, "Quod est nomen eius?"

Cui Valerianus, "Nomen eius invenire non poteris etiam si pennis
volaveris."

Prefectus dixit, "Jubiter ergo nomen Dei non est?"

155 Cui Valerianus, "Nomen est homicide et stupratoris."

Ad quem Almachius, "Ergo totus mundus errat et tu cum fratre tuo Deum
verum nosti?"

Valerianus respondit: "Nos soli non sumus, sed innumerabilis multitudo
hanc sanctitatem recipit."

160 Traduntur igitur sancti in custodia Maximi. Quibus ille ait, "O juventutis
flos purpureus, o germanus fraternitatis affectus, quomodo ad mortem quasi
ad epulas festinatis?"

Cui Valerianus ait, quod si crediturum se promitteret, gloriam animarum
eorum post mortem videret.

165 Et Maximus, "Fulminibus igneis consumar si non illum solum Deum
confitear, quem adoratis, si contingat quod dicitis."

Ipse igitur Maximus et omnis ejus familia et universi carnifices crediderunt
et a sancto Urbano, qui illuc occulte venit, baptisma susceperunt. Igitur dum
aurora finem daret, Cecilia exclamavit dicens, "Eya milites Christi, abicite
170 opera tenebrarum et induamini armis lucis."

Quarto igitur miliario ab urbe sancti ad statuam Jovis ducuntur, et dum
sacrificare nollent, pariter decollantur. Tunc Maximus cum juramento asseruit
se in hora passionis eorum angelos vidisse fulgentes, et animas eorum quasi
virgines de thalamo exeuntes, quas in gremio suo in celum angeli detulerunt.

175 Almachius vero, audiens Maximum Christianum effectum, eum plumbatis
tam diu cedi fecit quousque spiritum excussit. Cujus corpus sancta Cecilia
juxta Valerianum et Tyburcium sepelivit.

Tunc Almachius amborum facultates cepit inquirere, et Ceciliam tanquam
Valeriani conjugem coram se fecit astare, jussitque ut ydolis immolaret, aut
180 sentenciam mortis acciperet. Cum autem ad hoc ab apparitoribus urgeretur, et
illi vehementer flerent eo quod puella tam decora et nobilis ultro se morti
traderet, dixit ad eos, "Hoc, boni juvenes, non est juventutem perdere sed
mutare, dare lutum et accipere aurum, dare vile habitaculum et accipere
preciosum, dare brevem angulum et accipere forum perlucidum. Si quis pro
185 nummo solidos daret, nonne velocius festinaretis? Deus autem quod acceperit
simplum reddet centuplum. Creditis hiis que dico?"

169–70 Cecilia's exhortation echoes the words of St. Paul in Romans 13:12. On the symbolism that
may be present here, see the note to lines 134–7 of the Roman curia/ Franciscan abridgement.

And they answered, "We believe Christ is the true God, since He has such a hand-maid." Then Bishop Urban was called, and over 400 people were baptized.

Then Almachius, summoning Saint Cecilia before him, asked, "What is your condition?"

And she answered, "I am free-born and noble."

Almachius said, "I am asking you about religion."

And Cecilia said, "Your questioning begins foolishly, since it tries to elicit two answers with one question."

Almachius asked, "What is the source of such an impertinent answer?"

Then she said, "A good conscience and genuine faith."

Almachius asked, "Don't you know how powerful I am?"

And she said, "Your power is like a bag full of wind. If pricked by a needle, all its firmness gives way at once, and its appearance of solidity collapses."

Almachius said, "You began with harmful statements, and with harmful statements you continue."

Cecilia replied, "Statements cannot be called harmful unless they are untrue. Therefore, either show the harm, if I have spoken falsely, or blame yourself for bringing a dishonest accusation. But we who know the holy name of God cannot deny it at all. For it is better to die blessedly than to live miserably."

Almachius asked, "Why do you speak with such pride?"

And she said, "It is not pride but constancy."

Almachius said, "Miserable one, don't you know that the power of giving life and death has been entrusted to me?"

And she said, "I [will] show that you are now lying against manifest truth. You have the power to take life away from the living, but you have no power to give life to the dead. Therefore you are an agent of death, not of life."

Almachius said, "Now put aside your folly and sacrifice to the gods."

Cecilia replied, "I do not know where you lost your eyes; for what you say are gods we all see to be mere stones. Reach out your hand, then, and learn by touching what your eyes cannot see."

Then Almachius, full of anger, ordered her to be brought back to her house, and he ordered that she be burned there for a whole night and day in a boiling bath. But she remained as if in a cold place, and did not feel even a little sweat. When Almachius heard that, he ordered her to be beheaded in the bath. The executioner struck her on the neck with three blows, but still was not able to cut off her head; and since there was a law that a person being beheaded should not receive a fourth stroke, the blood-thirsty executioner left her there half-dead.

She survived, however, for three days, during which time she gave all her possessions to the poor. She entrusted to Bishop Urban all those whom she had converted to the faith, saying, "I asked for a respite of three days so that I might entrust these people to your Blessedness and so that you might consecrate this house of mine as a church."

192   **sumit** sumpsit C3 H.
193   **putat** putas B.
198   **pallescit** *corr to* follescit B; tabescit C1.
210   **dare** *add* vitam B C1 C2 F.
221   **seminecem** semivivam B C1 C2 F R T2.
225   **inducias** *add* a Domino C1 C3 L.

Et illi, "Credimus Christum verum esse Deum, qui talem possidet famulam." Vocato igitur Urbano episcopo, cccc et amplius baptizati sunt.

Tunc Almachius sanctam Ceciliam ad se vocans ait, "Cujus condicionis es?"

190 Et illa, "Ingenua sum et nobilis."

Cui Almachius, "Ego te de religione interrogo."

Et Cecilia, "Interrogacio tua stultum sumit inicium, que duas responsiones una putat inquisicione concludi."

Cui Almachius, "Unde tibi tanta presumpcio respondendi?"

195 At illa, "De consciencia bona et fide non ficta."

Cui Almachius, "Ignoras cujus potestatis sum?"

Et illa, "Potestas vestra est quasi uter vento repletus, quem si acus pupugerit omnis protinus rigor pallescit, et quicquid in se rigidum habere cernitur incurvatur."

200 Cui Almachius, "Ab injuriis cepisti et in injuriis perseveras."

Cecilia respondit: "Injuria non dicitur nisi quod verbis fallentibus irrogatur. Unde aut injuriam doce si falsa locuta sum, aut te ipsum corripe, calumpniam inferentem. Sed nos scientes sanctum Dei nomen omnino negare non possumus. Melius est feliciter mori quam infeliciter vivere."

205 Cui Almachius, "Ut quid cum tanta superbia loqueris?"

Et illa, "Non est superbia sed constancia."

Almachius dixit, "Infelix, ignoras quia vivificandi et mortificandi est tradita potestas mihi?"

Et illa, "Contra veritatem publicam probo te nunc esse mentitum, vitam

210 enim viventibus tollere potes, mortuis (fol. 321v) autem dare non potes. Es igitur minister mortis, non vite."

Cui Almachius, "Jam depone amenciam et sacrifica diis."

Cui Cecilia, "Nescio ubi oculos amiseris. Nam quos tu deos dicis, omnes nos saxa esse videmus. Mitte igitur manum et tangendo disce quod oculis non

215 vales videre."

Tunc iratus Almachius jussit eam ad domum suam reduci, ibique tota nocte et die jussit eam in bulliente balneo concremari. Que quasi in loco frigido mansit, nec modicum saltem sudoris persensit. Quod cum audisset Almachius, jussit eam in ipso balneo decollari. Quam spiculator tribus ictibus in collo

220 percussit, sed tamen caput ejus amputare non potuit. Et quia decretum erat ne quartam percussionem decollandus acciperet, eam seminecem cruentus carnifex dereliquit.

Per triduum autem supervivens, omnia que habebat pauperibus tradidit, et omnes quos ad fidem converterat Urbano episcopo commendavit, dicens,

225 "Triduanas mihi inducias postulavi, ut hos tue beatitudini commendarem, et hanc domum meam in ecclesiam consecrares."

---

225 *Tue Beatitudini* was an honorary title used in addressing a bishop.

Then Saint Urban buried her body among the bishops and consecrated her house as a church, as she had requested. She suffered her martyrdom around the year of our Lord 225, in the time of the Emperor Alexander. Elsewhere, however, it is recorded that she died in the time of Marcus Aurelius, who ruled around the year of our Lord 220.

V

On the feast of St. Cecilia

The illustrious virgin Cecilia always carried the gospel of Christ hidden in her breast and was constantly occupied with divine conversation and prayer, both by day and by night. She had a fiancé, a young man named Valerian; and when this young man importunately urged his suit, out of desire for the virgin, the wedding date was set. Beneath her garments woven of gold, however, Cecilia wore a hair shirt next to her flesh. The resolve of her family and fiancé was raging around her with such force that she could not reveal the desire of her heart or disclose by clear indications that she loved only Christ.

Why prolong the story? The day came when the wedding chamber was prepared. And while the musical instruments played, she sang in her heart to God alone, saying, "O Lord, keep my heart and my body undefiled, lest I be overcome." And she fasted for two or three days at a time, always praying, and entrusted to God what she feared. She summoned the angels with prayers, disturbed the apostles with tears, and prevailed upon the entire holy procession serving Christ, that with their prayers they would help her commend her chastity to the Lord.

After these things had been done, however, the night came when she had to confront the secret silence of the bed, alone with her husband, and this is what she said to him: "O dearest and most loving young man, I have a secret to tell you if you will swear to do everything in your power to keep it hidden." Valerian swore not to reveal it for any consideration or under any circumstances. Then she said, "I have an angel of God as my lover, who guards my body with extreme jealousy. If he should see any indication that you touch me with unclean love, he will immediately release his rage against you, and you will lose the best part of your wonderful youth. But if he knows that your love for me is pure and spotless and that you keep my virginity completely unimpaired, then he will love you just as he loves me and will show you his favor."

By the will of God Valerian was seized with fear, and he said, "If you want me to believe your words, show me this angel; and if I determine that he is truly an angel of God, then I will do as you say. But if you love another man, I will run you both through with my sword."

16   **nox** *written over erasure and followed by* nox *canc* N.

Sanctus autem Urbanus corpus ejus inter episcopos sepelivit, et domum
suam in ecclesiam, ut rogaverat, consecravit. Passa est autem circa annos
Domini cc xxv, tempore Alexandri imperatoris. Alibi tamen legitur quod
230 passa sit tempore Marcii Aurelii, qui imperavit circa annos Domini cc xx.

V

In festo Sancte Cecilie virginis et martyris

(from Paris, Bibl. Nationale, ms. latin 3278, later 13th century)

(fol. 300) Lectio i. Cecilia virgo clarissima absconditum semper
evangelium Christi gerebat in pectore suo, et non diebus neque noctibus a
colloquiis divinis et oratione cessabat. Hec Valerianum quendam juvenem
habebat sponsum. Qui juvenis in amorem virginis perurgens animum, diem
5 constituit nuptiarum. Cecilia vero subtus a carne cilicio induta erat, desuper
auro textis vestibus tegebatur. Parentum enim tanta vis et sponsi circa illam
erat exestuans, ut non posset amorem sui cordis ostendere, et quod solum
Christum diligeret indiciis evidentibus aperire.

Quid multa? Venit dies in qua thalamus collocatus est. Et cantantibus
10 organis, illa in corde suo soli Domino decantabat, dicens, "Fiat cor meum et
corpus meum immaculatum, ut non confundar." Et biduanis ac triduanis
jejuniis orans, commendabat Domino quod timebat. Invitabat angelos
precibus, lacrimis interpellabat apostolos, et sancta agmina omnia Christo
famulantia exorabat, ut suis eam deprecationibus adjuvarent suam Domino
15 pudicitiam commendantem.

Lectio ii. Set cum hec agerentur, venit nox in qua suscepit una cum sponso
suo secreta cubilis silentia, et sic eum alloquitur, "O dulcissime atque
amantissime juvenis, est secretum quod tibi confitear, si modo tu juratus
asseras tota te illud observantia custodire." Jurat Valerianus sponsus se illud
20 nulla ratione, nulla necessitate detegere. Tunc illa ait, "Angelum Dei habeo
amatorem, qui nimio zelo custodit corpus meum. Hic si vel leviter senserit
quod tu me polluto amore contingas, statim contra te suum furorem exagitabit,
et amittes florem tue (fol. 300v) gratissime juventutis. Si autem cognoverit
quod me sincero et immaculato amore diligas et virginitatem meam integram
25 illibatamque custodias, ita te quoque diliget sicut et me, et ostendet tibi
gratiam suam."

Tunc Valerianus nutu Dei timore correptus ait, "Si vis ut credam
sermonibus tuis, ostende michi ipsum angelum. Et si probavero quod vere
angelus Dei sit, faciam quod hortaris. Si virum autem alium diligis, te et illum
30 gladio feriam."

228–30 These dates vary somewhat in the manuscripts, and the second one is frequently omitted.

Cecilia answered, "If you promise to follow my advice, permit yourself to be purified in the unfailing wellspring, and believe there is one God in heaven, living and true, then you will be able to see him."

Valerian asked, "Who will be able to purify me so that I can see the angel?"

Cecilia answered, "There is an old man who knows how to purify people so that they deserve to see an angel."

Valerian asked her, "And where should I look for this old man?"

Cecilia answered, "Go to the third milepost from the city on the road called the Appian Way. There you will find some destitute people begging passers-by for assistance. These are people I have always tried to look after, and they are well aware of my secret. When you see them, give them my blessing and say, 'Cecilia has sent me to you so that you will show me the holy old man Urban, since I have secret messages to give him from her.' Once you have found him, tell him everything I have said. When he has purified you, he will clothe you in new, white garments. As soon as you return to this chamber, wearing those garments, you will see the holy angel, who will also love you, and you will receive everything you ask from him."

Then Valerian went out and, following the directions he had been given, found the holy bishop Urban, who had already been made a confessor twice, hiding among the martyrs' tombs. And when he had told him all of Cecilia's words, Urban rejoiced greatly. Kneeling on the ground, he raised his hands toward heaven and said with tears, "Lord Jesus Christ, good shepherd, sower of chaste purposes, receive the fruit of the seeds which you sowed in Cecilia. Lord Jesus Christ, good shepherd, your handmaid Cecilia zealously serves you like an ingenious bee. For her spouse, whom she received as a fierce lion, she has sent to you as a very gentle lamb. This man would not have come here if he did not believe. Therefore, Lord, open the gate of his heart to your words, that he may recognize you as his Creator and renounce the devil with all his vainglorious displays and idols."

When Saint Urban had said these and some further prayers, suddenly before their faces appeared an old man dressed in snow-white garments, holding in his hands an inscription written with golden letters. Seeing him, Valerian was seized with great fear and fell to the ground, where he lay as if dead. Then the old man lifted him up, saying, "Read and believe the words of this document, so that you may deserve to be purified and to see the face of the angel as the most faithful virgin Cecilia promised you."

Then Valerian, paying close attention, began to read to himself. This is what the inscription said: "One God, one faith, one baptism; one God and Father of all, who is above all and in us all."

When Valerian had read this to himself, the old man asked him, "Do you believe this to be true, or do you still have doubts?"

Then Valerian cried out in a loud voice, "There is nothing under the sky that can more truly be believed."

55   **huc** hic *apparently canc* N.

Lectio iii. Tunc beata Cecilia dixit ei, "Si consiliis meis promittis te acquiescere, et permittas te purificari fonte perhempni, et credas unum deum esse in celis vivum et verum, poteris illum videre."

Dicit ei Valerianus, "Et quis erit qui me purificet, ut ego angelum videam?"

35   Respondit Cecilia ei, "Est senior qui novit purificare homines ut mereantur videre angelum."

Dicit ei Valerianus, "Et ego ubi requiram hunc senem?"

Respondit ei Cecilia, "Vade in tertium miliarium ab urbe, via que Apia nuncupatur; illic invenies pauperes a transeuntibus petentes auxilium. De hiis

40   enim michi semper cura fuit, et optime mei secreti conscii sunt. Hos tu dum videris, dabis eis benedictionem meam, dicens, 'Cecilia me misit ad vos, ut ostendatis michi sanctum senem Urbanum, quoniam ad ipsum habeo eius secreta mandata que perferam.' Hunc tu dum videris, indica ei omnia verba mea. Et dum te purificaverit, induet te vestimentis novis et candidis. Cum

45   quibus mox ut ingressus fueris istud cubiculum, videbis angelum sanctum etiam tui amatorem effectum, et omnia que ab eo poposceris impetrabis."

Lectio iv. Tunc Valerianus perrexit, et secundum ea signa que acceperat invenit sanctum Urbanum episcopum, qui iam bis confessor factus, intra sepulchra martirum latitabat. Cui cum dixisset omnia verba Cecilie, gavisus

50   est gaudio magno. Et ponens genua sua in terram, expandit manus suas ad celum (fol. 301) et cum lacrimis dixit, "Domine Jesu Christe, pastor bone, seminator casti consilii, suscipe seminum fructus quos in Cecilia seminasti. Domine Jesu Christe, pastor bone, Cecilia famula tua quasi apis tibi argumentosa deservit. Nam sponsum quem quasi leonem ferocem accepit, ad

55   te quasi agnum mansuetissimum destinavit. Iste [huc] nisi crederet, non venisset. Aperi, Domine, januam cordis huius sermonibus tuis, ut te creatorem suum esse cognoscens, renuntiet dyabolo et pompis eius et ydolis eius."

Hec et hiis similia orante sancto Urbano episcopo, subito ante faciem ipsorum apparuit senior indutus niveis vestibus, tenens tytulum in manibus,

60   scriptum aureis litteris. Quem videns Valerianus, nimio terrore corripitur, cadensque in terram factus est quasi mortuus. Tunc senior levavit eum, dicens, "Lege huius libri textum, et crede, ut purificari merearis, et videre angelum cuius tibi aspectum Cecilia virgo devotissima repromisit."

Lectio v. Tunc Valerianus respiciens cepit intra se legere. Scriptura autem

65   tituli hec erat: "Unus deus, una fides, unum baptisma; unus deus et pater omnium, qui est super omnia et in omnibus nobis."

Cumque intra se legisset, dicit ei senior, "Credis ita esse, an adhuc dubitas?"

Tunc Valerianus clamavit voce magna, dicens, "Non est aliud quod verius

70   credi possit sub celo."

---

48   In this context *confessor* means one who has publicly proclaimed the Christian faith in the face of persecution, and probably endured torture, imprisonment or some other kind of punishment as a result.

53–4   For possible interpretations of *apis argumentosa*, see the note to line 47 of the *Legenda* chapter on Cecilia.

58–71 On the identity of the mysterious old man, see the note to lines 49–53 of the *Legenda* chapter.

65–6   Cf. Ephesians 4:5–6. One phrase from the Biblical text is omitted in this version, but very few of the manuscripts correct it by supplying the missing words.

The old man vanished from their sight as soon as Valerian had said this. Then Saint Urban baptized him, taught him the whole rule of faith, and sent him back to Cecilia well instructed.

When Valerian came back, wearing his white garments, he found Cecilia praying in their chamber, and standing beside her an angel of God with wings of shining feathers and a fiery bright countenance. In his hands the angel carried two crowns of shimmering roses and gleaming lilies. He gave one of these to Cecilia and the other to Valerian, saying, "Preserve these crowns with a clean heart and a pure body, for I have brought them to you from God's Paradise. And this will be a sign for you: no withered flower will ever be seen in them, their sweet fragrance will never diminish, and they will not be visible except to those who value chastity as much as you have proved you do. And Valerian, since you have agreed to the counsel of chastity, Christ the son of God has sent me to you so that you may request whatever you wish."

Hearing this, Valerian did homage and said, "Nothing in this life has been dearer to me than the affection of my brother, and it is intolerable for me, now that I am free, to see my brother in danger of damnation. Therefore I make this one request before all others: I humbly ask Christ to free my brother Tiburce along with me and make us both perfect in the confession of His name."

In response the angel said with a very glad face, "You have asked for something that Christ is even more joyful to grant than you to receive. Just as the Lord won you through His handmaid Cecilia, so He will win your brother through you, and together the two of you will attain the palm of martyrdom." As soon as these words were spoken, the visible manifestation of angelic power departed to heaven.

While Cecilia and Valerian were rejoicing [literally, feasting] and conversing about sacred knowledge, Valerian's brother Tiburce arrived. On entering, he greeted Cecilia as a kinswoman, with a kiss on the forehead, and said, "I wonder where this fragrance of roses and lilies is coming from, at this time. Even if I were holding those roses or those lilies in my hands, their perfumes could not fill me with such sweetness. I confess to you, I am so refreshed that I think I have suddenly been renewed altogether."

Valerian said to him, "You have been entitled to receive their fragrance through my intercession; but very soon, if you believe, you will also be able to delight in the sight of these roses. For we have crowns which your eyes are powerless to see, blooming with rosy color and snowy whiteness."

Tiburce answered, "Am I hearing this in dreams or are things really as you claim?"

Valerian said, "We have lived in dreams until now, but now we are in truth and there is no deception in us. In fact, the gods whom we worshipped are proved beyond all doubt to be demons."

Tiburce asked him, "Where did you learn these things you are saying?"

Valerian said, "An angel of God taught me, whom you too will be able to see if you are purified from all filth of idols."

Tiburce said, "If it can enable me to see the angel, why delay purification?"

---

102 **gaudere** *add* et intelligere cuius in rosis sanguis florescit et in liliis cuius corpus albescit Co Ca2 Ch P V2 V3 *and many other mss; same addition canc* As.

103 **roseo colore** *corr from* roseo calore N; *corr from* floreo rubore As; floreo rubore Ca2 Ch P V3 *and frequently elsewhere*; roseo rubore V2; flores roseo rubore M.

112 **ydolorum** ydorum N.

Cumque hec dixisset Valerianus, ille senex ab oculis eorum elapsus est. Tunc sanctus Urbanus baptizavit eum, et docens illum omnem fidei regulam, remisit illum ad Ceciliam diligenter instructum.

Veniens igitur Valerianus, indutus candidis vestimentis, Ceciliam intra
75 cubiculum orantem invenit, et stantem juxta eam angelum Domini, pennis fulgentibus alas habentem et flammeo aspectu radiantem, duas coronas ferentem in manibus, choruscantes rosis et liliis albescentes. Quique unam dedit Cecilie, alteram Valeriano, (fol. 301v) dicens, "Istas coronas mundo corde et immaculato corpore custodite, quia de paradyso Dei eas ad vos attuli.
80 Et hoc vobis signum erit: numquam aspectus sui marcidum adhibent florem, nunquam sui minuunt suavitatem odoris, nec ab aliis videri possunt nisi ab his quibus ita castitas placuerit, sicut et vobis probata est placuisse. Et quia tu, Valeriane, consensisti consilio castitatis, misit me Christus filius Dei ad te, ut quam volueris petitionem insinues."
85 At ille audiens adoravit et dixit, "Nichil michi dulcius in ista vita extitit quam fratris mei affectus, et impium michi est ut, me liberato, germanum meum in periculo perditionis aspiciam. Hoc solum omnibus petitionibus meis antepono et deprecor, ut fratrem meum Tyburtium sicud me liberare dignetur, et faciat nos ambos in sui nominis confessione perfectos."
90 Lectio vi. Audiens hec angelus, letissimo vultu dixit ad eum, "Quoniam petisti hoc quod melius quam te Christum implere delectat, sicut te per famulam suam Ceciliam lucratus est Dominus, ita per te quoque tuum lucrabitur fratrem et cum eodem ad martyrii palmam pertinges." Hiis itaque finitis sermonibus, aspectus angelici numinis migravit ad celos.
95 Et illis epulantibus atque in eruditione sancta sermocinantibus, Tybu[r]tius Valeriani frater advenit. Et ingressus quasi ad cognatam suam, osculatus est capud sancte Cecilie. Et ait, "Miror hoc tempore, roseus hic odor et liliorum unde respiret. Nam si tenerem ipsas rosas aut ipsa lilia in manibus meis, nec sic poterant odoramenta tante suavitatis michi infundere. Confiteor vobis, ita
100 sum refectus ut putem me totum subito renovatum."

Dicit ei Valerianus, "Odorem iam meruisti me interpellante suscipere, sed modo te credente, promereberis etiam in ipso roseo aspectu gaudere. Coronas enim habemus quas tui oculi videre non prevalent, roseo colore et niveo candore vernantes."
105 Dixit ei Tyburtius, "In sompnis (fol. 302) hec audio, an ita sunt in veritate ut asseris?"

Respondit Valerianus, "In sompnis huc usque viximus, modo in veritate sumus, et fallacia in nobis nulla est. Dii enim quos coluimus, ad omnem fidem demonia comprobantur."
110 Dicit ei Tyburtius, "Unde hec que narras nosti?"

Respondit Valerianus, "Angelus Domini docuit me, quem et tu videre poteris, si purificatus fueris ab omni sorde yd[ol]orum."

Dicit ei Tyburtius, "Et si potest fieri ut videam angelum, que mora est purificationis?"

After this Saint Cecilia kissed his breast and said, "Today I truly declare you my kinsman; for just as God made your brother my spouse, so your repudiation of idols will make you a member of my family."

Then Valerian took him to Pope Urban, who gave thanks to God and baptized him with great joy; and when he had been completely instructed, Urban consecrated him as a knight for Christ. Thereafter Tiburce received so much grace from the Lord that he saw angels every day, and everything he asked from God was granted right away.

In fact, it would take a long time to describe in order all the miracles, and how many, the Lord worked through them [Valerian and Tiburce]. Finally they were arrested by officers of the government [*apparitores*] and brought before Almachius, the prefect of the city. After a number of things had been said by them and by him, he ordered the executioners to lead them to a country district where there was a small statue of Jupiter, and if they refused to sacrifice both were to receive capital punishment.

Then the glorious martyrs were taken into custody by Maximus, the prefect's assistant [*cornicularius*], to be led to the aforesaid district. But he began to weep over them, and after the saints told him many things he got the executioners' permission to take them to his own house, where even the executioners and Maximus with his whole household listened to their preaching and became believers. Then Saint Cecilia came to them at night, bringing priests, and everyone was baptized.

When dawn put an end to that night, a great silence fell and Cecilia said, "Come on, soldiers of Christ, cast away the works of darkness and put on the armor of light. You have fought the good fight, you have finished the race, you have kept the faith. Go to the crown of life, which the righteous Judge will give you."

When the saints came to the designated place, they refused to make the offering of incense; instead, they knelt down and were put to death by the sword. Then with tears Maximus said, "I saw shining angels of God carry their souls to heaven," and many believed. Therefore, Almachius ordered him to be beaten with leaded whips until he breathed forth his spirit. Cecilia buried him next to Tiburce and Valerian, whom she had also buried, in his own tomb.

After this the prefect Almachius ordered Saint Cecilia to be constrained, and the officers began urging her to make an offering of incense. But at last they too were converted by her teaching; they spoke up with tears, believing what Saint Cecilia had said, and all declared to her with one voice, "We believe Christ, the son of God, is the true God, since He has such a handmaid as you."

When Almachius heard that these things had happened, he ordered Cecilia to be brought before him and, questioning her, he asked, "What is your condition?"

Cecilia answered, "Free-born, noble, and illustrious."

Almachius said, "I am asking you about religion."

---

121 **angelos** angelus V1.
144 **precepit** cepit Co.

115   Post hec sancta Cecilia pectus eius obsculata est, et dixit, "Hodie te fateor
esse vere meum cognatum. Sicut enim michi Deus fratrem tuum conjugem
fecit, ita te michi cognatum contemptus faciet ydolorum."
        Tunc Valerianus perduxit eum ad papam Urbanum. Qui gratias referens
Deo, cum omni gaudio baptizavit eum, et perfectum in doctrina sua Christo
120   militem consecravit. Tantam quoque Tyburtius deinceps gratiam consecutus
est Domini, ut et angelos Dei videret cotidie, et omnium que poposcisset a
Deo protinus eveniret effectus.
        Lectio vii. Verum, multum est omnia per ordinem prosequi, que et quanta
per eos Dominus mirabilia fecerit. Denique tenti ab apparitoribus, prefecto
125   urbis Almachio presentantur. Qui post plurima audita et responsa jussit
carnificibus ut ab eis ducerentur ad pagum ubi erat staticulum Jovis, et si
noluissent sacrificare ambo sententiam capitalem exciperent.
        Tunc gloriosi martyres, tenti a Maximo corniculario prefecti, ducebantur ad
pagum. Qui cepit flere super eos, et post multa que a sanctis audivit, cum
130   impetrasset a carnificibus, duxit eos in domum suam. Ad quorum
predicationem carnifices ipsi et Maximus cum omni domo sua crediderunt.
Tunc sancta Cecilia venit ad eos nocte cum sacerdotibus, et universi baptizati
sunt.
        Igitur cum aurora nocti finem daret, facto magno silentio Cecilia dixit, "Eya
135   milites Christi, abicite opera tenebrarum (fol. 302v) et induimini arma lucis.
Bonum certamen certastis, cursum consumastis, fidem servastis. Ite ad
coronam vite, quam dabit vobis justus judex."
        Venientibus ergo sanctis ad pagum, thura offerre recusant, recusantes
genua ponunt, gladio feriuntur. Tunc cum lacrimis narrante Maximo, quia vidi
140   angelos Dei fulgentes animas eorum ferentes ad celos, plurimi crediderunt.
Igitur Almachius jussit eum tam diu plumbatis tundi, quam diu spiritum
redderet, quem sancta Cecilia juxta Tyburtium et Valerianum, quos ipsa
sepelierat, in suo sarcophago sepelivit.
        Post hec sanctam Ceciliam prefectus Almachius precepit artari, que ut ipsa
145   quoque thura poneret ab apparitoribus cepit impelli. Denique et illi ad eius
doctrinam conversi, dabant voces cum fletu et sancte Cecilie dictis credentes,
omnes una voce dixerunt, "Credimus Christum filium Dei verum Deum esse,
qui te talem possidet famulam."
        Lectio viii. Almachius hiis que gerebantur auditis, Ceciliam sibi presentari
150   jubet, quam interrogans ait, "Cuius conditionis es?"
        Cecilia respondit, "Ingenua, nobilis, et clarissima."
        Almachius dixit, "Ego te de religione interrogo."

134–7 Cf. Romans 13:12 and 2 Timothy 4:7–8. Some manuscripts continue the speech, "non solum
vobis, sed et omnibus qui diligunt adventum ejus," as in 2 Timothy and the *Passio*. Thomas
Connolly suggests a larger symbolic reading of this speech and the imagery that surrounds it in
the legend (*Mourning into Joy*, pp. 75–6 and 206–11).

142–3 In the *Passio* there is no ambiguity at this point; Cecilia buries Maximus next to Tiburce and
Valerian, in a "novo sarcofago" on which she has the emblem of a phoenix carved, as an
indication of his faith in the resurrection (see ch. 24 in Delehaye's edition of the *Passio*, *Étude sur
le légendier romain*, p. 214). The vaguer wording in the Roman curia/ Franciscan account, on the
other hand, can be translated either "his own tomb" or "her tomb" (if one invokes the rule from
classical Latin and makes *suo* refer to the subject of the main verb).

Cecilia answered, "Your questioning has begun foolishly, since it tries to elicit two answers with one question."

Almachius asked, "What is the source of such an impertinent answer?"

Cecilia said, "A good conscience and genuine faith."

Almachius asked, "Don't you know how powerful I am?"

Cecilia answered, "All human power is like a bag full of wind. If pricked by a single needle, its appearance of solidity collapses."

Almachius said, "You began with harmful statements, and do you continue with harmful statements? Don't you know that our most invincible princes have decreed that all those who do not deny being Christians will be punished, while those who do deny it will be set free?"

Cecilia answered, "Your emperors are mistaken, just as your nobility is. From you in your rage comes a judicial decision that imposes on us, whom you know to be innocent, the crime of the name 'Christian.' But we who know that name to be holy cannot deny it at all."

Almachius said, "Choose one of these two things. Either sacrifice to the gods or deny that you are a Christian, so that you may have a means of escape."

Then Cecilia said, laughing, "O judge, perplexed by necessity! He wants me to deny that I am innocent, in order to make me guilty. He [alternately] spares and rages, dissimulates and threatens."

Almachius said, "Miserable one, don't you know that our most invincible princes have given me the power of granting life or death? Why do you speak with such pride?"

Cecilia answered, "I have spoken firmly, not proudly, for we deeply detest pride. However, if you are not afraid to hear the truth, I will show how you are lying against manifest truth. You said your princes have given you the power to grant death or life; but you can only take away life from the living, not give it to the dead. Say therefore that your emperors have allowed you to be an agent of death. If you claim anything more, you will be seen to be lying uselessly."

Almachius said, "Now lay aside your impudence and sacrifice to the gods. For I have philosophically disregarded the wrongs done to me, but I cannot endure those done to the gods."

Cecilia answered, "From the time you opened your mouth, there has not been a word that I have not shown to be unfair, silly, and worthless. But, lest anything be lacking, you show yourself to be blind even in your outward eyes; for what we all see is stone, you declare to be a god. If you wish, I [will] give you some advice: reach out your hand and know that it is rock by touching if you cannot tell by seeing. It is a terrible thing that all the people laugh at you. For they all know that God is in the heavens, and these images are useless both to you and to themselves."

When Cecilia had said these things and others like them, Almachius was violently angry and ordered her to be brought back to her house and in her house to be burned in the flames of the bath. When she was shut up in the heat of the bath,

157   **sim** sum A U Co.
161   **injuriis** in injuriis A U Co Cal.
163   **qui** et qui U.
172   **advertit** avertit U.
189   **si** quod U.
192   **hiis** aliis B.

Cecilia respondit, "Interrogatio tua stultum sumpsit initium, que duas responsiones una putat inquisitione concludi."

155 Almachius dixit, "Unde tibi tanta presumptio respondendi?"

Cecilia dixit, "De conscientia bona, et fide non ficta."

Almachius dixit, "Ignoras cuius potestatis sim?"

Cecilia respondit, "Omnis potestas hominis sic est, quasi uter vento repletus. Quem si una acus pupugerit, quicquid in se rigidum habere cernitur

160 incurvatur."

Almachius dixit, "Ab injuriis cepisti, et injuriis perseveras? Ignoras quia invictissimi principes jusserunt ut qui non se negaverint esse Christianos puniantur, qui vero negaverint dimittantur?"

Cecilia respondit, "Sic imperatores (fol. 303) vestri errant, sicut et nobilitas

165 vestra, ex quorum sententia sevientes nobis quos innocentes scitis, nominis tantum Christiani crimen impingitis. Set nos scientes sanctum nomen, omnino negare non possumus."

Almachius dixit, "Elige tibi unum e duobus. Aut sacrifica diis aut nega te esse Christianam, ut copiam evadendi suscipias."

170 Tunc ridens beata Cecilia dixit, "O judicem necessitate confusum. Vult ut negem me esse innocentem, ut ipse me faciat nocentem. Parcit et sevit, dissimulat et advertit."

Almachius dixit, "Infelix, ignoras quoniam mortificandi et vivificandi michi ab invictissimis principibus potestas data est? Quare cum tanta superbia

175 loqueris?"

Cecilia respondit, "Ego constanter locuta sum, non superbe, quia superbiam et nos fortiter execramus. Tu autem si verum audire non times, contra veritatem publicam te docebo esse mentitum. Dixisti principes tuos mortificandi et vivificandi tibi copiam tribuisse, qui tantum vitam viventibus

180 tollere potes, mortuis dare eam non potes. Dic ergo, quia imperatores tui mortis te ministrum esse voluerunt. Nam si quid plus dixeris, videberis frustra mentitus."

Lectio ix. Almachius dixit, "Depone iam audaciam tuam, et sacrifica diis. Nam meas injurias phylosophando contempsi, sed deorum ferre non possum."

185 Cecilia respondit, "Ex quo os aperuisti, non fuit sermo quem non arguerem injustum, stultum et vanum. Sed ne quid desit, etiam exterioribus oculis te cecum ostendis, quia quod omnes lapidem esse videmus, tu deum esse testaris. Do si jubes consilium. Mitte manum tuam et tangendo nosce saxum esse si videndo non nosti. Nefas enim est, ut totus populus de te ridiculum

190 habeat. Omnes enim sciunt Deum in celis esse, istas autem figuras neque tibi neque sibi prodesse."

Hec et hiis similia dicente beata Cecilia, iratus vehementer Almachius (fol. 303v) jussit eam ad domum suam reduci, et in domo sua flammis balneariis concremari. Cumque fuisset in calore balnei inclusa, et subter incendia nimia

---

164–72 The ultimate source behind Cecilia's two speeches in these lines is Tertullian's long, complex argument in the *Apology*, 2.4–20, against the tactics that were used to prosecute Christians. The original points are considerably obscured even in the *Passio* because Tertullian's statements have been greatly reordered and condensed, and some of them simply misunderstood by copyists; and the sense is even cloudier in this later, still more abbreviated version.

underneath it a great fire was fed with wooden fuel for a complete day and a whole night. As if she had been in a cold place, however, she remained so completely unharmed that no part of her body showed even a sign of sweat.

When Almachius heard that, he sent someone to behead her right there in the bath. The executioner struck her with three blows, but could not cut off her head; and since it was stipulated by law at that time that a person being beheaded should not receive a fourth stroke, the ferocious executioner left her there half-dead. All the Christians she had converted came and wiped up her blood with cotton or linen cloths.

During the three days that she survived, she never stopped teaching those whom she had nourished and strengthening them in the Lord's faith. She also gave them all her possessions, and she committed all these followers to the care of Saint Urban, pope of the city of Rome. She told him, "I asked for a respite of three days for this reason, so that I might entrust these souls to your Blessedness and dedicate this house of mine in perpetuity to the ownership of the church."

Then Saint Urban with his deacons removed her body and buried it by night among his associates, the bishops, where all the confessors and martyrs were placed. He also dedicated her house in perpetuity to the ownership of holy church, and it is filled with blessings of the Lord, in memory of Saint Cecilia, down to the present day. The most blessed virgin of Christ, Cecilia, was martyred on the tenth day of the kalends of December, in the reign of our Lord Jesus Christ, to whom belong honor and glory forever and ever, Amen.

195 **ministrarentur** ministrarent A Co Ca2 Ch P V4.
196 **nulla** *apparently corr from* null *plus a suspension mark* N.
207 **michi ad hoc** a domino As Ca2 Ch M P V4.
208 **nomini** nomine A As Ca2 Ch P V4.
211 **sunt** sancti A.
212 **nomini sancte ecclesie** nomine sancte cecilie As Ca2 P; nomine sancte ecclesie Ch M V4.

195 lignorum pabula ministrarentur, die integro et tota nocte quasi in loco frigido sic illibata perstitit sanitate, ita ut nulla pars membrorum eius saltem sudoris signa laxasset.

Quod cum audisset Almachius, misit qui eam ibidem in ipsis balneis decollaret. Quam spiculator tertio ictu percussit, et caput eius amputare non
200 potuit. Et quia legibus tunc cautum erat, ne quartam decollandus percussionem acciperet, sic seminecem truculentus carnifex dereliquit, cuius sanguinem omnes Christiani qui per eam crediderant bibleis linteaminibus extergebant.

Per triduum autem quod supervixit, non cessavit omnes quos nutrierat
205 perdocere et in fide dominica confortare. Quibus etiam divisit universa que habuit, et omnes urbis Rome sancto pape Urbano tradidit commendatos. Cui et dixit, "Triduanas michi ad hoc poposci indutias, ut et istas animas tue beatitudini commendarem, et hanc domum meam in eternum ecclesie nomini consecrarem."
210 Tunc sanctus Urbanus corpus eius auferens cum diaconibus nocte sepelivit eam inter collegas suos episcopos, ubi omnes sunt confessores et martyres collocati. Domum autem eius in eternum nomini sancte ecclesie consecravit, in qua beneficia Domini exuberant ad memoriam sancte Cecilie usque in hodiernum diem. Martirizata est autem beatissima virgo Christi Cecilia sub
215 die decimo kalendarum Decembrium, regnante domino nostro Jesu Christo, cui est honor et gloria in secula seculorum, amen.

---

202 The Latin word *linteaminibus* means linen cloths. Its modifier, *bibleis*, comes either from *bibulus*, meaning "thirsty, absorbent," or from *bibleus*, a term used in medieval Latin to mean papyrus or, more obscurely, fabrics made from hemp or cotton, perhaps woven in a pattern resembling rushes.

208 In this construction, *nomen* evidently means "legal title." In the manuscripts that have *nomen* in the ablative rather than the dative case, the phrase can be translated "consecrate my house forever in the name of the church," or "on behalf of the church."

213 The term *beneficia* had a wide range of meanings in medieval Latin, including "good works," "donations," and "liturgical services" or "sacraments."

The Parson's Tale

RICHARD NEWHAUSER

The textual sources for the *Parson's Tale* may be usefully differentiated in three classes: the illustrative sources for biblical, patristic, and classical quotations used with or without attribution throughout the treatise, derived either directly from the source texts or indirectly through intermediaries in the following two classes: the contextual sources which provided the initial penitential, aretological, and hamartiological contexts represented in Chaucer's work; and the verbal sources of a more immediate nature which approximate, as nearly as can now be reconstructed, the material which Chaucer drew on more directly for his own presentation of penitential and moral-theological concepts and the verbal formulations in which the reader finds them in the *Parson's Tale*. The illustrative sources of the *Parson's Tale* are diverse, but as in many medieval works of moral and pastoral intent, and as is indicated by the texts which Chaucer drew on more directly and which are indexed below (see pp. 612–13), the *Parson's Tale* is above all indebted to the inspiration of the Vulgate Bible for many of its ideas in direct quotations and paraphrased statements. A wide range of patristic thought is represented in the treatise, as well, in particular that of Augustine of Hippo, Jerome, Gregory the Great, Isidore of Seville, the *Glossa ordinaria* on the Vulgate bible, Gratian's *Decretum*, and Bernard of Clairvaux. Classical sources are far less apparent in the *Parson's Tale*, though Seneca, in particular, has a place here, as he does in many later-medieval treatises on moral theology, and the much more indirect influence of Aristotle stands out, as well. The history of scholarship on the sources of the tale reveals an increasing precision in the identification of the illustrative sources for particular quotations and the intellectual traditions which they represent. In the treatment of the sins, for example, the Parson quotes "the Philosophre" in defining wrath as "the fervent blood of man yquyked in his herte" (ParT X,536).[1] Robert C. Fox first identified the ultimate source of this definition as Seneca's *De ira*,[2] but as A. V. C. Schmidt then demonstrated, the definition is derived from Aristotle's *De anima*, which influenced Seneca's formulation.[3] Finally, as Siegfried Wenzel established, the quotation is found with the same attribution to the "Philosophus" in a text which represents one of Chaucer's more direct sources for material on the vices.[4]

This chapter was completed with the assistance of grants from the Gladys Krieble Delmas Foundation – American Council of Learned Societies and the National Humanities Center, through the Lilly Endowment. I gratefully acknowledge the generous support of these foundations here. I am grateful to Professor Siegfried Wenzel for his help in preparing this chapter.

[1]   All citations from Chaucer are from Larry D. Benson, gen. ed., *The Riverside Chaucer*, 3rd ed. (Boston, 1987).

[2]   Robert C. Fox, "The Philosophre of Chaucer's Parson," *Modern Language Notes* 75 (1960): 101–2. In an earlier note, Fox had understood Chaucer's reference to "the Philosophre" at ParT X,484 to refer to Aristotle, *Rhetorica*, 2.10: Robert C. Fox, "Chaucer and Aristotle," *Notes and Queries* N.S. 5 [203] (1958): 523–4, but see Siegfried Wenzel's note on ParT X,484 in "Fragment X: The Parson's Prologue, The Parson's Tale, Chaucer's Retraction," in *The Riverside Chaucer*, p. 960, where it is suggested that the reference is to Johannes Damascenus. Compare, however, text IV.1 below, one of Chaucer's closer verbal sources, where the *auctoritas* involved here is identified as Aristotle, and see Aristotle, *Topica*, 2.2 (trans. Boethius) (AL 5,1–3:33).

[3]   A. V. C. Schmidt, "Chaucer's 'Philosophre': A Note on 'The Parson's Tale,' 534–7," *Notes and Queries* N.S. 15 [213] (1968): 327–8.

[4]   Siegfried Wenzel, "The Source of Chaucer's Seven Deadly Sins," *Traditio* 30 (1974): 362.

As has been known since the work of Kate Oelzner Petersen, there are in large part only two contextual sources of the *Parson's Tale*: the first fourth and the last eighth of the Middle English prose text (lines 80–386, 958–1080) are drawn from the chapter "De paenitentiis et remissionibus" of Raymund of Pennaforte's *Summa de paenitentia*, while the long treatment of the seven deadly sins and their remedies (lines 390–955) which has been inserted between the sections taken from Pennaforte is derived in large part from William Peraldus's double *Summa de vitiis et virtutibus*, though to a much greater degree from the *summa* on the vices.[5] Pennaforte composed his *Summa* on penitence between the years c. 1225–27 and then reworked it to reflect the *Decretals* of Pope Gregory IX between the years c. 1235 and 1236. Peraldus published his treatment of the vices c. 1236, and put it into circulation together with his *summa* on the virtues by 1249 or 1250.[6] The double *summa* remained one of the most copied, adapted, translated, and reworked sources of information on the vices and virtues in Latin and the vernacular to the end of the Middle Ages.[7] Both Pennaforte and Peraldus were Dominicans; their works testify to the role of this fraternal order as one of the important institutional vehicles in carrying out the penitential and pastoral canons of the Fourth Lateran Council (1215). The basis for Chaucer's penitential and moral theology in the *Parson's Tale*, thus, has a conservative foundation, for it is derived from contextual sources

---

5   Kate Oelzner Petersen, *The Sources of the Parson's Tale*, Radcliffe College Monographs 12 (Boston, 1901; repr. New York, 1973). Petersen's work was rightfully criticized insofar as she insisted on direct borrowing from Peraldus for the entirety of the material on the sins in the *Parson's Tale*. See, for example, Alfred L. Kellogg, "St. Augustine and the 'Parson's Tale,' " *Traditio* 8 (1952): 424–30; repr. in Alfred L. Kellogg, *Chaucer, Langland, Arthur: Essays in Middle English Literature* (New Brunswick, NJ, 1972), p. 344.

6   For the date of composition of Raymund's work and its redactions, see S. Raimundus de Pennaforte, *Summa de paenitentia*, ed. Xaverio Ochoa and Aloisio Diez, Universa Bibliotheca Iuris 1B (Roma, 1976), pp. lxiii–lxxxi; Joh. Friedrich von Schulte, *Die Geschichte der Quellen und Literatur des canonischen Rechts*, vol. 2: *Von Papst Gregor IX. bis zum Concil von Trient* (Stuttgart, 1877; repr. Union, NJ, 2000), pp. 408–13; for Peraldus's work, see Carla Casagrande and Silvana Vecchio, *I peccati della lingua. Disciplina ed etica della parola nella cultura medievale*, Bibliotheca Biographica, Sezione Storico-Antropologica (Roma, 1987), pp. 103–35; William C. McDonald, "The Nobility of Soul: Uncharted Echoes of the Peraldean Tradition in Late Medieval German Literature," *Deutsche Vierteljahrsschrift für Literaturwissenschaft und Geistesgeschichte* 60 (1986): 543–71; Michael Evans, "An Illustrated Fragment of Peraldus's Summa of Vice: Harleian MS 3244," *Journal of the Warburg and Courtauld Institutes* 45 (1982): 14–68; Franco Mancini, "Un' 'auctoritas' di Dante," *Studi danteschi* 45 (1968): 95–119; Siegfried Wenzel, *The Sin of Sloth* (Chapel Hill, NC, 1967), esp. pp. 75–82; Morton W. Bloomfield, *The Seven Deadly Sins* ([East Lansing, MI, 1952]; repr., 1967), pp. 124–7; Antoine Dondaine, "Guillaume Peyraut, vie et œuvres," *Archivum Fratrum Praedicatorum* 18 (1948): 162–236. The popularity of both works has been documented by Morton W. Bloomfield, Bertrand-Georges Guyot, Donald R. Howard, and Thyra B. Kabealo, *Incipits of Latin Works on the Virtues and Vices, 1100–1500 A.D.*, The Mediaeval Academy of America, Publication 88 (Cambridge, MA, 1979), no. 5054 (Raymund), and nos. 1628 and 5601 (Peraldus); Raymund, *Summa*, ed. Ochoa and Diez, vol. 1B, pp. xciii–xciv; Thomas Kaeppeli, "Guillelmus Peraldus (Peyraut)," in Thomas Kaeppeli, *Scriptores Ordinis Praedicatorum Medii Aevi*, vol. 2 (Roma, 1975), no. 1622, pp. 133–42.

7   Richard Newhauser, *The Treatise on Vices and Virtues in Latin and the Vernacular*, Typologie des sources du moyen âge occidental 68 (Turnhout, Belgium, 1993), pp. 127–30; Siegfried Wenzel, "The Continuing Life of William Peraldus's *Summa vitiorum*," in M. D. Jordan and K. Emery, Jr., eds., *Ad litteram. Authoritative Texts and Their Medieval Readers*, Notre Dame Conferences in Medieval Studies 3 (Notre Dame, London, 1992), pp. 135–63.

which were roughly 150 years old by the time he adopted them for this treatise.[8]

As Petersen demonstrated, Chaucer took his treatment of penitence more directly from Pennaforte's chapter in the *Summa de paenitentia*, which, thus, belongs to the verbal as well as the contextual sources of the tale.[9] For the more immediate verbal form in which he found the material derived ultimately from Peraldus, Chaucerian scholarship is indebted to the research of Siegfried Wenzel. The treatment of the sins which Chaucer used is largely found in two redactions of Peraldus's *Summa de vitiis* which are commonly known by the opening words of their respective texts: the very extensive *Summa de vitiis "Quoniam"* and the briefer *Summa vitiorum "Primo"*, both unedited.[10] The remedies for the sins are represented in closest form in a work likewise indebted to Peraldus's treatment of the virtues, though in a much more indirect way, the *Summa virtutum de remediis anime*, influenced by Peraldus's *Summa de virtutibus* but substantively independent of it.[11] The basis for the aretological and hamartiological considerations in these more direct sources was apparently also quite traditional by the time Chaucer worked with them, for the *Summa vitiorum "Primo"* may have been produced very shortly after the publication of Peraldus's *Summa de vitiis*. As Wenzel has argued, this redaction contains a reference not found in Peraldus's treatise to Pope Gregory IX (d. 1241) that may indicate he was the ruling pontiff at the time it was written, which would place its period of composition in the years c. 1236–41, that is to say, sometime after the completion of Peraldus's work on the vices and before Gregory's death. The companion piece to the redaction on the vices, the *Summa virtutum de remediis anime*, was perhaps composed shortly after this period.[12] Since the *Summa de vitiis "Quoniam"* also contains the same text with the reference to Gregory IX as *dominus papa* which is found in the briefer treatise on the vices, a similar hypothesis may be advanced for its date of composition as was developed for the *Summa vitiorum "Primo."*[13] Whether or not the reference to Pope Gregory IX is conclusive as evidence for the date of composition of the treatises, it is not likely that these redactions of Peraldus's *summa* on the vices were composed later than the third quarter of the 13th century, because both of them contain a short narrative about a certain Stephen, rector of the church of Caldecote, which was borrowed for use in the *Liber exemplorum*, composed between the years

---

[8] Richard Newhauser, "*The Parson's Tale* and Its Generic Affiliations," in L. T. Holley and D. Raybin, eds., *Closure in The Canterbury Tales: The Role of The Parson's Tale* (Kalamazoo, MI, 2000), pp. 45–76.

[9] Petersen, pp. 2–34; see also Germaine Dempster, "The Parson's Tale," in W. F. Bryan and G. Dempster, eds., *Sources and Analogues of Chaucer's Canterbury Tales* (New York, 1941), pp. 729–41.

[10] Wenzel, "The Source of Chaucer's Seven Deadly Sins," pp. 351–78.

[11] *Summa virtutum de remediis anime*, ed. Siegfried Wenzel, The Chaucer Library (Athens, GA, 1984). See Siegfried Wenzel, "The Source for the *Remedia* of the Parson's Tale," *Traditio* 27 (1971): 433–53; and the introduction to the *Summa virtutum*, ed. Wenzel, pp. 2–30.

[12] *Summa virtutum*, ed. Wenzel, p. 12.

[13] *Summa de vitiis "Quoniam"* (Durham, Cathedral Library MS B.I.18, fols. 93b–va): "Restat enim uidere, quibus personis hoc sit licitum, quia non solum excluduntur ab exercicio legum plebani, idest majores ecclesie, ut in illa decretali *Super specula*, set eciam omnes curam animarum habentes, ut in / rescripto, quod mandauit dominus Papa episcopo Aurelianensi."

1275 and 1279.[14] Though the *Summa de vitiis "Quoniam"* and the *Summa vitiorum "Primo"* are, thus, also chronologically distant from the period in which Chaucer may have used them by at least a century, they are geographically closer to him than the contextual sources, for the redactions on the vices contain English verses and references to English place-names, as seen, for example, in the setting of Caldecote for the narrative just mentioned. In this way, the more immediate sources Chaucer drew on for his moral theology already demonstrate a process of localization in an English environment of the material presented originally by Peraldus.

The precise relationship between the redactions on the vices and their relative proximity to the *Parson's Tale* remains unclear; the *Summa de vitiis "Quoniam"* contains a certain number of passages which are closer to Chaucer's Middle English than what is found in the *Summa vitiorum "Primo,"* but the reverse is also true and, in fact, a few passages in Peraldus's *Summa de vitiis* are closer to Chaucer's text than what is presented by either of the Latin redactions of Peraldus. The treatment of penitence in the *Parson's Tale* also demonstrates some differences from what is found in the critical edition of Raymund's work, including added imagery and a certain amount of confusion in the schematics of presentation.[15] It is, of course, entirely possible that Chaucer himself combined, condensed, and made additions to the more direct verbal sources for the *Parson's Tale*, though he may also have found them in this form in a yet undiscovered treatise. It is clear, in any case, that the material contained in the Middle English text is considerably shorter than what the treatises which have been identified as its more direct verbal sources offer. There are a number of ways in which Chaucer's text represents an abbreviation of the *summae* by Pennaforte, Peraldus, and the redactions of Peraldus. Only a minute examination of all parts of Chaucer's text and its sources, including manuscripts which may represent an English redaction of Raymund's *Summa de paenitentia*, will allow a final determination in this matter, but in general one can say that Chaucer borrows from his sources those passages which provide him with the framework of the treatment of penitential and moral-theological matters without drawing on the inner-ecclesiastical and technical discussions intended for the use of the clergy involved in the sacrament of penitence, or in many cases without making use of the full range of the expansion of this material through quotations from Scripture and patristic or classical authorities in which his source texts abound. Within this framework, his treatise often represents additional material of its own, but the abbreviations generally reflect only the beginnings of major divisions of the text as they are found in his sources. He supplies transitions where necessary, but does not follow the often extended discussions

---

[14] For the *exemplum* and its use in the *Liber exemplorum*, see *Summa virtutum*, ed. Wenzel, pp. 11–12; Wenzel, "The Source of Chaucer's Seven Deadly Sins," p. 352.

[15] See the addition of the image of the tree of penitence noted below in passage II among the texts, and for evidence of confusion in the presentation of penitential material, see ParT X,1073, for example, where Chaucer refers to the second type of despair when he means the second cause of the first type of despair.

in his sources beyond their initial phase. Excerpts from both redactions of Peraldus's *summa* and Peraldus's original are represented below, as well as excerpts from the relevant chapter of Raymund of Pennaforte's *Summa de paenitentia*.

The *Parson's Tale* has many analogues among what W. A. Pantin has termed the "great mass of anonymous mystical and devotional writings" which were produced for the instructional needs of both the clergy and the laity in later-medieval England in response to the pastoral demands of English synodal decrees following the Fourth Lateran Council.[16] As a partial treatment of the seven deadly sins and their remedies in the vernacular dependent contextually on Peraldus and intended above all for a secular audience, the Parson's text can be related to such Middle English pastoral treatises as the anonymous, late 14th- or early 15th-century *Book for a Simple and Devout Woman*, an adaptation of Peraldus's double *Summa de vitiis et virtutibus* and Friar Laurent's *Somme le Roi*,[17] or to the *Memoriale Credencium*, a Middle English instructional handbook on religion for the laity from the first half of the 15th century in which material on the virtues derived from the *Summa virtutum de remediis anime* is arranged after each one of the vices to which it corresponds as a remedy.[18] As a treatise on penitential and moral theology in the vernacular, the *Parson's Tale* can also be associated with the compendia and handbooks which promulgated in more popular form teachings on penance, confession, and related catechetical matters in England, such as the Anglo-Norman *Manuel des péchés* and its many English derivatives, including Robert Mannyng of Brunne's *Handlyng Synne* and the late 14th-century prose translation of the *Manuel* entitled *Of Shrifte and Penance*.[19] Yet, the Parson's text is not a treatise on the vices and virtues, nor a

---

[16] W. A. Pantin, *The English Church in the Fourteenth Century* (Cambridge, Eng., 1955), p. 247. On pastoral literature in medieval England, see Joseph Goering, *William de Montibus (c. 1140–1213). The Schools and the Literature of Pastoral Care*, Studies and Texts 108 (Toronto, 1992), pp. 58–99; Robert R. Raymo, "Works of Religious and Philosophical Instruction," in A. E. Hartung, ed., *A Manual of the Writings in Middle English 1050–1500*, vol. 7 (New Haven, CT, 1986), pp. 2255–378, 2467–582; Leonard E. Boyle, "The Fourth Lateran Council and Manuals of Popular Theology," in T. J. Heffernan, ed., *The Popular Literature of Medieval England*, Tennessee Studies in Literature 28 (Knoxville, TN, 1985), pp. 30–43; Durant W. Robertson, Jr., *A Preface to Chaucer: Studies in Medieval Perspectives* (Princeton, 1962); Gerald R. Owst, *Literature and Pulpit in Medieval England*, 2nd rev. ed. (New York, 1961); idem, *Preaching in Medieval England* (Cambridge, Eng., 1926; repr. New York, 1965).

[17] *Book for a Simple and Devout Woman*, ed. F. N. M. Diekstra, Mediaevalia Groningana 24 (Groningen, 1998).

[18] *Memoriale Credencium. A Late Middle English Manual of Theology for Lay People Edited from Bodley MS Tanner 201*, ed. J. H. L. Kengen ([Nijmegen], 1979). For the use of material from the *Summa virtutum de remediis anime* in this text, though not the same material used earlier by Chaucer, see the review of Kengen's edition by Siegfried Wenzel in *Anglia* 99 (1981): 511–13.

[19] *Roberd of Brunnè's Handlyng synne (written A.D. 1303) with the French Treatise on which it is founded, Le Manuel des Pechiez by William of Wadington*, ed. Frederick J. Furnivall, Printed for the Roxburgh Club (London, 1862); partially re-edited in *Robert of Brunne's "Handlyng Synne," A.D. 1303, with those parts of the Anglo-French Treatise on which it was founded, William of Wadington's "Manuel des Pechiez,"* re-ed. Frederick J. Furnivall, 2 vols., EETS OS 119, 123 (London, 1901, 1903; repr. as one vol., 1973); *Robert Mannyng of Brunne, Handlyng synne*, ed. Idelle Sullens, Medieval and Renaissance Texts and Studies 14 (Binghamton, NY, 1983); *Of Shrifte and Penance*, ed. Klaus Bitterling, Middle English Texts 29 (Heidelberg, 1998).

compendium in the vein of the *Manuel des péchés*, nor does it evince the features which would place it in the genre of the sermon in any technical sense of that term, though the framework of the *Canterbury Tales* provides indications for a fictional setting of oral delivery in the *Parson's Tale* similar to that found in other links and tales throughout the collection.[20] The Parson's text belongs, rather, to the genre of the penitential manual, a literary form which is well represented in Latin from the 13th century onwards and, by the late Middle Ages, in all European vernaculars, as well. The penitential manual was designed in particular to address both the sacramental and the psychological-pedagogic functions involved in penitence, preparing the confessor to hear confession and instructing the penitent's conscience in what to confess, and it was calculated to do so with some degree of exclusiveness. The meditative function involved in the examination of the conscience opened the genre to the influence of late-medieval meditative prose, yet as Thomas Bestul has acknowledged, the major objects of a text which both the Parson and the host describe as a "meditacioun" (ParT X,55 and 69) are the vices and virtues which form the bulk of the work.[21] As the studies of H. G. Pfander and, more recently, Lee Patterson have demonstrated, many of the closer analogues to the *Parson's Tale* combine the two main ingredients in the penitential manual, that is to say, teachings on penitence and material on the vices and virtues, with a number of further catechetical elements, such as material on the decalogue, creed, gifts of the Holy Spirit, or the like.[22] Chaucer's work, however, remains focused on the two core elements in the penitential manual to the exclusion of extensive treatment of any extraneous matter. Patterson has emphasized the uniqueness of this trait of the *Parson's Tale* among Middle English penitential manuals which, like most of their French equivalents, use the occasion provided by a presentation of penitence, sin, and virtue to inform their readers of more general catechetical materials as well.[23] Yet Chaucer's work is not without any analogue in comparable vernacular penitential manuals of the later Middle Ages. Perhaps the closest equivalent can be found in Middle High German in Heinrich of Langenstein's *Erchantnuzz der Sund*, a manual which is just as bare of catechetical elaboration as Chaucer's and, if anything, even more doctrinally focused than the *Parson's Tale* and which, furthermore, draws on the same two texts which served as the contextual sources for Chaucer's work.[24] Although the German and English

---

[20] Siegfried Wenzel, "Notes on the *Parson's Tale*," *Chaucer Review* 16 (1982): 248–51.

[21] Thomas H. Bestul, "Chaucer's Parson's Tale and the Late-Medieval Tradition of Religious Meditation," *Speculum* 64 (1989): 600–11.

[22] Lee Patterson, "The 'Parson's Tale' and the Quitting of the 'Canterbury Tales,'" *Traditio* 34 (1978): 331–80; H. G. Pfander, "Some Medieval Manuals of Religious Instruction in England and Observations on Chaucer's Parson's Tale," *Journal of English and Germanic Philology* 35 (1936): 243–58.

[23] Patterson, "The 'Parson's Tale,'" pp. 339–40.

[24] Heinrich von Langenstein, *Erchantnuzz der Sund*, ed. Rainer Rudolf, Texte des späten Mittelalters und der frühen Neuzeit, vol. 22 (Berlin, 1969); see Thomas Hohmann and Georg Kreuzer, "Heinrich von Langenstein," *Die deutsche Literatur des Mittelalters. Verfasserlexikon*, 2nd ed., vol. 3 (Berlin, New York, 1981), cols. 768–9; Thomas Hohmann, "Initienregister der Werke Heinrichs von Langenstein," *Traditio* 32 (1976): 419, no. 232. On Langenstein, see also Michael H. Shank, *"Unless You Believe, You Shall Not Understand"* (Princeton, NJ, 1988). A more detailed comparison of the German and

treatises were both composed at the end of the 14th century, there is no question of textual borrowing between them, and I have not included extracts from the *Erchantnuzz der Sund* below.

Because the contextual and verbal sources which have been identified for Chaucer's work on the *Parson's Tale* lie much closer to his text than any of its several analogues, including the *Somme le Roi*, which was represented among the quotations in Dempster's work,[25] the passages presented here focus mainly on the more direct sources of the text. Nevertheless, the background for a few of the particular images found in Chaucer's text is provided from works which belong to the analogues and illustrative sources for the Parson's treatise where the contextual and verbal sources contain nothing closer. As illustrations of the sources for the *Parson's Tale*, the passages found below are taken from seven works and are arranged in four sections which exemplify the contents and functions of the Parson's treatise. In these sections I have reproduced the edition of Pennaforte's work by Xaverio Ochoa and Aloisio Diez (see above, n. 6) and the edition and translation of the *Summa virtutum de remediis anime* by Siegfried Wenzel (see above, n. 11); all other editions and translations are my own.

A. Penitence

I.   Raymund of Pennaforte, *Summa de paenitentia*, covering some of the presentation of the six items announced for treatment at ParT X,82–3:

   1.–2. Introductory material on penitence, including the initial material announced in ParT X,82–3: the definition of penitence and its actions and species, as well as what is necessary for true penitence;

   3.–4. On contrition, including the four items announced for treatment at ParT X,128: what contrition is, and what are its causes, qualities, and effects;

   5.–6. On confession, covering the items announced for treatment at ParT X,317: what confession is, whether it should be made by necessity, and what is appropriate for true confession, as well as the seven circumstances of sin discussed in ParT X,961–78;

   7.   On satisfaction, including two of the actions in which satisfaction consists: almsgiving and tormenting of the flesh, announced in ParT X,1029;

   8.   The impediments to penance, including the four impediments given in ParT X,1057: shame, fear, hope, and despair.

These eight passages provide a cross-section of the treatment of penitence and its continuity in Pennaforte's chapter, while also illustrating some of Chaucer's

---

Middle English texts' treatments of their sources can be found in Newhauser, "*The Parson's Tale* and Its Generic Affiliations."

[25] Dempster, "The Parson's Tale," pp. 759–60. Notice, however, Dempster's qualification of the use of this text, pp. 728–9.

choices in selecting which parts of Pennaforte's work to include in the *Parson's Tale*.

II. *Compileison de Seinte Penance*, presenting a more closely analogous treatment of the image of the tree of penitence presented in ParT X,112–16 than what is found in Pennaforte's treatise, though it is clear that the *Compileison* is an analogue and not a source for Chaucer's work. This section of the *Compileison* is edited from Cambridge, Trinity College MS R.14.7.[26] For a description of this codex and its contents, as well as of the other manuscripts used in the editions here, see the references in the notes to the list of abbreviations of manuscripts and early printed editions below.

B. Vices

III. William Peraldus, *Summa de vitiis*, edited from three of the earliest manuscripts of the work and a 16th-century imprint, and covering the treatment of material for which Peraldus's text is closer to Chaucer's Middle English than is either of the Latin redactions of Peraldus's treatise:

1.–3. From the treatment of the sin of pride, covering the source of pride in the goods of nature, fortune, and grace, as well as material dealing with the question of true nobility and the foolishness of pride in bodily freedom, all three areas examined in a continuous passage from ParT X,450 to ParT X,473 and illustrating some of Chaucer's technique of compression of his source text.

IV. *Summa de vitiis "Quoniam,"* edited from all three known manuscripts of the text and covering material for which this redaction of Peraldus's *Summa de vitiis* is closer to Chaucer's text than the other redaction or Peraldus's original:

1.–7. From the treatment of the sin of envy, which is a continuous passage in the *Parson's Tale* (ParT X,484–514), and represents another view of Chaucer's compression and selection of material from this source text.

V. *Summa vitiorum "Primo,"* edited from seven of the known manuscripts of the text and covering material for which this redaction of Peraldus's *Summa de vitiis* is closer to Chaucer's text than the other redaction or Peraldus's original:[27]

---

[26] Wenzel, "Notes on the *Parson's Tale*," pp. 241–2; W. H. Trethewey, ed., *The French Text of the Ancrene Riwle*, EETS OS 240 (London, etc., 1958), pp. xviii–xxv; Dempster, "The Parson's Tale," pp. 726–8. A passage from the *Compileison de set morteus pecches*, which immediately precedes the *Compileison de Seinte Penance* in MS C, was edited by W. H. Trethewey, "The Seven Deadly Sins in the Devil's Court in the Trinity College French Text of the *Ancrene Riwle*," *PMLA* 65 (1950): 1233–46.

[27] Not included in this partial edition are London, British Library MS Additional 5667 and Oxford, Corpus Christi College MS 231 because they are defective at this point and do not contain the relevant portion of the text.

1.–2. From the treatment of the sin of lust, which is a brief, continuous passage in the *Parson's Tale* (ParT X,850–3), and again represents a view of Chaucer's compression and selection of material from this source text.

C. Remedial Virtues

VI.   *Summa virtutum de remediis anime*, which is excerpted from the edition and translation by Siegfried Wenzel, with variants from a new manuscript of the text discovered after the publication of this edition: Graz, Universitätsbibliothek MS 1458 (14th century):[28]

1.   From the treatment of the virtue of humility, covering the remedy for the sin of pride treated in ParT X,476–83;

2.–3. From the treatment of the virtue of mercy, covering part of the remedy for the sin of avarice, treated in ParT X,804–10.

D. Meditative Prose

VII. Anselm of Canterbury, *Meditatio ad concitandum timorem*, presenting the illustrative source of the quotation in Chaucer's text, though it was a commonplace and was also excerpted by a number of other authors where Chaucer may have found it.[29]

Abbreviations

I. *Printed Sources*

AL   Aristoteles Latinus. Corpus Philosophorum Medii Aevi. Roma, etc., 1951– .

Decretum   *Corpus iuris canonici*. Ed. Emil Friedberg. 2 vols. Leipzig, 1879; repr. Graz, 1959.

Glossa   *Biblia latina cum glossa ordinaria*. Facsimile Reprint of the Editio Princeps, Adolph Rusch of Strassburg 1480–1. Intro. Karlfried Froehlich and Margaret T. Gibson. 4 vols. Turnhout, 1992.

Lombard,   *Petri Lombardi Libri iv sententiarum studio et cura PP. Collegii S. Sententiae Bonaventurae*. Second ed. 2 vols. Ad Claras Aquas, 1916.

---

[28] The variants show the close relationship between MSS E and Gr in the transmission of the text.

[29] See, for example, William Peraldus, *Summa de virtutibus*, 4.3.4, in *Summa virtutum ac vitiorum Guilhelmi Paraldi Episcopi Lugdunensis de ordine predicatorum*, vol. 1 (Paris, 1512), fol. 238a (attrib. Gregory); Robert Holkot, *Super Libros Sapientiae* (Hagenau, 1494; repr. Frankfurt/Main, 1974), lectio 7D, fol. 2va–vb (attrib. Anselm); a Lenten sermon of the late 14th century in Latin in Cambridge, Pembroke College MS 199, fol. 128vb (attrib. Anselm); Dives and Pauper, 8.14 (ed. Priscilla Heath Barnum, vol. 1.2, EETS OS 280 [Oxford, etc., 1980], pp. 243–4 [attrib. Gregory]); an English passage in a Latin sermon in Oxford, Merton College MS 248, fol. 66a (attrib. Anselm); an English and Latin passage of the *Ancrene Wisse* (ed. Mabel Day in *The English Text of the Ancrene Riwle*, EETS OS 225 [London, 1952], p. 137 [attrib. "Aunselme"]). See also E. J. Dobson, *Moralities on the Gospels: A New Source of Ancrene Wisse* (Oxford, 1975), p. 157.

SP   S. Raimundus de Pennaforte. *Summa de paenitentia*. Ed. Xaverio Ochoa and Aloisio Diez. Universa Bibliotheca Iuris, 1B. Roma, 1976.

SBO   *Sancti Bernardi opera*. Ed. Jean Leclercq, C. H. Talbot, and H. M. Rochais. 8 vols. Roma, 1957–77.

Tubach   Frederic C. Tubach. *Index exemplorum*. FF Communications 204. Helsinki, 1969.

Walther, *IC* Hans Walther. *Initia Carminum ac versuum medii aevi posterioris latinorum*. Carmina medii aevi posterioris latina 1. Göttingen, 1959.

Walther, *PS* Hans Walther. *Proverbia sententiaeque latinitatis medii aevi*. Carmina medii aevi posterioris latina 2. 6 vols. Göttingen, 1963–9.

II. *Manuscripts and Early Printed Editions*

A   London, British Library MS Additional 5667, fols. 3r–38v (13th century, second half) [*Summa vitiorum "Primo"*].[30]

C   Cambridge, Trinity College MS R.14.7, fols. 36a–115va (13th century, end) [*Compileison de seinte penance*].[31]

Du   Durham, Cathedral Library MS B.I.18, fols. 14a–136va (14th century) [*Summa de vitiis "Quoniam"*].[32]

E   Einsiedeln, Stiftsbibliothek MS 275, fols. 1a–91vb (13th century, second half) [*Summa vitiorum "Primo"*].[33]

F   Cambridge, University Library MS Ff.1.17, fols. 1r–74v (13th century, second half) [*Summa vitiorum "Primo"*].[34]

G   London, Gray's Inn MS 12, fols. 261r–286v (13th century, end) [*Summa virtutum de remediis anime*].[35]

Gr   Graz, Universitätsbibliothek MS 1458, fols. 87r–168v (14th century) [*Summa virtutum de remediis anime*].[36]

H   London, British Library MS Harley 406, fols. 1r–68v (15th century) [*Summa vitiorum "Primo"*].[37]

---

[30] http://molcat.bl.uk; *Summa virtutum*, ed. Wenzel, p. 30; Neil R. Ker, *Medieval Libraries of Great Britain*, 2nd ed. (London, 1964), p. 266; *Index to the Additional Manuscripts . . . Acquired in the Years 1783–1835* (London, 1849), p. 448 (q.v. Theology).

[31] Trethewey, ed., *The French Text of the Ancrene Riwle*, pp. xii–xiv; Montague Rhodes James, *The Western Manuscripts in the Library of Trinity College, Cambridge. A Descriptive Catalogue*, vol. 2 (Cambridge, Eng., 1901), pp. 289–91.

[32] Wenzel, "The Source of Chaucer's Seven Deadly Sins," p. 352.

[33] *Summa virtutum*, ed. Wenzel, pp. 31–2; Gabriel Meier, *Catalogus codicum manuscriptorum qui in bibliotheca Monasterii Einsidlensis O.S.B. servantur*, vol. 1 (Einsiedeln, 1899), p. 266.

[34] *Summa virtutum*, ed. Wenzel, p. 32; *A Catalogue of the Manuscripts Preserved in the Library of the University of Cambridge*, vol. 2 (Cambridge, Eng., 1857), pp. 305–7.

[35] *Summa virtutum*, ed. Wenzel, pp. 32–3; Neil R. Ker, *Medieval Manuscripts in British Libraries*, vol. 1: *London* (Oxford, 1969), pp. 59–60.

[36] http://www-ub.kfunigraz.ac.at/SOSA/katalog/index.html; Anton Kern, *Die Handschriften der Universitätsbibliothek Graz*, vol. 2, Handschriftenverzeichnisse österreichischer Bibliotheken, B.2 (Wien, 1956), p. 327.

[37] *Summa virtutum*, ed. Wenzel, p. 33; J. A. Herbert, *Catalogue of Romances in the Department of Manuscripts in the British Museum*, vol. 3 (London, 1910), p. 221; *A Catalogue of the Harleian Manuscripts in the British Museum*, vol. 1 (London, 1808), p. 235.

Ha   London, British Library MS Harley 3823, fols. 50r–407v (14th century, beginning) [*Summa de vitiis "Quoniam"*].[38]

I   Cambridge, University Library MS Ii.4.8, fols. 147r–171v (14th century, beginning) [*Summa virtutum de remediis anime*].[39]

J   Cambridge, Jesus College MS 20, fols. 1a–87b (13th century, end) [*Summa vitiorum "Primo"*].[40]

L   Oxford, Bodleian Library MS Laud Misc. 171, fols. 7r–49r (13th century, end) [*Summa virtutum de remediis anime*].[41]

Lu   Lucca, Biblioteca statale MS 1396, pp. 508–895 (14th century, beginning) [William Peraldus, *Summa de vitiis*].[42]

Ly   Lyon, Bibliothèque municipale MS 678, fols. 12a–152b (13th century, middle) [William Peraldus, *Summa de vitiis*].[43]

M   Manchester, John Rylands Library MS Lat. 201, fols. 159r–212r (15th century, first half) [*Summa vitiorum "Primo"*].[44]

Mz   Paris, Bibliothèque Mazarine MS 794, fols. 1a–235va (13th century, middle) [William Peraldus, *Summa de vitiis*].[45]

O   Oxford, Corpus Christi College MS 231, fols. 38r–59v (15th century) [*Summa vitiorum "Primo"*].[46]

Pr   *Summa virtutum ac vitiorum Guilhelmi Paraldi Episcopi Lugdunensis de ordine predicatorum*. Vol. 2. Paris: Johannes Petit, Johannes Frellon, Franciscus Regnault, 1512 [William Peraldus, *Summa de vitiis*].

R1   London, British Library MS Royal 8.A.x, fols. 54r–144r (14th century, beginning) [*Summa vitiorum "Primo"*].[47]

R2   London, British Library MS Royal 11.B.iii, fols. 226v–276r (14th century, first half) [*Summa vitiorum "Primo"*].[48]

[38] Wenzel, "The Source of Chaucer's Seven Deadly Sins," pp. 352–3; C. E. Wright, *Fontes Harleiani* (London, 1972), p. 211.

[39] *Summa virtutum*, ed. Wenzel, p. 33; Ker, *Medieval Libraries of Great Britain*, p. 137; *A Catalogue of the Manuscripts Preserved in the Library of the University of Cambridge*, vol. 3 (Cambridge, Eng., 1858), pp. 447–8.

[40] *Summa virtutum*, ed. Wenzel, p. 33; Ker, *Medieval Libraries of Great Britain*, p. 61; M. R. James, *A Descriptive Catalogue of the Manuscripts in the Library of Jesus College, Cambridge* (London, Cambridge, 1895), p. 21; J. Raine, *Catalogi veteres librorum Ecclesiae Cathedralis Dunelmensis*, Surtees Society Publications 7 (London, 1838), pp. 24, 100.

[41] *Summa virtutum*, ed. Wenzel, p. 34; H. O. Coxe, *Catalogi codicum manuscriptorum Bibliothecae Bodleianae. Pars secunda Codices Latinos et Miscellaneos Laudianos complectens*, ed. R. W. Hunt (Oxford, 1973), cols. 155–7 and p. 550.

[42] Kaeppeli, "Guillelmus Peraldus (Peyraut)," *Scriptores Ordinis Praedicatorum*, vol. 2, p. 137.

[43] *Catalogue général des manuscrits des bibliothèques publiques de France: Départements*, vol. 30,1 (Paris, 1900), pp. 184–5; cf. also the brief mention in Kaeppeli, "Guillelmus Peraldus (Peyraut)," *Scriptores Ordinis Praedicatorum*, vol. 2, p. 137.

[44] Moses Tyson, "Hand-list of Additions to the Collection of Latin Manuscripts in the John Rylands Library, 1908–1928," *Bulletin of the John Rylands Library Manchester* 12 (1928): 583; Robert Fawtier, "Hand-list of Additions to the Collection of Latin Manuscripts in the John Rylands Library, 1908–1920," *Bulletin of the John Rylands Library Manchester* 6 (1921–22): 193.

[45] Auguste Molinier, *Catalogue des manuscrits de la Bibliothèque Mazarine*, vol. 1 (Paris, 1885), pp. 384–5.

[46] H. O. Coxe, *Catalogus codicum mss. qui in collegiis aulisque Oxoniensibus hodie adservantur*, vol. 2 (Oxford, 1852), pp. 93–4.

[47] http://molcat.bl.uk; Sir George F. Warner and Julius P. Gilson, *Catalogue of Western Manuscripts in the Old Royal and King's Collections*, vol. 1 (London, 1921), p. 212.

[48] http://molcat.bl.uk; Warner and Gilson, *Catalogue of Western Manuscripts*, vol. 1, pp. 344–6.

Tr   Dublin, Trinity College MS 306, fols. 1a–121vb (14th century, beginning) [*Summa de vitiis "Quoniam"*].[49]

III. *Editorial Abbreviations*

*	Variant reading closer to Chaucer's text.
add	Variant added.
attrib.	Attribution of authorship.
marg	Variant written in the margin.
om	Text omitted.

---

[49] Marvin L. Colker, *Trinity College Library Dublin. Descriptive Catalogue of the Mediaeval and Renaissance Latin Manuscripts*, vol. 1 (Aldershot, Eng.; Brookfield, VT, 1991), pp. 619–21.

A. Penitence

I

Raymund of Pennaforte, *Summa on Penitence*

1. (ParT X,80–92)

After we called to mind some things further above as a precaution concerning the bottomless pit and the snares of Babylon – namely, so that they might be known and, being known, better avoided – it remains for us to hasten anxiously to the calm haven and eternal serenity which, indeed, is penitence, seeking the proper, necessary, and unerring path there. Concerning this matter one should understand what it is and from where it takes its name, the three actions of penitence, its three species, what things are necessary for true penitence, the keys, remissions, and hindrances to penitence, and we will introduce some other matters which need to be cleared up concerning this material.

WHAT IS PENITENCE

1. Penitence, as Ambrose says, is "to bewail past evils, and not to commit again deeds which ought to be bewailed."[1] Likewise Augustine: "Penitence is a certain chastisement of someone who grieves, punishing in himself that which he grieves to have done."[2] Now it is called penitence as if it were "the comprising of punishment" (*poenae tentio*) by one who ought to be punished, since through penitence a person punishes the illicit things which he has committed.

2. By reason of this phrase which is found in the authoritative statement by Ambrose, "and not to commit again deeds which ought to be bewailed," some have said that if someone truly does penance, he will never commit a deadly sin afterwards; and if it happens that he commits a sin afterwards, it is proven in this way that his previous penance was not true penance. Likewise, they defend themselves with many other authoritative statements. Isidore: "He is a mocker and not one doing penance who still commits the deeds for which he ought to be doing penance, nor does he appear to pray to God as His subject, but to mock Him as an arrogant man."[3] Likewise Augustine: "That penitence is empty which the next misdeed pollutes."[4] Idem: "Laments are of no benefit if the sins are repeated."[5]

To this it should be said that the words found in the authoritative statement by Ambrose mentioned above, and in similar ones, should not be taken as referring to

A. Penitence

I

Raimundus de Pennaforte, *Summa de paenitentia*

(from S. Raimundus de Pennaforte, *Summa de paenitentia*, 3.34, ed. Xaverio Ochoa
and Aloisio Diez [Roma, 1976], cols. 793–882)

1. (ParT X,80–92)

Post abyssum et laqueos Babylonis, de quibus superius aliqua col. 795
memoravimus ad cautelam, videlicet ut cognoscantur, et cognita
melius evitentur, restat ut ad portum quietis ac serenitatis aeternae,
solliciti festinemus, inquirentes viam rectam, necessariam et
5   infallibilem, quae quidem est paenitentia. Circa quam videndum /
quid ipsa sit et unde dicatur; de tribus actionibus paenitentiae; de col. 796
tribus speciebus ejusdem; quae sint necessaria in vera paenitentia;
de clavibus; de remissionibus; de impedimentis paenitentiae, et
aliqua alia dubitabilia interponemus circa istam materiam.
10 QUID SIT PAENITENTIA
    1. Paenitentia est, ut ait Ambrosius, "mala praeterita plangere, et
plangenda iterum non committere."[1] Item Augustinus: "Paenitentia
est quaedam dolentis vindicta puniens in se quod dolet
commississe."[2] Dicitur autem paenitentia, quasi poenae tentio, a
15 puniendo, quia per illam quis punit illicita quae commisit.
    2. Occasione illius verbi positi in auctoritate Ambrosii "et plangenda
iterum non committere," dixerunt quidam quod si aliquis vere
paenitet, numquam postea peccabit mortaliter; et si contingerit
ipsum peccare postea, probatur per hoc quod prima non fuit vera
20 paenitentia. Item muniunt se aliis auctoritatibus multis. Isidorus:
"Irrisor est et non paenitens qui adhuc agit quod paenitet, nec
videtur Deum poscere subditus sed subsannare superbus."[3] Item
Augustinus: "Inanis est paenitentia quam sequens culpa coinquinat."[4] Item
Idem: "Nihil prosunt lamenta si replicantur peccata."[5]
25 Ad hoc dicendum quod verba posita in auctoritate praedicta Ambrosii
et similibus, non ad diversa tempora, sed ad illud in quo quis paenitet

---

1. Ps.-Ambrose, *Sermones*, 25.1 (PL 17:677A); Gratian, *Decretum*, 2.33.3.3.1 (1:1211); Lombard, *Sententiae*, 4.14.2 (2:820); **2.** Ps.-Augustine of Hippo, *De vera et falsa poenitentia*, 8.22 (PL 40:1120) – Robert M. Correale, "The Sources of Some Patristic Quotations in Chaucer's The Parson's Tale," *English Language Notes* 19 (1981): 96; cf. Lombard, *Sententiae*, 4.14.2 (2:823); **3.** Isidore of Seville, *Sententiarum libri*, 2.16.1 (CCL 111:128) – Correale, "The Sources," p. 96; cf. Lombard, *Sententiae*, 4.14.2 (2:820); **4.** Isidore of Seville, *Synonyma de lamentatione anime peccatricis*, 1.77 (PL 83:845A); cf. Gratian, *Decretum*, 2.33.3.3.12 (1:1213); cf. Lombard, *Sententiae*, 4.14.2 (2:820–1); **5.** Isidore of Seville, *Synonyma de lamentatione anime peccatricis*, 1.77 (PL 83:845A); cf. Lombard, *Sententiae*, 4.14.2 (2:821).

unspecified times, but to that one time during which someone should do penance, namely, so that at the time when he bewails the evils he has committed, he will not commit anything, in will or in deed, which he ought to weep for. And this is clearly what Gregory means when he says: "To do penance is to bewail former evils and not to commit deeds which ought to be bewailed; for whoever thus weeps bitterly for some things while he nevertheless is committing others either does not understand that he is doing penance or is only pretending to do so. For what benefit is it if someone bemoans the sins of lust and nevertheless is still panting with the passions of avarice?"[6] Likewise, after the words "he is a mocker," etc., Isidore immediately added an explanation of what he was saying: "For many people shed tears incessantly and do not leave off sinning; those are the ones I perceive to be satisfied with tears as penitence, but without possessing the inner disposition of penitence."[7]

2. (ParT X,95–111)

ON THE THREE ACTIONS OF PENITENCE
5. "Now the actions of penitence," as Augustine says, "are three."[1]
The first one gives birth to a new human being, and this happens before baptism. For unless the person to be baptized repents of his former life, he cannot begin a new life, and if he is baptized, he receives a sign, but not grace or the remission of sins until deception leaves his heart. Nevertheless, he is not held to do external penance, since internal penance suffices for him. Only children are exempt from this penitence when they are baptized, because they are not capable of exercising a free will.
Now a person does the second penance, or action of penitence, for deadly sins after baptism.
The third one is done for venial and daily sins. Concerning this one, Augustine: "Penance for the humble and the good among the faithful is to suffer daily."[2] These are gifts and a divine calling, since in baptism God's grace does not require an act of moaning or wailing or something else, but faith alone, and it gives all things freely.
Now as far as the present material is concerned, we will focus primarily on the second action.
ON THE THREE SPECIES OF PENITENCE
6. There are three species of penitence, for one is solemn, one public, one private.
Solemn penance is carried out at the height of Lent with a ceremony. It is also called solemn, although not in such a strict sense, when someone who is unwilling to do penance is sent to a monastery. This penitence ought to be imposed only by a bishop or, on his orders, by a priest, and it ought to be imposed for a public and widely notorious crime which has stirred up the entire city. Likewise, it ought not to be imposed on a cleric, unless he has been removed from office. Whoever has once

sunt referenda, scilicet, ut tempore quo plangit commissa mala, non committat, voluntate vel opere, flenda. Et hoc aperte innuit Gregorius / dicens: "Paenitentiam agere est praeterita mala plangere et col. 797
30 plangenda non committere; nam qui sic alia deplorat ut tamen alia committat, adhuc paenitentiam agere, aut ignorat, aut dissimulat. Quid enim prodest si peccata luxuriae quis defleat et tamen adhuc avaritiae aestibus anhelat?"[6] Item Isidorus, post illa verba "irrisor est" etc., statim subjunxit, exponens quod dixerat: "Multi enim lacrimas
35 indesinenter fundunt et peccare non desinunt; quosdam accipere lacrimas ad paenitentiam cerno et affectum paenitentiae non habere."[7]

2. (ParT X,95–111)

DE TRIBUS ACTIONIBUS PAENITENTIAE   col. 800
5. "Actiones autem paenitentiae," ut ait Augustinus, "sunt tres."[1]
Una est quae novum hominem parturit, et fit ante baptismum. Nisi enim baptizandus paeniteat vitae veteris, novam vitam inchoare non
5 potest, et, si baptizetur, recipit characterem, sed non gratiam, nec peccatorum remissionem, donec recedat fictio de corde suo. Non tamen tenetur iste ad exteriorem paenitentiam agendam, quia sufficit ei paenitentia interior. Ab hac paenitentia, cum baptizantur, soli parvuli sunt immunes, eo quod non possunt uti libero arbitrio.
10 Altera vero paenitentia est, sive actio paenitentiae, quam quis facit post baptismum de mortalibus peccatis.
Tertia est quae fit de peccatis venialibus et cotidianis. De hac Augustinus: "Paenitentia humilium et bonorum fidelium poena cotidiana."[2] Dona sunt et vocatio Dei, quia gratia Dei in baptismo
15 non requirit gemitum, neque planctum vel opus aliquod, sed solam fidem, et omnia gratis condonat.
Circa secundam autem actionem est quantum ad praesentem materiam principaliter insistendum. /
DE TRIBUS SPECIEBUS PAENITENTIAE   col. 801
20 6. Species paenitentiae sunt tres, nam alia est sollemnis, alia publica, alia privata.
Sollemnis est quae fit in capite Quadragesimae cum sollemnitate. Dicitur etiam sollemnis, licet non ita proprie, quando aliquis invitus ad paenitentiam agendam mittitur in monasterium. Haec debet
25 imponi ab episcopo tantum, vel de mandato ejus a sacerdote. Et debet imponi pro crimine publico et vulgatissimo quod totam

---

6. Gregory the Great, *Homiliae in Evangelia*, 2.34.15 (PL 76:1256B) – cf. Siegfried Wenzel, "Fragment X: The Parson's Prologue, The Parson's Tale, Chaucer's Retraction," in *The Riverside Chaucer*, 3rd ed., gen. ed. Larry D. Benson (Boston, 1987), p. 957; cf. Lombard, *Sententiae*, 4.14.2 (2:820); 7. Isidore of Seville, *Sententiarum libri*, 2.16.2 (CCL 111:129); cf. Lombard, *Sententiae*, 4.14.2 (2:820).

1. Augustine of Hippo (?), *Sermones in diversis*, 351.2.2 (PL 39:1537); cf. Gratian, *Decretum*, 2.33.3.1.81 (1:1181); cf. Lombard, *Sententiae*, 4.16.4 (2:843–4); 2. Augustine of Hippo, *Epistolae*, 265.8 (PL 33:1089); cf. Gratian, *Decretum*, 2.33.3.1.81 (1:1181); cf. Lombard, *Sententiae*, 4.16.4 (2:843–4).

done this penance ought not to be promoted afterwards, nor ought he help at the mass in the order which he has entered. Likewise, he ought not to enter into matrimony; however, if he is already married, he will remain so.

Sometimes what was called solemn above is called public, for the reason that it is done publicly. Nevertheless, strictly speaking, public penitence occurs before the congregation of the Church, not with the ceremony mentioned above, but when the penitent is enjoined to go on a pilgrimage through the world with pilgrim's staff and scapular or other clothing customary for this purpose. It should be possible for any priest to impose this penance on one of his parishioners since I do not find that he is prohibited from doing so, unless there is a contrary custom in a particular church. Likewise, it ought not to be imposed on a cleric, unless he has been removed from office, nor ought it be imposed at all except for an enormous and clearly evident crime. Likewise, solemn penance ought not to be repeated, but any other penance can and ought to be repeated as often as a person sins.

That penitence is called private which, unlike the previous two species, happens daily, when someone confesses his sins in private to a priest.

WHAT IS NECESSARY FOR TRUE PENITENCE

7. Next, one should understand what is necessary for true and perfect penitence, and in fact there are three things, namely: contrition of the heart, confession by mouth, and satisfaction in deed. John Golden-mouth: "Perfect penitence compels the sinner to suffer all things willingly, for contrition in one's heart, confession in one's mouth, and complete humility in one's deeds – this makes for fruitful penitence."[3]

For since we offend God in three ways, namely: by delight in a thought, by shamelessness in speech, and by pride in a deed, then according to the rule that diseases are cured by their opposites, we should make amends in three opposing ways. Concerning these also Jerome, explaining the words of Amos, "For three transgressions of Damascus and for four I will not alter it:"[4] "We can say this according to the tropological level of exegesis. The first sin is to have had evil thoughts. The second, to have acquiesced to the perverse thoughts. The third, to have completed in deed what you have decided on mentally. The fourth, not to do penance after the sin and to be very pleased with oneself for one's transgression."[5]

3. (ParT X,128–283)

ON CONTRITION

8. The first day's journey is contrition, about which there are four things to consider, namely: what it is, what the causes are which lead to it, what qualities it ought to have, and what its effect is.

Contrition is the sorrow that one accepts for one's sins, with the intention of confessing and making amends. It is taught by God through His prophet where it is said: "Rend your hearts," etc.[1]

---

37 **aliqua** aliquia *SP*.

commoverit urbem. Item non debet imponi clerico, nisi deposito.
Qui semel egerit eam, non debet postea promoveri, nec ministrare in
ordine suscepto. Item non debet contrahere matrimonium; si tamen
30   contraxerit, tenebit.

Publica dicitur quandoque quae supra est dicta sollemnis, ideo quia
publice fit. Proprie tamen dicitur illa quae fit in facie Ecclesiae, non
cum praedicta sollemnitate, sed cum injungitur peregrinatio per
mundum cum baculo cubitali et scapulari, vel veste alia ad hoc
35   consueta. Hanc posset imponere quilibet sacerdos suo parochiano,
quia non invenio sibi prohibitum, nisi consuetudo esset contraria in
[aliqua] ecclesia. Item non debet imponi clerico, nisi deposito, nec
debet imponi nisi pro crimine enormi et manifesto. Item sollemnis
paenitentia non debet iterari, / sed alia quaelibet potest et debet col. 802
40   iterari quoties homo peccat.

Privata dicitur illa paenitentia quae singulariter fit cotidie, cum quis
peccata sua secrete sacerdoti confitetur.

QUAE SUNT NECESSARIA AD VERAM PAENITENTIAM

7. Sequitur videre quae sint necessaria in paenitentia vera et
45   perfecta. Et quidem tria, videlicet: cordis contritio, oris confessio,
operis satisfactio. Joannes, Os aureum: "Perfecta paenitentia cogit
peccatorem omnia libenter sufferre; in corde enim contritio, in ore
confessio, in opere tota humilitas, haec est fructifera paenitentia."[3]

Quia enim tribus modis Deum offendimus, scilicet: delectatione
50   cogitationis, impudentia locutionis et superbia operis, secundum
regulam ut contraria contrariis curentur, tribus modis oppositis
satisfaciamus. De his etiam Hieronymus, exponens verba Amos,
"Super tribus sceleribus Damasci et super quattuor non convertam
eum:"[4] "Juxta tropologiam hoc possumus dicere. Primum peccatum
55   est cogitasse quae mala sunt. Secundum, cogitationibus acquievisse
perversis. Tertium, quod mente decreveris opere complesse.
Quartum, post peccatum non agere paenitentiam et suo sibi
complacere delicto."[5]

3. (ParT X,128–283)

DE CONTRITIONE   col. 803

8. Prima diaeta est contritio. Circa quam quattuor sunt consideranda,
scilicet: quid ipsa sit, quae sint causae inductivae ipsius, qualis
debeat esse, et quis ejus effectus.
5   Contritio est dolor pro peccatis assumptus cum proposito confitendi
et satisfaciendi. Haec praecipitur a Domino per prophetam, ubi
dicitur: "Scindite corda vestra" etc.[1]

3. Ps.-Johannes Chrysostomus, *Sermo de Poenitentia* (John Chrysostom, *Opera omnia* [Antwerp, 1614], 5:361b) – Robert M. Correale, "The Source of the Quotation from 'Crisostom' in 'The Parson's Tale,'" *Notes and Queries* N.S. 27 [225] (1980): 101–2; cf. Gratian, *Decretum*, 2.33.3.1.40 (1:1168), 2.33.3.3.8 (1:1212); cf. Lombard, *Sententiae*, 4.16.1 (2:839); **4.** Amos 1:3; **5.** Jerome, *Commentariorum in Amos prophetam libri*, 1.1.4/5 (CCL 76:219).

1. Joel 2:13.

This sorrow ought to be threefold, as Bernard says: "harsh, harsher, harshest. Harsh, since we commit an offense against the Lord and Creator of all. Harsher, since it is against our heavenly Father, who nourishes us in many ways. Harshest, since it is against our Redeemer, who freed us with his own blood from the chains of sin, the cruelty of demons, and the harshness of hell."[2]

9. The causes that lead to it are six: thought, and from thought a shame for the sins one has committed; hatred of the vileness of sin itself; fear of the day of judgment and of punishment in hell; sorrow for losing the kingdom of heaven and for a manifold affront to the Creator; and a threefold hope, namely: for forgiveness, for grace, and for glory. For forgiveness, through which sins are forgiven. For grace, through which one will behave correctly. For glory, through which one still will be repaid for a good deed.

Concerning the first, namely concerning thought, Hezekiah: "I will reflect upon all my years in the bitterness of my soul."[3]

Concerning the second, namely shame, Job: "They turn worthy affairs to a matter for blushing."[4] Hosea 2: "I will reveal your private parts before your face."[5] Jeremiah in Lamentations: "Their faces have been made blacker than pieces of coal."[6]

Concerning the third, namely the hatred of sin, the vileness of which has made the sinner himself vile, Jeremiah: "How immeasurably vile you have become, repeating your ways again and again."[7] John in the Gospel: "Whoever commits a sin is a slave to sin."[8] Augustine: "Consider that you are of value, lest you become worthless to yourself."[9] Aristotle: "I am greater and I have been born for greater things than to be a slave to my body."[10] Seneca: "If I knew that the gods were going to pardon it, or that human beings would never find out about it, nevertheless I would still abhor sin."[11]

Concerning the fourth, namely fear of the day of judgment and of punishment, Jerome: "Whenever I consider that day, my entire body trembles."[12] Idem: "Whether I am eating or drinking or doing anything else, always that terrible roar seems to sound in my ears," etc.[13] Augustine: "Let a person climb up on the judgment seat of his own mind," etc.[14] Gregory: "What can the little twig of the desert do where the cedar of paradise is quaking with fear?"[15] Peter in the canonical epistle: "If the person who is just will barely be saved, where will the impious and the sinner be?"[16] Revelations 19: "The beast was captured and with it false prophets, and those who had received the token of the beast and those who had worshipped its image – these two were thrown into the lake of fire," etc.[17] Likewise, Revelations 21: "The fearful and the unbelieving and the cursed and the murderers and the fornicators and the sorcerers and the idolaters and all the liars, their portion will be in the

Iste dolor debet esse triplex, ut ait Bernardus: / "acer, acrior, col. 804
acerrimus. Acer, quia offendimus Dominum et Creatorem omnium.
10   Acrior, quia Patrem nostrum caelestem, qui nos pascit multipliciter.
Acerrimus, quia Redemptorem nostrum, qui nos liberavit proprio
sanguine a vinculis peccatorum, crudelitate daemonum et acerbitate
gehennae."[2]
9. Causae inductivae sunt sex: cogitatio, et ex ea pudor de peccatis
15   commissis; detestatio vilitatis ipsius peccati; timor de die judicii et
de poena gehennae; dolor de amissione caelestis patriae et multiplici
offensa Creatoris; et spes triplex, scilicet: veniae, gratiae et gloriae.
Veniae, qua peccata remittuntur. Gratiae, qua bene operabitur.
Gloriae, qua pro bono opere adhuc remunerabitur.
20   De primo, scilicet de cogitatione, Ezechias: "Recogitabo omnes
annos meos in amaritudine animae meae."[3]
De secundo, scilicet, pudore, Job: "Res dignas confusione agunt."[4]
Oseas 2: "Revelabo pudenda tua in facie tua."[5] Jeremias in Threnis:
"Denigrata est super carbones facies eorum."[6]
25   De tertio, scilicet detestatione peccati, propter cujus vilitatem
peccator vilis factus est, Jeremias: "Quam vilis facta es nimis iterans
vias tuas."[7] Joannes in Evangelio: "Qui facit peccatum servus est
peccati."[8] Augustinus: "Appende te ex pretio ne tibi vilescas."[9]
Philosophus: "Maior sum et ad maiora natus quam ut fiam
30   mancipium corporis mei."[10] Seneca: "Si scirem deos ignoscituros,
homines autem ignoraturos tamen abhorrerem peccatum."[11]
De quarto, scilicet timore de die judicii et poena, Hieronymus:
"Quoties diem illum considero toto corpore contremisco."[12] Idem:
"Sive comedo, sive bibo, sive aliquid aliud facio, semper videtur in
35   auribus meis illa tuba terribilis insonare" etc.[13] Augustinus:
"Ascendat homo tribunal mentis suae" etc.[14] Gregorius: "Quid faciet
virgula deserti ubi concutietur cedrus / Paradisi?"[15] Petrus in col. 805
canonica: "Si justus vix salvabitur, impius et peccator ubi
parebunt?"[16] Apocalipsis 19: "Apprehensa est bestia et cum illa
40   pseudoprophetae et qui acceperunt characterem bestiae et qui
adoraverunt imaginem ejus, missi sunt hi duo in stagnum ignis"
etc.[17] Item Apocalipsis 21: "Timidis et incredulis et exsecratis et
homicidis et fornicatoribus et veneficis et idolatris et omnibus

---

2. Cf. Ps.-Hugh of St. Victor, *Miscellanea*, 6.100 (PL 177:857B); cf. Nicholas of Clairvaux, *Sermo in festo Sancti Andreae*, 8 (PL 184:1052D–1053A) – Robert M. Correale, "Nicholas of Clairvaux and the Quotation from 'Seint Bernard' in Chaucer's *The Parson's Tale*, 130–2," *American Notes and Queries* 20,1 (1981): 2–3; **3.** Isa 38:15; **4.** Cf. Job 8:22; Prov 12:4; **5.** Nah 3:5, cf. Hos 2:10; **6.** Lam 4:8; **7.** Jer 2:36; **8.** John 8:34; **9.** Cf. Augustine of Hippo, *Enarrationes in Psalmos, Ps 32*, 2.1.4 (CCL 38:249) – cf. Wenzel, "Fragment X," in *The Riverside Chaucer*, p. 957; **10.** Seneca, *Epistulae morales*, 65.21; **11.** Cf. Werner II de Küssenberg, *Libri deflorationum sive excerptionum*, 2.22 (De remissione peccatorum) (PL 157:1205C) – cf. Wenzel, "Fragment X," in *The Riverside Chaucer*, p. 957; **12–13.** Cf. Jerome, *Epistulae*, 66.10 (CSEL 54:660); cf. Ps.-Jerome, *Regula monacharum*, 30 (PL 30:417B); **14.** Augustine of Hippo (?), *Sermones in diversis*, 351.4.7 (PL 39:1542); Augustine of Hippo, *In Iohannis Evangelium tractatus*, 33.5 (CCL 36:308); **15.** Cf. Peter Comestor, *Sermones*, 20 (*In Quadragesima sermo primus*) (PL 171:431C); cf. Peter Lombard, *Commentaria in Psalmos*, Ps. 42:1 (PL 191:424D); **16.** 1Pet 4:18; **17.** Rev 19:20.

lake burning with fire and brimstone, which is the second death."[18] Likewise Paul, Romans 6: "The wages of sin are death."[19]

Concerning the fifth, Revelations 3: "Hold onto what you have so that no one will take your crown."[20] In the same book 16: "Blessed is the one who remains awake and guards his clothing lest he walk about naked and they see his disgrace."[21]

Concerning the sixth, namely concerning hope, the Lord himself: "Behold, I stand at the door and I knock; if anyone hears me and opens the gate for me, I will come in to him and I will dine with him and he with me. Whoever is victorious, I will give him a place to sit with me on my throne."[22] Likewise, both he and his precursor call out at the beginning of their preaching, "Do penance."[23] And immediately they add something to it concerning a reward, saying: "For the kingdom of heaven is at hand."[24] Likewise: "I have not come to call the righteous, but sinners" to penitence.[25]

4. (ParT X,292–313)

The qualities which contrition ought to have

10. Next, what the nature of contrition ought to be, namely that it be universal and continuous, having the purpose of confessing and making amends.

These things are proven in the authoritative statement mentioned above: "I will reflect for you upon all the years," etc.[1] Likewise: "Every night I will wash my bed, with my tears I will moisten my couch."[2] Likewise: "Since I am ready for the lashes and my sorrow is always before my eyes."[3]

On the effect of contrition

11. Next, what its effect is. Now in part its effect is evident from the sense of its designation. For it is called "contrition" as if it were a whole or complete grinding up (*tritio*), which is to be understood both passively and actively.

Passively, since the entire heart is literally ground up, as it were, and torn to pieces by excessive distress, sorrow, wrath, and indignation which it has conceived against the sins themselves. Whence the Lord through His prophet: "Rend your hearts and not your vestments."[4] Likewise, the Psalm: "The sacrifice to God – a soul much afflicted, a heart contrite and humbled," etc.[5] Therefore, pierce and smite your heart, even if it were necessary to do so with the thorns, nails, and the lance, and the other instruments by which Christ himself was pierced for you on the cross.

Actively, since it acts like a very powerful engine of war, destroying the mass of sins which used to separate us from God, like a rampart. Isaiah: "Our iniquities have made a division between us and God."[6] Likewise this engine of war destroys the devil's snares and chains. The Psalm: "The snare has been destroyed and we have been set free."[7] Likewise, it tears down the infernal dungeon which the demons have prepared in hell for the sinful soul, and it weakens the demons' powers. Whence, after his hair had grown back and his strength had been restored, Samson shattered two columns and caused the building to collapse, so that he was killed together with the Philistines.[8] In the same way, when the sinner regains his hair (that is, the gifts

mendacibus pars illorum erit in stagno ardenti igne et sulphure,
45   quod est mors secunda."[18] Item Apostolus ad Romanos 6:
"Stipendia peccati mors."[19]
De quinto, Apocalipsis 3: "Tene quod habes ut nemo accipiat
coronam tuam."[20] In eodem 16: "Beatus qui vigilat et custodit
vestimenta sua ne nudus ambulet et videant turpitudinem ejus."[21]
50   De sexto, scilicet, de spe, ipsemet Dominus: "Ecce ego sto ad
ostium et pulso; si quis audierit me et aperuerit mihi januam,
introibo ad illum et cenabo cum illo et ille mecum. Qui vicerit, dabo
ei sedere mecum in throno meo."[22] Item tam Ipse quam praecursor
ejus clamant in suae praedicationis exordio: "Paenitentiam agite."[23]
55   Et statim subjungunt de praemio dicentes: "Appropinquabit enim
regnum caelorum."[24] Item: "Non veni vocare justos sed peccatores"
ad paenitentiam.[25]

4. (ParT X,292–313)

Qualis debeat esse contritio   col. 807
10. Sequitur qualis debeat esse contritio, scilicet, quod sit universalis
et continua, habens propositum confitendi et satisfaciendi.
Haec probantur in auctoritate praedicta: "Recogitabo tibi omnes
5   annos" etc.[1] Item: "Lavabo per singulas noctes lectum meum,
lacrimis meis stratum meum rigabo."[2] Item: "Quoniam ego in
flagella / paratus sum et dolor meus in conspectu meo semper."[3]   col. 808
De effectu contritionis
11. Sequitur quis sit ejus effectus. Patet autem effectus ejus in parte
10   ex vi ipsius nominis. Dicitur enim contritio quasi simul vel ex toto
tritio. Quod et passive intellegendum est, et active.
Passive, quia totum cor ad litteram quasi teritur et scinditur prae
nimia angustia, dolore, ira et indignatione quae concepit contra ipsa
peccata. Unde Dominus per prophetam: "Scindite corda vestra et
15   non vestimenta vestra."[4] Item Psalmus: "Sacrificium Deo spiritus
contribulatus, cor contritum et humiliatum" etc.[5] Punge igitur et
percute cor tuum, etiam si necesse fuerit spinis, clavis et lancea et
aliis quibus ipse Christus fuit pro te punctus in cruce.
Active, quia ista tamquam fortissima machina conterit congeriem
20   peccatorum quae quasi quidam murus separabant nos a Deo. Isaias:
"Iniquitates nostrae diviserunt inter nos et Deum."[6] Item haec
conterit laqueos et catenas diaboli. Psalmus: "Laqueus contritus est
et nos liberati sumus."[7] Item haec destruit carcerem infernalem
quem daemones paraverant in inferno animae peccatrici, et vires
25   daemonum enervat. Unde Samson, postquam creverant capilli ejus,
viribus restitutis, concussit duas columnas et corruit domus ita quod
ipse cum philisthaeis mortuus est.[8] Sic peccator, cum recuperaverit

---

18. Rev 21:8; 19. Rom 6:23; 20. Rev 3:11; 21. Rev 16:15; 22. Rev 3:20–1; 23. Matt 3:2, 4:17; 24. Matt 10:7; 25. Matt 9:13.

1. Isa 38:15; 2. Ps 6:7; 3. Ps 37:18; 4. Joel 2:13; 5. Ps 50:19; 6. Cf. Isa 59:2; 7. Ps 123:7; 8. Cf. Judg 16:22–30.

of the Holy Spirit) through contrition, his strength is restored to him, so that he destroys two very evil columns (that is, lust of the flesh and the pride of life), kills the former self within him, tears down the house of hell, and weakens the demons' strength. This engine of war destroys the arm of the sinner and of the evil one (that is, of the devil). Likewise, it repairs the walls of Jerusalem which Nebuchadnezzar had torn down. The Psalm: "Do good, oh Lord, in Your good will (i.e., in the contrition which has been or will be given freely by You alone) to Zion (i.e., the soul), so that in this way the walls of Jerusalem may be rebuilt" (namely, through penitence).[9]

And, briefly, contrition cleanses the soul of the accusation of blame and frees it from the punishment of hell, from the terrifying company of demons, and from the most vile slavery to sin. It restores the spiritual goods which the soul had lost through sin, the company and the spiritual communion of the church, and participation in all the good things which are done in the church. From a child of wrath[10] it creates a child of grace, from a child of the devil, a child of God and, as a result, someone enjoying an eternal inheritance.

Whether sin is forgiven in contrition without confession

12. Now in what way this ought to be understood, namely whether contrition removes sins by itself without confession or whether this happens by contrition with confession, there are diverse opinions.

5. (ParT X,316–19)

Likewise, about these matters observe for what reason confession or penitence is called a sacrament. For there are three things to be noted here, namely confession, contrition, and cleansing. Confession is only a sign, namely of contrition. Contrition is an object and a sign: the object denoted by the sign of confession, and the sign of cleansing. Cleansing is only an object denoted by a sign, namely that of contrition.

ON CONFESSION

14. The second day's journey is confession, about which there are seven things which must be taken into consideration, namely what it is, whether it should be made by necessity, and to whom; what things are necessary for a true confession; whether and by whom and in what way confessional questions are to be posed, and concerning the punishment of a priest who discloses a confession.

Confession is the lawful declaration of sins to a priest. And it is called "confession" as if it were a whole or complete or ubiquitous acknowledging (*fassio*); for whoever confesses, acknowledges everything.

The penitent is required to confess his sins by necessity. And, briefly, these three things, contrition, confession, and satisfaction, are in the law. Contrition is commanded in Joel: "Rend your hearts."[1] Confession in Lamentations: "Pour out your heart like water."[2] Likewise, the Psalm: "Pour out your hearts to God,"[3] and James: "Confess your sins to one another."[4] Satisfaction in John: "Bear fruits worthy of penitence."[5] Likewise, all of these matters are commanded by the Lord when he says: "Do penance," etc.[6]

capillos, id est, dona Spiritus Sancti per contritionem, vires sibi
restituuntur, ita quod duas pessimas columnas, id est,
30 concupiscentiam carnis et superbiam vitae concutit, veterem
hominem in se interficit, domum infernalem diruit, daemonum vires
enervat. Ista conterit brachium peccatoris et maligni, id est, diaboli.
Item / ista reparat muros Hierusalem quos destruxerat Nabuzardam. col. 809
Psalmus: "Benigne fac Domine, in bona voluntate tua (id est, in
35 contritione a te solo gratis data vel danda) Sion (id est, animae), ut
sic aedificentur (scilicet, per eam) muri Hierusalem."⁹
Et breviter ista mundat animam a reatu culpae, liberat a poena
gehennae, ab horrenda daemonum societate, et a vilissima peccati
servitute; restituit bona spiritualia quae amiserat per peccatum,
40 societatem et spiritualem communionem Ecclesiae bonorumque
omnium quae in ea fiunt participationem; de filio irae¹⁰ filium
gratiae, de filio diaboli filium efficit Dei et per consequens
participem hereditatis aeternae.
Utrum in contritione remittatur peccatum sine confessione
45 12. Qualiter autem hoc sit intellegendum, utrum scilicet sola
contritio sine confessione tollat peccata, an contritio cum
confessione, variae sunt opiniones.

5. (ParT X,316–19)

Item circa ista nota quare confessio sive paenitentia dicitur col. 811
sacramentum. Sunt enim ibi tria notanda, scilicet, confessio, contritio
et mundatio. Confessio est signum tantum, scilicet, contritionis.
Contritio est res et signum: res signi confessionis, signum
5 mundationis. Mundatio est res signi tantum, scilicet, contritionis.
DE CONFESSIONE
14. Secunda diaeta est confessio, circa quam sunt septem
consideranda, videlicet, quid ipsa sit, an necessario sit facienda, et
cui; quae sint necessaria ad veram confessionem; utrum et de quibus
10 et qualiter sint interrogationes faciendae, et de poena sacerdotis
revelantis confessionem.
Confessio est legitima coram sacerdote peccatorum declaratio. Et
dicitur confessio quasi simul vel ex toto vel undique fassio; nam ille
confitetur qui totum fatetur.
15 Tenetur paenitens peccata sua necessario confiteri. Et breviter: haec
tria, contritio, confessio et satisfactio, sunt in praecepto. Contritio
praecipitur in Joele: "Scindite corda vestra."¹ Confessio in Threnis:
"Effunde sicut aquam cor tuum."² Item Psalmus: "Effundite coram
illo corda vestra,"³ et Jacobus: "Confitemini alterutrum peccata
20 vestra."⁴ Satisfactio in Joanne: "Facite dignos fructus paenitentiae."⁵
Item omnia haec praecipiuntur a Domino cum dicit: "Paenitentiam
agite" etc.⁶

---

9. Ps 50:20; **10.** Cf. Eph 2:3.

1. Joel 2:13; **2.** Lam 2:19; **3.** Ps 61:9; **4.** Jas 5:16; **5.** Luke 3:8; **6.** Matt 4:17.

6. (ParT X,960–78)

On confessional questioning

31. As for the second matter, namely what the questions should be concerned with, this is already clear from the material mentioned above, that is, they should be concerned with sins and their circumstances. Moreover, take note in these verses of the circumstances to which the priest ought to pay special attention:

Who, what, where, through whom, how often, why, in what way, when.

Let everyone take heed of these when giving remedies.[1]

Who: namely, whether the sinner is a man or a woman; young or old; of high or low birth; free or a servant; appointed to an office or a position of honor, or a private individual without office; of sound mind or insane; knowledgeable or ignorant; single or married; in a monastic order, a cleric, or a member of the laity; related by blood, by marriage, or a stranger; a Christian, a heretic, or a pagan; and the like.

What: namely, whether the sinner committed adultery, or fornication, or murder, and so on. Likewise, whether the sin which the penitent has committed is grave, average, or minor. Likewise, whether it is known in public or is hidden. Likewise, whether it is four days old and festering, or recent, and the like.

Where: namely, whether in a holy place or in a profane one; in a home belonging to the nobility, or elsewhere.

Through whom: namely, through mediators and go-betweens, since all such people partake in the crime and its punishment, and the penitent himself is answerable and responsible for their sins. Likewise, through whom, i.e., with whom, for whom, and against whom.

How often: For, if it is possible, the sinner ought to confess, and the priest to ask about, not only the sins themselves, but also the number of times the sin has been committed and repeated, so that he should recount how often he has slept with a prostitute or an adulteress, and whether it has been with one or many, how often he has spoken quarrelsome words to his neighbor, how often he has repeated the offenses, and the like, because when an injury is repeated, the wound heals more slowly.

Why: namely, with what kind of temptation he has committed the deed, and whether he overcame this temptation, or was overcome by it; whether by his own free will or under constraint, and with what kind of constraint, namely conditional or absolute. Likewise, whether out of greed or out of poverty; whether in jest, or with a design to cause injury, and the like.

In what way: namely, actively or passively, because he is better known by his actions than by his speech.

When: whether during a consecrated time, for instance festivals, Lent, or other fast days, or during one which is not consecrated, as on other regular workdays. Likewise, whether before having received penitence, or even afterwards, by breaking the penitence.

6. (ParT X,960–78)

De interrogationibus col. 828

31. Ad aliud, scilicet, de quibus sint faciendae interrogationes, jam patet ex praemissa, quia de peccatis et circumstantiis eorumdem. Circumstantias autem istas, quas praecipue debet sacerdos 5 attendere, nota in his versiculis:

Quis, quid, ubi, per quos, quoties, cur, quomodo, quando.
Quilibet observet medicamina dando.[1]

Quis, scilicet, utrum ipse peccator fuerit masculus vel femina; juvenis vel senex; nobilis an ignobilis; liber vel servus; in dignitate seu officio 10 constitutus an privatus; sanae mentis vel insanus; sciens vel ignarus; solutus vel conjugatus; claustralis, clericus vel laicus; consanguineus, affinis an extraneus; christianus, haereticus vel paganus, et similia.

Quid, scilicet, utrum commisit adulterium, vel fornicationem, vel homicidium, et similia. Item, utrum peccatum quod perpetravit sit 15 enorme, mediocre vel parvum. / Item, utrum sit manifestum vel col. 829 occultum. Item, utrum quatriduanum et foetens, an recens, et similia.

Ubi, scilicet, utrum in loco sacro, an in profano; in domo dominorum, aut alibi.

20 Per quos, scilicet, mediatores et internuntios, quia omnes tales sunt participes criminis et damnationis, et ipse est reus et obligatus pro peccatis eorum. Item, per quos, id est, cum quibus, et pro quibus, et contra quos.

Quoties. Debet enim, si potest, peccator confiteri, et sacerdos 25 interrogare, non solum ipsa peccata, sed et vices et iterationes, ut dicat quoties cognovit fornicariam vel adulteram, et utrum unam vel plures, quoties dixit proximo verba contumeliosa, quoties iteravit injurias, et similia. Quia vulnus iteratum, tardius sanatur.

Cur, scilicet, quali tentatione hoc fecerit, et utrum praevenit ipsam 30 tentationem, vel fuit praeventus ab ea; utrum sponte vel coactus, et quali coactione, conditionali, videlicet, an absoluta. Item, utrum cupiditate, an paupertate; utrum, ludo, an nocendi animo, et similia.

Quomodo, scilicet, de modo agendi vel patiendi, quod melius actu, quam locutione scitur.

35 Quando, utrum, in tempore sacro, puta festis, quadragesima et aliis jejuniis, aut in non sacro, ut in aliis diebus profestis. Item, utrum ante acceptam paenitentiam, an etiam post, frangendo ipsam paenitentiam.

---

1. Walther, *PS* 25429a.

7. (ParT X,1029–56)

ON SATISFACTION

36. It remains for us to add some words concerning satisfaction, which is called external penance. Let us see, therefore, what the elements of satisfaction are; afterwards, we will see how the priest ought to proceed in applying them.

Satisfaction consists in three things, namely prayer, fasting, and almsgiving, in such a way that this threesome can be set against the abominable threesome of the devil:[1] prayer against pride, fasting against lust of the flesh, alms against avarice. It can also be stated otherwise, namely that satisfaction consists in two things, that is to say, the free dispensing of alms and the tormenting of the flesh.

On alms

Now alms are threefold. The first kind consists in contrition of the heart, when someone offers himself to God, according to the verse: "Pleasing God, have mercy on your own soul."[2] Concerning this kind of alms, the verse in Ecclesiasticus: "Just as water puts out fire," etc.[3] The second kind consists in compassion for one's neighbor, by which we have compassion for others' adversities as we do for our own. Concerning this kind of alms, Job: "Pity grew up with me, and it came out of my mother's womb with me."[4] The third kind consists in giving alms with one's hands, in legal assistance, in bodily and spiritual care and, in a word, in any kind of advice and support which we extend to our neighbor. Concerning this kind of alms, the Lord in the Gospel: "Give alms, and behold, all things are clean for you."[5] And Ambrose: "Feed the person dying of hunger; unless you have nourished him, you have killed him."[6]

The first kind of alms is greater than the others, for in it a person offers himself to God as a burnt offering, that is, as one consumed totally by fire, but in the other two he offers himself, as it were, as a sacrificial offering, that is, as a partial sacrifice.

On the tormenting of the flesh

37. Now the tormenting of the flesh consists of four elements, namely prayers, vigils, fasts, and flagellations. Concerning the first, Paul to the Thessalonians: "Pray without interruption,"[7] that is, without an interruption in the canonical hours, concerning which the Psalm: "Seven times a day I have praised you."[8] Or else this: pray without interruption, that is, always live justly and be desirous of eternal goods. Haymo: "The person who is just never ceases to pray, unless he ceases to be just; he always prays who always does good deeds."[9] Likewise Augustine: "The very desire for the good is prayer, and if it is a continual desire, it is continual prayer."[10]

On prayer

Now prayer is a pious movement of the mind directed to God which breaks out in speech, frequently so that the heart might not grow lazy. Or thus: Prayer is a collection of vocal sounds directed to God entreating Him for something.

Now, temporal matters ought not to be requested in prayer, at least not principally, but things which are spiritual, eternal, and which are pertinent to salvation. For this

13 **Deo** Deum *SP*.

7. (ParT X,1029–56)

DE SATISFACTIONE

36. Restat ut de satisfactione, quae paenitentia exterior dicitur, aliqua supponamus. Videamus ergo in quibus consistat satisfactio; deinde visuri qualiter sacerdos debeat procedere circa ipsius impositionem.

5 Consistit satisfactio in tribus, scilicet, oratione, jejunio et eleemonsyna, ut iste ternarius contra illum nefarium diaboli ternarium opponatur:[1] oratio contra superbiam, jejunium contra carnis concupiscentiam, eleemosyna contra avaritiam. Aliter etiam potest dici, videlicet, quod satisfactio consistit in duobus, scilicet, in

10 largitione eleemosynae et carnis maceratione.

De eleemosyna

Eleemosyna autem est triplex. Prima consistit in cordis contritione, quando aliquis seipsum offert [Deo], juxta illud: "Miserere animae tuae placens Deo."[2] De hac in Ecclesiastico: "Sicut aqua extinguit

15 ignem" etc.[3] Secunda consistit in compassione proximi, qua compatimur alienis adversitatibus tamquam nostris. De hac Job: "Mecum convaluit miseratio et ab utero matris meae egressa est mecum."[4] Tertia consistit in largitione manuali, advocatione, cura corporali et spirituali, et breviter in quocumque consilio et subsidio

20 quod impendimus proximo. De hac Dominus in Evangelio: "Date eleemosyna et ecce omnia munda sunt vobis."[5] Et Ambrosius: "Pasce fame morientem; nisi paveris, occidisti."[6]

Prima eleemosyna major est aliis, nam in illa offert se homo Deo tamquam holocaustum, id est, totum incensum. Sed / in aliis duabus

25 offert se quasi sacrificium, id est, hostiam particularem.

De carnis maceratione

37. Carnis autem maceratio consistit in quattuor, scilicet, orationibus, vigiliis, jejuniis et flagellis. De primo Apostolus ad Thessalonicenses: "Sine intermissione orate,"[7] id est, non

30 intermissis canonicis horis, de quibus Psalmus: "Septies in die laudem dixi tibi."[8] Alias, sine intermissione orate, id est, semper juste vivite et aeterna desiderate. Aymo: "Justus numquam desinit orare, nisi desinat justus esse; semper orat, qui semper bene agit."[9] Item Augustinus: "Ipsum desiderium boni oratio est, et si continuum

35 est desiderium, continua est oratio."[10]

De oratione

Est autem oratio pius affectus mentis in Deum tendens, plerumque ne animus pigritetur, in vocem prorumpens. Vel sic: Oratio est congeries vocum ad aliquid impetrandum in Deum tendentium.

40 Item non debent peti in oratione temporalia, saltem principaliter, sed spiritualia, aeterna et ad salutem pertinentia. Unde Dominus in

---

1. Cf. Matt 4:3–11, 1John 2:16; **2.** Sir 30:24; **3.** Sir 3:33; **4.** Job 31:18; **5.** Luke 11:41; **6.** Cf. Gratian, *Decretum*, 1.86.21 (1:302); **7.** 1Thes 5:17; **8.** Ps 118:164; **9.** *Glossa ordinaria*, 1Thes 5:15 (PL 114:620A); **10.** Cf. Augustine of Hippo, *Enarrationes in Psalmos, Ps 37*, 14 (CCL 38:392).

reason, the Lord in the Gospel: "Seek first of all the kingdom of God, and everything will be given to you."[11] Moreover, in the seven petitions the Lord and Master himself included those things which should be requested, when he taught us how to pray, saying: "Our Father," etc.[12] Likewise, elsewhere he restricted the number of those things which should especially be requested to three, namely faith, hope, and charity. Luke 11: "Now who among you is a father who will give his son a stone instead of the bread he asks for? or when he asks for fish, instead of the fish will give him a serpent? or if he were to ask for an egg, will offer him a scorpion instead?"[13] For the bread, charity is to be understood; for the fish, faith; for the egg, hope.

Now, these thirteen things are demanded from one's prayer, namely that it be faithful, untroubled, humble, discerning, devout, modest, private, pure, tearful, attentive, fervent, painstaking, and constant. I will not pursue these matters any further since they are commonplaces.

Moreover, prayer is chiefly efficacious against spiritual vices, for which reason on the passage: "This kind of demon is not expelled except in prayer and fasting,"[14] Jerome says as follows: "Medicine is to be employed for every type of ailment, but that medicine does not cure the eye which cures the heel; the diseases of the body are cured by fasting, but the diseases of the mind are cured by prayer."[15]

On vigils

38. On the second element, namely vigils, the Lord in the Gospel: "Watch and pray so that you will not enter into temptation."[16] Likewise: "And in that region there were shepherds keeping watch at night over their flock."[17] Likewise, this passage: "Be sober and watchful" in your prayers, etc.[18] Likewise, Luke 12: "Let your loins be girded and the lamps lit which you hold in your hands. And you should be like men waiting for their lord to return from his marriage feast," etc.[19] And further on: "And if he arrives during the second watch, or even if he arrives during the third, and he finds them in such a state, blessed are those servants."[20]

On fasts

39. Concerning the third element, namely fasts, note that fasting is threefold. The first type is corporeal, refraining from material food; the second is by affliction, refraining from temporal joy; the third is spiritual, refraining from deadly sin. And with this threefold fasting we ought to punish our beast of burden. For it is of little benefit to abstain from eating food if one does not abstain from sin. Isaiah 58: "Why have we fasted and you have not seen it; why have we humbled our souls and you have no knowledge of it?" etc.[21] And further on: "Behold, you have fasted and it has led to arguments and quarrels, and you have dealt wicked blows in the fight," etc.[22] And further on: "Is such the fast which I have chosen? Is not this rather the fast which I have chosen: Undo the bonds of wickedness, untie the oppressive bundles, and dash to pieces every burden? Break off a piece of your bread for the hungry," and so on. "Then your light will break forth as if at dawn," etc.[23]

Likewise, note that the Lord instituted fasting first in paradise, and afterwards he

65 **praecincti** praecinti *SP*.

Evangelio: "Primum quaerite regnum Dei et omnia adicientur vobis."[11] Conclusit autem ista, quae petenda sunt, ipse Dominus et Magister in septem petitionibus, cum docuit nos orare dicens: "Pater

45   noster" etc.[12] Item alibi restrinxit ad tria, scilicet, fidem, spem, caritatem, quae praecipue sunt petenda. Lucas 11: "Quis autem ex vobis / patrem petit panem, numquid lapidem dabit illi? aut piscem,   col. 837 numquid pro pisce serpentem dabit illi? aut si petierit ovum, numquid porriget illi scorpionem?"[13] In pane caritas, in pisce fides,

50   in ovo spes intellegitur.

Item exiguntur in oratione ista decem et tria scilicet: quod sit fidelis, secura, humilis, discreta, devota, verecunda, secreta, pura, lacrimosa, attenta, fervida, operosa et assidua. Quae non prosequor ultra, quia trita sunt.

55   Valet autem oratio praecipue contra vitia spiritualia; unde Hieronymus super illum locum: "Hoc genus daemonii non eicitur nisi in oratione et jejunio,"[14] ait sic: "Medicina cuilibet morbo est adhibenda; non sanat oculum, quod sanat calcaneum; jejunio sanantur pestes corporis; oratione vero sanantur pestes mentis."[15]

60   De vigiliis

38. De secundo, scilicet, de vigiliis, Dominus in Evangelio: "Vigilate et orate ne intretis in tentationem."[16] Item: "Et erant in regione illa pastores custodientes vigilias noctis super gregem suum."[17] Item illud: "Sobrii estote et vigilate" in oratione etc.[18] Item Luca 12: "Sint

65   lumbi vestri [praecincti] et lucernae ardentes in manibus vestris. Et vos similes hominibus exspectantibus dominum suum quando revertatur a nuptiis" etc.[19] Et infra: "Et si venerit in secunda vigilia, et si in tertia vigilia venerit, et ita invenerit, beati sunt servi illi."[20]

De jejuniis

70   39. De tertio, scilicet, de jejuniis, nota quod est triplex jejunium. Primum est corporis, a cibo materiali; secundum afflictionis, a gaudio temporali; tertium spirituale, a peccato mortali. Et hoc triplici jejunio debemus castigare jumentum nostrum. Parum enim prodest / jejunare a cibo nisi jejunetur a peccato. Isaias 58: "Quare   col. 838

75   jejunavimus et non aspexisti; humiliavimus animas nostras et nescisti" etc.[21] Et infra: "Ecce ad lites et contentiones jejunatis et percutitis pugno impie" etc.[22] Et infra: "Numquid tale est jejunium quod elegi? Nonne hoc est magis jejunium quod elegi: Dissolve colligationes impietatis, solve fasciculos deprimentes et omne onus

80   dirumpe? Frange esurienti panem tuum" et cetera. "Tunc erumpet quasi mane lumen tuum" etc.[23]

Item nota quod Dominus instituit primo jejunium in paradiso, et

---

11. Matt 6:33; **12.** Cf. Matt 6:9–13; **13.** Luke 11:11–12; **14.** Matt 17:20; **15.** Ps.-Jerome, *Commentarius in Marcum*, 9 (PL 30:616C) – cf. Robert M. Correale, "The Sources of Some Patristic Quotations in Chaucer's The Parson's Tale," *English Language Notes* 19 (1981): 98; *Glossa ordinaria*, Mark 9:28 (PL 114:215A); **16.** Matt 26:41; **17.** Luke 2:8; **18.** 1Pet 5:8; **19.** Luke 12:35–6; **20.** Luke 12:38; **21.** Isa 58:3; **22.** Isa 58:4; **23.** Cf. Isa 58:5–8.

sanctified it when he fasted forty days and forty nights in the desert.

Likewise, these four things ought to accompany fasting, namely largess, joyfulness, the proper time, and measure. Concerning the first, namely largess, Jerome: "Give to the poor what you would have eaten up, if you had not been fasting, so that your fast may be the satiety of your soul, not the profit of your purse."[24] Concerning the second, namely concerning joyfulness, the Lord in Matthew: "When you fast, do not be like mournful hypocrites."[25] Concerning the third, namely the proper time, one reads in the book of Kings that since Jonathan went before the proper time, he was judged to death, and many things like this.[26] Concerning the fourth, namely measure, Augustine: "A mind exhausted by the desire for food loses the virtue of prayer."[27]

On tribulations

40. On the fourth and final element, namely on tribulations, note that they are divided into four parts. The first consists in penitential equipment, namely in ashes, a hairshirt, and tears. The second, in beating of the breast, bowing to the yoke, and lashes. The third, in the affliction of a pilgrimage. The fourth, in torment and the affliction of any kind of illness, the kind of tribulations which Job endured. Concerning these, also Solomon: "The Lord whips every son whom he receives."[28] For this reason, the priest ought to say to the penitent that all of these works of satisfaction form a part of his penitence and they will all be efficacious if his penitence remains devout.

8. (ParT X,1057–75)

ON OBSTACLES TO PENITENCE

69. After we have seen what penitence is and what its parts are, it is appropriate that we add a few words on the obstacles to penitence, since the ancient serpent is ready to hinder penitence and human beings, moreover, are frequently heedless in resisting the serpent.

Now, there are four chief obstacles, namely shame, fear, hope, and despair. Each one of these should be examined in order.

Shame, namely of confessing. Indeed, shame holds many people back from penitence, but chiefly hypocrites and the proud, who would like to appear to people as healthy and beautiful, although they are actually sick and most foul; as externally handsome and adorned, although internally they are filled with impurity.

This obstacle is opposed by a triple remedy, namely a reasonable consideration, the power of divine discernment, and a comparison with future disorder. A reasonable consideration, since it is reasonable that because of shame you should not put off confessing your sins, which is honest and useful, you who did not hesitate because of shame to commit them, which is dishonest and useless or, even more, harmful. Concerning the second, Paul to the Hebrews, chapter 4: "All things are laid bare and open to the eyes of him to whom we speak."[1] Thus, he should not make you

postea sanctificavit cum jejunavit quadraginta diebus et quadraginta noctibus in deserto.

85 Item jejunium debent semper haec quattuor concomitari, scilicet: largitas, laetitia, hora et mensura. De primo, scilicet, largitate, Hieronymus: "Quod manducaturus eras, si non jejunares, da pauperibus, ut jejunium tuum sit saturitas animae, non marsupii lucrum."[24] De secundo, scilicet, de laetitia, Dominus in Matthaeo:

90 "Cum jejunatis nolite fieri sicut hypocritae tristes."[25] De tertio, scilicet, hora, legitur in libro Regum, quod Jonathas, quia praevenit horam, adjudicatus fuit morti, et similia multa.[26] De quarto, scilicet, mensura, Augustinus: "Mens aviditate ciborum lassata perdit orationis virtutem."[27]

95 De flagellis
40. De quarto et ultimo, scilicet de flagellis, nota quod quadripartita sunt. Prima consistunt in armis paenitentialibus, scilicet, in cinere, cilicio et lacrimis. Secunda, in pectoris tunsione, jugi genuflexione, et disciplinis. Tertia, in afflictione peregrinationis. Quarta, in

100 tribulatione, et cujuslibet aegritudinis afflictione, qualia flagella sustinuit Job. De his / etiam Salomon: "Flagellat Deus omnem   col. 839 filium quem recipit."[28] Unde sacerdos debet dicere paenitenti, quod omnia ista satisfactionis opera sunt ei pro parte paenitentiae, et valebunt omnia si adsit devota paenitentia.

8. (ParT X,1057–75)

DE IMPEDIMENTIS PAENITENTIAE   col. 877
69. Postquam vidimus quid sit paenitentia, et quae partes ejus, consequenter, quia serpens antiquus paratus est ad impediendam paenitentiam, homo autem incautus plerumque ad resistendum, de

5 impedimentis paenitentiae pauca supponamus.
Sunt autem quattuor praecipua impedimenta, scilicet: Pudor, timor, spes et desperatio. De singulis per ordinem videndum.
Pudor scilicet confitendi. Hic quidem pudor retrahit multos a paenitentia, sed praecipue hypocritas et superbos, qui vellent

10 apparere hominibus sani et pulchri, cum tamen sint infirmi et turpissimi; exterius ornati et picti, cum sint intus spurcitia repleti.
Contra hoc impedimentum opponitur triplex remedium, scilicet, consideratio rationis, virtus divinae intuitionis, comparatio futurae confusionis. Consideratio rationis, quia rationabile est ut propter

15 pudorem non differas confiteri peccata tua, quod honestum et utile est, qui propter pudorem non dubitasti ea committere, quod inhonestum et inutile, immo perniciosum est. De secundo, Apostolus ad Hebraeos 4: "Omnia nuda sunt et aperta oculis ejus ad quem nobis sermo."[1] Non ergo te pudeat confiteri, immo potius

---

24. Martin of Léon, *Sermones*, 10 (PL 208:646D); **25.** Matt 6:16; **26.** Cf. 1Sam 14:24–45; **27.** Cf. Defensor, *Liber scintillarum*, 10.8 (CCL 117:47); **28.** Heb 12:6.

1. Heb 4:13.

ashamed to confess, or even more to confess to God, whose deputy he is, since by divine power He already perceives you without your confession. Concerning the third, Solomon: "There is a disorder leading to disgrace and there is a disorder leading to glory."[2] Augustine: "There is a temporal disorder which is temporary, which indeed is beneficial, namely a disturbance of the heart reviewing its own sins and being terrified by the review, and being embarrassed by the terror, and correcting itself because of this shame."[3] I want the sinner to be thrown into a state of confusion by this disorder, not by an eternal disorder, from which I, a sinner, want to be set free. Zephaniah: "I shall examine Jerusalem with lamps, and I shall send punishment over the people held fast in their wine dregs."[4] Likewise, Nahum: "I will reveal your private parts, and to the peoples I will show your nakedness and to the kingdoms your shame."[5] Likewise, Jeremiah: "They will be greatly shamed who do not understand the eternal dishonor which will never come to an end."[6]

70. Fear, namely of making amends. For they think they cannot bear the punishment which will be imposed on them.

Three things are employed in the same way to remove this obstacle, namely the moderateness, lightness, and momentary brevity of punishment here and now. Opposed to this, however, the incomparable magnitude, the unbearable bitterness, and the unending eternity of future punishment. The Gospel: "Depart, cursed ones, to the eternal fire," etc.[7] Job: "He who flees from iron arms meets up with a bronze bow."[8] Job: "He who fears hoar frost," that is temporal punishment, "snow will blow over him," that is eternal punishment.[9] Likewise, Isaiah 33: "Who among you can dwell with the devouring fire, and who among you will dwell with eternal burnings?"[10] Idem, 30: "Thophet has been prepared since yesterday, prepared, given a foundation, and enlarged by the king. Its nourishment is fire and much wood, the breath of the Lord, like a torrent of brimstone, kindling it."[11] Thophet is the prison of hell, and it is interpreted to mean the inferno of dread, or the complete punishment of fools.

71. Hope, namely a threefold one: of living for a long time; of acquiring temporal wealth in which one might find peace; and of God's boundless mercy, which does not want to condemn anyone.

Against the first one James applies a remedy in chapter 4: "What is your life? It is a mist appearing for a short time, and then it will be dissipated."[12] Job: "Humankind, born of woman, lives a brief life filled with many troubles," etc.[13] Paul, 1st Epistle to the Thessalonians, 5: "The day of the Lord will come like a thief in the night: for when they say there is peace and security, then sudden destruction will overtake them, like labor comes to a woman carrying a child in her womb, and they will not be able to flee."[14] Likewise, the Lord in Mark 13: "Watch, for you do not know when the Lord is coming, whether at midnight, or at cock-crow, or in the morning, lest when he comes suddenly, he will find you asleep."[15] Likewise, Job 20: "The fame of the impious is short lived, and the joy of the hypocrite like a brief moment. Even if his pride were to ascend to heaven, and his head were to touch the clouds, in the end he will be destroyed like dung."[16]

Against the second one the Lord himself gives the remedy in Luke 12: "Of a certain man with riches," etc.[17] And further on: " 'My soul, you have a great deal of goods

24 **respicientis** respicientia *SP*. 62 **ipse** ipsae *SP*.

20   Deo, cujus vicarius est, cum Ipse virtute divina sine tua confessione jam videat. De tertio Salomon: "Est confusio adducens ignominiam et est confusio adducens gloriam."² Augustinus: "Est confusio temporalis quae est ad horam, quae quidem prodest, scilicet perturbatio animi [respicientis] peccata sua et respectione horrentis,
25   et horrore erubescentis, et rubore corrigentis."³ Tali confusione volo confundi, non aeterna, a qua peccator cupio liberari. Sophonias: "Scrutabor Hierusalem in lucernis, et visitabo super viros defixos in faecibus suis."⁴ Item Nahum: "Revelabo / pudenda tua et ostendam col. 878 gentibus nuditatem tuam et regnis ignominiam tuam."⁵ Item Jeremias:
30   "Confundantur vehementer qui non intellexerunt opprobrium sempiternum quod numquam delebitur."⁶

    70. Timor scilicet satisfaciendi. Cogitant enim quod non possent ferre poenam, quae eis imponeretur.

    Ad tollendum hoc impedimentum, tria similiter adhibentur, scilicet,
35   praesentis poenae modicitas, levitas, et momentanea brevitas. Ex opposito, vero, futurae poenae incomparabilis magnitudo, intolerabilis acerbitas, et infinalis aeternitas. Evangelium: "Ite, maledicti, in ignem aeternum" etc.⁷ Job: "Qui fugit arma ferrea incidit in arcum aeneum."⁸ Job: "Qui timet pruinam," id est
40   temporalem poenam, "irruet super eum nix," id est poena aeterna.⁹ Item Isaias 33: "Quis poterit habitare de vobis cum igne devorante, et quis habitabit ex vobis cum ardoribus sempiternis?"¹⁰ Idem 30: "Praeparata est ab heri Thophet, a rege praeparata, fundata et dilatata. Nutrimenta ejus ignis et ligna multa; flatus Domini sicut
45   torrens sulphuris succendens eam."¹¹ Thophet est carcer inferni, et interpretatur gehenna pavoris, vel plena poena stultorum.

    71. Spes, scilicet, triplex: diu vivendi, acquirendi temporales divitias, in quibus quiescat, et de nimia Dei misericordia, quae neminem vult damnare.
50   Contra primum, apponit remedium Jacobus in c. 4: "Quae est vita vestra? Vapor est ad modicum parens et deinceps exterminabitur."¹² Job: "Homo natus de muliere brevi vivens tempore repletur multis miseriis" etc.¹³ Apostolus, 1a ad Thessalonicenses 5: "Dies Domini sicut fur in nocte ita veniet: cum enim dixerint pax et securitas, tunc
55   repentinus eis superveniet interitus, sicut dolor in utero / habenti, et col. 879 non effugient."¹⁴ Item Dominus in Marco 13: "Vigilate, nescitis enim quando Dominus veniat, an media nocte, an galli cantu, an mane, ne cum venerit repente, inveniat vos dormientes."¹⁵ Item Job 20: "Laus impiorum brevis est, et gaudium hypocritae ad instar
60   puncti. Si ascenderit usque ad caelum superbia ejus, et caput ejus nubes tetigerit, quasi sterquilinium in fine perdetur."¹⁶

    Contra secundum, dat remedium [ipse] Dominus in Luca 12: "Hominis cujusdam divitis" etc.¹⁷ Et infra: "Anima mea, habes

---

2. Sir 4:25; **3.** Augustine of Hippo, *Enarrationes in Psalmos, Ps 30*, 2.1.5 (CCL 38:194); **4.** Zeph 1:12; **5.** Nah 3:5; **6.** Jer 20:11; **7.** Matt 25:41; **8.** Cf. Job 20:24; **9.** Job 6:16; **10.** Isa 33:14; **11.** Isa 30:33; **12.** Jas 4:15; **13.** Job 14:1; **14.** 1Thes 5:2–3; **15.** Mark 13:35–6; **16.** Job 20:5–7; **17.** Luke 12:16.

laid away for several years; rest, eat, drink, carouse.' But God said to him, "Fool, this night they," namely demons, "will take away your soul from you. Now those things you have prepared, whose will they be?' "[18] Job 27: "When the rich man sleeps, he takes nothing with himself; he will open his eyes and will find nothing. Indigence will overcome him like water, a storm will overtake him at night. The parching wind will lift him up, and it will bear him off, and like a whirlwind it will snatch him from his place," etc.[19]

Against the third one, Gregory: "It is characteristic of the great justice of the one passing judgment that those people never be without penalty who in this life never want to be without sin."[20]

These two obstacles, namely fear and hope, hold back in particular usurers and the avaricious, who never want to make restitution and would like to acquire without end, for which reason they are compared to hell. In Proverbs: "Hell and the infernal pit will never be filled, and in the same way the eyes of human beings are insatiable."[21]

72. Despair, namely a double one: the first, of forgiveness; the second, of remaining steadfast after forgiveness has been obtained. Three things bring on the first one, namely the quantity, the frequency, and the long duration of sinning.

Against the first of these is the passion of Christ, which is stronger in undoing sins than any sin is in binding them together. Job: "Oh that my sins would be weighed, and the calamity which I suffer put on the scales. They would be heavier than the sands of the sea."[22]

Against the second, Jerome, *On Penitence*, distinction 3: "Seven times the just man falls," etc.[23] And further on: "Not merely seven times, but even seventy seven times are a transgressor's sins forgiven, if he turns to penitence. The more He is abandoned by a sinner, the more He loves him," etc.[24]

Against the third, the Psalm: "But the mercy of the Lord is from everlasting to everlasting for those who fear Him."[25] Likewise: "At whatsoever hour the sinner turns," etc.[26] Likewise, Pope Leo: "A penitence which has been put off should not be denied when it has been requested very zealously, so that in this way the wounded soul might attain the medicine of remission."[27] "Likewise Augustine, explaining this passage in the Psalm: 'Do not let the depths swallow me up nor the pit close its mouth above me,'[28] says as follows: The pit is the depth of human iniquity; if you fall into it, it will not close its mouth above you unless you close yours. Therefore, confess and say: 'From the depths I called to you, Lord,' "[29] and you will escape.

Likewise, against the second despair, namely that of remaining steadfast after forgiveness has been obtained, three remedies are applied. The first, the weakness of the enemy. The second, the special vigor received from joy, freedom, armor, and fellowship. The third, God Himself, enlightening, protecting, and saving.

Concerning the first, an enemy is weak who can only defeat someone who wishes to be defeated; and indeed, a troop of demons was unable to enter even a herd of swine

---

94 **absorbeat** absolbeat *SP*.

multa bona posita in annos plurimos; requiesce, comede, bibe,
65   epulare. Dixit autem illi Deus: Stulte, hac nocte repetent, scilicet
daemones, animam tuam a te. Quae autem parasti, cujus erunt?"[18]
Job 27: "Dives, cum dormierit, nihil secum affert, aperiet oculos
suos et nihil inveniet. Apprehendet eum quasi aqua inopia, nocte
opprimet eum tempestas. Tollet eum ventus urens, et auferet, et
70   velut turbo rapiet eum de loco suo" etc.[19]
Contra tertium, Gregorius: "Ad magnam justitiam judicantis pertinet
ut numquam careant supplicio, qui in hac vita numquam voluerunt
carere peccato."[20]
Haec duo impedimenta, scilicet timor et spes, retrahunt praecipue
75   usurarios et avaros, qui nihil volunt restituere, et sine fine vellent
acquirere: unde comparantur inferno. Parabolis: "Infernus et
perditio non replebuntur: similiter et oculi hominum insatiabiles."[21]
72. Desperatio, scilicet, duplex: prima veniae; secunda,
perseverandi post veniam obtentam. Primam inducunt tria, scilicet,
80   peccandi quantitas, frequentia et diuturnitas.
Contra primum, opponitur Passio Christi, quae fortior est ad
dissolvendum, / quam peccatum aliquod ad ligandum, Job: "Utinam   col. 880
appenderentur peccata mea, et calamitas quam patior in statera.
Quasi arena maris haec gravior appareret."[22]
85   Contra secundum, Hieronymus, *De paenitentia*, dist. 3: "Septies
cadit justus" etc.[23] Et infra: "Non solum septies, sed etiam
septuagies septies delinquenti, si convertatur ad paenitentiam,
peccata donantur. Cui plus dimittitur, plus diligit" etc.[24]
Contra tertium, Psalmus: "Misericordia Domini ab aeterno et usque
90   in aeternum super timentes eum."[25] Item: "Quacumque hora
peccator conversus fuerit" etc.[26] Item Leo Papa: "Paenitentia quae
dilata est, cum studiosius petita fuerit non negetur, ut eo modo ad
indulgentiae medicinam anima vulnerata perveniat."[27] "Item
Augustinus, exponens illud locum Psalmi: 'Non [absorbeat] me
95   profundum neque urgeat super me puteus os suum,'[28] ait sic: Puteus
est profunditas humanae iniquitatis, in quam, si cecideris, non
claudet super te os suum, nisi tu clauseris tuum. Confitere ergo et
dic: 'De profundis clamavi ad te Domine,' "[29] et evades.
Item, contra secundam desperationem, scilicet, perseverandi post
100   veniam obtentam, apponuntur tria remedia. Primum, hostis
debilitas. Secundum, vigor proprius ex gaudio, libertate, armatura et
societate conceptus. Tertium ispe Deus illuminans, protegens et
salvans.
De primo, debilis est hostis qui non potest vincere, nisi volentem;
105   immo legio daemonum non potuit intrare etiam gregem porcorum,

18. Luke 12:19–20; **19.** Job 27:19–21; **20.** Gregory the Great, *Dialogorum libri*, 4.44 (PL 77:404A) – cf. Wenzel, "Fragment X," in *The Riverside Chaucer*, p. 965 ; **21.** Prov 27:20; **22.** Job 6:2–3; **23.** Prov 24:16; **24.** Gratian, *Decretum*, 2.33.3.3.23 (1:1216); Jerome, *Epistolae*, 122.3 (CSEL 56,1:66); cf. Luke 7:47; **25.** Ps 102:17; **26.** Ezek 33:12; **27.** Pope Leo I, *Epistolae*, 167, inquisitio 9, resp. (PL 54:1206A); cf. Gratian, *Decretum*, 2.33.3.1.62 (1:1176–7); **28.** Ps 68:16; **29.** Alan of Lille, *Liber poenitentialis* (PL 210:301A); cf. Augustine of Hippo, *Enarrationes in Psalmos, Ps 68*, 2.1 (CCL 39:917); Ps 129:1.

without permission to do so by the Lord.[30] For this reason Isaiah, using the words of the enemy, says to the soul, "Bow down, so we can walk over you."[31] Thus, fight against the devil and he will run away from you.

Concerning the second, namely concerning vigor, it is obvious that the greatest vigor is produced and nourished when someone rejoices after the weight of sin has been taken from him. Solomon: "A heart which rejoices makes the season bloom with flowers, but a sad spirit dries up the bones."[32] Likewise: "An untroubled mind is like a perennial feast; all the days of the sinner are evil."[33] Likewise, when someone is snatched away from the shackles and slavery of the devil, he turns to the freedom of God, which happens when Pharaoh is drowned in the Red Sea with all the Egyptians,[34] that is, in the bitter liquid of tears, colored red by the memory of Christ's passion. Likewise, since at first one is unarmed, and then one is soon outfitted with the armor of God. Paul to the Ephesians: "Put on the armor of God, so that you can stand up to the snares of the devil, since we are not contending against flesh and blood, but against the principalities and the powers, against the world rulers of this darkness, against the spiritual matter of wickedness within the heavens, etc. Stand, therefore, having girded your loins with truth, and having put on the breastplate of justice, and having shod your feet with the preparation of the Gospel of peace; taking up in all battles the shield of faith with which you can extinguish all the fiery darts of the evil one; and put on the helmet of salvation and the sword of the spirit (which is the word of God)," etc.[35] Likewise, to the Thessalonians, chapter 5: "Let us be sober, having put on the breastplate of faith and charity, and as a helmet the hope for salvation."[36] Likewise, since at first one is alone, and then one is soon united with the army of all the just, who are in the church, and with all the saints and the angels, who are in heaven. Concerning this company, Judith 15: "Since the Assyrians were not united, they ran headlong in flight, but the children of Israel, pursuing them in one line of march, vanquished all those whom they were able to find."[37]

113 **mali** mala *SP*.
117 **modo armatus** modoarmatus *SP*.
122 **succincti** succinti *SP*.

nisi permissa a Domino.[30] Unde Isaias in persona hostis ad animam:
/ "Incurvare ut transeamus."[31] Resistite ergo diabolo, et fugiet a col. 881
vobis.

De secundo, scilicet, de vigore, patet, quia vigor maximus
110 concipitur et nutritur, cum quis gaudet, deposito peccati pondere.
Salomon: "Animus gaudens aetatem floridam facit: spiritus vero
tristis desicat ossa."[32] Item: "Secura mens quasi juge convivium;
omnes dies peccatoris [mali]."[33] Item, cum quis de catena et
servitute diaboli eripitur, in libertatem Dei convertitur, quod fit
115 quando Pharao cum omnibus Aegyptiis[34] submergitur in mari rubro,
id est in amara aqua lacrimarum, rubricata per memoriam Passionis
Christi. Item, quia primo inermis, [modo armatus] armatura Dei.
Apostolus ad Ephesios: "Induite vos armatura Dei ut possitis stare
adversus insidias diaboli; quia non est nobis colluctatio adversus
120 carnem et sanguinem, sed adversus principes et potestates, adversus
mundi rectores tenebrarum harum, contra spiritualia nequitiae in
caelestibus etc. State ergo [succincti] lumbos vestros in veritate, et
induti loricam justitiae, et calceati pedes vestros in praeparatione
evangelii pacis; in omnibus sumentes scutum fidei, in quo possitis
125 omnia tela nequissimi ignea exstinguere; et galeam salutis assumite
et gladium spiritus (quod est verbum Dei)" etc.[35] Item ad
Thessalonicenses 5: "Sobrii simus induti loricam fidei et caritatis, et
galeam spem salutis."[36] Item, quia primo solus, modo associatus
exercitui omnium justorum, qui sunt in Ecclesia, et omnium
130 sanctorum et angelorum, qui sunt in caelo. De hac societate in Judith
15: "Quoniam assyrii non adunati in fugam ibant praecipites: filii
autem Israel, uno agmine persequentes, debellabant omnes quos
invenire poterant."[37]

---

30. Cf. Matt 8:30–2; **31.** Isa 51:23; **32.** Prov 17:22; **33.** Cf. Prov 15:15; **34.** Cf. Exod 14:28; **35.** Eph 6:11–17; **36.** 1Thes 5:8; **37.** Jth 15:4.

II

Compilation on Holy Penance

(ParT X,112–16)

On the Tree of Penance
This penance, therefore, bears the good fruit by which the soul is restored, as St.
John with the Golden Mouth, says.[1] And he correctly says that penance bears good
fruit because penance is like a tree, the root of which is contrition in the heart of one
who is repentant, and from this root grows the stock of penance, which is a firm
resolve to confess one's sins to a priest and to correct oneself. The leaves of this tree
are the words of confession, and its fruits are the deeds of satisfaction. Of this fruit
the Gospel speaks and admonishes us to carry out what it says to us: "Create," it
says, "worthy fruits of penance."[2] These fruits are the deeds of penance. "Create
fruits," it says, and not leaves, for a tree is not truly known by its root nor by its
leaves, but it is known by its fruit, because often there is bitterness in the leaves and
in the root while there is sweetness in the fruit. And for this reason our Lord says:
"By their fruits you shall know the trees."[3]

B. Vices

III

William Peraldus, *Summa on the Vices*

1. (ParT X,450–61)

From which goods pride is born.
We have set down the first division of pride and have described each of its sections
in order. It follows now logically that we set down the second division and describe
its sections in order. This division is arranged according to those things from which

Lu, pp. 779b–781b; Ly, fols. 109vb–110vb; Mz, fols. 158va–160b; Pr, fols. 161b–162vb.

1 **Ex ... superbia** de ... superbia Mz; unde et quomodo oritur superbia et ex quibus bonis Pr.
4 **ita** ista Pr.

II

Compileison de Seinte Penance

(from Cambridge, Trinity College MS R.14.7 [C])

(ParT X,112–16)

De le arbre de penaunce   fol. 40b
Ceste penance donc est portant le bon fruit paront le alme est refete,
si come dit seint Jehan oue la bouche orine.[1] E bien dit il / ke fol. 40va
penance porte bon fruit, kar penance est ansi come un arbre, de ki la
5   racine est contricion en le quer du repentant, de la quele racine sourt
la souche de penance, cest ferm purpos de regehir ses pecchiez au
prestre e de sei amender. De ki les foilles sunt les paroles de confession, e les fruiz sunt les oueres de satisfaccion. De queu fruit parout
la euangelie e nus amoneste de fere le quant ele nus dit: "Fetes," dit
10 ele, "dignes fruiz de penance."[2] Ces fruiz sunt les oueres de
penance. "Fetes fruiz," dit ele, e ne mie foilles, kar arbre ne est mie
veraiement conu per la racine ne par les foilles, mes est par le fruit,
pur ceo ke meintes fez est amertume en les foiz e en la racine e
doucour est en la fruit. E pur ceo dit nostre seignur: "Par lour fruiz
15 les arbres conoistrez."[3]

B. Vices

III

Guilelmus Peraldus, *Summa de vitiis*

(from Paris, Bibliothèque Mazarine MS 794 [Mz]; collated with Lucca, Biblioteca
statale MS 1396 [Lu]; Lyon, Bibliothèque municipale MS 678 [Ly]; *Summa
virtutum ac vitiorum Guilhelmi Paraldi Episcopi Lugdunensis de ordine
predicatorum*, vol. 2 [Paris, 1512] [Pr])

1. (ParT X,450–61)

[Ex quibus bonis nascitur superbia].   fol. 158va
Posuimus primam divisionem superbie et prosecuti sumus membra
ejus. Nunc consequens est, ut ponamus / secundam et prosequamur. fol. 158vb
Divisio vero [ita] sumitur secundum ea, ex quibus oritur superbia.

---

1. Ps.-Johannes Chrysostomus, *Sermo de Poenitentia* (John Chrysostom, *Opera omnia* [Antwerp, 1614],
5:362a); **2.** Matt 3:8; **3.** Matt 7:19–20 – cf. Wenzel, "Fragment X," in *The Riverside Chaucer*, p. 957.

pride arises. Thus, it should be noted that pride sometimes arises from the goods of nature, sometimes from the goods of fortune, sometimes from the goods of grace. Now, some of the goods of nature belong to the body, others belong to the soul. Belonging to the body are these: health, strength, agility, beauty, nobility, freedom. The natural goods belonging to the soul, on the other hand, are these: an accurate and nimble wit, a good memory, the power to endure spiritual exercise, a natural disposition to be virtuous, or a natural virtue. Now, the goods of fortune are external goods which are under human control and can be squandered by human beings, such as riches, charms, honors, praise or glory, and popular esteem. The goods of grace are knowledge and virtues. From these goods pride can be born.

Pride is born from beauty, for which reason the poet says:

Haughtiness dwells in those who are pretty, and pride comes with beauty,[1]

or it is born from nobility, for which reason Sallust says: "The common fault of nobility is pride."[2] Likewise it is born from other goods of nature. Further, it is born from the goods of fortune, such as from riches, for which reason Augustine says: "The worm of the rich is pride."[3] Ecclesiasticus 40: "Ability and power make the heart exalted."[4] Further, it is born from the goods of grace, as from knowledge. "For knowledge puffs up," according to Paul.[5] Nevertheless one must note that whoever becomes proud because of the goods mentioned above is extremely foolish.

That the wicked person who becomes proud because of his goods is foolish.

And first we should show in general that the wicked person who becomes proud because of his goods is extremely foolish. Then we will show on the basis of each one of the goods mentioned above that it is extremely foolish to be proud because of them. And five arguments can be developed to show why the wicked person who becomes proud because of his goods is foolish. First, since in a certain way he is inferior even to irrational creatures insofar as they have to endure only the misery of suffering, but the human being himself must endure the misery of guilt and suffering. Beyond that, irrational creatures have to die only once, and after that they will experience absolutely no evil; a wicked human being, however, is liable for a double death, since after a fleeting death, he will have an eternal one. For this reason, the sinner who is proud because of his goods, considering himself to be better than other human beings while in a certain sense he is inferior to animals, is not just a little foolish. Second, he is foolish since he becomes proud because of those goods in which even animals exceed him, such as bodily strength and agility. Even the Jews and Saracens and other evil human beings have more of these goods than he has. Even demons appear to have more knowledge than the wicked themselves have, though knowledge appears to be one of the chief goods which the wicked possess. For this reason, a person is extremely foolish to be proud of those goods in which he is outdone by demons. Third, the wicked person is foolish who is proud because of his goods, since these goods belong to him more truly for modesty than for glory. For this reason, Augustine, speaking to a wicked person, says, "Do

---

11 **dispositio** *add* se habet Ly. 14 **sunt scientia** est scientia Lu; sunt scientie Mz. 16 **superbia** *om* Ly, *add* enim Pr. 18 **vel** item Pr. 22 **exaltant** exultant Ly. 23 **Apostolum** *add* i ad Corintheos viij Pr. 24 **quod** *add* cum fatuus sit impius qui de bonis suis superbit Pr. 25 **Quod** quinque rationes quare Ly. **impius** nimis Lu; christianus Mz. **bonis** donis Pr. 26 **ostendamus** ostendemus Pr **impius** *om* Lu; christianus Mz. 27–30 **Deinde . . . superbit** *om* Lu. 33 **irrationales** irrationabiles LuPr. 39 **alii** *om* Lu. 40 **de** *add* bonis LyPr. 41 **videtur** *add* esse LyPr. 42 **impii** *om* Lu.

5   Notandum ergo, quod superbia oritur quandoque ex bonis nature, quandoque ex bonis fortune, quandoque ex bonis gratie. Bona vero nature quedam sunt corporis, quedam anime. Corporis sunt ista: sanitas, fortitudo, agilitas, pulcritudo, nobilitas, libertas. Bona vero anime naturalia sunt ista: rectitudo ingenii et velocitas, bonitas

10   memorie, potestas tolerandi exercicium spirituale, naturalis [dispositio] ad virtutes, sive virtus naturalis. Bona vero fortune sunt bona exteriora, que sunt in potestate hominum, que ab hominibus possunt auferri, ut sunt divicie, delicie, dignitates, laus sive gloria, et gracia humana. Bona gratie [sunt scientia] et virtutes. Ex istis bonis

15   nasci potest superbia.

[Superbia] nascitur ex pulcritudine, unde poeta:

Fastus inest pulchris, sequiturque superbia formam,[1]

[vel] nascitur a nobilitate, unde Salustius: "Commune malum nobilitatis est superbia."[2] Similiter nascitur ex aliis bonis nature.

20   Item nascitur ex bonis fortune, sicut ex diviciis, unde Augustinus: "Vermis divitum est superbia."[3] xl Ecclesiastici: "Facultates et virtutes [exaltant] cor."[4] Item nascitur ex bonis gratie, ut a scientia. "Scientia enim inflat," secundum [Apostolum].[5] Notandum tamen, [quod] valde fatuus est, qui de bonis predictis superbit.

25   [Quod] fatuus sit [impius], qui de [bonis] suis superbit.

Et primo generaliter [ostendamus], quod valde fatuus est [impius], qui de bonis suis superbit. [Deinde ostendemus de unoquoque predictorum bonorum, quod valde / fatuum sit inde superbire. Et   fol. 159a possunt v rationes assignari quare fatuus sit impius, qui de bonis

30   suis superbit]. Primo, quia ipse quodammodo inferior est etiam irrationabilibus creaturis in hoc, quod ille sint tantum in miseria pene, homo ipse vero est in miseria culpe et pene. Preterea, creature [irrationales] unicam debent mortem, post quam nichil omnino mali sencient; homo vero impius debitor est duplicis mortis, quia post

35   transitoriam habebit eternam. Unde non parum fatuus est peccator, qui de bonis suis superbit, superiorem se aliis hominibus reputando, qui quodammodo brutis inferior est. Secundo vero fatuus est, quia de illis bonis superbit, in quibus ipsa bruta eum excedunt, sicut est fortitudo corporis et agilitas. Ipsi etiam Judei et Sarraceni et [alii]

40   pessimi homines plus habent [de] illis quam ipse habeat. Etiam ipsi demones de scientia, que [videtur] unum de maximis bonis, que habent impii, plus videntur habere, quam ipsi [impii] habeant, unde valde fatuus est, qui de bonis illis superbit, in quibus a demonibus superatur. Tertio fatuus est impius, qui de bonis suis superbit, cum

45   bona illa sint ei ad verecundiam verius quam ad gloriam. Unde Augustinus loquens ad impium inquit: "Nonne vides te debere

---

1. Ovid, *Fasti*, 1.419; **2.** Sallust, *Bellum Iugurthinum*, 64; **3.** Augustine of Hippo, *Sermones de scripturis*, 39.2.4 (PL 38:242); **4.** Sir 40:26; **5.** 1Cor 8:1.

you not see that you ought to be embarrassed by your goods if your home is filled with goods and evil possesses you?"[6] Fourth, the wicked person is foolish who is proud because of his goods, since his goods are not goods for him. Seneca: "Nothing good belongs to a human being unless it itself is good. Is something good for a person which makes him ill and is a stumbling block to his salvation?"[7] The wise man: "All things which are goods external to us, which have belonged to human beings by chance, are not praised because someone has possessed them, but because he has used them honestly."[8] Thus Seneca says that "a fool does not need anything, for he does not know how to use anything."[9] Fifth, the wicked person is foolish who is proud because of his goods since he has only stewardship over them, and a twofold danger threatens him from them, for there is a danger to him if he loses the principal and there is also a danger to him if he does not report a profit, and concerning both a strict account is required from him.[10] For this reason, whoever is proud because of the multitude of these goods is proud because of the magnitude of his burden.

That it is foolish to take pride in the goods of one's body, such as health and things of this kind.

Now, it is particularly foolish to take pride in the health of one's body. First, since this health is transitory, for today one is healthy, tomorrow sick or dead, James 4: "What is your life? It is a mist appearing only for a while," etc.[11] Second, since the body is an intimate enemy, and thus very injurious, "for no plague is more effective in injuring than an intimate adversary," says the wise man.[12] Thus, no one should take pride in bodily health, but rather should fear it, for one is in greater danger, since health is one's enemy. Third, whoever takes pride in this health is foolish, since very frequently health itself is the occasion of the soul's illness, just as is written from the opposite point of view in Ecclesiasticus 23: "A grave illness furthers the sobriety of the soul."[13] There is no reason why someone would take pride in the health of his foot if he has a deadly illness in his head; thus, one ought not to take pride in the health of the body which is the source of deadly illness in the soul. A man who is healthy in his body but mentally infirm is like an apple which is whole on the outside but rotten within. It is also foolish to be proud of bodily strength, since it is written in Wisdom 6 that "Worse torments await those who are stronger,"[14] and since there is a continuous wrestling match between the soul and the body: "For the flesh sets its desire against the soul and the soul against the flesh."[15] For this reason, the greater one's bodily strength, the more one must fear for the soul. And we see this often literally, because those who have greater bodily strength are weaker mentally, for they are less able to resist wrath and lust and the other vices. It is also foolish to be proud of one's ability to run fast, since the body is like a horse on which hellish enemies frequently lead the spirit to its death, and even more frequently, the faster that horse is, the more easily its spirit is captured by its enemies. Beyond this, in speed we are surpassed by dogs, for which reason it is foolish for a human being to take pride in something in which he sees that he is inferior to dogs. It is also foolish to be proud of corporeal beauty, since the body is like

---

47 **habeat** habebit Lu; habet Ly; habetat Mz. 52 **bona** dona LuLy. **contigerint** contingerint Lu; contigunt Pr. 54 **res** re Pr. **opus** apostolus Ly. **re** *om* Mz. 61 **sui** *om* Lu; **de . . . sui** *om.* Ly. **ut** *om.* Ly; videlicet Pr. **sanitate** *add* et velocitate corporis Ly, *add* fortitudine velocitate et pulchritudine etc. Pr. 68 **inimicus** *add* sicut Ly. 70 **est** *add* homo Pr. 73 **xxiii** xxxiij Lu; xxxi Pr. 76 **est** *add* usque Lu. 84 **mente** anime Lu. 87 **ut** et et Ly; ut Mz.

erubescere de bonis tuis, si domus tua plena est bonis et te [habeat] malum?"[6] Quarto fatuus est impius, qui de bonis suis superbit, quia bona ipsius ei bona non sunt. Seneca: "Nihil est homini bonum sine
50   se bono. Estne bonum homini, quod est ei materia / infirmitatis et   fol. 159b impedimentum salutis?"[7] Sapiens: "Omnia, que extra nos sunt [bona], quecumque hominibus forte [contigerint], non ideo laudantur, quod habuit quis ea, sed quod hiis honeste sit usus."[8] Ideo dicit Seneca, quod "stulto nulla [res] est [opus], nulla enim [re] scit
55   uti."[9] Quinto fatuus est impius, qui de bonis suis superbit, quia ipse tantum habet dispensationem in eis, et periculum imminet ei inde duplex. Periculum est enim ei, si sortem amiserit, periculum etiam est ei, si lucrum non reportaverit. Et de utroque districta ratio exigetur ab eo.[10] Unde qui de multitudine istorum bonorum superbit,
60   ipse superbit de magnitudine oneris sui.

Quod fatuum sit [de bonis corporis sui] superbire, [ut] de [sanitate] et hujusmodi.

Specialiter vero fatuum est superbire de sanitate corporis. Primo, quia ista sanitas momentanea est. Hodie enim quis sanus est, cras
65   infirmus vel mortuus, Jacobi iiii: "Que est vita vestra? Vapor est ad modicum parens," etc.[11] Secundo, quia corpus hostis familiaris est, et ideo multum nocivus. "Nulla enim pestis efficacior ad nocendum quam familiaris [inimicus]," ait Sapiens.[12] Non debet ergo aliquis superbire propter sanitatem corporis, sed potius timere. In majori
70   enim periculo [est], cum hostis ejus sanus sit. Tertio fatuus est, qui de hac sanitate superbit, cum ipsa sanitas ut frequencius occasio sit infirmitatis anime, sicut econtrario scriptum est in Ecclesiastici [xxiii]: "Infirmitas gravis sobriam reddit animam."[13] Non est, quare aliquis superbiat de sanitate pedis, si in capite infirmitatem habeat
75   ad mortem, sic non est superbiendum de sanitate corporis, ex quo / in anima infirmitas [est] ad mortem. Homo sanus corpore, infirmus   fol. 159va mente, similis est pomo exterius sano, interius putrido. De fortitudine etiam corporis fatuum est superbire, cum scriptum sit Sapientie vi, quod "Forcioribus forcior instat cruciatio,"[14] et cum
80   continua lucta sit inter spiritum et corpus: "Caro enim concupiscit adversus spiritum, et spiritus adversus carnem."[15] Unde quanto corpus forcius, tanto magis spiritui timendum est. Et ad literam hoc videmus frequenter, quod forciores corpore infirmiores sunt [mente]. Minus enim resistere possunt ire et luxurie et ceteris viciis.
85   Fatuum etiam est superbire de corporis velocitate, cum corpus sit velud equs quidam, in quo hostes infernales ut frequenter ducunt spiritum ad mortem ipsius, [ut et] frequencius, quanto iste equs velocior est, tanto facilius spiritus ab hostibus suis capitur. Preterea in velocitate ista a canibus superamur, unde fatuum est, quod homo
90   de hoc superbiat, in quo a canibus inferiorem se videt. De pulchritudine etiam corporis fatuum est superbire, cum corpus sit

---

6. Augustine of Hippo, *Sermones de scripturis*, 72.4.5 (PL 38:469); **7.** unidentified; **8.** unidentified; **9.** Seneca, *Epistulae morales*, 9.14; **10.** Cf. Matt 25:14–30; **11.** Jas 4:15; **12.** Boethius, *De consolatione Philosophiae*, 3pr5 (CCL 94:45); **13.** Sir 31:2; **14.** Wis 6:9; **15.** Gal 5:17.

a tomb. Augustine: "The body of a sinner is the tomb of a dead soul."[16] For this reason, when a sinner is proud of corporeal beauty, it is just as if a dead person were proud of the image of his tomb, and it is also just as if someone were proud of the beauty of a dung-pit when it is covered by snow.

Why one should not pay attention to nobility of the flesh.

It is also foolish to be proud of one's nobility, since that nobility is extremely contemptible. Many reasons can be adduced why this nobility is extremely contemptible. First, it ought to be despised, since frequently nobility of the flesh robs one of a greater nobility, namely a nobility of the mind. The wise man: "No one deludes himself about the nobility of his family if he is a servant in the better sense. It is much more unworthy to be a servant in mind than in body."[17] Second, it ought to be despised, since we are all from the same father and the same mother: One does not read that the Lord made one Adam of silver from whom the nobles come, and one of clay from whom the common people come, but only one Adam, and he molded him from the clay from which we have all emerged. For this reason, if someone is noble only because he comes from a noble father and noble mother, either we are all noble, or we are all common, since our first parents were either noble or common. If, moreover, they were noble, then for that reason we, too, are all noble, and also equally noble, since we were born from those who were equally noble, and they must be judged as equally noble. If, however, they were common, all of us are common, and equally common, since we were born from those who are equally common. Malachi 2: "Do we not all have one father? Did not one God create us? Why, therefore, does each one of you hate his brother?"[18] Third, nobility of the flesh ought to be despised since God himself hated it, for He did not want to choose kings from the nobles at the beginning of the synagogue; indeed, he took the first king, namely Saul, following after donkeys, and he selected the second king, namely David, who was looking after foul-smelling animals.[19] During the time of grace, too, He wanted to choose commoners more than nobles, for which reason 1 Corinthians 1: "God has chosen the common and contemptible things of the world."[20] Fourth, moreover, nobility of the flesh ought to be despised since it does not belong to him who glories in it, but rather to those from whom he is descended. For this reason, Seneca: "No one lived for our glory, nor do the things which came before us belong to us: the soul makes someone noble."[21] Fifth, moreover, the nobility of the flesh ought to be despised since the natural material which someone inherits from his parents, the reason for his belief that he is noble, is something vile and unclean and a cause for embarrassment, and it issues from them through an unclean and embarrassing deed. For this reason, why will someone possess nobility because of that material, when that material itself was vile? Why does someone dare to call himself noble by birth when everyone could say on the example of Job: "I said to putridity: 'You are my father' "?[22] Thus, by right nobility of the flesh ought to be despised; indeed, it ought to be abhorred. For this reason Luke 16: "Whatever is exalted

---

97 **Quare . . . reputanda** octo raciones ad hoc quod nobilitas carnis sit contempnenda Ly; quod fatuum sit de nobilitate generis superbire Pr. 100 **valde** *om* LuPr. 103 **nobilitate** *add* corporis vel generis Pr. 103–4 **Multo . . . corpore** *om* Pr. 107 **unicum** *add* fecit Ly. 112 **nobiles** *add* sumus Pr. 113 **fuerunt** fuerint Ly; *add* ergo Pr. 114 **sumus** simus Ly. 115 **ignobilibus** nobilibus LuPr. 119 **in principio** et principes Ly. 125 **Unde Seneca** *om* Mz. 127 **facit** *add* hominem Ly. 128 **a** cum Ly. 132 **fuit** fuerit Pr. 133 **dixi** *om* LuLy.

velut quoddam sepulchrum. Augustinus: "Corpus peccatoris anime
mortue est sepulchrum."[16] Unde cum peccator de pulcritudine
corporis superbit, simile est acsi mortuus de pictura sepulcri
95 superbiat, simile est etiam acsi aliquis superbiat de pulcritudine
sterquilinii nive cooperti.

[Quare nobilitas carnis non sit reputanda].   fol. 159vb

De nobilitate etiam / carnis fatuum est superbire, cum illa nobilitas
valde contemptibilis sit. Multe autem cause possunt assignari, quare
100 ista nobilitas [valde] contemptibilis sit. Primo contempnenda est,
quia ut frequenter nobilitas carnis meliorem nobilitatem aufert, scilicet mentis nobilitatem. Sapiens: "Non est, quo sibi aliquis de
[nobilitate] generis blandiatur, si ex meliori parte sit famulus. [Multo
indignius est mente servire quam corpore]."[17] Secundo contemnenda
105 est, quia omnes sumus ex eodem patre et eadem matre: non legitur
Dominus fecisse unum Adam argenteum, unde essent nobiles, et
unum luteum, ex quo essent ignobiles, sed [unicum], et illum de luto
plasmavit, ex quo omnes exivimus. Unde si aliquis ex hoc solo
nobilis est, quia ex nobili patre et nobili matre, aut omnes erimus
110 nobiles aut omnes ignobiles, quia aut parentes primi fuerunt nobiles
aut ignobiles. Si autem ipsi fuerunt nobiles, ergo et nos omnes
nobiles sumus, et etiam eque [nobiles], cum geniti ex eque nobilibus
et eque nobiles judicentur. Si vero ignobiles [fuerunt], nos omnes
ignobiles sumus, et eque ignobiles, cum geniti [sumus] ex eque
115 [ignobilibus]. Malachie ii: "Numquid non pater unus omnium
nostrum? Numquid non Deus unus creavit nos? Quare ergo despicit
fratrem suum unusquisque vestrum?"[18] Tertio contempnenda / est fol. 160a
nobilitas carnis, quia ipse Deus contempsit eam. Noluit enim ex
nobilibus reges eligere [in principio] synagoge, immo primum
120 regem post asinas assumpsit, scilicet Saul, secundum regem, scilicet
David, de post fetantes accepit.[19] In tempore etiam gratie pocius
voluit ignobiles eligere quam nobiles, unde i Ad Corinthios i:
"Ignobilia et contemptibilia mundi elegit Deus."[20] Quarto vero
contemnenda est nobilitas carnis, quia non est illius, qui de ea
125 gloriatur, sed potius illorum a quibus ipse descendit. [Unde Seneca]:
"Nemo in gloriam nostram vixit, nec quod ante nos fuit nostrum est:
animus nobilem [facit]."[21] Quinto vero contempnenda est nobilitas
carnis, quia materia, quam [a] parentibus contrahit aliquis, ratione
cujus nobilem se credit, vile quid est immundum et erubescibile, et
130 opere immundo et erubescibili procedit ab eis. Unde quomodo
ratione illius materie habebit quis nobilitatem, cum illa materia vilis
[fuit]? Quomodo aliquis audet dicere se nobilem generatione, cum
quilibet exemplo Job possit dicere: "Putredini [dixi], 'Pater meus
es' "?[22] Ideo merito nobilitas carnis contemnenda est, immo
135 abhominanda. Unde Luce xvi: "Quod altum est hominibus,

---

16. Cf. Eucherius of Lyons, *Formularum liber*, 6 (PL 50:757A); Hrabanus Maurus, *De universo*, 7.6 (PL
111:195B); **17.** Pelagius (?), *Epistolae*, 17.22 (PL 33:1115; PL 30:36D–37A); **18.** Mal 2:10; **19.** Cf. 1Sam
9:3–16, 1Sam 16:11–12; **20.** 1Cor 1:28; **21.** Seneca, *Epistulae morales*, 44.5; **22.** Job 17:14.

among human beings is an abomination before God."[23] Sixth, nobility of the flesh ought to be despised, or even more it should not be considered at all, since in truth it is not nobility, just as the philosophers themselves discovered. Seneca: "No one is more noble than another unless his natural talents are better and more fittingly endowed with good skills."[24] Likewise: "Nobility is nothing other than ancient riches."[25] Likewise Seneca: "What is a nobleman or a servant or a freedman? They are titles, born from ambition or injury."[26] Likewise Seneca: "Plato says that there is no king not descended from servants, no servant not descended from kings. A continuing inconstancy has blended all these things together and fortune has turned whoever was on top to a position on the bottom."[27]

2. (ParT X,462–69)

On the twofold nobility of the heart

Moreover, the nobility of the heart is twofold. One is natural, on which Seneca: "Who is well-born? The one who has been well fitted by nature for virtue."[1] The other nobility is given freely when someone possesses God's grace, which makes him a son of God; it watches over him so that he does not serve the interests of moral turpitude. Cicero: "Someone should be considered free when that person does not serve the interests of moral turpitude."[2] In the same way, a wise man: "You should pride yourself on that nobility which makes people sons of God and His co-heirs. A person should think of himself as preserving his nobility in an irreproachable state if he refuses to be a servant to the vices and to be overcome by them, 'for when someone is bested by another person, he also acts as that person's servant.' "[3] Bernard: "Is someone not a servant, who is ruled by evil?"[4] No matter how noble a person's descent, he is still a commoner if he hates God and does not wish to serve Him; and no matter how common someone's descent, he is still noble if he serves God. For this reason in 1 Samuel 2 the Lord says to Eli: "I will have none of it, but whoever honors me, I will glorify him, but those who hate me will be commoners."[5]

On the six signs of true nobility.

One should also note that there are six signs of true nobility. The first is generosity. For this reason God, who is the most noble being, is Himself the most generous, for His generosity is such that He gives not only what belongs to Him, but also His very self, He gives not only to those serving Him, but also to His enemies. "For He makes His sun rise over the good and the evil, and He causes it to rain over the just and the unjust," Matthew 5.[6] Out of His generosity He created whatever has been created, for whatever He created, He created for the purpose of being given. He created rational creatures so that he could give things to them, and He created the other creatures so that they could be what He gives. The lion, too, which is said to be the king of the beasts and a noble animal, is generous. For this reason Aristotle says that it is a communicative animal.[7] And just as generosity is a sign of nobility,

---

138 **deprehenderunt** reputaverunt Pr. 140 **Item** idem LuPr. **quam** nisi Lu. **antiquate** antique Ly. 141 **eques** equs LuLyMz. **libertinus** add nisi Pr. 143 **regibus** add oriundum esse Ly.

Lu, pp. 782b–784a; Ly, fol. 111a–vb; Mz, fols. 161a–162a; Pr, fols. 163b–164va.

1 **duplici** duplice Ly; *om* Mz. 6 **quidam** *om* Pr. 12 **nolit** noluerit Pr. 13 **ex . . . ignobilibus** econtrario . . . ignobilis Pr. 14 **I** *om* LyMz. **Hely** Helyam Ly. 17 **De . . . signis** de vii signis Lu; quod sex sunt signa Pr. 20 **ejus** enim Mz. 21 **nec** non Ly. 25 **rationales** rationabiles Lu. **facit** fecit Pr. 26 **ut** non Ly.

abhominatio est ante Deum."²³ Sexto contempnenda est nobilitas
carnis, immo pocius non est reputanda, cum in veritate nobilitas non
sit, sicut etiam ipsi philosophi [deprehenderunt]. Seneca: "Nemo
altero nobilior, nisi cui rectius est ingenium et bonis artibus apcius."²⁴
140 [Item]: "Nichil aliud est nobilitas [quam] [antiquate] divicie."²⁵ Idem:
"Quid / est [eques], aut servus, aut [libertinus]? Nomina ex ambitione   fol. 160b
vel injuria nata."²⁶ Idem: "Plato ait neminem regem non ex servis
oriundum esse, neminem servum non ex [regibus]. Omnia ista longa
varietas miscuit, et sursum deorsum fortuna versavit."²⁷

2. (Part X,462–9)

De [duplici] nobilitate animi.   fol. 161a
Animi vero nobilitas duplex est. Quedam naturalis, de qua Seneca:
"Quis est generosus? Ad virtutem bene a natura compositus."¹ Alia
nobilitas est gratuita, quando aliquis gratiam Dei habet, qua Dei
5 filius est, que custodit eum, ut nulli turpitudini serviat. Tullius:
"Liber existimandus est, qui nulli turpitudini servit."² Item [quidam]
sapiens: "De illa nobilitate glorieris, que filios Dei et coheredes
facit. Tunc ille nobilitatem suam integram servare se putet, si
dedignetur servire viciis et ab illis superari. 'A quo enim quis
10 superatur, ejus et servus est.' "³ Bernardus: "An non servus, cui
dominatur iniquitas?"⁴ Quantumcunque aliquis ex nobilibus ortus
sit, tamen ignobilis est, si Deum contempnat et [nolit] ei servire, et
[ex quantumcumque ignobilibus] ortus sit, nobilis tamen est, si Deo
serviat. Unde [I] Regum ii dicit Dominus ad [Hely]: "Absit hoc a
15 me, sed quicumque honorificaverit me, glorificabo eum; qui autem
contempnunt me, erunt ignobiles."⁵
[De vi signis] vere nobilitatis.
Et notandum, quod vi sunt signa vere nobilitatis. Primum est
liberalitas. Unde Deus, qui nobilissimus est, ipse est liberalissimus.
20 Liberalitas [ejus] tanta est, ut non solum sua det, sed etiam seipsum,
[nec] solum servientibus sibi dat, sed etiam hostibus suis. "Ipse
enim solem suum oriri facit super bonos et malos, et pluit super
justos et injustos," Matthei v.⁶ Ipse propter liberalitatem suam fecit
quecumque facta sunt. Ad dandum enim fecit, quecumque fecit.
25 Creaturas / [rationales] [facit], ut eis daret, alias autem creaturas,   fol. 161b
[ut] eas daret. Leo etiam, qui dicitur esse rex animalium, quod
animal nobile est, liberale est. Unde Aristoteles dicit ipsum esse
animal communicativum.⁷ Et sicuti liberalitas signum est nobilitatis,

23. Luke 16:15; **24.** unidentified; **25.** Cf. Aristotle, *Politics*, 4.6.5 (1294a21–2); **26.** Seneca, *Epistulae morales*, 31.11; **27.** Seneca, *Epistulae morales*, 44.4 (cf. Plato, *Theaetetus* 174D–175A).

1. Seneca, *Epistulae morales*, 44.5; **2.** Ps.-Cicero, *Rhetorica ad Herennium*, 4.17.24; **3.** Pelagius (?), *Epistolae*, 17.22 (PL 33:1115; PL 30:36D); 2Pet 2:19; **4.** Bernard of Clairvaux, *De consideratione*, 1.4.5 (*SBO* 3:399); **5.** 1Sam 2:30; **6.** Matt 5:45; **7.** Cf. Aristotle, *Analytica priora*, 2.27 (trans. Boethius, rec. Flor.) (AL 3,1–4:139).

so is rapine a sign of boorishness. For this reason those who are considered to be noble are the most boorish when they do not cease to steal from the poor and from those who cannot defend themselves, just as master Alanus demonstrated to some knights. Master Alanus was lecturing near Montpellier, and knights who were nearby heard that an important cleric was present and that he would answer everything that was asked of him. After consulting each other, they came to him for this purpose and asked him what is the greatest act of courtliness. He responded to them that the most courtly act is to give. When they heard that, all of them agreed with his answer. He, however, said to them that after speaking about the matter among themselves, they should tell him which one out of a number of possibilities is the more boorish act. They spoke about the matter among themselves and were unable to arrive at a single conclusion. Thus, they returned to him and said that they were not able to agree on the matter. When he heard this, he upbraided them saying: "I set you on the path on which you could have discovered the answer to the question I posed, for if the most courtly act is to give, then to steal, which is the opposite of it, is the most boorish. For this reason you who unceasingly steal from the poor are the most boorish."[8]

The second sign of nobility is gratitude, or a recollection of kindness, and on the other hand, ingratitude, or not remembering kindnesses, is a sign of boorishness. For this reason, it is obvious that those who are thought to be noble have been honored by God above all other human beings, and yet they, more than any others, dishonor Him. These nobles also unceasingly oppress their subjects who toil greatly to make a profit which the nobles themselves live from and because of whom the nobles are in a position of honor. Such people also seem to be worse than the most uncivilized wild beasts, for even wild beasts feel a sense of duty and kindness, as Seneca says.[9]

The third sign of generosity is mildness and mercy towards whatever is under someone's rule. This is also one matter which is extremely appropriate in those who have power. For which reason, Seneca: "Of all human beings, none is more distinguished by mercy than a king or a prince."[10] Again: "The angriest and the most warlike animals, given their capacity, are bees, and they leave their stinger behind in the wound. The king himself, however, is without a stinger; Nature did not want him to be savage or to seek a revenge which would exact a great cost, and so it removed his spear and left his anger unarmed, which is a powerful example for all kings. It would be shameful not to draw a moral lesson from these tiny animals."[11] Christian kings are anointed in a sign of this mildness or mercy. The wise man: "Someone possessing the greatest power ought to imitate the creator of power as far as this is possible for him."[12] Now, he will imitate God to the maximum extent if he judges nothing to be more precious than to show mercy. And just as mildness towards one's subjects is a sign of nobility, so is cruelty towards one's subjects a sign of boorishness and slavery. For this reason, Proverbs 30: "At three things the earth shakes, and there is a fourth which it cannot endure: at a servant who begins to act as a king."[13] *The Eunuch:*

---

29 **illi** multi hoc die Pr.   31 **se** *add* exemplum Lu.   32 **magister** *om* Pr.   34 **accedentes** accesserunt Pr. 37 **ejus** *add* ideo dicit Dominus quod beatius est dare quam recipere quia dare ficit siimilem Deo qui omnibus dat et a nemine recipit Pr.   38 **alias** omnes Pr.   42 **vobis** *om* Mz.   43 **dare** *om* Ly; dari Pr. 46 **recogitacio** recognitio Pr.   48 **recogitacio** recognitio LyPr.   55 **nobilitatis** liberalitatis LuLyMz. 61 **detraxit** destruxit Mz.   63 **ingens** inquens Mz; linquens Pr.   65 **Sapiens** Philosophus Pr.   68 **subjectos** subditos Lu.   69 **subditos** subiectos Ly.   71 **per** scilicet Ly.   **Eunuchus** Ethnicus Lu; unde Alexander Ly; Ovidius Pr.

ita rapina signum rusticitatis. Unde [illi], qui nobiles reputantur,
30   rusticissimi sunt, cum non cessent auferre pauperibus et illis, qui
non possunt defendere [se], sicut magister Alanus ostendit
quibusdam militibus. Legebat [magister] Alanus apud Montem
Pessulanum, et audierunt milites vicini, quod tantus clericus esset et
quod ad omnia interrogata responderet. Unde [accedentes] ad eum
35   de communi consilio quesierunt ab eo, que esset maxima curialitas.
Qui respondit eis, quod dare curialissimum esset. Quo audito omnes
consenserunt responsioni [ejus]. Ipse vero dixit eis, ut habito
consilio ad invicem dicerent ei, que inter [alias] rusticitates major
esset. Qui habuerunt ad invicem consilium et non potuerunt in idem
40   convenire. Unde revertentes ad eum dixerunt, quod non poterant
concordare. Quo audito ipse increpavit eos dicens: "Ego posueram
vos in via per quam possetis solutionem questionis [vobis] proposite
cognoscere. Si enim [dare] curialissimum est, auferre, quod est ei
contrarium, rusticissimum est. Unde vos, qui incessanter aufertis a
45   pauperibus, rusticissimi estis."[8]

Secundum signum nobilitatis est gratitudo sive [recogitacio]
beneficii. Et per contrarium, ingratitudo seu beneficiorum non
[recogitacio] signum rusticitatis est. Unde patet, quod illi, qui
nobiles reputantur, qui Deum, qui eos pre ceteris hominibus /
50   honoravit, pre ceteris hominibus inhonorant, subditos etiam suos,   fol. 161va
qui multo sudore lucrantur, unde ipsi vivunt, et propter quos ipsi
sunt in honore, incessanter opprimunt. Rusticissimis feris etiam
videntur tales deteriores esse. "Fere enim officia sive beneficia
senciunt," sicut ait Seneca.[9]

55   Tercium signum [nobilitatis] est mansuetudo et misericordia in ea,
que sunt ei subiecta. Et hoc est unum, quod valde decens est in hiis,
qui potestatem habent. Unde Seneca: "Nullum ex omnibus magis
clemencia quam regem et principem decet."[10] Idem: "Iracundissime
ac pro captu pugnacissime sunt apes et aculeum in vulnere
60   relinquunt. Rex ipse sine aculeo est. Noluit ipsum natura nec sevum
esse nec ultionem, que magno constaret, petere, telumque [detraxit],
et iram ejus inhermem reliquit, exemplar hoc omnibus regibus
[ingens]. Pudeat ab exiguis animalibus non trahere mores."[11] In
signum hujus mansuetudinis vel misericordie inunguntur reges
65   Christiani. [Sapiens]: "Maximam potestatem habens creatorem
potestatis juxta possibilitatem suam debet imitari."[12] In hoc autem
Deum maxime imitabitur, si nichil judicaverit quam misereri
preciosius. Et sicuti mansuetudo in [subjectos] signum est nobilitatis,
sic crudelitas in [subditos] signum est rusticitatis et servitutis. Unde
70   Proverbiorum xxx: "Per tria movetur terra, et quartum quod non
potest sustinere: [per] servum cum regnare ceperit."[13] / [*Eunuchus*]:   fol. 161vb

---

8. Cf. Tubach 1296; **9.** unidentified; **10.** Seneca, *De clementia*, 1.3.3; **11.** Seneca, *De clementia*, 1.19.3–4;
12. unidentified; **13.** Prov 30:21–2.

Nothing is so cruel than when a man of humble origins soars to the heights.
He strikes out at all things while he fears all things, he rages against everyone
So that they will think he is powerful, nor is any monster more offensive
Than the fury of a slave raging against those born free.[14]

The fourth sign of nobility is manliness or decisiveness against one's opponents. As a sign of this quality, a sword is given to new knights which they are supposed to use against their enemies, not against their subjects. Many of them, however, use this sword against their subjects whom they ought to care for greatly, for they are the ones who assist them. Sometimes brothers even fight against their own brothers, but in fact they have united themselves with the enemies of God and the church, namely with sins, demons, or even the very people persecuting the church. Such impiety is a diabolical impiety, for the devil acts wickedly towards those who serve him.

The fifth sign of nobility is to fear the disgrace either of slavery or of treachery or of some other wickedness. We see, however, that many of those who are considered noble do not fear the worst slavery to their vices or demons and are not embarrassed to confess that they are slaves to their most vile bodily parts, namely those which serve the ends of lust. This servitude, without a doubt, is worse than the servitude of lepers. They are not even embarrassed to treacherously attack their own lord from whom they possess all things, and at whose expense they live and clothe themselves. Nor are they even embarrassed to expose themselves to every uncleanliness of sin. From this fact it is obvious that they are not noble but extremely boorish.

The sixth sign of nobility is magnitude of the heart, by which someone disdains what is mediocre and seeks what is grand. On the other hand, however, it is a sign of boorishness to place one's love in what is mediocre and to turn one's back on what is grand. For this reason, it is obvious that those fine ladies who would rather give their love to one miserable knight than to the King of Glory are not truly noble. Moreover, knights cannot be seen as noble who place their love on this earth in contempt of the kingdom of heaven, when nevertheless the entire earth is nothing but a dot in relation to the heavens. Since they have more from the earth than others do, they want to have nothing from heaven. If the land of a poor knight belonged to someone from his mother's side, but the kingdom belonged to him from his father's side, would he be wretched if out of contempt for the kingdom he held onto the land which came to him from his mother's side? Thus, these knights are wretched who do not care for the kingdom of heaven, which belongs to them from their heavenly father's side, but are eager for that land of poverty which belongs to us from the side of our mother, Eve. David was not acting in this way, for which reason the Psalm: "What is there for me in heaven, and what did I want from you on the earth?"[15]

---

78 **subjectos** subditos Lu. 79 **subditos** subiectos Pr. 80 **proprios** proprii eos LuMz; proprii Ly. 82 **ipsis** *om* Lu. **uniti** iuncti LuLy. 85 **Multos** multis Mz. 87 **suorum** *om* Lu; scilicet Ly. 90 **proditione** proditiose Pr. 98 **quod** quare Ly. 102 **nichil volunt** nolunt aliquid Pr. 104 **numquid** *add* non Pr. 105 **eum** ei Ly. 107 **contenti** contempta Ly. **nos** illos Ly. 108 **nostre** *add* scilicet Ly. **Eve** *add* pater noster Deus est mater nostra Eua Pr. **unde** *add* ipse Ly; *om* Pr.

Asperius humili nichil est, cum surgit in altum.
Cuncta ferit, dum cuncta timet, desevit in omnes,
Vt se posse putant, nec belua tetrior ulla est
75   Quam servi rabies in libera terga furentis.[14]

Quartum signum nobilitatis est virilitas seu strenuitas in eos, qui
repugnant. In signum hujus datur ensis militibus novis, quo gladio
uti debent in hostes, non in [subjectos]. Multi vero ex eis gladio isto
in [subditos] utuntur, quos deberent valde diligere. Hii enim sunt,
80   qui juvant eos. Quando etiam fratres eorum [proprios] impugnant,
hostibus vero Dei et ecclesie, peccatis scilicet, demonibus vel etiam
[ipsis] persecutoribus ecclesie [uniti] sunt. Impietas talis impietas
diabolica est. Diabolus enim impius est in eos, qui sibi serviunt.
Quintum signum est nobilitatis timere opprobrium vel servitutis vel
85   proditionis vel alicujus turpitudinis. [Multos] tamen ex illis, qui
nobiles reputantur, videmus, qui non timent pessimam servitutem
viciorum [suorum] vel demonum, qui non erubescunt confiteri se
servos vilissimorum membrorum illorum, scilicet que libidini
deserviunt. Que servitus pejor est indubitanter servitute leprosorum.
90   Non erubescunt etiam [proditione] impugnare dominum illum, a quo
omnia possident, cujus expensis vivunt et vestiuntur. Et non
erubescunt etiam omni immundicie peccati se exponere. Ex quo
patet eos non esse nobiles sed valde rusticos.
Sextum signum / nobilitatis est cordis magnitudo, qua quis modica   fol. 162a
95   contempnit et magna appetit. Econtrario vero signum rusticitatis est
amorem suum in modicis ponere, magna vero negligere. Unde patet
dominas illas, que pocius volunt amorem suum ponere in uno
misero milite quam in Rege Glorie, [quod] ipse vere nobiles non
sunt. Milites etiam non videntur nobiles esse, qui amorem suum in
100   terra ponunt contempto regno celorum, cum tamen tota terra quasi
punctum sit respectu celi. Et quia plus habent de terra quam alii,
[nichil volunt] habere de celo. Si ad aliquem pertineret terra unius
pauperis militis ex parte matris, regnum vero ex parte patris,
[numquid] infelix esset, si contempto regno adhereret illi terre, que
105   [eum] contingeret ex parte matris? Sic infelices sunt illi milites, qui
de regno celorum non curant, quod ad eos pertinet ex parte patris
celestis, [contenti] ista terra paupertatis, que ad [nos] pertinet ex
parte matris [nostre] [Eve]. Non sic faciebat David, [unde] in
Psalmo: "Quid mihi in celo, et a te quid volui super terram?"[15]

14. Claudianus, *In Eutropium*, 1.181–4 (Walther, *IC* 1576; Walther, *PS* 1565); **15.** Ps 72:25.

3. (ParT X,470–73)

That it is foolish to be proud of bodily freedom and glory and things of this kind.
Now that we have seen that it is foolish to be proud of the nobility of the flesh, it
follows logically to see that it is foolish to be proud of the other goods which were
named earlier. Thus, one should note that it is foolish to be proud of the freedom of
the body, since the body is an ill-disposed servant and thus worthy of torture and
shackles, according to the passage in Ecclesiasticus 33: "For an ill-disposed servant
there should be torture and shackles," etc.[1] It is, moreover, foolish to be proud of the
natural goods of the soul since a person can possess these goods for his own evil just
as well as for his good. For this reason, Bernard: "A person new to the religious
vocation is skillful in his way of thinking if he is esteemed for his skill and if he
excels through his intellect. These are the tools both of vices and of virtues. Thus,
one should not flee from being taught to use something for good which also can be
used for evil."[2] It is also foolish to be proud of riches, for this is to be proud of the
fact that one has a larger millstone around his neck than others do. It is foolish to be
proud of power, since it is written in Wisdom 6 that: "The powerful will suffer
severe torments."[3] In the same passage one reads that: "The harshest judgment will
be reserved for those who are powerful."[4] And Augustine says that: "The higher the
position one has, the greater the danger he is in."[5] It is also foolish to be proud of
one's human charm since it is written at the end of Proverbs that: "Charm is decep-
tive."[6] It is also foolish to be proud of the glory of this world since such glory is a
drooping flower, for which reason Isaiah 28: "The glory of their rejoicing will be a
drooping flower."[7] It is a characteristic of children to gather flowers which hang
down from trees and to take joy in this. Thus, those people are childish who find joy
in the glory of this world. It is also foolish to be proud of one's knowledge since it is
written in Ecclesiastes 1: "Whoever adds knowledge also adds sorrow."[8] To be
proud of knowledge is to be blinded by the light. It is also foolish to be proud of
one's virtues, for this is to be wounded by medication. Gregory: "Whoever is
exalted by the virtues which he possesses, it is as if he were wounded by medicine."[9]

Lu, pp. 785b–786a; Ly, fol. 112b–va; Mz, fol. 163b–va; Pr, fol. 165va–vb.

1–2 **de . . . hujusmodi** de libertate corporis et scientia et gloria et huiusmodi bonis naturalibus anime
Lu; de libertate corporis de bonis naturalibus anime de beneficiis potestate [?] gracia uel gloria de
humana scientia vel virtut<. . .> [*margin cropped*] Ly; generaliter de qualibet re temporali scilicet
libertate corporis etc. et bonis naturalibus anime Pr. 3 **quod** quomodo Lu. 6 **servus malivolus** maliuolum
Ly. 9 **suum** *om* Ly. 10 **Bernardus** *add* si Pr. 12 **Instrumenta** instituta Ly. 21 **ultimo** v Lu. 28 **enim** *add*
superbire Ly. **medicacione** medicamine LyPr.

3. (ParT X,470–3)

Quod fatuum sit superbire [de libertate corporis et gloria et fol. 163b hujusmodi].

Viso [quod] fatuum sit superbire de nobilitate carnis, consequens est videre, quod fatuum sit superbire de aliis bonis, que prius nominata
5   sunt. Notandum ergo, quod fatuum est superbire de libertate corporis, cum corpus sit [servus malivolus] et ideo tortura et compedibus dignus, juxta illud Ecclesiastici xxxiii: "Servo malivolo tortura et compedes," etc.[1] De bonis vero naturalibus anime fatuum est superbire, quia bona illa potest homo habere ad malum [suum]
10 sicut ad bonum. Unde [Bernardus]: "In professione religionis novus homo callidus est ingenio, si viget arte, si preeminet intellectu. [Instrumenta] sunt hec tam viciorum quam virtutum. Non ergo refugiat doceri uti eo in bono, quo et in malo uti potest."[2] Fatuum est etiam superbire de diviciis. Hoc enim est superbire de hoc, quod
15 homo habet majorem molam ad collum quam alii. Fatuum est de potestate superbire, cum scriptum sit Sapientie vi, quod: "Potentes potenter tormenta pacientur."[3] Ibidem legitur, quod: "durissimum judicium hiis, qui presunt, fiet."[4] Et Augustinus dicit, quod: "Quanto quis in loco superiori, tanto in periculo majori versatur."[5] Fatuum est
20 etiam superbire de gratia humana, cum scriptum sit Proverbiorum [ultimo], quod: "Fallax gratia."[6] Fatuum est etiam superbire de gloria hujus mundi, cum gloria talis flos sit decidens. Unde Ysaie xxviii: "Erit flos decidens gloria exultationis."[7] Puerorum est flores colligere, / qui ex arboribus decidunt et inde letari. Sic pueriles sunt, fol. 163va
25 qui de gloria hujus mundi letantur. Fatuum etiam est superbire de scientia, cum scriptum sit Ecclesiaste i: "Qui addit scientiam, addit et dolorem."[8] De scientia superbire est de lumine excecari. Fatuum etiam est de virtutibus superbire. Hoc [enim] est de [medicacione] vulnerari. Gregorius: "Qui de virtutibus habitis extollitur, quasi de
30 medicamento vulneratur."[9]

1. Sir 33:28; **2.** William of St.-Thierry, *Tractatus ad fratres de Monte Dei*, 1.6.17 (PL 184:319C–D); **3.** Wis 6:7; **4.** Wis 6:6; **5.** Isidore of Seville, *Sententiarum libri*, 3.50.5 (CCL 111:302); **6.** Prov 31:30; **7.** Isa 28:1; **8.** Qoh 1:18; **9.** Gregory the Great, *Moralia in Iob*, 33.12.25 (CCL 143B:1695) – Robert M. Correale, "The Sources of Some Patristic Quotations in Chaucer's The Parson's Tale," *English Language Notes* 19 (1981): 97.

IV

Summa on the Vices, "Quoniam"

1. (ParT X,484–90)

Next, concerning envy, which according to the wise man is "sorrow proceeding from someone else's happiness leading the heart astray into contrary matters,"[1] and according to Aristotle it is "sadness at the success of any among those who are good-natured,"[2] that is, "it rejoices in someone else's misfortune and is unhappy at his good fortune";[3] these words are according to the blessed Gregory. And according to Augustine: "Envy is sorrow at another's happiness."[4] And this vice is extremely hateful, for it is appropriately called a sin against the Holy Spirit, since even if every sin is committed against the Holy Spirit (since "it creates an insult to grace," Hebrews 10[5]), envy in particular opposes goodness by itself, appropriately enough, for envy comes from a self-created malice. This malice has two species: one is hard-heartedness, the other is aggression.

Now, hard-heartedness is obstinacy in evil or a blindness of mind by which someone does not consider that he has sinned, or he does not care that he has, but rather he rejects the grace offered to him. This evil is seen in condemned angels and human beings; concerning it, Hebrews 3: "Be watchful, lest one of you be hardened by the deceitfulness of sin."[6]

And the sinner is hardened in a number of ways: First, by the creation of an inborn malice, Job 41: "His heart will become as hard as stone."[7] Second, by the creation of an implanted malice which is from without, that is to say, by the suggestion of the devil, Ecclesiasticus 43: "The north wind blew and the water froze to ice."[8] In the third way, by the withdrawal of grace, Gregory: "God does not harden someone by bestowing malice, but by withdrawing grace."[9] In the fourth way, by the ingratitude of one who has been hardened against God, just as the Jews were, Deuteronomy 32: "Stiffnecked," etc.[10] In the fifth way, by a perverse habit, as in Judges 5. f: "The children of Israel walked by a most difficult way,"[11] to which they had become accustomed. A habit is also like another nature, as the *exemplum* goes, and as is

---

Du, fol. 40a–b; Ha, fols. 136v–137r; Tr, fol. 16a–va.

2 **retorquens** torquens Du. 4 **mitium** vicini Du. 5 **secundum . . . etiam** Gregorii et Du. 7 **quia** *om* Tr. 8 **peccatum** *om* Du. 9 **gratie** *add* eius Du. **invidia** *add* tamen Du. 10 **ex creata** excusata HaTr. 11 **est** *om* Du. 14 **sed** si HaTr. 23 **ingratitudine** magnitudine HaTr. **sicut** sit Tr.

IV

Summa de vitiis "Quoniam"

(from Durham, Cathedral Library MS B.I.18 [Du]; collated with London, British Library MS Harley 3823 [Ha], and Dublin, Trinity College MS 306 [Tr])

1. (ParT X,484–90)

Sequitur de invidia, que secundum Sapientem est "dolor ex alterius   fol. 40a
felicitate proveniens, animum ad contraria [retorquens],"[1] et
secundum Aristotelem est "tristicia de prosperitate alicujus
[mitium],"[2] id est, "gaudet de malo alterius et dolet de bono,"[3] hec
5   [secundum beatum Gregorium. Et etiam] secundum Augustinum:
"Invidia est dolor aliene felicitatis."[4] Et est valde detestabile hoc
vicium, [quia] est peccatum in Spiritum Sanctum appropriate
sumpto vocabulo, / quia licet omne [peccatum] fiat contra Spiritum   fol. 40b
Sanctum, quia "[gratie] contumeliam facit," Hebreorum x,[5] [invidia]
10 specialiter obviat appropriate sibi bonitati, cum sit invidia [ex creata]
malicia. Que malicia habet duas species: una est obduracio, alia [est]
inpungnacio.

Est autem obduracio obstinacio in malo sive cecitas mentis, qua quis
non avertit se peccasse vel non curat, [sed] oblatam sibi gratiam
15 repellit. Hec est in reprobis angelis et hominibus, de qua Ad
Hebreos 3: "Videte, ne quis vestrum obduretur fallacia peccati."[6]
Et induratur peccator pluribus modis: Primo, concreacione innate
malicie, Job xli: "Indurabitur cor ejus quasi lapis."[7] Secundo,
concreacione seminate malicie, que est ab extrinseco, scilicet a
20 suggestione diabolica, Ecclesiastici 43: "Flavit aquilo et congellavit
cristallus ab aqua."[8] Tertio modo, subtractione gratie, Gregorius:
"Non indurat Deus inperciendo maliciam, set subtrahendo gratiam."[9]
Quarto modo, [ingratitudine] obdurati, [sicut] fuerunt Judei,
Deuteronomii 32: "Dura cervice," et cetera.[10] Quinto modo, prava
25 consuetudine, ut in Judicum 5. f: "Filii Israel ambulaverunt viam
durissimam,"[11] quam consueverant. Est etiam consuetudo quasi

---

1. Cf. Publilius Syrus, *Sententiae*, Proverbia.112 (ed. Woelfflin, p. 107); **2.** Cf. Aristotle, *Topica*, 2.2 (trans. Boethius) (AL 5,1–3:33) and Aristotle, *Rhetorica*, 2.10 (trans. anon.) (AL 31,1–2:87; trans. Guillelmus de Moerbeka, p. 244); cf. Wenzel, "Fragment X," in *The Riverside Chaucer*, p. 960; cf. Robert C. Fox, "Chaucer and Aristotle," *Notes and Queries* N.S. 5 [203] (1958): 523–4; cf. Charles A. Owen, "Relationship Between the *Physician's Tale* and the *Parson's Tale*," *Modern Language Notes* 71 (1956): 86; **3.** Cf. Gregory the Great, *Moralia in Iob*, 6.46.84 (CCL 143:281); **4.** Cf. Augustine of Hippo, *De Genesi ad litteram*, 11.14.18 (PL 34:436); cf. Augustine of Hippo, *Enarrationes in Psalmos, Ps 104*, 17 (CCL 40:1545); cf. Augustine of Hippo, *Sermones in diversis*, 353.1.1 (PL 39:1561); **5.** Heb 10:29; **6.** Heb 3:12–13; **7.** Job 41:15; **8.** Sir 43:22; **9.** Cf. Bandinus, *Sententiarum libri*, 1.40 (PL 192:1019B); **10.** Cf. Deut 31:27; **11.** Cf. Judg 5:10.

clear enough in examples from art and from nature.

The other species is aggression, which is twofold. The first is aggression against a recognized truth, which is seen in heretics and in brothers like them, who endeavor to destroy the truth of life and doctrine in the church, concerning whom Job 24: "These people are rebels against the light."[12] The other is aggression against grace in one's neighbor, Galatians 4. f: "Even as he who was born according to the flesh persecuted him who was born according to the spirit, so also now."[13]

It is clear in another manner how hateful this sin is because while any other vice might be opposed to one vice or one virtue, as prodigality is opposed to liberality and miserliness, envy is opposed to every virtue and nearly every vice, for nearly any kind of vice entails some enjoyment, actually existing or appearing to the sinner as such, and yet envy entails none, but rather it is opposed to every virtue with the greatest amount of anxiety and sadness, since it is made sad by every good thing which happens to a neighbor. Therefore, envy is more opposed to the greatest goodness (*bonitas*), although the greatest good (*bonum*) does not have a contrary, since the greatest evil cannot be said to exist. And beyond that the greatest good does not exist in a class of things, but it is an essence (*ens*) greater than every essence and a substance greater than every substance, according to what John of Damascus says.[14] Nevertheless, at times it is said to be a thing contrary to God, since in the desire and deeds of a perverse creature envy discovers a resistance to God, when what is forbidden happens, or what is commanded is hated.

2. (ParT X,491–93)

Next, on the species of envy, of which the first is sadness at another's good fortune. Since good fortune is the basic ingredient of joy according to nature, it is obvious that envy is also contrary to nature, Ecclesiasticus 11: "One slaves and sorrows, without faith."[1] The second is joy at a neighbor's bad fortune, in which the envious person is in particular an imitator of the devil "who rejoices when he does evil," etc., Proverbs 2.[2] And the exultation of the envious person is like the exultation of the delirious, for they are happy about something which should cause sorrow, since concerning bad fortune and its opposite, as is said in Proverbs 24, "When your enemy falls, do not rejoice."[3] If one ought not to rejoice at the downfall of enemies, all the more so at the downfall of a just person. The third is slander, by which someone maliciously defames and wounds one who is not present. And slander is a hateful union between Herod and Pilate.[4] As Paul says in Romans 1: "Slanderers, hateful to God."[5] This slander, in fact, should be advised against, Leviticus 19: "You shall not curse the deaf nor put a stumbling block before the blind, but you shall fear the Lord your God" to the letter.[6] It is exceedingly wicked to curse a deaf

30 **agnite** agnitorum Tr. **similibus** falsis Du. 35 **quam** quod Du. 36 **vicium** *add* aliquod Ha; *add* alio Tr. 39 **maxima anxietate** maximam anxietatem DuTr. **tristitia** tristitiam Tr. 41 **cum** tamen Du. 42 **habet** licet Tr. 43 **ens** genus Du.

Du, fol. 42a; Ha, fols. 139v–140r; Tr, fols. 17vb–18a.

2 **bonum** *om* HaTr. 3 **sit** etiam est Du. 5 **specialis** * specialiter Tr. 6 **2 5** Du. **invidi** inuida Du. 9 **inimicorum** inimici Du. 10 **magis** minus est gaudendum Du. 11 **odiosa** *add* eciam Du. 12 **Apostolus** Bernardus Du. 14 **pones** ponas HaTr.

altera natura, ut exemplum est et per exempla satis patet in artificialibus et in naturalibus.

Alia species est inpungnacio, que est duplex. Prima est inpungnatio
30 veritatis [agnite], que est in hereticis et in [similibus] fratribus, qui veritatem vite et doctrine in ecclesia nituntur destruere, de quibus Job 24: "Ipsi rebelles fuerunt lumini."[12] Alia est inpungnatio gratie in proximo, Galatharum 4. f: "Quomodo is, qui secundum carnem natus est, persequebatur eum, qui secundum spiritum, ita et nunc."[13]
35 Aliter patet, [quam] detestabile sit hoc peccatum, quia cum aliquod [vicium] uni vicio opponatur vel uni virtuti, ut prodigalitas largitati et tenacitati, invidia omni virtuti opponitur et fere omni vicio, quia fere quodlibet vicium habet aliquam voluptatem existentem vel apparentem set invidia nullam, set [maxima anxietate] et [tristicia]
40 omni virtuti opponitur, quia de omni bono proximi tristatur, et ideo summe bonitati magis adversatur, [cum] summum bonum non [habet] contrarium, cum nihil sit summe malum. Et preterea summum bonum non est in genere, set est ens supra omne [ens] et substantia supra omnem substantiam, secundum quod dicit
45 Damascenus.[14] Dicitur tamen quandoque aliquod Deo contrarium, quia in voluntate et opere perverse creature invenit resistenciam, dum sit, quod prohibetur, vel contempnitur, quod precipitur.

2. (ParT X,491–3)

Sequitur de speciebus invidie, quarum prima est dolor de alieno fol. 42a bono. Cum [bonum] naturaliter sit materia gaudii, patet, quod invidia [sit] contraria nature, Ecclesiastici xi: "Est laborans et dolens, impius."[1] Secunda est gaudium de malo proximi, in quo invidus
5 [specialis] est imitator dyaboli, "qui letatur, cum malefecerit," et cetera, Proverbiorum [2].[2] Et est exultacio [invidi] sicut exultacio freneticorum. Gaudent enim, unde dolendum esset, quia de malo et econtrario, cum dicatur Proverbiorum 24: "Cum ceciderit inimicus tuus, ne gaudeas."[3] Si non est gaudendum de ruina [inimicorum],
10 multo [magis] de ruina justi. Tertia est detractio, qua quis maliciose absentem diffamat et dilacerat. Et est detractio [odiosa] collacio inter Herodem et Pilatum.[4] Ut dicit [Apostolus], Romanorum i: "Detractores, Deo odibiles."[5] Que quidem detractio dissuadetur Levitici 19: "Non maledices surdo neque coram ceco [pones]
15 offendiculum, set timebis Dominum Deum tuum" ad litteram.[6] Valde inpium est surdo maledicere, cum ipse non audiat nec contra

---

12. Job 24:13; 13. Gal 4:29; 14. unidentified.

1. Sir 11:11; 2. Prov 2:14; 3. Prov 24:17; 4. Cf. Luke 23:12; 5. Rom 1:30; 6. Lev 19:14.

person, since he cannot hear nor can he say anything in response to accusations. It is also exceedingly wicked to put a stumbling block before a blind person, since he cannot see nor can he take precautions, but according to the *Gloss*: "Whoever slanders someone not present curses the deaf."[7] A man who is not present can hear a slanderer less well even than if he were deaf, since sometimes a deaf person hears when he is shouted at loudly. The one not present, however, who is sometimes two leagues or more distant, would not hear a slanderer however much he was shouting. The slanderer also puts a stumbling block before the blind when he is listened to by a person who is blind or simple-minded or unfamiliar with the person who is being slandered, and tells another detail by which this person is offended. Whence the slanderer acts wickedly and treacherously both towards the person he is slandering and towards the person before whom he commits slander. For this reason it follows in the same chapter, Leviticus 19: "You shall not be a calumniator and a tale-bearer among the people."[8] That person is a calumniator, which is a slanderer, who takes delight in another's misdeed, Ecclesiasticus 5: "Do not be called a tale-bearer on your way, and do not be ensnared by your tongue,"[9] and James 4: "Do not slander" etc.[10]

3. (ParT X,493–98)

And of slander there are five species. The first is simply to speak evil of someone, with the result being that he is in no way "a good man, but rather leads the people astray," John 7.[1] The second is to pervert the intention of someone who is listening or speaking. Ecclesiasticus 11 is said concerning this slanderer: "He changes good into evil."[2] Isaiah 5: "Woe to those who call good evil," etc.[3] The third is to diminish a good deed; even if it is done well, nevertheless it is defective. Ecclesiasticus 11 is said concerning this slanderer: "He maintains there is fault in those who are excellent."[4] The fourth is to disparage one person by a comparison with someone who is better, as in the Psalm: "You have destroyed him by a cleansing,"[5] that is, in the manner of the rhetorical figure of antonomasia, by cleansing a good person, i.e. by commending him, you have destroyed the guilty one, i.e., you have disparaged the one who was spoken about earlier. The fifth is to agree improperly with those things which have been spread about, Augustine: "Whoever willingly slanders or willingly listens to a slanderer, each one bears the devil on his tongue."[6]

17 **etiam** *om* Du. 20 **potest** *om* Du. **quam** *add* etiam Du. 21 **alte** *add* dicatur HaTr. **vero** *om* Du. 24 **ille** illum HaTr. 25 **vel** *om* Ha. 27 **prodiciose** prodigiose Ha; prodisiose Tr. **in eum** Deo Ha. 29 **et nec** Du. 31 **via** vita Du.

Du, fol. 42a–b; Ha, fol. 140r–v; Tr, fol. 18a.

1 **simpliciter** simplex Tr. **malum** *om* HaTr. 3 **audientis** * agentis Du. 4–7 **de detractore . . . detractore dicitur** de detractore . . . dicitur detractore Ha; detractione Tr. 9 **antonomasice** anotomasice Du; antonomagice Ha; antonomatice Tr. 10 **bonum** (?) Ha; (?) Tr. **reum** reliquum Du. 11 **depresisti** *add* illum Du.

objecta aliquid possit respondere. Valde [etiam] impium est coram
ceco ponere offendiculum, cum ille non videat nec possit cavere, set
secundum *Glossam*: "Surdo maledicit, qui absenti detrahit."[7] Homo
20 absens minus [potest] audire detrahentem, [quam] si surdus esset,
quia quandoque audit, quando sibi [alte] clamatur. Absens [vero],
qui quandoque distat per duas leucas vel amplius, non audiret
detrahentem, quantumcumque clamaret. Detrahens etiam coram
ceco ponit offendiculum, dum [ille], qui eum ascultat, qui cecus est
25 vel simplex [vel] quia non noscit personam, cui detrahitur, narrat
alienum factum, unde ipse scandalizatur. Unde detractor impie agit
et [prodiciose] tam in eum, cui detrahit, quam [in eum], coram quo
detrahit. Ideo sequitur eodem capitulo Levitici 19: "Non eris
criminator [et] susurro in populis."[8] Criminator idem est, quod
30 detractor, qui alieno crimine delectatur, Ecclesiastici 5: "Ne
appelleris susurro in [via] tua, et lingua tua ne capiaris,"[9] et Jacobi 4:
"Noli detrahere," et cetera.[10]

3. (ParT X,493–8)

Et sunt detractionis quinque species. Prima est [simpliciter] [malum] fol. 42a
de aliquo dicere, ut nequaquam "bonus est, set seducit populum,"
Johannis vii.[1] Secunda est pervertere intencionem [audientis] vel
dicentis. Ecclesiastici xi dicitur [de detractore: "Bonum in malum
5 convertit";[2] Ysaie 5: "Ve, qui dicunt bonum malum," et cetera.[3]
Tercia est minuere bonum; etsi bene sit factum, tamen cum defectu.
Ecclesiastici xi de detractore dicitur]: "In electis ponit maculam."[4]
Quarta est comparacione melioris alium deprimere, ut in Psalmo:
"Destruxisti eum ab / emundacione,"[5] id est ita [antonomasice] fol. 42b
10 mundando [bonum], id est commendando, destruxisti [reum] (id est
[depresisti]), de quo prius fiebat sermo. Quinta est assentire prelatis
male, Augustinus: "Qui libenter detrahit vel detractorem libenter
audit, uterque diabolum in lingua gerit."[6]

---

7. Geoffrey Babion, *Sermones de diversis*, 94 (PL 171:778A); cf *Glossa* 1:253–4 (Lev 19:14); **8.** Lev 19:16; **9.** Sir 5:16; **10.** Jas 4:11.

1. John 7:12; **2.** Sir 11:33; **3.** Isa 5:20; **4.** Sir 11:33; **5.** Ps 88:45; **6.** Cf. Paulinus of Aquileia, *Liber de salutaribus documentis*, 26 (PL 40:1056).

4. (ParT X,499–505)

The fourth is grumbling (*susurrum*), that is, a hidden murmuring. To buzz (*susurrire*), however, is a characteristic of bees, but metaphorically *susurrire* is to detract, and "for the rumor monger (*susurrator*) there is hatred, enmity, reproach," Ecclesiasticus 5. f.[1] Now, murmuring is slander performed without just cause against the words or deeds of someone else, but one can only call it murmuring when it is against God or a prelate, which is objected to in Wisdom 1: "Guard yourselves against murmuring, which is not beneficial,"[2] but rather injurious. For unhappiness does not end because of murmuring, but something which could have been praiseworthy is made damnable because of murmuring. For a man is defiled by what should have cleansed him; he is destroyed by what should have chastized him. The Psalm: "You have destroyed him by a cleansing."[3] John 6: "Do not murmur one after the other."[4] Corinthians 10: "Do not murmur"[5] one after the other. Philippians 2: "Do everything without murmurings."[6] Peter 4: "Be hospitable to one another without murmurings."[7]

To create abhorrence for murmuring there is the example of Jesus, Isaiah 53: "Like a sheep before the shearer," etc.[8] And likewise that of God's saints, because no murmuring, no sounds of complaint, came from them. Concerning Zechariah and his wife one reads that "both of them were upright before God, following all the commandments and ordinances of the Lord without complaint."[9] Beyond that, murmuring bears the curse of God, Ecclesiasticus 28: "A curse on the tale-bearer and the deceitful, for he has been the ruin of many possessing peace."[10] He represents something hateful to God, Romans 1: "Rumor mongers and detractors – hateful to God."[11] And since we do not know what might be of use to us, murmuring is senseless, for sometimes adversity is more beneficial than prosperity. Thus, no one ought to murmur about adversity, Ecclesiasticus: "No one should say, 'This is better than that,' for all things prove good at their proper time."[12] And since we belong to the Lord, now by reason of being created, now by reason of being revived, we should not murmur about anything which it pleases Him to do to us, Proverbs 12: "Nothing will sadden the one who is just, no matter what happens to him."[13] Bernard: "Justly does he claim my life for himself, who laid down his for me."[14] Romans 14: "Whether we live or whether we die, we belong to the Lord."[15] Thus, Isaiah 45: "Woe to them who speak against their maker," and after this passage: "Does the clay say to the potter, 'What are you making?' "[16]

Arguing against the sin of murmuring is the punishment meted out for it by the Lord, for Miriam, the sister of Moses, was struck with leprosy, Exodus c.[17] The bodies of Dathan and Abiram were swallowed up living by the earth, Numbers 16;[18] Korah was consumed by fire, as one reads in the same section.[19] Because of this sin

Du, fols. 43vb–44b; Ha, fols. 144v–146r; Tr, fols. 20b–21a.

1 **Quarta** octaua DuHaTr. 2 **proprium** proprie Du. **apium** apum Tr. 5 **dicendum** *add* est quod Du. **Deum** dictum Du. 11 **Johannis** Jeronimus Du. 13 **murmuracionibus** murmuracione Du. 13–14 **Petri ... murmuracionibus** *om* Ha. 17 **non** nec Du. 18 **ejus** *add* Luce i Tr. **quod** quia Du. 20 **Dei** *om* Du. **induit** inducit Tr. 22 **et** *om* Du. 26 **Ecclesiastici** *add* 3.a Du. **enim** *add* in Ha. 27 **Domini sumus** Deum scimus Ha. 28 **tum ... racione** tum racione recreacionis Tr; *om* Ha. 29 **Proverbiorum 12** Sapientie Ha. 31–2 **Ad Romanos 14** Colossensium iij Du; Apostolus Ha. 32 **sive** *add* etiam Du. 33 **contradicunt** contradicit Ha. 36 **Exodi c** Exodi Ha; Numeri 12 Tr. 37 **terra** *add* sunt Du.

4. (ParT X,499–505)

[Quarta] est susurrum, id est occultum murmur. Susurrire tamen fol. 43vb
[proprium] est [apium], translative vero susurrire est detrahere, et
"susurratori odium, inimicicia, contumelia," Ecclesiastici 5. f.[1] Est
autem murmur oblocucio indebito modo facta contra dictum vel
5 factum alicujus, set de illo solum [dicendum] contra [Deum] vel
contra prelatum, quod dissuadetur Sapientie 1: "Custodite / vos a fol. 44a
murmuracione, que nichil prodest,"[2] immo obest. Non enim propter
murmur cessat tribulacio, set quod potuit esse meritorium, propter
murmur fit dampnosum. Inquinatur enim homo, unde debuit
10 mundari; destruitur, unde debuit emendari. Psalmi: "Destruxisti eum
ab emundacione."[3] [Johannis] 6: "Nolite murmurare invicem";[4]
Corintheorum x: "Neque murmuraveritis"[5] invicem; Philippensium
ii: "Omnia facite sine [murmuracionibus]";[6] [Petri iiii: "Hospitales
invicem sine murmuracionibus]."[7]
15 Ad detestacionem murmuris est exemplum Christi, Ysaie 53: "Quasi
agnus coram tondente se," et cetera.[8] Iterum et sanctorum Dei, quia
de eis non murmur resonat, [non] querimonia. De Zaccharia et uxore
[ejus] legitur, [quod] "erant justi ante Deum ambo incedentes in
omnibus mandatis et justificacionibus Domini sine querela."[9]
20 Preterea murmur maslediccionem [Dei] [induit], Ecclesiastici 28:
"Susurro et bilinguis maledictus. Multos enim turbavit pacem
habentes."[10] Deo odibilem reddit, Romanorum i: "Susurratores [et]
detractores, Deo odibiles."[11] Et quia nescimus, quid nobis expediat,
murmurare est insanire. Aliquando enim magis prodest adversitas
25 quam prosperitas. Ideo de adversitate nullus debet murmurare,
[Ecclesiastici]: "Non est dicere: 'Hoc melius illo.' Omnia [enim]
tempore suo comprobuntur."[12] Et quia [Domini sumus] tum racione
creacionis [tum recreacionis racione], non debemus murmurare,
quicquid sibi de nobis placeat facere, [Proverbiorum 12]: "Non
30 contristabit justum, quicquid ei acciderit."[13] Bernardus: "Juste sibi
vendicat vitam meam, qui pro mea posuit suam."[14] [Ad Romanos
14]: "Sive vivimus, [sive] morimur, Domini sumus."[15] Ideo Ysaie
45: "Ve, qui [contradicunt] factori suo," et post: "Nunquid dicit
lutum figulo: 'Quid facis?' "[16]
35 Contra peccatum murmuris est vindicta pro eo a Domino sumpta.
Maria enim soror Moysi est lepra percussa, [Exodi c].[17] Corpora
Dathan et Abiron viva a [terra] absorta, Numeri 16;[18] Chore igne
consumptus, ut ibidem legitur.[19] Propter istud peccatum filii Israel

1. Sir 5:17. **2.** Wis 1:11; **3.** Ps 88:45; **4.** John 6:43; **5.** 1Cor 10:10; **6.** Phil 2:14; **7.** 1Pet 4:9; **8.** Isa 53:7;
9. Luke 1:6; **10.** Sir 28:15; **11.** Rom 1:29; **12.** Sir 39:40; **13.** Prov 12:21; **14.** Cf. Bernard of Clairvaux,
Sermones de diversis, 22.5 (*SBO* 6.1:173); **15.** Rom 14:8; **16.** Isa 45:9; **17.** Cf. Num 12:10; **18.** Cf. Num
16:32–3; **19.** Cf. Num 16:35.

the children of Israel were struck by fiery serpents and the greater part of the children of Israel was destroyed in the desert,[20] Numbers 14: "All of you who have murmured," etc.[21] When the people also murmured against God because of the hardships, "fire devoured them at one end of the camp," Numbers 11.[22] "All of you from 20 years old and upwards who have murmured against me will not enter the land over which I have raised my hand in order to make a dwelling place for you, except Caleb son of Jephunneh and Joshua son of Nun."[23] And, briefly, as the authority says, by no deed is this people said to have offended the Lord more than by murmur, or rather by murmuring.[24]

Jude also speaks about the future punishment for murmuring in his epistle: "They are complaining murmurers, acting according to their lusts."[25] And he lays out their punishment before them: "For whom the tempest of the dark regions has been reserved forever."[26] Gregory: "The kingdom of heaven receives no one who is a murmurer; no one who receives it can murmur."[27] And note that there is a murmuring from envy, Matthew 20: "And on receiving it they murmured against the head of the house, saying: 'These last ones came one hour ago,' " etc.[28] There is also a murmuring from pride, Luke 7: "Seeing this, the Pharisee who had called him said to himself, 'If this man were a prophet,' " etc.[29] There is also a murmuring from avarice, John 12: "Why is this ointment not sold for three hundred denarii?"[30] A murmuring from impatience, Numbers 11: "A murmuring against the Lord arose from the people, as from those who are lamenting, because of their hardships."[31] And there is a murmuring arising from one's conscience, that is, when someone who is forced into a deed by another person murmurs about committing an act against God, as in Numbers 22: "The Lord opened the mouth of the ass and it spoke, 'What have I done to you, why are you beating me? See, already now the third time.' "[32] Balaam wanted to force the donkey to do something which was against the Lord's will. And note that murmuring arising from one's conscience is divided into a murmuring about the good things which we bestow and into a murmuring about the evils which we ought to endure. The first one is argued against in Ecclesiasticus 18, where one reads about good things: "Do not complain, and let there not be the sadness of an evil word with every gift."[33] Of the other murmuring, Ecclesiasticus 19, so that the prudent and disciplined person will not murmur when he is corrected.[34] The prudent person is the one who makes provision for the future, that is for rewards and punishments. Someone like this does not murmur about the scourge, for he gladly endures the switch in order to preserve himself from the scourge of eternal punishment; witness the *exemplum* of the boy who gladly endures a blow with the rod in order to avoid a beating with the switch. The disciplined person is one who has been instructed about the usefulness of adversities. And finally there is a murmuring against God and against one's neighbor, against God for a variety of reasons, that is because of illness or poverty or the untimeliness of the season or about the prosperity of those who are evil or the suffering of those who are good.

39 **ab ignitis** ambiguis Du. 40 **estis** essent Ha. 41 **Dominum** Deum Du. **de labore** *om* Ha. 42 **Domini** eum Du. 43 **supra** *add* videtur HaTr. 44 **in** *om* Du. 45 **Jephene** Jophone Du. 47 **populus ille** post HaTr. **sicut** *om* Ha. 55 **novissima** novissimi Ha. **una** *om* Du. 57 **Est** *add* etiam Du. 59 **venundatur** uenundetur Tr; uenundentur Ha. 61 **Dominum** Deum Du. **Et est** est autem Ha; et autem Tr. 62 **Deum** Dominum Du. 64 **quare** cur Du. 67 **sustineamus** sustinemus Du. 70 **ut** ubi Ha; uir Tr. **correctus** coactus Ha; correptus Tr. 71 **est** *om* Du. 74 **sustinet** accipit Ha. 75 **tribulacionum** *add* est Du. 77–8 **vel . . . malorum** *om* Tr. 78 **vel** et Du.

[ab ignitis] serpentibus percussi et major pars filiorum Israel in
40   deserto deperdita,²⁰ Numeri 14: "Omnes, qui murmurati [estis]," et
cetera.²¹ Murmurante etiam populo contra [Dominum] [de labore]
"ignis [Domini] devoravit extremam partem castrorum," Numeri
xi.²² "Omnes, qui a xx annis et [supra] murmurastis contra me, non
intrabitis [in] terram, super quam levavi manum meam, ut habitare
45   vos facerem preter Caleph filium [Jephene] et Josue filium Nun."²³
Et breviter, sicut dicit auctoritas, de nulla re magis offendisse dictus
est [populus ille] Dominum [sicut] de murmure vel quam
murmurando.²⁴
Pena eciam murmuris futura dicit Judas in epistola sua: "Hii sunt
50   murmuratores querulosi, secundum desideria sua ambulantes."²⁵ Et
premittit penam: "Quibus procella tenebrarum in eternum servata
est."²⁶ Gregorius: "Regnum celorum / nemo, qui murmurat, accipit;   fol. 44b
nemo, qui accipit, murmurare potest."²⁷ Et nota, quod est murmur
invidie, Mathei 20: "Et accipientes murmurabant adversus
55   patremfamilias dicentes: 'Hii [novissima] [una] hora venerunt,' " et
cetera.²⁸ Est etiam murmur superbie, Luce 7: "Videns Phariseus, qui
vocaverat eum, ait intra se: 'Hic si esset propheta,' " et cetera.²⁹
[Est] murmur avaricie, Johannis xii: "Quare hoc unguentum non
[venundatur] trecentis denariis?"³⁰ Murmur inpaciencie, Numeri xi:
60   "Ortum est murmur populi quasi dolencium pro labore contra
[Dominum]."³¹ [Et est] murmur consciencie, scilicet quando aliquis
murmurat facere, quod contra [Deum] est, ab alio coactus, sicut
Numeri 22: "Aperuit Dominus os asine et locuta est: 'Quid feci tibi,
[quare] percutis me? Ecce jam tercio.' "³² Volebat Balam cogere
65   asinam ad id, quod erat contra Domini voluntatem. Et nota, quod
murmur consciencie dividitur in murmur de bonis, que conferimus,
et in murmur de malis, que [sustineamus]. Primum dissuadetur
Ecclesiastici 18, ubi legitur de bonis: "Ne des querelam, et in omni
dato, ne des tristiciam mali verbi."³³ De alio murmure, Ecclesiastici
70   19, [ut] prudens et disciplinatus non murmurabit [correctus].³⁴
Prudens [est], qui providet futura, scilicet premia et tormenta, et
talis non murmurat de flagello. Libenter enim virgam tolerat, qui
eum a flagello pene eterne servat. Exemplum de puero, qui libenter
[sustinet] ictum ferule, ut evadat verberacionem virge. Disciplinatus
75   est, qui circa utilitates [tribulacionum] instructus. Est et ultimo
murmur contra Deum et contra proximum. Contra Deum
multipliciter, scilicet vel pro infirmitate [vel paupertate vel temporis
inoportunitate vel de prosperitate malorum] [vel] adversitate
bonorum.

---

20. Cf. Num 21:6; **21.** Cf. Num 14:2, 14:29; Deut 1:29; **22.** Num 11:1; **23.** Num 14:29–30; **24.** Cf. *Glossa*
1:143 (Exod 16:1, marginal); **25.** Jude 16; **26.** Jude 13; **27.** Gregory the Great, *Homiliae in Evangelia*,
1.19.4 (PL 76:1156B); **28.** Matt 20:11–12; **29.** Luke 7:39; **30.** John 12:5; **31.** Num 11:1; **32.** Num 22:28;
33. Sir 18:15; **34.** Cf. Sir 19:28.

5. (ParT X,509)

Next, the fifth species of envy, which is hidden hatred lying concealed in the heart so long that it nourishes rancor. Against this hatred is Leviticus 19: "You shall not hate your brother in your heart, lest you bear sin because of him,"[1] since "more serious is the enemy who lies concealed in the heart," as Seneca says.[2]

6. (ParT X,510–12)

The sixth species of envy is bitterness, which produces a sickness of the soul and makes every good thing unpalatable. In the likeness of bile, which spoils the taste and the tongue, it fills one up with a corrupted fluid. The Philosopher: "To those laboring, that is to say, to the sick, all things seem bitter,"[1] for the tongue is filled with its fluid. On this bitterness, Ecclesiasticus 21: "There is no sense where there is bitterness."[2]

The seventh is discord, which is the opposite of friendship and disturbs the harmony of hearts, Proverbs 17: "He who studies discord loves strife."[3] That the sin of discord is hateful to God, Proverbs 6: "There are six things which God hates: haughty eyes," etc; "and a seventh one His soul abhors, namely he who sows discord among brothers."[4] He places this person in the final position as the one who is more greatly detested. Now, the union of peace in Matthew 5 refers to Jesus and his servants: "Blessed are the peacemakers," etc.;[5] the dispersion in John 10 refers to the devil and his servants: "He who scatters the sheep," etc.[6] But note that there should be a great unity among all people due to their origin from one source, namely Adam, from whom every type of human being has been spread over the earth, something which one does not read about concerning other living beings, for not all cows are from one cow, nor are all sheep from one sheep. For this reason, if a cow which gores with its horns attacks another one, "is it for cattle that God is concerned?" Corinthians 9.[7] For this reason, with nature itself teaching us, we ought to live in harmony. There ought to be an even greater harmony among the faithful, since in them a harmony of faith and grace is added to the harmony of nature, Acts 4: "They were one heart and one soul"[8] before God. There ought to be the greatest harmony among those in religious orders, since in them the harmony of discipline and observance under a rule, as in habit, food, and other matters of this kind, is added to the harmony of nature, faith, and grace. Augustine: "For this purpose you have been gathered together into one: so that you will be of one mind" etc.,[9] since as Seneca says: "With harmony small things grow, with disharmony even large things fall apart."[10] On this nature, see below.

Du, fol. 47vb; Ha, fol. 157r; Tr, fol. 26a.

Du, fol. 57a–b; Ha, fol. 184r–v; Tr, fols. 37vb–38a.

2 **facit** *add* anime Du. **insipidum** *add* et Du. 4 **omnia** *om* Du. 12 **discordiam** discordias Du. 14 **diabolum** *add* vero Du. **ad servos** suos Du; *add* eius Tr. 17 **Adam** ab Adam Tr. 17–18 **omne . . . humanum** omnes gentes hominum Du. 19 **nec** ne Du. 20 **cornipeta** cornupeta Tr; corrupta Ha. 22 **autem** *om* Du. 24 **Maxima** maxime Du. 25 **eis** *om.* Du. 26 **ceteris** *om* HaTr. **Augustinus** *om* Du. 27 **et cetera** *om* Ha; sitis Tr. 28 **discordia** *add* etiam Du. 29 **natura** materia Du.

5. (ParT X,509)

Sequitur de quinta specie invidie, que est odium occultum adhuc fol. 47vb
latens in pectore, quod rancorem nutrit. Contra quod Levitici 19:
"Non oderis fratrem tuum in corde tuo, ne habeas super eum
peccatum,"[1] quia "gravior est inimicus, qui latet in pectore," ut dicit
5   Seneca.[2]

6. (ParT X,510–12)

Sexta species invidie est amaritudo, que nauseam anime generat et fol. 57a
omne bonum [facit] [insipidum]. Ad similitudinem fellis, que inficit
gustum et linguam, replet humore corrupto, Philosophus:
"Laborantibus, id est infirmantibus, [omnia] videntur amara."[1]
5   Lingua / enim plena est humore hujus. De hac amaritudine, fol. 57b
Ecclesiastici 21: "Non est sensus, ubi est amaritudo."[2]
Septima est discordia, que est amicicie contraria et pacem cordium
perturbans, Proverbiorum 17: "Qui meditatur discordias, diligit
rixas."[3]   Quod   peccatum   discordie   sit   Deo   abhominabile,
10   Proverbiorum 6: "Sex sunt, que odit Deus: oculos sublimes," et
cetera; "et septimum detestatur anima ejus, scilicet eum, qui seminat
inter fratres [discordiam]."[4] Illum ponit ultimum tanquam magis
exosum. Ad Christum autem et ad servos ejus pertinet pacis unio,
Mathei 5: "Beati pacifici," et cetera;[5] ad [diabolum] et [ad servos]
15   pertinet dispersio, Johannis x: "Qui dispergit oves," et cetera.[6] Sed
nota, quod magna unitas debet esse inter omnes homines propter
egressionem ab uno principio, scilicet [Adam], a quo [omne genus
humanum] disseminatum est, quod de aliis animantibus non legitur.
Non enim omnes boves sunt ab uno, [nec] omnes oves ab una. Unde
20   si bos [cornipeta] alium impeteret, "nunquid de bobus cura est Deo,"
Corintheorum 9?[7] Unde ipsa natura edocente in unitate debemus
vivere. Major [autem] unitas debet esse inter fideles, quia unitati
nature superadditur eis unitas fidei et gratie, Actuum 4: "Erat eis cor
unum et anima una"[8] in Deo. [Maxima] inter claustrales, quia unitati
25   nature, fidei et gratie superadditur [eis] unitas regularis discipline et
observancie, ut in habitu, victu et [ceteris] hujusmodi. [Augustinus]:
"Propter quod in unum congregati estis, ut unanimes," [et cetera],[9]
quia ut dicit Seneca: "Concordia res minime crescunt, [discordia]
res magne dilabuntur."[10] De hac [natura], infra.

---

1. Lev 19:17; 2. Publilius Syrus, *Sententiae*, 200 (ed. Woelfflin, p. 79).

1. unidentified; 2. Sir 21:15; 3. Prov 17:19; 4. Prov 6:16–19; 5. Matt 5:9; 6. John 10:12; 7. 1Cor 9:9; cf. Exod 21:29, 21:36; 8. Acts 4:32; 9. Augustine of Hippo, *Epistolae*, 211.5 (PL 33:960); Augustine of Hippo, *Regula ad servos Dei*, 1 (PL 32:1378); 10. Seneca, *Epistulae morales*, 94.46.

The eighth is mockery, which scoffs not only at evil, but also at good deeds, Job 12: "The simple faith of the just person is mocked."[11] Of him, however, Gregory says that: "Simple faith is judged to be folly by the craftiness of the duplicitous."[12] Against mockery, Esdras 4, when Tobiah the Ammonite mocked the Jews who were building a wall, saying: "If a fox goes up on it, he will overcome their stone wall." "Hear, our God," says [Nehemiah], "that we are made an object of contempt. Turn their taunting back upon their own heads." And the following is added: "Do not cover their evil and let their sins not be blotted out in your sight, they who have mocked the builders."[13]

The ninth is accusation, which always seeks an occasion to act maliciously against a neighbor, and this is in reference to the customary activity of the devil, who is "the accuser of brethren," Revelations 12.[14]

The tenth is reproaching or chiding . . .

7. (ParT X,513–14)

The eleventh is malice, by which "someone undertakes something evil or cursed in secret," as the *Gloss* on Romans 1 says.[1]

The twelfth is villany, by which someone heedlessly dares to do what he is unable to do.[2] Against both it is said in Corinthians 5: "Not with the old leaven nor" etc.[3] The leaven is envy, the mother of both, and it is truly leaven, since it changes what is bitter into what is swollen, and it corrupts the pascal feast.

The thirteenth is malignity, which has an evil will although it cannot perform evil deeds, or as the *Gloss* on Romans 1 says: "Malignity is not giving thanks for assistance which has been received."[4] This evil includes the rich and powerful of the world who say, Wisdom 5: "In our malignity we have been consumed. They who have sinned said such things in hell."[5]

30 **malum** *om* Ha; male acta Tr. 33 **duplicium** simplicitatis Du. 34 **irrideret** irriderent DuTr; irritent Ha. **dicens** dicentes Du. 38 **qui** quia Du.

Du, fol. 57va–vb; Ha, fols. 185v–186r; Tr, fol. 38va.

1 **occulte** in occulto Tr. 3 **est** *om* Du. **temere** tenere Tr. 6 **pascam** pascit Du. 9 **acceptis** *om* Tr. 11 **peccaverunt** in peccato Ha; positi sunt et cetera Tr.

30   Octava est derisio, que non solum [malum] set etiam bene gesta
insultat, Job xii: "Deridetur justi simplicitas."[11] Hujus tamen dicit
Gregorius, quia: "Simplicitas estimatur fatuitas ab hastucia
[duplicium]."[12] Contra dirisionem, Esdre 4, cum Tobias Amonites
[irrideret] Judeos edificantes [dicens]: "Si ascenderit vulpes, transiret
35   murum eorum lapideum." "Audi," inquid, "Deus noster, quod facti
sumus despeccio. Converte obprobrium super capud eorum." Et
subditur: "Ne operias iniquitatem eorum et peccata eorum coram
facie tua non deleantur, [qui] irriserunt edificantes."[13]
        Nona est accusacio, que semper querit occasionem malignandi in
40   proximo, et ipsa pertinet ad officium diaboli, qui est "accusator
fratrum," Apocalypsis xii.[14]
        Decima est convicium vel depravacio . . .

7. (ParT X,513–14)

Undecima est malicia, qua "quis malum vel dampnum [occulte]   fol. 57va
molitur," ut dicit *Glossa*, Romanorum i.[1]
        Duodecima [est] nequicia, qua quis [temere] presumit, quod nequit.[2]
Contra utrumque dicitur Corintheorum 5: "Non in fermento veteri /
5   neque," et cetera.[3] Fermentum est invidia, utriusque mater, et bene   fol. 57vb
fermentum, quia amarum tumidum mutat, [pascam] et corrumpit.
        Terciadecima est malignitas, que malam voluntatem habet, cum
mala non possit, vel ut dicit *Glossa*, Romanorum i: "Malignitas est
de [acceptis] beneficiis gratias non referre."[4] Hec concludit mundi
10   potentibus et divitibus dicentibus Sapientie 5: "In malignitate nostra
consumpti sumus. Talia dixerunt in inferno hii, qui [peccaverunt]."[5]

11. Job 12:4; 12. Cf. Gregory the Great, *Moralia in Iob*, 8.50.86 (CCL 143:450); 13. Neh 4:3–5; 14. Rev
12:10.

1. *Glossa ordinaria*, Rom 1:29 (PL 114:474A); 2. Cf. *Glossa ordinaria*, Rom 1:29 (PL 114:474A);
3. 1Cor 5:8; 4. *Glossa ordinaria*, Rom 1:29 (PL 114:474A); 5. Wis 5:13–14.

V

Summa on the Vices, "Primo"

1. (ParT X,850–51)

This sin is very pleasing to the devil, since through it he deceives and holds onto an infinite multitude, Habacuc 1: "He will give burnt offerings to his snare and will sacrifice to his net, since with them a part of him is fattened and his food is chosen."[1] The devil's snare is avarice, his net is lust, which is called a "net" (*sagena*) as if it were "full of blood" (*sanguine plena*), for just as a net catches and holds back both the larger fish and the smaller ones, so does lust overwhelm at one and the same time the young and the old, the rich and the poor, clerics and laymen, married and single men. Bernard: "Lust lies hidden under the purple cloth of kings and under the ragged clothing of the poor."[2] A merchant rejoices more in that business transaction from which he earns more, as the devil rejoices in fornication, the *Gloss* on Leviticus: "Although demons rejoice in every sin, their chief joy is in fornication."[3] Beyond that, demons are like scarabs which take pleasure in excrement and filth. It has been said above that lust is Greek fire since it is nourished by fluids, such as by drunkenness and inebriation, and it is not extinguished. This is the fire which burns beyond the power of water, Wisdom at the end of the book.[4] Likewise, "fire quickly passes through a conflagration when an estate or a castle is burned, and nevertheless the damage remains for a long time," as Gregory says.[5] Thus, lust bursts into flame in a moment and its defilement endures.

E, fol. 74va–vb; F, fols. 59vb–60a; H, fol. 55r; J, fols. 69vb–70a; M, fol. 200r–v; R1, fol. 126vb–127a; R2, fol. 266v.

2 **multitudinem** *add* populorum R2. **sagene sue** sanguinem suum M. 3 **reti suo** et cetera MR1. 4 **est** *om* F; et H. **ejus** *om* HM. 5 **enim** *add* maiora F. 6 **majores . . . minores** uarios pisces R1. 7 **solutos** absolutos R2. 8 **latet** latet vel iacet J. **sub** super E. 10 **negociacione** mercacione E. 12 **fornicacioni** *add* ut patet infra per exemplum capitulo de incontinentia religiosorum. Item quantum placeat diabolo et cetera F. 13 **et fetore** *om* E. 14 **supra** *add* columpna 230 ante e F. 15–16 **Hic . . . fine** *om*. F. 17 **durat** manet R1. 19 **perseverat** *add* Job 31 F.

V

Summa vitiorum "Primo"

(from Einsiedeln, Stiftsbibliothek MS 275 [E]; collated with Cambridge, Jesus
College MS 20 [J]; Cambridge, University Library MS Ff.1.17 [F]; London, British
Library MS Harley 406 [H]; London, British Library MS Royal 8.A.x [R1];
London, British Library MS Royal 11.B.iii [R2]; Manchester,
John Rylands Library MS Lat. 201 [M])

1. (ParT X,850–1)

Valde placet dyabolo hoc peccatum, quia per illud decipit et detinet fol. 74va
infinitam [multitudinem], Abacuc primo: "Immolabit [sagene / sue] fol. 74vb
et sacrificabit [reti suo], quia in ipsis incrassata est pars ejus et cibus
ejus electus."[1] Rete dyaboli [est] avaricia, sagena [ejus] est luxuria,
5   que dicitur "sagena" quasi "sanguine plena." Sagena [enim]
[majores pisces et minores] recipit et retinet, sic luxuria juvenes et
senes, divites et pauperes, clericos et laicos, conjugatos et [solutos],
simul involvit. Bernardus: "Luxuria [latet] [sub] purpura regum et
sub panniculis pauperum."[2] Mercator magis gaudet de illa
10 [negociacione] per quam magis lucratur, sic dyabolus de
fornicacione, *Glossa* super Levitici: "Cum de omni peccato gaudeant
demones, precipue congaudent [fornicacioni]."[3] Preterea demones
sunt similes scarabeis, qui in fimo [et fetore] delectantur. Dictum est
[supra], quod luxuria ignis grecus est, quia humidis nutritur, ut
15 ebrietate et crapula, et non extinguitur. [Hic est ignis, qui ardet super
virtutem aque, Sapiencie in fine].[4] Item "cito transit ignis
incendium, cum incenditur villa vel castrum, et tamen diu [durat]
dampnum," ut dicit Gregorius.[5] Sic libido ad momentum cremat et
ejus inquinacio diu [perseverat].

---

1. Hab 1:16; **2.** Cf. Peraldus, *Summa de vitiis*, 3.1.3 (attrib. Jerome); **3.** *Glossa ordinaria*, Lev 18:24 (PL
113:348C); **4.** Cf. Wis 19:19; **5.** unidentified.

2. (ParT X,852–53)

Now, in which ways women can attract men is described in this verse in which the five fingers of the devil are touched upon:

Sight and speech, touching and kisses, the deed.[1]

She attracts men through sight like the basilisk which kills with a poisoned glance,[2] or like the wolf which makes a man hoarse, Ecclesiasticus 9: "Do not look at a woman with many desires, lest by chance you fall into her traps."[3] A woman is said to be of many desires (*multivola*) since she wants (*vult*) many men and many things, or she hastens (*volat*) through many places. For this reason according to Isidore she is called "of two desires" (*dyavolaris*), and if the letter "v" were transformed into a "b," she could be called "diabolic-like" (*diabolaris*). And Gregory teaches by an example how much we ought to restrain sin caused by sight, saying: "One should consider how much we who are living mortals ought to restrain sight, since the mother of the living came to death through her eyes."[4] Likewise, the concupiscence of the heart follows the concupiscence of the eyes, for which reason in the book *On Animals* it is said that in the womb the eyes are formed after the heart,[5] and therefore there is a great affinity between the heart and the eyes, and because of this Gregory forbids anyone to look upon what it is not lawful to desire.[6]

E, fols. 75vb–76a; F, fol. 60vb; H, fol. 56r; J, fol. 71a–b; M, fol. 201r–v; R1, fol. 128a–b; R2, fol. 267v.

1 **alliciant** alliceant ER2; alliciantur H; alliciunt J. **mulieres** miseros E. **describitur . . . versu** scribuntur per hunc versum R2. 2 **v** *om* H. **diaboli** *add* notantur et R1. 3 **factum** *add* sunt fomes veneris hos fuge tutus eris J. 4 **visu venenato** visu venenoso E; visu venenatu J; per visum venenatum R1. 6 **multivolam** maliuolam M. 6–7 **ne . . . illius** ne incidas in laqueos illius E; ne . . . laqueum eius F; ne . . . lacus eius J; *om* MR1. 7 **multivola** maliuola M. **et multa** *om* F. 8 **loca** *om* E. 9 **v** quinta FH; quarta MR2. **transeat** transit HJ. 10 **debeamus . . . visus** debeamus cohibere peccatum visus F; debemus peccatum visus restringere J; debeamus uitare peccatum visus M; debeamus uitare peccatum visus R1; fugere debeamus peccatum huius R2. 11 **per exemplum** *om* E. 12 **mortaliter** molliter E. 12–13 **per . . . mortem** ad mortem per oculos E. 14 **unde** ut E. **libro** primo J. 15 **quod** quia E. 16 **propter hoc** ideo R1. 17 **concupiscere** concupisci E.

2. (ParT X,852–3)

Quibus autem modis [alliciant] [mulieres] [describitur hoc versu], in fol. 75vb
quo [v] digiti [dyaboli] tanguntur:

Visus et alloquium, contactus et oscula, [factum].[1]

Per visum allicit similis basilisco, qui [visu venenato] interficit,[2] vel
5   similis lupo, qui raucum hominem reddit, Ecclesiastici ix: "Ne
respicias / mulierem [multivolam], [ne forte incidas in laqueos fol. 76a
illius]."[3] Mulier [multivola] dicitur, quia multos vult [et multa], vel
quia per multa [loca] volat, unde secundum Ysidorum "dyavolaris"
dicitur, et si "[v]" littera [transeat] in "b," potest dici "dyabolaris."
10   Et quantum [debeamus restringere peccatum visus], docet Gregorius
[per exemplum] dicens: "Pensandum est, quantum debeamus visum
restringere, qui [mortaliter] vivimus, quia mater vivencium [per
oculos ad mortem] venit."[4] Item concupiscentiam oculorum sequitur
concupiscentia cordis, [unde] in [libro] *De animalibus* dicitur,
15   [quod] post cor in ovo effigiantur oculi,[5] eo quod magna sit vicinitas
inter cor et oculos, et [propter hoc] prohibet Gregorius intueri, quod
non licet [concupiscere].[6]

1. Cf. Walther, *PS* 33819 – Lionel J. Friedman, "Gradus Amoris," *Romance Philology* 19 (1965): 167–77; cf. Gregory M. Sadlek, "The Image of the Devil's Five Fingers in the South English Legendary's 'St. Michael' and Chaucer's Parson's Tale," in Klaus P. Jankofsky, ed., *The South English Legendary: A Critical Assessment* (Tubingen, 1992), p. 55; 2. Cf. Bartholomaeus Anglicus, *De proprietatibus rerum*, 18.16 (trans. John Trevisa, 2:1153); 3. Sir 9:3; 4. Gregory the Great, *Moralia in Iob*, 21.2.4 (CCL 143A:1066); 5. Cf. Aristotle, *De generatione animalium*, 2.6 (trans. Guillelmus de Moerbeka) (AL 17,2.5:70–1); 6. Gregory the Great, *Moralia in Iob*, 21.2.4 (CCL 143A:1066).

C. Remedial Virtues

VI

Summa of Virtues on Remedies for the Soul

1. (ParT X,476–83)

ON HUMILITY

After having spoken of the virtues in general, we will now discuss them individually and begin with humility, for it is the remedy for pride – not because it is the first in the order of the virtues but in their preservation. Charity is the first as their "mistress" and form,[1] for it gives to all others the power to gain merit. Faith is the first in terms of their origin, because it is the first habit of grace by which the other virtues exist in man. Therefore is faith called "substance," Hebrews 11;[2] the *Gloss*: "that is, one foundation of believers."[3] Even though faith is the first virtue in origin, nevertheless all virtues are simultaneous in time; Gregory: "The virtues fly in one flock."[4] Humility is the first in the safekeeping of the virtues; Gregory: "Whoever gathers all the other virtues without humility, carries as it were dust into the wind."[5] Bernard: "The religious life is built on poverty and is kept safe by humility."[6]

Humility is either true or false. True humility is defined by Bernard as follows: "Humility is the virtue by which through perfect self-knowledge one becomes of small value to oneself."[7] Another definition says: "Humility is the voluntary bending down of the mind when it considers its Creator or its own weakness."[8] And this definition touches on the causes of becoming humble. True humility is divided into: humility of heart, of mouth, and of deed. Humility of heart has four aspects, the first of which is self-abasement. Matthew 8: "He who will come after me, let him deny," etc.[9] Gregory: "He abases himself who, after trampling upon the swelling of pride, shows himself in God's eyes to be a stranger to himself."[10] The second aspect is to despise no man in one's mind; Jerome: "The humble man despises no one, the meek man hurts no one."[11] Moreover, Michol despised David for his humil-

---

Gr, fols. 94r–95v; additional variants from ed.

1 **De humilitate** De humilitate contra superbiam. Rubrica. Gr. 7 **est** *om* Gr. 11 **Gregorius** cuius EGr. 13 **humilitate** *add* sibi Gr. **ventum** vento Gr. 18 **Alia . . . humilitas** Item EGr. 23 **Matthei . . . etc.** *om* EGr. 28 **recepit** recipit Gr.

C. Remedial Virtues

VI

Summa virtutum de remediis anime

(from *Summa virtutum de remediis anime*, ed. and trans. Siegfried Wenzel [Athens, GA, 1984]; with variants from Graz, Universitätsbibliothek MS 1458 [Gr])

1. (ParT X,476–83)

[DE HUMILITATE] p. 77

Postquam dictum est de virtutibus in genere, dicendum est de eis in specie, et primo de humilitate, quia ipsa est remedium superbie – non quod ipsa sit prima in ordine virtutum set in earum
5   conservacione. Caritas est prima tanquam "magistra virtutum"[1] et forma, quia omnibus aliis dat efficaciam merendi. Fides est prima origine, quia ipsa [est] primus habitus gratuitus quo mediante cetere virtutes insunt. Ideo dicitur fides "substancia," Hebreorum xi;[2] *Glossa*: "idest unum credencium fundamentum."[3] Et licet fides sit
10   prima origine, omnes tamen virtutes sunt simul tempore; [Gregorius]: "Virtutes gregatim volant."[4] Humilitas est prima in conservacione virtutum; Gregorius: "Qui ceteras virtutes sine [humilitate] congregat, quasi in [ventum] pulverem portat."[5] Bernardus: "Religio in paupertate fundatur, in humilitate
15   custoditur."[6]

Alia est humilitas vera, alia ficta. Humilitas vera sic diffinitur secundum Bernardum: "Humilitas est virtus qua quis verissima sui cognicione sibi ipsi vilescit."[7] [Alia est hujusmodi: "Humilitas] est voluntaria mentis inclinacio intuitu Conditoris vel proprie
20   fragilitatis."[8] Et hec tangit causas humiliacionis. Vera humilitas sic dividitur: Alia est cordis, alia oris, alia operis. Illa que est cordis consistit in quatuor, quorum primum est semetipsum abnegare. [Matthei viii: "Qui vult post me venire, abneget," etc].[9] Gregorius: "Semetipsum abnegat, qui calcato typo superbie ante Dei oculos sese
25   a se alienum demonstrat."[10] Secundum est ut neminem in animo contempnat; Jeronimus: "Humilis neminem contempnit, mansuetus neminem ledit."[11] Preterea Michol contempsit David propter suam

---

1. Gregory the Great, *Moralia in Iob*, 23.13.24 (CCL 143B:1162); **2.** Heb 11:1; **3.** Cf. *Glossa ordinaria*, Heb 11:1 (PL 114:663C); **4.** Cf. Gregory the Great, *Moralia in Iob*, 21.3.7 (CCL 143A:1069); **5.** Gregory the Great, *Homiliae in Evangelia*, 1.7.4 (PL 76:1103A); **6.** Ps.-Bernard of Clairvaux, *Sermo "Ecce nos reliquimus omnia,"* 7 (PL 184:1132A); **7.** Bernard of Clairvaux, *De gradibus humilitatis et superbiae*, 1.2 (*SBO* 3:17); **8.** Cf. Peraldus, *Summa de virtutibus*, 5.4.1 (attrib. Augustine of Hippo); **9.** Matt 16:24; **10.** Gregory the Great, *Moralia in Iob*, 33.6.13 (CCL 143B:1682); **11.** unidentified.

ity and was punished with perpetual sterility, 2 Kings 6.[12] This means: those who despise others become less able to receive grace and more prone to commit sins; Proverbs 28: "He that is easily stirred up to wrath, shall be more prone to sin."[13] The third is to despise being despised, and this will arise from one's own deficiency when one notices that one is in no way self-sufficient but has all things from God's generosity. Thus one will always flee to God's help, the support of the saints, and the advice of one's neighbors. Such are the "poor in spirit," Matthew 5;[14] the Greek text has "God's beggars or needy,"[15] that is, the humble who recognize that they need God in all things; and to them is promised the kingdom of heaven. The humble person trusts in God, the proud in himself. Therefore, he is like the bull who in his pride bellows against the thunder and is struck by lightning in the field; to whom it is said, Ecclesiasticus 6: "Do not extol yourself in the thoughts of your soul like a bull."[16] Such a man is not poor in spirit but very rich and puffed up; to him Job 15 says: "Why does your spirit swell against God?"[17] The proud of heart is like a bladder which swells up with the wind of vanity; that is, he becomes "puffed up by the sense of his flesh," Colossians 2.[18] The fourth aspect is not to grieve when one is put down, but rather to "lay down one's greatness without tribulation," Job 36.[19] One cannot do this as long as one is puffed up with the wind of pride, for one will yet burst in the furnace, that is, in tribulation, as Gregory says.[20] Impure gold, which is alloyed with some other metal, bursts in the furnace; thus pride in tribulation. Ecclesiasticus 2: "Gold and silver are tried in the fire, but acceptable men in the furnace of humiliation."[21]

Humility of mouth has four aspects, the first of which is to keep silence "until one is asked," according to Bernard.[22] And Ecclesiasticus 32: "If you are asked twice, let your answer have an end";[23] that is, in addition bow your head out of humility, or let your speech begin discreetly and end with due measure, so as not to be superfluous. But many people are like the jackdaw or the parrot, which are very garrulous birds that learn human words and talk to themselves, ask and answer and greet passers-by without being themselves addressed. Of these it is said in Proverbs 18: "He that answers before he hears shows himself to be a fool and worthy of confusion."[24] The second is to report one's deeds with humble words and not to praise them; and even when we have done all things well, let us say that "we are unprofitable servants," Luke 18,[25] for the Lord threatens those who enlarge their own fringes.[26] Zephaniah 3: "I will take away your proud boasters."[27] The third is to confess oneself low and impure. Such was the law for the leper, who signifies the sinner, Leviticus 13.[28] The fourth is to praise other people's good without belittling it; Gregory: "True humility thinks little of itself and praises another man's good without malice."[29]

31 **erit** *add* ex defectu Gr. 34 **suffragium** suffragia EGr. 35 **consilium** consilia EGr. 36 **mendici** medici Gr. 37 **istis** isti Gr. 43–4 **vanitatis scilicet** sic iste uento uanitatis sue EGr. 48 **adultero** adulterino AGrI. 53 **usque** ut EGrJ. 57 **que** qui Gr. 60 **respondit** respondet Gr. 61 **et . . . dignum** *om* EGrL. 65 **magnificantibus** *add* auferre EGr. 69 **sine** *add* diminutione Gr.

humilitatem et [recepit] in penam perpetuam sterilitatem, II Regum
vi.[12] Hoc est: qui alios contempnunt, minus habiles ad graciam fiunt
30 et proniores ad peccandum; Proverbiorum xxviii: "Qui ad
indignandum facilis est, [erit] ad peccata proclivior."[13] Tercium est
ut contempnat se contempni, et hoc erit ex defectu sui si se conspiciat
in nullo sibi sufficere et omnia ex largitate / Dei possidere. Ita p. 79
semper confugiet ad Dei adjutorium et sanctorum [suffragium] et
35 proximorum [consilium]. Tales sunt "pauperes spiritu," Matthei v;[14]
Grecus habet "Dei [mendici] vel egeni,"[15] idest humiles qui in
omnibus se recognoscunt Deo indigere; et [istis] promittitur regnum
celorum. Humilis confidit in Deo, superbus in seipso. Unde similis
est thauro qui pre superbia contra tonitruum mugiens fulminatur in
40 agro; cui dicitur Ecclesiastici vi: "Non te extollas in cogitacione tua ut
thaurus."[16] Talis non habet pauperem spiritum set valde divitem et
inflatum; cui dicit Job xv: "Quid tumet contra Deum spiritus tuus?"[17]
Superbus corde similis est vesice que tumet vento [vanitatis; scili-
cet] "inflatus sensu carnis sue," Colossensium ii.[18] Quartum est ut
45 non contristetur in sua dejectione, set ut "deponat magnitudinem
suam sine tribulacione," Job xxxvi.[19] Hoc non posset quamdiu tumet
vento superbie, quia adhuc crepabit in fornace, idest in tribulacione,
ut dicit Gregorius.[20] Aurum enim non purum de [adultero] metallo
habens interceptum crepat in fornace; sic superbia in tribulacione.
50 Ecclesiastici ii: "Aurum et argentum in igne probatur, homines vero
receptibiles in camino humiliacionis."[21]
Humilitas oris consistit in quatuor, quorum primum est taciturnitas
"[usque] ad interrogacionem," secundum Bernardum.[22] Et
Ecclesiastici xxxii: "Et si bis interrogatus fueris, habeat capud
55 responsum tuum";[23] idest, adhuc inclina capud propter humilitatem,
vel sermo tuus discretum sumat inicium et cum moderamine finem,
ne sit superfluus. Set multi sunt similes graculo et siccato, [que] sunt
aves multe garrulitatis et humana addiscunt verba et cum seipsis
locuntur, querunt, et respondent, et salutant transeuntes non salutati.
60 De talibus dicitur Proverbiorum xviii: "Qui prius [respondit] quam
audiat, stultum se esse demonstrat [et confusione dignum]."[24]
Secundum est propria facta humili verbo referre, non extollere; et
eciam cum omnia bene fecerimus, dicamus quod "servi inutiles
sumus," Luce xviii,[25] quia Dominus comminatur proprias fimbrias
65 [magnificantibus].[26] Sophonie iii: "Auferam magniloquos superbie
tue."[27] Tercium est seipsum vilem et contaminatum proclamare. Hec
enim fuit lex leprosi, qui peccatorem signat, Levitici xiii.[28] Quartum
est aliena bona sine diminucione commendare; Gregorius: "Vera
humilitas est que parva de se estimat et alterius bona [sine] livore
70 commendat."[29] /   p. 81

---

12. Cf. 2Sam 6:16–23; **13.** Prov 29:22; **14.** Matt 5:3; **15.** Ps.-Johannes Chrysostomus, *Opus imperfectum
in Matthaeum*, hom. 9 (PG 56:680); **16.** Sir 6:2; **17.** Job 15:13; **18.** Col 2:18; **19.** Job 36:19; **20.** Gregory
the Great, *Moralia in Iob*, 16.32.39 (CCL 143A:822–3); **21.** Sir 2:5; **22.** Benedict of Nursia, *Regula*, 7.56
(CSEL 75:50); **23.** Sir 32:11; **24.** Prov 18:13; **25.** Luke 17:10; **26.** Cf. Matt 23:5; **27.** Zeph 3:11; **28.** Cf.
Lev 13:45; **29.** Cf. Gregory the Great, *Moralia in Iob*, 26.40.72 (CCL 143B:1320).

Humility in deed has five aspects, the first of which is to place others above oneself or to give them greater honor; Romans 12: "With honor anticipating one another."[30] The second is to choose the lower place; Luke 14: "Sit down in the lowest place."[31] The third is to agree easily with the view or counsel of other people. For this teaches us "the wisdom that is from above"; for it is "easy to be persuaded and consenting to the good," James 3.[32] The fourth is to submit oneself willingly to one's superiors and obey them; Jerome glosses Matthew 4 as follows: "Humility is true when obedience does not abandon it as its companion."[33] And notice that humility is threefold: one is lesser, to submit oneself to people of higher standing; the second is greater, to submit oneself to one's equals; the third is the greatest and most perfect, namely, to submit oneself to one's inferiors.

2. (ParT X,804–9)

ON MERCY AND PITY

In the fifth place follows the remedy for avarice, which is mercy or pity; and these are one and the same virtue, except that mercy is in one's affection, pity in the deed. Mercy is defined by the Philosopher as follows: "Mercy is the virtue through which one's mind is moved over the misfortune of afflicted people."[1] But pity is threefold. The first kind is called *theosebia*, that is, worship of God, according to Augustine, *On the Trinity*.[2] The second kind stands for the works of mercy; Timothy 4: "Exercise yourself unto pity."[3] The third is the veneration or obedience or kindness that we owe our parents, which the Philosopher describes as follows: "Through pity we render service and diligent care to those who are joined by blood and are devoted to our country."[4]

The Lord taught us mercy by his words in Matthew 5: "Blessed are the merciful,"[5] that is, those whose heart is made miserable by another person's want, as Bernard explains;[6] those are the ones who understand their neighbors' need from their own disposition, Ecclesiasticus 31.[7] The Lord also taught this virtue by his example, when he gave us not only what belonged to him but himself. Galatians 1: "He gave himself for our sins, that he might deliver us from this wicked world."[8] This lesson the Apostle had in mind when he said: "I most gladly will spend and be spent myself for your souls," near the end of 2 Corinthians.[9]

Mercy is commendable for many reasons. First because as God created out of his goodness, so he restored out of mercy. That he created out of goodness is clear from the definition of the good: "The good spreads or communicates its own being," as Augustine says in his book *On the Nature of the Good*.[10] And Boethius in the *Consolation* speaks of the Creator as follows:

---

79 **subdere** subire Gr. 80 **se** *add* de Gr.

Gr, fols. 146v–147r; additional variants from ed.

1 **De . . . Pietate** *om* FGGrL. 2 **loco** *om* EFGGrL. 6 **theosebia** theosibia Gr. 9 **beneficium debitum** obsequium beneficium Gr. 10 **describit** de sic Gr. 11 **officium** affectum Gr. **cultus** clericus Gr. 15 **xxxi** *om* Gr. 18 **nequam** *add* et superinpendar Gr. 23 **enim** *om* EGr. 24 **vel** *add* ex Gr. **Augustinus** *add* in EGr.

Humilitas operis consistit in quinque, quorum primum est alios sibi preponere sive honore prevenire; Romanorum xii: "Honore invicem prevenientes."[30] Secundum est inferiorem locum eligere; Luce xiiii: "Recumbe in novissimo loco."[31] Tercium est aliorum sensui vel
75 consilio facile assentire. Hoc enim docet "sapiencia que desursum est"; est enim "suadibilis et bonis consenciens," Jacobi iii.[32] Quartum est libenter subici majoribus et obedire; *Glossa* Jeronimi super Matthei iiii: "Vera humilitas est quam non deserit obediencia comes."[33] Et nota quod est triplex humilitas: una minor, [subdere] se
80 majoribus; alia major, subdere [se] equalibus; tercia maxima et perfectissima, scilicet subdere se minoribus.

2. (ParT X,804–9)

[DE MISERICORDIA ET PIETATE]   p. 247
Quinto [loco] sequitur de remedio avaricie, idest de misericordia sive pietate; et sunt eadem virtus, set misericordia est in affectu, pietas in effectu. Misericordia sic diffinitur a Philosopho: "Misericordia est
5 virtus per quam movetur animus super calamitate afflictorum."[1] Pietas autem triplex est. Prima dicitur [theosebia], idest cultus Dei, secundum Augustinum *De Trinitate*.[2] Alia sumitur pro operibus misericordie; Thymothei iiii: "Exerce teipsum ad pietatem."[3] Tercia est veneracio sive obsequium sive [beneficium debitum] parentibus,
10 quam sic [describit] Philosophus: "Pietas est per quam sanguine junctis et patrie benivolis [officium] et diligens tribuitur [cultus]."[4] Misericordiam docuit Dominus verbo, Matthei v: "Beati misericordes,"[5] idest, ob alienam indigenciam miserum cor habentes, secundum Bernardum;[6] tales enim sunt qui ex seipsis necessitatem
15 proximorum intelligunt, Ecclesiastici [xxxi].[7] Docuit eciam illam exemplo, non solum dans nobis sua set eciam seipsum. Galatarum i: "Dedit semetipsum pro peccatis nostris, ut nos eriperet a seculo [nequam]."[8] Cujus leccionem memoriter tenuit Apostolus cum dixit: "Libenter inpendam et superinpendar pro animabus vestris," II
20 Corinthiorum ultimo.[9] Misericordia in multis est commendabilis. Primo quia sicut Deus ex bonitate creavit, ita ex misericordia recreavit. Quod autem creavit ex bonitate, patet ex boni diffinicione: "Bonum [enim] est diffusivum sui esse [vel] communicativum sui," sicut dicit [Augustinus] libro
25 *De natura boni*.[10] Et Boecius in *Consolacionibus* de Creatore sic loquitur:

---

30. Rom 12:10; **31.** Luke 14:10; **32.** Jas 3:17; **33.** *Glossa* 4:13 (Matt 3:11 marginal).

1. *Moralium dogma philosophorum* (ed. Holmberg, p. 27, ll. 17–18); **2.** Augustine of Hippo, *De civitate Dei*, 10.1 (CCL 47:273); **3.** 1Tim 4:7; **4.** *Moralium dogma philosophorum* (ed. Holmberg, p. 25, ll. 3–4); Cicero, *De inventione*, 2.53.161; **5.** Matt 5:7; **6.** Bernard of Clairvaux, *De gradibus humilitatis et superbiae*, 3.6 (*SBO* 3:21); **7.** Cf. Sir 31:18; **8.** Gal 1:4; **9.** 2Cor 12:15; **10.** Cf. Dionysius Areopagita, *De divinis nominibus*, 4.1 (PG 3:694); *De caelesti hierarchia*, 4.1 (PG 3:178).

No external causes impelled you to make
this work from chaotic matter, rather it was the form
of the highest good.[11]

And the Philosopher: "The beginning of all things is love and desire."[12] From these words can be seen that as he created out of goodness, so did he restore from mercy; Titus 2: "According to his mercy he saved us."[13] Further, mercy bent the heavens and drew God down from heaven, as Augustine says;[14] add: from heaven into the Virgin's womb, from the cross into the sepulcher. But his soul it drew into hell. Of this mercy is written in Jeremiah 31: "I have loved you with an everlasting love, therefore have I drawn you, having mercy on you";[15] and 2, where the Lord speaks to the assembly of the first believers: "I have remembered you, having mercy on your youth and the love of your espousals."[16] In this can be seen that it was mercy which bound him to our forefathers, which has now united him in the flesh with the Church of the Gentiles. Likewise, mercy sold the Redeemer himself for the redemption of the prisoners, so that it might be said of her what is written in Wisdom 10: "She forsook not the just when he was sold but delivered him from sinners."[17] Though this applies literally to Joseph, yet his selling prefigured the selling of Christ, which Zechariah 11 foretold: "They weighed for my price thirty pieces of silver."[18] Further, just as mercy has bought the miserable ones back, so does it protect them from both sin and punishment; Lamentations 3: "Many are the mercies of the Lord, that we are not consumed."[19]

3. (ParT X,810)

Mercy has five species, which are derived from the Gospel. The first is to give; Luke 6: "Give, and it shall be given to you."[1] The second is to lend, as in the same chapter: "Lend, hoping for nothing thereby."[2] The third is to pardon, as in the same: "Forgive, and you shall be forgiven."[3] The fourth is to show compassion, as the Lord taught when he wept over the city, Luke 19,[4] and on another occasion over Lazarus, John 11.[5] And compassion, by which one gives of oneself, is greater than an external bestowing by which one gives of one's possession, as Gregory says.[6] The fifth species is correction; Matthew 18: "If your brother offends against you, rebuke him between," and so forth;[7] the *Gloss*: "lest he lose face if he were rebuked in public."[8] From such a work of mercy sometimes follows the bond of friendship; Proverbs 28: "He that rebukes a man shall afterward find favor with him, more than he that by a flattering tongue deceives him."[9]

---

28 **fluitantis** fluctuantis Gr. 31 **sicut** *marg* E; *om* Gr. 32 **ii** iiii sed Gr. **misericordiam** *om* Gr. 36 **xxxi** xiii Gr. 36–7 **te . . . ii** id est attraxi te iiii te et ii eodem Gr. 38 **sum** siue Gr. 41 **univit eum** induit eam E; induit cum Gr. 42 **ut** ubi Gr. 46 **qua** quo Gr. 49 **consumpti** *om* GGr.

Gr, fol. 152r.

2 **Date** dare Gr. 9–10 **corripe . . . inter** *om* Gr.

Quem non externe pepulerunt fingere cause
Materie [fluitantis] opus, verum insita summi
Forma boni.[11]

30   Et Philosophus: "Principium omnium, amor et desiderium."[12] Ex
hiis patet quod [sicut] ex bonitate creavit, sic ex misericordia
recreavit; Ad Thytum [ii]: "Secundum suam [misericordiam] salvos /   p. 249
nos fecit."[13] Item misericordia celos inclinavit et Deum de celo
deposuit, ut dicit Augustinus;[14] suple: de celo in Virginis uterum, de

35   cruce in sepulcrum. Animam vero deposuit in abyssum. De hac
misericordia Jeremie [xxxi]: "Caritate perpetua dilexi [te, ideo attraxi
te miserans te";[15] et ii], ubi alloquitur Dominus ecclesiam primorum
fidelium dicens: "Recordatus [sum] tui, miserans adolescenciam
tuam et caritatem desponsacionis tue."[16] Ubi apparet quod

40   misericordia copulavit eum antiquis patribus, que modo per carnem
[univit eum] Ecclesie de Gentibus. Item misericordia ipsum
Redemptorem vendidit pro redempcione captivorum, [ut] posset de
ea dici quod legitur Sapiencie x: "Hec venditum justum non
dereliquit set a peccatoribus liberavit illum."[17] Licet hoc ad litteram

45   conveniat Joseph, tamen ejus vendicio Christi vendicionem
prefiguravit, de [qua] predixit Zacharie xi: "Appenderunt precium
meum triginta argenteis."[18] Item sicut misericordia redemit, sic ipsa
miseros custodit et a peccato et a supplicio; Trenorum iii:
"Misericordie Domini multe, quia non sumus [consumpti]."[19]

3. (ParT X,810)

Quinque sunt species misericordie que ex Ewangelio colliguntur.   p. 265
Prima est dare; Luce vi: "[Date] et dabitur vobis."[1] Secunda est
commodare, ut in eodem capitulo: "Date mutuum, nichil inde
sperantes."[2] Tercia est condonare, ut in eodem: "Dimittite, et

5   dimittetur vobis."[3] Quarta est conpati, quam Dominus docuit flens
super civitatem, Luce xix,[4] et iterum flendo super Lazarum,
Johannis xi.[5] Et est conpassio major per quam dat de seipso quam
exterior largicio per quam dat de suo, ut dicit Gregorius.[6] Quinta est
correpcio; Matthei xviii: "Si peccaverit in te frater tuus, [corripe eum

10   inter]," etc;[7] *Glossa*: "Ne publice correptus verecundiam perdat."[8]
Et ex tali opere misericordie solet quandoque sequi fedus amicicie;
Proverbiorum xxviii: "Qui corripit hominem, graciam postea
inveniet apud eum magis quam ille qui per lingue blandimenta
decipit."[9]

---

11. Boethius, *De consolatione Philosophiae*, 3m9.4–6 (CCL 94:52); **12.** Cf. Aristotle, *Metaphysica*, 1.4
(trans. composita) (AL 25,1–1a:97); **13.** Tit 3:5; **14.** Cf. Ps.-Augustine of Hippo (Ps.-Geoffrey of Bath),
Sermones ad fratres in eremo, 6 (PL 40:1246–7); **15.** Jer 31:3; **16.** Jer 2:2; **17.** Wis 10:13; **18.** Zach 11:12;
19. Lam 3:22.

1. Luke 6:38; **2.** Luke 6:35; **3.** Luke 6:37; **4.** Luke 19:41; **5.** John 11:35; **6.** Cf. Gregory the Great, *Moralia
in Iob*, 20.36.70 (CCL 143A:1055); **7.** Matt 18:15; **8.** *Glossa* 4:60 (Matt 18:15, interlinear); **9.** Prov 28:23.

D. Meditative Prose

VII

Anselm of Canterbury, *Meditation on the Last Judgment*

(ParT X,169–73)

Oh torments! On this side will be the accusing sins; on that, the terrifying justice; below, the horrid chasm of hell lying open; above, the wrathful judge; within, a stinging conscience; without, the burning world. "Scarcely will the righteous person be saved."[1] If the sinner is overtaken in this way, in what place can he hide himself? Bound fast, where will I hide, how will I show myself? To hide will be impossible, to show myself intolerable. I will desire the one, and it will never be; the other I will curse, and it will be everywhere.

D. Meditative Prose

VII

Anselm of Canterbury, *Meditatio ad concitandum timorem*

(from Anselmus Cantuariensis, *Meditationes, I: Meditatio ad concitandum timorem*, in *S. Anselmi Cantuariensis archiepiscopi Opera omnia*, ed. F. S. Schmitt, 2nd ed., 6 vols. [Stuttgart, 1984], 3:76–9)

(ParT X,169–73)

O angustiae! Hinc erunt accusantia peccata, inde terrens justitia; p. 78
subtus patens horridum chaos inferni, desuper iratus judex; intus
urens conscientia, / foris ardens mundus. "Justus vix salvabitur,"[1] p. 79
peccator sic deprehensus in quam partem se premet? Constrictus ubi
5   latebo, quomodo patebo? Latere erit impossibile, apparere
intolerabile. Illud desiderabo, et nusquam erit; istud execrabor, et
ubique erit.

---

1. 1Pet 4:18.

List of Citations

Citations are identified by the page number on which they occur in the texts above and the footnote number on that page.

593n30; **Acts** *4:32*: 595n8; **Rom** *1:29*:
591n11; *1:30*: 587n5; *6:23*: 551n19; *12:10*:
607n30; *14:8*: 591n15; **1Cor** *1:28*: 575n20;
5:8: 597n3; *8:1*: 571n5; *9:9*: 595n7; *10:10*:
591n5; **2Cor** *12:15*: 607n9; **Gal** *1:4*: 607n8;
4:29: 587n13; *5:17*: 573n15; **Eph** *2:3*:
553n10; *6:11–17*: 567n35; **Phil** *2:14*: 591n6;
Col *2:18*: 605n18; **1Thes** *5:2–3*: 563n14; *5:8*:
567n36; *5:17*: 557n7; **1Tim** *4:7*: 607n3; **Tit**
3:5: 609n13; **Heb** *3:12–13*: 585n6; *4:13*:
561n1; *10:29*: 585n5; *11:1*: 603n2; *12:6*:
561n28; **Jas** *3:17*: 607n32; *4:11*: 589n10;
4:15: 563n12, 573n11; *5:16*: 553n4; **1Pet** *4:9*:
591n7; *4:18*: 549n16, 611n1; *5:8*: 559n18;
2Pet *2:19*: 577n3; **1John** *2:16*: 557n1; **Jude**
13: 593n26; *16*: 593n25; **Rev** *3:11*: 551n20;
3:20–1: 551n22; *12:10*: 597n14; *16:15*:
551n21; *19:20*: 549n17; *21:8*: 551n18
Boethius, *De consolatione Philosophiae*, 3pr5:
573n12; 3m9.4–6: 609n11
Cicero, *De inventione*, 2.53.161: 607n4
Ps.-Cicero, *Rhet. ad Herennium*, 4.17.24: 577n2
Claudianus, *In Eutropium*, 1.181–4: 581n14
Defensor, *Liber scintillarum*, 10.8: 561n27
Dionysius Areopagita, *De caelesti hierarchia*, 4.1:
607n10; *De divinis nominibus*, 4.1: 607n10
Eucherius of Lyons, *Formularum liber*, 6: 575n16
Glossa ordinaria, Exod 16:1: 593n24; Lev 18:24:
599n3; Lev 19:14: 589n7; Matt 3:11: 607n33;
Matt 18:15: 609n8; Mark 9:28: 559n15; Rom
1:29: 597n1–2, n4; Heb 11:1: 603n3; 1Thes
5:15: 557n9
Gratian, *Decretum*, 1.86.21: 557n6; 2.33.3.1.40:
547n3; 2.33.3.1.62: 565n27; 2.33.3.1.81:
545n1–2; 2.33.3.3.1: 543n1; 2.33.3.3.8:
547n3; 2.33.3.3.12: 543n4; 2.33.3.3.23:
565n24
Gregory the Great, *Dialogorum libri*, 4.44:
565n20; *Homiliae in Evangelia*, 1.7.4: 603n5;
1.19.4: 593n27; 2.34.15: 545n6; *Moralia in
Iob*, 6.46.84: 585n3; 8.50.86: 597n12;
16.32.39: 605n20; 20.36.70: 609n6; 21.2.4:
601n4, n6; 21.3.7: 603n4; 23.13.24: 603n1;
26.40.72: 605n29; 33.6.13: 603n10; 33.12.25:
583n9
Hrabanus Maurus, *De universo*, 7.6: 575n16
Ps.-Hugh of St. Victor, *Miscellanea*, 6.100: 549n2

Isidore of Seville, *Sententiarum libri*, 2.16.1:
543n3; 2.16.2: 545n7; 3.50.5: 583n5;
Synonyma de lamentatione anime peccatricis,
1.77: 543n4–5
Jerome, *Comment. in Amos prophetam libri*,
1.1.4/5: 547n5; *Epistulae*, 66.10: 549n12–13;
122.3: 565n24
Ps.-Jerome, *Comment. in Marcum*, 9: 559n15;
Regula monacharum, 30: 549n12–13
Ps.-Johannes Chrysostomus, *Opus imperfectum in
Matthaeum*, hom. 9: 605n15; *Sermo de
Poenitentia*: 547n3, 569n1
Leo I, Pope, *Epistolae*, 167, inquisitio 9, resp.:
565n27
Martin of Léon, *Sermones*, 10: 561n24
Moralium dogma philosophorum (ed. Holmberg),
p. 25: 607n4; p. 27: 607n1
Nicholas of Clairvaux, *Sermo in festo Sancti
Andreae*, 8: 549n2
Ovid, *Fasti*, 1.419: 571n1
Paulinus of Aquileia, *Liber de salutaribus
documentis*, 26: 589n6
Pelagius (?), *Epistolae*, 17.22: 575n17, 577n3
Peraldus, William, *Summa de virtutibus*, 5.4.1:
603n8; *Summa de vitiis*, 3.1.3: 599n2
Peter Comestor, *Serm.*, 20 (*In Quadragesima
sermo primus*): 549n15
Peter Lombard, *Commentaria in Psalmos*, Ps.
42:1: 549n15; *Sententiae*, 4.14.2: 543n1–5,
545n6–7; 4.16.1: 547n3; 4.16.4: 545n1–2
Plato, *Theaetetus* 174D–175A: 577n27
Publilius Syrus, *Sententiae*, 200: 595n2 (IV.5);
Proverbia.112: 585n1
Sallust, *Bellum Iugurthinum*, 64: 571n2
Seneca, *De clementia*, 1.3.3: 579n10; 1.19.3–4:
579n11; *Epistulae morales*, 9.14: 573n9;
31.11: 577n26; 44.4: 577n27; 44.5: 575n21,
577n1; 65.21: 549n10; 94.46: 595n10
Tubach, 1296: 579n8
Walther, *IC* 1576: 581n14; *PS* 1565: 581n14;
25429a: 555n1; 33819: 601n1
Werner II de Küssenberg, *Libri deflorationum
sive excerptionum*, 2.22 (De remissione
peccatorum): 549n11
William of St.-Thierry, *Tractatus ad fratres de
Monte Dei*, 1.6.17: 583n2

Contributors and Editors

William Askins, Professor of English and Humanities, Community College of Philadelphia

Peter Beidler, Lucy G. Moses Distinguished Professor of English, Lehigh University

Thomas H. Bestul, Professor of English, University of Illinois at Chicago

Helen Cooper, Professor of English Language and Literature, University of Oxford, and Tutorial Fellow in English, University College, Oxford

Robert M. Correale, Professor of English, Wright State University, Ohio

Vincent DiMarco, Professor of English, University of Massachusetts (Amherst)

Robert Edwards, Distinguished Professor of English and Comparative Literature, The Pennsylvania State University

Thomas J. Farrell, Professor and Chair of English, Stetson University

Amy W. Goodwin, Associate Professor of English, Randolph-Macon College

Mary Hamel, Professor of English, Mt St Mary's College, Maryland

Richard Newhauser, Professor of English and Medieval Studies, Trinity University, Texas

Peter Nicholson, Professor of English, University of Hawaii at Manoa

Sherry L. Reames, Professor of English, University of Wisconsin, Madison

John Scattergood, Professor of Medieval and Renaissance English at Trinity College, Dublin

Edward Wheatley, Associate Professor of English and Chair of the Medieval and Renaissance Studies Program, Hamilton College

General Index

Index of Manuscripts

CHAUCER STUDIES